1 PETER
FOR PASTORS

JOHN A. KITCHEN

1 Peter for Pastors
© 2023 by John A. Kitchen

ISBN: 978-1-934952-83-2

Published by Kress Biblical Resources
The Woodlands, TX 77393
www.kressbiblical.com

All rights reserved. No portion of this book may be reproduced in any form without the written permission of the publisher except for brief excerpts quoted in critical reviews.

Unless otherwise noted, Scripture quotations are taken from the NEW AMERICAN STANDARD BIBLE7, 1960, 1962, 1963, 1968, 1971, 1972, 1973, 1975, 1977, 1995 by The Lockman Foundation. Used by permission. www.Lockman.org

The Greek text used is *Novum Testamentum Graece*, Nestle-Aland 27th Edition. Copyright © 1993 Deutsche Bibelgesellschaft, Stuttgart, Germany.

Other versions used:
    Scripture quotations marked (ASV) are from the American Standard Version.
    Scripture quotations marked (CEV) are from the Contemporary English Version, Copyright © 1991, 1992, 1995 by American Bible Society. Used by Permission.
    Scripture quotations marked (CSB) have been taken from the Christian Standard Bible®, Copyright © 2017 by Holman Bible Publishers. Used by permission. Christian Standard Bible® and CSB® are federally registered trademarks of Holman Bible Publishers.
    Scripture quotations marked (ESV) are taken from The Holy Bible, English Standard Version™, copyright © 2001 by Crossway Bibles, a division of Good News Publishers. Used by permission. All rights reserved.
    Scripture quotations marked (HCSB) are from the Holman Christian Standard Bible®. HCSB®. Copyright ©1999, 2000, 2002, 2003 by Holman Bible Publishers. Used by permission. Holman Christian Standard Bible®, Holman CSB®, and HCSB® are federally registered trademarks of Holman Bible Publishers.
    Scripture quotations marked (KJV) are taken from the King James Version.
    Scripture quotations marked (NASB) are taken from the NEW AMERICAN STANDARD BIBLE7, 1960, 1962, 1963, 1968, 1971, 1972, 1973, 1975, 1977 by The Lockman Foundation. Used by permission.
    Scripture quotations marked (NASU) are taken from the NEW AMERICAN STANDARD BIBLE7, 1995 by The Lockman Foundation. Used by permission.
    Scripture quotations marked (NCV) are taken from the New Century Version®. Copyright © 2005 by Thomas Nelson. Used by permission. All rights reserved.
    Scripture quotations marked (NEB) are taken from the New English Bible, copyright © Cambridge University Press and Oxford University Press 1961, 1970. All rights reserved.
    Scripture quotations marked (NET) are from The NET Bible® Copyright © 2005 by Biblical Studies Press, L.L.C. www.bible.org All rights reserved.
    Scripture quotations marked (NIV) are taken from the New International Version®. Copyright © 1973, 1978, 1984 by International Bible Society. Used by permission of Zondervan Publishing House. All rights reserved.
    Scripture quotations marked (NKJV) are taken from *The New King James Version*. Copyright © 1979, 1980, 1982 by Thomas Nelson, Inc. Used by permission. All rights reserved.
    Scripture quotations marked (NLT) are taken from the *Holy Bible*, New Living Translation, copyright © 1996. Used by permission of Tyndale House Publishers, Inc., Wheaton, Illinois 60189. All rights reserved.
    Scripture quotations marked (NRSV) are taken from the New Revised Standard Version. Copyright © 1989 by the Division of Christian Education of the National Council of the Churches of Christ in the United States of America. All rights reserved.
    Scripture quotations marked (Phillips) are taken from The New Testament in Modern English, copyright © 1958, 1959, 1960 J.B. Phillips and 1947, 1952, 1955, 1957 The Macmillian Company, New York. Used by permission. All rights reserved.
    Scripture quotations marked (RSV) are taken from the Revised Standard Version of the Bible, Copyright © 1952, 1946, 1971 by the National Council of Churches of Christ in America.
    Scripture quotations marked (TEV) are taken from the Good News Translation in Today's English Version- Second Edition Copyright © 1992 by American Bible Society. Used by Permission.
    Scripture quotations marked (YLT) are taken from Young's Literal Translation of the Holy Bible 1862/1887/1898, by J. N. Young. ASCII version Copyright © 1988–1997 by the Online Bible Foundation and Woodside Fellowship of Ontario, Canada. Licensed from the Institute for Creation Research. Used by permission.

In memory of
Dr. David L. Larsen

ποιμάνατε τὸ ἐν ὑμῖν ποίμνιον τοῦ θεοῦ
—1 Peter 5:2

CONTENTS

Acknowledgements	9
Abbreviations	11
How to Use this Book	15
1 Peter	17
Introduction	19
1 Peter 1	45
1 Peter 2	155
1 Peter 3	277
1 Peter 4	377
1 Peter 5	459
Appendix A: Preaching and Teaching 1 Peter	523
Appendix B: A Topical Index to the Ministry Maxims	545
Appendix C: Annotated Bibliography	551

ACKNOWLEDGEMENTS

I extend my gratitude to Rick Kress of Kress Biblical Resources for believing in the value of this kind of study and for partnering to put tools in the hands of God's servants—tools that help them engage God's Word more deeply that they might know and love God more genuinely and serve Him more effectively. My thanks also go to Charles Audino for his assistance in editing the text.

Always, I am grateful for my wife, Julie. Her support and encouragement mean the world to me and free me to serve God more fully. Her friendship makes the journey immeasurably more enjoyable.

I am grateful for those who shepherd local churches across the globe, serving in many cases in obscurity and with little to no remuneration. I am thankful to stand among you as a brother in service to our Savior. My prayer is that this contribution will help us be more faithful to "the Great Shepherd of the sheep," who "through the blood of the eternal covenant" redeemed us and made us His own (Heb. 13:20).

ABBREVIATIONS

Old Testament

Gen.	Genesis	Eccl.	Ecclesiastes
Exod.	Exodus	Song of Sol.	Song of Solomon
Lev.	Leviticus	Isa.	Isaiah
Num.	Numbers	Jer.	Jeremiah
Deut.	Deuteronomy	Lam.	Lamentations
Josh.	Joshua	Ezek.	Ezekiel
Judg.	Judges	Dan.	Daniel
Ruth	Ruth	Hos.	Hosea
1 Sam.	1 Samuel	Joel	Joel
2 Sam.	2 Samuel	Amos	Amos
1 Kings	1 Kings	Obad.	Obadiah
2 Kings	2 Kings	Jonah	Jonah
1 Chron.	1 Chronicles	Mic.	Micah
2 Chron.	2 Chronicles	Nah.	Nahum
Ezra	Ezra	Hab.	Habakkuk
Neh.	Nehemiah	Zeph.	Zephaniah
Esth.	Esther	Hag.	Haggai
Job	Job	Zech.	Zechariah
Psa.	Psalm	Mal.	Malachi
Prov.	Proverbs		

New Testament

Matt.	Matthew	1 Tim.	1 Timothy
Mark	Mark	2 Tim.	2 Timothy
Luke	Luke	Titus	Titus
John	John	Philem.	Philemon
Acts	Acts	Heb.	Hebrews
Rom.	Romans	James	James
1 Cor.	1 Corinthians	1 Peter	1 Peter
2 Cor.	2 Corinthians	2 Peter	2 Peter
Gal.	Galatians	1 John	1 John
Eph.	Ephesians	2 John	2 John
Phil.	Philippians	3 John	3 John
Col.	Colossians	Jude	Jude
1 Thess.	1 Thessalonians	Rev.	Revelation
2 Thess.	2 Thessalonians		

Bible Translations

ASV	American Standard Version
CEV	Contemporary English Version
CSB	Christian Standard Bible
ESV	English Standard Version
HCSB	Holman Christian Standard Bible
KJV	King James Version
NASB	New American Standard Bible (1977)
NASU	New American Standard Bible: Updated Edition (1995)
NCV	New Century Version
NEB	New English Bible
NET	New English Translation
NIV	New International Version
NKJV	New King James Version
NLT	New Living Translation
NRSV	New Revised Standard Version
RSV	Revised Standard Version
TEV	Today's English Version
YLT	Young's Literal Translation

Miscellaneous

A.D.	*Anno Domini*, in the year of our Lord
B.C.	Before Christ
c.	*circa*, about
cf.	*confer*, compare
contra	contrary to
e.g.	*exempli gratia*, for example
etc.	*et cetera*, and the like
ff.	following (verses, pages, etc.)
ibid.	*ibidem*, in the same place
i.e.	*id est*, that is
LXX	Septuagint
n.	Footnote
n.d.	no date
NT	New Testament
OT	Old Testament
rpt.	reprint

Footnotes

BDAG	*A Greek-English Lexicon of the New Testament and Other Early Christian Literature*, 3rd ed.
NIDNTTE	*The New International Dictionary of New Testament Theology and Exegesis*
NIDNTT	*The New International Dictionary of New Testament Theology*
TDNT	*Theological Dictionary of the New Testament*, 10 vols.

HOW TO USE THIS BOOK

Allow me to share a word about how you may use this volume for your personal growth and for that of your congregation. Like the other commentaries in this series, the present work weaves three distinct features into the fabric of one volume. It will serve your needs in a number of different ways. Three of the most obvious ways it will serve you are as a commentary, a counselor, and a coach.

Commentary: You will find that *1 Peter for Pastors* provides a wealth of exegetical information regarding the text of this NT epistle. I suggest you read the commentary with your Greek (or Interlinear Greek/English) New Testament open to the passage and follow the development of the passage. This, I trust, will aid you in personally understanding God's Word, in preaching and teaching these texts, and in explaining the meaning of these Scriptures to the people whom you shepherd.

Counselor: You will find generously dispersed throughout the text what I call Ministry Maxims. These are pithy, pointedly stated principles of ministry which arise from or are suggested by the verse. The maxims distill the wisdom of the given Scripture into a pointed—and sometimes provocative—statement of principle which applies in ministry contexts of all cultures and times. Do you wonder if that is possible? Have a debate with one of the Ministry Maxims? Then they have served their purpose. They are thought-provoking, aimed at stimulating your mind and rousing you to interact with the truth. While the commentary speaks facts into your mind, the Ministry Maxims are designed to speak truth into your heart.

Coach: This companion never allows you to leave a section of Scripture without stopping to ponder how its truth applies to your life and ministry. It provides bridges of application from the truths found in the text of Scripture to the work of ministry in your local church. You will find Digging Deeper questions dispersed throughout the text. I hope these will stimulate reflection on how the truths of 1 Peter apply to life and local church ministry. If the commentary is designed to speak facts into your mind and the Ministry Maxims are designed to speak truth into your heart, then these Digging Deeper questions are intended to put skill into your hands as you serve the Lord by serving His people. The appendices also provide practical ideas on how to use 1 Peter in personal ministry growth, counseling, and preaching/teaching.

Finally, may I suggest that *1 Peter for Pastors*, like the other commentaries in this series, is suitable for diving, wading, and dipping. That is to say, you may want to dive in and immerse yourself in the fullness of its content. Or you may want to wade into a particular section of the epistle by studying the commentary on the corresponding text. Or you may simply want to dip into its contents by perusing the Ministry Maxims and only then stop to examine the exegetical work behind the statements that pique your interest. The deeper you dive, the better, but there is benefit in all these approaches.

1 PETER

INTRODUCTION

Four threads weave the fabric of the Apostle Peter's first letter. They are not the only strands of thought found here but form the letter's substance and weight. Together the four threads weave a pattern of Christ-exalting, gospel-centered exhortation to faithfulness under pressure.

The first thread is suffering. Christ's and therefore our own.
The second thread is holiness. Christ's and therefore our own.
The third thread is glory. Christ's and therefore our own.
The fourth thread is mission. Christ's and therefore our own.

Peter points us consistently to Jesus Christ and, in the wonder of His resurrection life, to that of which our lives consist in union with Him.

Could we say that suffering speaks to our pain, holiness to our passion, glory to our hope, and mission to our purpose? Pain, passion, hope, and purpose. Does Christ have something to say to us about these realities? He does. And because He does, He transforms them for us. In Christ, pain is not what it first appears to be. Christ recasts our hope. Christ ignites passion within us. Christ provides us a purpose, one that matters not only in this life but forever.

All this is to say, 1 Peter speaks to earthly life's most essential elements. In its lines, we meet Christ, and because we do, we come into life-altering, life-giving, life-defining grace (1 Peter 5:12).

Later in this introduction, we will review how Peter develops each of these threads and then weaves them together into a God-glorifying pattern of life. But for now, let us concern ourselves with basic questions regarding what we hold in our hands as we open the letter known to us as 1 Peter.

Authorship: Who Wrote 1 Peter?

The letter claims to have been written by "Peter, an apostle of Jesus Christ" (1:1a). Some, however, not content with the letter's witness, have looked elsewhere for proof of its authorship and to others as possible authors.

Evidence of non-Petrine Authorship

Often, those who doubt Peter as the letter's author cite the following reasons to look elsewhere for its author.

1. The vocabulary and level of writing are beyond a simple Galilean fisherman like Peter.

Some claim that Peter—a poor, uneducated Galilean fisherman—could not have produced a letter in Greek of the intellectual and literary quality of 1 Peter. However, at that time, in Peter's home-region of Galilee, Aramaic, Hebrew, and Greek were all in common use. Moreover, Peter was a businessman and likely would have acquired the languages necessary to conduct prudent and efficient business with whoever wished for his goods, whatever language they spoke. Furthermore, we do not know with certainty where all Peter may have traveled and all that he may have faced in the decades between the last references we have to him in Acts and the time of this letter's composition. He may well have broadened his horizons not only geographically but culturally and linguistically. It is not unreasonable to believe that during those decades, Peter had opportunities to acquire greater skill in the Greek language.[1] Furthermore, it is nothing less than prejudice and class pride to assume the imbecility of first-century Galileans.

2. The vocabulary and theology of the letter sound too much like Paul to have come from Peter's hand.

Some object that the letter has too many echoes of Pauline thought and expression to have come from the hand of Peter. True, Peter and Paul did not generally run in the same circles. Also true, the letter contains theology that is in harmony with that of Paul. Neither of these points require a

---

1 Note, for example, Peter's love for alliteration (1:4, 19; 2:15, 21; 3:17, 20).

non-Petrine authorship. On the contrary, several lines of evidence suggest just the opposite. First, Peter and Paul were reared in the same faith and ingrained with the same Scriptures. Second, both were redeemed by the same Lord and preached the same gospel. Third, while Peter and Paul circulated in different ministry circles, Peter clearly was aware of Paul's message and theology (cf. Gal. 1:18; 2:1–21; 2 Peter 3:15–16). Finally, while Peter was more focused on believers of Jewish extraction and Paul on those of Gentile birth, the redemption all experienced was the same.

3. The letter extensively quotes or alludes to the LXX, something deemed unimaginable for a first-century Galilean fisherman.

Some assume that a Galilean Jew would not have had the level of familiarity with the LXX necessary to produce a document so thoroughly dependent upon it. By this time, however, the LXX had existed for approximately 250 years. Its circulation was widespread, and it is not unthinkable that copies of it circulated throughout Galilee. Furthermore, Peter's travels in the decades following Jesus' resurrection and ascension surely took him to locales and circles of fellowship where he would have enjoyed extensive exposure to the LXX.

4. The description of persecution sounds out of date with the known chronology of Peter's life.

Some demand that the persecution described in 1 Peter is of a kind that could only have happened after Peter's death. Such thinking assumes, however, that the persecution addressed in the letter is official, Empire-wide, and arose primarily from the state. The level of persecution read into the document is said to have been possible only under Domitian (A.D. 81–96), who reigned well after the traditional date of Peter's martyrdom, somewhere in the middle to later part of the A.D. 60s. But, as we shall see below, such a conclusion is based on assumptions that are by no means certain and does not take in the actual evidence of the letter itself. What the letter actually describes regarding the persecution of its readers fits well within what we know of the reign of Nero (A.D. 54–68).

5. If Peter were the author, one would expect the letter to reflect more directly on Jesus' life and ministry.

Some assume that if the letter was written by Peter, it would include more evidence of the author's relationship with Jesus during His earthly ministry. Yet the text of the letter itself seems to indicate otherwise. As we shall see below, there is significant evidence of the author's immediate relationship with Jesus. For example, the author claims to have been a "witness of the sufferings of Christ" (5:1). The description regarding shepherding God's people under God's "chief shepherd," Jesus (5:2–4), sounds precisely like what Peter would have written in view of John 21:15–17.

Evidence of Petrine Authorship

The previously stated objections stand in the face of the evidence found in the letter. Note the following signs that Peter was indeed the author.

1. The letter claims Peter as the author.

The letter opens with the claim that it comes from "Peter, an apostle of Jesus Christ" (1 Peter 1:1a). No evidence has emerged to compel an objective reader to disregard this simple, straightforward, plainly stated assertion of authorship.

The letter's closing also makes a claim about authorship: "Through Silvanus, our faithful brother (for so I regard him), I have written to you" (5:12a). When the author says it was "through [Διὰ] Silvanus … I have written to you" it could refer to his service to the author as an amanuensis in taking down the letter, or it could refer to his role as a courier of the letter to its recipients in Asia Minor (1:1). The traditional understanding has been that Silvanus served as amanuensis for Peter in taking down this letter. This practice was not unheard of in the first century. Sometimes the Apostle Paul employed the services of another in penning down the words of his letters (e.g., Rom. 16:22). Perhaps something similar took place with this letter. If this was indeed the case, we possess no clear answer as to the level of involvement Silvanus may have had in forming and shaping the letter. Whether he took down the words in dictation or was given a freer hand in framing the author's thoughts cannot now be known.

More recent scholarship tends to read this as a signal that Silvanus served as the carrier of the letter to its addressees.[2] Support is found in the actions of the Jerusalem Council. After reaching an agreement about their response to the question of the Law (and circumcision in particular) as it relates to Gentile believers in Jesus, the leaders composed a letter to express their decision. Then, along with Paul and Barnabas, they selected "Judas called Barsabbas, and Silas, leading men among the brethren" (Acts 15:22) and "They wrote this letter by them" (γράψαντες διὰ χειρὸς αὐτῶν, v.23a, NKJV). Note the use of διὰ ("by") particularly. It is clear from the context that none of the four men named penned the letter but that it was delivered "by" their hands to its intended audience. Thus, Peter may have used similar language to describe how Silvanus was employed with the letter known to us as 1 Peter.

Still others suggest that Silvanus may have served both as amanuensis and courier.[3] Wherever one deems the weight of evidence to lie, we can be confident that, whatever the details of Silvanus' role, as with "All Scripture," 1 Peter "is breathed out by God and profitable for teaching, for reproof, for correction, and for training in righteousness" (2 Tim. 3:16, ESV). As with the OT Scriptures, so too with this letter: "men moved by the Holy Spirit spoke from God" (2 Peter 1:21).

2. The letters contents and the nature of the writing point to Peter's authorship.

The contents of the letter and the nature of the writing point to Peter's authorship. 1 Peter 5:1 says the author was a witness to the sufferings of Christ (Matt. 26:58, 67–69; Mark 14:54; Luke 22:54, 61). In that regard, 1 Peter 2:23 may be read as the remembrances of an eyewitness. Further, we may read 4:13 in light of Peter's previous rebuke of Jesus for speaking of His sufferings (Matt. 16:21–23). Perhaps 1 Peter 5:1–2 fulfills Jesus' command for Peter to "feed my sheep" (John 21:15–17, ESV). Is 5:5 an echo of Jesus washing Peter's feet (John 13:3–15)? The author may be

---

[2] E.g, Dubis, 173; Forbes, 183; Grudem, 206–207; Hiebert, 326–327; Jobes, 320; Lenski, 229; Michaels, 306; Schreiner, 248–249.

[3] E.g., Bigg, 195; MacArthur, 228; Raymer, 2:857; Robertson, *Word Pictures*, 6:134; Stibbs, 175.

speaking as one who was present on the day of Pentecost (1 Peter 1:12). The mention of Mark in 1 Peter 5:13 may early Christian tradition which associated Mark with Peter.

3. The earliest witnesses understood Peter to be the author of the letter.

From the letter's earliest days, it was universally accepted as coming from Peter. The earliest reference to 1 Peter comes in 2 Peter: "This is now, beloved, the second letter I am writing to you in which I am stirring up your sincere mind by way of reminder" (2 Peter 3:1). There exists no evidence, historical or otherwise, from the first centuries of 1 Peter's existence of any suspicion of different authorship.

The earliest witnesses among the Church Fathers support Peter as the author. The witness of the church for its first eighteen centuries was that Peter was the author of this letter. This was largely unchallenged until the skepticism of the critical school of thought arose in the nineteenth century. The earliest witnesses and church leaders affirmed Peter as the author.

1 Peter was quoted without specific comment on its authorship by Clement of Rome (*The Epistles of Clement of Rome to the Corinthians*, A.D. 95–96). Eusebius said that Papias (A.D. 60–130) quoted an epistle of Peter. Polycarp, a disciple of the Apostle John, references 1 Peter when he writes to the Philippians. Irenaeus (*Against the Heresies*, A.D. 180) was the first to identify Peter as the letter's author.[4] Tertullian testified to Peter as the author (*De Oratione*, c. A.D. 200–206). In the fourth century Eusebius said the letter was universally recognized as authentically Petrine. According to Eusebius, Clement of Alexandria (A.D. 150–220) wrote a commentary on 1 Peter.[5] Origen (A.D. 185–253) added his witness to Peter's authorship of the letter.

Grudem notes, "There seems to have been no doubt anywhere in the early church that I Peter was written by the apostle Peter" and "from the earliest time the letter circulated in the church, it was known and accepted as a letter by Peter."[6]

---

4 Hiebert, 12.

5 Ibid.

6 Grudem, 22, 23.

Further, the reference to Mark as "my son" (1 Peter 5:13) is consistent with the tradition recounted by Eusebius that Mark served as Peter's "interpreter." "Writing in A.D. 325, Eusebius includes I Peter among those books everywhere recognize as belonging to the New Testament. Wherever it was circulated, it was accepted as genuine."[7]

4. *The early church consistently rejected any writing that appeared pseudepigraphic.*

If one rejects Petrine authorship of the letter, the options are slim. It must have been either a pseudonymous letter (purposefully written by another hand and attributed to Peter) or an anonymous letter later ascribed to the Apostle.[8]

But the early church gave no leniency in the matter of pseudepigraphic writers. For example, Tertullian tells of elders from Asia Minor who removed a man from his post because for "love of Paul," he penned the apocryphal *Acts of Paul* which included *3 Corinthians*. The man protested that he had written from good motives, yet he was removed from office for composing a work that "fictitiously bore Paul's name or for composing a fiction about the apostle."[9] Similarly, Eusebius tells of how Serapion, who served as bishop of Antioch, denied the use of the *Gospel of Peter* because it was deemed pseudepigraphic and heretical.[10]

If the early church had any hint that the writings of the NT were pseudepigraphic, they would have applied similar measures against the letters and their authors. Instead, the entire testimony of the early church stands in favor of understanding Peter as the author of 1 Peter.

It is neither wise nor academically superior to deny the early, consistent, sustained, and enduring witness of the Scriptures, its first readers, and the early church. It is hubris to believe that someone twenty-plus centuries removed knows better than the Scriptures and its earliest witnesses. A letter that clearly claims the authorship of Peter and yet is deemed untrue

---

7   Ibid., 23.

8   Hiebert, 18, 19.

9   Wilder, 42.

10 Ibid.

in this claim cannot then be trusted in anything else it sets forth. We take the witness of the letter, the whole of Scripture, the earliest witnesses, the Church Fathers, and the majority of scholarship throughout the last two millennia to be true—Peter is the author of the letter we know as 1 Peter.

Unity of the Letter

Some divide 1 Peter into two parts, 1:1–4:11 and 4:12–5:14. They posit that what we know as 1 Peter is the synthesis of two originally separate documents.[11] The presence of two doxologies (4:11; 5:11) within the text is offered as evidence. But looking across the landscape of the entire NT, we find other letters which contain doxologies at points within the documents themselves (e.g., Rom. 11:33–36; Eph. 3:20–21).

Kelly identifies the epistle's teaching on suffering as a unifying theme running through the whole.[12] But others contend that the letter contains two differing views of suffering: in the first part suffering is viewed as a possibility, while in the second part, it is treated as actuality. But if we compare, for example, 1:6 and 4:12, we discover that both halves sound quite alike in their description of the suffering under consideration.

Some hold to the basic unity of the letter but suggest that the bulk of the letter originally existed as a sermon and that 1:1–2 and 5:12–14 were added later to make it serve as a letter. Some believe that the sermon was prepared for the occasion of baptism.[13] But the letter only refers explicitly to baptism on one occasion (3:21). Other lines of evidence set forth by the proponents are, in the end, unconvincing.

Despite such attacks on the integrity of the letter, 1 Peter demonstrates unity and bears signs of being one document as originally written by the Apostle Peter. Consult the detailed exegetical outline in Appendix A for evidence of the development of thought throughout the letter.

---

11 Hiebert, 20.

12 Kelly, 20.

13 E.g., Perdelwitz (37), Preisker (156), and Cross (31).

Origin: From Where Was 1 Peter Written

Eusebius, the early historian of the church, said that Peter wrote the letter from Rome. Both Tertullian (A.D. 203) and Eusebius (A.D. 325) attest to Peter's presence and ministry in Rome late in his life.

The letter itself places Peter in Rome. With his last drops of ink Peter says, "She who is in Babylon, chosen together with you, sends you greetings, and so does my son, Mark" (1 Peter 5:13). There has long been speculation as to the identity of this "Babylon." But the choices are limited.

The ancient empire of Babylon had long since come to nothing, and the renowned city of Babylon had been reduced to a mere shell of its former glory, now mainly irrelevant to the powers that shaped the world in the first century. The Jewish population there had been reduced to almost nil, and we have no record of Peter ever traveling there.

There was a tiny military outpost in Egypt called "Babylon," but it seems to have been too small and insignificant to mention here. We likewise have no record of Peter ever visiting that location.

Some suggest the city of Jerusalem, in its present apostate state, might have been symbolically called "Babylon." But there is little evidence to suggest this was common enough practice for Peter to refer so cryptically to it here, expecting his readers to discern his intent.

The earliest tradition tells us Peter referred to Rome in this way. References to "Babylon" in Revelation may have represented the city of Rome (Rev. 14:8; 16:19; 17:5; 18:2). The "seven mountains on which the woman sits" (17:9) appears to reference the famed seven hills of Rome.[14] It was not uncommon in pseudepigraphical writings of the era for "Babylon" to be a code for Rome. Eusebius indicated that Papias (c. A.D. 80–155) and Clement of Alexandria (c. A.D. 155–215) both thus used the word.[15] As already noted, early tradition puts Peter in Rome toward the end of his life. For these reasons, it is best to conclude that Peter wrote his letter from the Empire's capital.

---

14 Grudem, 34–35.
15 Hiebert, 27.

Like Babylon of old, first-century Rome was the most powerful nation on earth, and their capital cities were the seat of their culture and power. Rome, like ancient Babylon, was the center of ungodliness. As Babylon was for ancient Jewish exiles, Rome was for Peter a place of dislocation and even exile (cf. 1 Peter 1:1; 2:11).[16] Like Babylon of old, Rome would fall and fade from the scene. Peter may have been motivated in his cryptic reference by the fact that he wanted to conceal his location from the authorities who would have loved to lay hands on one of Jesus' apostles. Yet he knew that the letter's recipients would recognize the place from which he wrote and the spiritual implications of his designating it "Babylon." To the people being persecuted by the powers of Rome, Peter's designation was a signal that the persecutors would not ultimately win but that God's Kingdom would prevail. To those finding themselves "aliens and strangers" (1 Peter 2:11) living in exile away from their true homeland in God's presence, Peter's reference to Babylon signaled that he, too, understood their heavenly homesickness. Peter's reference would fortify his readers to remain faithful under the painful trials brought upon them by representatives of Rome.

Recipients: To Whom Was 1 Peter Written?

The author writes "To those who reside as aliens, scattered throughout Pontus, Galatia, Cappadocia, Asia, and Bithynia, who are chosen…" (1 Peter 1:1b).

But why these areas? Who lived in these localities? How did the gospel come to them?

People from these regions were in Jerusalem at Pentecost when the Spirit of God was given to the people of God (Acts 2:9–11). It is possible that at this time they heard the gospel preached by Peter (vv.14–36) and were among those who pleaded with the apostles, "Brethren, what shall we do?" (v.37). Did they hear Peter's plea to repent and be baptized in

---

16 Forbes, 185; In Βαβυλῶνι ("Babylon") we may have another inclusion, matching διασπορᾶς ("the dispersion," ESV) in 1:1 (Goppelt, 375; Jobes, 323; Michaels, 311).

Jesus' Name (v.38)? Were they among the "three thousand souls" who responded in faith (v.41)? If so, they may have returned to their homelands bearing the gospel. But we have no definite witness to this fact.

We know that Paul ministered in some of these general locations (cf. Acts 16:6; 18:23; 19:10, 26). But we encounter challenges in trying to connect his ministry directly to the peoples of these specific regions. He was known, for example, to have ministered in the provinces of Galatia and Asia (cf. Acts 16:6; 18:23; 19:8–10), but it is not possible to fix his connection to these specific localities and people.

In the end, we must admit that we do not know with certainty just how the gospel arrived in these locations. We are grateful for the Scriptural witness of the book of Acts (supplemented by the Epistles) and what they tell us of the gospel's progress in the Roman Empire. Yet we must admit that in this we possess a selective history of the fulfillment of Jesus' mission in the first century. We have no direct Scriptural testimony for much gospel ministry. We find simple reports of the reality of the gospel and its saving power in these places, but we do not always possess the details of how it advanced there. And this is encouraging, for it is a testimony to the power of the gospel in the hands of ordinary people empowered by God's Spirit as they faithfully "give an account for the hope that is in" them (1 Peter 3:15).

Peter mentions those who preached the gospel to them (1:12) but gives no indication of who they were or when they arrived. Peter reports the act of preaching the gospel to his readers in a way that appears to assign that preaching to others, rather than to himself. We can safely conclude, therefore, that otherwise unknown but faithful servants of Christ ventured into these regions, spreading the hope of Christ wherever they went. They gathered believers. They established churches. They equipped and designated leaders. And at some point, Peter came to know of these believers and felt pastoral concern for them, leading him to pen this letter. Specifics beyond these simple lines of evidence lead us into speculation.

What can be known about these regions generally?

The areas represented were diverse in nearly every way. Topographically, they included "coastal regions, mountain ranges, plateaux, lakes and river systems."¹⁷ As for the peoples themselves, they represented "different origins, ethnic roots, languages, customs, religions, and political histories."¹⁸ Yet, for all the uniqueness, God had drawn them together into one unified people through His Son Jesus Christ (2:9–10, 17; 5:9).

Were the recipients primarily Jewish or Gentile? Or were they made up of both?

Michaels can say, "No NT letter is so consistently addressed, directly or indirectly, to 'Israel,' that is (on the face of it) to Jews" (1:1; 2:6, 9).¹⁹ Those outside the believers addressed are described as "Gentiles" (2:12; 4:3). Yet alongside this lies consistent evidence that the recipients were predominantly Gentile in ethnicity, with perhaps, a sprinkling of Jewish believers. Previously, Peter told them, you lived "in your ignorance" (1:14), and you were redeemed "from your futile way of life inherited from your forefathers" (1:18). Peter would have been unlikely to have used such expressions of ethnic Jews. They fit precisely with how Gentiles are described elsewhere in the Scriptures. They once were "not a people," but now are "the people of God" (2:10, NASB). He warned them that "the time already past is sufficient for you to have carried out the desire of the Gentiles, having pursued a course of sensuality, lusts, drunkenness, carousing, drinking parties and abominable idolatries" (4:3). And now that they have turned to Christ, "In all this, they are surprised that you do not run with them into the same excesses of dissipation" (v.4). But, if they were Jews, the Gentiles surely would not have been surprised at their refusal to participate any longer in the Gentile way of life.

It seems most likely, that the largest portion of the believing community was ethnically Gentile. Yet there were probably among them some who were ethnically Jewish, for we know that some from "Cappadocia, Pontus and Asia" were present in Jerusalem at Pentecost and heard Peter preach the gospel (Acts 2:9).

---

17 Clowney, 17.

18 Elliot, *Home*, 61.

19 Michaels, xiv.

It is not clear whether Peter intends us to understand these designations politically or geographically. If the latter, then the area would have been somewhat smaller. We are left to wonder, but the understanding of the text is not affected either way.

Is there something to be discerned from the order in which Peter lists these areas? Many today agree with the suggestion initially made by Hort[20] and its further refinement by Hemer,[21] that the order in which Peter presents the locales follows a roughly circular pattern, one that might be the natural course along which the carrier of the letter would travel.[22] Presumably, copies of the letter would have been made at each significant stopping point, with copies then disseminated to smaller locales surrounding each area named here. In this way, Peter's letter would have spread widely and rapidly throughout Asia Minor.

Occasion: What Circumstances Gave Rise to the Writing of 1 Peter?

What were the circumstances of those to whom Peter wrote? What were their lives like? What was demanded of them as followers of Christ?

Even a cursory reading of the letter reveals a people facing significant and painful pressure for their faith in Jesus Christ. What remains to determine is the precise nature of that pressure. Was this official persecution coming down from the top of the Empire? Was this more regional and situation-specific? What prompted and drove this persecution?

A careful reading suggests that the persecution was primarily verbal (1 Peter 2:12, 15; 3:9, 16; 4:4, 14) and not physical abuse or the immediate threat of martyrdom.

---

20 Hort, 157–84.

21 Hemer, 239–43.

22 E.g., Abernathy, 12; Bigg, 69; Goppelt, 3–5; Grudem, 53–54; Hiebert, 49; Kelly, 41–42; Marshall, 31; Michaels, 9–10; Schreiner, 52. Jobe thinks otherwise, suggesting that "… it seems more likely that the list of regions simply represents the author's mental map of Asia Minor, probably using the names of regions as he first learned them, even if Roman administration had subsequently altered the map" (66).

The vocabulary Peter uses throughout the letter to describe the opposition his readers faced helps us significantly: λοιδορέω ("to revile"; 2:23), λοιδορία ("reviling," 3:9 [2x]), ἐπηρεάζω ("to mistreat," 3:16), καταλαλέω ("to speak against," 2:12; 3:16), καταλαλιά ("slander," 2:1), and ὀνειδίζω ("to revile," 4:14).[23] This verbal abuse was socially ostracizing. There is little to prove that the readers were facing the active threat of martyrdom, though that possibility could never be entirely removed.

As to what is known about the circumstances of the Apostle Peter as he wrote, the letter provides us with almost nothing. We have seen already that it appears Peter wrote from the city of Rome. Beyond that, we must piece together bits of evidence from the wider landscape of the New Testament and history generally. All of this affects one's attempt at establishing a tentative date for the letter's composition.

History attests to Peter's presence in the city of Rome toward the end of his life. Indeed, he is said to have given his life up in martyrdom in that city. Paul also spent the latter part of his life incarcerated for the second time in Rome. It seems safe to assume that if they had been together at the time of writing this letter, Peter would have mentioned Paul, especially given that Paul had ministered in a few of the places to which this letter was addressed. Peter does mention Paul's writings in his second letter (2 Peter 3:15–16). As the Book of Acts closes, Paul is under house arrest in Rome (Acts 28:16–31). Paul was released from his first Roman imprisonment in approximately A.D. 62. He then entered a period of freedom and continued ministry (A.D. 62–67). Toward the end of that time, Paul was rearrested, incarcerated in Rome for a second time, and eventually martyred.

Working on the assumption that Peter would have probably mentioned Paul in his letter if either he was present in the city or had recently been martyred, it seems best to place Peter's presence there sometime between the end of Paul's first Roman imprisonment (A.D. 62), his rearrest and second imprisonment, and eventual martyrdom (A.D. 66–67). Therefore, 1 Peter was written between A.D. 63–66.

---

23 Forbes, 156.

The persecution of the letter's recipients appears to be largely verbal, and consequently social, and therefore local and sporadic rather than official and Empire-wide. An official, more intense, and deadly kind of persecution began under Nero in the fall of A.D. 64. Nero himself died June 9, A.D. 68. Early church tradition tells us Peter himself died under Nero's reign, so the letter, if genuinely from his hand, must have been written before that date. Given Peter's counsel regarding how to relate to governing authorities (1 Peter 2:13–17), it seems unlikely that the official and more violent form of persecution had yet broken out.

For these reasons it seems best to place the writing of this letter somewhere between A.D. 62 and 63. This would leave time for Peter to pen his second letter somewhere in late A.D. 63 or 64, shortly before his martyrdom.

Purpose: Why did Peter Write 1 Peter?

Peter set out his purpose in penning the letter: "I have written to you briefly, exhorting and testifying that this is the true grace of God. Stand firm in it!" (5:12). This compact statement reveals several objectives behind Peter's letter. First, Peter had more that he could have shared ("I have written to you briefly"). Second, Peter was not writing simply to inform, but to call to action ("exhorting," "Stand firm"). Third, Peter was writing to give personal attestation to the truth he enunciated ("testifying"). Finally, Peter wrote to extend grace through the unfolding of the gospel ("this is the true grace of God").

Peter wrote to clarify his readers' identity in Christ, individually (1:1–12) and corporately (2:4–10), and then to lay out how that grace ought to find expression in their lives, lived out in an opposing world (1:13–2:3; 2:11–5:12).

Theology: What does 1 Peter Teach Us?

The first order of theology is the doctrine of God. Thus, first we ask what God reveals about Himself in 1 Peter.

Peter, a Jewish monotheist to the core, is nevertheless free to describe God as Triune (1 Peter 1:2). The Father elects, the Son secures, and the

Spirit applies the work of salvation (1:2). The Triune God is holy (1:15, 16), "mighty" (5:6), possesses eternal "dominion" (5:11), and is to be feared (1:17). He is the Creator of all things (4:19). He is light, shining forth "excellencies" that are beyond human understanding (2:9). His will rules all things (2:15; 4:2; 5:11). Sometimes His will includes the suffering of His people (3:17; 4:19). He alone possesses unqualified authority. He appoints earthly rulers, putting them in place according to His will (2:14).

This same God acts in kindness (2:3) and is gracious in ways too numerous to recount (4:10). Indeed, He is "the God of all grace" (5:10). He extends His favor (2:20), calling His people to share "His eternal glory in Christ" (5:10). His word stands forever (1:25) and He demands obedience to "the gospel of God" (4:17). To those who believe, He promises to personally "perfect, confirm, strengthen and establish" them to the end (5:10). He is, thus, the object of His peoples' hope (3:5). He observes every detail of their lives and hears their every prayer (3:12). God sets Himself against those who do evil (3:12) and opposes the proud (5:5). He gives grace to the humble (5:5), lifting them up at the proper time (5:6). "He cares for" His people, inviting them to cast their cares upon Him (5:7). He supplies strength to His people (4:11). He makes His people "the household of God" (4:17) and "the flock of God" (5:2). As such they are His glad "bondslaves" (2:16) who seek to glorify Him in all things (4:16).

God the Father is "Blessed" above all else (1:3). He is the "Father of our Lord Jesus Christ" (1:3). He raised Jesus from the dead (1:21). He acts in sovereign, electing grace according to His determinative foreknowledge (1:2), extending "mercy" (1:3) to those He chooses. He "caused us to be born again" (1:3). As the Father of His children, He grants and protects their inheritance (1:4). By His power, He keeps them as His own (1:5). He tests their faith to refine and reveal its genuineness (1:7). He is patient (3:20), but He is also the Judge of all (1:17). When He judges He does so "impartially" (1:17) and "righteously" (2:23). He rightly receives our worship and service (2:5).

God the Son is the "Lord Jesus Christ" (1:3). As "Lord," He is fully divine. As the man "Jesus," He is fully human. As the "Christ," He fulfills all the Father's work of salvation under the anointing of the Spirit. He was "foreknown before the foundation of the world" (1:20). He was the subject of the OT prophets preaching and the object of their longing (1:8–9). He was incarnated as God on earth (1:20) and lived a sinless life (2:22). Being rejected by men (2:4, 7), He suffered on our behalf (4:1; 5:1) and died in our place (2:24). He shed His blood to redeem us (1:2), thus serving as the perfect sacrifice for sin (1:19; 3:18). By these sufferings He heals us (2:24), bringing us to the Father and reconciling us (3:18). He was raised from the dead (1:3; 3:18, 21) and ascended to heaven, being seated victoriously at the Father's right hand (3:22). Now to Him "belongs the glory and the dominion forever and ever" (4:11).

The Son is, thus, the cornerstone of God's saving work (2:7, 8), "the Chief shepherd" of His people, keeping them as His own until He appears to complete their salvation (5:4). As such, "obedience" is due Him (1:2) and all "will give account to Him" (4:5). Salvation is realized in union with Him (3:16; 5:14). His people offer spiritual sacrifices to God through Him (2:5). He is His people's example in suffering (2:21). His own set Him apart as "Lord" in their hearts (3:15).

Jesus will return to earth (1:13) to be revealed in His glory (4:13) and to share it with His own (5:10).

The Spirit is fully divine (4:14). He was operative in and through the OT prophets (1:11; cf. 2 Peter 1:21). The Spirit was "sent" by the Father and the Son (1:12) and is, therefore, both "the Spirit…of God" (4:14) and "the Spirit of Christ" (1:11). He enables those who proclaim the gospel (1:12) and regenerates the elect to eternal life (1:3). The Holy Spirit sanctifies the child of God (1:2). He communicates the glory of God to the child of God and through that child to the world about him (4:14).

What then does 1 Peter teach us about humankind? The answer is found both by direct statement and by implication as Peter describes the change the redeeming work of Christ accomplishes in believers. Unredeemed humanity is spiritually dead (1:3, 23), living in spiritual darkness (2:9), separated from God (3:18), and passing away (1:24). Apart God's redemption we are mortal and perishable, without rights before God (1:4). We are unaware of and unprepared for the return of Christ and the judgment we will face at that time (1:7, 13, 17; 4:5, 17). We do not fear God (2:17). We are spiritually ignorant (1:14) and thus foolish (2:15). If presented with the claims of Christ, we have refused to believe them (1:21; 2:7), are disobedient to the gospel (2:8; 3:1), having rejected Christ (2:7), stumbling over Him through taking offense at Him (2:8). We are subject to the sinful nature and its practices (2:1, 11; 4:3). In all of this, we stand outside the people of God (2:10, 12).

Having touched upon what we learn in 1 Peter about theology, Christology, pneumatology, and anthropology, we now consider just how God and humanity may be reconciled. We ask, what does 1 Peter teach us about soteriology?

A review of Peter's teaching on salvation brings us back to the four threads in 1 Peter that weave a pattern of Christ-exalting, gospel-centered exhortation to faithfulness under pressure. The primary threads that form the substance of Peter's exhortation are suffering, holiness, glory, and mission. In all cases, both Christ's and ours.

Jesus' suffering is both efficacious and exemplary. Jesus suffered and died to atone for the sin that separates us from God and to reconcile us by His grace (2:24; 3:18). In His suffering Jesus also provided an example for their suffering (2:21–23; 4:1–2). At the heart of this rich theme lies Peter's extensive use of the noun πάθημα (1:11; 4:13; 5:1, 9) and the verb πάσχω (2:19, 20, 21, 23; 3:14, 17, 18; 4:1 [2x], 15, 19; 5:10). God calls His people to suffer (2:21), to actually "share the sufferings of Christ" in this world (4:13). Suffering is part of God's will for His own (3:17; 4:19). Christ's suffering and death rescues us not from all suffering, but from useless suffering in this life (2:21) and eternal suffering in the next (2:8; 3:19; 4:5, 17–18).

As a part of God's sovereign will for His people (3:17; 4:19), He uses suffering to refine His peoples' faith (1:7; 4:12) and purify their lives in holiness (3:13–17; 4:17–19). It is through the refining fires of suffering that the believer's faith is proved genuine, and the beauty of holiness brought forth (1:7). Jesus suffered and died "so that we might die to sin and live to righteousness" (2:24). One's willingness to suffer demonstrates one has "ceased from sin" (4:1). The essence of holiness is conformity to God's character (1:14–16). Holiness, thus, is more than good deeds. The evidence of holiness is in the goodness of one's actions. Peter contrasts believers doing good (2:15, 20; 3:6, 11, 17; 4:19) with those who do evil (2:12, 14; 3:17; 4:15). Peter uses ἀγαθ- words a total of thirteen times throughout the letter (ἀγαθοποιός, "doing good," 2:14; ἀγαθοποιέω, "to do good," 2:15, 20; 3:6, 17; ἀγαθοποιΐα, "doing what is right," 4:19; ἀγαθός, "good," 2:18; 3:10, 11, 13, 16 [2x], 21).[24]

The faithful stay the course of suffering and holiness because of the promise of glory, Christ's own resurrected glory revealed to the world at His Coming and shared with and manifested in His people (1:7, 11, 21, 24; 4:11, 13, 14; 5:1, 4, 10). For Jesus, suffering and glory are inextricably bound together, the former leading unfailingly to the latter. Indeed, in God's economy, suffering and glory are never far apart (1:11; 4:13, 16; 5:1, 10). The sustaining power fueling holy obedience is the promised demonstration of God's glory in Christ at His Coming (1:11, 13; 2:12; 4:11, 13; 5:1) and the promise that His people will share with Him in that revelation of His glory (1:5, 7, 13; 4:13; 5:1, 4, 10). The noun δόξα ("glory") is prominent throughout the letter (1 Peter 1:7, 11, 21, 24; 4:11, 13, 14; 5:1, 4, 10). Peter employs the verb δοξάζω to call his readers to "glorify" God in all things (1:8; 2:12; 4:11, 16).

This final triumph in glory was behind God's mission laid upon His Son (1:3–5, 10–11, 20). Jesus' victorious fulfillment of the Father's mission was sealed through His death (3:18a), resurrection (v.18b), ascension (vv.19–20), and session (v.22). Jesus will be completely vindicated, and the already-accomplished triumph will be fully realized at His Coming. The mission of His people is to live and love in such a way that they bring others into this triumphant salvation in Christ, which is enjoyed in this life (1:3, 8–9, 23; 2:9–10; 3:10–12; 4:2, 14) and entered into entirely at His Coming (1:7, 13; 4:13; 5:1, 4, 10). For citizens (2:13–17), slaves (vv.18–20), wives (3:1–6), and all believers (vv.8ff) the path of obedience is held forth in missional terms: "they may because of your good deeds, as they observe them, glorify God in the day of visitation" (2:12), "silence the ignorance of foolish men" (v.15), "even if any of them are disobedient to the word, they may be won without a word" (3:1), "always be ready to make a defense to everyone who asks you to give an account for the hope that is in you" (v.15), "they may live in the spirit according to the will of

---

24 Cf. Peter's use of καλός ("beautiful"/"good") in 2:12 [2x] and 4:10.

God" (4:6). The Holy Spirit empowers God's people in their proclamation of the gospel (1:12).

The call of God is to live faithfully in relationship to Jesus amid suffering by the enabling of the Holy Spirit. Such suffering becomes God's means of refining us in holiness, displaying His glory in us, and accomplishing His mission through us.

Suffering brings forth God's holiness in us, displays His glory in us, and advances His mission through us.

Holiness is refined through our suffering, God's glory displayed through us, and His mission fulfilled in us.

Glory is God's answer to our suffering, the display of His holiness in us, and the goal of His mission accomplished through us.

God's mission is fulfilled through suffering, aimed at His glory, and the dissemination of holiness.

All of this will be realized only by God's freely given grace (1 Peter 1:2, 10, 13; 2:19, 20; 3:7; 4:10; 5:5, 10). Indeed, the entire letter unfolds "the true grace of God" (5:12).

Bibliography

Abernathy, David. *An Exegetical Summary of 1 Peter*. 2nd ed. Dallas: SIL International, 2008.

Achtmeier, Paul J. *1 Peter*. Philadelphia: Fortress Press, 1996.

Alford, Henry. *Alford's Greek Testament: An Exegetical and Critical Commentary*, vol. IV. Grand Rapids: Baker Book House, revised edition, 1875, reprinted, 1980.

Barclay, William. *The Letters of James and Peter*. The Daily Study Bible.

Edinburgh: The Saint Andrew Press, 1958, 1060, 1961, 1964.

Bauer, Walter, *A Greek-English Lexicon of the New Testament and Other Early Christian Literature*. William F. Arndt and F. Wilbur Gingrich, Trans. 2nd edition. Chicago: The University of Chicago Press, 1979. (BAGD)

Bauer, Walter. *A Greek-English Lexicon of the New Testament and Other Early Christian Literature.* Edited by Frederick W. Danker. 3rd ed. Chicago: University of Chicago Press, 2000. BibleWorks. v.9. (BDAG)

Bigg, Charles. *A Critical and Exegetical Commentary on The Epistles of St. Peter and St. Jude.* The International Critical Commentary. Edinburgh: T.&T. Clark Limited, 1903.

Blum, Edwin A. *1, 2 Peter and Jude.* The Expositor's Bible Commentary, v.12. Grand Rapids: Zondervan Publishing House, 1981.

Brooks, James A. and Carlton L. Winbery. *Syntax of New Testament Greek.* Lanham, Maryland: University Press of America, 1979.

Brown, Colin, ed. *The New International Dictionary of New Testament Theology.* 3 vols. Grand Rapids, Michigan: Zondervan Publishing House, 1975.

Clowney, Edmund. *The Message of 1 Peter: The Way of the Cross.* The Bible Speaks Today. Downers Grove, Illinois: InterVarsity Press, 1988.

Cross, F.L. *I Peter, A Paschal Liturgy.* London: A.R. Mowbray, 1954.

Dana, H.E. and Julius R. Mantey, *A Manual Grammar of the Greek New Testament.* Toronto: The MacMillan Company, 1927, 1955.

Davids, Peter H. *The First Epistle of Peter.* The New International Commentary on the New Testament. Grand Rapids: William B. Eerdmans Publishing Company, 1990.

Davids, Peter H. *The Letters of 2 Peter and Jude.* The Pillar New Testament Commentaries. Grand Rapids: William B. Eerdmans Publishing Company, 2006.

Davids, Peter H. *2 Peter and Jude: A Handbook on the Greek Text.* Baylor Handbook on the Greek New Testament, Martin M. Culy, Gen. Ed. Waco, Texas: Baylor University Press, 2011.

Draper, Edythe. *Draper's Book of Quotations for the Christian World.* Wheaton, Illinois: Tyndale House Publishers, 1992.

Dubis, Mark. *1 Peter: A Handbook on the Greek Text*. Waco: Baylor University Press, 2010.

Duguid, Iain M. *ESV Expository Commentary – Hebrews-Revelation: Volume XII*. Wheaton, Illinois: Crossway Books, 2018. WORD*search* CROSS e-book.

Elliot, John H. *A Home for the Homeless; A Sociological Exegesis of 1 Peter, Its Situation and Strategy*. Minneapolis: Fortress Press, 1981; SCM Press, 1982.

Elliot, John H. *I Peter*. New Haven: Yale University Press, 2007.

Fleagle, Arnold R. *First Peter: Strategic Imperatives for Suffering Saints*. The Deeper Life Pulpit Commentary. Camp Hill, Pennsylvania: Christian Publications, 1997.

Forbes, Greg W. *1 Peter*. Exegetical Guide to the Greek New Testament. Nashville: B&H Publishing Group, 2014.

Forsyth, Peter Taylor. *Director of Souls*. London: Epworth Press, 1948.

Friberg, Timothy, Barbara Friberg and Neva F. Miller. *Analytical Lexicon of the Greek New Testament*. Victoria, British Columbia: Trafford Publishing, 2005.

Gangel, Kenneth O. "2 Peter." *The Bible Knowledge Commentary: New Testament*, John F. Walvrood and Roy B. Zuck, Editors. Colorado Springs: Victor Books, 1983.

Gilbrant, Thoralf, ed. *The Complete Biblical Library – Hebrews-Jude*. Springfield, IL: World Library Press, Inc., 1989. WORD*search* CROSS e-book.

Goppelt, Leonhard. *A Commentary on 1 Peter*. Grand Rapids: William B. Eerdmans Publishing Company, 1993.

Grudem, Wayne A. *1 Peter: An Introduction and Commentary*. Tyndale New Testament Commentaries, vol. 17. Downers Grove, Illinois: InterVarsity Press, 1988, 2009.

Harris, Murray J. *Prepositions and Theology in the Greek New Testament.* Grand Rapids: Zondervan, 2012.

Hiebert, D. Edmond. *First Peter.* Chicago: Moody Press, 1984, 1992.

Hellerman, Joseph H. *Philippians.* Exegetical Guide to the Greek New Testament. Nashville: Broadman and Holman Publishing Group, 2015.

Hemer, C.J. "The Address of 1 Peter," *ExpTim* 89 (1978–79): 239–43.

Henry, Matthew. *Matthew Henry's Commentary on the Whole Bible: Complete and Unabridged in One Volume.* Peabody, Massachusetts: Hendrickson Publishers, Inc. 1991.

Hort, F.J.A. *The First Epistle of St Peter: I.1–11.17.* New York: Macmillan, 1898.

Jobes, Karen H. *1 Peter.* Baker Exegetical Commentary on the New Testament. Grand Rapids: Baker Academic, 2005.

Kelly, J.N.D. *The Epistles of Peter and Jude.* Black's New Testament Commentaries. London: Adam & Charles Black, 1969, 1976.

Keener, C. S. *The IVP Bible Background Commentary: New Testament.* Downers Grove, IL: InterVarsity Press, 1993.

Kistemaker, Simon J. *James, Epistles of John, Peter, and Jude.* New Testament Commentary. Grand Rapids, Michigan: Baker Book House, 2002.

Kitchen, John A. *Proverbs: A Mentor Commentary.* Fearn, Tain: Christian Focus Publications, 206.

Kittel, Gerhard and Gerhard Friedrich. *Theological Dictionary of the New Testament.* Translated by Geoffrey W. Bromiley. Grand Rapids, Michigan: William B. Eerdmans Publishing Company, 1964–1976.

Lenski, R.C.H. The *Interpretation of the Epistles of St. Peter, St. John and St. Jude.* Minneapolis: Augsburg Publishing House, 1966.

Liddell, Henry George, and Robert Scott. *A Greek-English Lexicon: With a Revised Supplement.* Edited by Sir Henry Stuart Jones and Roderick McKenzie. 9th ed. Oxford: Clarendon, 1996. BibleWorks, v.9.

Louw, Johannes E., and Eugene A. Nida. *Greek-English Lexicon of the New Testament: Based on Semantic Domains.* 2 vols. 2nd ed. New York: United Bible Societies, 1989. BibleWorks, v.9.

Luther, Martin, *Commentary on the Epistles of Peter and Jude* (Grand Rapids: Kregel Publications, 1982).

MacArthur, John. *MacArthur New Testament Commentary—1 Peter.* Chicago: Moody Press, 2004. WORDsearch CROSS e-book.

Machen, J. Gresham. *New Testament Greek for Beginners.* Toronto: The Macmillan Company, 1923.

MacLeay, Angus. *Teaching 1 Peter: Unlocking 1 Peter for the Bible Teacher.* Fearn, Ross-shire, Scotland: Christian Focus Publications, 2008.

Marshall, I. Howard. *1 Peter.* The IVP New Testament Commentary Series. Downers Grove, Illinois: InterVarsity Press, 1991.

Michaels, J. Ramsey. *1 Peter.* Word Biblical Commentary, vol. 49. Waco, Texas: Word Books, 1988.

Moulton, J. H., and G. Milligan. *Vocabulary of the Greek Testament.* London: Hodder and Stoughton, 1930. BibleWorks, v.9.

Mounce, William D. Gen. Ed. *Mounce's Complete Expository Dictionary of Old and New Testament Words.* Grand Rapids: Zondervan, 2006.

Motyer, J. Alec. *The Prophecy of Isaiah: An Introduction and Commentary.* Downers Grove: IVP Academic, 1993.

Newman, Jr., Barclay M. *A Concise Greek-English Dictionary of the New Testament.* Stuttgart: Deutsche Bibelgesellschaft, 1993. BibleWorks, v.9.

Perdelwitz, R. *Die Mysterienreligion und das Problem des I. Petrusbriefes: Ein literarischer und relgionsgeschichtlicher Versuch.* Gieseen: Töppelmann, 1911.

Piper, John, "Hope as the Motivation of Love: 1 Peter 3:9–12," NTS 26 (1979–80), 212–231.

Presker, H. Die *katholischen Briefe: Erklärt von Hans Windisch.* 3rd edition. Revised and augmented. Tübigen: Mohr-Siebeck, 1951.

Rienecker, Fritz. *A Linguistic Key to the Greek New Testament.* Translated by Cleon L. Rogers, Jr. Grand Rapids, Michigan: Zondervan Publishing House, 1976, 1980.

Raymer, Roger M. "1 Peter." *The Bible Knowledge Commentary: New Testament*, John F. Walvrood and Roy B. Zuck, Editors. Colorado Springs: Victor Books, 1983.

Reicke, Bo. *The Epistles of James, Peter, and Jude.* The Anchor Bible. Garden City, N.Y.: Doubleday, 1964.

Robertson, Archibald Thomas. *Grammar of the Greek New Testament in the Light of Historical Research.* London: Hodder & Stoughton. Third edition, 1919.

_____. *Word Pictures in the New Testament.* 6 vols. Grand Rapids, Michigan: Baker Book House, reprint n.d. from 1930 Sunday School Board of the Southern Baptist Convention.

Schreiner, Thomas R. *1, 2 Peter, Jude.* The New American Commentary, v.37. Nashville: B&H Publishing Group, 2003.

Stibbs, Alan M. *The First Epistle General of Peter.* Tyndale New Testament Commentaries. Grand Rapids: William B. Eerdmans Publishing Company, 1959, 1981.

Tenney, Merrill C. *New Testament Times.* Grand Rapids: William B. Eerdmans Publishing Company, 1965.

Thayer, Joseph H. *Thayer's Greek-English Lexicon of the New Testament.* Peabody, Massachusetts: Hendriksen Publishers, Inc., reprinted 2003 from the 4th edition originally published by T&T Clark, Edinburgh, 1896.

Tozer, A.W. *The Best of A. W. Tozer*. Harrisburg, PA: Christian Publications, Inc., 1981.

Trench, Richard Chenevix, *Synonyms of the New Testament*, London: Macmillan and Company, 1880.

Vincent, Marvin R. *Word Studies in the New Testament*, vol. 1. McLean, Virginia: Macdonald Publishing Company, n.d.

Vine, W.E. *Vine's Expository Dictionary of New Testament Words*. McLean, Virginia: MacDonald Publishing Company, n.d.

Wiersbe, Warren W. "1 Peter." *The Bible Exposition Commentary*, New Testament, vol. 2. Colorado Springs: Victor, 2001.

Wiersbe, Warren W. *Live Like a King*. Grand Rapids: Kregel Publications, 1995.

Wilder, Terry L. "A Brief Defense of the Pastoral Epistles' Authenticity." Midwestern Journal of Theology, 2.1. Fall 2003.

1 PETER 1

Verse 1 – Peter, an apostle of Jesus Christ, To those who reside as aliens, scattered throughout Pontus, Galatia, Cappadocia, Asia, and Bithynia, who are chosen

The author identifies himself with the first word of the text. He does so differently here than he will do in his second letter. There he identifies himself as "Simon Peter" (Συμεὼν Πέτρος). The first (more literally and according to the best manuscripts, "Simeon," ESV, NET, NRSV) was his given name. Jesus notably changed his name to "Peter" (Matt. 16:18). The name Πέτρος ("Peter") means "a stone." The act of naming was a signal of lordship, dominion, rule, and authority. Repeatedly throughout Scripture, the changing of a person's name is held out as a prerogative that belongs to God (e.g., Abram to Abraham, Gen. 17:5; Sarai to Sarah, v.15; Jacob to Israel, 32:28). Jesus demonstrated His deity and authority in changing Simeon's name to Peter. In this way, He also indicated the way the transforming power of His grace would be made evident in this man's life. Simeon would be transformed from the volatile, impetuous individual so often seen early in the Gospels to a man of rock-solid character and conviction, able, as Christian tradition teaches us, to lay his life down in martyrdom for his Lord.

Having stated his name, Peter identifies himself as "an apostle of Jesus Christ" (ἀπόστολος Ἰησοῦ Χριστοῦ). The word "apostle" (ἀπόστολος) refers to one sent with a message and endowed with the full authority of the sender in delivering it. Peter had been one of the original twelve chosen by Jesus to be with Him and to be sent out by Him to preach, heal, and minister (Matt. 10:2–4; Mark 3:14–19). Peter quickly became the man at the head of the group of disciples. In every listing of the Apostles, Peter is mentioned first (Matt. 10:2; Mark 3:16; Luke 6:13–14; Acts 1:13). The noun is qualified by the genitive "of Jesus Christ" (Ἰησοῦ Χριστοῦ). The genitive is subjective—Jesus is the one who commissioned and sent Peter.

With a lengthy and detailed series of clauses, Peter identifies those to whom he addresses the letter. He designates them with a combination of two adjectives (ἐκλεκτοῖς παρεπιδήμοις, "those who reside as aliens...who are chosen"). One or the other of the adjectives is nominalized (i.e., functioning as a noun). But which did Peter intend to be viewed in this way? Was he thinking "aliens who are elect by God" or "the elect of God who are aliens"? Competent and compelling arguments have been advanced for both views.

Some have opted to see "aliens" as the nominative and "chosen" as the qualifying adjective.[1] Others have chosen to see "chosen" as the nominative and "aliens" as the qualifying adjective.[2] Still others have suggested that one need not be subordinate to the other but that the second (παρεπιδήμοις, "who reside as aliens") stands in apposition to the first (ἐκλεκτοῖς, "who are chosen").[3]

What is clear is that followers of Jesus Christ are, at the same time, wanted, chosen, and elect and yet also unwanted, rejected, and alien. The latter is the view

Ministry Maxim

Believers live with the tension of being wanted, chosen, and elect, and yet unwanted, rejected, and alien.

of the present culture and the people who make it up. The former of the One who rules and overrules all that takes place in this present world. The

---

1 Bigg, 90; Dubis, 2; Goppelt, 64; Grudem, 52–53; Hiebert, 46; Schreiner, 50; ESV, NKJV, NRSV.

2 Hart, 39; Michaels, 7; NLT.

3 Forbes, 12; Jobes, 75.

latter's voice is heard more immediately, but that of the former is eternal. The latter may have the audible voice, but God's verdict is decisive, fundamental, and final.

In the end, perhaps it is best to say both are true, and neither misses Peter's overall intention. As Christ's followers we are "aliens" (παρεπιδήμοις) and we are "elect" (ἐκλεκτοῖς). Each helps us understand the other. To be chosen by God means that we are "aliens" to this present world. Likewise, to be "aliens" to this world is the mark of having been chosen of God.

In this two-fold collective identity the recipients of the letter are called "scattered" (διασπορᾶς). The translators have chosen to render the noun with a verbal expression ("scattered"). The word originally referred to the Jewish people who had spread beyond Jerusalem and Judea and lived in the larger Gentile world. The scattering followed God's discipline, wherein the Jewish people were removed from their homeland by Assyria and Babylon. Jewish leaders, during a period of controversy with Jesus, asked: "He is not intending to go to the Dispersion [διασπορὰν] among the Greeks, and teach the Greeks, is He?" (John 7:35). The expression was transferred then by Peter about Christians who lived as strangers to this world, not yet gathered "home" to the presence of God.[4] This and ἐκλεκτοῖς ("who are chosen") are opening examples of Peter's proclivity to employ words initially assigned to Israel as a nation and apply them now to the New Covenant people of God. Luke used the verbal form of the word to describe God dispersing His people beyond Jerusalem and Judea (in fulfillment of Jesus' missional words in Acts 1:8) to bear witness to Christ and His gospel to the ends of the earth (Acts 8:1, 4; 11:19).

Peter specified the breadth of their dispersion as "throughout Pontus, Galatia, Cappadocia, Asia, and Bithynia" (Πόντου, Γαλατίας, Καππαδοκίας, Ἀσίας καὶ Βιθυνίας). These five genitive nouns relate to διασπορᾶς ("scattered") as either genitives of place (the locales where the people are "scattered") or stand in apposition ("the dispersion which

---

4   BDAG, 1914.2.

consists in these places").[5] Each constituted a definable region within the Roman province of Asia Minor north of the Taurus Mountains, located in what is the modern country of Turkey. There seems to be general agreement that the original suggestion of Hort[6] and its further refinement by Hemer[7] is correct, that the order in which Peter presents them follows a roughly circular pattern that might be the natural course along which the carrier of the letter might travel.[8] Presumably the letter was copied at each major stopping point, and then disseminated to smaller locales surrounding "Pontus, Galatia, Cappadocia, Asia, and Bithynia." In this way, Peter's letter would have spread widely throughout Asia Minor.

Just when the gospel arrived in these locales is not known with precision. Still we do know that there were representatives from some of these regions present on the Day of Pentecost: "Parthians and Medes and Elamites, and residents of Mesopotamia, Judea and Cappadocia, Pontus and Asia, Phrygia and Pamphylia, Egypt and the districts of Libya around Cyrene, and visitors from Rome, both Jews and proselytes" (Acts 2:9–10). Many of these may have been converted at that time and returned home with the gospel in their hearts and on their lips. We have no other scriptural record of how the gospel may have come to many of these regions. It underscores that the historical record of Scripture, while accurate and trustworthy, is selective. There was more gospel work going on in the first century than we know. Speculation about the relationship of Peter and Paul to the various churches in the different regions of Asia Minor is just that.

---

5   Forbes, 12; cf. Jobes, 75; contra. Dubis, 2–3.
6   Hort, 157–84.
7   Hemer, 239–43.
8   E.g., Abernathy, 12; Bigg, 69; Goppelt, 3–5; Grudem, 53–54; Hiebert, 49; Kelly, 41–42; Marshall, 31; Michaels, 9–10; Schreiner, 52. Jobe thinks otherwise, suggesting that "… it seems more likely that the list of regions simply represents the author's mental map of Asia Minor, probably using the names of regions as he first learned them, even if Roman administration had subsequently altered the map" (66).

Consult the Introduction for more about these specific areas, the history of the gospel in them, and their relationship to other gospel ministers and ministries, like those of the Apostle Paul. But we should pause to ask why the Holy Spirit would specifically name these locations. He identifies these specific geographical locations, not because that is the only place Peter's words have significance. Instead, the locations are named because each of us resides in some specific place, with peculiar features, oddities, and characteristics that make followers of Christ realize this world is not their home and in which the electing grace and love of God set them apart from the other residents of the region. God and His love define us, but we are affected by the earthly realities of where we live. We cannot rely upon the latter to define who we are; only the former can do that. But we cannot live out our heavenly calling anywhere other than within the realities of our earthly sojourn. Your earthly realities are not precisely like mine. God has called you to Himself and to live in fellowship with Him right where you are. Where you reside is not as determinative as who set His love on you and chose you. But where you live is significant as you live out the reason His love and call has planted you there.

Verse 2 – according to the foreknowledge of God the Father, by the sanctifying work of the Spirit, to obey Jesus Christ and be sprinkled with His blood: May grace and peace be yours in the fullest measure.

As the phrase "throughout Pontus, Galatia, Cappadocia, Asia, and Bithynia" enlarged upon and fleshed out the noun διασπορᾶς ("scattered throughout") so the combination ἐκλεκτοῖς παρεπιδήμοις ("aliens... who are chosen") is developed further by the three prepositional phrases that open verse 2 and continue the sentence begun in verse 1. The phrases develop the role of each member of the Trinity in the electing work of God. Both their standing before God ("chosen") and, therefore, their condition in this world ("aliens") are the product of the Triune God's grace.

The first prepositional phrase is "according to the foreknowledge of God the Father" (κατὰ πρόγνωσιν θεοῦ πατρὸς). The preposition (κατὰ, "according to") points to the standard by which the recipients of the letter became "aliens... who are chosen."[9] In this sense, it means "*in agreement with, corresponding to, in conformity with*"[10] or signifies "congruence"[11] with another reality. The reality in which the election of God's saints finds "conformity" or "congruence" is "the foreknowledge" (πρόγνωσιν) of the first member of the Trinity. The noun form is found in the NT only here and in Acts 2:23, where on the day of Pentecost, Peter declared that Jesus was "delivered over by the predetermined plan and foreknowledge [προγνώσει] of God." Paul uses the verbal cognate in theologically significant passages such as Romans 8:29 and 11:2. Peter also employs it in 1 Peter 1:20 and 2 Peter 3:17 (cf. Acts 26:5). The English translation ("foreknowledge") can imply information grasped before an event or reality. But the Greek word is more potent than this and includes the notion not simply of awareness but intention, predetermination[12] and prearrangement.[13] It carries the idea of choice predating other realities.[14] Thus the word sets before us "the moving cause of election."[15] It describes God's "effective choice."[16] To this end the NLT says God the Father "knew you and chose you long ago" and the NRSV renders it "chosen and destined by God the Father." This determinative foreknowledge was specifically "of God the Father" (θεοῦ πατρὸς). He holds this standing in relationship to Jesus

> **Ministry Maxim**
>
> The Father initiated, the Son procured, and the Spirit actualizes the salvation in which we live.

---

9   Dubis, 3.
10 Friberg, 216.
11 Abernathy, 13.
12 BDAG, 6173.2.
13 Thayer, 538; cf. TDNT, 1:715; NIDNTT, 1:692–693.
14 NIDNTT, 1:693.
15 Alford, 4:331.
16 Kelly, 43; Rienecker, 743.

Christ (1:3). All who are His children through Christ are also privileged to "call on him as Father" (1:17, ESV). The first person of the Godhead designed and initiated the redemptive plan.

The second prepositional phrase is "by the sanctifying work of the Spirit" (ἐν ἁγιασμῷ πνεύματος). The preposition ἐν ("by") is used to express the means or instrumentality by which the readers became "aliens...who are chosen."[17] What was determined in eternity past by God the Father became a living reality in time and space as the Holy Spirit brought into experience the saving grace of God purchased by the Son of God (see the next phrase). The English "the...work of the Spirit" renders but one word in the Greek text (πνεύματος). The genitive (lit., "of [the] Spirit") is subjective, pointing to the sanctification which the Spirit produces (cf. 2 Thess. 2:13).[18] The anarthrous, genitive noun could be rendered "of spirit" and thus understood as referring to a reality performed upon or in the human spirit. But that it should be rendered as definite and understood as a reference to the Spirit of God ("the Spirit") is clearly Peter's intent. It was common practice in the Greek language to drop the definite article, allowing the reader to assume the noun is definite because of context. The context here clearly is bent on identifying the work of the Trinity in the work of salvation. That "work of the Spirit" (πνεύματος) is "sanctifying" (ἁγιασμῷ), a word Paul used extensively (Rom. 6:19, 22; 1 Cor. 1:30; 1 Thess. 4:3, 4, 7; 2 Thess. 2:13; 1 Tim. 2:15). The only other usages are by the author of Hebrews (Heb. 12:14) and here by Peter. The noun refers to holiness, consecration, or sanctification. It may refer to the process of becoming holy, but, in the NT, it more often describes the state of being sanctified or consecrated.[19] The Spirit takes up the electing will of the Father and sets the chosen one apart unto Him, applying the atoning work of Christ to that life and marking them as thus cleansed, sanctified, set apart, and holy unto God. The child of God is thus sanctified unto God already ("By this will we *have been sanctified* through the offering of

---

17 BDAG, 2581.5.b.

18 Dubis, 3; Forbes, 13; Hart, 40; Rienecker, 743; Robertson, *Word Pictures*, 6:80.

19 BDAG, 57.

the body of Jesus Christ once for all," Heb. 10:10) and yet continues to be led by the Spirit through the sanctifying work of becoming holy in experience ("For by a single offering he has perfected for all time those who *are being sanctified*" (Heb. 10:14, ESV; emphases added).

The third prepositional phrase is "to obey Jesus Christ and be sprinkled with His blood" (εἰς ὑπακοὴν καὶ ῥαντισμὸν αἵματος Ἰησοῦ Χριστοῦ). The preposition εἰς ("to") signifies the purpose or goal behind their being made "aliens … who are chosen."[20] In this case, there is a dual goal or purpose. Both are related to the second member of the Trinity: "Jesus Christ" (Ἰησοῦ Χριστοῦ). The designation of our Lord is pushed to the end of the phrase, though it relates to both purpose statements. The genitive form functions as a possessive genitive in relationship to "blood" (αἵματος; Jesus' own blood) and as an objective genitive to "obey" (ὑπακοὴν; obedience to Jesus).[21]

The first purpose of their election is "to obey" Jesus (ὑπακοὴν). The word itself came from the verb ὑπακούω, which properly was used "of one who on a knock at the door comes to listen who it is."[22] It came then, by popular usage, to describe one who hearkened to the voice of another, or, that is, listened to *and obeyed* instructions or commands. Believers are to listen to Jesus, to hear and respond actively to what He says. Listening and obeying marks the entire existence of followers of Christ. This is their reason for existence. They always have an ear to their Master (Mark 4:9, 23; Rev. 2:7, 11, 17, 29; 3:6, 13, 22), listening with their will already engaged and their disposition already set to move when His voice makes His will clear (John 7:17). God the Father purposed from before the foundation of the world (1 Peter 1:20) to call out for His Son a listening, obedient people. Thus, Peter later identifies them as "obedient children" (v.14; cf. v.22).

The Father willed this to become a reality by choosing them to "be sprinkled by His blood" (ῥαντισμὸν αἵματος). The noun ῥαντισμός ("sprinkled") is found just five times in the LXX, all in Numbers 19,

---

20 Harris, 88–90.

21 Dubis, 3; contra Forbes, 13.

22 Thayer, 637–638.

where it describes the holy cleansing water prescribed by God to wash clean those guilty of a variety of offenses (vv.9, 13, 20, 21 [2x]). However, ῥαντισμός ("sprinkled") is also more pointedly and conceptually linked to Moses' act of sprinkling the people with the blood of the sacrifices in Exodus 24:3–8. It is found elsewhere in the NT only in Hebrews 12:24, where it also refers to Jesus' blood atonement (cf. Heb. 9:11–28 and 10:22 for insight on Peter's intent here). The blood of Jesus, the Lamb of God (John 1:29, 36), sprinkles clean and sanctifies to God those who submit themselves to Him in repentance and faith. Peter elsewhere uses the noun αἷμα ("blood") only in v.19, where he calls it "precious blood, as of a lamb unblemished and spotless." Thus, God the Father willed that those upon whom He set His electing love would become related to Him through the atoning death of His Son, Jesus Christ. In this way, their sins would find atonement and forgiveness and they would be cleansed to stand before and live in relationship to Him as obedient children.

To this, Peter adds an opening prayer/wish for those to whom he writes: "May grace and peace be yours in the fullest measure" (χάρις ὑμῖν καὶ εἰρήνη πληθυνθείη). "Grace" (χάρις) both declares and reminds us that all which comes to us from God in salvation is a free, unmerited gift. The word "peace" (εἰρήνη) resounds with echoes of the Hebrew *shalom* (שָׁלוֹם). The stress is not so much on an inward tranquility of heart but the full-orbed wholeness of a life at rest with God. This peace the Apostle extends "to you" (ὑμῖν), using the plural form to address all those just classified in verse 1.

Peter prays that this grace and peace will be his readers "in the fullest measure" (πληθυνθείη). The optative mood expresses the Apostle's prayer or wish for his readers.[23] The passive voice looks to God to work in and upon Peter's readers so that their trials of faith yield multiplied graces. The aorist tense seeks concrete expression of this fruit in their lives in time and space. This verb is used elsewhere in NT salutations only in 2 Peter 1:2 and Jude 2. The verb means to increase, grow, or multiply.[24] Thus the

---

23 Wallace, 481–482.

24 Mounce, 356.

ESV renders the phrase "be multiplied to you." The verb is found twelve times in the NT. It is used frequently in Acts to describe the growth of the word of God (6:7; 12:24), the disciples who believed it (6:1), and "the church" that resulted (9:31). And all this reflects the pattern of the supernaturally exponential reproduction of Hebrew children in Egypt (Acts 7:17). Paul used the verb of God's ability to "multiply" the Corinthian believers' resources for excellence in giving (2 Cor. 9:10). It was in the mouth of Jesus as He described the increase of lawlessness in the last days (Matt. 24:12). And it is doubled up for emphasis in God's original promise, given by God to Abraham for his obedience, that God would "surely multiply" (πληθύνων πληθυνῶ; a Hebraic idiom meaning literally, "multiplying I will multiply") Abraham in vast future generations and nations (Heb. 6:14, quoting Gen. 22:17). In English the word "multiplying" may imply something greater and more expansive than mere "adding." To add to something is to make it bigger. But to multiply it is to do so in entirely different ways and with greater magnitude, volume, and speed. The Greek word does not necessarily have these same inherent ideas. Yet, as shown above, its use in the NT speaks, in every case but one, of supernatural growth and expansion—something only God could bring about. Thus, the expectations are raised, not by the philology of the Greek word itself, but by the way the Spirit of God has directed the writers of Scripture in its use. Peter is looking for a remarkable advance in both "grace and peace" in a way that only God could bring about; the kind of thing that the Apostle Paul would say "surpasses all comprehension" (Phil. 4:7). The singular form of the verb, when applied to two nouns, seems to speak of the experience of "grace and peace" as a unitary matter.[25] Peter desires that "grace and peace are multiplied to match the growth of hostility with which the Christians addressed are confronted."[26]

---

25 Hiebert, 38.
26 Hart, 41.

Digging Deeper:
1. Describe the ways you feel the tension of being wanted, chosen, and elect by God and yet also unwanted, rejected, and alien to the world (v.1).
2. How does the three-fold work of salvation by the Triune God (v.2) reassure and steady you as one who lives in this tension (v.1)?

Verse 3 – Blessed be the God and Father of our Lord Jesus Christ, who according to His great mercy has caused us to be born again to a living hope through the resurrection of Jesus Christ from the dead,

Peter here begins a sentence that extends through verse 12. Before he can tell us why, he erupts into an exclamation of praise: "Blessed" (Εὐλογητὸς)! The clause possesses no verb, leaving the reader to provide the appropriate verb. But should we understand the implied verb to be indicative ("is," thus stating a fact) or optative ("be," thus putting forth a prayer/wish)? Virtually all modern English translations render it "be," which seems fitting given that Peter has just employed the optative at the end of verse 2 ("May grace and peace be yours in the fullest measure").²⁷ The adjective (Εὐλογητὸς, "Blessed") depicts that which is "praised" or worthy to be thus "blessed." The NT only uses Εὐλογητὸς to describe God (Luke 1:68; Rom. 1:25; 2 Cor. 1:3; 11:31; Eph. 1:3) and His Son (Rom. 9:5). In fact, it is used as a periphrasis for God: "the Blessed" (Mark 14:61). Not surprisingly this harkens to familiar Jewish expressions rooted in the Old Testament (e.g., Gen. 9:26; 14:20; 24:27; Exod. 18:10; Josh. 22:33; 2 Sam. 18:28; 22:47; 1 Kings 1:48; 5:7; 8:15, 56; Ezra 7:27; Neh. 9:5; Psa. 18:46; 28:6; 31:21; 41:13; 66:20; Dan. 2:20). The familiar Jewish, "Blessed, art Thou O Lord" is here given a distinctively Christian ring: "the God and Father of our Lord Jesus Christ." The entire expression "Blessed

---

27 NET Bible.

be the God and Father of our Lord Jesus Christ" (ὁ θεὸς καὶ πατὴρ τοῦ κυρίου ἡμῶν Ἰησοῦ Χριστοῦ) is found verbatim in 2 Corinthians 1:3 and Ephesians 1:3.

God the Son is given the full, three-fold designation that is rightly His. He is "the Lord" (τοῦ κυρίου). Note the definite article, specifying and designating Him as singular and unique. The noun κύριος is used throughout the LXX to identify Yahweh. He is thus designated as fully divine. Yet, at the same time, He is "Jesus" (Ἰησοῦ), the character of human history who lived in time and space, making the unique and fullest revelation of God to His creation, and offering Himself as the final sacrifice for sin. Jesus is not only fully divine, but, at the same time, fully human. And He is the "Christ" (Χριστοῦ), the anointed of God. He is rightly acclaimed as the fulfillment of all God's promises of a coming Redeemer and of His salvation. Peter is sparing throughout this letter with his use of plural pronouns (cf. 1:3; 2:24; 4:17), so the fact that he designates Jesus as "our" (ἡμῶν) Lord Jesus Christ is a significant confessional statement. He stands alongside his readers on level ground as they relate to the Lord.

Him to whom Peter directs our worship is called "the God and Father" of our Lord Jesus Christ. One definite article (ὁ, "the") assigned to two nouns (θεὸς καὶ πατὴρ, "God and Father") indicates Peter is thinking of but one unified Being who rightly bears both designations.[28] Calling Him "the God" (ὁ θεὸς) of Jesus does not imply that Jesus' divinity is lesser (cf. John 20:17; 2 Cor. 1:3; 11:31; Eph. 1:3; Rev. 1:6; 3:12). In the outworking of our salvation, it is God the Father who *initiates* ("God so loved the world, that He gave His only begotten Son," John 3:16), God the Son who *procures* ("in order that the world might be saved through Him," John 3:17) and God the Spirit who *actualizes* ("everyone who is born of the Spirit," John 3:8). Jesus broke new ground in referring to God as His "Father" (πατὴρ), something little known among the Jews until that time (though cf. Deut. 32:6; Psa. 89:26; Isa. 63:16; 64:8; Jer. 3:4, 19). It spoke of the intimacy of Jesus' relationship to God and hinted at His divine nature as the unique Son of God. "For this reason therefore the Jews were

---

28 Wallace, 270–290.

seeking all the more to kill Him, because He not only was breaking the Sabbath, but also was calling God His own Father, making Himself equal with God" (John 5:18). "For Jesus according to his human nature God is his God, and for Jesus in his deity God is his Father; his God since the incarnation, his Father from all eternity."[29]

It is He "who...has caused us to be born again" (ὁ...ἀναγεννήσας ἡμᾶς). The participle is substantive ("who...has caused us to be born again," emphasis added). It stands in apposition to "the God and Father of our Lord Jesus Christ," thus introducing us more fully to Him who is "Blessed" above all. The aorist tense pictures the event of God thus bringing His people to new birth. He is the active agent in regeneration. He brings forth new life. It is a solely divine work. A child does not birth itself, nor even contribute to bringing about its birth (thus: "who...*has caused us* to be born again," emphasis added). By using the plural pronoun (ἡμᾶς, "us"), Peter includes himself with everyone who is a part of God's family. The verb is a compound comprised of ἀνά ("again") and γεννάω ("be/become the parent of," "to give birth to," "bear," "beget"). The compound verb is found in the NT and LXX only here and 1:23 (ἀναγεγεννημένοι, "you have been born again"). In verse 23 the perfect tense is used, denoting one's standing resulting from the new birth, and the passive voice again underscores the active agency of God in bringing His people to new birth. Though the verb is only used twice in the NT, the NT uses different words to communicate the same reality. In John 3:3 and 7, Jesus speaks of the same reality using the same root verb along with an adverb (ἄνωθεν) meaning "above" ("born from above," NRSV; NET). The Holy Spirit brings about the birth from above: "he saved us...by the washing of regeneration [παλιγγενεσίας] and renewal of the Holy Spirit" (Titus 3:5). Like Peter's verb, Paul's choice is a compound: πάλιν ("again") and γένεσις ("beginning/birth," lit., "genesis," cf. Matt. 1:1, 18; Luke 1:14). Paul (2 Cor. 5:17; Gal. 6:15;

> **Ministry Maxim**
>
> Hope lives because Jesus lives.

---

29 Lenski, 30.

Eph. 2:10), James (James 1:18) and John (1 John 5:1–4) all join Peter in following their Jesus' insistence on the reality and necessity of the new birth. Some find here a link to baptism[30], though nowhere is it mentioned in the text. Schreiner is correct: "The focus is not on baptism but conversion."[31] Some have sought the roots of Peter's imagery in this verb, locating it variously in the pagan mystery religions[32], Judaism generally[33] or Qumran specifically.[34] It seems more likely that Peter is taking cues from Jesus' and the other Apostles' teachings.[35]

The participle is qualified by four prepositional phrases, the first three in verse 3 and the fourth in verse 4. First, tucked into the attributive position between the definite article (ὁ, "who") and the participle (ἀναγεννήσας, "has caused … to be born again") is the clause, "according to His great mercy" (κατὰ τὸ πολὺ αὐτοῦ ἔλεος). The attributive position emphasizes the qualitative nature of God's actions in thus bringing His people to new birth. God's gift of the new birth is "according to" (κατὰ) something that lay beyond our desire, will, or ability. The preposition serves as a "marker of norm of similarity or homogeneity," but in this case, "the norm is at the same time the reason, so that *in accordance with* and *because of* are merged."[36] This is the only time in either of Peter's letters that he makes mention of "mercy" (ἔλεος). The word points to the kindness, concern, compassion, and pity[37] within God's heart that moved Him to take the initiative to relieve our sorry estate, floundering in alienation from Him. The definite article (τὸ) appears to specify that "mercy" which is in view. Between the noun and the definite article is tucked "His great,"

---

30 E.g., Goppelt, 84; Kelly, 48.

31 Schreiner, 61; cf. Grudem, 60.

32 Davids, 51.

33 Selwyn, 306.

34 Goppelt, 82–83.

35 Jobes, 83; Kelly 50.

36 BDAG, 3938.B.5.δ.

37 Ibid., 2488.

the adjective πολὺ ("great") and the personal pronoun αὐτοῦ ("His"), emphasizing the qualitative nature of the "mercy" in view. That which initiated our new birth is both massive and personal. Our new start began not in our heart but in God's heart, from which came a mercy far greater than the need—so much greater that it overwhelmed, inundated, and buried our need.

The second prepositional phrase to qualify "who ... has caused us to be born again" (ὁ ... ἀναγεννήσας ἡμᾶς) is "to a living hope" (εἰς ἐλπίδα ζῶσαν). This clause is the first of three that begin with εἰς ("to") in vv. 3–5. Here the preposition depicts motion toward a goal, "the end to which a thing reaches or extends" and thus indicates "measure or degree."[38] But it may be more than simply a goal. It may be a goal *realized* ("*and so we have a living hope*").[39] The target of the new birth is bringing the resulting child of God into "hope" (ἐλπίδα), and the "measure of degree" of that hope is nothing less than "living" (ζῶσαν). The new birth is first conceived in the heart of God ("His ... mercy") but is not complete until "hope" is alive in the heart of the new creature He has brought forth. Mercy is something that resides within God and is the point of genesis for the new birth, while hope is something that resides within the child of God (ἐν ὑμῖν, "in you" 3:15) and is the product of the new birth brought about by God in His mercy. Eternal life is truly a gift from God's heart to ours.

"Hope" (ἐλπίδα) means an expectation of something beyond oneself (εἰς θεόν, "in God" 1:21) and beyond one's immediate environment and circumstances. Just as "God ... raised [Jesus] from the dead and gave Him glory" (1:21) after He had died on our behalf, so we who live and die in faith may confidently expect that the new life God has given us will outlive this life and result in our resurrection from the dead. Indeed, it is precisely because our faith and hope rest in "God, who raised [Jesus] from the dead" that this expectation is "living" (ζῶσαν). The participle is present tense, underscoring the abiding and unending nature of the life in view. The participial form is used qualitatively to depict the nature of

---

38 Thayer, 1604.B.II.3.

39 Harris, 101.

the "hope" under consideration. Peter is fond of this verb, using it seven times in this letter (1:3, 23; 2:4, 5, 24; 4:5, 6, cf. Acts 9:41 and 10:42). The word group generally depicts the transcendent life of eternity in relationship with God (ζωή) as opposed to that which describes life on the horizontal, earthly plane (βίος). The "hope" is "living" in our experience now because it rests upon and is of the same substance as the resurrection life of Jesus, the life of eternity (1 Peter 1:21).

Little wonder then that the third prepositional phrase to qualify "who...has caused us to be born again" (ὁ...ἀναγεννήσας ἡμᾶς) is "through the resurrection of Jesus Christ from the dead" (δι' ἀναστάσεως Ἰησοῦ Χριστοῦ ἐκ νεκρῶν). Grammatically, this clause could qualify the participle "living" (ζῶσαν). While possible, it seems unlikely given that in verse 23, the same preposition (διά) is used with the only other occurrence of the verb ἀναγεννάω ("caused us to be born again"). It is best to see the preposition (δι') here pointing to "the instrumental cause" of the new birth.[40] The means by which new life becomes possible and actual for the children of God is "the resurrection of Jesus Christ from the dead." Here is another compound, this time a noun: ἀνά ("again") joined to στάσις ("existence/standing"). The prefixed preposition (ἀνά) was also used in "caused...to be born again": ἀνά ("again") and γεννάω ("be/become the parent of," "to give birth to," "bear," "beget"). The means by which we are "born *again*" is Jesus' being brought *again* to life through the "resurrection." While Peter only uses the noun one other time (1 Peter 3:21), he demonstrates an affinity to compounds beginning with ἀνά, employing them more than twenty times in his two letters. One wonders if this is due to the profound grace by which Peter came again to the favor and service of Jesus after his denials. Was Peter forever bent toward offering others the new start he had received from His Lord?

The NT uses the precise phrase ἐκ νεκρῶν ("from the dead") over forty times, all but one (Rom. 11:15) designating resurrection "from the dead." The plural substantive form of the adjective νεκρῶν "has in view all of

---

40 Thayer, 1286.A.III.2.

those who have died."[41] This is now the fourth time in the opening three verses that Peter has specifically named "Jesus Christ" (Ἰησοῦ Χριστοῦ). He signals early and often that his readers are to interpret the whole of their experience and hope Christologically.

Verse 3, then, sets before us the norm and reason (κατὰ), the goal and measure (εἰς), and the instrument and cause (διά) of the new birth. The sentence continues (through verse 12), and the fourth prepositional phrase waits in the next verse.

Verse 4 – to *obtain* an inheritance *which is* imperishable and undefiled and will not fade away, reserved in heaven for you,

Peter now adds the fourth prepositional phrase modifying "who…has caused us to be born again" (ὁ…ἀναγεννήσας ἡμᾶς) in verse 3. It is "to an inheritance" (εἰς κληρονομίαν). This is the second of three prepositional phrases beginning with εἰς ("to"). Here the preposition points to one of God's goals or purposes[42] for the new birth—the giving of "an inheritance" (κληρονομίαν) to His children.

The word κληρονομία ("inheritance") points most naturally to that which passes to an heir after another's death (Matt. 21:38; Mark 12:7; Luke 20:14), which might include property (Acts 7:5) or other goods. It describes what is promised or has already been possessed. The word echoes OT language related to the promise of the land of Canaan to Israel (e.g., Numb. 32:19; Deut. 2:12; 12:9; Josh. 11:23; Psa. 105:11). Each Israelite received an "inheritance" of land, kept in perpetuity. The Levites were exempt in this, for the Lord Himself was their inheritance (Numb. 18:20, 23). This promise of an inheritance drove the first generations of those brought out of Egypt to enter and possess the land of Canaan (e.g., Josh. 1:15; 11:23; 13:1–7). The hearts of future generations broke when taken from the land into exile. Though a remnant was physically restored to the

---

41 Dubis, 7.
42 Harris, 101.

land of promise they failed to realize all that their physical inheritance of land had held before them.

As the redemptive plan of God further unfolded, it became clear that the "inheritance" of God's people is God Himself (Psa. 16:5–6; 73:26; Lam. 3:24). Thus, in the NT, when all God's children are made "a kingdom and priests to our God" (Rev. 5:10; cf. 1 Peter 2:5, 9) it is no surprise to hear Peter emphasize the reality of God's New Covenant realized in an "inheritance" that is found in Christ Himself. The NT uses κληρονομία metaphorically of "transcendent salvation" itself (Gal. 3:18; Col. 3:24; Heb. 9:15).[43] The Holy Spirit, through His present indwelling presence and ministry, "is the guarantee of our inheritance" (Eph. 1:14, ESV; cf. 2 Cor. 1:22; 5:5). Through His ministry already we "have tasted...the powers of the age to come" (Heb. 6:5). The opening preposition (εἰς, "to") may hint at a present, partial enjoyment of the "inheritance."[44] Still, in a moment, Peter will describe the inheritance as "reserved in heaven for you" and thus seems to primarily view this salvation-as-"inheritance" as the full, eternal, heavenly realization of the salvation we already enjoy by faith on earth.[45]

Our "inheritance" is described by three verbal adjectives strung together in parallel with one another by two uses of the coordinating conjunction καὶ ("and...and"). Each of the adjectives uses the alpha-privative for negation; this makes for an alliterative effect that arrests the reader's attention (cf. 1 Peter 1:19; 2:15, 21; 3:17, 20).

Our inheritance is "imperishable" (ἄφθαρτον). The alpha-privative negates the verb φθείρω ("to ruin," "to corrupt," "to spoil") and the resulting adjective thus points to that which is "not corruptible," "not liable to pass away" or die.[46] It is a fundamental attribute of God's nature (Rom. 1:23; 1 Tim. 1:17). It is then the nature of that which He gives, whether the Gospel (1 Peter 1:23), the beauty of "a gentle and quiet spirit"

---

43   BDAG, 4271.

44   Grudem, 61.

45   DNTT, 2:300.

46   Rienecker, 744.

(1 Peter 3:4), believers' resurrection bodies (1 Cor. 15:52) or rewards (1 Cor. 9:25). Christ, having died and having been raised (1 Peter 1:3) in the power of an indestructible life (Heb. 7:16) is no longer liable to death. Salvation is sharing in Christ's life and thus is by nature "imperishable."

Our inheritance is "undefiled" (ἀμίαντον). The alpha-privative negates the verb μιαίνω ("to stain," "to defile") so that, in the NT, the resulting adjective is used only figuratively of that which is pure in a religious or moral sense.[47] It might apply to things such as the marriage bed (Heb. 13:4), religion (James 1:27) or, as in the present case, salvation itself. Our salvation/inheritance can be thus because Jesus our High Priest is "undefiled" by sin or imperfection (Heb. 7:26).

> **Ministry Maxim**
>
> The new birth triumphs over old threats.

Our inheritance "will not fade away" (ἀμάραντον). The root verb μαραίνω ("to quench," "to destroy") was used literally of plants "losing beauty and vitality," and thus they "fade away," dry up, or wither.[48] It is found in the NT only in James 1:11 where it describes a rich person who fades away and, in the end, possesses nothing. Here the adjective, as with the previous two, is negated by the alpha-privative. Our salvation/inheritance is not subject to processes or powers that would cause it to fail and come to nothing. Positively stated, our salvation/inheritance will be preserved and fulfilled in all its promise-filled glory. In other literature, the verb could be used for flowers whose blooms never wilt, droop, or fade in their beauty.[49] "'All flesh is like grass and all its glory like the flower of grass. The grass withers, and the flower falls, but the word of the Lord remains forever'" (1 Peter 1:24–25a). The inheritance will be fulfilled in a world that knows no decline, death, or disappointment.

Together the three adjectives "indicate that the inheritance is 'untouched by death,' 'unstained by evil,' 'unimpaired by time'; it is

---

47 BDAG, 407.
48 Friberg, 253.
49 BDAG, 373.

compounded of immortality, purity, and beauty."[50] Our inheritance "is in its *substance*, incorruptible: in *purity*, undefiled: in *beauty*, unfading."[51] Thus Jesus calls: "Do not store up for yourselves treasures on earth, where moth and rust destroy, and where thieves break in and steal. But store up for yourselves treasures in heaven, where neither moth nor rust destroys, and where thieves do not break in or steal; for where your treasure is, there your heart will be also" (Matt. 6:19–21). Trench is insightful when he says, "it is a remarkable testimony to the reign of sin, and therefore of imperfection, of decay, of death throughout this whole fallen world, that as often as we desire to set forth the glory, purity, and perfection of that other, higher world toward which we strive, we are almost inevitably compelled to do this by the aid of negatives; by the denying to that higher order of things the leading features and characteristics of this."[52]

Because of Israel's repeated willfulness and sin, the earthly land of Canaan, as Israel's inheritance, was subject to all three. It was the scene of bloody battles, the place of repeated spiritual adultery through idolatry, and again and again, faced drought and famine. The prophets had warned it would be so.

When Isaiah warned, "The earth will be completely laid waste and completely despoiled, for the LORD has spoken this word" (Isa. 24:3), the phrase "completely laid waste" is a doubling up of the cognate noun and root verb (φθορᾷ φθαρήσεται) Peter uses here for "imperishable" (ἄφθαρτον).[53] And he uses the cognate adjective in 1 Peter 1:18: "knowing that you were not redeemed with perishable [φθαρτοῖς] things like silver or gold from your futile way of life inherited from your forefathers." And again, "For you have been born again not of seed which is perishable [φθαρτῆς] but imperishable, that is, through the living and enduring word of God" (1:23).

---

50 Rienecker, 744.

51 Alford, 4:333.

52 Trench, 254.

53 Clowney, 48.

Through Ezekiel, God said, "I will also turn My face from them, and they will profane [μιανοῦσιν] My secret place; then robbers will enter and profane it" (Ezek. 7:22). He here used the verbal form of the root he used here to say our inheritance is "undefiled" (ἀμίαντον). God told His people, "I brought you into the fruitful land To eat its fruit and its good things. But you came and defiled [ἐμιάνατε] My land, And My inheritance you made an abomination" (Jer. 2:7).[54]

And finally, Peter's concern echoes warnings that sounded as far back as Job. The hopefulness of inheritance that "will not fade away" (ἀμάραντον) is set against a background where one of Job's friends warned concerning the wicked: "He will not escape from darkness; The flame will wither [μαράναι] his shoots, And by the breath of His mouth he will go away" (Job 15:30). Job himself later agreed, saying, "They are exalted a little while, then they are gone [ἐμαράνθη]; Moreover, they are brought low and like everything gathered up; Even like the heads of grain they are cut off" (Job 24:24).[55]

Indeed, the people of Israel eventually were removed by God from their "inheritance" by exile to Assyria and Babylon. During that time, the land became the stage for unspeakable acts of impurity (e.g., defilement of the Temple by Antiochus IV Epiphanies, Dan. 11:31; 12:11). And when God's agents of discipline came, they found "The land … like the garden of Eden before them" but would leave "a desolate wilderness behind them" (Joel 2:3).

How indescribably wonderful to possess in Christ "an inheritance which is imperishable and undefiled and will not fade away" and "treasures in heaven, where neither moth nor rust destroys, and where thieves do not break in or steal" (Matt. 6:20)!

Peter adds another descriptor of our inheritance, this time employing a participial phrase. The inheritance is "reserved in heaven for you" (τετηρημένην ἐν οὐρανοῖς εἰς ὑμᾶς). The verb means to watch over, to guard, to keep. The perfect tense points to its state of being held;

---

54 Ibid.

55 Ibid.

emphasizing that it has already been procured, presently exists, and is actively being preserved for us. The passive voice pictures God's active and personal vigilance in watching over our inheritance to present it to us in due time. Two prepositional phrases qualify the participle. The inheritance is being thus kept "in heaven" (ἐν οὐρανοῖς) and "for you" (εἰς ὑμᾶς). Note the interplay of the prepositions—it resides "in" (ἐν) the sphere of God's presence in "heaven," and it is being kept there "for" (εἰς) you. In the case of the former, "in heaven" (ἐν οὐρανοῖς) indicates that the inheritance is not simply the believer's arrival "in heaven," but that heaven is the vault of the inheritance's assured security.[56] In the case of the latter preposition, Peter could have easily used a simple dative but chose this more "graphic" means of pointing out that the inheritance is being guarded and kept "*with reference to* you."[57] It may underscore that "this inheritance was intended for his readers from the very beginning."[58] They did not simply stumble into the good fortune but were its object from the beginning. The plural pronoun (ὑμᾶς, "you") points to the common salvation all of God's people enjoy together in Christ. The pronoun will be enlarged upon in the next verse. The second-person plural form departs from the first-person plural forms of verses 3 and 4.[59] The second person plural will dominate the rest of the letter.

Verse 5 – who are protected by the power of God through faith for a salvation ready to be revealed in the last time.

Peter continues his lengthy sentence (vv.3–12) by enlarging upon the second person plural pronoun ὑμᾶς ("you") that closed out verse 4. By "you" (ὑμᾶς), Peter means specifically his readers and, by application, all believing persons who take up this letter. He does so now utilizing a participle used as a substantive (τοὺς ... φρουρουμένους, "*who* are protected,"

---

56 Hiebert, 62.
57 Vincent, 1:631; cf. Harris, 101; Robertson, *Word Pictures*, 6:82; Robertson, *Grammar*, 535.
58 Hiebert, 62.
59 Grudem, 62; Michaels, 22.

emphasis added) and which stands in apposition to the previous pronoun. The present tense underscores the continual, unceasing nature of the protection. The voice is a divine passive, indicating it is God who acts upon and for the benefit of His people. The verb could be used for the literal guarding of a city (2 Cor. 11:32). Moulton and Milligan explain the imagery as "a garrison keeping ward over a town."[60] It is a military word and would likely have carried strong and emotion-laden images in the minds of Peter's readers as they were scattered abroad through the Roman province of Asia Minor, facing at times the stern and even hostile arm of the Roman army. Though the persecution was scattered and localized, for many readers either facing actual persecution or hearing worrying reports of it, the sight of Roman legions would have inspired fear, not comfort. But here it is "the LORD of hosts," to use OT language, who personally protects His people, keeping them for His purposes and according to His promises.

Our "inheritance" is "reserved" for us in heaven (v.4) and we are being continuously "protected" here on earth to ensure our coming into that "inheritance" (v.5). "The inheritance is kept; the heirs are guarded."[61] Peter and Jude both use the verb τηρέω ("to keep," "to guard") similarly, describing fallen angels being kept for judgment (2 Peter 2:4; Jude 6) and judgment being held for them (2 Peter 2:17; Jude 13).[62] Here the two verbs (τετηρημένην, "reserved" and τοὺς ... φρουρουμένους, "who are protected") may be considered roughly synonymous in meaning.

Three prepositional phrases then qualify the participle. First, believers are being thus protected "by the power of God" (ἐν δυνάμει θεοῦ). The phrase is in the attributive position between the participle and its definite article, thus with the force of an attributive adjective.[63] The preposition ἐν ("by") is used instrumentally to describe the fundamental means by which believers "are protected." The word translated "power" (δυνάμει) speaks of the potentiality of the power under consideration. God (θεοῦ) possesses

---

60   Moulton and Milligan, 4595.
61   Bengel, quoted in Robertson, *Word Pictures*, 6:82.
62   Michaels, 22.
63   Hiebert, 63.

all power, and He is ready to deploy it on behalf of His own. Whatever threat may arise, God has at hand more than enough power to counter and overcome it.

Secondly, believers are kept by God "through faith" (διὰ πίστεως). The preposition (διὰ, "through") signals the secondary means by which believers enjoy this protection. God's power keeps the believer, but it happens as one rests in faith in His care. The noun "faith" (πίστεως) designates restful dependence or "firm commitment."[64] No object of the trust is stated, but clearly, such "faith" rests upon the "God" (θεοῦ) mentioned in the previous prepositional phrase (cf. also "through Him are believers [πιστοὺς] in God ... your faith [πίστιν] and hope are in God," 1:21). With one's faith resting upon God it is automatically set against the Evil One and all the resistance he may bring (5:8–9). Little surprise then that "faith" will be tested to prove it genuine (1:7). The outcome of such "faith" is the salvation of one's soul (1:9). God's protection does not become more certain by increased effort, whether emotionally, mentally, or spiritually. The believer's role is simply to rest. Ours is simply to repose upon God's keeping grace as held before us in the promise.

> **Ministry Maxim**
>
> In Jesus hope, inheritance, and salvation all coalesce as one abiding experience.

Thirdly, God's protection of His people is "for a salvation (εἰς σωτηρίαν). This phrase has the third of three consecutive uses of εἰς (vv.3, 4, 5). Together the three εἰς clauses signal that Peter is discussing one great grace from God, understood variously as a "living hope" (v.3), a secure "inheritance" (v.4), and a readied "salvation" (v.5).[65] Here the preposition (εἰς, "for") points to the purpose of God's protection of His people or to that goal being realized ("so acquire a salvation").[66] By "salvation" (σωτηρίαν) Peter means all that our Father has given us as our

---

64 BDAG, 5941.2.d.α.

65 Forbes, 19.

66 Harris, 101; contra Jobes who sees it as temporal, 88–89.

"inheritance" (v.4) in Christ. By His grace, believers are "heirs of God and fellow heirs with Christ" (Rom. 8:17). In living union with Christ by the Holy Spirit (2 Cor. 1:22; 5:5; Eph. 1:14), we already enjoy a foretaste of that full "salvation" that will be ours in the end. The "salvation" we now enjoy in union with Christ the prophets of old "made careful searches and inquiries" into (1 Peter 1:10). Though it is a present reality, it is something one "may grow up into" (2:2, ESV) more and more throughout this life. Yet "salvation" is something to be fully realized only in the future.

Peter tells us our salvation/inheritance is "ready to be revealed" (ἑτοίμην ἀποκαλυφθῆναι). This salvation/inheritance was given for a particular purpose. In conformity to that purpose, God has prepared or made it 'ready' (ἑτοίμην). Nothing more needs to be done for its unveiling. Jesus Christ finished the work "once for all" (Heb. 7:27; 9:12, 26; 10:10; Jude 3) during His first advent. Our salvation/inheritance has been fully, divinely put "in a state of readiness."[67] That for which it has been prepared is "to be revealed" (ἀποκαλυφθῆναι). In a literal sense, the verb means "*to uncover*" or to "*lay open what has been veiled or covered up*" and thus "*to disclose*" or "*make bare.*"[68] Jesus uses it to describe His second coming (Luke 17:30). Paul similarly uses the cognate noun of Jesus' return (1 Cor. 1:7; 2 Thess. 1:7) and uses the verb of many of the attending realities attached to it, such as the revealing of the antichrist (2 Thess. 2:3, 6, 3), the quality of each man's work in this life (1 Cor. 3:13), and glory for Christ's followers (Rom. 8:18). Peter similarly uses the noun of Jesus' return (1 Peter 1:7, 13) and both the noun (4:13) and the verb of the glory in which His people will share (5:1). The infinitive is used to express purpose.[69] By employing the aorist tense, Peter points to that moment in time when Jesus Christ will return in glory to bring all His redeemed into their "inheritance/salvation." The passive voice pictures God unveiling this "salvation" for those who are His heirs by grace.

---

67   Louw-Nida, 77.2.
68   Thayer, 62.
69   BDAG, 3192.a.

The revelation of Jesus and the salvation/inheritance He will bring for His people will take place within (ἐν, "in") the boundaries of what Peter designates "the last time" (καιρῷ ἐσχάτῳ). The word for "time" (καιρός) indicates an opportune or seasonal time; a "time" that is advantageous for the fulfillment of some purpose.[70] Note the singular form, "time" (cf. 1 Peter 4:17) rather than "times" (e.g., 1 Thess. 5:1; 1 Tim. 4:1; 2 Tim. 3:1). Here, it points to "a particular moment, not a duration of time … the end itself … the precise moment when [salvation] actually will be revealed."[71] It is thus to be accounted the "last" (ἐσχάτῳ) time, that moment beyond which this present age will not continue. Indeed, the word typically points to the last in a series of things beyond which nothing else will be found.[72]

Viewing the three prepositional phrases, then, we have set before us "the efficient cause" ("the power of God"), "the effective means" ("through faith"), and "the end and limit of" ("a salvation") our preservation by God.[73] Similarly, we have, "*By*, indicating the efficient cause; *through*, the secondary agency; *unto*, the result."[74]

> **Digging Deeper:**
> 1. How does Peter's insistence that new birth originates in divine initiative, not human action, challenge your understanding of evangelism? (v.3)
> 2. Why do you think Peter resorted to negative terms in describing the believer's inheritance? (v.4)
> 3. In dealing pastorally with troubled souls why is it important to emphasize along with Peter (v.5) the primary and the secondary means of one's spiritual security?

---

70 Thayer, 318.
71 Michaels, 15–16.
72 BDAG, 3168.2.b.
73 Alford, 4:334.
74 Vincent, 1:632.

Verse 6 – In this you greatly rejoice, even though now for a little while, if necessary, you have been distressed by various trials,

Though most English translations[75] begin a new sentence with verse 6, Peter's winding sentence (begun in v. 3) continues to make its way to its conclusion (v.12). The continuity of his thought is signaled by the relative pronoun ᾧ ("this"). The great challenge is identifying its antecedent.[76] The form can be read as either masculine or neuter. The nouns "hope" (ἐλπίδα, v.3), "inheritance" (κληρονομίαν, v.4), and "salvation" (σωτηρίαν, v.5) are all feminine nouns and are thus ruled out as possible antecedents.[77] If read as masculine, ᾧ ("this") could connect to "Christ" (Χριστοῦ) in verse 3 or "God" (θεοῦ) in verse 5, but they are probably too far removed from verse 6 to be considered as serious candidates. Also, reading ᾧ ("this") as masculine, its antecedent could be ἐν καιρῷ ἐσχάτῳ ("in the last time") at the end of verse 5. Peter did the same at the end of verse 4 and the beginning of verse 5 in picking up on the last item he had just mentioned to continue his complex sentence. But it is perhaps wisest to read the form as neuter and to see it as referring generally to all that is set forth in verses 3 through 5.

"In [ἐν] this" salvation to be entirely inherited at Christ's revelation, Peter says, "you greatly rejoice" (ἀγαλλιᾶσθε). The verb is stronger than the more frequently used χαίρειν. It may emphasize "the external expression and exuberant triumph" of the joy[78], and the NT ties it most precisely to the final acts of divine salvation at Jesus' return.[79] Does the preposition signal a temporal connection (i.e., "when you have arrived in the last time")? Or does it set forth a more anticipatory connection of the

---

75 As well as the Nestle-Aland[27] text.

76 This won't be the last time the combination ἐν ᾧ ("In this") raises questions regarding its antecedent (cf. 2:12; 3:16, 19; 4:4).

77 Abernathy, 21.

78 Alford, 4:335.

79 Mounce, 573.

object of one's joy (i.e., rejoicing now in anticipation of the last time)? Coupled with the present tense verb, it seems best to read it in the latter way, "an anticipatory joy experienced even now."[80] The middle voice "is best taken...to describe an emotional state."[81] The relative pronoun (ᾧ) with the preposition (ἐν) "connects w[ith] the situation described in what precedes *under which circumstances = under these circumstances*."[82] That is to say, the rejoicing under consideration takes place in the present partial installment of salvation and the anticipation of a fully revealed and realized salvation at Jesus' Coming.

Peter uses a participle to set forth a concession ("*even though...* you have been distressed" (λυπηθέντες; emphasis added). The verb means to be "sad, sorrowful, distressed."[83] It distinguishes the "mental effect of suffering."[84] The passive voice pictures the believer being acted upon by events and circumstances that create such pain. The aorist tense sees these experiences as occurring not continually but at specific times. They are not the abiding experience of the child of God, but they are real. The emotional scars are fresh. Being under God's protective hand (v.5) does not rule out all painful circumstances (v.6). We find as God's children on this side of Jesus' Second Coming that life is mingled regularly with rejoicing and sadness, joy, and pain. Such circumstances may come precisely because one is in the grip of God's grace. The wonder is not why we sorrow as God's children in this life but why we are privileged to own such joy.

> **Ministry Maxim**
>
> This side of Jesus' Second Coming the believer's life is mingled regularly with rejoicing and sadness, joy and pain.

---

80   Davids, 55; cf. Dubis,10; Forbes, 23; contra. Goppelt, 88–89 and Michaels, 27–29.
81   Ibid.
82   BDAG, 5391.1.k.γ.
83   Ibid., 4624.2.a.
84   Rienecker, 745; cf. Bigg, 103.

This distress is a present reality for Peter's first-century readers (ἄρτι, "now"), though, on the eternal continuum, it will be seen to have lasted only "for a little while" (ὀλίγον). Peter's only other use of the adverb ἄρτι ("now") is in verse 8 where he reminds them that they do not "now" see Jesus. They do not presently see their Savior, but they do presently experience distress because of bearing His name. Though there is true rejoicing in the present experience of faith, its full payout awaits the revelation of Jesus Christ.

The adjective (ὀλίγον, "for a little while") is used here as an adverb, also qualifying "you have been distressed" (λυπηθέντες).[85] It is so used again in 5:10, forming an inclusion for the letter that speaks so much to the pain and suffering of God's people. There Peter assures them that their suffering for Christ will last only "a little while" (cf. 3:20 and 5:12, where it is used as an adjective). Paul, too, can assure his fellow believers that what difficulties they experience on behalf of Christ are only "momentary, light affliction" and that they are "producing for us an eternal weight of glory far beyond all comparison" (2 Cor. 4:17; cf. Rom. 8:18).

The distress is caused "by various trials" (ἐν ποικίλοις πειρασμοῖς). The preposition ἐν ("by") sets forth "the state or condition in which anything is done or anyone exists, acts, suffers."[86] The noun (πειρασμοῖς, "trials") may depict either a temptation to fall into sin or a trial by which the true character and nature of something is to be revealed. In Peter, it always appears in this latter sense (1 Peter 4:12; 2 Peter 2:9). Indeed, this is Peter's first mention of the difficulties that his readers face on behalf of Christ, a theme that will dominate this letter. The adjective (ποικίλοις, "various") originally described that which is many-colored. It points to the variety and diversity of the "trials" that may befall a follower of Christ. Pain may present itself in a believer's life in many forms and from every conceivable angle. Peter uses it again in 4:10 to insist that just as varied as the trials of life may be, so is the multitude of ways God pours His grace into our lives.

---

85 Wallace, 293.
86 Thayer, 210; cf. BDAG, 2581.2.b.

But these sufferings are only permitted to fall upon a believer "if necessary" (εἰ δέον). The present participle (δέον, "necessary") couples with the conditional particle (εἰ, "if") to cast the condition as determined as to fulfillment—it is "necessary" in their present case that they suffer hardship for Christ's sake. The participle points to that which is fitting, needful, or proper. There may even be a hint of inevitability about the word.[87] The sovereign hand of God determines the occurrence of such suffering to fulfill His redemptive plan for humanity. God never tempts His own (James 1:13), but He does permit us to be tested (2 Cor. 12:7–10), that we might "come forth as gold" (Job 23:10). There is, then, nothing random or haphazard about that which befalls the child of God. All our experiences are determined by necessity, and necessity is measured against a goal—the revelation of God's glory in Jesus Christ to all creation.

For the believer, the grief caused by suffering is turned to joy because whatever befalls them is limited by time ("for a little while") and controlled in divine sovereignty ("if necessary").

> **Verse 7 – so that the proof of your faith, *being* more precious than gold which is perishable, even though tested by fire, may be found to result in praise and glory and honor at the revelation of Jesus Christ;**

Peter now provides the purpose (ἵνα, "so that" with the distantly separated subjunctive εὑρεθῇ, "may be found") of the "various trials" (v.6) in the midst of which his readers rejoice. Those hardships draw out "the proof of your faith" (τὸ δοκίμιον ὑμῶν τῆς πίστεως). The articular noun τὸ δοκίμιον ("the proof") is used only one other time in the NT. There too, it designates "the testing [τὸ δοκίμιον] of your faith" (James 1:3). It points to an effort "to learn the genuineness of something by examination and testing," and doing so "through actual use" of that which is being tested.[88] And thus, the "trials" expose the genuineness of the faith by means

---

87   Louw-Nida, 71.34.

88   Louw-Nida, 27.45.

of demanding its use. It may refer to the test itself or the process of the testing (as in James 1:3) or, as here, to the result of the testing ("the tested genuineness," ESV).[89] The definite article marks this as "the" definitive genuineness of one's faith. The hardships and trials of life are a believer's proving ground, and thus one can find purpose in the difficulties.

That which is being tested is "your faith" (ὑμῶν τῆς πίστεως). The genitive plural pronoun (ὑμῶν, "your") points to that common faith that is the unique possession of all true believers. The pronoun is placed before the articular noun, stressing the personal nature of this faith. The definite article marks this "faith" as that which is aroused by God's promises and is exercised upon them. The articular noun can be used to designate that objective body of truth that comprises the gospel (e.g., 1 Tim. 3:9; 4:1, 6), but here it points to the subjective, active, personal trust a believer rests upon that truth. Peter's readers possess this faith (1:5, 9, 21), but their hardships bring it into the realm of observation.

The "trials" are endurable because of the surpassing value of the certified "proof" of faith. It is "more precious than gold" (πολυτιμότερον χρυσίου). There is some debate as to whether that which is "more precious than gold" is "faith" itself or "the proof" of that faith drawn out for heaven and earth to witness. The adjective (πολυτιμότερον, "more precious than") is neuter in form, which links it to "the proof of" faith (also neuter in form) rather than "faith," which is feminine in form. But of course, "the proof" is only valuable because the thing being proven is treasured. The adjective is used only two other times in the NT, once to describe "the pearl of great price" (Matt. 13:46, KJV) and the other of the "very costly perfume" (John 12:3) with which Mary anointed Jesus before His passion. It is a compound made up of πολύς ("much," "many," "great") and τιμή ("price," "value"). It can mean "oppressively expensive," "rare and luxurious," and even "sumptuous."[90] It depicts that which is precious because of the high cost of procuring it.[91] Proving one's faith carries a high price tag.

---

89 Friberg, 119.

90 Spicq, 3:134.

91 Ibid.

The adjectival root (πολύς) injects a comparative ("more ... than") element into the imagery. Gold was the most highly valued precious metal of the ancient world, so in referring to it, Peter tops all the very best that this world has to offer by way of value.

Unlike faith, gold is something "which is perishable" (τοῦ ἀπολλυμένου). The verb is a compound comprised of ἀπό ("from") and λύω ("to loose/untie"). It is used frequently in the NT with a meaning ranging from "to destroy," "to perish," "to ruin," and "to lose."[92] As it does here, it can mean the destruction of something. Jude uses it of God's judgment of the wilderness generation of Israel (Jude 5, 11). In his second letter, Peter uses it of the judgment of everything outside of Noah's ark (2 Peter 3:6) as evidence of the coming eternal realities of hell (v.9). A fiery judgment is coming in which "the heavens will pass away with a roar and the elements will be destroyed with intense heat, and the earth and its works will be burned up" (v.10). Even the highest and best of earth's treasures will prove "perishable." Here the participial form functions as an attributive adjective ("is perishable").[93] The middle voice may point to the inherently transitory nature of gold. The present tense depicts this as abidingly so. No matter how the world may claw after gold, it remains something "which is perishable." Gold was never made to last forever. It will "be lost," "pass away," "be ruined."[94] Peter will say so again in 1 Peter 1:18. He will counsel women not to put their hope in "gold" but in that which is of "imperishable quality" (3:3–4). In all this Peter is reflecting the testimony of the Scriptures (Prov. 16:16), Jesus (Matt. 6:19–20), and the other apostles (1 Tim. 6:17; James 5:1–3).

But like gold, the value of faith remains "even though tested by fire" (διὰ πυρὸς δὲ δοκιμαζομένου). The conjunction δὲ is rendered as having concessive force ("even though"). Despite being "tested" (δοκιμαζομένου), the value remains. The verb has both the sense of testing and approving something or approving something after testing. The word was used in

---

92 BDAG, 958.

93 Wallace, 618.

94 BDAG., 958.1.b.β.

metallurgy to describe the scrutiny employed to test the genuineness of metal. As such, it was used to describe both the scrutiny and the resulting approval of the genuine article.[95] Here it means to "draw a conclusion about worth based on testing."[96] The means or instrument (διὰ, "by")[97] of this proving is "fire" (πυρὸς). The passive voice of the participle sees the gold as being acted upon by the heat of "fire," which serves to both refine and reveal its worth.

Time will render gold worthless, but testing will not. Time cannot diminish the value of faith, and testing

> **Ministry Maxim**
>
> Jesus' certification of one's faith is of higher value than any other thing in heaven or on earth.

only causes it to shine more brightly. Indeed, the "trials" of "faith" are necessary so that its value "may be found" (εὑρεθῇ). The noun (τὸ δοκίμιον, "the proof") and its verb (εὑρεθῇ, "may be found") are separated by the double-participial clause (πολυτιμότερον χρυσίου τοῦ ἀπολλυμένου διὰ πυρὸς δὲ δοκιμαζομένου, "being more precious than gold which is perishable, even though tested by fire"). The verb can mean something as simple as "happen upon" or "come across" and range from there to discovering something through study or examination.[98] Peter uses it here in this latter sense. The aorist tense aims "at the revelation of Jesus Christ" when all the trials and tests of this life stand behind us, and once and for all, their proven faith is "found" by God to be genuine and beyond compare in value. The passive voice pictures one's faith set out before all, awaiting the verdict of the Judge. The subjunctive mood coupled with ἵνα ("so that') sets forth the purpose of their rejoicing amid trials (v.6)—their proven faith as valuable above all things.

What is thus "found" after all the testing of one's faith? The testing is "to result in praise and glory and honor" (εἰς ἔπαινον καὶ δόξαν καὶ τιμὴν).

---

95 Thayer, 154.

96 BDAG, 2065.2.a.

97 Ibid., 1823.3.a; Gingrich, 1516.III.1; Thayer, 133.

98 Friberg, 180.

The preposition εἰς ("to result in") points to the outcome of the "testing." That is to say, the grade received after taking the test. The great grader registers three marks to examine the believer's faith.[99]

First, "praise" (ἔπαινον). The noun is used eleven times in the NT, and only by Paul and Peter. Paul used the term of what God deserves in view of His glory (Eph. 1:6, 12, 14; Phil. 1:11). But he also used it of praise which comes to us from God (Rom. 2:29; 1 Cor. 4:5) or others (Rom. 13:3; 2 Cor. 8:18). In the later sense both Paul (Rom. 13:3) and Peter (1 Peter 2:14) use it of praise that comes to law-abiding citizens from divinely appointed political leaders. It is used here of the positive affirmation and confirmation that comes from God for His child who has successfully come through the testing of faith in this life.

Added (καὶ, "and") to this is "glory" (δόξαν). The essence of δόξα ("glory") is a shining forth or brilliance (cf. the reference to Jesus' Transfiguration in 2 Peter 1:16–18 and to the "prophetic word" being like "a lamp shining in a dark place" and like the sun at the dawn of a new day in 1:19). Spicq calls it "the splendor of his majesty and the omnipotence of his interventions."[100] Strictly speaking, "glory" rightly belongs to God alone (Isa. 42:8; 48:11). Yet in the mystery of His grace, He has purposed that through Christ at His revelation, His children might share that "glory" with Him (Phil. 3:21; Col. 3:4). Indeed, at Jesus' return His children will find that that which has been "sown in dishonor" will be "raised in glory" (1 Cor. 15:43). Truly, our present suffering "is producing for us an eternal weight of glory far beyond all comparison" (2 Cor. 4:17).

To "praise" and "glory" is added (καὶ, "and") "honor" (τιμὴν). The word generally depicts the value ascribed or assigned to something or someone.

---

99 It seems clear that the "praise and glory and honor" is given by God at the time of Jesus' coming to His own who are shown to have genuine faith. But these are matters normally ascribed to God by His people. Thus, Michaels may be correct when he observes: "In honoring he is honored, in glorifying he receives glory, and in praising he is praised. There is a certain ambiguity in the three unmodified nouns, 'praise, glory, and honor,' with the hint of a double reference that cannot be overlooked. Yet the priority is clear. Peter has in mind *explicitly* the praise, glory, and honor that God bestows on his servants, and only implicitly the praise, glory, and honor that is his in the act of giving" (Michaels, 31).

100 Spicq, 1:370.

It is related to the root (τιμή, "price," "value") of the compound adjective previously rendered "more precious than" (πολυτιμότερον). Clearly, God deserves all "honor" (Rev. 4:9). His people must offer that to Him in glad worship (Rev. 4:11). To hear God the Father honor Jesus as His Son at the Transfiguration (2 Peter 1:17) was revealing concerning just who was among them. But we also find elsewhere that honor should be extended horizontally in human relationships: citizens are to honor their governing authorities (Rom. 13:7), husbands are to honor their wives (1 Peter 3:7), and Christians are to honor one another (Rom. 12:10). But here we discover that there is "honor" awaiting the faithful children of God, an honor which will come down to them from God Himself (cf. 1 Peter 2:7).

Technically it is to "the proof" (τὸ δοκίμιον) that this "praise and glory and honor" is ascribed. But "the proof" is the resulting evidence of "your faith" (ὑμῶν τῆς πίστεως). So ultimately, it becomes needlessly pedantic to distinguish between the faith, the proof/genuineness of the faith, and the one who has lived in that faith.

All this is to be realized "at the revelation of Jesus Christ" (ἐν ἀποκαλύψει Ἰησοῦ Χριστοῦ). The precise phrase will be used again in verse 13, where Peter will draw a logical (Διὸ, "Therefore") inference from all he says in this long sentence (vv.3–12). The noun is used again in 4:13, where it is called simply "the revelation (τῇ ἀποκαλύψει). It is the first word of the book of Revelation (Ἀποκάλυψις) which is for this reason often referred to as The Apocalypse. It is a compound made up of ἀπὸ ("from") and κάλυμμα ("a covering," "a veil"). Literally it means "a lying bare" or "making naked" (cf. 1 Sam. 20:30, LXX). But used figuratively, as it is here, it refers to an unveiling of something that heretofore has been unseen.[101] The word may imply that Jesus is present spiritually at this moment, though unseen (Matt. 28:20). His "revelation" will simply bring into the realm of sight what has already been true.[102] The preposition (ἐν, "at") is used as a marker of a period of time, in this case, the moment

---

101 Thayer, 62.

102 Hiebert, 69; Michaels, 32; Schreiner, 69; Stibbs, 78–79.

when "the revelation" takes place.¹⁰³ The genitive (Ἰησοῦ Χριστοῦ, "of Jesus Christ") is probably to be considered objective, that is to say, Jesus is that which is revealed. But at the unveiling of Jesus' Person at His glorious coming, all else will be disrobed in the light of His appearing. God the Father is the assumed agent of "the revelation."

All of creation holds its breath for the moment when Jesus Christ returns. Our "living hope" (v.3) is calibrated to this end. At that time, the fullness of our "inheritance" (v.4) will become ours in unmeasured experience. It is for this time that we have been given "a salvation ready to be revealed in the last time" (v.5). At that moment, the trials of faith in this life will be exposed as having been only "for a little while" (v.6). It is at that point that the proving heat of the "fire" of our "trials" of faith will have achieved the fullness of its refining and revealing processes and "the proof of your faith" will become obvious (v.7).

Verse 8 – and though you have not seen Him, you love Him, and though you do not see Him now, but believe in Him, you greatly rejoice with joy inexpressible and full of glory,

In the two relative clauses that now follow, both uses of the relative pronoun (ὅν, "Him") find their antecedent in "Jesus Christ" (v.7). Both are followed by participial forms of the common NT verb ὁράω ("to see"). Both participles have concessive force ("though"). The first is "you have not seen" (οὐκ ἰδόντες). The aorist tense indicates that they have never been fortunate enough to see Jesus physically. The second participle is "you do not see" (μὴ ὁρῶντες). The tense now is present, signifying that they do not presently have that privilege. This is underscored by the addition of the temporal adverb ἄρτι ("now"). It also implies that while "now" they do not see Jesus, they await the promised moment when they and all believers will behold Jesus gloriously coming again (1 John 3:2; Rev. 1:7).¹⁰⁴

---

103 BDAG, 2581.10.b.

104 Hiebert, 70.

Peter uses two different forms of negation with the participles. The first participle is negated by οὐκ ("not") which serves to mark a simple denial of their having ever seen Jesus. The second participle is negated by μὴ ("not"). Thayer notes the difference between the two: "οὐ denies the thing itself (or to speak technically, denies simply, absolutely, categorically, directly, objectively), but μή denies the thought of the thing, or the thing according to the judgment, opinion, will, purpose, preference, of someone."[105] Thus we can categorically eliminate any notion of Peter's readers ever having contact with Jesus when He ministered on earth and should affirm that they do not presently have that opportunity.

To each of these concessions, Peter adds a positive and actual action attributed to his readers. First, he says, "you love Him" (ἀγαπᾶτε). And this even though they have never at any time "seen Him." The present tense underscores the abiding, ongoing, continuing nature of their "love" for Jesus. Peter also says that despite not having current visual confirmation of Jesus, you "believe in Him" (εἰς ὃν ... πιστεύοντες). The NASU, as with most English translations, rightly reads εἰς ὃν ("in Him") with πιστεύοντες ("believe") rather than with ἀγαλλιᾶσθε ("you greatly rejoice").[106] The combination of εἰς with πιστεύω is original to the NT writers, not being found elsewhere in ancient Greek literature. John used the combination most extensively (thirty-six of the forty-five NT usages are found in Johannine literature).[107] It gives a sense of one believing "into" Jesus. This may sound strange to our ears but is used to signal an utter abandonment of oneself to Jesus, of the foundational, unalterable, and unshakable trust

> **Ministry Maxim**
>
> Those who suffer for Christ taste already the sweetness of the glory He will display at His return.

---

105 Thayer, 408; Robertson says, "Here οὐ ν harmonizes with the tense of ἰδόντες as an actual experience, while μὴ with ὁρῶντες is in accord with the concessive idea in contrast with πιστεύοντες" (*Grammar*, 1138).

106 Bigg, 105; BDAG, 5939.2.a.β; Forbes, 26; Grudem, 70; Harris, 236; Lenski, 41; Michaels, 33; Robertson, *Word Pictures*, 6:84; Stibbs, 79; Thayer, 511; contra Dubis, 15.

107 Harris, 236.

being placed in Him. The present tense of the verb again sets forth the ongoing nature of their faith in Jesus. Whereas ἀγαπᾶτε was an indicative, πιστεύοντες is in a participial form. We, like the original recipients of Peter's letter, have Jesus' own word of blessing spoken to Thomas upon his great confession: "Because you have seen Me, have you believed? Blessed are they who did not see, and yet believed" (John 20:29). Peter, having been forgiven and restored by Jesus, had professed his love for Jesus three times (John 21:15, 16, 17), but his was a love by sight. Lenski says, "Peter silently places himself below his readers. It is more praiseworthy to love as they do than to love as Peter does."[108]

Despite the potential setback of a lack of visual evidence for Jesus (set out by the concessive participles), believers nevertheless "love" and "believe in" Him. Neither love nor faith rests on a personal eyewitness experience, but upon the veracity of the record of Jesus' life, death, and resurrection (Rom. 10:17). Truly, "we walk by faith, not by sight" (2 Cor. 5:7).

In contrast (δὲ, "but") to the potential negatives, Peter says, "you greatly rejoice" (ἀγαλλιᾶσθε). The present tense again pictures the rejoicing as an abiding course of life.[109] The middle voice pictures the inward "consciousness of joyful pride expressed in the whole attitude."[110] The verb is the same one just used by Peter of his readers' joy over their protection for a salvation ready to be revealed at Jesus' coming (v.6). It will be theirs in fullest measure at the unveiled glory of Jesus at His return (4:13). It is used of rejoicing of Mary (Luke 1:47), Jesus in prayer to the Father (Luke 10:21), the crowds in response to John the Baptist (John 5:35), Abraham (John 8:56), David (Acts 2:26; cf. Psa. 16:9), the newly converted Philippian jailer (Acts 16:34), and the multitudes of the faithful at Jesus' glorious coming (Rev. 19:7). The verb depicts a stronger expression

---

108 Lenski, 41.

109 Some want to read the present tense as having a future reference, but it is their present rejoicing while in the midst of suffering to which Peter points. It is precisely this that makes their joy "inexpressible" and beyond human comprehension.

110 TDNT, 1:19.

of rejoicing that the simple and more frequently used χαίρειν. It may emphasize the outward and exuberant expression of the joy experienced.

They thus rejoice "with joy inexpressible" (χαρᾷ ἀνεκλαλήτῳ). Though the verb and noun are not cognates by form (ἀγαλλιάω and χαρά), they are cognates in meaning, the dative emphasizing the action of the verb.[111] The adjective ἀνεκλαλήτῳ ("inexpressible") is found only here in the New Testament.[112] It is a compound comprised of a prefix for negation (ἀν, "in-") and ἐκλαλέω ("to speak out," found in the NT only in Acts 23:22), itself a compound comprised of ἐκ ("out") and λαλέω ("to speak").[113] The resulting compound depicts that for which words are inadequate and is thus "unspeakable" (KJV). It "contains the sense of a divine mystery exceeding the powers of speech and thought."[114] Paul understood the conundrum of human speech being a feeble carrier for heavenly realities, for well after his heavenly encounter with Christ, he had to say he had "heard inexpressible words, which a man is not permitted to speak" (2 Cor. 12:4).

To this is added (καὶ, "and") "full of glory" (δεδοξασμένη). The participle is used to attribute this "glory" to the "joy" of which Peter speaks[115] and thus further intensifies the "joy" he describes.[116] The perfect tense pictures the "joy" being imbued with "glory" at a point in the past and that "joy" now abiding in that state of "glory." The participle (δεδοξασμένη, "full of glory") harkens back to δόξαν ("glory") in verse 7 and indicates this is the glory of heaven[117]; the glory that awaits them now fills their lives even as they suffer for Christ. The passive voice pictures God acting to

---

111 Wallace, 168–169.

112 Though cf. a similar construction in Romans 8:26: ἀλάλητος: "too deep for words."

113 Compare the similar compound: ἀν ("in-") + ἐκ ("out") + διηγέομαι ("to tell," to describe") in 2 Cor. 9:15: "Thanks be to God for His indescribable [ἀνεκδιηγήτῳ] gift!" And compare: ἀ ("not") + λαλητός ("spoken") in Rom. 8:26: "too deep for words."

114 Rienecker, 745.

115 Dubis, 16.

116 Forbes, 26.

117 Schreiner, 70.

bestow His "glory" upon their "joy." Indeed, Peter will soon tell them, "If you are reviled for the name of Christ, you are blessed, because the Spirit of glory and of God rests on you" (1 Peter 4:14). Hart well says, "Their faith enables them to pass beyond their present sufferings to the joy which belongs to the subsequent glories" and "… this joy is *glorified* because it is an earnest of the glory which shall be revealed."[118]

Verse 9 – obtaining as the outcome of your faith the salvation of your souls.

Peter's winding sentence continues with a participle (κομιζόμενοι, "obtaining") that modifies ἀγαλλιᾶσθε ("rejoice") in verse 8. The verb is used ten times in the NT, most of the time in an eschatological context related to receiving or obtaining as it does here (Matt. 25:27; 2 Cor. 5:10; Eph. 6:8; Col. 3:25; Heb. 10:36; 1 Peter 5:4). In the active voice it simply means "to bring" (Luke 7:37), but in the middle voice, as we have it here, it means to "carry off," "get (for oneself)" or "receive."[119] Thus the idea of "personal appropriation and enjoyment" is involved.[120] It is used of receiving wages, a return on an investment (Matt. 25:27), and the fulfillment of a promise (Heb. 10:36; 11:39). It is also used for recompense or reward—either positively (Eph. 6:8; 1 Peter 5:4) or negatively (Col. 3:25) or either (2 Cor. 5:10). The present tense indicates that already they are "obtaining… the salvation of [their] souls." The full consummation awaits Christ's return, but even now, they experience a foretaste of that fullness of deliverance. Some view the participle as pointing out the cause of their rejoicing (v.8) even while suffering.[121] Others believe the participle to be temporal in nature, indicating that they rejoice "when they obtain" the outcome of their faith at the time of Christ's

---

118 Hart, 45.

119 BDAG, 4337.3.

120 Stibbs, 80.

121 Bigg, 106; Schreiner, 70; cf. NET, NIV, NRSV.

return.¹²² This, however, misreads the present tense participle as having futuristic overtones. It seems better to view it as setting forth the circumstances which attend such present "rejoicing" (v.8).¹²³ As one experiences, while suffering, the inexplicable joy of God's salvation, one more and more lays hold of and experiences in greater depth the reality of that salvation which in its fullness awaits the revelation of Jesus Christ. Here the verb has the sense of receiving for oneself something as recompense, in this case, "the outcome of your faith" (τὸ τέλος τῆς πίστεως ὑμῶν). The noun translated "the outcome" (τὸ τέλος) points to the designed and ultimate end of a thing. Peter uses it elsewhere in this letter in ultimate terms: "The end [τὸ τέλος] of all things" (1 Peter 4:7) and "the outcome [τὸ τέλος] for those who do not obey the gospel of God" (4:17).¹²⁴ Here the presence of the definite article marks "the outcome" or ultimate goal toward which one's "faith" aims. The genitive pronoun (ὑμῶν, "your") is a subjective genitive, making it the "faith" (τῆς πίστεως) which you exercise or possess.¹²⁵ The one who remains faithful to Christ in suffering has every confidence of arriving safely at the designed goal of the faith they have placed in Him. The present joy that God gives to him despite his suffering is a foretaste of that ultimate salvation.

> **Ministry Maxim**
>
> Faith yields real-time benefits, but its full worth won't be seen until the last day.

Peter puts "the salvation of your souls" (σωτηρίαν ψυχῶν) in apposition to (as an explanation of) "the outcome of your faith" to state clearly that ultimate goal. In speaking of "your souls," he does not think of some

---

122 Forbes, 26–27; Michaels, 25, 35.

123 Grudem, 71–72; cf. ESV, NASU, NKJV.

124 Peter also uses it in another sense in 1 Peter 3:8, signaling a transition in his letter.

125 Wallace, 116; this assumes that ὑμῶν ("your") is genuine. Some manuscripts do not contain the pronoun, though its inclusion is well attested.

subset or part of an individual but uses "souls" in the Semitic sense of the person himself.[126]

> **Digging Deeper:**
> 1. How does knowledge that griefs that enter the believer's life are limited in time ("for a little while") and controlled in divine sovereignty ("if necessary") help in persevering under trial? (v.6)
> 2. Why isn't having faith enough; why does it have to be proven at the cost of great pain? (v.7)
> 3. How does present suffering grant a taste of the joy to be found fully at Jesus' Return? (v.8)
> 4. How does keeping "the outcome of your faith" in view during earthly troubles help sustain the believer? (v.9)

Verse 10 – As to this salvation, the prophets who prophesied of the grace that *would come* to you made careful searches and inquiries,

For the fourth time in this winding sentence, Peter has begun a new clause with a relative pronoun (cf. vv.6, 8 [twice]). He thus continues his thoughts on the topic of "the salvation of your souls" (v.9) by using the relative pronoun (ἧς, "this"), the gender and number agreeing with the noun there. But he also repeats the noun here, though changing the case to meet the need of this new clause (σωτηρίας, "salvation."). The preposition περὶ ("As to") with the genitive noun designates the object around which the action operates ("Concerning," ESV, NET, NIV, NRSV). It is "salvation" (σωτηρίας) that is at the heart of Peter's concern (vv.5, 9, 10).

That "salvation" which Peter and the other Apostles proclaim through Christ is the very same for which "the prophets" of old longed and of

---

126 TDNT, 9:652.

which they spoke. They are "the prophets who prophesied" (προφῆται οἱ ... προφητεύσαντες). The noun (προφῆται, "the prophets") and the articular participle used as a substantive (οἱ ... προφητεύσαντες, "who prophesied") doubles up the emphasis, stressing both their identity ("prophets") and their activity ("who prophesied"). The aorist tense of the participle is best read as Peter describing the work of the collective body of the prophets of the Old Testament era who anticipated the "salvation" provided by God. In their day, they spoke "of the grace that would come to you" (περὶ τῆς εἰς ὑμᾶς χάριτος). The preposition (περὶ, "about," ESV; "concerning," YLT) with the genitive noun indicates the center (τῆς ... χάριτος, "the grace") around which the activity ("prophesied") took place. The NLT translates the articular noun τῆς ... χάριτος ("the grace") as an adjective modifying "salvation," thus rendering it "this gracious salvation." It would be preferable to consider the two nouns as complementary in some way, perhaps "grace" being another way of saying "salvation." Between the noun and its definite article is the prepositional phrase εἰς ὑμᾶς ("that would come to you"). The preposition (εἰς) points to "the end" for which this "grace" has been extended[127] or, we might say, the destiny for which it was granted.[128] Verse 11 uses the same preposition about "the sufferings of [εἰς] Christ." The grace destined for us came at the high cost of "the sufferings" destined for Christ. This prepositional phrase will be echoed by τὰ εἰς Χριστὸν παθήματα ("the sufferings of Christ") in verse 11. The "grace" that is "yours" (ὑμᾶς, v.10) is precisely so because of the "sufferings" that were Christ's (v.11).

These prophets, by the Spirit, granted a foretasting of God's good "grace" in "salvation" through Jesus. In their day they "made careful searches and inquiries" (ἐξεζήτησαν καὶ ἐξηραύνησαν) as to it what it could mean. The first verb (ἐξεζήτησαν, "made careful searches") is a compound comprised of ἐκ ("out," "from,") and ζητέω ("to seek"). The

> **Ministry Maxim**
>
> We live in the most privileged moment of redemptive history.

---

127 BDAG, 2291.4.d.

128 Harris, 162.

preposition in compound intensifies the word ("*out* from a secret place, from all sides"[129]). The aorist tense and plural form emphasize the multiple individual acts of searching undertaken by "the prophets" throughout the ages. No one so searches unaided by God (Rom. 3:11). Such searching is at the heart of faith (Heb. 11:6). To this is added (καὶ, "and") the "inquiries" (ἐξηραύνησαν), a verb found only here in the NT. It, too, is a compound beginning with ἐκ ("out," "from"), which again serves to intensify the root verb (cf. the uncompounded form below in verse 11: ἐραυνῶντες, "seeking to know"). It thus means "to search out, search anxiously and diligently"[130] and "as making a thorough investigation *search out diligently, inquire carefully, seek intently.*"[131]

Verse 11 – seeking to know what person or time the Spirit of Christ within them was indicating as He predicted the sufferings of Christ and the glories to follow.

Peter continues his theme uninterrupted, saying the "prophets" were "seeking to know" (ἐραυνῶντες) more about this salvation. The participle enlarges upon what Peter meant by "careful searches and inquires" (v.10), the latter of which is a compounded form of this same verb. All their effort was in a quest, "seeking to know." The word describes an "attempt to learn something by careful investigation or searching"; that is to say, "to try to learn, to search, to try to find out, to seek information."[132] It underscores the thoroughness and care taken in the search.[133] The present tense depicts their ongoing efforts at discovery and discernment; again and again, their hearts sent them back to God in a desire to understand.

That which the prophets were "seeking to know" was "what person or time" (εἰς τίνα ἢ ποῖον καιρὸν) was to usher in this salvation. The

---

129 Thayer, 195.
130 Ibid., 222.
131 Friberg, 155.
132 Louw-Nida, 27.34.
133 BDAG, 3102.

preposition (εἰς) introduces that upon which their search centered. Two words set that forth. The first (τίνα) demands the reader make several decisions. Is this a masculine form that stands alone as a substantive ("what person") or a plural neuter that serves to qualify καιρὸν ("the time," NIV; "what time," NLT)? Is it an interrogative adjective ("what," KJV, NKJV, YLT) or an interrogative pronoun ("what person," NASU, ESV, NET, NRSV)? It is unlikely that it serves as an adjective because, in its over one thousand NT usages, it functions as an adjective in less than twenty.[134] Also, in every other occurrence in 1 Peter, it functions as a pronoun.[135] Thus we seem safe in assuming here, too, Peter intends us to read this as a pronoun. The prophets were diligently searching to discover the "person" who would usher in the salvation they had seen with prophetic insight from afar. A substantial case can be made, however, for viewing it as a plural neuter that, along with (ποῖον, "what"), qualifies καιρὸν ("time"). In such a case, the first (τίνα) questions what "time" this salvation would come and the second (ποῖον) the general "circumstances" (NIV) or "situation" (NLT) under which it would become reality. Some argue this makes for an awkward and unlikely redundancy, but the second broadens the first from a specific time to a general set of conditions. This sounds a good deal like the question the Disciples asked Jesus: "Tell us, when will these things be, and what will be the sign when all these things are going to be fulfilled?" (Mark 13:4).[136] The immediate context suggests nothing about the prophets questioning the "who" of God's salvation, but that the "when" was their great concern. Yet the matter is difficult. Commentators are divided. In the end, it seems more likely that Peter uses τίνα as a masculine substantive ("what person").[137] The prophets asked "what person" could bring about such a promised salvation.

Not only so, but they were also (ἢ, "or") seeking to know at "what time" (ποῖον καιρὸν) this salvation would become a reality. The interrogative

---

134 Jobes, 101–102.

135 Forbes, 30.

136 Hiebert, 76.

137 Cf. Grudem's excellent summary of the evidence, 78–80.

(ποῖον, "what") points to the class or kind of a thing.[138] In this case, the question is, what kind of "time" (καιρὸν) would be fit to bring forth the promised salvation and the Savior who would usher it in? What series of events? What combination of circumstances? What alignment of conditions?

The prophets' quest was the result of a divine work, for these questions were being prompted by "the Spirit of Christ within them" (τὸ ἐν αὐτοῖς πνεῦμα Χριστοῦ). We find here a mysterious combination of divine initiative ("the Spirit ... indicating as he predicted") and human effort ("made careful searches and inquiries ... seeking to know"), which Peter feels no compulsion to untangle for inquiring minds. The prophets wrote God's Word under the direction of God's Spirit (2 Peter 1:21), but the Spirit worked in such a way that it did not bypass their own human personalities and involvement. Mystery surrounds the process even while we confidently hold the completed Word of God in our hands.

By "the Spirit" (τὸ ... πνεῦμα), Peter clearly means the third person of the Trinity, who moved in the prophets to bring forth God's Word (2 Tim. 3:16; 2 Peter 1:21). He qualifies the expression in two ways. The first is by the genitive Χριστοῦ ("of Christ"). Should the genitive be understood as pointing to the Spirit, which is Christ's (Acts 16:7), or to the Spirit which Christ gives (John 15:26; 16:7)? While the latter is true, the former is the more likely point here. In referencing the giving of the Spirit after His ascension, Jesus said: "I will come to you" (John 14:18, 28; emphasis added). Paul can speak of "the Spirit of Jesus Christ" (Phil. 1:19) for it was "the Spirit of Jesus" that directed his course of life and ministry (Acts 16:7). It is "the Spirit of His Son" that God has set within each of His children (Gal. 4:6). Christ gives us of His very own Spirit. There is a great mystery in the makeup and function of the members of the Trinity. We must not confound the second person of the Trinity (God the Son)

> **Ministry Maxim**
>
> For Christ and for His followers, suffering always precedes glory.

---

138 BDAG, 6026.1.a.α.

and the third person of the Trinity (God the Spirit), yet Scripture itself tells us of their complete unity (along with God the Father). We must affirm what Scripture declares and tread carefully in our logical extensions of what God has spoken. But note that Christ, before His incarnation, was, by His Spirit, at work in the OT prophets. This clearly implies the preexistence of Christ.

The second qualification Peter makes regarding "the Spirit" employs the prepositional phrase (ἐν αὐτοῖς, "within them"). It sits in the attributive position, tucked between the noun and its definite article. This serves to emphasize the quality of "the Spirit" under consideration. Woodenly representing the original word order, it reads: "the in them Spirit." This was an internal work initiated by the very Spirit of Christ Himself. Christ by His Spirit provoked an inward, intense curiosity in OT prophets about Himself ("what person") as the coming Savior. This underscores the correctness of reading τίνα as a masculine pronoun ("what person"). It was "the Spirit of Christ" moving them to wonder about Christ Himself and the conditions of the time of His saving work.

The Spirit is described as undertaking two actions with the OT prophets. First, He was "indicating" (ἐδήλου) something to them. The verb is used in the LXX of God making known his name (Exod. 6:3), his purposes (33:12), his ways (1 Kings 8:36; 2 Chron. 6:27), his mysteries (Dan. 2:28–30), his covenant (Psa. 25:14), and his power (Jer. 16:21).[139] Out of the thirty-nine usages in the LXX, fourteen are found in Daniel 2, where it conveys the sense of expounding or interpreting something.[140] In the NT, it continued, at times, to be used for special revelations (1 Cor. 3:13), as it is here.[141] Peter will use the same verb again in 2 Peter 1:14 to say Christ "has made clear" (ἐδήλωσέν) to him that his death is imminent. Here the imperfect tense depicts this as an ongoing work of the Holy Spirit as He moved in the prophets. He gifted the prophets with a curiosity-burden that would not easily or quickly be satisfied.

---

139 NIDNTT, 3:316–317.

140 Ibid.

141 Reinecker, 771.

The second action the Holy Spirit undertook in the prophets of old is that he "predicted" (προμαρτυρόμενον) certain realities about Christ and the time in which He would procure and bring about our salvation. The verb occurs only here in the NT. It is a compound word comprised of πρό ("before") and μαρτύρομαι ("to testify/bear witness"). The resulting meaning is "to state with assurance what is to happen in the future."[142] The participial qualifies the previous verb (ἐδήλου, "indicating"). Most English translations understand it as indicating a temporal relationship: "when" (ESV, NET, NIV, NRSV, NLT), "as" (NASU). It could also point to how the Spirit was "indicating" what He was saying to them.[143] The present tense also underscores the ongoing ministry of the Spirit at work in the prophets.

The Holy Spirit was so working in the OT prophets that He was solemnly and assuredly telling them two things about the coming Messiah: "the sufferings of Christ and the glories to follow" (τὰ εἰς Χριστὸν παθήματα καὶ τὰς μετὰ ταῦτα δόξας).

Consider first "the sufferings of Christ" (τὰ εἰς Χριστὸν παθήματα). The articular noun (τὰ ... παθήματα, "the sufferings") points to the definite, predetermined sufferings appointed to Jesus by His Father (Acts 2:23; cf. 3:18; 26:22–23). It "was the will of the LORD to crush him," to "put him to grief" so that His "soul makes an offering for guilt" (Isa. 53:10, ESV). The plural form points to the multiplicity and variety of ways Jesus suffered—physically, yes, but spiritually, emotionally, mentally, relationally, and more—to take upon Himself the full effects of sin and remove it from His people forever. In the attributive position, between the noun and its definite article, is the prepositional phrase εἰς Χριστὸν ("of Christ"). Its position suggests the qualitative nature of "the sufferings." The preposition (εἰς) can serve in place of the genitive and this appears to be the position of the translators of the NASU ("of").[144] But here, it more likely acts as "a marker of an involved experiencer" and thus has the

---

142 Louw-Nida, 33.282.

143 Dubis, 19.

144 TDNT, 2:434.

sense of "to, toward, for."[145] This again underscores the divinely appointed nature of Jesus' sufferings. Therefore, it may be rendered "the sufferings *appointed for* Christ" (NET) or "the sufferings *destined for* Christ" (NRSV, emphases added).[146] These were not just any sufferings undertaken by just anyone, but divinely appointed, endured by God's appointed Savior, atoning, saving, redeeming "sufferings" unique among all the sufferings of time. See the same preposition used above in verse 10 regarding the grace of God destined to be ours because of the sufferings destined to be Christ's.

What sort of person could usher in this kind of salvation? Not a conquering military Messiah, but a *suffering* Messiah! Only a humble, meek, obedient, suffering Messiah could save His people from their true enemy; one who would bear the consequences of the sins of others, making atonement for them through His own death. As the resurrected Jesus unfolded the truth for his traveling companions on the road to Emmaus, he exhorted them, "O foolish men and slow of heart to believe in all that the prophets have spoken! Was it not necessary for the Christ to suffer these things and to enter into His glory?" (Luke 24:25–26). Later, to His disciples, he explained, "Thus it is written, that the Christ should suffer and on the third day rise from the dead" (Luke 24:46). It was Paul's pattern of ministry to give "evidence that the Christ had to suffer and rise again from the dead" (Acts 17:3). His gospel proclaimed that "Christ died for our sins according to the Scriptures" (1 Cor. 15:3). These "Scriptures" written by the prophets included portions such as Psalm 22, Isaiah 53, Zechariah 12:10 and 13:7, among others. It was to these that the religious leaders of Jesus' day were blind, finding in His sufferings proof that He could not possibly be the Messiah (Matt. 27:42).

Then also (καὶ, "and") the Holy Spirit revealed to the prophets something of "the glories to follow" (τὰς μετὰ ταῦτα δόξας). Once again, a prepositional phrase appears in the attributive position, stressing the qualitative nature of "the glories" under consideration. The plural form

---

145 Louw-Nida, 90.59.

146 Harris, 89.

(τὰς ... δόξας, "the glories") matches the plural form of "the sufferings." As "the sufferings" of Jesus extended to all levels of His life and body and to His suffering the full extent of sin's consequences on the cross, so "the glories" that His sufferings and death ushered in extend to the farthest reaches of God's glory and grace. Harris suggests a translation of "splendors," meaning "glorious events" or "majestic results."[147] He further says, "That concrete instances of δόξα are in mind is shown by the use of the article ... and of the plural."[148] Indeed, the plural form "suggests the multiplicity and the greatness of the glorious events following the passion: resurrection, appearances, ascension, session 'at the right hand of the Majesty on high' (Heb 1:3; 1 Pet 3:22)."[149] The prepositional phrase μετὰ ταῦτα ("to follow") might more literally be rendered "with these" and designate specifically "the sufferings of Christ." Peter intends to tell us that the glories that come to Christ follow upon His sufferings. There is to be no glory without suffering (cf. Rom. 8:18–25; 2 Cor. 4:17; Rev. 2:10–11).

Indeed, throughout this letter, Peter builds upon the themes of suffering and glory, the former always the precursor to the latter (1 Peter 4:13; 5:1, 6). To a persecuted people, feeling the weight of suffering, the hope of glory is held out as a reward. Peter personally beheld Christ's sufferings (1 Peter 5:1) and called Christ's people to share in them (4:13; 5:9). But he also reminds them that Christ's people are called to share in His glory (5:10). The faithfulness of His people will enable them to share in His glory now (4:14) and one day it will "result in praise and glory and honor at the revelation of Jesus Christ" (1:7). Peter was already "a partaker also of the glory that is to be revealed" (5:1). He calls his readers to so live now that they will, at Christ's coming, receive "the unfading crown of glory" (5:4).

We should not miss Peter's clear witness of the continuity of God's plan and purposes. What NT believers experience now and forever was clearly initiated and predicted by God, as the witness of His Spirit to the

---

147 Harris, 162.

148 Ibid.

149 Spicq, 1:371.

OT prophets testifies. God is "the King of ages" (1 Tim. 1:17, ESV) and rules and guides them to His appointed ends and to the fulfillment of His "eternal purpose," which "he has realized in Christ Jesus our Lord" (Eph. 3:11, ESV). Jesus "appeared once for all at the end of the ages to put away sin by the sacrifice of himself" (Heb. 9:26, ESV). He did this "to bring to light what is the administration of the mystery which for ages has been hidden in God who created all things" (Eph. 3:9), "the mystery which has been hidden from the past ages and generations, but has now been manifested to His saints" (Col. 1:26). Indeed, we are those upon whom "the end of the ages has come" (1 Cor. 10:11, ESV). The salvation and calling which are ours in Jesus Christ were "granted us in Christ Jesus from all eternity" (2 Tim. 1:9). It was "promised before the ages began" (Titus 1:2, ESV). Jesus and His salvation constitute "the consummation of the ages" (Heb. 9:26).

> **Verse 12 – It was revealed to them that they were not serving themselves, but you, in these things which now have been announced to you through those who preached the gospel to you by the Holy Spirit sent from heaven—things into which angels long to look.**

Peter now ends the lengthy and complex sentence begun back in verse 3. The dative plural relative pronoun οἷς ("to them") finds its antecedent in "the prophets" (προφῆται) in verse 10. While the prophets were never entirely satisfied in their impassioned pursuit of understanding "what person or time" was involved in the arrival of God's salvation (vv.10–11), "It was revealed" (ἀπεκαλύφθη) that they played an essential role in the bringing forth of that Savior and the salvation He would provide. The verb means to uncover, unveil, or pull back the cover that has kept something hidden. Peter uses the same word of the final salvation and glory to be revealed at Jesus' Second Coming (1 Peter 1:5; 5:1). Peter uses the noun form of "the revelation [ἀποκαλύψει] of Jesus Christ" (1:7, 13) and "of His glory" (4:13). The prophets were made to realize (note the passive voice of the verb) by the Holy Spirit that while they were not yet to meet God's Savior face to face on earth or immediately to enjoy the fullness of the "glories" that would follow His sufferings (v.11), they were in an essential linkage of events that would serve to bring these realities to pass.

The OT prophets were made to see "that they were not serving themselves, but you" (ὅτι οὐχ ἑαυτοῖς ὑμῖν δὲ διηκόνουν). The verb is pushed to the end of the clause (διηκόνουν, "they were ... serving"). The imperfect tense sets forth the ministry of the prophets as an ongoing, unfolding matter. Through all the trials (and in some cases martyrdom) of the prophets (cf. Matt. 23:37; Luke 11:47–51; 13:34; Acts 7:52; Rom. 11:3; Heb. 11:32–38), they were exercising faith in the fact that God was using them to serve subsequent generations of believers. As the author of Hebrews puts it, "having gained approval through their faith, [they] did not receive what was promised, because God had provided something better for us, so that apart from us they should not be made perfect" (Heb. 11:39–40). The negation (οὐχ, "not") "denies the thing itself (or to speak technically, denies simply, absolutely, categorically, directly, objectively)."[150] Their service had no innate, immediate benefit to "themselves" (ἑαυτοῖς). Rather (δὲ, "but") the prophets were serving "you" (ὑμῖν). Interestingly Peter does not say "us"[151] but "you." He found himself with his readers (and all other NT believers) in a position as a beneficiary of the ministry of the OT prophets. But perhaps because Peter had beheld "the person" of Jesus and understood more experientially the "time" and "circumstances" (NIV) of His suffering and death and had beheld Him in His glory, he was highlighting how believers who did not share these privileges relate to the ministry and messages of the prophets. He had the personal opportunity to behold that for which the prophets had longed. This put his readers more in company with the prophets than even himself.

The prophets thus served Peter's readers and all NT believers "in these things" (αὐτά). The neuter plural pronoun gathers up all aspects of

---

150 Thayer, 408.

151 Some manuscripts have ἡμῖν (dative plural; "us") and the KJV, NKJV, and YLT follow this, but the weight of evidence points to ὑμῖν (dative plural; "you") as being the original reading.

the message of "the gospel" that Peter's readers had heard, especially focusing on "the sufferings of Christ and the glories" that would be His because of those sufferings (v.11). These, Peter says, are those things "which now have been announced to you" (ἃ νῦν ἀνηγγέλη ὑμῖν). The temporal adverb νῦν ("now") sets the experience of Peter's readers in contrast to that of the OT prophets and their efforts long ago to perceive and peer into the matters of which they spoke (v.11). Peter's readers are living in the fulfillment of that which the prophets could only gaze into from afar with limited insight. Someone (Peter does not identify them personally, only the role they played) had "announced" (ἀνηγγέλη) the gospel to them. The aorist tense points to the gospel proclamation event among Peter's readers. The passive voice sees the subjects as acting upon the gospel by proclaiming it. The verb means "to provide information"¹⁵² and may insinuate doing so in "considerable detail."¹⁵³ If that is the case here this could be another way Peter may subtly be comparing the level of information and insight afforded his readers (and all NT believers) in comparison to the limited insight and information of the OT prophets. "The least disciple of Christ is in a better position to understand Old Testament revelation than the greatest prophet before Christ came."¹⁵⁴ Ponder that level of grace and privilege.

> **Ministry Maxim**
>
> The preacher's confidence is in the enabling of the Spirit who inspired the Scriptures he preaches.

This announcement took place "through those who preached to gospel to you" (διὰ τῶν εὐαγγελισαμένων ὑμᾶς). The preposition (διὰ, "through") points to the agency by which the announcement came. At the human level, that was "those who preached the gospel to you." The participle is used substantively ("*those who* preached the gospel," emphasis added). Peter does not identify who these evangelists were. They

---

152 BDAG, 450.2.

153 Louw-Nida, 33.197.

154 Clowney, 59–60.

should not be limited to the apostles because Peter does not so limit them. Yet they may have included the apostles. The aorist tense pictures the event of proclamation and that their experience turns on its definitive nature. The means by which ([ἐν], "by")[155] this proclamation came was "the Holy Spirit sent from heaven" (πνεύματι ἁγίῳ ἀποσταλέντι ἀπ' οὐρανοῦ). Here Peter demonstrates the flexibility of his terms: He who was just called "the Spirit of Christ" (v.11) is now identified simply as "the Holy Spirit." The Spirit that was at work in the OT prophets as they searched, inquired, and longed to discern "the person or time" of God's salvation (v.11) is the same Spirit that moved the servants of God in his day to proclaim the gospel of Jesus Christ to his readers. Indeed, He was "sent from heaven" (ἀποσταλέντι ἀπ' οὐρανοῦ) for both ministries, but particularly in a new and unique way upon the followers of Jesus after His ascension to the Father's right hand (John 7:39; 16:7; Acts 2:33). The participle (ἀποσταλέντι, "sent") is attributive[156] and the passive voice signals that God the Father is the author of the gospel and how it has come to man—all is grace. The aorist passive may point to the outpouring of the Holy Spirit at Pentecost (Acts 2), an event in which Peter participated. The fact that the Spirit is described as sent "from heaven" (ἀπ' οὐρανοῦ) is another effort to highlight this as a gracious act of God. It may further hint at the unique way the Spirit operates in and through His people in the NT era compared to the way He came upon the prophets in the OT era, even while underscoring the continuity of God's purpose throughout.

The same Spirit who inspired the prophets of old fills and works through the one expounding those Scriptures in witness to the unbelieving today. In this, we are emboldened, not because of self-confidence, but because of the promise of the Spirit's enabling. This is also a

---

155 The dative preposition ἐν does not occur in some significant manuscripts. Doubt as to whether it is original has led to the brackets being placed around it in our text. Whether or not it is original the dative case of "the Holy Spirit" (πνεύματι ἁγίῳ) assures the point that the means (Dubis, 21; Forbes, 32) of the proclamation of the gospel to Peter's readers was the Holy Spirit (Michaels, 38).

156 Dubis, 22.

reminder that we not only may preach the gospel from the text of the OT but that we should do so. They "are able to give you the wisdom that leads to salvation through faith which is in Christ Jesus" (2 Tim. 3:15). In Peter's words, a Christocentric hermeneutic with the OT is not only authorized but demanded (Rom. 15:4; 1 Cor. 10:11; Luke 24:25–27).

We live in the midst of "things into which angels long to look" (εἰς ἃ ἐπιθυμοῦσιν ἄγγελοι παρακύψαι), which highlights the honor of the NT believers' position in God's redemptive plan. The relative pronoun in the neuter plural form (ἃ, "things") finds its point of reference in the previous personal pronoun also in the neuter plural form (αὐτά, "these things"), which in turn gathered up in itself the message of the gospel, particularly focusing upon the sufferings of Jesus and the glories that would come to Him because of those sufferings. These saving realities are matters "into which" (εἰς) "angels long to look." The preposition εἰς ("into") "denotes entry" being attempted or made.[157] The "angels" (ἄγγελοι) of God, who have resided in His glorious presence since their creation and have had the closest access to His throne and observed His actions from creation (Job 38:7) down through time, are described as seeking entry "into" the wonders of God's grace extended in the gospel. They who have beheld God in His glory, who presumably have observed Father, Son, and Holy Spirit in their deliberations and actions and delighted over each one, look upon the gracious salvation we are privileged to enjoy and wonder over it, gasp over it, marvel because of it. That God the Son would become human, live on the earth He created, among the rebellious and sinful race of humans who have spurned Him, suffering at their hands, and even dying in their place, bearing their sins that He might redeem them and reconcile them to His Father is simply more than the angels can enter "into" and understand. Press as they might in their exalted nature to comprehend such love, such grace is simply more than even angels can quite attain.

The inward pressure they feel (ἐπιθυμοῦσιν, "long") throbs within them, a consuming desire that refuses to be extinguished, thrusting

---

157 Harris, 83.

them ever forward (present tense) despite their repeated inability "to look" (παρακύψαι) with understanding and insight upon such divine grace and love. The verb means "to stretch forward the head" as through a window[158] or door. The angels, who are not subject to redemption, yearn to understand this grace in which we live (Luke 15:7, 10; 1 Cor. 4:9; Eph. 3:10; 1 Tim. 3:16; Heb. 2:16). The aorist tense of the infinitive (παρακύψαι, "to look") contrasts with the present tense of the verb for which it serves as the object (ἐπιθυμοῦσιν, "long"). They continuously "long" after penetrating insight and comprehension of the kind of love God has demonstrated to us in "this salvation" (v.10) procured for us through the death and resurrection of His Son (v.11). They wondered over it when God the Spirit spoke of it through the prophets of the OT (vv.10–11). They marvel over it still as the ambassadors of Christ speak it today and people find life anew through the gospel (v.12).

Something of the angels' inextinguishable quest is evident even in Peter's lengthy and complex sentence, which now comes to an end (vv.3–12). The subject is God's great mercy and grace that He should, through His own Son's sufferings, death, and resurrection, redeem us and grant us an eternal and untouchable inheritance as His children. But Peter, as it were, gets lost in wonder, love, and praise as he seeks to hold it before his readers. The sentence rushes along, the linkage complex from one clause to the next, the syntax intense, but the worship pervasive. Apostles (through Peter), prophets, evangelists, and angels together call us to shout, "Oh what privilege is ours in Christ!" In a similar emphasis, Jesus said to His disciples, "Blessed are your eyes, because they see; and your ears, because they hear. For truly I say to you that many prophets and righteous men desired to see what you see, and did not see it, and to hear what you hear, and did not hear it" (Matt. 13:16–17; cf. Luke 10:23–24).

---

158 "… the windows of heaven from which angels peer (cf. 1 *En.* 9:1)," (Dubis, 22).

> **Digging Deeper:**
> 1. The hunger and curiosity of the OT prophets (v.10) remind us that we could not live at a better time in history. How does this make you think differently about things going on around you at this moment?
> 2. Can you explain how Christ's experience with suffering and glory (v.11) helps us with our present sufferings?
> 3. If you could audibly hear the urging of the prophets of old and the angels of heaven as you open God's Word today, how would it change your reading and study? (v.12)

Verse 13 – Therefore, prepare your minds for action, keep sober *in spirit*, fix your hope completely on the grace to be brought to you at the revelation of Jesus Christ.

In light of the surpassing grace of God to us in Christ (vv.3–12), Peter calls his readers to some logical (Διὸ, "Therefore") moral implications. The breathtaking panorama of the glories of gospel grace laid the foundation for the rest of the epistle to present gospel responsibilities, particularly for a people suffering precisely because of that gospel. The indicatives of doctrine do not entirely disappear in the remainder of the epistle, but the clear emphasis from this point on will be upon the duties of grace received. Praise for God's grace in Christ (vv.3–12) sets us up to rightly understand the practice such grace demands. Most immediately in the remainder of this first chapter, five commands follow (one here in verse 13 and four more in verses 15, 17, 22, and 2:2) along with a prohibition (v.14). In addition to these commands, there are several other forms which may carry imperatival force.

The primary verb is the command "fix your hope" (ἐλπίσατε). As Peter begins his ethical exhortations, he returns immediately to the object of his attention in the previous description of God's saving grace (ἐλπίδα, "hope," v.3, the noun form of our verb). This will serve then as an inclusion for this subsection of the letter (cf. ἐλπίδα, v.21). Here, the aorist imperative marks the first command given in this epistle that sets forth many of them. Peter demands the action be undertaken with urgency, immediacy and decisively—thus the rendering "*fix* your hope" (emphasis added).[159] While the verb appears over thirty times in the NT, this is the only occurrence in the imperative mood. This one is to undertake "perfectly" (τελείως, YLT). The adverb means "fully," "completely," or "altogether."[160] The adverb is rightly connected to the imperative (ἐλπίσατε, "fix your hope") rather than the participle νήφοντες ("keep sober").[161] The KJV renders it "to the end"; the ESV, NKJV, and RSV translate it "fully"; the NASU and NET render it "completely"; while others do not translate it at all (NIV). This also is the only occurrence of this adverb in the NT. This doubly unique phrase underscores the challenging plight of Peter's original readers. They are in difficult straits because of their faith; thus the apostle calls upon them to confirm, strengthen, and anchor their hope beyond this world.

Two participial phrases qualify the main verb. They may be taken as expressing attendant circumstances (that which accompanies a fixed hope), manner/instrumental (the way in which one fixes one's hope) or means (the way by which one fixes one's hope). The effect on the meaning between these is sometimes marginal, and it appears that Peter's point is not significantly changed by which we choose. We should also consider that the participles pick up an imperatival force from the main verb (cf. KJV, NASU, NRSV, NLT, NKJV). The first is an aorist indicating a decisive action; the second is a present tense calling for an abiding state.[162]

---

159 In 1 Peter the number of present imperatives (10) is outpaced by the number of aorist imperatives (25), perhaps a sign of the urgency of Peter's instructions to those suffering for their faith in Christ. But we are wise to heed the counsel of Forbes when he says, "it is important not to force all of the aorist imperatives in this epistle into a single paradigm" (Forbes, 4–6).

160 Friberg, 377.

161 Dubis, 23; Forbes, 37; Goppelt, 107; Hiebert, 91–92; Jobes, 109; Kelly, 67; Lenski, 52; Schreiner, 77; contra Bigg, 112; Marshall, 51; Michaels, 55.

162 Lenski, 52; One need not agree with Lenski when he argues that the tenses determine the order: "in a sober state of mind the readers are to make up their mind." The tenses do not seem to be so decisive. It is as easy to picture Peter insisting that from a decisive decision an abiding state is to arise (cf. Grudem, 82; Jobes, 110–111).

The first of these is "prepare your minds" (ἀναζωσάμενοι τὰς ὀσφύας τῆς διανοίας ὑμῶν). A more literal translation would be, "having girded up the loins of your mind" (YLT). The verb is a compound word comprised of ἀνά ("up") and ζώννυμι ("to gird"), the prefixed preposition giving direction to the movement. In the ancient Middle East, a man would gather the flowing lengths of his robes, pulling them up (to "the loins," τὰς ὀσφύας, where his belt would be) and tucking them into his belt for work, battle, or travel (cf. Exod. 12:11; 1 Kings 18:46; 2 Kings 9:1; Job 40:7; Jer. 1:17). Peter may be reflecting Jesus' imagery in Luke 12:35. This is an apt metaphor for those Peter depicts as "aliens" (1:1; 2:11) sojourning through the foreign land of this world toward their homeland in heaven.[163] That Peter uses the word figuratively is clear in that Peter refers to "the loins of your minds" (τῆς διανοίας ὑμῶν, emphasis added). The noun is a compound composed of διά

> **Ministry Maxim**
>
> A hope anchored in the promise of future grace becomes faithfulness in the present.

("through") and νως ("mind").[164] Thus the emphasis is upon "think through" and depicts a "meditative and reflective mind thinking through a matter."[165] One's "mind" is to be dedicated, along with the whole of one's being, to loving God (Matt. 22:37; Mark 12:30; Luke 10:27). It is the place God longs to place His Law (Heb. 8:10; 10:16). Yet in rebellion against God humanity has become "darkened in their understanding [τῇ διανοίᾳ]" (Eph. 4:18) and "indulging the desires of the flesh and of the mind [τῶν διανοιῶν]" (Eph. 2:3). The word here describes a kind or way of thinking. It is descriptive of one's disposition[166] or the way one thinks. It is, then, "the psychological faculty of understanding, reasoning, thinking, and deciding."[167] In the LXX διάνοια most often is used where the

---

163 Vincent, 1:636.

164 Thayer, 140.

165 Hiebert, 138.

166 BDAG, 1887.2.

167 Louw-Nida, 26.14.

Hebrew has לֵב ("heart"). The noun is in the singular form, despite the plural rendering in English ("minds"). While Peter addresses many believers across broad regions (1:1–2) and specifically denotes them here with the plural pronoun (ὑμῶν, "your"), the "mind" (τὴν...διάνοιαν) he calls them to is singular, underscoring and reinforcing at one and the same time the singularity of Christ as their life and their unity in Him. The aorist tense of the verb depicts the definitive nature of the action. The middle voice pictures the act as being taken upon oneself. The participial form sets out how one's hope may be fixed. Several English translations attribute imperatival force to the participle (e.g., KJV, NASB, NASU, NET, NRSV, NLT), which, if we are careful to retain its support role to the main imperative ("fix your hope"), is not unjustified.

The second action to be undertaken to "fix your hope" is "keep sober" (νήφοντες). Half of the six appearances of the verb in the NT are found here in 1 Peter (1:13; 4:7; 5:8; cf. 1 Thess. 5:6, 8; 2 Tim. 4:5). The literal sense of the word is to be free from intoxicants. But the NT usages are all figurative, meaning "be free fr[om] every form of mental and spiritual 'drunkenness', fr[om] excess, passion, rashness, confusion, etc." and thus to be "be well-balanced" and "self-controlled."[168] Therefore, the translators added "in spirit." It denotes "the alertness required in the light of an imminent parousia."[169] Schreiner aptly notes, "There is a way of living that becomes dull to the reality of God, that is anesthetized by the attractions of this world. When people are lulled into such drowsiness, they lose sight of Christ's future revelation of himself and concentrate only on fulfilling their earthly desires."[170] The present tense underscores the perpetual need and vigilant watchfulness demanded. It stands in contrast to the aorist tense of the previous participle. The call is to take definitive action to "prepare your minds," settling and establishing them once for all and then to vigilantly, continuously "keep sober" in one's watch for all threats.

---

168 BDAG, 5098.

169 NIDNTTE, 3:391.

170 Schreiner, 79.

Hope is only as good as the object upon (ἐπὶ, "on") which it rests.¹⁷¹ The only sure foundation for hope is "the grace to be brought to you at the revelation of Jesus Christ" (τὴν φερομένην ὑμῖν χάριν ἐν ἀποκαλύψει Ἰησοῦ Χριστοῦ). The believer's only hope is the "grace" (χάριν) of God. Grace is a present reality for the believer (1 Peter 1:2; 2:19, 20; 4:10; 5:5, 12), though it is "varied" (4:10, ESV) in its measure and form in each of our lives. But we serve "the God of all grace" (5:10) who has given us present grace to sustain us (2:19, 20) and motivate us to hold out for the fullness of His grace to be brought to us at Christ's Coming. We are thus heirs (3:7) of an even fuller, more pervasive grace that is yet "to be brought" (τὴν φερομένην) to us. The participle is thrust forward for emphasis—this "grace" is not yet fully present, but its fullness is guaranteed to God's people. This requires waiting in faith for its sure arrival. The present tense may underscore the current, even if partial, reality of this grace and its current movement toward Peter's readers and its continual progress toward its certain fulfillment.¹⁷² Alternatively, some read the present tense as a future.¹⁷³ The passive voice is a divine passive, indicating that it is God who is moving this "grace" along to its arrival. God, who rules all things (5:11), providentially is controlling all things so that they make steady progress toward the day of Jesus' Coming (ἐν ἀποκαλύψει Ἰησοῦ Χριστοῦ, "at the revelation of Jesus Christ"). The precise phrase was used above in verse 7; see our comments there. Peter repeatedly held before his suffering readers the glory, praise, honor, and grace that every believer will share when Jesus is unveiled to all of creation (1:7, 13; 4:13).

In all this, Peter seems to be intentionally calling upon the imagery of the Hebrew people setting out in pilgrimage after God following the redemption of the Passover. The Hebrews were to eat the Passover meal "with your loins girded, your sandals on your feet, and your staff in your hand" (Exod. 12:11). If so, Peter may continue to build on this parallelism with the experience of the ancient people of God as he depicts his

---

171 Robertson suggests the preposition here may "express one's emotions" (*Grammar*, 602).
172 Lenski, 53.
173 Michaels, 56; Schreiner, 78.

readers as redeemed by the blood of the lamb who is without spot or blemish (vv.18–19) and as setting forth on pilgrimage (v.17), "having girded up the loins of [their] mind" (v.13, YLT).[174]

> **Digging Deeper:**
> 1. Describe someone you know who seems to have a mind prepared for action. What makes them so? What have they done to be considered so?
> 2. Likewise, describe someone whom you consider to be "sober in spirit."
> 3. In practical terms how does someone "fix" their hope?

Verse 14 – As obedient children, do not be conformed to the former lusts *which were yours* in your ignorance,

The dam having been opened (v.13), the imperatives begin now to come one upon another. The sentence Peter begins here runs through verse 16, with the main verb, an imperative, being found in verse 15 (ἅγιοι ... γενήθητε, "be holy"). These imperatives fall upon Peter's readers, and their response to them arises from them "As obedient children" (ὡς τέκνα ὑπακοῆς). The comparative particle (ὡς, "As") typically introduces a metaphorical comparison. But here, it marks the perspective from which Peter's readers view themselves, emphasizing the quality inherent in their role as "obedient children."[175]

The noun "children" (τέκνα) is neuter and thus refers to both males and females. Though he does not state it definitively here, it is clear from the context that his readers are considered "children" in relationship to God their Father (1 Peter 1:2, 17). Adam was designated the son of God

---

174 TDNT, 5:901.

175 BDAG, 8075.3.a.α.

(Luke 3:38). Israel was designated God's firstborn son (Exod. 4:22; Isa. 1:2–3; 43:6–7; 49:14–15; 54:1–3; Jer. 3:19–20; Hosea 1:10). David was called God's son (2 Sam. 7:14). The prophets promised a son of David who would reign over God's people (e.g., Isa. 7:13–14; 9:1–7; Jer. 23:5–6; Ezek. 34:23–24; 37:24–28; Zech. 12:7–10). This came to full bloom in the NT, where Jesus is both the Son of David (Matt. 1:1–17; 15:22; 20:30–31; 21:9) and the Son of God (Matt. 3:17; Mark. 15:39; Luke 4:41; John 1:34; Rom. 1:4; Heb. 4:14). Those who belong by grace through faith to Jesus are likewise children of God. Jesus called His disciples to live uprightly before the unbelieving world "so that you may be sons of your Father who is in heaven" (Matt. 5:45). In this case, Peter designates them "obedient" (ὑπακοῆς) children. It is possible to be the opposite, "sons of disobedience" (Eph. 2:2; 5:6; Col. 3:6), "children of the devil" (1 John 3:10), and thus "accursed children" (2 Peter 2:14), "children of wrath" (Eph. 2:3). But God calls His children to be "obedient" to their Father. It is to this end that God chose them (εἰς ὑπακοὴν, "to obey" 1 Peter 1:2). The noun arose from the verb ὑπακούω, which properly was used "of one who on a knock at the door comes to listen who it is."[176] It came then, by popular usage, to describe one who hearkened to the voice of another, or, that is, listened to and obeyed what they were told—in this case, their Father and His Son, Jesus Christ (v.2). Obedience is measured by its response to and conformity to "the truth" (v.22) as our Father has made it clear through His Word. The genitive form of the noun (ὑπακοῆς, lit., "children *of obedience*") is attributive, describing their nature as children in relation to the Father.[177] It expressed "an essential property, a mode of being. We could say that the neophytes are obedient by nature, devoted to

> **Ministry Maxim**
>
> The fabric of a child of God's being is woven with threads of obedience and submission to the Father.

---

176 Thayer, 637–638.

177 Robertson, *Grammar*, 496–497.

obeying God, made to obey."[178] Believers "are those whose mother is obedience, in whom is the spirit of obedience."[179] English translations render the expression "obedient children" rather than a more literal "children of obedience." The difference, however, is profound. "Obedient children" focuses on one's behavior, while "children of obedience" points to one's nature.[180] The call to holiness (vv. 14–15) resonates with the believer at the core of his being as a new creature in Christ. He who lays claim to the hope of Christ (v.13) hears and heeds Christ's call to holiness (v.15).

To be "children of God" is to bear the Father's likeness and share His mind, mission, values, and perspective. Peter thus instructs his readers: "do not be conformed" (μὴ συσχηματιζόμενοι) to other influences and powers. The negation (μὴ, "not") combines with the adversative ἀλλὰ ("but") in verse 15 to set forth a stark and powerful contrast in responsibilities and resulting actions. That which they are not to do is "be conformed" (συσχηματιζόμενοι). The root of the compound word is cognate to the noun σχῆμα ("scheme"), which is used significantly in the description of Christ's incarnation in Philippians 2. There it is contrasted with μορφή ("form," vv.6–7) and ὁμοίωμα ("likeness," v.7). There, σχῆμα is rendered "appearance" (v.8). The noun μορφή ("form") emphasizes the essence of a thing, ὁμοίωμα ("likeness") the resemblance of a thing to its original, and σχῆμα ("appearance") denotes the outward presentation of the thing. Thus, σχῆμα denotes "the form or nature of something, with special reference to its outer form or structure."[181] It refers to "the generally recognized shape or form in which someth[ing] appears."[182] The σχῆμα is what is observable to the senses.[183] Thus σχῆμα may be subject to change. As such, here in 1 Peter, it powerfully

---

178 Spicq, 1:452,

179 Bigg, 113.

180 Hiebert, 93–94.

181 Louw-Nida, 58.7.

182 BDAG, 7204.1.

183 TDNT, 7:954.

depicts the endless pursuit of unredeemed "lusts," forever chasing an ever-changing and unattainable goal. In Peter's compound verb, the prefix (σύν, "with") depicts "a personal assimilation to, or conformity with, the pattern" of one's lusts.[184] The only other use of the verb in the NT is when Paul commands the believers in Rome, "do not be conformed to this world" (Rom. 12:2). The verb means "to fashion in accordance with,"[185] to "mould" or "form after"[186] the pattern/shape of something.

The NASU renders the participial form as an imperative ("do not be conformed"; cf. also ESV, NET, NIV, NRSV, NLT; compare to KJV, NKJV, YLT) and, while it may be true (as it was in verse 13) that the participle carries some imperatival power, it does none the less qualify the main verb, an imperative, (γενήθητε, "be") in verse 15. The participle here may relate to the main verb as instrumental (depicting the opposite, negative side of how one must "be holy").[187] The present tense calls for continual resistance to the pull and pressure of that which would otherwise conform one to its mold. This underscores the constant battle in which believers find themselves. The voice may be either middle or passive. If passive, it pictures the believer as acted upon by the unholy pressures ("do not be conformed," ESV, NASU, NRSV)[188]; if middle, it pictures the believer acting upon himself to resist these pressures ("not conforming yourselves to," NKJV; "not fashioning yourselves to," YLT). If we choose to read it as a passive form, we must remember that Peter presses this upon us with some imperatival force; we are not helpless victims of the pressures of "the former lusts" of our lives. Suppose we choose to read it as a middle voice. In this case, we must realize that in conforming ourselves to "the former lusts" of our lives, we are not simply making a dry, intellectual choice but are giving way to powerful forces that

---

184 Hiebert, 94.

185 Mounce, 1285.

186 NIDNTT, 1:708.

187 Forbes, 38.

188 Rienecker says this may be an example of a permissive middle, "do not allow yourselves to be fashioned" (747).

exert their pressure and demand our conformity. Peter demands personal responsibility in the face of real pressures.

That to which they are to resist conformity in Romans 12:2 is "this world" (τῷ αἰῶνι τούτω; "to this age," YLT). Here it is "to the former lusts" (ταῖς πρότερον ... ἐπιθυμίαις), upon which the powers of "this age/world" play and which they feed. The noun ἐπιθυμία is a morally neutral term, designating any strong and overwhelming desire. Paul uses the noun nineteen times in his letters, always in a negative sense (except in Philippians 1:13 and 1 Thessalonians 2:17). Peter uses the noun eight times, always in a negative sense (former and in ignorance, 1 Peter 1:14; fleshly, 2:11; human, 4:2; unredeemed, 4:3; worldly, 2 Peter 1:4; corrupt, 2:10; fleshly, 2:18; personal, 3:3). The plural form designates powerful desires in their variety and combined power. The presence of the definite article with the noun makes these "lusts" specific, particular, and identifiable.

These "lusts" are identified as "former" (πρότερον), meaning they characterized the lives of Peter's readers before their redemption in Jesus Christ. At that time, Peter says, you indulged these lusts "in your ignorance" (ἐν τῇ ἀγνοίᾳ ὑμῶν). While the noun "ignorance" (τῇ ἀγνοίᾳ) could refer to Jews in their dealings with Christ (Acts 3:17), it seems here to indicate that largely Peter's readers are Gentiles, as it is more regularly used in the NT to describe the pre-Christian condition of the unredeemed of the nations (Acts 17:30; Eph. 4:18). This "ignorance" is not primarily an intellectual problem, but a moral and spiritual one.[189] Peter's use of the definite article with the noun signals that he has in mind the unredeemed state ("ignorance") which marked his readers (ὑμῶν, "your") in their former life without Christ. Prior to their new life through Christ, they lived "in" (ἐν) this state—the preposition depicting the sphere of their existence as unredeemed. This entire prepositional phrase is in the attributive position between the noun and its definite article, thus emphasizing the nature of the "lusts" that seek their conformity: they were those which characterized their past, unredeemed life (πρότερον, "former") when they operated "in ... ignorance" of God's revelation and grace in Jesus.

---

189 Michaels, 58.

Verse 15 – but like the Holy One who called you, be holy yourselves also in all *your* behavior;

In stark contrast (ἀλλὰ, "but") to "the former lusts" that characterized Peter's readers in their pagan "ignorance" (v.14), he calls them to "be holy" (ἅγιοι … γενήθητε). The verb generally depicts coming into being/existence and, therefore, might be translated "become" (NET, YLT). But most English versions translate it as a substitute for the common verb εἰμί ("to be"), which does not appear in the aorist tense, as we have here. The command thus echoes the oft-repeated call of God to His people throughout the OT (e.g., Lev. 11:44–45; 20:7, 26; Numb. 15:40), which will be quoted from Leviticus 19:2 in the next verse. This call is issued to God's New Covenant people (1 Cor. 7:34; Eph. 1:4; 5:27; Rev. 22:11). The aorist imperative demands action at once. There must be no debate or delay in the heart of the believer when it comes to the clear will of God. The imperative stands at the end of the clause to emphasize its urgency.[190] The passive voice may be deponent and thus translated with an active sense.[191] It may also be read as a middle voice, picking up on the "emphasis upon the recipients' ethical responsibility" and underscoring the action as taking place upon oneself.[192] In this, however, we want to avoid any sense "that holiness is something dependent upon human behavior."[193] As Israel was made holy (i.e., set apart to God) and thus called to live up to what God had graciously enacted in their lives, so New Covenant believers in Jesus Christ have already been made holy (i.e., been set apart, sanctified to God; 1 Cor. 1:2; 6:11; Heb. 10:10; 1 Peter 2:9) and are now called to "be" in every expression of life what God has, in fact, made them by His grace.

The standard for their holiness is: "like the Holy One who called you" (κατὰ τὸν καλέσαντα ὑμᾶς ἅγιον). This prepositional phrase is placed before the main verb, emphasizing it. In this context, the preposition

---

[190] Hiebert, 96.

[191] Abernathy, 39.

[192] Dubis, 27–28.

[193] Forbes, 39.

(κατά, "like") serves as a "marker of norm of similarity or homogeneity" and thus means "*in accordance with, in conformity with, according to.*" It serves "to introduce the norm which governs" something.[194] This may lay bare a comparison Peter is making with what he has just ordered not to take place. We are prohibited from being "conformed to the former lusts [ἐπιθυμίαις]" (v.14) but are now told to be conformed to the holiness of the God who has called us to Himself. That to which our holiness is to conform is the nature of God Himself. Little wonder, then, that Peter, in his second letter, will call his readers to live by faith in the promises of God "so that by them you may become partakers of the divine nature, having escaped the corruption that is in the world by lust [ἐπιθυμία]" (2 Peter 1:4).

One must decide whether the definite article (τὸν) is to be read with the participle that immediately follows it (καλέσαντα, "calls") or with the more distant adjective (ἅγιον, "holy"). Opinions are divided, but it seems best to take it with the adjective (ἅγιον, "holy") and read it here as a substantive ("the Holy One," cf. NET).[195] God is designated "the Holy One" forty-five times in the OT. In the NT, the title appears eight times, used of both the Father (Rev. 16:5) and of Jesus (Mark 1:24; Luke 4:34; John 6:69; Acts 2:27; 13:35). It is not entirely clear whether the use of the title in 1 John 2:20 refers to God the Father or God the Son. But here, it is clearly a reference to the Father, for tucked in the attributive position is καλέσαντα ὑμᾶς ("who called you"). In the NT epistles, God the Father calls (1 Cor. 1:9; 7:15, 17; 1 Peter 5:10) through His Son (Gal. 1:6) by the Spirit. It bespeaks the divine initiative in salvation and the powerful and effective nature of God's call. Peter's letters reveal his persistent concern with the call of God upon the lives of his readers. They are here called to holiness of life (1 Peter 1:15), "out of darkness into his marvelous light" (2:9), to endure suffering patiently (2:21), to receive God's blessing (3:9), to God's "eternal glory in Christ" (5:10), and "by his own glory and

---

194 BDAG, 3938.5.a.

195 Alford, 4:340; Best, 114; Dubis, 26–27; Hiebert, 95; Michaels, 51, 58; As opposed to a predicate adjective as per the ESV, NIV, NKJV, NLT, and NRSV: "as he who called you is holy."

excellence" (2 Peter 1:3). The participle is attributive[196], characterizing "the Holy One" as Him "who called" (καλέσαντα).

This is stunning! Given the inability of too highly exalting "the Holy One" over all His creatures, He is nevertheless the One who calls people into relationship with Himself through His Son by the working of the Spirit, setting them apart by grace as His very own. The aorist tense looks either to the decisive moment of their call to salvation in Jesus Christ when they heard the gospel or, if it is an ingressive aorist, to God's initial call that continues now in its effect as they continue being called by Him to Himself through Jesus. In the NT, the call of God to His people through the gospel is viewed as both a past (e.g., Gal. 1:6; Eph. 4:1; 1 Peter 2:9) and a present, ongoing reality (Gal. 5:8; 1 Thess. 2:12; 5:24). Peter always refers to the call upon the lives of his readers using the aorist tense.

The gracious, divine "call" is not some detached theological premise but a highly personal event. For, Peter reminds them, it came to "you" (ὑμᾶς). Just as personal, then, is the demand for holiness befitting this call, for it is underscored and made emphatic by the presence of the plural pronoun αὐτοὶ ("yourselves").

The "also" (καὶ) points not to "be holy" in addition to something else required of you, but to "be holy" as "also" God Himself is holy. The call of the Holy One is a call to join Him in His holiness. The arena where this holiness is to be found is "in all your behavior" (ἐν πάσῃ ἀναστροφῇ). The preposition sets forth the arena or sphere (ἐν, "in") where their holiness is to be found. The entire prepositional phrase sits between the adjective (ἅγιοι, "holy") and the verb (γενήθητε, "be"), stressing the

> **Ministry Maxim**
>
> The Holy One begets holy ones.

nature of the holiness being sought. The noun (ἀναστροφῇ, "behavior") is found thirteen times in the NT, eight of which are by Peter (1 Peter 1:15, 18; 2:12; 3:1, 2, 16; 2 Peter 2:7; 3:11; cf. the verbal cognate ἀναστρέφω in 1:17). It literally means "a turning about in place" and then came to

---

196 Dubis, 27; Michaels, 58.

designate one's daily behavior[197], though that moment-by-moment conduct is pictured as driven by certain principles[198], for good (1 Tim. 4:12; Heb. 13:7; James 3:13; 1 Peter 1:15; 2:12; 3:1, 2, 16; 2 Peter 3:11) or ill (Gal. 1:13; Eph. 4:22; 1 Peter 1:18). Just as the wickedness of the residents of Sodom and Gomorrah drove their behaviors (2 Peter 2:7) so the holiness of the One who called them drives the believer. Peter has no room for a professed faith that finds no expression in how one lives. What is in the heart and in the mind finds its way out through words and actions. This is to extend to "all" (πάσῃ) one's conduct and actions—"all or every manner of conduct, whether in business or pleasure, labor or rest, joy or sorrow, easy or difficult situations."[199] The whole of one's life is the stage upon which the holiness of the One who called us is held before the world. This is Peter's repeated refrain throughout both of his letters. We are called to become "a holy priesthood" so we can "offer up spiritual sacrifices acceptable to God through Jesus Christ" (1 Peter 2:5). God, through Christ, has made us a "holy nation … so that you may proclaim the excellencies of Him who has called" us (1 Peter 2:9, NASB). "Since all these things are to be destroyed in this way, what sort of people ought you to be in holy conduct and godliness" (2 Peter 3:11).

Verse 16 – because it is written,
"YOU SHALL BE HOLY, FOR I AM HOLY."

Peter now gives the ground (διότι, "because") for his call to "be holy" (v.15). The conjunction is formed from διά ("because of") and ὅτι ("that")[200] and is used here to indicate that what has just been commanded is a reasonable demand.[201] It is used three times by Peter, each time introducing a quotation from the OT (1 Peter 1:16, 24; 2:6). The reason why Peter's demand

---

197 Friberg, 52.
198 BDAG, 566.
199 Lenski, 56.
200 Friberg, 117.
201 BADG, 2028.3.

is legitimate is Scripture demands it ("it is written," γέγραπται). The perfect tense of the verb indicates that what was penned at a point in time in the past continues to stand as authoritatively "written" now. It depicts the continuing and binding authority of God's revealed Word, the Scriptures. The passive voice indicates the written product was the work of another: there are human authors, to be sure, but behind and over them stands the Holy Spirit as the ultimate author of Scripture (2 Tim. 3:16). Indeed, as Peter will say in his second letter, "men ... spoke," but they did so "from God" as "moved by the Holy Spirit" (2 Peter 1:21).

In this case, the specific Scriptural statement authenticating and justifying Peter's imperatives (vv.14–15) is set forth as he quotes from the OT: "YOU SHALL BE HOLY, FOR I AM HOLY" (ἅγιοι ἔσεσθε, ὅτι ἐγὼ ἅγιός [εἰμι]). Peter quotes oft-repeated lines from Leviticus (11:44, 45; 19:2; 20:26; 21:8). Just which passage he may be quoting is often debated, but the theme is a consistent one, and it matters little to pin Peter's quotation on just one of its expressions. The future imperative (ἔσεσθε, "YOU SHALL BE") carries a unique imperatival force. In the NT it most often shows up in quotations of the OT. The result is a more emphatic and solemn form of command.[202]

The ground (ὅτι, "FOR")[203] of believers' hope of holiness is the holiness of the one who calls them (ἐγὼ ἅγιός [εἰμι], "I AM HOLY"). Some manuscripts include the verb (εἰμι, "AM"), and others do not. The textual experts are divided as to whether it should be considered original. But surely, if not original, Peter intended that the reader mentally supplies the verb. What is clear is that God is being emphatic, signaled by using the first-

> **Ministry Maxim**
>
> It is impossible for one who comes into relationship to Him who is holy to remain unholy.

---

202 Wallace, 452–453, 569–570, 718–719.

203 The ὅτι is missing in several manuscripts. Perhaps διότι ... ὅτι ... ὅτι seemed redundant to scribes who then dropped the first ὅτι. Michaels says, "The ὅτι should probably be retained but left untranslated (the imperative with which the quotation begins makes it virtually untranslatable in English)" (Michaels, 51).

person pronoun ἐγώ ("I"). Let there be no mistaking who is making the declaration. And the self-assertion is that He is "HOLY" (ἅγιός). This is the fourth time in this sentence that the word is used (two in verse 15 and two here in verse 16). Holiness is not simply one among numerous attributes or perfections of God. Holy is what God is in His essential being. The seraphim in Isaiah's exalted vision cry out, "Holy, Holy, Holy, is the LORD of hosts" (Isa. 6:3). The four living creatures in John's vision of the throne room do the same (Rev. 4:8). No other attribute of God is depicted in this three-fold manner anywhere in the Scripture. The self-assertion of God, "I AM HOLY," is Him simply telling the truth about Himself and graciously bringing us into the most intimate and authentic revelation of who and what He is. Holiness is God being God. His being "HOLY" has unavoidable ethical and moral implications for those brought into relationship with Him.

This brings us into the awesome wonder of being called to be "holy" as God is holy. What God is (vv.15a, 16b) those whom He calls by His grace are (1 Peter 2:9) and must be (v.15b, 16a). Peter presses upon New Covenant believers in Jesus the moral imperative of God's holiness first set upon the Old Covenant people, Israel. The imperative of holiness unto God remains binding, even while the specifics of the civil, ceremonial, and dietary laws do not.

> **Digging Deeper:**
> 1. In what way is sin fundamentally a matter of ignorance (v.14)?
> 2. How does measuring holiness according to God's nature (rather than a list of actions) change your conception of sanctification (v.15)?
> 3. Why does being called by One utterly holy demand our holiness (v.16)?

Verse 17 – If you address as Father the One who impartially judges according to each one's work, conduct yourselves in fear during the time of your stay *on earth*;

Peter begins a new, extended sentence that will run through verse 21. He opens the sentence with καὶ (not translated in NASU, NIV, NRSV, but cf. "And" in ESV, KJV, NASB, NET, NKJV, RSV, YLT). While beginning a new sentence, it continues the string of ethical exhortations that started in verse 13.

The main verb, an imperative, is held off until the end of verse 17, piling up the qualifiers before the command is unveiled. The command is to "conduct yourselves" (ἀναστράφητε) in a particular way (cf. the noun ἀναστροφῇ, "behavior," v.15). The verb is a compound made up of ἀνά ("up/upon") and στρέφω ("to turn") and connotes changing direction by turning on a particular point, based on specific principles.[204] It can be used literally (Acts 5:22). When used in a metaphorical sense, it might describe sinful living (Eph. 2:3; 2 Peter 2:18), but primarily it is used in the NT of the Christ-ordered life of His followers (2 Cor. 1:12; 1 Tim. 3:15; Heb. 13:18). It is in this latter sense that Peter uses it here. Here the aorist imperative underscores the urgency with which the readers are to undertake the life of faith. No time can be wasted, and no equivocation is permitted in getting on with their discipleship to Christ. The passive (or middle) form may have a present tense meaning.[205] Or it may be used reflexively, meaning "to turn back and forth,"[206] perhaps indicating the obedience necessary at each decision point of life.

This pattern of living is to be undertaken "in fear" (ἐν φόβῳ). The preposition (ἐν, "in") is used to indicate the manner in which one is to conduct one's life.[207] The noun can have a meaning along a spectrum from terror to worshipful reverence. Just how is it to be understood in the

---

204 BDAG, 565.3.

205 Ibid.

206 Friberg, 52; Thayer, 42.

207 Louw-Nida, 89.84; cf. Abernathy, 43–44.

present passage? The same phrase (ἐν φόβῳ, "in fear") is used five other times in the NT. Paul uses it of "the fear of God" (2 Cor. 7:1) or Christ (Eph. 5:21). Peter appears to use it similarly (1 Peter 3:2). Jude uses it regarding our ministry of mercy to those in sin (Jude 23). In what sense, then, are we to fear God? He is here presented as both our "Father" and the Judge before whom we will stand. We should thus live "in fear" before Him without severing that spectrum of meaning and moving to either end to exclude the other. We dwell safely in His grace through Jesus Christ. He is our Father. We are loved, cared for, kept, and cherished. He is our Judge.

> **Ministry Maxim**
>
> My Father is my Judge—I live now in the balance of intimacy and awe, security and accountability.

We will stand before Him and have no answer for our crimes but the provision He has made for us through His Son. We need not worry or reside in terror, for we are objects of His infinite divine grace. We should not grow presumptuous or slack, for we will stand before Him to account for our lives. We thus need to order our lives "in fear" before Him—reverently, respectfully, righteously, and humbly living under both His free grace and His moral demands.

This is required "during the time of your stay on earth" (τὸν τῆς παροικίας ὑμῶν χρόνον). Generally, the noun καιρός (already used in 1:5, 11; cf. 4:17; 5:6) depicts an opportune or seasonal time; a "time" that is advantageous for the fulfillment of some purpose.[208] The noun used here (τὸν ... χρόνον, "the time"; cf. 1:20; 4:2, 3) designates a finite space or span of time, whether that be specific or indefinite.[209] That meaning is seen here where Peter thinks of his readers' typical lifespans within the period lying between Jesus' first and second advents. The noun (τῆς παροικίας, "stay ... on earth") is used in the NT only here and in Acts 13:17, where it refers to the period of Israel's living in Egypt. It designates a period of time spent living as a foreigner in another land. Here it is applied to New

---

208 Thayer, 318.
209 Mounce, 732.

Covenant believers in this present world. The kindred verb παροικέω, which as a compound (παρά, "beside" + οἰκέω, "to live/dwell") means "to live beside," gives the sense of "sojourning" (cf. πάροικος in 1 Peter 2:11 where Peter calls his listeners "sojourners"). Peter is thus picking up the theme with which he began, calling his readers "those who reside as aliens, scattered throughout" the lands where they reside (1:1). Here, in verse 17, Peter tucks the articular noun (τῆς παροικίας, "stay...on earth") in the attributive position between the noun and its article (τὸν...χρόνον, "the time") to signal just how his readers are to view the span of their (ὑμῶν, "your") lives lived out between Jesus' first and second coming. Our entire earthly existence is a sojourn in a foreign land. This world is not our home but the training ground to prepare us for our eternal home.

Peter fronted all this with a conditional clause (εἰ πατέρα ἐπικαλεῖσθε τὸν ἀπροσωπολήμπτως κρίνοντα, "If you address as Father the One who impartially judges"). The condition (εἰ + indicative) signals that which is assumed true for the sake of the point being made. Wallace argues against translating with "since" (NIV) but retaining the weight of the conditional statement so the force of the point is not missed.[210] Peter believes that his readers do indeed "address as Father the One who impartially judges," but he also wants to allow them to answer this in the affirmative, even if only in their hearts and minds.

The assumption is that Peter's readers "address" (ἐπικαλεῖσθε) God. The present tense pictures their regular practice. The verb, in the active and passive voices, can mean simply to address another, and this seems to be how the NASU understands it: "address as Father" (cf. NET).[211] But it seems best here to regard the form as the middle voice, where the word means "to call upon a deity," to invoke God for something.[212] Peter characterizes the one upon whom his readers call as both "Father" (πατέρα) and as "the One who...judges" (τὸν...κρίνοντα). Commentators are not at one over which of these is considered primary and the other

---

210 Wallace, 692–694.

211 Hiebert, 98.

212 BDAG, 2963.1.

complementary. Is it that they call "Father" the one who is also Judge? Or that they call upon the One who is Judge as their Father? Those who put the primary emphasis upon "Father" (πατέρα) note that it is thrust forward for emphasis. The absence of the definite article is not consequential, for either the reader is to understand it as definite ("the Father," KJV, NKJV, NLT, YLT) or as qualitative, emphasizing God's nature "as Father" (ESV, NASU, NET, NRSV). The participle (τὸν ... κρίνοντα) is substantive ("the *One who* ... judges," emphasis added). The present tense may be read as having future orientation (e.g., "He will judge or reward you," NLT) or as depicting the present, ongoing nature of God already dealing with His people in discipline and justice (e.g., "is judging," YLT). Peter emphasizes both the present (1 Peter 4:17) and future aspects of God's judgment (4:5; 2 Peter 2:4, 9; 3:7). Here, Peter seems to have in view a future and final judgment since it will take place "according to each one's work" (κατὰ τὸ ἑκάστου ἔργον). The preposition κατὰ ("according to") "specifies the criterion, standard, or norm in the light of which" God will judge (cf. Matt. 16:27; Rom. 2:6; 1 Cor. 3:8; Rev. 2:23).[213] The noun (τὸ ... ἔργον, "work") can be used broadly of all that humanity does upon the earth (2 Peter 3:10). These may be good (1 Peter 2:12) or evil (2 Peter 2:8) in nature.

The adjective (ἑκάστου) is used to specify "each one" within an affinity group. Personal responsibility falls upon all people but will be accounted from each one individually. This is further underscored by the fact that the adjective is in the attributive position between the noun and its definite article (τὸ ... ἔργον, "work"). The span of one's life on this earth, sitting between the first and second coming of the Lord, is to be filled with "work." The singular form is noteworthy. The more usual form in the NT is the plural, and all of Peter's other uses are in the plural form (1 Peter 2:12; 2 Peter 2:8; 3:10). The plural form emphasizes each of the works under consideration. The singular summarizes and views the whole output of an individual's life – "the real sum and substance of each

---

213 Harris, 152.

man's life."²¹⁴ That work is to be undertaken in the clear awareness of one's responsibility and accountability before "the One who ... judges" all that we do with the time and resources He has allotted to us. What I do is truly *my* work, and I am accountable to God for it.

God undertakes judgment "impartially" (ἀπροσωπολήμπτως). The adverb depicts just how God "judges." It is in the attributive position between the participle and its definite article, further emphasizing God's nature in judgment. The word is found only here in the NT. It is formed from the alpha-privative (as a negation), πρόσωπον ("face"/"countenance"), and λαμβάνω ("to receive").²¹⁵ Peter, bearing witness to God's inclusion of the Gentiles in the salvation found in Jesus, used the root compound word: "I most certainly understand now that God is not one to show partiality [προσωπολήμπτης]" (Acts 10:34; cf. Rom. 2:11; Gal. 2:6, Eph. 6:9; Col. 3:25; James 2:1). We are called to be God's "obedient children" (v.14), and if we should fail to so live, we should not think our position as His children will influence His role as Judge.

In the final analysis, whether the primary emphasis rests upon "Father" or "the One who ... judges" may be left open to debate. We may be confident that the One upon whom we call for aid is both our Father and final Judge. By His doing, the One who will act as Judge is already my Father. The One before whom I will stand in final accountability is the very One upon whom I call now for aid that I might, in that final day, stand before Him with favor. Peter thus mingles intimacy and awe, security and accountability as he calls each one "to conduct yourselves in fear during the time of your stay" in this world. If we read the love of God in Christ in a way that moves us to approach Him in a casual, flippant, or presumptuous way, then we have not rightly understood the gospel. If we cower in fearful anxiety over whether we will be accepted before God when we genuinely call upon Him through Jesus Christ, then we have not rightly understood the gospel. The biblically informed Christian lives in the balance of intimacy with and awe before God through His Son, Jesus.

---

214 Lenski, 60.

215 Thayer, 70, 550.

Verse 18 – knowing that you were not redeemed with perishable things like silver or gold from your futile way of life inherited from your forefathers,

The sentence continues as Peter adds a long participial clause that will run through verse 19. The command of verse 17 to "conduct yourselves" (ἀναστράφητε) is to be undertaken in the knowledge (εἰδότες, "knowing") of something specific. The participle is used to express the cause underlying why they should live in the prescribed way. Their daily conduct and deportment are to be undertaken with a fully engaged mind. They are to "be holy" (v.16) and "conduct" (v.17) themselves in godly fear because they know something to be true. The perfect tense of the verb has the force of the present tense. Peter uses οἶδα twice as often (1 Peter 5:9; 2 Peter 1:12, 14; 2:9) as γινώσκω (2 Peter 1:20; 3:3; but cf. the compounded forms in 1 Peter 1:20 and 2 Peter 3:17). Scholars often debate whether there is an intended difference between οἶδα (used here) and γινώσκω. The words can be used interchangeably without significant variance in meaning, but at times the former emphasizes cognitive knowledge which "is present to the mind," while the latter "denotes ... a knowledge grounded in personal experience."[216] Peter seems to emphasize that knowledge which "is present to the mind" as they live their lives.

> **Ministry Maxim**
> The price of redemption and the purity of the redeemed can never be separated.

The pattern of their thinking is set before us in an extended clause that begins with ὅτι ("that"), indicating the content that they are to hold consciously in their minds. Of central concern is the fact that they "were ... redeemed" (ἐλυτρώθητε). The verb means to be freed from bondage by means of a λύτρον, a ransom price. The verb is used often in the LXX of the redemption of the Hebrews out of their slavery in Egypt (e.g., Exod. 6:6; 15:13; Deut. 7:8; 9:26), of the ransom of the firstborn (e.g., Exod. 13:13, 15; 34:20; Numb. 18:15), of property lost through

---

216 Thayer, 118.

poverty (Lev. 25:25), of one enslaved through indebtedness (Lev. 25:48–49), etc. It would also have been a vivid metaphor for the largely Gentile believers to whom Peter wrote as they had often seen slaves bought and sold on the auction block. A slave could be redeemed by payment made into the treasury of a pagan temple. Thereafter, the individual would be freed from his/her former owner, now to be considered a slave of the god or goddess of the temple. Peter may have this in mind, for he will soon enough call his readers "bondslaves of God" (1 Peter 2:16).[217]

Somewhat surprisingly, the verb is used only two other times in the NT (Luke 24:21; Titus 2:14) though the concept is found throughout the pages of the NT. Of note are two compounded forms of the root. The compound form ἀπολύτρωσις emphasizes the release *from* (note the prefix ἀπό, "from") bondage through the payment of the ransom price (e.g., Rom. 3:24; 8:23; 1 Cor. 1:30; Eph. 1:7; Col. 1:14). The compound ἀντίλυτρον (ἀντί, "instead of"/"in place of") underscores the ransom offered in the place of the one being redeemed (1 Tim. 2:6). Peter and Paul agree, "You have been bought with a price: therefore glorify God in your body" (1 Cor. 6:20). Jesus used the cognate noun when He said, "the Son of Man did not come to be served, but to serve, and to give His life a ransom [λύτρον] for many" (Matt. 20:28; Mark 10:45). Here the aorist tense again points to the events of Christ's suffering and death which accomplished our redemption. The passive voice reminds us that all the power of redemption lay on Christ's side, and we were the helpless objects of His perfect redeeming work. It is what is sometimes referred to as a divine passive—God is the active agent, and Christ's life is the price that was paid. We are the beneficiaries of this grace. No mention is made of to whom the price of redemption was paid.

Peter speaks both of that *from which* and that *by which* they were "redeemed." He sets forth that by which they were redeemed by way of a stark contrast (οὐ ... ἀλλὰ, "not ... but," vv.18–19). The first side of the contrast is set forth here, and the second side is set forth in verse 19. They have not been redeemed "with perishable things like silver or gold"

---

217 Kelly, 73; Jobes, 116.

(οὐ φθαρτοῖς, ἀργυρίῳ ἢ χρυσίῳ). The negation (οὐ, "not") is categorical and absolute.[218] Such redemption was not and could not be accomplished through "perishable things" (φθαρτοῖς). The adjective, used here as a substantive, designates that which is liable to decay, decomposition, and destruction. That includes the whole of physical creation, including this world's most precious things, "like silver or gold" (ἀργυρίῳ ἢ χρυσίῳ).[219] The two mark the most costly and valuable of precious metals, the latter being surpassingly so. Yet Peter has already said that the believer's faith is "more precious than gold [χρυσίου] which is perishable" (1 Peter 1:7). And will say that it is nothing compared to "the imperishable [ἀφθάρτῳ] quality of a gentle and quiet spirit" (3:3, 4). Indeed, an "imperishable" (ἄφθαρτον) inheritance (1:14) could not be secured by "perishable things" (φθαρτοῖς). It could come about "not of seed which is not perishable [φθαρτῆς] but imperishable [ἀφθάρτου]" (1:23). Being thus redeemed, our hearts and spirits ought to take on an "imperishable quality" (τῷ ἀφθάρτῳ, 3:4). The price of our redemption establishes the nature of our redeemed life. The price paid to free us is to be stamped both upon our inward person (3:4) and our outward conduct (1:17–19).

If it is argued that neither silver nor gold is susceptible to such destruction, Peter will later say that "by His word the present heavens and earth are being reserved for fire, kept for the day of judgment and destruction of ungodly men" and that on that day "the heavens will pass away with a roar and the elements will be destroyed with intense heat, and the earth and its works will be burned up" (2 Peter 3:7, 10). Indeed, on that day, "the heavens will be destroyed by burning, and the elements will melt with intense heat" (v.12).

Between the two sides of this contrast regarding how they were redeemed (vv.18a, 19), Peter reminds them of that from which they were redeemed: "from your futile way of life inherited from your forefathers"

---

218 Thayer, 408.

219 Many look to Isaiah 52:3 for the background to Peter's words here: "For thus says the LORD, 'You were sold for nothing and you will be redeemed without money.'"

(ἐκ τῆς ματαίας ὑμῶν ἀναστροφῆς πατροπαραδότου). The redemption through Christ snatched them out of the midst of (ἐκ, "from") a "futile way of life" (τῆς ματαίας ... ἀναστροφῆς). The noun was just used by Peter in verse 15 (which see for more on the meaning of the word) when he called his readers to "be holy yourselves also in all your conduct [ἀναστροφῇ]." The cognate verb was also just used in verse 17 (which also see), where Peter called to his readers: "conduct yourselves [ἀναστράφητε]" as aliens in exile on this fallen earth. The adjective (ματαίας, "futile") sits between the noun and its definite article in the attributive position, emphasizing the character or quality of this "way of life." The word describes that which is of "no use, *idle, empty, fruitless, useless, powerless,* lacking *truth.*"[220] In the OT, idols often are described in this way (e.g., Isa. 2:20; Jonah 2:8),[221] and the NT continues that theme (Acts 14:15; cf. Rom. 1:21; Eph. 4:17). But the NT tends to use the term more broadly of thoughts (1 Cor. 3:20), misplaced faith (1 Cor. 15:17), quarrels (Titus 3:9), and false religion (James 1:26). Peter makes this deeply personal by reminding his readers that it was "your" (ὑμῶν) experience. The personal pronoun is, like the adjective, in the attributive position emphasizing the personal nature of their experience.

Their empty and humanly inescapable past was "inherited from your fathers" (πατροπαραδότου). The word is found only here in both the LXX and NT. It is a compound made up of πατήρ ("father") and παραδίδωμι ("to hand/give over," cf. Luke 22:48; 1 Cor. 15:24), which in turn is a compound of παρά ("alongside") and δίδωμι ("to give"). Folly runs in the family, and we have each born the family resemblance in our daily lives. But through Jesus the Father has plucked us from the midst of that fruitless, folly-filled, damnable way of life. Peter highlights the "inheritance" his readers have received through Christ (1:4) and that over against the way of life "inherited from [their] fathers."

---

220 BDAG, 4737.

221 And note the use of the cognate noun (ματαιότης) 39 times in Ecclesiastes.

Verse 19 – but with precious blood, as of a lamb unblemished and spotless, *the blood* of Christ.

Peter continues the long participial clause begun in verse 18 to describe the reason ("knowing") they are to "conduct" themselves in the fear of God (v.17) and holiness (v.16). We have here the second half of a stark contrast (οὐ … ἀλλὰ, "not … but," vv.18–19). The first half underscored that their redemption did not occur "with perishable things like silver or gold." Rather (ἀλλὰ, "but") it took place "with precious blood" (τιμίῳ αἵματι).

The reference to "blood" is shorthand for lifeblood poured out in sacrificial death. Peter has already said the purpose for which God chose his readers was to "be sprinkled with His blood" (1 Peter 1:2). It stands as fact that "without shedding of blood there is no forgiveness" (Heb. 9:22). But "it is impossible for the blood of bulls and goats to take away sins" (10:4b). Therefore, Jesus, "through His own blood … entered the holy place once for all, having obtained eternal redemption" (9:12). As a result, "we have confidence to enter the holy place by the blood of Jesus" (10:19). The blood of Christ is the instrument or means by which He secured our salvation.[222]

Peter denotes the blood of Jesus as "precious" (τιμίῳ). The adjective designates that which is of "exceptional value."[223] It describes that which "Babylon" used in her rebellion against God (Rev. 17:4; 18:12 [2x], 16). But it is also used to describe the very appearance of the New Jerusalem itself (Rev. 21:11) as well as the stones used in her foundations (21:19). In Peter's only other use, it describes the value of the promises of God (1 Peter 1:4). Jobes notes that Peter may be employing a play on words here, given that the "price" (τιμή, cf. 1 Cor. 6:20) of redemption for a slave or prisoner of war sounds very much like our present adjective (τιμίῳ, "precious").[224] What is certainly clear is that Peter is holding in

---

222 Brooks and Winbery, 42–43.

223 BDAG, 7368.1.

224 Jobes, 116–117.

juxtaposition that which is most precious in their world ("silver or gold," v.18) and that which is "precious" both in this world and the next—the blood of Christ. To be cleansed by His blood is beyond all earthly valuation. This fires the ceaseless, eternal worship of God's people in heaven (Rev. 5:9). All that is precious in this world will perish (1 Peter 1:18), but Christ's blood secured an "eternal redemption" (Heb. 9:12) and established an "eternal covenant" (13:20).

Christ's blood shed on the cross was "as of a lamb" (ὡς ἀμνοῦ). The noun is found only four times in the NT (John 1:29, 36; Acts 8:32 1 Peter 1:19), though it is used over ninety times in the LXX. In the OT, the bulk of its appearances occurs in the Pentateuch, particularly in Leviticus and Numbers in prescriptions for the ritual worship of Israel. The offering of a lamb in sacrifice was a part of Israel's worship daily (Exod. 29:38–42), weekly at the Sabbath (Numb. 28:9), monthly at the New Moon (Numb. 28:11), yearly at its annual feasts (Tabernacles, Numb. 29:13–40; Pentecost, Lev. 23:18–20; Passover, Exod. 12:5), and at other times as well (e.g., the dedication of the Tabernacle, Numb. 7; Aaron's ordination, Lev. 9:3; purification after childbirth, Lev. 12:6; sins of ignorance, Lev. 4:32). The lamb was symbolic of that which is innocent, meek, and humble (Isa. 11:6; 65:25; Luke 10:3; John 21:15). At the sight of Jesus, John the Baptist openly proclaimed, "Behold, the Lamb of God who takes away the sin of the world!" (John 1:29; cf. v.36). This was doubtless a part of the report Peter's brother Andrew brought to Him about Jesus (vv.40–41). While John used the word as a title for Jesus, Peter emphasizes His role as the "lamb" who secured our salvation. When the eunuch from Ethiopia read of one who "AS A LAMB BEFORE ITS SHEARER IS SILENT" and "DOES NOT OPEN HIS MOUTH" before its slayer (Acts 8:32; cf. Isa. 53:7), he wondered to Philip, "… of whom does the prophet say this?" (8:34). In response Philip, "preached Jesus to him" (v.35). Paul directly identified Jesus as the fulfillment of Israel's sacrifice of a lamb in their Passover experience in Egypt: "Christ our Passover also has been sacrificed" (1 Cor. 5:7). It is best to see the entire broad landscape of OT imagery for the lamb behind Peter's words here.

Jesus' blood served "as" (ὡς) a lamb's blood. The conjunction is used to introduce "a characteristic quality."[225] It thus serves as a "marker introducing the perspective from which a pers[son], thing, or activity is viewed or understood as to character, function, or role," focusing particularly upon the "quality, circumstance, or role" that things bear.[226] But here, clearly, Peter intends us to understand not exact correspondence, for that which Jesus achieved through the shedding of His blood far surpasses that which took place under the Levitical system of worship. "For if the blood of goats and bulls and the ashes of a heifer sprinkling those who have been defiled sanctify for the cleansing of the flesh, how much more will the blood of Christ, who through the eternal Spirit offered Himself without blemish to God, cleanse your conscience from dead works to serve the living God?" (Heb. 9:13–14).

> **Ministry Maxim**
>
> The truth of our redemption is seen in the value we place upon our Redeemer.

As Peter continues the imagery, he likens Jesus' blood, not to the blood of just any lamb but to one "unblemished and spotless" (ἀμώμου καὶ ἀσπίλου). Note the assonance of the two adjectives and the alliteration of αἵματι ("blood"), ἀμώμου ("unblemished"), and ἀσπίλου ("spotless"), adding rhetorical effect for those listening to or reading Peter's words (cf. 1:4; 2:15, 21; 3:17, 20).[227] The first adjective (ἀμώμου, "unblemished") is comprised of the alpha-privative affixed as a negation to the noun μῶμος ("blemish," "defect" or "flaw"[228]; found in the NT only in 2 Peter 2:13). The resulting word is used eight times in the NT, often being paired with the adjective "holy" (ἅγιος, Eph. 1:4; Eph. 5:27; Col. 1:22). The word is used extensively throughout the LXX and stands as the inviolable requirement for any sacrifice made to God. It is used here not in a cultic or ritualistic sense but bespeaks "the perfect moral blamelessness ... of

---

225 Friberg, 416.

226 BDAG, 8075.3.a.

227 Dubis, 32; Forbes, 44; Michaels, 66.

228 Friberg, 267.

the Redeemer who sacrifices Himself."²²⁹ Because Jesus "offered Himself without blemish [ἄμωμον] to God" on our behalf, His "blood" is able to "cleanse your conscience from dead works to serve the living God" (Heb. 9:14). He did this because we were chosen by God in Christ "before the foundation of the world, that we should be … blameless [ἀμώμους] before Him" (Eph. 1:4). Christ's sacrifice reconciled us to God "in order to present you before Him holy and blameless [ἀμώμους] and beyond reproach" (Col. 1:22). He is presently sanctifying us so He can present His Church to Himself "blameless" (Eph. 5:27). Thus, in our daily conduct we are to prove ourselves "to be blameless and innocent, children of God above reproach [ἄμωμα] in the midst of a crooked and perverse generation" (Phil. 2:15). Revelation sets before us worshipers around God's throne, who have been preserved "blameless" (ἄμωμοί) to live in His presence forever (Rev. 14:5).

Added (καί, "and") to this is a second adjective (ἀσπίλου, "spotless"). The adjective is comprised of the noun σπίλος ("a spot/blemish")²³⁰ with the alpha-privative added for negation. It comes then to be used of "untainted character"²³¹ that is, therefore, "free from censure" and "irreproachable."²³² It, too, "includes the thought of the sinlessness of Jesus."²³³ Christ's blood is not liable to failure regarding our redemption. The combined force of the two adjectives underscores Peter's valuation of Christ's blood as "precious" and beyond compare. Unlike the first adjective, the present word appears only in the NT and then only three other times. In each of those references, it is descriptive of the sanctified lives of the people of God. What is true here of the blood that redeems becomes the characteristic of life for the redeemed. True believers live in line with

---

229 TDNT, 4:831.

230 cf. 2 Peter 2:13 where Peter calls the false teachers "blots [σπίλοι] and blemishes" and Ephesians 5:27 where Christ labors to present the Church to Himself as a Bride "having no spot [σπίλον] or wrinkle or any such thing." These are the only two other NT usages of the adjective.

231 BDAG, 1200.2.

232 Thayer, 81.

233 TDNT, 1:502.

that by which they have been redeemed, being "diligent to be found by Him in peace, spotless [ἄσπιλοι] and blameless" (2 Peter 3:14). Bought and owned by Christ, we are not our own (1 Cor. 6:19–20) so we strive to "keep the commandment without stain [ἄσπιλον]" (1 Tim. 6:14) and to "keep oneself unstained [ἄσπιλον] by the world" (James 1:27).

Now the comparison fades, and the stark means of that redemption is set before us. It was the blood "of Christ" (Χριστοῦ). The noun is pushed to the end to emphasize it and set up the qualifying participial clauses that follow in verses 20 and 21.[234] The genitive form of the noun is far more than a simple identifier. In Peter's first sermon on Pentecost, he addressed the Jewish leaders and said, "all the house of Israel [should] know for certain that God has made Him both Lord and Christ-- this Jesus whom you crucified" (Acts 2:23, 36). In essence, Peter told them, "The Messiah for which you say you long came to you and you crucified Him!" But, irony of all ironies, "If you repent (cf. Acts 2:38) that blood for which you are humanly responsible will be the means by which God blots out your sin and redeems you to Himself."

Verse 20 – For He was foreknown before the foundation of the world, but has appeared in these last times for the sake of you

Peter's extended sentence continues from its beginning in verse 18. The genitive noun Χριστοῦ ("of Christ") was held to the end of the last clause both for emphasis and to position it for the present enlargement upon it by two participial phrases here in verse 20. The two participial phrases are set against one another by contrast ("but"). This contrast is set before us by the combination μὲν ... δὲ, which can woodenly be set forth as "on the one hand ... and on the other."[235] Both participles serve as attributives "of Christ" (Χριστοῦ, v.19).

---

234 Michaels, 66; Robertson, *Word Pictures*, 6:91; Vincent, 1:638.
235 Machen, 262.

So, on the one hand (μὲν), Peter can say of Christ, "He was foreknown" (προεγνωσμένου). The verb is a compound made up of πρό ("before") and γινώσκω ("to know"). The compounded verb is used only five times in the NT, twice of God's foreknowledge (Rom. 8:29; 11:2), once by Paul in his defense before Agrippa noting what the accusing Jews had known about him for a long time (Acts 26:5), and again by Peter in his second letter, reminding his readers that they were aware "beforehand" of the challenges coming and the faith necessary to meet them (2 Peter 3:17). Here Peter has already used the cognate noun (πρόγνωσις, "foreknowledge") in verse 2 to designate the foundation of his reader's election unto salvation. As we noted in our comments, the noun speaks not merely of prior awareness but of intention, predetermination, and prearrangement; it denotes choice that takes place before other realities. Similarly, the verb used here means to "select in advance, choose or appoint beforehand."[236] God's "foreknowledge...is an [act] of election or foreordination."[237] In verse 2 believers were the object of God's foreknowledge; here, it is Christ as the sacrificial lamb who the Father foreknew. Here the perfect tense views the divine choice as made in the past and continuing in its effect in the present. The passive tense pictures the divine choice of the Father being set upon Christ.

Peter gives us a peek into the eternal decree of the Father, choosing to send His Son into the world to redeem the humans He would create, for here, the Father's divine choice is said to have taken place "before the foundation of the world" (πρὸ καταβολῆς κόσμου). The preposition πρό ("before"; just used in compound in the verb, see above) is used temporally, pointing to a time prior to an additional point of time. It signals that this divine choice was made before "the world" (κόσμου) and all that fills it, including the human race, had been created. The noun κόσμος ("world") designates the ordered reality (cf. its use in 1 Peter 3:3) God originally created, as opposed to the chaos that ensued after the Fall. It is

---

236 Friberg, 327; cf. BDAG, 6171.2.

237 TDNT, 1:715.

used here of "the sum total of everything here and now."²³⁸ It is particularly "the foundation" (καταβολῆς) of this ordered creation that is in view. The noun is related to the compound verb of κατά ("down") and βάλλω ("to sow/cast/throw"). It thus designates that which has been laid down to serve as the "foundation" or the beginning of something. In ten of the noun's eleven appearances in the NT, it is coupled with κόσμος in the precise phrase we have here (καταβολῆς κόσμου, "the foundation of the world." The phrase is sometimes preceded by ἀπό ("from"; Matt. 13:35; 25:34; Luke 11:50; Heb. 4:3; 9:26; Rev. 13:8; 17:8) and, as here, with πρὸ ("before"; John 17:24; Eph. 1:4; 1 Peter 1:20). In all these occasions it points to the beginning of the created order.

Before the creation of the earth and all that fills it, particularly humans, God knew that He would send His Son as the Lamb, who would redeem us at the cost of His own life. Prior to our creation, the Father saw our fall. Prior to our fall, the Father had already chosen to redeem us. The Father's redeeming love was set upon us not only before we had done anything good or bad, not only prior to our birth but before the existence of the human race. When we were but a thought in His mind, the Father already loved us, infinitely, at the cost of sending the Second Person of the Trinity with whom He had enjoyed eternal loving relationship into the world He would create and of all that would be required of Him here and of all that would become His experience in this world, particularly His death. This only begins to get at what it means to be the object of God's love. This pre-temporal choice is the foundation of our very identity as God's people. Indeed, Christ is "the Lamb who was slain from the creation of the world" (Rev. 13:8, NIV; cf. KJV, NKJV, YLT). As Lenski says, "Christ's sacrifice was seen by God as eternally present."²³⁹

Little wonder Paul prayed for the believers in Ephesus to "know the love of Christ which surpasses knowledge" (Eph. 3:19). Only a work of God the Spirit will enable us to begin to comprehend "the breadth and

---

238 BDAG, 4371.3.

239 Lenski, 67.

length and height and depth" of such love (v.18). But it is the Spirit's assignment and joy to pour out this love of God into our hearts (Rom. 5:5).

In contrast (δὲ, "but") to the pre-creation decision of the Father in the shadowy confines of eternity past, Christ actually "has appeared" (φανερωθέντος) in time and space upon the earth. The verb is used frequently throughout the NT and depicts the act of making visible that which has heretofore been unseen.[240] Peter uses it to speak both of Christ's first advent, as he does here, and of His Second Advent (1 Peter 5:4). Whereas the previous participle was perfect tense, depicting the divine act of foreknowing as a past action with continuing results, the aorist tense of this participle depicts Christ's incarnation as the decisive event which manifested God's eternal plan in time and space.

> **Ministry Maxim**
>
> God had you in mind before creation and has worked all things toward your ultimate salvation.

As with the previous participle, the passive form here also designates this as God's doing. In sending His Son, the Father pulled back the veil of His eternal plan of salvation. Again, both participles serve as attributives "of Christ" (Χριστοῦ, v.19). Paul similarly used the present verb to speak of "the mystery which has been hidden from the past ages and generations, but has now been manifested [ἐφανερώθη] to His saints" (Col. 1:26). The fact that Christ "has appeared" in this created order through His incarnation implies He existed prior to His revelation to the world. It was "when the fullness of the time came" that "God sent forth His Son" (Gal. 4:4). The Son already was—from eternity—but as God unfolded His redemptive plan in time and space, there came a moment when He revealed His Son to the world.

This unveiling appearance "of Christ" took place "in these last times" (ἐπ ἐσχάτου τῶν χρόνων). Peter has already spoken of "the last time" (1:5), where he also used the combination of ἔσχατος ("last") and καιρός ("time"), though in a different fashion (cf. the use of the preposition ἐν ["in"] rather than ἐπί ["in"] which he uses here). He will also speak of

---

240 Mounce, 439.

"the last days," combining ἔσχατος ("last") with ἡμέρα ("day"; 2 Peter 3:3). The preposition (ἐπ', "in") is used as a marker of temporal significance and means "in the time of," designating the "time within which an event or condition takes place."[241] Peter is comfortable in speaking of these "last" days as both already present (1 Peter 1:20; cf. Acts 2:16–17; Gal. 4:4; Heb. 1:2) but in some sense not yet fully arrived (1 Peter 1:5). Indeed, the first Advent of Christ inaugurated "the last days" and His Second Advent will be their terminus point. The age between the Advents is "the last days." The word for "time" (καιρός) designates an opportune or seasonal time; a "time" that is advantageous for the fulfillment of some purpose.[242] The plural form here might better be rendered "times." It is the "last" (ἐσχάτου) of multiple times that have made up the course of history. Presently, in Christ, we have arrived at that final season beyond which this present age will not continue. Indeed, the word typically points to the last in a series of things beyond which nothing else will be found.[243] The phrase might be rendered the "last of the times." Davids thus comments, "Of all the periods of time determined by God this is the last."[244] Thus Peter effectively reaches from eternity past to the final flickering moments of history as we know it—emphasizing that from pole to pole, God has been actively, sovereignly, and lovingly initiating and fulfilling His redemption of His people.

Christ made His appearance "for the sake of you" (δι' ὑμᾶς). The preposition with the accusative denotes the cause of Jesus' incarnation and means "because of" or, as here, "for the sake of."[245] The plural pronoun shows that Peter has the whole body of his believing readers in mind. All believers and each believer can know that God's pre-creation choice to send His Son to redeem them, and its actual outworking in His first Advent, was undertaken with them in His mind. We may be scattered

---

241 BDAG, 2922.18.a.

242 Thayer, 318.

243 BDAG, 3168.2.b.

244 Davids, 74.

245 BDAG, 1823.B.2.a.

exiles journeying through this present spiritual wasteland, but we were and are central to God's intended redemption from before creation. The hard, earthly realities that make the life of faith in this world so difficult must not blind us to the privilege that is ours as objects of God's eternal love and grace in Jesus Christ our Savior. If God has thus sovereignly directed all things from eternity past to the end of time for the appointed ends of our salvation, how infinitely "precious" (v.19) is the blood of Christ, shed in sacrificial death for us? Let us live in the holy fear of such a sovereign, loving God.

Verse 21 – who through Him are believers in God, who raised Him from the dead and gave Him glory, so that your faith and hope are in God.

Now, at last, Peter concludes the sentence he began in verse 17. Just as Peter held Χριστοῦ ("of Christ") to the end of verse 19 to set up the attributive participles connected to it so here he pushed ὑμᾶς ("you") to the end of verse 20 so that the development of it here in verse 21 would be clear. Thus τοὺς ... πιστοὺς ("who ... are believers") stands in apposition to ὑμᾶς ("you"), that is, the readers of Peter's letter. The plural articular adjective is used as a substantive, further expounding upon how the apostle views his readers. Debate has ensued as to whether the verbal adjective should be understood in a passive ("faithfulness," "trustworthy") or active sense as in the NASU ("are believers") and most English translations.[246] The active sense seems to be most in accord with God as the object of the verbal idea of the adjective (εἰς θεὸν, "in God"). The prepositional phrase δι' αὐτοῦ ("through Him") is in the attributive position between the adjective and its definite article, emphasizing the nature of how they came to have their standing as "believers" (cf. Peter's words in Acts 3:16). The personal pronoun αὐτοῦ ("Him") finds its reference in the distant αὐτοῦ ("of Christ")

---

[246] The adjective is somewhat unusual here; this is the only NT occurrence of the adjective with εἰς ("in"). Numerous manuscripts have a participle (whether present or aorist) instead of the adjective. These appear to be attempts at smoothing an otherwise unusual expression. The adjective, for this reason, is more likely to be the original reading.

at the end of verse 19. The preposition (δι') denotes the instrument or agency "through" which they became "believers."

Their faith rests "in God" (εἰς θεὸν). The preposition (εἰς, "in") denotes movement toward and "into" something. It is somewhat unusual that their faith is depicted as "through" (δι') Christ and "into" (εἰς) God. In the NT, Christ is more frequently made the object of one's faith than is the Father (e.g., 1 Peter 1:8, though cf. John 12:44c; 14:1a; Acts 16:34; Rom. 4:3, 5, 17; Gal. 3:6; 1 Thess. 1:8; Titus 3:8; Heb. 6:1). Harris is correct: "it is in Christ that God meets the individual in salvation. There are not two competing objects of human faith."[247] They are "believers in God," not in some generalized sense, as though they had moved from atheism to theism. Even in their pre-Christian paganism they would have been considered theists. No, they had become "believers" in the one true God and arrived at their faith in Him "through" Christ and in the uniqueness of the gospel call. He in whom they believed "is specifically the God of the Christian gospel, not merely the Creator, or the God of the Jews."[248]

Their faith thus rests in the one "who raised Him from the dead" (τὸν ἐγείραντα αὐτὸν ἐκ νεκρῶν). The NT most frequently attributes Jesus' resurrection to the Father. Jesus could speak of the power He possessed to lay His life down and to take it up again (John 2:19; 10:17, 18), but even this was from the Father (10:18b; cf. 5:19, 30; 8:28). Similarly, the Spirit is said to have raised Jesus from the dead (1 Peter 3:18; cf. Rom. 1:4; 8:11), yet in the end, it is the Father who willed it and made it so through the Son's obedient death and the Spirit's powerful operation (cf. Peter's Pentecost sermon, Acts 2:24, 32). Here it is clearly the Father who is in view. The participle is accompanied by the definite

> **Ministry Maxim**
>
> The Father's faithfulness to glorify His Son is our assurance He will do the same for us.

---

247 Harris, 237.

248 Hiebert, 106.

article and used as a substantive (τὸν ἐγείραντα, "*who* raised," emphasis added). The aorist tense looks back to that reality-altering moment early on the third day when Jesus (αὐτὸν, "Him") was reanimated and brought forth from the tomb. That moment serves as the hinge of history. The door of eternity swung open to all who will repent and believe in the triumphant Christ. In that moment Jesus came forth "from the dead" (ἐκ νεκρῶν). The preposition emphasizes movement outward "from" a place or state. Jesus was thus in the grip of death but came forth from that in utter triumph over death and over him who holds its power in this world (Heb. 2:15).

In addition (καὶ, "and") to raising Jesus from the dead, the Father "gave Him glory" (δόξαν αὐτῷ δόντα). The one definite article (τὸν) serves both participles which are held in parallel (καὶ, "and") with one another. This participle is also in the aorist tense, underscoring those triumphant events that followed Jesus' resurrection from the dead. The theme of "glory" (δόξα) is prominent in Peter's view of reality (1 Peter 1:7, 11, 21, 24; 4:11, 13, 14; 5:1, 4, 10; 2 Peter 1:3, 17; 2:10; 3:18). As the cross drew near Jesus was motivated by the prospects of the glory that awaited Him, of His return to the glory He has openly shared with the Father from eternity and prior to His incarnation (John 17:5, 24; cf. Heb. 12:2) and which He gives to His followers (John 17:22). As in 1 Peter 1:11 ("the glories to follow" Christ's sufferings) "glory" (δόξαν) here includes all that flowed from the Father to the Son after His willing, sacrificial death—encompassing everything from resurrection to triumph at His Second Coming (cf. Peter's testimony in Acts 3:13; cf. also 2:33; 5:31). Peter has effectively surveyed the vast landscape of Christ's saving work: His being made the object of His Father's *eternal decree of salvation* ("He was foreknown before the foundation of the world," v.20a), His *incarnation* ("has appeared in these last times for the sake of you," v.20b), His *death* as a substitutionary sacrifice ("with precious blood, as of a lamb unblemished and spotless, the blood of Christ," v.19), His *resurrection* from the dead ("raised Him from the dead," v.21a) and His *ascension*, *session* and *glorification* at the Father's right hand ("gave Him glory," v.21b).

The result (ὥστε, "so that")[249] of the resurrection, ascension, and session of Christ was that Peter's readers' (ὑμῶν, "your) "faith and hope are in God" (τὴν πίστιν … καὶ ἐλπίδα εἶναι εἰς θεόν). God's redemptive plan had borne fruit in their lives. He just said they are believers "in God" (εἰς θεόν). So now he again says their "faith and hope" are both "in God" (εἰς θεόν). As Jesus came out of death (ἐκ νεκρῶν) by the Father's doing, so now through Him, Peter's readers have come out of spiritual death and through the resurrection of Christ have moved their faith and hope into God (εἰς θεόν). God has effectively changed their spiritual dwelling place. The article (τὴν) serves both "faith" (πίστιν) and "hope" (ἐλπίδα), marking them as definite and specific. The conjunction (καὶ, "and") is coordinate and holds "faith" and "hope" in parallel relationship.[250] Peter so intertwines the themes of "faith" and "hope" in this letter that it is impossible to divide them from one another. Both rest upon the past, finished work of Christ (1:18–20), and both look forward to the fulfillment of God's promises through Him (1:5, 13). Rooted in the finished work of redemption, faith is active hope and hope is trusting anticipation. The present tense infinitive (εἶναι, "are") underscores the present and ongoing reality of their active trust and hope in God. Hope serves as an inclusion for the whole of Peter's instruction thus far (1:3, 21) and the exhortations he has been making (1:13, 21).[251]

---

249 BDAG, 8083.2.a.β; Dubis, 35; Forbes, 45; Jobes, 119; contra those who read it as a purpose statement, e.g., Michaels, 70; Schreiner, 89.

250 The rendering "that your faith is also hope in God" (TDNT, 6:208) is statistically unlikely (Grudem, 91–92).

251 Lenski, 69; Schreiner, 89.

> **Digging Deeper:**
> 1. Which carries more emotional power in your life, thinking of God as Father or as Judge (v.17)?
> 2. If the price paid defines the life lived (vv.18–19) how are you demonstrating the worth of the One who gave Himself for you?
> 3. All God's work from eternity past to eternity future has gone into allowing you to live with Him in *this* moment (v.20)—how does this change your view of God and life with Him?
> 4. How does the Father's faithfulness to glorify His Son assure His promise to glorify us with His Son (v.21)?

Verse 22 – Since you have in obedience to the truth purified your souls for a sincere love of the brethren, fervently love one another from the heart,

The sentence that comprises verses 22 and 23 demands "love" (ἀγαπήσατε). The aorist imperative underscores the urgency of the command and demands that action is undertaken without delay. Peter's command to "love" is added to his call to establish their hope (v.13), walk in holiness (v.15), and the fear of the Lord (v.17). Peter's readers already love Christ (1:8), now they must love "one another" (ἀλλήλους). What is true vertically must be true horizontally. Indeed, the horizontal proves the reality of the vertical. The reciprocal pronoun depicts back-and-forth relationships. Love is to flow in both directions. Love is not only to be received, but given; not only given, but received.

This love must be exercised "fervently" (ἐκτενῶς). The adverb appears only here and Acts in 12:5, where it describes the prayers of God's people on behalf of Peter during his imprisonment. The word derives from the verb ἐκτείνω ("to stretch out") and points to "an unceasing activity, normally involving a degree of intensity and/or perseverance."[252] It and its cognates

---

252 Louw-Nida, 68.12.

"express tautness and, in a moral sense, an effort that can be understood either as perseverance ('without respite, without letting up, assiduously') or as intensity ('with fervor, urgently')."[253] At times both senses may meld into one. Peter uses the cognate adjective (ἐκτενής, "fervent") in 4:8 to qualify the cognate noun of our present verb (ἀγάπη, "love"): "keep fervent in your love." The adjective, like the adverb, is used elsewhere in the NT only of prayer, in this case, Jesus' prayers in the Garden (Luke 22:44). Prayer and love—God and man—must receive the same fervent, persevering love and pursuit. Here the adverb is placed last for emphasis.

It comes as no surprise then that this love must arise "from the heart" (ἐκ...καρδίας). The preposition ἐκ depicts outward movement "from" a point of origin. In this case, that is "the heart" (καρδίας) of the believer. This is Peter's first mention of the "heart," though he will soon enough speak of "the hidden person of the heart" (3:4). He will speak of the "heart" as the place where we must "sanctify Christ as Lord" (3:15). It is the place where the light of God's saving truth in Christ must arise (2 Peter 1:19). It is possible to have one's heart "trained in greed" (2 Peter 2:14). But when Jesus saves, He reorients the "heart," from coveting ("greed") to giving ("love"). Believers deliver their hearts over to Jesus, and setting Him apart as Lord. Love reveals the truth of one's "heart," but it must never be merely for show. Love is driven from within. Love arises from an internal work of God. God arises "from the heart" because "the love of God has been poured out within our hearts through the Holy Spirit" (Rom. 5:5).

The Greek text has placed καθαρᾶς ("pure," ESV, KJV, NKJV, NET, YLT) in brackets, indicating uncertainty as to its authenticity. The NASU does not translate it (as also the NIV and NRSV). It is easy to see why a scribe's eyes may have skipped over it as his eyes glanced back and forth from the original to his copy since καθαρᾶς and καρδίας are very close to one another visually. If original it adds emphasis to the theme of purity along with "purified" (ἡγνικότες, see just below). In that case, both their "souls" (Τὰς ψυχὰς) and their "heart[s]" (καρδίας) are to be pure before

---

253 Spicq, 1:457.

the Lord. In view of God's love and costly redemption (vv.18–21), the believer is gladly His, heart and soul (i.e., entirely, completely, thoroughly).

The command is qualified by two participial clauses, one before the imperative (here in v.22) and the second after (v.23). Both participles are to be understood as causal. The reason for their love for one another is first: "Since you have ... purified your souls" (Τὰς ψυχὰς ὑμῶν ἡγνικότες). Peter now further develops his thoughts on sanctification (v.2) and holiness (v.15). The verb occurs seven times in the NT, four of which describe ritual cleansing (John 11:55; Acts 21:24, 26; 24:18). The remaining three prescribe moral purity (James 4:8; 1 Peter 1:22; 1 John 3:3). Because of the verb's use in ritual contexts within Judaism and because it is at times connected there to ritual washings, some claim this as a reference to Christian baptism.[254] Nothing, however, in the context of Peter's letter suggests a connection to baptism. The perfect tense views their consecration as having happened in the past and continuing into the present. True, obedient faith in the gospel leaves one "purified" by God and before God.

As in verse 9, when Peter speaks here of his readers' "souls" (Τὰς ψυχὰς), he is not speaking of a subset or part of an individual but uses "souls" in the Semitic sense of the person himself (cf. Peter's other uses of ψυχή, 1 Peter 1:9; 2:11, 25; 3:20; 4:19; 2 Peter 2:8, 14). It is not that they have "purified" some portion of their lives and not others, but the whole of who they are has been cleansed by and come under the lordship of Jesus Christ.

This they had done "in obedience to the truth" (ἐν τῇ ὑπακοῇ τῆς ἀληθείας; "in the obedience of the truth," YLT). The preposition ἐν ("in") denotes how their purification took place.[255] Peter only uses the noun ἀλήθεια ("truth") three times in his letters, always with the definite article (τῆς ἀληθείας, "*the* truth," emphasis added). It serves as shorthand for the apostolic gospel as held before us in the written Word of God (2 Peter 1:12; 2:2). It thus stands as the opposite of their former "ignorance"

---

254 E.g., Spicq, 1:75, 135, 451; 2:33; 3:413, 425; Kelly, 78–79.
255 Dubis, 37; Louw-Nida, 89.76.

(v.14) and "futile way of life" (v.18) when they operated in unbelief and disobedience.[256]

The truth/gospel issues a call that demands "obedience" (τῇ ὑπακοῇ). The definite article again makes the nouns particular and specific—that unique obedience the gospel demands or requires. The genitive (τῆς ἀληθείας) is objective (i.e., obedience to the truth set forth in the gospel). Peter thus continues the theme of obedience begun earlier: "to obey Jesus Christ" (1:2); "As obedient children" (1:14). He will soon enough question the destiny of "those who do not obey the gospel of God" (1 Peter 4:17; cf. 2:8; 3:1; 3:20). Paul demands that the gospel is something not just to believe, but to obey (Rom. 1:5; 10:16; 16:26; 2 Cor. 9:13; 2 Thess. 1:8).

> **Ministry Maxim**
>
> The gospel is to be obeyed, not just believed.

Many manuscripts include διὰ πνεύματος ("through the Spirit," KJV) at this point. However, the oldest and best manuscripts omit the phrase. It bears the marks of a scribe's efforts to conform Peter's statement here to verse 2.[257]

Their obedience has been "for a sincere love of the brethren" (εἰς φιλαδελφίαν ἀνυπόκριτον). Whereas the preposition ἐν ("in") marked how their souls found purification (i.e., obedience to the truth of the gospel) here the preposition εἰς ("for") emphasizes purposeful movement into the result of that purification of their souls.[258] Obedient faith in the gospel always leads to "love of the brethren" (φιλαδελφίαν). The word originally referred to the love shared with a family member of common physical descent (brother or sister). It became, then, something of a technical term for the affection shared between those joined together in common relationship to the Father by Christ through the work of the Holy Spirit (Rom. 12:10; 1 Thess. 4:9; Heb. 13:1; 2 Peter 1:7). Peter will use the

---

256 Spicq, 1:75.

257 Michaels, 72; NET Bible.

258 It denotes "extension toward a special goal," (Louw-Nida, 84.16) and thus may serve as "a marker of intent, often with the implication of expected result" (89.57).

noun in a list of seven realities that if actively a part of a believer's life will render them "neither useless nor unfruitful in the true knowledge of our Lord Jesus Christ" (2 Peter 1:8). Some want to see an implied difference between "love" and "love of the brethren." Marshall suggests that "love of the brethren" denotes a reciprocal love while "love" is a non-reciprocating love that, when practiced, may cause "love of the brethren" to result and flourish.[259] Kistemaker sees in the words the difference between liking and loving deeply.[260] Davids views "love of the brethren" as being taken deeper and intensified by the command to "love."[261] Grudem notes a progression from "love of the brethren" to "love," while noting that there is "considerable overlap" in the terms.[262] There may be some subtle nuance of meaning here, but it seems likely that in this case Peter uses ἀγαπήσατε ("love") and φιλαδελφίαν ("love of the brethren") as largely synonymous terms.

This love must be "sincere" (ἀνυπόκριτον), not feigned. The adjective refers to that which is without hypocrisy. The negation (alpha-privative) is added to the already compounded word (ὑπό, "under" and κρίσις, "judgment"). The noun "hypocrite" (ὑποκριτής) was commonly used to designate an actor, one playing a part that did not represent reality. Spicq, however, argues against translating "according to etymology ('without hypocrisy') or usage ('not competent to perform on the stage')" and particularly when it qualifies love. He suggests a translation of "authentic."[263] A "sincere love" is thus genuine and without pretense. It is never put on display. It functions from internal ("from the heart") motivations, not external ones. The gospel changes something inside us that then transforms our outward behavior.

---

259 Marshall, 59–60.

260 Kistemaker, 72.

261 Davids, 77.

262 Grudem, 94.

263 Spicq, 3:412–413.

Verse 23 – for you have been born again not of seed which is perishable but imperishable, *that is*, through the living and enduring word of God.

Peter now adds the second causal participle to the sentence he began in verse 22. The command "love one another" (v.22) is reasonable only because "you have been born again" (ἀναγεγεννημένοι). Like the first, this participle is in the perfect tense. At a point in time in the past, Peter's readers were "born again" and they remain in that state of new life as he writes. The passive voice means that their new birth was brought about by another who took action to bring them forth in new life. The Father gave them birth (1 Peter 1:3a) by the working of His Holy Spirit (John 3:6, 8; Titus 3:5) through Jesus Christ (1 Peter 1:3b). The verb is the same one used in verse 3, its only other appearance in the NT (see our comments there).

While the Father, by the Spirit and through Jesus, "has caused us to be born again" (v.3) He did so out "of seed" (ἐκ σπορᾶς). The preposition (ἐκ, "of") designates the source or origin of the new birth. The noun occurs only here in the NT, though the related verb (σπείρω, "sowing") occurs frequently. Our noun describes "a sowing" or that which is sown and thus rendered here as "seed." The "word of God," the gospel, is that "seed" as Peter will momentarily make clear. As seed is cast upon the ground or a man impregnates a woman,[264] by the doing of God, His word carries the power of life within it. James thus calls upon his readers to "receive the word implanted, which is able to save your souls" (James 1:21).

Like begets like; each reproduces after its kind (Gen. 1:11, 12, 21, 24, 25). Peter thus categorically denies (οὐκ, "not") that this "seed" is "perishable" (φθαρτῆς). Peter just used the adjective in verse 18 to say we "were not redeemed with perishable things [φθαρτοῖς] like silver or gold." The Word of God is not liable to decay, decomposition, and destruction, and what it brings forth is not subject to such processes. Instead, in stark

---

264 The talk of new birth points toward reproductive imagery while the Scripture quotations in verse 24 and 25 point toward an agricultural metaphor.

contrast (ἀλλὰ, "but"), their new birth came about by seed that is "imperishable" (ἀφθάρτου). Peter has already reminded his readers that their inheritance is "imperishable" (v.4), and that is precisely because it bears the incorruptible nature of the "seed" which brought it forth. The "seed" of the gospel is not vulnerable to death or its processes, nor are those begotten by God through it to eternal life. Indeed, "THE WORD OF THE LORD ENDURES FOREVER" (v.25).

Now Peter leaves behind metaphor and imagery and speaks plainly. Their new birth came about "through the living and enduring word of God" (διὰ λόγου ζῶντος θεοῦ καὶ μένοντος). The preposition διὰ ("through") points to the intermediate agency by which the new birth came about.[265] The Father caused the new birth to take place through Jesus Christ and by the power of the Spirit "through" the agency of "the living and enduring word of God" (i.e., the gospel). Note Peter's interplay between the prepositions ἐκ ("of") and διὰ ("through"). Harris is correct: "One should assume a writer chooses his prepositions with care."[266] In this regard, he notes that "regeneration is said to have its origin or source in an act of immortal procreation or in imperishable seed ... but is effected by means of the living and abiding word of God."[267]

> **Ministry Maxim**
>
> The nature of the Word is evidenced in the life it begets and the fellowship it creates.

This is the first reference Peter makes to the "word of God" (λόγου ... θεοῦ). He will later remind his readers that it was by "the word of God the heavens existed long ago and the earth was formed" (2 Peter 3:5) and that presently "by His word the present heavens and earth are being reserved for fire" (v.7). This is a most powerful word and those who "disobey the word" (1 Peter 2:8; 3:1) stumble over it to their own eternal

---

265 Louw-Nida, 90.4.

266 Harris, 40.

267 Ibid.

doom. But those who receive and believe this word are birthed by God's power into "imperishable" life.

The combination of λόγος ("word") and θεός ("God") is used by Peter in 1 Peter 4:11 (λόγια θεοῦ, "the utterances of God") and 2 Peter 3:5 (τῷ τοῦ θεοῦ λόγῳ, "the word of God"). In 1 Peter 1:25, he will speak of "the word of the Lord," using a different noun (τὸ ... ῥῆμα κυρίου). The combination ῥῆμα ("word") and θεός ("God") is not used by Peter but is found in Ephesians 6:17 (ῥῆμα θεοῦ, "the word of God"), Hebrews 6:5 (θεοῦ ῥῆμα, "the word of God"), and 11:3 (ῥήματι θεοῦ, "the word of God"). While ῥῆμα can be used to specifically designate a word spoken, it can also be used interchangeably with λόγος, more broadly referring to a word either written or spoken. It appears that Peter intended no major distinction between the two words as he used them in verses 23 and 25. The origin of everything is found in the simple fact that "God said" (Gen. 1:3, 6, 9, 11, 14, 20, 24, 26, 28, 29). Indeed, "By faith we understand that the worlds were prepared by the word of God, so that what is seen was not made out of things which are visible" (Heb. 11:3). The self-expression of God is inseparable from God Himself, for "In the beginning was the Word, and the Word was with God, and the Word was God" and "All things came into being through Him, and apart from Him nothing came into being that has come into being" (John 1:1, 3). That same powerful Word is sounded in the gospel and brings forth new life wherever it is spoken. Indeed, it brings forth "a new creature" (2 Cor. 5:17), "a new creation" (Gal. 6:15). God "brought us forth by the word of truth" (James 1:18).

Two present active participles qualify the expression here. There is some debate as to whether they qualify λόγου ("word") or θεοῦ ("God"). Michaels views them as qualifying the latter and he translates the phrase "the living and enduring God," arguing that we have here an echo of the oft-repeated OT phrase "the living God."[268] The following two verses emphasize, however, the enduring nature of the Word of God and that tips the evidence in favor of reading the participles as qualifying λόγου

---

268 Michaels, 72, 76–77.

("word"). Indeed, the bulk of commentators and most English translations read it this way. The present tense indicates what is always true of the gospel wherever and whenever it is found. The word order is somewhat unusual: λόγου ζῶντος θεοῦ καὶ μένοντος. A woodenly literal rendering might be: "[the] word living of God and enduring." The first participle is in the attributive position between "word" and "of God," stressing the qualitative nature of the divine word. This word is "living" (ζῶντος) in that it begets life wherever it is sounded and received in repentant faith. Peter loved using the verb to speak of God's actions through Jesus. He has already spoken of the "living hope" (ἐλπίδα ζῶσαν, 1 Peter 1:3) into which God births us through His Son. Jesus is "a living stone" (λίθον ζῶντα, 2:4), and all who believe in Him become "living stones" (λίθοι ζῶντες) in the new temple He is building (2:5). It is the express purpose of the gospel that people "may live" (ζῶσι, 4:6) spiritually; that we "may live to righteousness" (τῇ δικαιοσύνῃ ζήσωμεν, 2:24).

The second participle (καὶ, 'and') states that this word is "enduring" (μένοντος). This participle is found at the end of the clause to emphasize it. Indeed, this point is developed as Peter quotes from Isaiah 40:6–8 in the following two verses. Peter's only other use of the verb comes in verse 25, where "THE WORD OF THE LORD ENDURES [μένει]." There the endurance is an everlasting one (εἰς τὸν αἰῶνα, lit. "unto the age"). Many manuscripts added the phrase here as well (εἰς τὸν αἰῶνα), but it is not found in the oldest and best manuscripts of verse 23 and appears to be a scribal addition to the original text. "Heaven and earth will pass away, but My words will not pass away" (Matt. 24:35).

In verse 22, the emphasis lies upon the necessary human response to the gospel ("you have in obedience to the truth purified your souls"), while here the stress lies upon the sovereign, divine act of grace through the gospel ("you have been born again"). As Davids notes, "both are kept in creative tension."[269]

---

269 Davids, 78.

> **Digging Deeper:**
> 1. Why does the gospel always produce love for God and others (v.22)?
> 2. If the Word believed does not produce the life and love of Christ (vv.22–23) where should blame be placed?

Verse 24 – For, "ALL FLESH IS LIKE GRASS, AND ALL ITS GLORY LIKE THE FLOWER OF GRASS. THE GRASS WITHERS, AND THE FLOWER FALLS OFF,

Peter now offers a foundation (διότι, "For") for his assertion that the Word of God is "living and enduring" (v.23b), focusing especially upon the latter. As he does with each use of the conjunction (cf. 1 Peter 1:16; 2:6), Peter cites Scripture as the justification for his confidence. Here his confidence that "the word of God" (v.23) is "living and enduring" is set forth in a quotation from that Word, specifically Isaiah 40:6b-7a. In saying that God's Word is "living and abiding," he is confirming Scripture's testimony to itself.

The testimony is built off a double simile (ὡς, "AS"). The physical reality used for comparison is "GRASS" (χόρτος) and "THE FLOWER OF GRASS" (ἄνθος χόρτου). Regarding the former (χόρτος, "GRASS"), we should picture the fields of herbage that made up the landscape around them. Jesus used it often in His teaching (Matt. 13:26; Mark 4:28) and particularly as a symbol of the fleeting nature of life (Matt. 6:28–30; Luke 12:27–28). James used to illustrate those rich in this world (James 1:10–11). The latter (ἄνθος χόρτου, "THE FLOWER OF GRASS") calls to mind those grasses, wildflowers, and other herbage at the height of their fertility and beauty. The noun ἄνθος ("FLOWER") is used only twice outside this verse, both when James links the "flower" of the grass with its "beauty" (James 1:10–11). In the grand scheme of things, the springtime of man is as fleeting as the passing blossoms of the world around him.

That which is compared to these things is "ALL FLESH" (πᾶσα σὰρξ) and "ALL ITS GLORY" (πᾶσα δόξα αὐτῆς). While σὰρξ ("Flesh") can be used of both animals and humans (1 Cor. 15:39; Rev. 19:18), it is predominantly used in the NT of the latter, as is the case here. The addition of πᾶσα ("ALL") gathers up all humanity and likens the whole of our experience to the transitory existence of "GRASS." So also (καὶ, "AND") with "ALL ITS GLORY." Just what does Peter intend by referring to humanity's "GLORY" (δόξα)? The LXX of Isaiah 40:6 has δόξα ("glory"), but the Hebrew text has חֶסֶד ("loveliness"). This theologically rich word often points to God's unfailing covenant commitment to His people. Used of humans, however, it seems to point to the failed nature of our commitments. Thus, the NET renders it "all their promises are like the flowers in the field." The fact remains, however, that Peter seems to follow the LXX (δόξα, "GLORY") and thus seems to point to humanity at its best and highest. On humanity's best day, in all her best achievements, through all her greatest conquests, she remains transient and her "GLORY" shines only for a moment and is quickly gone. Jesus also used "glory" as a comparison, but in the opposite direction—moving from Solomon in his splendor to the grasses of the fields (Matt. 6:28–30; Luke 12:27–28). Peter perhaps recalls this but uses the illustration in reverse—from the "glory" of wildflowers to that of humanity. And Jesus and Peter used them to make different points. Jesus' point was to dispel worry—if God is so generous with the grasses of the fields, will He not take care of you as well? Peter's point (and Isaiah's before him) was the fragility and transitory nature of human existence—humanity in all its glory is no more lasting than the herbage of the field.

> **Ministry Maxim**
>
> Life at its highest and best is but a fleeting proving ground for eternity.

Earthly reality is reflected in the perishability of plant life: "THE GRASS WITHERS, AND THE FLOWER FALLS OFF" (ἐξηράνθη ὁ χόρτος καὶ τὸ ἄνθος ἐξέπεσεν). Alive as a plant may be in one moment, it eventually "WITHERS" (ἐξηράνθη) and often in a comparatively short time. Glorious as the beauty of plant life may be (and it often is), it "FALLS OFF" (ἐξέπεσεν). Both verbs are in the aorist tense, either emphasizing the suddenness of their perishing[270] or being considered gnomic, describing plant life's customary and axiomatic nature.[271] For all their life and beauty, they are suddenly dead. The first verb (ἐξηράνθη, "WITHERS") means "to dry out" and when passive, as it is here, "dry up."[272] It is used in the NT to depict the demise of rootless plants (Matt. 13:6; Mark 4:6; Luke 8:6), the fig tree cursed by Jesus (Matt. 21:19–20; Mark 11:20–21), a diseased hand (Mark 3:1), an unceasing issue of blood upon coming into Jesus' healing presence (Mark 5:29), demonic activity in the presence of Christ (Mark 9:18), a river dried up (Rev. 16:12), a branch detached from its trunk (John 15:6), and, as here, grass under the power of the sun (James 1:11) and crops at the end of their growing season (Rev. 14:15). The passive form is often taken as deponent (having an active meaning) but may also be read as a middle—the grass "WITHERS" of its own accord, as the natural progression of its existence.[273] The second verb (ἐξέπεσεν, "FALLS OFF") is a compound constructed of ἐκ ("out of," "away") and πίπτω ("to fall"). The first verb pictures the internal process, and the second the external result.

Peter's point is continued and brought to its end as he continues the quotation in the next verse.

Verse 25 – BUT THE WORD OF THE LORD ENDURES FOREVER." And this is the word which was preached to you.

Peter continues to cite Isaiah. Having just quoted (v.24) Isaiah 40:6b-7a, he skips a clause from the original text ("When the breath of the LORD blows upon it; Surely the people are grass. The grass withers, the flower

---

270 Hiebert, 117; Kelly, 81; Rienecker, 749; Vincent, 1:640.

271 Bigg, 123; Dana and Mantey, 197; Dubis, 40; Forbes, 51; Michaels, 78; Robertson, *Word Pictures*, 6:93; Wallace, 562.

272 Friberg, 275.

273 Dubis, 40.

fades…", Isa. 40:7b-8a)²⁷⁴ and ends with "BUT THE WORD OF THE LORD ENDURES FOREVER" (τὸ δὲ ῥῆμα κυρίου μένει εἰς τὸν αἰῶνα, Isa. 40:8b). The expression "THE WORD OF THE LORD" is found over 250 times in the Bible, mostly in the OT where it stands for the divine utterance given to humankind through His prophets. It is most often accompanied by the verb "came to" or the command to "listen." "THE WORD OF THE LORD" comes to us in the pages of Scripture (2 Peter 1:20–21), and we are under obligation to "listen" to God as He speaks to us there.

Humanity and the flowers of the field have in common their fleeting existence (v.24), "BUT" (δὲ) God's Word does not share in this quality. Rather it "ENDURES FOREVER" (μένει εἰς τὸν αἰῶνα). Peter uses the verb again from verse 23: "the … abiding [μένοντος] word of God" (ESV). Because it is "imperishable" and "living" (v.23), it is "abiding" and "ENDURES." Here too, the verb is in the present tense, underscoring its unceasing resilience. Indeed, nothing overcomes it "FOREVER" or, more literally, "unto the age" (εἰς τὸν αἰῶνα). The exact phrase is found twenty-eight times in the NT; here, as so often (cf. John 6:51, 58; Heb. 5:6; 6:20; 7:17, 21, 24, 28; 1 John 2:17), it designates that which is everlasting. Jesus declared, "Truly I say to you, until heaven and earth pass away, not the smallest letter or stroke shall pass from the Law until all is accomplished" (Matt. 5:18) and "Heaven and earth will pass away, but My words will not pass away" (24:35). "Forever, O LORD, Your word is settled in heaven" (Psa. 119:89).

Peter now adds (δέ, "And") an interpretation that specifies what is meant by "THE WORD OF THE LORD," saying, "this is the word which was preached to you" (τοῦτο … ἐστιν τὸ ῥῆμα τὸ εὐαγγελισθὲν εἰς ὑμᾶς).

> **Ministry Maxim**
>
> All Scripture finds its fulfillment in the gospel of Jesus Christ and provides the means for faithfully proclaiming it.

---

274 Which the LXX is also missing, thus confirming the suspicion that Peter quoted from it rather than the MT, though with a few slight alterations (Schreiner, 96).

Peter equates "THE WORD OF THE LORD" with the gospel of Jesus Christ, which had been proclaimed to them. What conclusions should we draw from the transition from λόγου ... θεοῦ ("the ... word of God," v.23) to τὸ ... ῥῆμα κυρίου ("THE WORD OF THE LORD," v.25)? The change from λόγου to τὸ ... ῥῆμα may be accounted for by the LXX's use of ῥῆμα at this point. The transition from θεοῦ to κυρίου, however, seems intentional and designed to carry a message, for the best LXX's manuscripts have θεοῦ at this point. Elsewhere Peter appears to refer to Jesus when using κύριος (e.g., 1:3; 2:3; 3:15). Peter is here again making Jesus the fulfillment of God's redemptive purposes set forth in the OT Scriptures. In this, we may see Peter's implicit testimony to the deity of Jesus Christ.

Deciding whether the genitive (κυρίου, "of the Lord") is to be read as subjective (the word Jesus proclaimed) or objective (the word about Jesus) is ultimately superfluous. Peter has already said his readers "have not seen Him" (1 Peter 1:8) and thus have not heard Jesus preach. But he now reminds them of the word Jesus spoke being preached to them (v.25a).[275]

The demonstrative pronoun (τοῦτο, "this") makes the direct connection—the "word of the Lord" of which Isaiah spoke in his day (Isa. 40:8b) was all along to find its fulfillment in the gospel of our Lord Jesus Christ.[276] The OT Scriptures "were written for our instruction, upon whom the ends of the ages have come" (1 Cor. 10:11). "Whatever was written in earlier times was written for our instruction, so that through perseverance and the encouragement of the Scriptures we might have hope" (Rom. 15:4). Having been raised from the dead, Jesus Himself taught that "all things ... written about Me in the Law of Moses and the Prophets and the Psalms must be fulfilled" (Luke 24:44). The prophets foretold that the Christ must suffer (Acts 3:18; 13:29) and rise again (Acts 13:33). The whole of Jesus' life, death, and resurrection were "according to the Scriptures" (1 Cor. 15:3–4). Paul quoted Genesis 15:6 regarding Abraham's faith being counted to him as righteousness. He then concluded, "Now not for his

---

275 Forbes, 52.

276 Wallace, 326.

sake only was it written that it was credited to him, but for our sake also, to whom it will be credited, as those who believe in Him who raised Jesus our Lord from the dead" (Rom. 4:23–24).

Isaiah spoke of the Servant of the Lord who would suffer an atoning death to redeem His people (Isa. 52:13–53:12). Peter already spoke of what "the Spirit of Christ within them [the prophets] was indicating as He predicted the sufferings of Christ and the glories to follow" (1 Peter 1:11). Peter now tells us Jesus is the fulfillment of Isaiah's prophecy and that His death accomplished our redemption. This is "an eternal gospel" (Rev. 14:6) which constitutes God's final word to humanity (Heb. 1:1–2). As such, it will never pass away.

Peter reminds his readers that this was the gospel "preached" (τὸ εὐαγγελισθὲν) to them. The same verb was used in verse 12, where Peter reminded them of "those who preached the gospel" (τῶν εὐαγγελισαμένων) to them. When indicating the gospel proclamation was "to you" (εἰς ὑμᾶς), he used the same phrase that occurs in verse 4 regarding their inheritance in Christ and in verse 10 of the grace that the prophets saw would come to them in Christ (cf. Peter's only other use in 2 Peter 3:9). When a simple dative (ὑμῖν, "to you"; cf. 1:2, 12, 13) would have sufficed Peter chose this more graphic expression to emphasize his readers' privilege in receiving the gospel.[277]

---

277 Michaels enlarges on the same thought, saying, "The placement of εἰς ὑμᾶς at the end of the section gives emphasis to what has been a major theme in the epistle's first chapter at least since the εἰς ὑμᾶς of v 4: everything that God planned from the beginning, everything that he accomplished through the death and resurrection of Jesus Christ, everything still waiting to be revealed, is for the sake of the Christians in Asia Minor who read Peter's words. From the εἰς ὑμᾶς of vv 4 and 10, to the δι' ὑμᾶς of v 20, to the εἰς ὑμᾶς of v 25, all of it, punctuated by the repetition of the pronouns ὑμῶν (vv 7, 9, 13, 14, 17, 18, 21, 22), ὑμῖν (vv 12, 13), and ὑμᾶς (vv 12, 15), is 'for you.' The repeated pronouns help build the readers' identity, and begin to call them to responsibility." (Michaels, 79–80)

Digging Deeper:

1. What counsel does verse 24 give regarding your use of time today?
2. How does verse 25 suggest you invest a good portion of your time today?

1 PETER 2

Verse 1 – "Therefore, putting aside all malice and all deceit and hypocrisy and envy and all slander,"

Peter continues the argument from the end of chapter 1 with a logical deduction (οὖν, "Therefore"). Since all that is human is frail and passing away (1:24) and since his readers have been implanted with eternal life through the imperishable word of the Lord, the gospel (vv.23, 25), they must take the actions outlined in the following verses. The free gift of eternal life carries ethical obligations. The main verb, a command, is found in verse 2: "long for" (ἐπιποθήσατε). Implanted with life through the seed of the Word, sharing in the Lord's own eternal and imperishable life, they must "long for" that "word."

But before we can reach that command, we are confronted with a participle that modifies it: "putting aside" (Ἀποθέμενοι, v.1). The participle depicts that which must take place for the command to be fulfilled, the action of the participle logically preceding that of the command.[1] The participle picks up something of the imperative

> **Ministry Maxim**
>
> To share in the life of God is to separate from all that would separate the people of God.

---

1   Davids, 80; Forbes, 55; Hiebert, 120–121.

and should be read as a pressing necessity that is not up for discussion. Thus, several English versions translate it as a command (cf. "put away," ESV; "get rid of," NET, NLT; "Rid yourselves of," NIV, NRSV). The aorist tense depicts the decisive nature of the act, though probably not understanding the action as a once-for-all or once-and-done proposition. The sins outlined must be dealt with repeatedly, as often as they show up to tempt us. But we must plant our feet and refuse to give way to them in any instance. Here, as in all its NT occurrences, it is in the middle voice, depicting the subject acting upon him/herself and stressing the inward nature of the decisive separation. The verb is a compound comprised of ἀπό ("from") and τίθημι ("to put/place"). It could be used literally of taking off clothing and setting it aside (Acts 7:58). But most often in the NT, as here, it depicts the moral action of setting aside sin and having nothing to do with it any longer (Rom. 13:12; Eph. 4:22, 25; Col. 3:8; Heb. 12:1; James 1:21).

Peter makes mention of five specific sins the believer must put away from one's life. Four occurrences of καὶ ("and") string these together. The first, second, and fifth items are accompanied by the appropriate form of πᾶς ("all"), indicating the wholesale denunciation of each and every form of the immoral practice under consideration. Every form, all that might be considered under its banner, everything to do with it, each occasion should be jettisoned. The fact that the adjective does not appear with the third and fourth items in Peter's list should not be taken as an indication they are of less concern but is probably a stylistic consideration on his part. The first two nouns are singular, and the last three are plural. The former may be considered collective nouns, gathering anything that might fit the category In each case, the latter may find multiple and varied expressions while still being failures that share the common root.[2] All five are chosen as representative of those things which war against the command to "love one another" (1:22).

---

2 "This use of the plural of abstract substantives does indeed lay stress on the separate acts." (Robertson, *Grammar*, 408).

The first sin that the believer must set aside is "all malice" (πᾶσαν κακίαν). It is moral depravity and is the opposite of ἀρετή ("virtue," cf. 1 Peter 2:9; 2 Peter 1:3, 5).³ It has "the quality of wickedness, with the implication of that which is harmful and damaging."⁴ Elsewhere Peter demanded that one must repent of this wickedness (Acts 8:22). Paul also lists it among other vices which must be "put away" (Rom. 1:29; Eph. 4:31; Col. 3:8), as does James (James 1:21). It was characteristic of the unconverted life of even Paul and Titus (Titus 3:3). Jesus said each day presents challenges of this sort (Matt. 6:34). Thus the decision to put it aside must be just as daily and at each occurrence of its threat.

The second is "all deceit" (πάντα δόλον). Principally it was bait used to catch fish. By extension and used metaphorically it then described any stratagem, plot, or trick used to take in the unsuspecting. It is craft, guile, and fraud. Its ploys often work through false words (1 Peter 3:10). It is what the religious authorities used in attempting to gain control over Jesus (Matt. 26:4; Mark 14:1). It operates in and arises out of the unredeemed heart (Mark 7:22). The devil is a liar (John 8:44). He is the ultimate source of all "deceit" (Acts 13:10). Jesus forsook deceit (1 Peter 2:22) and so must all who pledge allegiance to Him.

To this is added the third vice from which we are to be separated, "hypocrisy" (ὑποκρίσεις). The noun is used only six times in the NT and only here by Peter. But Peter was guilty of it when he withdrew from table fellowship with the Gentile believers of Galatia out of fear of other Jews' scorn (Gal. 2:13). In the Gospels, it is applied to the Pharisees (Matt. 23:28; Mark 12:15; Luke 12:1). The word originally described an actor on stage, wearing a mask and playing the part of someone else. In the NT, the word is always negative, referring to a person pretending to be one thing while being something quite different.

The fourth sin to flee is "envy" (φθόνους). Envy is a negative response prompted by the success of another. Paul frequently included the term in his lists of vices (Rom. 1:29; Gal. 5:21; 1 Tim. 6:4; Titus 3:3). It is used to

---

3   Friberg, 213.

4   Louw-Nida, 88.105.

describe the unregenerate (Rom. 1:29; Titus 3:3) and is one of the deeds of the flesh (Gal. 5:21). It is what motivated those who delivered over Jesus to be killed by the Jewish religious leaders (Matt. 27:18; Mark 15:10).

Finally, there is "all slander" (πάσας καταλαλιάς). The word is used only here and in 2 Corinthians 12:20, where Paul also used it in a list of vices. It is a compound comprised of ("down"/"from") and λαλιά ("speech"/"speaking"). It is, then, defamatory speech that defames, disparages, denigrates, and destroys others. Peter uses its cognate verb in 2:12 and 3:16, where it depicts unbelievers speaking evil of believers in both cases. Peter thus demands here "they must not repay in kind, with Christ functioning as the model (2:21–25)."[5]

Verse 2 – "like newborn babies, long for the pure milk of the word, so that by it you may grow in respect to salvation,"

After the long setup (v.1), now the command arrives (ἐπιποθήσατε, "long"). It is pushed to the end of Peter's line of reasoning for emphasis (all that follows it is a purpose statement and a conditional clause). The aorist imperative demands action with a punch of urgency and immediacy. The verb is a compound comprised of ἐπί ("on"/"upon") and ποθέω ("to long for"). The preposition may mark the intensity of the desire or give direction to the yearning.[6] The word is a strong one, describing an intense yearning after something (2 Cor. 5:2) or someone (Rom. 1:11; 2 Cor. 9:14; Phil. 1:8; 2:26; 1 Thess. 3:6; 2 Tim. 1:4). It is used in the LXX of one's longing for the Lord Himself: "As the deer pants [ἐπιποθεῖ] for the water brooks, So my soul pants [ἐπιποθεῖ] for You, O God" (Psa. 42:1); "My soul longed [ἐπιποθεῖ] and even yearned for the courts of the LORD" (Psa. 84:2a). And, significantly in relationship to Peter's present exhortation (see below), it depicts longing for the word of the Lord: "My soul is crushed with longing [ἐπεπόθησεν] After Your ordinances at all times"

---

5 Forbes, 56.

6 Spicq, 2:58.

(Psalm 119:20); "I opened my mouth wide and panted, For I longed [ἐπεπόθουν] for Your commandments" (Psalm 119:131; cf. also v.174).

That after which they are to long is "the pure milk of the word" (τὸ λογικὸν ἄδολον γάλα). The object of the desire is "milk" (τὸ ... γάλα). The imagery is of an infant with its mother. Paul (1 Cor. 3:2) and the author of Hebrews (Heb. 5:12–13) use the noun to describe elementary and initiatory teachings in the Christian faith. In both cases, "milk" is set over against "solid food," which is suitable for sustaining a mature believer. But Peter does not use the noun in precisely the same way. His present metaphor must control the meaning here. Peter is not discussing relative stages of maturity but the basic desire of a child for sustenance. Within the metaphor, the definite article identifies that "milk" only the mother (and within the metaphor itself, God) can supply the child. It is the only sustenance the child can stomach, and she the only source from which it can come. Apart from it, the child withers and death encroaches; with it the child thrives, and growth takes place. It is the nature of an infant to yearn after the mother's milk. The child grows desperate and will stop at nothing to see the need met, thrashing, crying, and demanding until the mother satisfies the need.

Two adjectives qualify "milk" (τὸ ... γάλα), both in the attributive position between the noun and its definite article. The first (λογικὸν, "of the word") is the subject of debate as to how it ought to be translated. The word could be used for what is rational (mental; thought-related) rather than physical or what is metaphorical rather than literal. Strictly speaking, the word depicts that which is "carefully thought through" and can thus be rendered "thoughtfully."[7] The adjective is found elsewhere only in Romans 12:1, where it describes the presentation of our bodies to God as one's "spiritual [λογικὴν] service of worship" (cf. "reasonable service," KJV, NKJV, NET; "intelligent service," YLT). Many modern English translations aim to capture this idea here in 1 Peter 2:2 and render it "spiritual" (e.g., ESV, NET, NIV, NLT, NRSV). But other translations detect a play on words and render it "of the word" (KJV, NKJV, NASU) or "the word's"

---

7   BDAG, 4599.

(YLT). The play on words is between the adjective λογικός and the noun λόγος (λόγου…θεοῦ, "the…word of God," 1:23) through which they were given new birth; just as ἄδολον ("pure") follows on δόλον ("deceit") of verse 1 (see below).[8] The adjective (λογικός) itself is derived from the noun (λόγος). Indeed, Liddell and Scott list the first meaning of the adjective as "*of* or *for speaking* or *speech*."[9] Likewise, Mounce assigns the meaning as "*pertaining to speech*."[10] When associated with λόγος, the emphasis of the adjective is "belonging to reason" or "rational."[11] The play on words is central to Peter's expression, and the local context must control our understanding of the word in this case. We should thus understand Peter as emphasizing the rational, mental priority in spiritual growth, with the nourishment for the believer's growth coming from the gospel as revealed and unfolded in the text of Scripture.

Schreiner is correct, "The means by which God sanctifies believers is through the mind, through the continued proclamation of the word. Spiritual growth is not primarily mystical but rational, and rational in the sense that it is informed and sustained by God's word."[12] It is only logical (οὖν, "Therefore," 2:1) that being born anew through the gospel as communicated through the Scriptures (1 Peter 1:23–25) that the new life implanted will drive the newly born one back to it again and again for sustenance, strength, and maturing. The attributive position of the adjective emphasizes, even more, its qualitative nature.

Isaiah cried out: "Ho! Every one who thirsts, come to the waters; And you who have no money come, buy and eat. Come, buy wine and milk Without money and without cost" (Isa. 55:1). Soon enough, he makes it clear that it is the Lord's own "word…which goes forth from My mouth" that is his concern. And the Lord assures us, "It will not return to Me

---

8   Goppelt, 131; Kelly, 85; Lenski, 79; Stibbs, 96; cf. NIDNTT, 3:118.
9   Liddell and Scott, 26640.
10 Mounce, 1201.
11 TDNT, 4:142.
12 Schreiner, 100.

empty, Without accomplishing what I desire, And without succeeding in the matter for which I sent it" (v.11).

Another adjective (ἄδολον, "pure") also qualifies the noun "milk." It appears only here in the NT. It is formed by the alpha-privative (for negation) and the noun δόλος ("guile," "deceit," "treachery"; cf. 1 Peter 2:22). Peter once again engages in wordplay, and the present adjective stands over against the "deceit" (δόλον) to be jettisoned according to verse 1. It designates that which is without fraud or deceit, and when applied to liquids, as it is here metaphorically, it means unadulterated, undiluted, and without compromise. It was not uncommon in the ancient world for merchants to water down their product, be it wine or milk, for the sake of profits. Sadly, some preachers do the same with their message (2 Cor. 2:17) and some people demand it so (2 Tim. 4:3). To the child there is no substitute for mother's milk. To the child of God there is no substitute for the word of the gospel extended in and expounded from the words of Scripture. It alone gives life, nourishes, matures, strengthens, and saves. Let us have it full-strength and undiluted!

> **Ministry Maxim**
>
> Present spiritual hunger is a sign of ultimate salvation.

This longing is to be "like newborn babies" (ὡς ἀρτιγέννητα βρέφη). The comparative particle (ὡς, "like") calls us to consider the nature of this longing. The noun βρέφη ("babies") is used in the NT of a baby still in the womb (Luke 1:41, 44) or just born (Luke 2:12, 16; Acts 7:19). The adjective "newborn" (ἀρτιγέννητα) is found only here in the NT. It is a compound comprised of ἄρτι ("now") and γεννητός ("begotten," "born"; found in the NT only in Matt. 11:11; Luke 7:28). A hungry newborn makes its demands known. A ravenous infant that catches the scent of mother and her milk will not be denied. So too was the craving of the child of God for the Word through which he was regenerated. Life depends upon that Word and the child of God cannot get enough of it. Peter's imagery should not lead us to conclude that his readers are all recent converts and, thus, still "babies" in the faith. Rather he is likening all believers—however long they may have known the Lord—to ever-hungry, ravenous babes who yearn after the "milk" that gives them life.

We can see then the notion that Peter here writes a baptismal catechism for new converts is misguided. This word is necessary sustenance for all God's people, newly converted and long in the faith.

The purpose (ἵνα + with a subjunctive verb, "so that") of this longing is that "by it you may grow" (ἐν αὐτῷ αὐξηθῆτε). The pronoun αὐτῷ ("it") finds its antecedent in γάλα ("milk"). The preposition ἐν ("by") denotes the means or instrument by which the growth takes place. Peter will later use the verb (αὐξηθῆτε, "you may grow") to command his readers to "grow in the grace and knowledge of our Lord and Savior Jesus Christ" (2 Peter 3:18). Luke used it to recount the advance of the gospel in the days of the early church (Acts 6:7; 12:24; 19:20). Paul employed it of the believer's advance in the things of Christ (e.g., 2 Cor. 10:15; Eph. 2:21; 4:15; Col. 1:10; 2:19). The passive voice views God working in the life of the believer through the means of His Word by His Spirit to bring about the growth of his people. Hiebert says, "Spiritual growth is not a direct act of human volition. The Christian's responsibility is to diligently appropriate the Word that produces the growth."[13]

This growth is to be "in respect to salvation" (εἰς σωτηρίαν).[14] The preposition (εἰς, "in respect to") marks the purpose or goal of God's work through His Word with the note of its resulting completion.[15] That goal is "salvation" (σωτηρίαν). Peter's emphasis has been on the culmination of God's saving work at the return of Jesus (1 Peter 1:5, 9), and it seems to be so used here as well, for the precise phrase (εἰς σωτηρίαν) is also found in 1:5. The life-long growth and progressing maturity that God causes in us by means of the Word of God finds its apex and fulfillment at the return of Jesus Christ and the final salvation His people. Peter writes to bolster his readers' faith that eventually, it "may be found to result in praise and glory and honor at the revelation of Jesus Christ" (v.7).

---

13 Hiebert, 125.

14 The phrase (εἰς σωτηρίαν) is not found in many later manuscripts (thus its absence from the KJV), but the earlier and best manuscripts include it. It seems likely that at some point it dropped out due to a scribe's discomfort with what may have sounded like one growing into rather than being gifted with salvation. The phrase should be included in the text as original.

15 BDAG, 2291.4.e.

Verse 3 – "if you have tasted the kindness of the Lord."

Peter closes out the sentence that began in verse 1 with a conditional statement: "if you have tasted the kindness of the Lord" (εἰ ἐγεύσασθε ὅτι χρηστὸς ὁ κύριος). The condition is assumed to be true. Because it is assumed true, the NIV moves away from translating it as a conditional statement and renders it with "Now that." Yet we should consider whether, though Peter assumed the condition to be true, any such rendering may supplant his desire to make his readers consider whether the condition is true for them personally.[16] Peter believes that his readers have indeed, through the gospel of Jesus Christ (1:25), "tasted of the kindness of the Lord." Let them prove him correct by craving after the Word by which they have tasted that kindness (v.2).

The verb (ἐγεύσασθε, "you have tasted") is in the aorist tense, pointing to the simple act. The middle voice pictures the inward nature of the taste. The verb has a range of meanings: "to taste, partake of, enjoy, come to know, experience."[17] Used metaphorically, as here, it means "to experience someth[ing] cognitively or emotionally"[18] or "come to know by experience."[19] It should not be read as merely sampling something instead of ingesting it. Nor should this be reduced to a partaking of the Eucharist.[20] The past tense cannot be reduced to ritual participation.

> **Ministry Maxim**
> One taste of grace creates a lifetime of hunger.

That (ὅτι, "that") which has been thus "tasted" is "the kindness of the Lord" (χρηστὸς ὁ κύριος). The fact that the adjective (χρηστὸς, "kindness") comes before the noun and its definite article (ὁ κύριος, "of the Lord")

---

16 Schreiner, 101; Wallace, 690–694.
17 NIDNTTE, 1:565.
18 BDAG, 1637.2.
19 Grudem, 102.
20 Davids, 83–84; Goppelt, 133; Kelly, 87.

makes the emphasis fall slightly more upon the adjective than the noun.[21] Yet Peter is not diminishing the Lord in any way, for the presence of the definite article marks Him out as that unique and only Lord who alone is God.[22] Peter focuses his readers on the sweet taste of the divine, exclusive "kindness" that has fallen upon the palate of their souls. Storms notes the assonance of χρηστὸς ("kindness") and Χριστός ("Christ"), which led to some variations among the manuscripts though the χρηστὸς must be considered original.[23] In Psalm 34, David speaks of Yahweh; Peter freely takes up his words and uses them of Jesus (as verse 4 makes explicit).

In all this Peter is quoting Psalm 34:8a (33:9, LXX).[24] The quotation is exact (ὅτι χρηστὸς ὁ κύριος, "that the Lord is good"), except Peter drops David's conjunction and second verb (καὶ ἴδετε, "and see") and uses the first verb in the imperative mood. Peter uses the indicative with the added conditional particle (εἰ, "if") to form the first-class condition that fits his present line of thought. The writer of Hebrews appears to refer to this same psalm: "have tasted the good word of God" (Heb. 6:5). But notice the substitution of "the word of God" (θεοῦ ῥῆμα) for "the kindness of the Lord." This is telling, for it forms yet another line of support for our understanding of λογικὸν above in verse 2 (cf. τὸ ῥῆμα, "the word," 1 Peter 1:25).

The command is to "long for the pure milk of the word," just like a baby longs after its mother's milk. In the word/gospel (1:23, 25), we "have tasted the kindness of the Lord." That "taste" is to incite a longing after more of that "word." The taste of God's goodness in the gospel/word (v.3) creates a longing (v.2a) that must be satisfied and when it is it results in final salvation (v.2b).

---

21 Wallace, 307–308.

22 Ibid., 223.

23 Hart, 55; Storms, 315.

24 In 1 Peter 3:10–12 Peter will again quote from Psalm 34, this time verses 12–16. See Schreiner for a detailed description of the parallels between the entire Psalm and 1 Peter (101–102).

> **Digging Deeper:**
> 1. Explain to someone the logical connection between the implanted life of God and our rejection of all that might separate one from the people of God (1 Peter 1:23; 2:1).
> 2. In what way is one's appetite for the written Word of God a barometer for one's spiritual health? (vv.2–3).

Verse 4 – "And coming to Him as to a living stone which has been rejected by men, but is choice and precious in the sight of God,"

Having completed a series of moral imperatives (1:13–2:3) based upon the grace given to his readers through Christ (1:1–12), Peter now repeats his strategy. While in 1:1–12, Peter focuses on the *individual* believer's identity in Christ, here in 2:4–10, he speaks to the *corporate* identity of his readers as believers in Jesus Christ. As Peter did in 1:13–2:3, in light of God's grace to make us new (2:4–10), he will issue commands for holy living (2:11–5:11). He establishes the corporate identity of Christ's followers using terms that originated under the Old Covenant with Israel and will now apply them to the New Covenant people of God. He has already used this strategy (cf. 1:16, 25; 2:3) but now indulges even more fully in the practice. In fact, before verse 10 is done, Peter will have quoted or alluded to ten different passages from the OT and applied them in Christ to his readers. We will work through the text and then synthesize and draw theological conclusions (see comments on verse 10).

The sentence begun here runs through verse 5, where the main verb is found (οἰκοδομεῖσθε, "are being built up"). A participial phrase here in verse 4 and an infinitive clause at the end of verse 5 modify the fact that Peter's readers "are being built up." Their being "built up" begins with their "coming to Him" (πρὸς ὃν προσερχόμενοι). The antecedent of the relative pronoun (ὅν, "Him"; cf. "whom," KJV, YLT) is "the Lord" (ὁ κύριος, v.3). In the Hebrew text of Psalm 34 (which is quoted in verse 4) "the Lord" is Yahweh, the personal, covenant name of God. Here, clearly,

Peter applies what is said of Him to Jesus. Peter's Christology is clear. The verb is a compound made up of πρὸς ("to") and ἔρχομαι ("to come"). To this is added here the same preposition in freestanding form (πρὸς, "to"). This serves to double the emphasis upon Jesus as the object of their "coming." Peter may have chosen the verb because Psalm 34:5 ([LXX, Psa. 33:6]; cf. the quotation from Psa. 34:8 [LXX, Psa. 33:9] here in verse 3) begins with the same verb. Peter, however, takes the line of thought in a different direction than the psalmist. The verb was used frequently in the LXX of Levitical priests approaching God in worship under the Mosaic covenant. It is frequently found in Hebrews to describe the present New Covenant privilege of all God's people "coming" before God into His very presence as priests (Heb. 4:16; 7:25; 10:1, 22; 11:6; 12:18, 22). The present tense participle emphasizes the ongoing, repeated, and habitual approach to faith. This describes the life of faith, not simply the pivot of repentance and trust, which must precede and open the door to this pattern of faith. As an infant comes to its mother repeatedly for life-giving sustenance (v.2), so the child of God comes again and again to Christ for life. The "coming" Peter has in mind envelops relationship with God the Son by the grace of God the Father and the working of God the Spirit. The participle may be describing circumstances attendant to[25] or the means[26] of "being built up" (v.5). The building process (v.5) depends upon coming and continuing to come to Jesus (v.4).

> **Ministry Maxim**
>
> Jesus elicits a binary response—either you treasure Him or trash Him.

But in what sense are they "coming to" Jesus? They approach as to "a living stone" (λίθον ζῶντα). In referring to Jesus as a "stone" (λίθον) Peter is anticipating his use of Isaiah 28:16 (in v. 6), Psalm 118:22 (in v.7), and Isaiah 8:14 (in v.8), all of which employ such imagery. Peter views all these as having the Messiah, Jesus, in view. He likely draws upon Jesus'

---

25 Forbes, .61.

26 Dubis, 45.

own application of these verses and this imagery to Himself (Matt. 21:42; Mark 12:10; Luke 20:17). Peter had already begun to apply them to Jesus early in His post-Pentecost ministry (Acts 4:11). The λίθον ("stone)" is a groomed stone, prepared and fit for building.²⁷ He is "living" (ζῶντα) both in the sense that Peter is speaking of a spiritual structure (temple) rather than a physical one (i.e., in Jerusalem) and because Jesus has been raised from the dead to life (1 Peter 1:3, 11b, 21) and thus gives new life to those he chooses (1:3, 23; 2:2). The participle qualifies the noun λίθον ("stone"). The present tense underscores not only the present life but the ongoing and, indeed, unending resurrection life of Jesus. It has been used twice already by Peter, and he appears to be developing a theme: "living hope" (ἐλπίδα ζῶσαν, 1:3), "living ... word" (λόγου ζῶντος, 1:23), "living stones" (λίθοι ζῶντες, 2:5).

Since Jesus is the sole source of life, it is tragic that He "has been rejected by men" (ὑπὸ ἀνθρώπων ... ἀποδεδοκιμασμένον). The prepositional phrase ὑπὸ ἀνθρώπων ("by men") is set before the participle for emphasis, just as its parallel (παρὰ ... θεῷ, "by God") will be in the next clause. This sets up an emphatic contrast between the actions of God and the response of people in relationship to Jesus Christ. The noun (ἀνθρώπων, "men") represents not males but the whole of humanity, male and female, young and old, across all racial, ethnic, and national lines. Of the nine NT usages of the verb, eight refer to the treatment afforded Jesus (cf., the exception in Heb. 12:17, which refers to Esau). The verb is a compound comprised of ἀπό ("from") and δοκιμάζω ("to put to the test/examine"; cf. 1:7, where this root verb is used, as is the cognate noun) and strictly speaking, it means "throw out as the result of a test."²⁸ It can have the sense of "declare useless."²⁹ Jesus was despised and repudiated by humankind. The perfect tense indicates that the rejection of Jesus took

---

27 Peter uses the noun λίθος ("stone") rather than πέτρος ("rock"; i.e., "Peter") which Jesus conferred upon him (Matt. 16:18). For this reason and because he makes no explicit connection of the two in our present passage it is unlikely that we should seek either connection or application to that pivotal moment in Peter's life and ministry.

28 Friberg, 66.

29 NIDNTTE, 756.

place in the past and continues at present. Thus "we do not yet see all things subjected to him." (Heb. 2:8). The passive voice pictures Christ the "living stone" being acted upon by humankind, whose volition was gifted to them by Him.

Rejection of Jesus is tragic and brings an everlasting effect, for He "is chosen and precious in the sight of God" (παρὰ ... θεῷ ἐκλεκτὸν ἔντιμον). The contrast ("but") between the rejection of men and the election and love of God the Father is set out emphatically in the formula μὲν ... δὲ. Rejection of Jesus has put them at enmity with God. The preposition παρὰ serves as a "marker of one whose viewpoint is relevant" and is thus translated "in the sight of."[30] There appears to be some interplay between the prepositions Peter chooses, by what is done "by" (ὑπὸ) humankind and what is true "in the sight of" (παρὰ) God. In the end, the only viewpoint that matters is that of "God" (θεῷ). The combination (παρὰ ... θεῷ) "indicates the ultimate standard—the purity of the divine life and the clarity of the divine vision—by which all aspects of human thought and conduct should now be assessed and will in the end be judged."[31] God the Father, aware of all the evidence, has valued Jesus Christ differently than "men" have—to their eternal undoing.

In God's sight, Jesus is "chosen" (ἐκλεκτὸν) and "precious" (ἔντιμον). Peter uses the first adjective in 1:1 of his readers ("elect exiles," ESV), here and in 2:6 of Christ the "stone," and in 2:9 of the whole of Christ's followers as "A CHOSEN RACE." It is a theologically rich term from an equally theologically rich word family. Here it may pertain "to being considered best in the course of a selection" and be thus rendered "excellent" or "choice."[32] Jesus is, as becomes clear as the imagery develops, the highest and best, indeed the very "cornerstone" (v.6, ESV, NET, NIV, NLT, etc.) of all God is doing in the unfolding of His redemption. This heightens the tragedy of His rejection at the hands of men. Humankind gave Jesus a grade of F; God the Father scored Him infinitely beyond an

---

30 BDAG, 5548.3.B.2.

31 Harris, 172–173.

32 BDAG, 2385.3.

A+. Indeed, in the Father's eyes, Jesus is "precious" (ἔντιμον). The adjective is used five times in the NT, of a highly valued servant (Luke 7:2), of a valued position at a wedding feast (Luke 14:8), and of the "honor" Epaphroditus, a valued servant of God, is due (Phil. 2:29). The other two usages are here and in verse 6, in reflections of Isaiah 28:16 and applied to Christ. The word is a compound made up of ἐν ("in") and τιμή ("honor") and designates that which is worthy of being held "in honor."

What a tragic and fatal estimation "men" have made when looking upon Jesus Christ! In so doing, they have not only devalued Him who is above all worth and treasure, but they have arrayed themselves in opposition to God the Father who has counted His Son above all else. Apart from the initiative and intervention of divine grace, there can be no recovery from such a miscalculation.

Verse 5 – "you also, as living stones, are being built up as a spiritual house for a holy priesthood, to offer up spiritual sacrifices acceptable to God through Jesus Christ."

The main verb of the sentence beginning in verse 4 now stands before us: "you ... are being built up" (οἰκοδομεῖσθε). The word is a compound comprised of οἶκος ("house") and δομάω ("to build"). It can be used of the physical construction of a structure (e.g., Matt. 21:33; Luke 7:5; John 2:20), a city (Luke 4:29), or a tomb (Matt. 23:29). It can also, as here, be used metaphorically. In such cases, it may describe personal strengthening in faith (1 Cor. 8:1, 10), corporate strengthening in faith (Acts 20:32; 1 Cor. 10:23; 14:4, 17; 1 Thess. 5:11), establishing of churches (Rom. 15:20), and numerical growth of the church (Acts 9:31). It is used of building a temple (Acts 7:47, 49). Jesus used this imagery of the resurrection of His body as the new temple (Matt. 26:61; 27:40). He also, significantly, used it in His pivotal promise to Peter: "I also say to you that you are Peter, and upon this rock I will build [οἰκοδομήσω] My church; and the gates of Hades will not overpower it" (Matt. 16:18). It is telling that Peter does not tie his present comments to that encounter, but to the promises and prophecies of the OT. Indeed, he uses the verb here in anticipation of his use of it in verse 7, where he will quote its use in Psalm

118:22. There, the participle will be used substantively (οἱ οἰκοδομοῦντες, "THE BUILDERS"). In this present passage, Peter seems to combine most of these metaphorical elements to describe the building and edification of the Church. The present tense pictures the ongoing construction and expansion of the Church, while the passive voice pictures the hand of God at work through His servants in thus establishing His new temple, the Church. As people come and keep coming to Jesus and side with God in His valuation of Him (v.4), God builds His Church as the new temple of His dwelling in this world (v.5). While the form of the verb can be read as an imperative ("be yourselves built," RSV; "let yourselves be built," NRSV; "let yourselves be used in building," TEV) contextually it is best read as an indicative, stating the fact of what God does as people come to Jesus.

Consider the materials for the construction project: "you also, as living stones" (καὶ αὐτοὶ ὡς λίθοι ζῶντες). In so identifying his readers, Peter is clearly building off calling Jesus "a living stone" (λίθον ζῶντα) in the previous verse. We saw there that by "living," Peter identified Jesus not only as a person but as alive forever from the dead "in the power of an indestructible life" (Heb. 7:16). So too as he identifies Christ's followers as "living" (ζῶντες), he marks them not merely as possessing a pulse, but as those who have been "born again" (1:3, 23) and presently reside in the eternal life that Jesus gives. As with Jesus (v.4), so "also" (καὶ) with His followers—the participle "living" is in the present tense to underscore the present, ongoing, unending reality of this life gifted to them by God through Christ. By being in relationship to Jesus the "living stone" (λίθον ζῶντα, 2:4), they have come to possess a "living hope" (ἐλπίδα ζῶσαν, 1:3) through the "living... word" (λόγου ζῶντος, 1:23) of the gospel. Jesus is the "stone" (λίθον) who will soon enough be identified as the cornerstone (v.6), and they, in relationship to Him, are individual "stones" (λίθοι) being fitted together into a new temple in which God will dwell and manifest Himself in this world. Every stone is fitted to Jesus the cornerstone, receiving from Him the eternal life that is His alone to give. The pronoun (αὐτοὶ) serves to intensify ("you yourselves," ESV, NET) what is also communicated through the second person plural form of the verb (οἰκοδομεῖσθε, "you... are being built up")—each one of Peter's readers and all of them together are in view. Let not even one child of God think this eternal life, this intimate connection to Jesus, this high honor, this holy calling has passed them by and does not apply to them. The conjunction ὡς ("as") does not so much mark Peter's word as metaphorical (that is already clear by the imagery he employs) but signals how his readers are to view themselves within the purposes and active hand of God as they come and keep coming to Jesus ("as living stones").

The goal of the building project is two-fold. First, they are being built up "as a spiritual house" (οἶκος πνευματικὸς). The Greek is abrupt. There is nothing in the Greek text to suggest the word "as," though most English translations provide either "as" (ESV, NASU, NET) or "into" (NIV, NLT, NRSV) in an effort at smoother English. It is, more literally, "being built a spiritual house" (KJV, NKJV; cf. YLT). The noun οἶκος (just used in compound [οἰκοδομεῖσθε, "built up"], see above) can be used of a physical dwelling (Matt. 9:6–7; 11:8; Mark 5:38; Luke 19:5), of the tabernacle (Matt. 12:4; Luke 6:4), the temple of God (Matt. 21:13; Mark 11:17), the nation of Israel (Matt. 10:6; 15:24; Acts 2:36; Heb. 3:2), a family (Acts 10:2; 11:14; 16:31; 18:8; 1 Tim. 3:4, 5, 12), a family dynasty (Luke 1:27, 33; 2:4), the Church (1 Tim. 3:15), and the Kingdom of God (Heb. 3:6). Here Peter uses it as descriptive of the temple of God, figuratively considered. The physical temple of Israel is desolate, and its system of worship is obsolete. Not many years after Peter penned this letter, it was destroyed at the hands of the Roman General Titus. Already Peter envisions a different, new temple comprised not of physical stone but by the redeemed of God. As Stephen said, "the Most High does not dwell in houses made by human hands" (Acts 7:48). He has now fashioned His people as the temple of His dwelling (1 Cor. 3:16; 2 Cor. 6:16; Eph. 2:21–22; Heb. 3:6; 10:21–22). The people of God comprise a "spiritual" (πνευματικὸς) house. The adjective depicts that which is "derived from or being about the Spirit – 'spiritual, from the Spirit'" and is used of things such as "gifts, benefits, teachings, blessings, and religious songs."[33] It can be used of "one who

---

33   Louw-Nida, 12:21.

has received God's Spirit and presumably lives in accordance with this relationship."³⁴ In this case, it seems to point to the people of God as made by the Spirit of God into a place fit for divine dwelling.

The second goal is that they are being built up "for a holy priesthood" (εἰς ἱεράτευμα ἅγιον). The preposition εἰς ("for") conveys a sense of movement "into" something. In this case, God's grace has intent behind it. From the beginning, He was looking to create a people for the role of "a holy priesthood." The noun (ἱεράτευμα, "priesthood") is found in the NT only here and in verse 9. Israel, too was a priesthood, called to an exclusive relationship with and role before the Lord: "a kingdom of priests and a holy nation" (Exod. 19:6). Peter declares this to be now the Church's privilege and part. Indeed, "He has made us to be a kingdom, priests to His God and Father" (Rev. 1:6a). The role of the "priesthood" is not simply to enjoy the status nor even the exclusive intimacy afforded them to God. It is to serve God by representing Him to the people and to serve the people by representing them to God. If the entire Church is a "priesthood," then to whom are they representing God, and whom are they representing before Him? The very ones who have been the focus of God's attention from the beginning—the nations. But they are not just any "priesthood," but a "holy (ἅγιον) one. Peter has already called them to share in and reflect the holiness of God in their lives (1 Peter 1:15–16). Now that unique distinction of God is to be the very nature and substance of their priestly role and service.

The outcome of the building project is "to offer up spiritual sacrifices" (ἀνενέγκαι πνευματικὰς θυσίας). The Church's role as a "priesthood" is not merely ornamental or titular. There is work to be done. Peter has already underscored clearly the unique and complete work of Christ's atoning sacrifice of Himself on the cross (1:18–20). This was a "once for all" (Rom. 6:10; Heb. 7:27; 9:12, 26; 10:10; 1 Pet. 3:18) atonement; the sacrifice to end all sacrifices (Heb. 7:27; 10:1–14). Christ's sacrifice was not only once-for-all, complete, and perfect in its eternal sufficiency, it

---

34 Ibid., 12.20.

was also physical, bloody, earthly, and made at a precise moment in time-space history.

What are these "sacrifices" that God's priest-Church is "to offer up"? We contribute nothing to the sufficiency and efficacy of Christ's sacrifice but rest upon its completeness and look to God's certification of its acceptability through the resurrection of our Savior from the dead. From this posture of faith, however, God calls for "sacrifices" (θυσίας) to be made from gratitude for and as an expression of faith in that singular, perfect, finished sacrifice of Christ. These "sacrifices" include the presentation of our bodies to God "as a living sacrifice, holy and acceptable to God" (Rom. 12:1), walking in love which is "an offering and sacrifice to God" (Eph. 5:2), offering our expressions of worship and gratitude as "a sacrifice of praise to God" (Heb. 13:15), our acts of goodwill and sharing simply because "such sacrifices are pleasing to God" (Heb. 13:16), our gifts of support for gospel workers as "a fragrant aroma, an acceptable sacrifice, well-pleasing to God" (Phil. 4:18). Indeed, all our obedience to God is regarded as "the sacrifice and service of [our] faith" (Phil. 2:17).

> **Ministry Maxim**
>
> Both our identity and our activity as the people of God are priestly.

From our posture of rest upon God's provision for us in Christ, our sacrifices are "spiritual" (πνευματικὰς). The adjective depicts that which is "pertaining to the Spirit" or "suited for the Spirit."[35] Our sacrifices are "spiritual" as opposed to physical and literal, like those under the Mosaic system of worship. Gone are the offerings of "bulls and goats" (Heb. 9:13; 10:4) in desperate hope of acceptance. We have our acceptance in the finished work of Christ. Now we offer sacrifices through the enabling of God's own Spirit. These are movements of cooperation with His enabling presence. They are God Himself moving in and through us to act in expressions of love and gratitude, made in the obedience of faith and worship. We have here the same adjective just used in this verse, though the gender,

---

35 Rienecker, 750; cf. BDAG, 5999.2.

case, and number differ. We are a "spiritual house" (οἶκος πνευματικὸς), and we offer "spiritual sacrifices" (πνευματικὰς θυσίας). Is anything to be made of the fact that in the former expression, the adjective follows the noun, while here, it precedes it? The effect is chiastic: house-spiritual-spiritual-sacrifices. Lenski suggests the construction "emphasizes the fact that everything in the relation of the readers to God through Christ is now altogether spiritual."[36]

All these expressions of sacrifice we are "to offer up" (ἀνενέγκαι) gladly to God. The verb is a compound comprised of ἀνά ("up") and φέρω ("to bear/carry"). It can describe the ascent of a mountain (Matt. 17:1; Mark 9:2) and Jesus' ascent into heaven after His resurrection (Luke 24:51). But more attuned to Peter's line of thought, it was the verb used frequently of a priest offering *up* a sacrifice to God on the altar (Lev. 3:11, 14, 16; 4:10, 19, 26, 31, etc.; Heb. 7:27a). It is used to describe Christ's sacrifice for us on the cross (Heb. 7:27b; 9:28; 1 Peter 2:24). It is also the verb used to call us to "offer up [ἀναφέρωμεν] a sacrifice of praise to God" (Heb. 13:15). Here the infinitive marks purpose and the aorist tense focuses on each act of service and worship as an individual expression of devotion and gratitude to God.

These sacrifices are deemed "acceptable to God" (εὐπροσδέκτους [τῷ] θεῷ) when they are offered in obedience to God, from the restful posture of faith upon Christ's singular, perfect sacrifice, out of love to God and man, relying upon the empowering of the Holy Spirit, and "through Jesus Christ" (διὰ Ἰησοῦ Χριστοῦ)[37] for the advance of His mission. The adjective is a double compound made up of εὖ ("good"), πρός ("to"), and δέχομαι ("to receive"). It designates "that which is particularly acceptable, and hence quite pleasing."[38] It is used only five times in the NT, three of those related to the acceptability to God of the gifts of Gentile believers to the suffering people of Judea (Rom. 15:16, 31; 2 Cor. 8:12). So too, here

---

36 Lenski, 90.

37 The phrase "through Jesus Christ" (διὰ Ἰησοῦ Χριστοῦ) may be attached to either "to offer up" (ἀνενέγκαι) or "acceptable" (εὐπροσδέκτους) or perhaps, better, to both.

38 Louw-Nida, 25.86.

the concern is with our "sacrifices" as a holy "priesthood" being "acceptable to God."

Note that believers are both the temple ("a spiritual house") and the "priesthood" that serves the One dwelling in the temple. The "priesthood" is not comprised merely of a few individuals or a select tribe within the larger whole of God's people. The whole of God's people now forms "a holy priesthood." It was a return to this "priesthood of all believers," which the reformers called God's people.

Digging Deeper:
1. What is it about Jesus that demands a binary response (v.4)?
2. Detail specifically how you are representing God to people and those people to God (v.5).
3. What sacrifices have you offering to Jesus Christ this week (v.5)?

Verse 6 – "For *this* is contained in Scripture: 'BEHOLD, I LAY IN ZION A CHOICE STONE, A PRECIOUS CORNER *stone*, AND HE WHO BELIEVES IN HIM WILL NOT BE DISAPPOINTED.'"

Having laid down the basics of the corporate identity of God's New Covenant people (vv.4–5), Peter begins a litany of Scriptural support that confirms and advances what he has said (vv.6–10). What he has said is true because (διότι, "For") Scripture tells us it is so. The conjunction is formed from διά ("because of") and ὅτι ("that")[39] and is used here to indicate what has just been stated is reasonable.[40] It is used three times by Peter, each time introducing a quotation from the OT (1 Peter 1:16, 24; 2:6). What Peter says, "is contained in Scripture" (περιέχει

---

39 Friberg, 117.
40 BADG, 2028.3.

ἐν γραφῇ). The verb is a compound made up of περί ("around") and ἔχω ("to have/hold"). It has the sense of envelope, wrap, or contain. Elsewhere in the NT, it is used only in Luke 5:9, describing people being rapt in astonishment. Here the truths Peter has been advancing about the corporate identity of God's people (vv.4–5) come wrapped "in Scripture" (ἐν γραφῇ); that is to say, in what we would call the OT. The present tense of the verb indicates that the OT continues to teach these things even after Jesus' death, resurrection, and glorification. Even as Peter writes NT Scripture, he says the OT Scripture still speaks. We should not set aside the OT in our study and preaching. We do so to the impoverishment of our souls and those of the people committed to our care. The combination of the noun and preposition (ἐν γραφῇ, "in Scripture") is found again when Paul begins his magisterial documentation of the gospel in the book of Romans. He declares that "the gospel of God" is something God "promised beforehand through His prophets in the holy Scriptures [ἐν γραφαῖς]" (Rom. 1:2).

Peter offers a Scriptural defense of his reference to Jesus as "a living stone" (v.4). His reasoning calls (vv.6–8) on three passages selected from Isaiah and the Psalms, all of which make use of the "stone" imagery. First, Peter supports his line of reasoning by quoting Isaiah 28:16. In the original context, God is condemning the rulers of Jerusalem for seeking a covenant with Egypt (Isa. 28:14–15) in the face of foreign armies rather than trusting in Him. The nation faced impending judgment by God for their sins. The divine threat came through the earthly nation of Assyria. The nation's leaders saw only earthly threats, not divine discipline. They believed their problem to be a military weakness, not a moral failure. So rather than turn to God in repentance and faith, they sought earthly, human remedies. They relied upon the arm of flesh rather than the mercy of God. In so doing, they "made falsehood [their] refuge (Isa. 28:15) and trusted in a "refuge of lies" (v.17). God promised them a deliverer, the Messiah. They chose a near-neighbor instead.

Taken alone, the text of Isaiah 28:16 could be read as indicating the "stone" and "foundation" as the city of Jerusalem itself, the Davidic line, or David's greater son. Peter tells his readers that Jesus is the ultimate fulfillment of that "CHOICE STONE," that "PRECIOUS CORNER *stone.*" In sending His Son, God has called all people everywhere to make their choice—whom will they trust? God's appointed Savior? Or their human ingenuity, efforts, and resources?

Peter does not cite the text of the LXX entirely or precisely but carries its substance. He may have been working from memory or purposefully adapting the text of the LXX to fit his present line of thought while retaining its original emphasis. Peter begins partway into the verse (omitting διὰ τοῦτο οὕτως λέγει κύριος, "Therefore, thus saith the Lord"). He picks up with ἰδοὺ ("see/behold") and then omits ἐγὼ ἐμβαλῶ εἰς τὰ θεμέλια ("I laying into the foundation") which he replaces with τίθημι ἐν ("I LAY IN"). The future of the LXX becomes a present tense at Peter's hand. The action that was prophetically looked forward to in Isaiah is now a present reality in Jesus. Peter picks up Σιὼν λίθον ("ZION A…STONE") but skips the next word of the LXX: πολυτελῆ ("precious"). Peter then rearranges the order of the LXX from ἐκλεκτὸν ἀκρογωνιαῖον ἔντιμον ("chosen," "corner," "precious") to ἀκρογωνιαῖον ἐκλεκτὸν ἔντιμον (simply inverting the first two terms). At this point, he omits εἰς τὰ θεμέλια αὐτῆς ("into the foundation itself") and finishes with the precise quotation of the remainder of the verse: καὶ ὁ πιστεύων ἐπ' αὐτῷ οὐ μὴ καταισχυνθῇ ("AND HE WHO BELIEVES IN HIM WILL NOT BE DISAPPOINTED").

> **Ministry Maxim**
>
> The safest bet in the universe is trust placed on the risen Christ.

All of this is represented below, with the bold type indicating text common to both the LXX and Peter, and the underlined word indicates Peter's movement of it within the sentence. The plain type indicates either words of the LXX Peter has omitted or words he has added to adapt the sentence to his present purposes and context.

LXX: διὰ τοῦτο οὕτως λέγει κύριος **ἰδοὺ** ἐγὼ ἐμβαλῶ εἰς τὰ θεμέλια **Σιων λίθον** πολυτελῆ **ἐκλεκτὸν** <u>ἀκρογωνιαῖον</u> **ἔντιμον** εἰς τὰ θεμέλια αὐτῆς **καὶ ὁ πιστεύων ἐπ' αὐτῷ οὐ μὴ καταισχυνθῇ** (Isa. 28:16).

NT: **ἰδοὺ** τίθημι ἐν **Σιὼν λίθον** <u>ἀκρογωνιαῖον</u> **ἐκλεκτὸν ἔντιμον καὶ ὁ πιστεύων ἐπ' αὐτῷ οὐ μὴ καταισχυνθῇ**. (1 Peter 2:6).

The adjective ("cornerstone") is a compound created by ἄκρος ("extreme") and γωνία ("corner," "angle"). The word is found only here and in Ephesians 2:20 in the NT and only in Isaiah 28:16 in the LXX, leading to the conjecture that the translators of the LXX may have originated the word. There is debate as to just what is intended by the word. Is it the "cornerstone" laid in the ground and from which the edifice rises, from which all its angles are determined, and which ties the entire structure together? Thus considered, "the stone is a foundation cornerstone."[41] Or is it better rendered "capstone"? As such, Jeremias calls it "The 'final stone' in a building, probably set over the gate" and adds, "Underlying the image is the lofty declaration of Jesus that He is the final stone in the heavenly sanctuary."[42] Other major lexicons cannot answer definitively and offer both definitions for the word.[43] But the LXX of Isaiah 28:16 twice makes clear that a foundation stone (τὰ θεμέλια, "the foundation") is what is under consideration, and it is unclear how one would stumble (v.8) over a stone that is not at ground level. Here the adjective depicts the "stone" (λίθον) laid at the corner of a building, which founds the rising walls, gives them their lines and direction, and ties them together as one whole.

We must wonder why Peter, whose very name, given by Jesus Himself (cf. Matt. 16:13–18), means "rock," makes no mention of it in this pivotal discussion of the church's corporate identity as founded upon Christ, the "cornerstone." Perhaps Jobes is correct in saying, "His silence here, where such a suggestion would be most natural, lends support to the understanding that the 'rock' of Matt. 16:18, on which Christ will build the church, is the confession of Jesus being the Christ, not Peter himself."[44]

The fact that this all is said to take place "in Zion" (ἐν Σιὼν) is a signal that the ultimate triumph of God is in view. In Hebrews, believers in Christ are told, "you have come to Mount Zion and to the city of the

---

41 NIDNTTE, 1:629; cf. Mounce, 1076; Thayer, 24.
42 TDNT, 1:792.
43 E.g., BDAG, 292; Friberg, 42; Louw-Nida, 7.44.
44 Jobes, 151.

living God, the heavenly Jerusalem" (Heb. 12:22). God has established our spiritual residence, and we journey now as sojourners anticipating arrival at our glorious home.

We have already met the adjective ἐκλεκτός ("chosen") in 1:1 and 2:4 and will again in 2:9. Similarly, we have already encountered the adjective ἔντιμος ("precious") in 2:4. See our comments on both words above on verse 4. The articular participle (ὁ πιστεύων) is used as a substantive ("HE WHO BELIEVES"). The present tense pictures present and ongoing trust in Christ. It is not simply faith "IN HIM," but more literally, faith which rests upon (ἐπ') Christ (αὐτῷ). The combination of ἐπί and πιστεύω in the dative occurs only four times in the NT, three of which are quotations of Isaiah 28:16 (Rom. 9:33; 10:11; 1 Peter 2:6; 1 Tim. 1:16). It "denotes the placing of one's complete reliance and trust on a person (Christ) who affords a firm support or a solid foundation (ἐπί = 'resting on')."[45] The personal pronoun (αὐτῷ, "HIM") indicates that the "CORNERSTONE" is not an inanimate object but a personal being.

The one who places all his trust in Christ "WILL NOT BE DISAPPOINTED" (οὐ μὴ καταισχυνθῇ). The LXX's (and thus Peter's) rendering is interpretive of the Hebrew (cf., "shall not make haste," KJV). Lenski explains, "... the one who must hurry away in flight does so because he is ashamed."[46] The double negation (οὐ μὴ, "WILL NOT") is emphatic, absolute, and complete. The combination of οὐ μὴ and the aorist subjunctive verb "denies a potentiality" it "rules out even the idea as being a possibility."[47] Never, under any condition, would one who puts his trust in Christ ever "BE DISAPPOINTED" (καταισχυνθῇ). The word is a compound derived from κατά ("down") and αἰσχύνη ("shame," "humiliation"). Here it designates "the shame and disappointment that come to one whose faith or hope is shown to be vain."[48] The passive voice pictures the one believing being acted upon by another, in this case, Christ.

---

45 Harris, 235.

46 Lenski, 95.

47 Wallace, 468–469.

48 BDAG, 3972.3.

But being disappointed by Him is an impossibility since "it is impossible for God to lie," and thus "we who have taken refuge would have strong encouragement to take hold of the hope set before us" (Heb. 6:18).

Peter is not alone in applying Isaiah 28:16 to Christ. Paul so quotes it in Romans 9:33. There, he wrestles over the matter "That Gentiles, who did not pursue righteousness, attained righteousness, even the righteousness which is by faith; but Israel, pursuing a law of righteousness, did not arrive at that law" (vv.30–31). Why was this so? "Because they did not pursue it by faith, but as though it were by works." (v.32a). This, simply stated, means "They stumbled over the stumbling stone" (v.32b). Paul then says this was no novel idea, but one prophesied by Isaiah, quoting 28:16. They stumbled over the matter of faith alone in Jesus Christ alone rather than in their concerted efforts at attaining righteousness before God through their law-keeping. He quotes the last portion of Isaiah 28:16 in Romans 10:11 again. Paul just declared that "if you confess with your mouth Jesus as Lord, and believe in your heart that God raised Him from the dead, you will be saved; for with the heart a person believes, resulting in righteousness, and with the mouth he confesses, resulting in salvation" (Rom. 10:9–10). He immediately underscores this certainty by saying, "For the Scripture says, 'WHOEVER BELIEVES IN HIM WILL NOT BE DISAPPOINTED'" (10:11).

Verse 7 – "This precious value, then, is for you who believe; but for those who disbelieve, 'THE STONE WHICH THE BUILDERS REJECTED, THIS BECAME THE VERY CORNER *stone*,'"

Before continuing with his second line of Scriptural evidence, Peter pauses to apply what he has just quoted in verse 6. He speaks logically (οὖν, "then") of what follows from the fulfillment of Isaiah 28:16 in Jesus.

How are we to understand ἡ τιμὴ ("This precious value")? Peter could use the noun of the proceeds from the sale of land (Acts 5:2–3). He used it to describe the manifested affirmation of the Father over His Son on the Mount of Transfiguration (2 Peter 1:17). He laid it alongside "praise and glory" as the "honor" the believer will share with Jesus at His return

(1 Peter 1:7). And he used it of the husband demonstrating "honor" to his wife "as a fellow heir of the grace of life" (3:7). In just what sense, then, does Peter use the noun here? Certainly, Jesus is of "precious value" as the "stone" who is "choice," "precious" (ἔντιμος from the same root as τιμή), and the "corner" stone of His temple. Being brought into union with the risen Christ, the church (vv.4, 6) receives the privilege[49] and honor of being "living stones" in the temple where He chooses to make Himself known. Jesus, the "living stone" (v.4), shares His "value"/honor with those who, by virtue of His resurrection life, are made "living stones" (v.5) in His new temple. But ultimately the honor is that bestowed upon believers presently and personally by God and then openly before all at the return of Jesus, vindicating their faith in Him amid opponents who will themselves ultimately be "put to shame" (v.6b, ESV, NIV, NKJV, NRSV).

This "value"/honor accrues, Peter says, "to you" (ὑμῖν), his readers and all who like them rest their trust upon Christ. Indeed, the treasure "is for you who believe" (τοῖς πιστεύουσιν). Peter repeats the verb from the previous verse (ὁ πιστεύων, "HE WHO BELIEVES"), except there it was in the singular (intending each believer) while here it is in the plural (addressing all believers as a group). Again, the articular participle is used as a substantive, and the present tense signals abiding, ongoing trust. They had "not seen Him," and they "do not see Him now," but they "believe in Him" and, as a result, "greatly rejoice with joy inexpressible and full of glory" (1 Peter 1:8).

While Peter's readers have their faith squarely upon Jesus, there is a contrasting (δὲ, "but") reality to be faced. It is "for those who disbelieve" (ἀπιστοῦσιν). The verb is identical to the preceding verb, except that the alpha-privative has been added for negation. Accordingly, it designates one who does not believe or refuses to believe. With τοῖς πιστεύουσιν ("you who believe") held to the end of its clause for emphasis, the contrast with ἀπιστοῦσιν ("those who disbelieve") is further emphasized by the juxtaposition of the two opposites. In this case, they refuse to believe in Jesus as the Christ, God's appointed Savior. Here too, though it lacks the

---

49 BDAG, 7367.4.

definite article, the participle is used substantively ("*those who* disbelieve," emphasis added). The absence of the definite article, in contrast to the preceding τοῖς πιστεύουσιν ("you who believe") "may be indicating that unbelievers are not a unified group"[50] or drawing attention to unbelief as their determinative quality.[51] The present tense presents their unbelief as a present and abiding reality.

The blessedness and future of those "who believe" was set forth in verse 6. Now the reality and future of "those who disbelieve" is set forth in a pair of quotations from the OT, the first here in verse 7 and the second in verse 8. Describing what they face requires both quotations.

First, Peter cites Psalm 118:22 (117:22 LXX)[52]: "THE STONE WHICH THE BUILDERS REJECTED, THIS BECAME THE VERY CORNER *stone*," (λίθος ὃν ἀπεδοκίμασαν οἱ οἰκοδομοῦντες, οὗτος ἐγενήθη εἰς κεφαλὴν γωνίας). This is one of the most frequently quoted OT passages in the NT, being found upon the lips of Jesus in all the Synoptic Gospels (cf. Matt. 21:42; Mark 12:10; Luke 20:17) and upon Peter's as he and John stood before the Jewish rulers (Acts 4:11). Jesus quoted these verses at the conclusion of His parable of the tenants, where He drew out from them a confession that the owner of the vineyard would give that vineyard to other tenants (Matt. 21:41). Then He used the words of Psalm 118 to drive home and personalize the point. Having done so, He flatly declared, "the kingdom of God will be taken away from you and given to a people, producing the fruit of it" (Matt. 21:43). Jesus continued, unambiguously, "And he who falls on this stone will be broken to pieces; but on whomever it falls, it will scatter him like dust" (v.44). Peter applied it just as boldly but from the vantage point of looking back upon the rulers' rejection of Jesus (Acts 4:11–12). In this present letter, Peter now works out the realities Jesus' announced. God had taken away from unbelieving Israel the privileges and honor of knowing Him and had conferred it upon a new people, to which

---

50 Forbes, 64.

51 Lenski, 95.

52 Peter quotes the LXX precisely except the LXX's λίθον ("a stone"; accusative, masculine, singular) in Peter's hand becomes λίθος ("a stone"; nominative, masculine, singular).

Peter applies the appellations and descriptions previously spoken over Israel (1 Peter 2:4–10). In God's eyes, the physical temple in Jerusalem is now defunct and would soon be destroyed at the hands of the Romans. God is crafting a new temple, one made up of "living stones" founded upon "the cornerstone" of His Son Jesus Christ. He is gifting His presence to a people "producing the fruit" that His presence and kingdom bring.

"THE STONE" (λίθος) continues the theme already begun and developed in verses 4, 5, and 6, where the noun also appears. Christ as the "stone" is "living" (v.4), "choice," "precious" (vv.4, 6), and a "corner" stone (v.6). Those who trust in Him become through Him "living stones" (v.5) in the new temple of His people. But He is that stone "WHICH" (ὃν, agreeing with λίθος in gender and voice) was "REJECTED" (ἀπεδοκίμασαν). The verb is the same one found in verse 4, where Peter began his theme (see our comments there). There the rejection was by "men" (ἀνθρώπων). Not males alone, but humanity. Here it is "THE BUILDERS" (οἱ οἰκοδομοῦντες) who reject the stone. In verse 4, the perfect tense pictured the settled state of rejection. Here the aorist tense looks particularly upon the pivotal, historical rejection of Christ by the Jewish leadership that was responsible as shepherds of the nation and who should have welcomed Him.

> **Ministry Maxim**
>
> Reject Christ, and God will reject your verdict.

Peter, standing before the "rulers and elders and scribes" (Acts 4:5) along with "Annas the high priest… and Caiaphas and John and Alexander, and all who were of high-priestly descent," addressed them as "Rulers and elders of the people" (vv.6, 8). He identified them as "THE BUILDERS" of whom Isaiah spoke and charged them with rejecting Jesus "the STONE" appointed by God to be "THE CHIEF CORNER" (v.11). Now, in this letter, "Peter applies the prophecy of the psalm to all who still repeat this disbelief and this rejection."[53] Indeed, "the rejecters are any and all people, whether Jew or Gentile, who reject Christ."[54]

---

53 Lenski, 96.

54 Jobes, 154.

At Jesus' Triumphal Entry, the religious leaders denounced the welcome given Him by the populace. Jesus confronted them with the words of Psalm 118:22 (Matt. 21:42; cf. Mark 12:10; Luke 20:17). He then added, "I say to you, the kingdom of God will be taken away from you and given to a people, producing the fruit of it. And he who falls on this stone will be broken to pieces; but on whomever it falls, it will scatter him like dust" (Matt. 21:43–44). In a series of woes later pronounced over the nation and its leaders, Jesus cried out, "But woe to you, scribes and Pharisees, hypocrites, because you shut off the kingdom of heaven from people; for you do not enter in yourselves, nor do you allow those who are entering to go in" (Matt. 23:13). This echoed Jesus' earlier denunciation, "Woe to you lawyers! For you have taken away the key of knowledge; you yourselves did not enter, and you hindered those who were entering" (Luke 11:52). Jesus lamented over the capital city, "Jerusalem, Jerusalem, who kills the prophets and stones those who are sent to her! How often I wanted to gather your children together, the way a hen gathers her chicks under her wings, and you were unwilling. Behold, your house is being left to you desolate!" (Matt. 23:37–38). In view of His rejection by "THE BUILDERS" of the nation, Jesus plainly foretold the destruction of the physical temple in Jerusalem (Matt. 24:1–2; Mark 13:1–2; Luke 21:5–6), making way for the establishment of the new temple, His body, the Church.

The horror of their actions is set before us in that "THIS" (οὗτος; agreeing with λίθος in case, gender, and number) very stone (Jesus Himself whom they rejected) "BECAME THE VERY CORNER stone" (ἐγενήθη εἰς κεφαλὴν γωνίας) of God's new temple. The demonstrative pronoun (οὗτος, "THIS") is both "emphatic and ironic."[55] It "emphasizes that the very One the builders rejected was placed in the very position they refused Him."[56] The verb (ἐγενήθη, "BECAME") is aorist, depicting the pivotal event of Christ's resurrection and exaltation whereby He was placed (εἰς denotes movement *into* the place prepared for it) by the Father (note the

---

55 Forbes, 65.

56 Hiebert, 139.

passive voice) as "THE VERY CORNER" stone of the dwelling of God with His people. By combining the two nouns (κεφαλὴν γωνίας; "the head of the corner," KJV, YLT) Peter makes clear that he has in mind not the capstone that is the last stone placed at the top of a temple/building or the keystone that fits in an archway and holds the whole together, but rather pictures the cornerstone, laid and founded and from which the entire edifice rises and by which it is controlled. The latter of the two nouns (γωνίας, "CORNER") appears only nine times in the NT, five of which are in quotations of Psalm 118:22 (Matt. 21:42; Mark 12:10; Luke 20:17; Acts 4:11; 1 Peter 2:7). In each of these five citations κεφαλὴν ("the head," KJV, YLT) appears with it.

Verse 8 – "and, 'A STONE OF STUMBLING AND A ROCK OF OFFENSE'; for they stumble because they are disobedient to the word, and to this *doom* they were also appointed."

Peter continues his sentence by referencing Isaiah 8:14.[57] The quotation effectively adds two more descriptors (καὶ … καὶ, "and … AND") of what Christ has become to "those who disbelieve" (v.7). In addition to "THE VERY CORNER" (v.7), Jesus is to the unbelieving "A STONE OF STUMBLING" (λίθος προσκόμματος). The noun (λίθος, "A STONE") has already been met in verses 4, 5, 6, and 7. As noted, it refers to a groomed stone prepared and fit for a particular spot in a building. The second noun (προσκόμματος, "OF STUMBLING") depicts the act of stumbling. The genitive is a genitive of product—the stone which causes stumbling.[58] The cognate verb will be used before the sentence is complete (προσκόπτουσιν, "they stumble"). It serves to remind us that it is

---

57 Peter snatches just a couple of phrases from Isaiah 8:14, adjusting the original to fit his present context. LXX: "λίθου προσκόμματι … πέτρας πτώματι"; Peter: "λίθος προσκόμματος καὶ πέτρα σκανδάλου." It might be fair to say Peter alludes to or paraphrases the Hebrew text of Isaiah 8:14 rather than quotes the LXX. Note also, in 3:14 Peter will quote Isaiah 8:12 and in 3:15 appears to still allude to the opening words of Isaiah 8:13. Clearly, Isaiah 8 was influential in shaping Peter's (and the early church's) understanding of what God has done in Christ.

58 Dubis, 54; Forbes, 65.

a ground-level "cornerstone" that Peter has had in view, not an elevated "capstone" or "keystone" high in the air. Jesus Christ became, to the Jews particularly and more generally to unbelieving Gentiles, a means of "stumbling" through unbelief.

Jesus is also, thirdly, called "A ROCK OF OFFENSE" (πέτρα σκανδάλου). The noun πέτρα ("A ROCK") is the very one chosen by Christ and given to Simon "Peter" (Πέτρος; cf. Matt. 16:18) as a name. Peter, however, does not make any connection to himself. He focuses on Christ and how unbelieving people relate to Him. We should probably not press the distinction between λίθος ("a stone") and πέτρα ("A ROCK") and look for subtleties of meaning within Peter's overall metaphor.[59] Christ is to the unbelieving "OF OFFENSE" (σκανδάλου). The noun literally described "the movable bait stick or trigger in a trap" and "by synecdoche, the trap itself."[60] It came then to be used metaphorically, as it is here, of "that which causes offense and thus arouses opposition."[61] The genitive is again a genitive of product—the rock which causes offense.[62] Interestingly, Jesus used this noun of Peter when he misinterpreted Christ and His role and stood in His way: "But He turned and said to Peter, 'Get behind Me, Satan! You are a stumbling block [σκάνδαλον] to Me; for you are not setting your mind on God's interests, but man's'" (Matt. 16:23). In relationship to unbelieving Jews, Paul spoke of "the stumbling block [σκάνδαλον] of the cross" (Gal. 5:11). The Jews had no room for a crucified Messiah. "For indeed Jews ask for signs and Greeks search for wisdom; but we preach Christ crucified, to Jews a stumbling block [σκάνδαλον] and to Gentiles foolishness, but to those who are the called, both Jews and Greeks, Christ the power of God and the wisdom of God" (1 Cor. 1:22–24).

In the context of Isaiah 8:14, the "STONE" (λίθος) and "ROCK" (πέτρα) refer to the Lord Himself. If they will trust in Him, He will be a

---

59 Robertson, *Word Pictures*, 6:98.

60 Friberg, 349.

61 Louw-Nida, 25.181.

62 Dubis, 54; Forbes, 65.

"sanctuary" to them (v.14a). But when met with unbelief, He becomes "A STONE OF STUMBLING" and "A ROCK OF OFFENSE." "It is the LORD of hosts whom you should regard as holy. And He shall be your fear, And He shall be your dread. Then He shall become a sanctuary; But to both the houses of Israel, a stone to strike and a rock to stumble over, And a snare and a trap for the inhabitants of Jerusalem" (Isa. 8:13–14). Motyer, commenting on the text of Isaiah, observes, "It is as if a rock were put across a road to block the traveler from danger but, in carelessness or scorn, he refuses the warning and stumbles to his death. The stress in these verses is upon the reality that whatever gives most offense to the sinner, and what at the same time constitutes his greatest danger, is the presence of the divine. The same God in his unchanging nature is both sanctuary and snare; it depends upon how people respond to his holiness."[63] Jesus, God incarnate, applied these verses to Himself. Having just quoted Psalm 118:22–23 (as Peter just did in verse 7 above; cf. Matt. 21:42; cf. Mark 12:10–11; Luke 20:16–17), He announced that the kingdom of God would be taken away from the Jews and given to a people who would produce its fruits (Matt. 21:43). Then, alluding to Isaiah 8:14, He announced: "He who falls on this stone will be broken to pieces; but on whomever it falls, it will scatter him like dust" (Matt. 21:44; cf. Luke 20:18). Christ is either the cornerstone upon which we are built or the one over whom we stumble and by whom we are then crushed.

Paul quoted the same passage in Romans 9:33, where he also cited Isaiah 28:16 (as did Peter above in verse 6). See our discussion above on verse 6 for Paul's purposes in quoting these passages.

The relative pronoun οἳ (lit. "who") identifies "those who disbelieve" (v.7) as those still under consideration. Having rejected Christ, "they stumble" (προσκόπτουσιν). The noun form of the word was just used earlier in the verse (προσκόμματος, "OF STUMBLING"). It is a compound made up of πρὸς ("against") and κόπτω ("to cut off," "to chop") and means literally "to strike, dash against."[64] It came to mean to "take offense at,"

---

63 Motyer, 95.

64 TDNT, 6.745.

"feel repugnance for," or "reject."⁶⁵ In this case, it is Christ over which one takes offense, trips, and falls. This stumbling comes about "because they are disobedient to the word" (τῷ λόγῳ ἀπειθοῦντες). As we discovered in 1 Peter 1:23, "the word" (τῷ λόγῳ) is a descriptor for the gospel, as extended and expounded in the written "word" of God. Note the presence of the article, designating that singularly unique "word," which is the revelation of God in the gospel. Peter has gone out of his way already to underscore that the gospel is something that must be obeyed (1:2, 14, 22). This is the first of four occurrences of the verb in this letter (ἀπειθοῦντες, "are disobedient"). Four of its fourteen NT uses are taken up by Peter here. It can describe unbelieving husbands (ἀπειθοῦσιν τῷ λόγῳ, "are disobedient to the word," 3:1) and fallen angels (ἀπειθήσασίν, "who once were disobedient," 3:20). Ultimately Peter uses it to speak of coming judgment and asks "what will be the outcome for those who do not obey the gospel of God? [ἀπειθούντων τῷ τοῦ θεοῦ εὐαγγελίῳ]" (4:17). Here the participle is used to express cause: "they stumble *because* they are disobedient" (emphasis added).

> **Ministry Maxim**
>
> God is sovereign in both salvation and judgment.

In closing his sentence, Peter adds a prepositional phrase (εἰς ὃ καὶ ἐτέθησαν, "and to this *doom* they were also appointed"). The Greek text has no equivalent to the English "and." It is more abrupt and stark, the more powerful for being so. Similarly, it has no equivalent for "doom" (thus the NASU's italics). The preposition εἰς ("to") is used here to "mark divine appointment, reflecting divine purpose."⁶⁶ Peter's choice of verb underscores this (ἐτέθησαν, "they were… appointed"). Peter just used the same verb to describe Christ's divinely appointed place in God's redemptive plan ("I LAY [τίθημι] … A CHOICE STONE," v.6).⁶⁷ Now He tells his readers that those who disbelieve come to their resulting judgment

---

65 BDAG, 6315.3.a.

66 Harris, 89.

67 The verb serves as an inclusion, wrapping verses 6–8 and setting them forth as one unit.

under the same sovereign hand of God. Just as Christ was "appointed" to His role and position as a finely prepared and placed stone in God's temple (2:6), so "also" (καὶ) those who fail through unbelief were "appointed" (ἐτέθησαν). The aorist tense views the action as complete. The passive voice indicates that they are acted upon, God Himself setting them in their place.

To just what were they "appointed"? Identifying the antecedent of ὅ ("this") is at the heart of answering the question. It could refer to the phrase that immediately precedes: "they are disobedient to the word" (τῷ λόγῳ ἀπειθοῦντες). In such a case, the individual's disobedience is in view. It could refer to "they stumble" (προσκόπτουσιν). In such a case, the individual's judgment is in view. Or it could refer to both, in which case it could be both their unbelief/disobedience and its resulting judgment, which God appoints.

The relative pronoun (ὅ, "this") is neuter singular in form. The only other neuter singulars in the sentence are προσκόμματος ("OF STUMBLING") and σκανδάλου ("OF OFFENSE") but making them the direct antecedent of the relative pronoun strains the syntax. Robertson says that here the pronoun ὅ ("this") "is used to refer to a verbal idea or to the whole sentence"[68] Thus the antecedent is surely προσκόπτουσιν ("they stumble") the verbal form of the noun (προσκόμματος, "OF STUMBLING"). It is thus not the unbelief itself to which they are appointed but the resulting judgment that is the necessary result of their unbelief. Grudem argues this is impossible because the plural form of the verb (ἐτέθησαν, "they were ... appointed") must point to persons, not to a principle (i.e., judgment must follow unbelief).[69] But Forbes points out that it is not the verb's subject that provides the point but the relative pronoun's antecedent.[70]

Christ, by virtue of His obedient death and powerful resurrection, was placed by God's sovereign hand as the cornerstone of His new people, the

---

68   Robertson, *Grammar*, 714.

69   Grudem, 114.

70   Forbes, 66.

temple of His dwelling. It is the very place God designed and chose for Him as the Savior of humankind. Those who believe are born again (1:3, 23) and elect (1:2). Conversely, those who disbelieve and stumble over Christ find their place under a resulting judgment, the very end to which God has "appointed" all who so reject His Son. What else could they receive? Having rejected the only Savior, they come to God's "appointed" end for all who disbelieve in Him—eternal judgment. Bigg comments, "Their disobedience is not ordained, the penalty of their disobedience is."[71] Hiebert agrees, "God has established Christ, the living stone, as His divinely appointed way for human salvation; He has also ordained that men cannot reject His provision with impunity."[72]

> **Digging Deeper:**
> 1. Why do you think that amidst all this talk of "stone" and "rock" Peter didn't make any reference to his name-change (vv.6–8)?
> 2. What/who determines whether Jesus and the Gospel issue in saving faith or disbelief (vv.6–8)?

Verse 9 – "But you are A CHOSEN RACE, A royal PRIESTHOOD, A HOLY NATION, A PEOPLE FOR *God's* OWN POSSESSION, so that you may proclaim the excellencies of Him who has called you out of darkness into His marvelous light;"

Now, in contrast (δὲ, "But") to the shame and ignominy of those who stumble over Christ (vv.6–8), Peter, by means of the emphatic plural personal pronoun (ὑμεῖς, "you"), sets forward the contrasting honor that belongs to his believing readers. In so doing, he lays upon them

---

71 Bigg, 133.
72 Hiebert, 141.

four markers of identity, each taken from the OT depiction of Israel and applied now to New Covenant believers in Jesus. Each noun is a collective singular, setting forth the corporate identity of God's people in Christ. The first and fourth are from Isaiah 43:20–21 and the second and third from Exodus 19:5–6.

> "The beasts of the field will glorify Me, The jackals and the ostriches, Because I have given waters in the wilderness And rivers in the desert, To give drink to My chosen people. The people whom I formed for Myself Will declare My praise." (Isa. 43:20–21)

> "'Now then, if you will indeed obey My voice and keep My covenant, then you shall be My own possession among all the peoples, for all the earth is Mine; and you shall be to Me a kingdom of priests and a holy nation.' These are the words that you shall speak to the sons of Israel." (Exod. 19:5–6)

Believers in Jesus Christ are "A CHOSEN RACE" (γένος ἐκλεκτόν). Peter appears to call upon Isaiah 43:20, where God promises to provide Israel "rivers in the desert, To give drink to My chosen people [τὸ γένος μου τὸ ἐκλεκτόν, LXX]" (cf. Deut. 10:15; 33:12). The noun γένος ("A…RACE") fundamentally has in view a familial, family lineage ("ancestral stock"), can be used of a larger unit such as a "nation" or "people" more generally, and can be extended further to "entities united by class or kind" (cf. our scientific term *genus*).[73] Paul used the noun when he identified himself as of "the people [γένους] of Israel" (Phil. 3:5) and of his youth "among my countrymen [τῷ γένει]" (Gal. 1:14). The risen Christ uses it of Himself as "the descendant [τὸ γένος] of David" (Rev. 22:16). It was used to describe a woman of "Syrophoenician race [τῷ γένει]" (Mark 7:26). But what binds the New Covenant people of God together is not their physical birth, DNA, or patrilineal origins. It is that they have been born again (1:3, 23) and are partakers of the resurrection

---

73 BDAG, 1629; cf. TDNT, 1:684–685.

life of Jesus. They have been birthed into a new, spiritual family. This is so because they are "CHOSEN" (ἐκλεκτόν). Their identity is purely a matter of divine grace and not of human effort or doing (John 1:13). Peter has sounded this note of sovereign grace from the beginning of his letter, regarding both his readers (1 Peter 1:2) and Jesus (2:4, 6).

In what sense can Peter use the terminology of Israel as God's "CHOSEN RACE" and apply it to New Covenant believers? Peter has shown his close affinity to the prophet Isaiah (1 Peter 1:24–25 = Isaiah 40:6, 8; 1 Peter 2:6 = Isaiah 28:16; 1 Peter 2:8 = Isaiah 8:14), and perhaps Isaiah helps us here again. Isaiah's servant songs begin by clearly referencing the nation of Israel as God's elect and chosen "servant" (Isa. 41:8; 44:1), but soon enough, it becomes clear that this "servant of the Lord" cannot be the nation as a whole but must be an individual within it (49:3–6), which will through His sufferings redeem a people to God as His unique and special people (Isa. 52:13–53:12). Jesus is the fulfillment of this "servant of the Lord," as Peter will soon enough make clear (1 Peter 2:22 = Isa. 53:9; 1 Peter 2:23 = Isa. 53:7; 1 Peter 2:24 = Isa. 53:4, 5, 11; 1 Peter 2:25 = Isa. 53:6). As "the Servant of the Lord" Jesus became all that God's people Israel should have been but failed to be. We share now in that standing by virtue of God's mercy and grace in bringing us into union with Him.

Believers in Jesus Christ are also accounted "A royal PRIESTHOOD" (βασίλειον ἱεράτευμα). Peter reflects on Exodus 19:6a: "you shall be to Me a kingdom of priests." Isaiah foresaw a day in which not only would the entire nation of Israel be constituted a priesthood (Isa. 61:6), but that redeemed peoples from the nations would join them in this priesthood (Isa. 66:21). The noun ἱεράτευμα ("PRIESTHOOD") is used elsewhere in the NT only in 1 Peter 2:5 where the New Covenant people are constituted "a holy priesthood." Again, we note that believers in Jesus Christ are not only the new temple in which God dwells but the priesthood that serves Him there. The adjective βασίλειον ("royal") may be read as a substantive (i.e., a kingdom) but clearly appears to qualify ἱεράτευμα ("PRIESTHOOD") and is best seen as serving adjectivally (i.e., "royal"). That being so, we should not lose the connection between "kingdom" and "royal," for the OT regularly connects the concept of "kingdom" and "priesthood." The rest of the NT does similarly. John worships Him who "has made us to be a kingdom, priests to His God and Father" (Rev. 1:6a). He depicts the four living creatures and the twenty-four elders around the throne of God singing "a new song, saying, 'Worthy are You to take the book and to break its seals; for You were slain, and purchased for God with Your blood men from every tribe and tongue and people and nation. You have made them to be a kingdom and priests to our God; and they will reign upon the earth" (Rev. 5:9–10; cf. 20:6). See our comments above on verse 5 for the function of God's New Covenant people as priests to God.

> **Ministry Maxim**
>
> Our privilege is granted for the fulfillment of our purpose—forget the purpose, forfeit the privilege.

Believers in Jesus Christ are "A HOLY NATION" (ἔθνος ἅγιον). As noted above, Exodus 19:6 combined "a kingdom of priests and a holy nation." The noun ἔθνος ("NATION") fundamentally designates a group bound together by "kinship, culture, and common traditions."[74] Whereas γένος ("RACE") majored on familial, patrilineal connections and broadened from there, ἔθνος ("NATION") seems to begin with cultural connectedness, while also being able to be narrowed to matters of physical kinship. Significantly, ἔθνος in the plural became the standard way for referring to non-Israelite peoples.[75] Now through Jesus Christ, God has fulfilled His intention from the beginning (Gen. 12:3)—calling out from all τὰ ἔθνη (the nations/Gentiles) of the world a people to Himself and making of them an ἔθνος, a people ἅγιον ("HOLY") to Himself. Peter has been building a theme of holiness throughout the opening portions of this letter (1 Peter 1:2, 15–16; 2:5). This holiness comes by virtue of union with Jesus and by the sanctifying work of the Spirit (1:2). His people can rightly be designated both "a holy priesthood" (2:5) and "A HOLY NATION" (2:9) set apart to God and His service.

---

74 BDAG, 2229.1.

75 Cf. Peter's use of the noun in 1 Peter 2:12 and 4:3 of unbelieving peoples in his day.

Believers in Jesus Christ are designated "A PEOPLE FOR *God's* OWN POSSESSION" (λαὸς εἰς περιποίησιν). Peter returns to Isaiah 43 for this fourth designation of God's New Covenant people: "The people whom I formed for Myself Will declare My praise" (Isa. 43:21). Whereas γένος ("RACE") began with concerns of familial and patrilineal connections and whereas ἔθνος ("NATION") started with issues of shared cultural and traditional foundations, λαός ("A PEOPLE") was a generalized term that became specific in the LXX as a designation for the uniqueness and identity of Israel. Outside the Bible, the term was broad and general, but its extensive use (over 2,000 occurrences) in the LXX brought a shift in meaning. There it became "a specific term for a specific people, namely, Israel, and it serves to emphasize the special and privileged religious position of this people as the people of God."[76] It designated "people as a union."[77] God is Lord over all the earth and the nations that fill it. But God uniquely chose Israel for Himself, to possess them as His own in a unique, exclusive, intimate, and missional relationship.[78] Israel was not chosen because of inherent value (Deut. 7:7), but in a free act of God's grace (v.8). But God warned Israel that if they turned from Him, they would be scattered among "the peoples" of the earth (Deut. 4:27).

In the NT λαός continued being used to designate Israel as God's peculiar and personal people (e.g., Matt. 2:6; Acts 26:47; 2 Peter 2:1), and in that sense λαός ("A PEOPLE") stands as the opposite of τὰ ἔθνη (the nations/Gentiles). But it came to be used of Christians—both Jewish and Gentile—as the new people of God as verse 10 makes explicit. James raised his voice to cite Peter's witness to God's grace upon the Gentiles. He said, "Simeon has related how God first concerned Himself about taking from among the Gentiles [ἐθνῶν] a people [λαὸν] for His name" (Acts 15:14). Paul, citing first Hosea 2:23 and then Hosea 1:10 (as Peter also does in 2:10), argued that this is exactly what God had done: "I will call those who were not My people, 'My people,' And her who was not

---

76 TDNT, 4:32.

77 Ibid., 4:33.

78 Ibid., 4:35.

beloved, 'beloved.' And it shall be that in the place where it was said to them, 'you are not My people,' There they shall be called sons of the living God" (Rom. 9:25–26, NASB). Zechariah prophesied this very thing: "Many nations will join themselves to the LORD in that day and will become My people" (Zech. 2:11). This is at the heart of Jesus' mission, for He "gave Himself for us to redeem us from every lawless deed, and to purify for Himself a people for His own possession" (Titus 2:14).

The people God has in mind is "FOR God's OWN POSSESSION" (εἰς περιποίησιν). The expression is more literally "a people for possession." The Greek text does not have an equivalent for "God's," but He is clearly the one in view. The preposition (εἰς, "FOR") points to the goal of God's pursuit of a people. The noun (περιποίησιν, "OWN POSSESSION") has the sense of acquisition for oneself and sees God as having "acquired a people… the church. He has become its acquirer and owner; he has exclusive rights to the redeemed; they are his personal property, the people whom he has acquired… The emphasis is on the original acquisition and the strictly guarded ownership of the" the people "over which God retains permanent mastery."[79] The point is that God pursued and acquired at the cost of His own Son (1 Peter 1:18–19) those who had no claim to His mercy, no place in His plan, no identity before Him and bestowed upon them by grace all this and more. Through Isaiah, God spoke of "The people whom I formed *for Myself*" (Isa. 43:21, emphasis added). There also seem to be echoes of Exodus 19:5–6 where he combined the concepts of a kingdom of priests, a holy nation, and a people who are God's "possession." So also, perhaps Malachi 3:17: "'They will be Mine,' says the LORD of hosts, 'on the day that I prepare My own possession, and I will spare them as a man spares his own son who serves him.'"

Lay side-by-side the four nouns transferred from Israel to the Church: "race" (γένος), "priesthood" (ἱεράτευμα), "nation" (ἔθνος), and "people" (λαός). The first depicts ethnicity, the second role, the third cultural identity, and the fourth possession and inclusion. All of them together bespeak

---

[79] Spicq, 3:100–101.

"honor" (1 Peter 1:7; 2:7; 3:7) rather than the "shame" (2:6; 3:16 ESV) their persecutors wish to heap upon them.

From the beginning, God sought a people for Himself who were constituted not based on physical DNA, culture, tradition, or social/political ideology. Rather by sovereign grace alone through Jesus Christ and by the working of His Spirit, God constituted a new people as His very own. They thus stand as a new "race" that includes individuals from across the globe, a "nation" from all the peoples of the earth, a new "people" from those previously excluded by their own rebellion and sin, and a kingdom of priests who worship and serve God as the new temple for His eternal dwelling.

There is a purpose (ὅπως + subjunctive, "so that") that stands behind being bestowed this honored standing. It is that we "may proclaim" (ἐξαγγείλητε) something. The verb is a compound comprised of ἐκ ("out") and ἀγγέλλω ("to announce"; in the NT only in John 20:18). In the LXX, it is most often found in the context of worship (e.g., Psa. 9:15; 55:9; 70:15; 72:28; 78:13) and thus some limit it to the proclamation made among the people of God. While not excluding this context, it must be noted that the entire purpose of God's choice of Israel was that they might sound His praise among the nations (e.g., Psa. 18:49; 57:9; 67:2; 96:3), so we ought not to limit this purpose to the circle of worship among God's people, but see it as including the missional proclamation of God's saving acts through Jesus to the peoples of the world. The verb is found only here in the NT (cf. Mark 16:8, 20). It means "to announce, with focus upon the extent to which the announcement or proclamation extends," so "to proclaim throughout."[80] The extension is to range throughout all the territories where they have been scattered (1 Peter 1:1) and beyond as far as they might let it be known, even to "all the world" and to "all creation" (Mark 16:15).

That which is proclaimed are "the excellencies of Him who has called you" (τὰς ἀρετὰς ... τοῦ ... ὑμᾶς καλέσαντος). The noun (τὰς ἀρετὰς, "the excellencies") is found only five times in the NT, four of them by Peter's

---

80 Louw-Nida, 33.204.

pen (1 Peter 2:9; 2 Peter 1:3, 5 [2x]; cf. Phil. 4:8). It is that which is preeminently true of God (1 Peter 2:9; 2 Peter 1:3; note the definite article in our present verse) but is also then to be found in His children (2 Peter 1:5). This should come as no surprise to those who are invited to "become partakers of the divine nature" (v.4). The noun had a broadly varied usage throughout Greek philosophy and Hellenistic Judaism.[81] The related verb means "to fit together." At its most basic root, the noun designated "the specific quality appropriate to an object or person."[82] Outside the NT the noun is "a term denoting consummate 'excellence' or 'merit' within a social context," the exhibition of which invites recognition, resulting in renown or glory."[83] It, then, in the NT is used of the "manifestation of divine power"—here exercised in the saving grace of salvation. In the LXX, it is found only a handful of times, one being Isaiah 43:21, which Peter seems to allude to here: "The people whom I formed for Myself Will declare My praise [τὰς ἀρετάς]." The context there seems to point to a recitation of God's mighty, saving acts. It would seem then that here it has in view particularly those things (note the plural) which God accomplished through Jesus Christ in the salvation of human beings.

In this case, the mighty acts of God's saving grace are bound up in and made effectual through the call of God in the gospel (τοῦ ... καλέσαντος, "of Him who has called"). The participle is used substantively ("*Him who* has called," emphasis added). The aorist tense looks back upon the moment when they heard the gospel, and God, by His Spirit, made it personal and effectual in their lives. The genitive ("*of* Him who has called," emphasis added) is subjective and designates the work accomplished by Him who called us.[84] It was not just a generalized call but highly personal and individual (ὑμᾶς, "you"). God has called them, so they call out as far and wide and to as many as possible this same good news. We who have

---

81 NIDNTT, 3:925–926.
82 Ibid, 3:925.
83 BDAG, 1088.
84 Forbes, 69.

been the object of God's gospel call are to be the means by which it reaches more and more people.

God's call on us is to arise "out of darkness" (ἐκ σκότους) and to step, by His grace, "into His marvelous light" (εἰς τὸ θαυμαστὸν αὐτοῦ φῶς). The "darkness" under consideration is a spiritual one. It is the natural state in which we arrive in this world (Eph. 5:8). All that takes place there and is generated from such a state is fruitless and damning (Eph. 5:11). It is a state brought about and ruled over by the devil himself (Eph. 6:12). It constitutes a rival kingdom (Col. 1:13). Peter speaks only one other time of "darkness" (σκότους) and there it is of the "the black darkness" of eternal judgment that "has been reserved" for those who do not heed the gospel call (2 Peter 2:17; cf. Jude 13). But those who take up the call of God in the gospel are "rescued…from the domain of darkness, and transferred…to the kingdom of His beloved Son" (Col. 1:13). And so, by God's mighty hand through Jesus Christ and His resurrection from death, God brings us "into His marvelous light" (εἰς τὸ θαυμαστὸν αὐτοῦ φῶς). Carefully note the contrast between ἐκ ("out of") εἰς and ("into"). The latter preposition (εἰς, "FOR") points to more than a simple direction ("into"); it "gives more the aim of the call, than its local result: to, i.e., to attain unto and be partakers of."[85] We are, to use Paul's word, "transferred" from one domain to another. Not just moved in a direction, but delivered into a state and standing— "His…light" (τὸ…αὐτοῦ φῶς). "Darkness" did not contain the definite article; it was general, broad, and all-encompassing. But the "light" (τὸ…φῶς) is that peculiar and singular light that is "His" (αὐτοῦ) alone.

The personal pronoun (αὐτοῦ, "His") is in the attributive position between the noun and its definite article, emphasizing the qualitative nature of the light under consideration. "God is Light, and in Him there is no darkness at all" (1 John 1:5). In the person of Christ, Isaiah's prophecy has come true: "The people who walk in darkness Will see a great light; Those who live in a dark land, The light will shine on them" (Isa. 9:2). Peter personally knew the dawning of this great light, even quite

---

85 Alford, 4:349.

literally. For once, in the nighttime darkness of a Roman prison cell, "an angel of the Lord suddenly appeared and a light shone in the cell; and he struck Peter's side and woke him up, saying, 'Get up quickly.' And his chains fell off his hands" (Acts 12:7). That physical deliverance was an outward manifestation of the spiritual deliverance Peter had already experienced. By His mercy, God through His Son makes us "sons of light and sons of day" so that we can truly say, "We are not of night nor of darkness" any longer (1 Thess. 5:5). Paul was sent to the Gentiles "to open their eyes so that they may turn from darkness to light and from the dominion of Satan to God" (Acts 26:18a).

And, indeed, Peter found that light to be "marvelous" (θαυμαστὸν). The word designates something which induces awe or causes one to marvel. The adjective is used only six times in the NT, two of those in quotations from Psalm 118:23 (Matt. 21:42; Mark 12:11). This is significant because Peter just cited Psalm 118:22 above in verse 7. He continues to weave the string of OT pearls together. Ironically, it was used by the man Jesus delivered from the darkness of blindness as the Jewish authorities continued to challenge him about the one who had delivered him: "Well, here is an amazing thing [τὸ θαυμαστόν], that you do not know where He is from, and yet He opened my eyes" (John 9:30). As he went on to instruct his religious leaders, only God can deliver a person from darkness, physical or spiritual (vv.31–33). Its final two NT usages occur in Revelation 15:1 and 3, where we meet a throng in heaven "who had been victorious over the beast and his image and the number of his name" (v.2). As God prepared to pour out the final expression of His wrath upon all evil and to deliver fully, finally, and forever His people, the throng sang "the song of the Lamb," saying, "Great and marvelous [θαυμαστὰ] are Your works, O Lord God, the Almighty; Righteous and true are Your ways, King of the nations!" (v.3).

Verse 10 – "for you once were NOT A PEOPLE, but now you are THE PEOPLE OF GOD; you had NOT RECEIVED MERCY, but now you have RECEIVED MERCY."

Peter has stated the high honors of being God's people (v.9a) and the resulting purpose that falls upon believers as such (v.9b). The sentence carries on by continuing the dramatic contrast put in motion by the call of God "out of darkness into His marvelous light" (v.9b). The same dramatic shift of salvation is still in view, though under different terms.

The first order of business is to determine just what Peter had in mind by οἵ. Did he intend it to be a relative pronoun, or was it intended as a definite article? If the former, it finds its antecedent in ὑμεῖς ("you") in verse 9. If the latter, it has attracted the accent mark from the following unaccented word (ποτε, "then"). In that case, it would be read as a parallel to the following definite article (οἱ οὐκ ἠλεημένοι, lit., "the ones not having been pitied"). Dubis, choosing the latter option, observes, "This article nominalizes the entire expression ποτε οὐ λαὸς νῦν δὲ λαὸς θεοῦ ('formerly-not-a-people-but-now-people-of-God ones'), which stands in apposition to the λαὸς in verse 9."[86] While this is possible grammatically, it is simpler to read the form as a relative pronoun.

Whatever one decides in this regard, Peter clearly continues to build off the last of his designations of the people as "A PEOPLE FOR God's OWN POSSESSION" (λαὸς εἰς περιποίησιν, v.9). There Peter referenced Isaiah 43:21, with echoes of Exodus 19:5–6, and Malachi 3:17. In verse 4 Peter used "stone" (λίθος) as the thread on which to string together various OT passages (Isa. 28:16; Psa. 118:22; Isa. 8:14), applying them all to Christ (vv.4, 6–8). Here too, he picks up on his use of λαὸς in v.9 (from Isa. 43:21; Exod. 19:5–6; Mal. 3:17) and uses it to allude to statements by the prophet Hosea (cf. Hosea1:6, 9, 10 and 2:23). He references these to stress the change in their status as "A PEOPLE," and that based upon their reception of "MERCY" from God.

Peter contrasts what his readers "once were" (ποτε) as Gentiles apart from Christ and what they are "now" (νῦν) as those included in Christ by God's mercy. Their former state (ποτε, "once were") was "NOT A PEOPLE" (οὐ λαὸς). The negation (οὐ, "NOT") is absolute and categorical.[87] On the noun (λαὸς, "A PEOPLE"), see our comments on verse 9

---

86 Dubis, 57.
87 Thayer, 408.

above. There is no verb in the Greek, the stark expression highlighting the bleak, solitary nature of their previous experience.

Here Peter begins his allusions to Hosea. God asked Hosea to live out a marriage and family life that served as a parable/illustration of God's relationship with Israel. Hosea married a woman who proved unfaithful, just as Israel had proven unfaithful to God (Hos. 1:2–3). Their children would bear names that reflected God's offense at Israel's unfaithfulness. Their second-born, a girl, was named Lo-ruhamah, meaning "No Mercy" (1:6, ESV), for God would no longer have mercy upon unfaithful Israel. Hosea's third child was named Lo-ammi, which meant "Not My People" (1:9, ESV), for God rejected unfaithful Israel as His unique, covenant people. Yet God promised salvation for Israel, saying, "I will sow her for myself in the land. And I will have mercy on No Mercy, and I will say to Not My People, 'You are my people'; and he shall say, 'You are my God'" (2:23, ESV).

Paul also cites Hosea 2:23 in Romans 9:25 and Hosea 1:10 in Romans 9:26.[88] Through Hosea, God promised mercy and standing to His wayward people Israel. Paul cites Hosea to show that God, through Christ, was showing mercy and giving standing to Jews and Gentiles alike ("us, whom He also called, not from among Jews only, but also from among Gentiles," Rom. 9:24). Peter calls on Hosea to underscore that what had been promised to Israel was now being applied to Gentiles who, by God's mercy, are in Christ by faith.

Peter's readers are reminded that not only had they once not been the people of God, but they had not even been a people. They were a disenfranchised, wayward amalgam of helpless individuals living under the wrath of God. But there came a transformation so fundamental that what they once were gave way to a new day and a new standing (νῦν δὲ, "but now"). As Peter wrote, they were constituted "THE PEOPLE OF GOD" (λαὸς θεοῦ; cf. Hos. 1:9; 2:23). Again, there is no verb in the Greek text,

---

88 There is no basis for concluding Peter was depending upon Paul here. Though they both turn to Hosea, their wording is different enough to eliminate the idea of literary dependence upon Peter's part.

but over against the stark expression of their former state, this serves to dramatically set forth their new reality.

How could this have ever come about? Peter explains. Previously they "had NOT RECEIVED MERCY" (οἱ οὐx ἠλεημένοι; cf. Hos. 1:6). The participle is substantive (i.e., "*the ones who* had not received mercy"). The negation (οὐx, "NOT") is again absolute and categorical. The perfect tense sets forth their merciless state as abiding and continuing. They continually lived as those "having no hope and without God in the world" (Eph. 2:12). They were aliens to God and foreigners to His mercy. The passive voice pictures them as solitary, left to themselves, and without any merciful, saving intervention from beyond themselves.

Yet this changed (νῦν δὲ, "but now"). Against all comprehension, somehow his readers have "RECEIVED MERCY" (ἐλεηθέντες; cf. Hos. 2:23). The prior definite article is to be read with both participles (οἱ οὐx ἠλεημένοι ... ἐλεηθέντες) and in this case might be read "*the ones who* received mercy." The aorist tense stands in contrast to the previous perfect. There they stood in an abiding state of merciless need. But God stepped in (note the passive voice again) through His Son Jesus Christ, and through the gospel, they "RECEIVED MERCY." The aorist tense points to the pivotal moment when they heard the call of God through the gospel and turned and trusted in Jesus Christ. That moment ended their previous existence as being not a people and as having no mercy and constituted them "THE PEOPLE OF GOD" who have "RECEIVED MERCY." The latter picks up the note with which Peter began the letter: "according to His great mercy" God "has caused us to be born again to a living hope through the resurrection of Jesus Christ from the dead" (1 Peter 1:3).

They who had been aliens and foreigners to God are now "aliens" to this world (1 Peter 1:1; 2:11). They had been "excluded from the commonwealth of Israel, and strangers to the covenants of promise" (Eph.

> **Ministry Maxim**
>
> Self-understanding not rooted in divine mercy is misguided.

2:12), but by the mercies of God "are no longer strangers and aliens, but you are fellow citizens with the saints, and are of God's household" (v.19). This is so for anyone from any ethnicity, nationality, language, culture, or people who will turn to God through His Son, the appointed Savior, Jesus Christ.

Let us return to that fundamental question first raised in our comments on verse 4. Does Peter equate the NT Church with the nation of Israel so that we might say the Church is now the "new Israel"? Is it correct to say these verses explicitly teach that the NT Church is the true Israel of God? Is there a distinction to be made between the Church and Israel? Is there a future for ethnic or national Israel? Or does Peter, in fact, point to Jesus as the perfect fulfillment of Israel and that through relationship to Him, all people, Jew or Gentile, may come into the grace of God promised and set in motion in the OT and fulfilled in the NT? Jesus is the "living stone" (v.4), and in relationship to Him believers become "living stones" (v.5). Or is he simply saying that in the unfolding plan of God, the grace of God that was always intended to go not just to ethnic or national Israel, but all the peoples of the earth, has now done so, despite Israel's unbelief? Is Peter saying God has permanently replaced Israel with the Church or that now, for His purposes, the Church takes up some of the functions previously assigned to Israel?

Many take the kinds of statements we meet here to say that what Israel once was, the Church now is. It is seen simply as the Church having replaced Israel. In response, we can say that the NT, at times, uses OT language once applied to Israel to speak now of the Church. And thus, when the question of the Church's identity is raised, some will insist, "We are the new Israel." I suggest, however, that the point Peter (and the rest of the NT) makes is not that the Church gets its identity from Israel but from Jesus Christ. Adam failed to be what God required him to be, as did Cain, Seth, Noah, and all who have followed from them. So, God started over with just one man, Abraham. God made of him a great nation, Israel. Israel failed to be what God required them to be. Jesus came and was everything Adam should have been but failed to be—the only perfect man to ever live, the head of a new humanity. Jesus fulfilled all righteousness. Likewise, Jesus came and fulfilled everything Israel should have been but failed to be. He is the perfect Prophet, Priest, and King. Christ is the second Adam, and as individuals, we find our identity now in Christ, no longer in Adam (Rom. 5:12–21). Christ is the perfection of all Israel ever was called to be, and collectively (as God's people, the Church), we find our identity in Christ, not Israel. Little wonder that the NT often uses OT language (originally referring to Israel) to speak of those who are in Christ, who is the perfect Israel. I am suggesting that Israel and the Church are not to be identified as the same entity, one replacing the other. God will raise up Israel again as a believing people (Rom. 11:25–27). The NT clearly uses OT "Israel" language to speak of the Church, not because the Church has replaced Israel, but because Jesus fulfilled everything Israel was ever supposed to be and because we find our identity, individually as Christians and corporately as the Church, in Him. Jesus was *chosen* (1 Pet 2:4), and thus all who are "in Him" constitute "A CHOSEN RACE" (v.9).

Digging Deeper:
1. How does the high value of independence in North American culture set us up to struggle with understanding the Bible's emphasis on corporate identity as the people of God (v.9)?
2. How has divine mercy reshaped your self-perception (v.10)?

Verse 11 – "Beloved, I urge you as aliens and strangers to abstain from fleshly lusts which wage war against the soul."

In 1:1–12 Peter used the indicatives of grace (applied to each as individual believers) to lay a foundation from which grew imperatives of moral action (1:13–2:3). Similarly, having laid a fresh foundation of grace received (2:4–10; applied this time to all believers corporately) he again establishes from their foundation imperatives for godly living (2:11–5:11). First Peter 2:11–12 serve to lay the foundation for the commands that follow. Christ's people must live well amid the lost around them, stressing first that which they must avoid (v.11) and then setting forth that which they must pursue (v.12).

Having settled his readers' personal (1:1–12) and corporate identity in Christ (2:4–10), Peter is free to address them now as the "Beloved" (Ἀγαπητοί) of God, and therefore of his own heart as well. Peter begins now to use this form of address freely (1 Peter 2:11; 4:12; 2 Peter 3:1, 8, 14, 17). Here again is another indicator of their identity—individually and corporately—they are the "Beloved" of God. They reside under His covenant of love through Jesus Christ. They are marked out from the rest of humanity as those chosen, favored, and determinatively dealt with by the grace of God. Only as the "Beloved" of God, the objects of His great grace, may the moral imperatives to follow be reasonably laid upon them.

As such a people, Peter is free to "urge" (παρακαλῶ) them to live in a way distinctive from all others. The verb is frequently used in the NT, but Peter will employ it again only in 1 Peter 5:1 and 12. Yet he characterizes the entire letter as such an exhortation (5:12). The verb is a compound, built from καλέω ("to call") and παρά ("beside"). The bare combination might mean "to call alongside," but its meaning may vary from encourage and comfort on one end of the spectrum to exhort and implore on the other end. The individual context must determine where an author intends to anchor a particular use of the verb on this continuum of meaning. Here Peter seems to use the verb in the stronger sense. The hour is too dark, the issues too significant, and the matters hanging in the balance are eternal—they must hear and heed his word of exhortation.

Though they are "Beloved" (Ἀγαπητοί) to God, and thus to Peter, they reside in the world "as aliens and strangers" (ὡς παροίκους καὶ παρεπιδήμους). Peter sounded this theme as he opened the letter, reminding his readers that they are "elect exiles" (1:1, ESV). To God, they are "elect." As to the world, they are "exiles." They must "conduct" themselves accordingly "during the time of [their] stay on earth" (1:17). But note, they *are* "Beloved"; this is their abiding identity. Peter must address them "*as* [ὡς] aliens and strangers" (emphasis added); this is their temporary role in the limited sphere of their earthly lives. Peter uses ὡς ("as") to introduce "the perspective from which" his readers are to be "viewed or understood as to character, function, or role."[89] Two adjectives, used as substantives, define them.

---

89 BDAG, 8075.3.a.α.

First, they are "aliens" (παροίκους). The word appears only four times in the NT. Twice Stephen used the word, once to recount the plight of the Hebrews in Egypt (Acts 7:6) and again to remind them of Moses' position in Midian, having fled Egypt (Acts 7:29). Paul reminded the Ephesian believers "that formerly you, the Gentiles in the flesh... were at that time separate from Christ, excluded from the commonwealth of Israel, and strangers to the covenants of promise, having no hope and without God in the world" (Eph. 2:11–12). Then he reminded them that in Christ "you are no longer strangers and aliens [πάροικοι], but you are fellow citizens with the saints, and are of God's household" (v.19). Peter used the kindred noun (παροικία) to denote "the time of your stay" on earth (1 Peter 1:17). The adjective describes a noncitizen; someone who resides as a resident alien in a foreign land.[90] Like Paul, this has been Peter's point. They had previously been "strangers and aliens" to God and at home in this world. Now, because of the redemption that is theirs in Jesus Christ, they are "strangers and aliens" to this world and now "A CHOSEN RACE, A royal PRIESTHOOD, A HOLY NATION, A PEOPLE FOR God's OWN POSSESSION" (1 Peter 2:9). They who once "were NOT A PEOPLE" now are "THE PEOPLE OF GOD" (v.10).

> **Ministry Maxim**
>
> You are either loved by the world and a stranger to God or loved by God and stranger to the world.

They also (καὶ, "and") are "strangers" (παρεπιδήμους). This is the word with which Peter first identified his readers: "elect strangers [παρεπιδήμοις]" (1 Peter 1:1). The only other NT use of the word describes all the people of faith listed in Hebrews 11, identifying them as "strangers and exiles [παρεπίδημοί] on the earth" (v.13). The word is largely synonymous with the previous adjective. It describes "a person who for a period of time lives in a place which is not his normal residence."[91]

---

90 Friberg, 301.
91 Louw-Nida, 11.77.

Peter may be recalling the words of Genesis 23:4 and/or Psalm 39:12 (38:13 LXX), where the same expression is found. Abraham identifies himself to the Hittites of Canaan as "a stranger and a sojourner" among them (Gen. 23:4). David tells God, "I am a stranger with You, A sojourner like all my fathers" (Psa. 39:12). Peter's readers stand in the heritage of the greats of the faith. They too, like their forefathers, can be faithful in a strange and hostile world.

While we physically reside in this world as the people of Christ, we are like Abraham, "looking for the city which has foundations, whose architect and builder is God" (Heb. 11:10). We "desire a better country, that is, a heavenly one" (11:16). "For here we do not have a lasting city, but we are seeking the city which is to come" (13:14). And this because "our citizenship is in heaven" (Phil. 3:20).

It is precisely because they live at one and the same moment as both the "Beloved" of God and thus as "aliens and strangers" in this world that Peter calls them "to abstain" (ἀπέχεσθαι) from certain aspects of life in this world. It is a compound verb constructed from ἀπό ("from," "away from," "out of") and ἔχω ("to have," "to hold"). The prefixed preposition can lend its meaning in two directions. The word can mean to have or hold something "from" another person. Thus, Paul uses the verb to acknowledge the receipt of the monetary gift from the Philippians (Phil. 4:18). But it can also mean to have or hold something "away from" yourself. And thus, it means, as it does here, "to abstain." It is used in this sense in Acts 15:20 when the Jerusalem Council called upon Gentile believers in Christ to "abstain [ἀπέχεσθαι] from things contaminated by idols and from fornication and from what is strangled and from blood" (cf. also v.29). Paul commanded the believers in Thessalonica "to abstain [ἀπέχεσθαι] from sexual immorality" (1 Thess. 4:3) and to "abstain [ἀπέχεσθε] from every form of evil" (5:22). The present tense here indicates that the believer must make it the pattern of life. The middle voice may mark the action as taken upon oneself and might be rendered, "holding yourselves off from."[92] Peter here picks up on his exhortation in 2:1 to "put aside" (Ἀποθέμενοι)

---

92 Hiebert, 155.

various sins. The verb there is also a compound with ἀπό ("from," "away from," "out of") as a prefix. Here he restates the basic orientation toward sin and the impulses that move us to them.

That from which they must hold themselves back are "from fleshly lusts" (τῶν σαρκικῶν ἐπιθυμιῶν). Peter has already addressed the problem of "lusts" (ἐπιθυμιῶν) in 1:14 (see our comments there) and will do so more and more (1 Peter 4:2, 3; 2 Peter 1:4; 2:10, 18; 3:3). In 1:14 these "lusts" were characterized as "former" (πρότερον) and undertaken "in … ignorance" (ἐν τῇ ἀγνοίᾳ) and unbelief. The noun ἐπιθυμία ("lusts") is morally neutral; it describes strong passions and urges of any kind (e.g., 1 Thess. 2:17; 1 Tim. 6:9). Here they are denoted as "fleshly" (σαρκικῶν). The adjective denotes those things "which move and stir in the ethical domain of the flesh, which have in that rebellious region of man's corrupt and fallen nature their source and spring."[93] They are, as such, those "which wage war against the soul" (αἵτινες στρατεύονται κατὰ τῆς ψυχῆς). Peter sets the "fleshly" (σαρκικῶν) over against "the soul" (τῆς ψυχῆς). The noun ψυχή ("soul") is one with a breadth of meaning, but here Peter uses it to designate "the seat and center of life that transcends the earthly."[94] Thus, he is presently concerned for what is oriented to and arises from merely a physical alignment to life versus what is oriented to and arises from a concern for the total person. That which is "fleshly" seeks to defile, debase, and destroy "the soul." God has saved the "soul" (ψυχή) through Christ (1 Peter 1:9). It must be purified through obedience (1:22), is overseen and shepherded by Jesus (2:25), and must be entrusted to God amid unjust suffering (4:19).

The pronoun (αἵτινες, "which") may be used categorically, sweeping up all "fleshly lusts" into a class all their own and denoting that there isn't one among them which doesn't "wage war against your soul."[95] Or it may be used qualitatively and intensively, meaning "the very things that."[96]

---

93 Trench, 273.
94 BDAG, 8046.2.d.
95 Vincent, 1:645; Alford, 4:350.
96 Wallace, 344.

Peter likens that battle to one who will "wage war" (στρατεύονται). The verb can be used as a substantive ("soldiers," Luke 3:14) and to describe the action of soldiering generally (1 Cor. 9:7; 2 Tim. 2:4). Metaphorically, it can describe the believer's spiritual battle (2 Cor. 10:3; 1 Tim. 1:18) or, as here, that which wars against the believer (James 4:1). James also notes the link between one's desires and the war against the soul: "What is the source of quarrels and conflicts among you? Is not the source your pleasures that wage war [στρατευομένων] in your members?" (James 4:1). Here Peter uses the present tense to denote the steady, unremitting assault of one's lusts against one's best interests and life. It is found only in the middle voice in the NT. The preposition κατά ("against") generally denotes downward movement. Thus the "lusts" are pictured as looming over "the soul" and threatening to destroy it. The preposition thus serves here as "a marker of opposition," setting forth the antagonism of "lusts" against "the soul."[97]

Observing that Peter speaks in the plural of "lusts" (τῶν ... ἐπιθυμιῶν) but uses the singular "soul" (τῆς ψυχῆς), Michaels notes that there are "many impulses besieging each individual soul."[98]

Verse 12 – "Keep your behavior excellent among the Gentiles, so that in the thing in which they slander you as evildoers, they may because of your good deeds, as they observe *them*, glorify God in the day of visitation."

The Greek sentence continues from verse 11. There Peter stated the matter negatively (what "to abstain from" and why), while verse 12 states the matter positively and missionally.

What the English states as an imperative ("Keep your behavior") is a participle ("having your behavior," YLT). The participle (ἔχοντες, lit., "having") modifies "to abstain from" (ἀπέχεσθαι) in verse 11 and is probably to be understood as setting forth the attendant circumstances, what

---

97 Louw-Nida, 90.31.

98 Michaels, 116.

takes place positively as one abstains from the lusts of the flesh,[99] or instrumentally, "by keeping your conduct good among the Gentiles."[100]

The participle may carry some imperatival force, for which most English translations opt (except cf. KJV, NET, NKJV, YLT). The present tense sets forth the necessity of constant vigilance over one's behavior. Louw-Nida defines the verb in this case as "to have or possess objects or property (in the technical sense of having control over the use of such objects)."[101] Thus you are to take rightful authority over and possess for gospel purposes "your behavior" (τὴν ἀναστροφὴν ὑμῶν). Eight of the thirteen times the noun appears in the NT are from the pen of Peter (1 Peter 1:15, 18; 2:12; 3:1, 2, 16; 2 Peter 2:7; 3:11; cf. also the verbal cognate ἀναστρέφω in 1:17). The noun means "a turning about in place" and then came to designate one's daily behavior[102], though that moment-by-moment conduct is pictured as driven by certain principles[103], for good (1 Tim. 4:12; Heb. 13:7; James 3:13; 1 Peter 1:15; 2:12; 3:1, 2, 16; 2 Peter 3:11) or ill (Gal. 1:13; Eph. 4:22; 1 Peter 1:18). It could be used metaphorically of walking in virtue, designating "a mode of existence, a way of behaving."[104] It became a technical term in Christian sanctification and pointed to "an unassailable comportment." "Whether with respect to bearing, dress, or behavior in family and social relations, every action and reaction in the context of the community, that is, the concrete life of the believer, should be noble and radiant."[105] The plural pronoun (ὑμῶν, "your") marks this as both a personal responsibility and a collective obligation.

---

99 Dubis, 61; Forbes, 75.

100 Schreiner, 121.

101 Louw-Nida, 57.1.

102 Friberg, 52.

103 BDAG, 566.

104 Spicq, 1:111.

105 Ibid., 1:112.

The context in which they are to so guard and shape their conduct is "among the Gentiles" (ἐν τοῖς ἔθνεσιν). The preposition (ἐν) means "in," but used with the plural noun (τοῖς ἔθνεσιν, "the Gentiles") has the sense of "among." Peter just used the singular form of the noun to refer to Christ's followers as "A HOLY NATION" (v.9). But in the plural, it often designated non-Jewish peoples. Here it has the sense of not simply non-Jewish peoples but of those who do not believe in, submit to, or obey God through Jesus Christ (cf. 4:3). Though there may have been some small Jewish communities within the region of Asia Minor where Peter's readers dwelt, it was predominantly Gentile in makeup. Though Peter would not label his readers as Jews (as opposed to Gentiles), he would consider them under the favor of the God who called the nation of Israel so He could bring forth His Son through that nation and demonstrate God's glory and extend God's grace to all the peoples of the earth. They are now a part of God's "HOLY NATION," and those who do not believe are outside His favor and thus can be termed broadly "the Gentiles."

The standard for their conduct is set at "excellent" (καλήν). The adjective refers to that which is morally positive and generally valued.[106] It designates that which is in accord with the highest level of a thing's purpose for existence.[107] Storms notes that Peter uses καλός instead of ἀγαθός.[108] He says καλός "goes beyond the idea of moral goodness or ethical righteousness and includes the element of aesthetic worth and beauty: a goodness that commends itself to the beholder by its nobility and attractiveness."[109] Peter will employ it again later in this verse to speak of his readers' "good [καλῶν] deeds." He will also use it to speak of being "good [καλοὶ] stewards" of God's manifold grace (1 Peter 4:10). Peter's call is not unlike Paul's exhortation to the believers of Ephesus "to walk in a manner worthy of the calling with which you have been called" (Eph. 4:1; cf. Phil. 1:27;

---

106 Louw-Nida, 88.4.

107 BDAG, 3900.2.

108 Though note that Peter uses ἀγαθός with the same verb (ἀναστροφή, "behavior") in 1 Peter 3:16 (Stibbs, 107).

109 Storms, 325.

Col. 1:10; 1 Thess. 2:12; 3 John 6). The general measure of "excellent" may be more than, but never less than what Peter will next outline for citizens (2:13–17), servants (2:18–25), wives (3:1–6), husbands (3:7), "all of" God's people (3:8–4:19), and elders (5:1–5).

Peter sets forth the purpose for his concern and their obedience (ἵνα + subjunctive, "so that"). The clause is complex but, simply stated, the purpose of living well among the unbelieving is that "they may ... glorify God" (δοξάσωσιν τὸν θεόν). The verb has the idea of accurately acknowledging and ascribing appropriate worth to the object in question. Since God is the object to be glorified, there is no limit to the glory that is due to Him. Finite humanity can never fully ascribe the glory due to the infinite God. But the quest to do so is the essence of worship. God's purpose is to make all of creation a mirror reflecting the greatness of its Creator and Redeemer. Humans, as the highest of God's created beings, have a unique and privileged place in this work of glorification. The believer's occupation is to seek that "in all things God may be glorified [δοξάζηται]" (4:11). As we do so, we experience joy that is "full of glory" (δεδοξασμένῃ, 1:8). Even when we suffer because we are Christians we are to "glorify" (δοξαζέτω) God (4:16). But we exist for more than rendering to God our personal worship. All things are being sovereignly moved to that time when "at the name of Jesus EVERY KNEE WILL BOW, of those who are in heaven and on earth and under the earth, and that every tongue will confess that Jesus Christ is Lord, to the glory of God the Father" (Phil. 2:10–11).

"Why did Christ come? Why was He conceived? Why was He born? Why was He crucified? Why did He rise again? Why is He now at the right hand of the Father? The answer to all these questions is, 'In order that He might make worshipers out of rebels.'"[110]

Ironically the unbelieving will glorify God precisely "in the thing in which they slander you as evildoers" (ἐν ᾧ καταλαλοῦσιν ὑμῶν ὡς κακοποιῶν) at the present time. The preposition (ἐν, "in") and relative pronoun (ᾧ, "which") assume the presence of a demonstrative pronoun

---

110 Tozer, 217.

("the thing"). Combined, the resulting meaning is "in that which."¹¹¹ It all points to something in which, at present, "they slander you" (καταλαλοῦσιν ὑμῶν). The verb is found only five times in the NT (James 4:11 [3x]; 1 Peter 2:12; 3:16). It is a compound made up of κατά ("against") and λαλέω ("to speak"). It means to speak evil of, to slander, to rail against,¹¹² "to criminate,"¹¹³ to speak ill of, degrade, or defame.¹¹⁴ The present tense pictures this as a pattern of speech. The party line is to defame and degrade that which you do not understand or with which you disagree. The slander is that in your exemplary living, they tag you "as evildoers" (ὡς κακοποιῶν). Again, we have a compound: κακόν ("evil") and ποιέω ("to make"). The adjective is found only here in 1 Peter (2:12, 14; 4:15). It designates "the one who does evil," "who acts badly," or "that which has harmful effects."¹¹⁵ It stands as the opposite of the "excellent" and "good" (καλός) conduct to which Peter calls his readers.

> **Ministry Maxim**
>
> Your conduct may be the difference between heaven and hell for one presently provoking you to live poorly.

Indeed, the irony is in the fact that the label of "evildoers" comes precisely "because of your good deeds" (ἐκ τῶν καλῶν ἔργων). The preposition ἐκ ("because of") designates the "effective cause" of their words and the source of their understanding.¹¹⁶ That source is the "good deeds" (τῶν καλῶν ἔργων) of Peter's readers (ὑμῶν, "your"). The definite article has specific acts and words in mind. The attributive position of the adjective (καλῶν, "good") stresses the qualitative nature of the "works" Peter calls to their attention. The concern for good works is one often sounded in

---

111 BDAG, 5396.1.b.α.
112 NIDNTTE, 3:78.
113 Thayer, 322.
114 BDAG, 3997.
115 TDNT, 3:485.
116 BDAG, 2317.3.g.β.

the PE (1 Tim. 2:10; 3:1; 5:10, 25; 6:18; 2 Tim. 2:21; 3:17; Titus 1:16; 2:7, 14; 3:1, 8, 14), but also elsewhere in the NT (e.g., Heb. 10:24). One is not saved "on the basis of deeds which we have done in righteousness" (Titus 3:5; cf. 2 Tim. 1:9), but true salvation produces a life of grateful obedience that shows itself in good deeds. As believers, we are to so live that our lives "will adorn the doctrine of God our Savior in every respect" (Titus 2:10b).

The juxtaposition of the adjective καλός ("good") over against the previously compounded adjective κακόν ("evil") is jarring. The words and actions of the unbelieving revilers prove their moral confusion. They are "those who call evil good, and good evil; Who substitute darkness for light and light for darkness; Who substitute bitter for sweet and sweet for bitter" (Isa. 5:20). They do not understand that "He who justifies the wicked and he who condemns the righteous" are both "alike are an abomination to the LORD" (Prov. 17:15).

The giving of glory to God will happen "as they observe" (ἐποπτεύοντες) those "good deeds." The verb occurs only here and in 3:2, where Peter instructs wives to live with their unbelieving husbands such that "they observe [ἐποπτεύσαντες] your chaste and respectful behavior." Peter uses the cognate noun to identify himself and James and John as "eyewitness" (ἐπόπται) of Jesus' glory on the Mount of Transfiguration (2 Peter 1:16). The verb itself implies both continuity and intent[117] and thus suggests that they have regularly observed their behavior and found it time and again to be "good." The present tense underscores and emphasizes this; it "indicates the covering of a longer period of time and includes the observer's memory and reflection upon the deeds."[118] They have regularly observed their lives and should have been able to see that "the Spirit of glory and of God rests on" them (1 Peter 4:14). The evidence is right before their eyes, yet they do not yet see it for what it is. Their "light" has become "darkness" (Luke 11:35). They condemn others to justify themselves. And

---

117 Louw-Nida, 24.45.

118 Rienecker, 752.

when they justify themselves in this way, they are "detestable in the sight of God" (Luke 16:15).

But "in the day of visitation" (ἐν ἡμέρᾳ ἐπισκοπῆς), their perception and words will change. This is now the third use of ἐν ("among," "in") in this verse. Peter is concerned with what is happening "in" the midst of the lost, "in" their defamation of God's people, and what will happen "in" the day of Christ's return. It is "in" the latter that the first two find their answer—rewards for those faithful with the commission of living out the gospel among the lost and judgment for those who reject the gospel and those who brought it to them.

The noun "day" (ἡμέρᾳ) is used by Peter to speak of not a solar day of twenty-four hours but of the dawn of a new era in God's dealings with man. Here it is characterized as a "visitation" (ἐπισκοπῆς). The word occurs only four times in the NT. It can designate an overseer (1 Tim. 3:1) or the "office" of leadership (Acts 1:20). But it also has the sense of a drawing near of divine presence, power, and opportunity and thus a "visitation." Jesus used it this way when He lamented over Jerusalem, "you did not recognize the time of your visitation [ἐπισκοπῆς]" (Luke 19:44). In Jesus, God came near; He visited those He created. Jesus is Immanuel, "God with us" (Matt. 1:23). But the Jewish national leadership and the populace as a whole did not recognize Him and take advantage of the opportunity of grace being extended to them in His "visitation." Thus, when Jesus returns, it will be for some "the day of judgment" (2 Peter 2:9; 3:7). It will set in motion "the day of the Lord" (3:10), "the day of God" (3:12), and will usher in "the day of eternity" (3:18).

Some want to make "the day of visitation" simply a breaking in of God by His Spirit to awaken hearts to the offer of the gospel and to call them to repentance and faith in Jesus.[119] Jobes, however, observes: "Contra this understanding, it should be noted that generally the visitation of God referred to elsewhere in Scripture is of a corporate, not individual nature, and that 1 Peter (1:5, 7, 13; 4:7, 13, 17; 5:1) often mentions the coming

---

119 E.g., Lenski, 109; Hiebert, 160; cf. also Calvin, Beare, Elliott, Reicke, and Selwyn.

day of judgment."[120] This and Peter's clear focus upon the return of Christ points to understanding "the day of visitation" as fulfilled in or at least inaugurated by the return of Jesus Christ.

Peter pictures that "day" as a time when those who deride Christ's people will "glorify God" for the very thing for which they slandered them in this life. Just how are we to understand Peter's intent?

Peter may be calling upon Isaiah 10:3, where the nation in its sin is questioned: "And what will ye do in the day of visitation, and in the desolation which shall come from far?" (Isa. 10:3, KJV).[121] If this is so, Peter sounds a warning of judgment. Davids bids us compare Joshua 7:19, "where 'give glory to God' is an exhortation to acknowledge God's justice and righteousness by a full confession before execution."[122] The day of Christ will bring universal confession of His lordship (Phil. 2:10–11), but for some, it will be as they make their parting exit to eternity apart from God in judgment.[123] As for the oppressors of Peter's readers, their tune will change when they behold the unveiled glory of Christ, which the believers had perceived already, and which has changed their lives.

But the point Peter seems to be making is the hope of salvation. This is underscored by his counsel to believing wives of unbelieving husbands. Peter uses the same verb to counsel that a wife of an unbelieving husband so live that "by the behavior [ἀναστροφῆς] of" her life her unbelieving husband "may be won" to faith in Christ (1 Peter 3:1). Peter's words here appear to be a clear recollection of Jesus' words: "Let your light shine before men in such a way that they may see your good works, and glorify your Father who is in heaven." (Matt. 5:16; cf. James 3:13). The point seems to be that godly living in the present, though for the moment reviled, will serve as a powerful witness over time to those who

---

120 Jobes, 172.

121 TDNT, 2:608.

122 Davids, 97.

123 Grudem says, "The forced acknowledgement of Christ's Lordship which then results in God's glory, in Phil. 2:11, is different from the active glorifying of God indicated by *doxazō*." But he offers no evidence to support his assertion.

now persecute you. Such living looks in hope to a time when those who presently oppose the believer will, by the gracious working of God, find their minds changed, repent and believe in Christ with the result that at Christ's return, they will be found together with those they now persecute worshiping God forever.

In this light, Peter's instruction is not unlike Paul's counsel to Titus. As already noted, a steady exhortation to good works runs through the brief letter (Titus 1:16; 2:7, 14; 3:1, 8, 14). The believers of Crete live among a notoriously difficult and unbelieving people (1:12). Titus is to teach the Cretan believers to "adorn the doctrine of God our Savior in every respect" (2:10). And this after giving specific instructions for behavior by specific groups within the church: older men (2:2), older women (2:3), younger women (2:4–5), younger men (2:6–8), and slaves (2:9). Then immediately Paul urges Titus to remind the people that the grace of God in Christ is for all peoples, including their unbelieving neighbors who make life difficult for them (2:11–14).

> ### Digging Deeper:
> 1. How are you feeling the tension between being "Beloved" to God and "aliens and strangers" to the world (v.11)?
> 2. How should a pastor respond to open slander against him (v.12)?
> 3. Does his response change if the slander comes from within the church as opposed to outside the church?

Verse 13 – "Submit yourselves for the Lord's sake to every human institution, whether to a king as the one in authority,"

Verses 11 and 12 serve as a thematic introduction to the moral instructions that now begin and run through most of the rest of the book. We do well to recall that Peter has labored to make clear that the moral imperatives he issues are founded upon the grace of God received in Christ (1 Peter 1:1–12; 2:4–10). What follows are not moralisms but moral imperatives that arise from divine grace received. Since Peter's readers find themselves as aliens and strangers in this world (1:1; 2:11) and persecution is rising (4:12ff), he begins with the Christian citizen's response to the state.

Christian citizens' response to the governing authorities under which they reside in this world begins with the command to "Submit yourselves" (Ὑποτάγητε). The verb is a compound comprised of ὑπό ("under") and τάσσω ("to order," "to appoint," "to arrange"). It carries the connotation of authority and the order that results from arranging life under it. Peter will use the verb five more times before he closes this letter (1 Peter 2:18; 3:1, 5, 22; 5:5). It forms the basic key to his understanding of God-glorifying conduct by slaves (2:18), wives (3:1, 5), and the younger generation (5:5). Similarly, Paul uses the word to describe the Church in subjection to Christ (Eph. 5:24), believers in subjection to one another (Eph. 5:21), wives to husbands (Eph. 5:24; Col. 3:18; Titus 2:5), slaves to masters (Titus 2:9), citizens to civic leaders (Rom. 13:1, 5; Titus 3:1), women in worship (1 Cor. 14:34), creation to futility (Rom. 8:20), and the spirits of the prophets to the prophets themselves (1 Cor. 14:32). Peter's use here of the aorist tense demands immediate and decisive action. The passive voice, in this case, has what Alford calls a "quasimiddle sense,"[124] and thus, "Submit yourselves" (i.e., take action upon yourself, so you are submitted). The intent is "subject oneself," "be subjected," or "be subordinated."[125]

This submission is owed "to every human institution" (πάσῃ ἀνθρωπίνῃ κτίσει). The noun κτίσις ("institution") appears nineteen times in the NT. In the other eighteen, it describes an act of creative expression or the result of such an act. Some argue for personalizing the reference here so that it means something like "every human creature."[126] It is argued that this is preparation for Peter's generalized command in verse 17: "honor all

---

124 Alford, 4:351; cf. Dubis, 64; Hiebert, 163; Lenski, 110.

125 BDAG, 7645.1.b.β.

126 E.g., Clowney, 105; Davids, 98–99; Goppelt, 182–183; Kelly, 107–108.

people." This, however, makes little sense when later in this sentence, Peter specifies examples of what he means by κτίσει – "a king" (βασιλεῖ) and "governors" (ἡγεμόσιν). Such a command would ultimately prove impossible, for how can one, in practical terms, submit to "every creature"?[127] Furthermore, the verb in question (ὑποτάσσω, "Submit") designates submission to *authority*, something "every creature" does not possess.[128] We possess ample proof that the noun (κτίσις) was used in ancient Greek of a creative act that brought into being "an authoritative or governmental body," and by extension, then that institution or authority itself.[129] Thus for Peter and his readers, it would have designated the Roman Empire and those who, at a variety of levels, would have functioned within it as leaders. This was no mere human construct but of divine creation. Neither Peter nor the NT generally endorses a given system of political governance. He emphasizes that government is of divine design. Order is better than chaos, governance than anarchy. It is no small thing to note that at the time of Peter's writing this would have meant the Roman Empire and, specifically, Nero himself.

Nero came to power at seventeen years of age. For the first eight years of his reign, the empire thrived, though Nero busied himself with racing chariots and singing in musicals, leaving the day-by-day business of running the empire to his advisors. Eventually, Nero determined to take a more hands-on approach to government. As he seized more and more control, Nero became increasingly brutal, insane, and immoral in his ways. He drained the treasury through his elaborate ventures. When finances got tight, he did what many rulers do.

> **Ministry Maxim**
>
> My submission in human relationships accomplishes God's divine plans.

He raised taxes. At one point, Agrippina, Nero's mother, attempted to manipulate more and more control over the empire. But being frustrated

---

127 Hiebert, 163.

128 Grudem, 126.

129 BDAG, 4433; cf. Grudem, 126.

in her efforts, she supported her son's cousin, Britannicus. To secure his position, Nero had Britannicus poisoned to death, and his mother banished to exile. He placed his mother on a ship designed to sink and end her life, though the plan failed. Thus, in A.D. 59, Nero called for his mother's return and then executed her for treason, having her abdomen laid open so that he might look upon the womb that bore him. In A.D. 64, riots broke out, resulting in much of the city of Rome being burned to the ground. Reportedly Nero had set the fire, but to avert attention from himself, he blamed the conflagration on the Christians. This started the severest of his persecutions upon Jesus' followers. Nero was known for throwing Christians to the lions, impaling them upon high stakes, and setting them on fire so that they might serve as torches to light up his royal gardens at night.[130] And let us not forget, Nero commanded that he be honored as divine, and it was under his hand that Peter would later be martyred for his faith in Jesus.

How could Peter call for subjecting oneself to such a ruler? To such an empire? To those who supported and advanced its cause? Because he saw behind their creation and existence not merely a political process that brought them to power but the creative, sovereign hand of God. He agreed with Paul, "Every person is to be in subjection to the governing authorities. For there is no authority except from God, and those which exist are established by God" (Rom. 13:1). Peter calls it a "human" (ἀνθρωπίνῃ) institution. But that describes the circle of its existence, not the genesis of its creation, the realm of its limited, delegated authority, not the locus of its origin. Human processes and decisions—often brutal and bloody in the Roman Empire—were certainly involved. But behind it all was God's sovereign, ruling hand.

The deference and submission commanded are due in "every" (πάσῃ) case, as Peter will delineate in the rest of verse 13 and 14. Here, the anarthrous noun designates "every" individual instance of human governance.[131] Lower officials are not exempt nor are the highest levels of civil

---

130 Tenney, 283–292.

131 Robertson, *Grammar*, 771–772.

leadership. The laws enacted are binding. The result is that "whoever resists authority has opposed the ordinance of God; and they who have opposed will receive condemnation upon themselves" (Rom. 13:2). Jesus Himself commanded His followers to give "to Caesar the things that are Caesar's; and to God the things that are God's" (Matt. 22:21). Of course, there may come a time when, like the Apostles, Christ's followers have to say to governing authorities, "We must obey God rather than men" (Acts 5:29; cf. 4:19; Exod. 1:17; Dan. 3:13–18; 6:10–24; Heb. 11:23). Discerning just when that time comes is no small challenge. To explore this matter further, I encourage you to consider my book *Embracing Authority*.[132] Not long after Peter penned his two NT epistles, the verdict came down from Roman power that he be executed for his faith in Jesus. Peter found the line that he could not cross, the line demarking the passage from obedience to God in submission to human authority and disobedience to God as the highest and only authority. In life, Peter lived what he preached; in death he proved who had his ultimate allegiance.

While submission to human authorities is often distasteful and difficult, the motive is to be pure and holy. We are to do so "for the Lord's sake" (διὰ τὸν κύριον). The singular noun with the definite article (τὸν κύριον) stands over against the all-encompassing anarthrous expression (πάσῃ ἀνθρωπίνῃ κτίσει, "every human institution"). Gather every individual expression of political, earthly authority, combine them together and they individually and collectively arise from, answer to, and ultimately fulfill the singular will of the solitary Lord of the universe. The preposition (διὰ) with the accusative form of the noun points to the cause or reason for our submission ("for the Lord's sake"). The Lord alone could rightly demand and justly expect such action. Submission to earthly authorities is fundamentally an act of submitting ourselves to God in love and worship. Such living not only fulfills His command but advances His cause—that the unbelieving might see the beauty of the Christian lives around them and one day come to glorify the Lord themselves. Our obedience to God's command to submit to earthly authorities is not simply a personal act of

---

132 John A. Kitchen, *Embracing Authority* (Fearn, Tain: Christian Focus Publications) 2002.

worship but a strategic act designed to multiply His worshipers and magnify His glory. Our present submission to the leaders of earthly kingdoms is ultimately service rendered to the only true King and an act designed to bring in His everlasting Kingdom. In this, we imitate Christ's example (1 Peter 2:21–23), obey His command (Matt. 22:21), and advance His mission (1 Peter 2:12).

Peter takes the rest of verse 13 and all of verse 14 to further define what he means by "human institution." He uses the formula εἴτε … εἴτε ("whether … or")[133] to set off two possibilities. The first is "to a king as one in authority" (βασιλεῖ ὡς ὑπερέχοντι). The noun "a king" (βασιλεῖ) designates the highest pinnacle of ruling authority within a given realm. Though it could be used of those who governed subdivisions of the Roman Empire (e.g., Matt. 2:1–3; Mark 6:22), in the case of Peter and his readers, it refers here to the Emperor of Rome (John 19:15; Acts 17:7), Nero. God is the King of all things (Matt. 5:35), and Jesus is the King of all other kings (Rev. 1:5; 19:16). But for the wise outworking of His plans for redemption and judgment God has delegated a measured portion of His absolute authority to those He places over peoples in any given area (e.g., Dan. 2:37; 4:32; 5:18). The "Most High is ruler over the realm of mankind and bestows it on whomever He wishes" (Dan. 4:25). "He removes kings and establishes kings" (2:21). Peter will use the noun again momentarily to command: "honor the king [βασιλέα]" (1 Peter 2:17).

Our submission to earthly rulers is not total, for absolute submission is due to God alone through Jesus Christ. Our submission is to one "as in authority" (ὡς ὑπερέχοντι). Peter uses ὡς ("as"), a "marker introducing the perspective from which" our submission is to be "viewed or understood."[134] The verb (ὑπερέχοντι, "in authority") is a compound made up of ὑπέρ ("over/above") and ἔχω ("to have," "to hold"). Literally,

---

[133] Used for "bringing together two objects in one's thoughts while keeping them distinct from each other" (Friberg, 134).

[134] BDAG, 8075.3.a.α.

it means "to hold above."¹³⁵ It designates one who holds the high ground over others and thus has an advantage, power, and authority. It designates the highest office in the land ("head of state," NLT). In Rome, that meant the Emperor. It appears only five times in the NT. Paul uses it to speak of considering others higher than yourself (Phil. 2:3), of the surpassing value of knowing Christ (3:8), and of God's peace that transcends all understanding (4:7). Most significant is its use in Paul's statement: "Let every soul to the higher [ὑπερεχούσαις] authorities be subject" (Rom. 13:1, YLT). Here the participial form is used substantively, "*one* in authority." The present tense indicates the one who, for the moment in God's providential workings, possesses measured authority over those living within a particular human realm. Such a one's "authority" is measured and temporary. They will be held accountable by God for how they use it (e.g., Psa. 82; Isa. 40:23–24; Dan. 5). Throughout their tenure of "authority" their heart remains squarely in God's hand (Prov. 21:1), and He can use them in His providence to achieve His sovereign purposes (Psa. 76:10; Rom. 8:28). Given God's command through Peter, our temporal submission to them is then a part of our eternal submission to God. We trust not the human ruler we can see, but the divine King who uses him or her for His purposes.

Verse 14 – "or to governors as sent by him for the punishment of evildoers and the praise of those who do right."

The sentence continues from verse 13 with the second (εἴτε … εἴτε, "whether … or") possible "human institution" to which Christian citizens should submit: "to governors" (ἡγεμόσιν). Peter's use of the noun is the only NT usage outside the Gospels and Acts. While "king" (βασιλεῖ, v. 13) was used of the pinnacle of power in Rome, the Emperor, this noun is used of those who, under the Emperor's authority, exercise authority in limited portions of the Roman Empire and thus were thus "governors"

---

135 Friberg, 390.

over a Roman province. In the NT, it is used of Pilate (Matt. 27:2), Felix (Acts 23:24), and Festus (26:30).

Submission (v.13) is due to such "as sent by him" (ὡς δι' αὐτοῦ πεμπομένοις). Peter uses ὡς ("as") as he did in the parallel statement in verse 13, see our comments there. The present participle (πεμπομένοις, "sent") pictures the appointment happening as each situation deems it necessary, "from time to time."[136] At first glance, "him" (αὐτοῦ) seems to point back to the "king" (βασιλεῖ, v.13). The preposition διά ("by") with a genitive noun (αὐτοῦ, "him") indicates the agency by which "governors" are sent. When so used, it normally designates an intermediate agency, "through" (e.g., Rom. 2:16; 2 Tim. 2:2). It can be used to express primary agency and mean "by," though the occasions in the NT where it is thus used of human action are exceedingly rare (cf. 2 Cor. 1:11).[137] Upon closer examination the referent of "him" (αὐτοῦ) could be either the Roman Emperor (βασιλεῖ, "king") or God as the one who created (κτίσει, v.13) the office and the ultimately the one who appoints a person to it. Given the rarity with which the preposition with a genitive noun signals a human, it seems more likely that Peter intends us either to read his intent as God sending the "governors" or that he uses it of a "king" as a secondary, human agent "through" (NASU margin) whom God appoints the "governors" to their post.[138] This, then, sounds very much like Romans 13:1ff. As Jesus told Pilate, "You would have no authority over Me, unless it had been given you from above" (John 19:11a). Indeed, "The king's heart is like channels of water in the hand of the LORD; He turns it wherever He wishes" (Prov. 21:1). Thus, our submission to God is primary and absolute while our submission to earthly authorities, who hold a measured authority over us by divine appointment, is secondary.

God's purpose (εἰς + infinitive) in establishing these offices and appointing those who fill them is twofold. God gives governments and those who serve their roles within them their authority, first, "for the punishment of

---

136 Bigg, 140; Hiebert, 166.
137 BDAG, 1823.4; cf. Louw-Nida, 90.4.
138 Cf. Grudem, 127; Hart, 60; Hort, 141; Stibbs, 110.

evildoers" (εἰς ἐκδίκησιν κακοποιῶν) "and" (δὲ) correspondingly for "the praise of those who do right" (ἔπαινον ... ἀγαθοποιῶν).

Two adjectives used as substantives contrast one another: "evildoers" (κακοποιῶν) and "those who do right" (ἀγαθοποιῶν). The former was just used, ironically enough, to describe what the people of this world call believers (v. 12). Peter alone uses the word in the NT, and its other appearance will come in 4:15. It is a compound made up of κακόν ("evil") and ποιέω ("to make"). See our comments on verse 12 for more on the word's meaning. Contrasting this are "those who do right" (ἀγαθοποιῶν). The word appears only here in the NT.[139] It is a compound derived from ἀγαθός ("good") and ποιέω ("to do"). Peter will further develop what doing right in a society contrary to the Christian faith requires (1 Peter 3:10–17).[140] Peter has in mind more than living within the established laws of the land; he pictures good works done for the benefit of the larger society. Christians are to live so as to make their environment better. "Seek the welfare of the city where I have sent you into exile, and pray to the LORD on its behalf; for in its welfare you will have welfare" (Jer. 29:7).

> **Ministry Maxim**
>
> Earthly governments are to be moral agents of punishment and reward.

Thus, the roots κακόν ("evil") and ἀγαθός ("good") stand in contrast against one another while the verbal root (ποιέω, "to do") is held in common. The "excellent" and "good" (καλός) conduct to which Peter calls his readers (v. 12) and the "right" (ἀγαθός) he depicts here all stand over against the "evil" (κακόν) of some citizens.

Peter is strictly binary in his description of those who live within any given locale. They are either "evildoers" or "those who do right." He allows no middle ground. Earthly political authorities must discern "evil" and "good" and deal with them accordingly. "A [wise] king who

---

139 But ἀγαθοποι—prefixed words appear from Peter's pen six out of their eleven appearances in the NT: 1 Peter 2:14, 15, 20; 3:6, 17; 4:19 (Forbes, 81).

140 Michaels, 126.

sits on the throne of justice Disperses all evil with his eyes" (Prov. 20:8). But woe comes upon a nation led by "those who call evil good, and good evil; Who substitute darkness for light and light for darkness; Who substitute bitter for sweet and sweet for bitter" (Isa. 5:20). Peter realized the injustice of both the Jewish and Roman leadership concerning Jesus (Acts 2:22–23; 5:30;1 Peter 2:22–24) and with respect to James (Acts 12:2).

A just ruler deals out "punishment" (ἐκδίκησιν) to the one and "praise" (ἔπαινον) to the other. The former describes justice dispensed in retribution and vengeance for wrongdoing. It belongs to God alone (Luke 18:7–8; 21:22; Rom. 12:19; 2 Thess. 1:8; Heb. 10:30), but for temporal purposes, He delegates measured use of it to leadership in both the church (2 Cor. 7:11) and government (1 Peter 2:14). There is in the term no hint of that which is remedial or transformative. Peter is not looking for rehabilitation of offenders but for their punishment for wrongs done.[141] Of course, his instructions do not prohibit that desirable end. Restoration is always the goal of church discipline (Matt. 18:15–17; Gal. 6:1–5; James 5:19–20) and ultimately of all correction (Prov. 13:1; 15:5, etc.). Peter simply underscores that there is a legitimate place for enacting a price for a wrong done. The offender is not ultimate; the public good is. The latter term describes "praise" (ἔπαινον) due to and offered up to God (Rom. 2:29; Eph. 1:6, 12, 14; Phil. 1:11) as well as "praise" given by God (1 Cor. 4:5; 1 Peter 1:7), the church (2 Cor. 8:18), or the government (Rom. 13:3; 1 Peter 2:14) for worthy actions. This will only be worked out perfectly on the last day, but God intends for there to be justice and honor within the fabric of society during this age. Leaders in both government and the church fail in this primary assignment when they do not deal with evil and fail to recognize and honor good within their midst. But even faulty, failing human government provides more stability than anarchy. God consistently condemns unjust laws, but even imperfect and unjust law is better than lawlessness.

---

141 Gruden, 128.

Verse 15 – "For such is the will of God that by doing right you may silence the ignorance of foolish men."

There is a reason (ὅτι, "For") behind Peter's instruction for believers to render submission (v.13a) to earthly governmental leaders (vv.13b-14). That reason is "that…you may silence the ignorance of foolish men" (φιμοῦν τὴν τῶν ἀφρόνων ἀνθρώπων ἀγνωσίαν). The verb (φιμοῦν, "you may silence") is used in the NT literally of muzzling an ox (1 Tim. 5:18; cf. 1 Cor. 9:9), but elsewhere it is used metaphorically of putting to silence. Jesus silenced the storm-tossed sea (Mark 4:39), demons (Mark 1:25; Luke 4:35), and the Sadducees (Matt. 22:34, cf. v.12). As Jesus' actions silenced the Sadducees, so Peter calls for submission to governing authorities that will quiet "the ignorance of foolish men." Peter's readers are slandered by their neighbors (1 Peter 2:12). Peter now enlarges on what he said there about how they can be silenced.

The noun ἀγνωσία ("ignorance") is a compound made up of γνῶσις ("knowledge") and the alpha-privative for negation. It speaks of a lack of knowledge, not primarily in an intellectual sense, but spiritually. In the only other NT usage, Paul says, "some have no knowledge [ἀγνωσίαν] of God" (1 Cor. 15:34). The articular noun (τὴν…ἀγνωσίαν, "the ignorance") identifies their ignorance as specific to this particular realm. They abide in that state because they are spiritually "foolish men" (τῶν ἀφρόνων ἀνθρώπων). The entire phrase is set in the attributive position between ἀγνωσίαν ("ignorance") and its definite article (τὴν), emphasizing the type of ignorance that is in view. The term was used in Hellenistic gnostic philosophy of "lack of the knowledge essential to the salvation of the soul" and "If someone was living without knowledge, it was either because the person had not been granted the revelation or had refused it. Those who did receive it were freed from their ignorance of their origin."[142] While the Biblical word-view differs significantly from that of the Greek Gnostics, this reveals to us the essentially religious essence of the knowledge under

---

142 NIDNTTE, 1:135.

review. Peter earlier reminded his readers to leave behind the former "ignorance" (ἀγνοίᾳ) in which they lived before Christ (1 Peter 1:14).

The noun "foolish" (ἀφρόνων) is a compound comprised of φρήν and the negating alpha-privative. The noun designated the diaphragm or midriff muscle, which divided the heart and lungs from the lower abdominal organs. This was thought to be the seat of man's thoughts.[143] It may point then to a "culpable ignorance rather than mere lack of knowledge."[144] Such ignorance is "because of the hardness of their heart" (Eph. 4:18).[145] Because they refuse to honor God, they have become "futile in their speculations, and their foolish heart was darkened" (Rom. 1:21). The noun ἄνθρωπος ("men") is not gender specific to males but points to humans generally ("people," NET, NIV). Men and women, boys and girls who have no knowledge of God often rail against those who know Him. They practice "reviling where they have no knowledge" (2 Peter 2:12). They "revile the things which they do not understand" (Jude 10). Jesus spoke in parables, "because while seeing they do not see, and while hearing they do not hear, nor do they understand" (Matt. 13:13). "A natural man does not accept the things of the Spirit of God, for they are foolishness to him; and he cannot understand them, because they are spiritually appraised" (1 Cor. 2:14). Alliteration (note the repletion of the opening α: τὴν τῶν ἀφρόνων ἀνθρώπων ἀγνωσίαν) adds rhetorical punch to Peter's point (cf. 1:4, 19; 2:21; 3:17, 20).[146]

Peter pictures this happening "by doing right" (ἀγαθοποιοῦντας). The verb appears only nine times in the NT, four of which are by Peter's hand (1 Peter 2:15, 20; 3:17, 20). It is the verbal cognate of the adjective ἀγαθοποιός in verse 14 ("those who do right"), signaling he is continuing to develop the thought he began there. It is thus a compound comprised of ἀγαθός ("good") and ποιέω ("to do"). When the Jewish leaders opposed Him, Jesus asked if it was lawful "to do good [ἀγαθοποιῆσαι] or to do

---

143 Liddell-Scott, 95941.

144 Rienecker, 753.

145 Storms, 327.

146 Forbes, 81; Raymer, 2:847; Robertson, *Word Pictures*, 6:101.

harm" (Luke 6:9). He used it to speak of not simply reciprocating good deeds done to you (Luke 6:33), but of doing good to those counted as your enemies (v.35). John characteristically simplifies it all by saying, "The one who does good [ὁ ἀγαθοποιῶν] is of God; the one who does evil has not seen God" (3 John 11). In our present passage, the present tense signals that such acts are to be done regularly, habitually, as a pattern of the believer's life. The participle signals the manner or means "by" which the opposing unbelievers are silenced.

> **Ministry Maxim**
>
> A well-lived life is the best answer to religious bigotry.

Peter says, "such is the will of God" (οὕτως ἐστὶν τὸ θέλημα τοῦ θεοῦ). Peter fronts this clause, the adverb οὕτως ("such") pointing forward to what would follow it. It generally means "in this way," "in this manner," or "thus." The present tense of the verb (ἐστὶν, "is") signals God's abiding desire regarding His followers' relationship to earthly rulers. Peter speaks here for the first time of "the will of God" (τὸ θέλημα τοῦ θεοῦ), though he will begin to do so more and more (1 Peter 3:17; 4:2, 19; cf. 2 Peter 1:21). Submission to God is paramount for the believer. A believer's general posture toward earthly rulers is that of submission and the doing of good for the welfare of the larger nation because it serves as an expression of one's submission to "the will of God." The will of God is to be chosen over freedom from suffering (1 Peter 3:17; 4:19) and the following of one's desires (1 Peter 4:2). Thus "the will of God" rules over all things, both those external to and those internal to the believer's life. Peter's instructions here are a more specific application of his instructions in verse 12. It is "the will of God" that, by doing good for the larger society, the ignorant slander of the unbelieving is silenced.

Verse 16 – "*Act* as free men, and do not use your freedom as a covering for evil, but *use it* as bondslaves of God."

There is no main verb expressed for this clause,[147] and there is debate about where to connect the words found here. Some link them to the

---

147 Most English translations insert a verb in the imperative (though cf. KJV, NKJV, YLT); "Act," (NASU), "Live" (ESV, NET, NIV, NRSV).

participle ἀγαθοποιοῦντας ("doing right") in verse 15. Michaels connects them to the four imperatives that follow in verse 17.[148] Others see this verse as something of an ellipsis or independent statement.[149] But overall, it seems best to see it reaching all the way back to the command to "be subject" (v.13) to the governing leaders in office. Submission silences "the ignorance of foolish men" (v.15) when believers live "as free men" (ὡς ἐλεύθεροι). In ancient secular Greek, "The 'free' person is the full citizen who belongs to the πόλις ... the city state, in contrast to the slave, who did not enjoy the rights of citizenship. Freedom consists in the right to participate fully in public debates over civic matters. It is the right to speak freely and to decide about one's own affairs within the city-state."[150] Peter encourages the believers not to withdraw in self-protection but to enter fully into life within the Empire and the specific locations where they reside, contributing fully to the well-being of their society and cities. But freedom is never absolute. It is always bounded by law. This is why Peter can combine the command to "be subject" with the insistence they do so "as free men." This may sound contradictory to modern ears unfamiliar with the Bible's teachings. Subject yourselves "as free men." Not as enslaved people, who have no rights and power of self-determination. Not as those who have no other choice. Not as those who have no other options. But as those truly set free by Christ, with the liberty that comes from being redeemed, made new, and now indwelt and empowered by His omnipotent Spirit. Such freedom is something the natural-born but spiritually dead citizens of the Roman Empire knew nothing about.

On the earthly plane, to be "free men" (ἐλεύθερος) is the opposite of being a δοῦλος ("servant").[151] But the NT intertwines liberty and obligation, freedom and submission, to underscore the unique freedom into which the believer in Jesus Christ has come. Paul can say, "He who was

---

148 Michaels, 121, 128.

149 Cf. Dubis, 68; Forbes, 81.

150 NIDNTTE, 2:173.

151 Liddell-Scott, 13915.

called in the Lord while a slave [δοῦλος], is the Lord's freedman; likewise he who was called while free [ἐλεύθερος], is Christ's slave [δοῦλος]" (1 Cor. 7:22). He can assert, "For though I am free [Ἐλεύθερος] from all men, I have made myself a slave [ἐδούλωσα] to all, so that I may win more" (1 Cor. 9:19). God through Christ sets free the slave to sin so that he needs to serve it no more. But divine emancipation creates a new servitude—slavery to God. But now, the shackles are formed of grace, and the bonds are held in place by love. The believer in Jesus Christ becomes a glad captive of God, His purposes, and His commands. He is free from all other obligations and bondage, freed to be and do what he ought. Nevertheless, he is bound by the strictures of love to fulfill his Liberator's will freely and gladly. Thus, Peter seeks to underscore for his readers their unique position within their earthly locations—they are free in a way that their unbelieving neighbors are not. Socially and politically, they are as free and may participate just as fully as their neighbors; spiritually they are freer and uniquely positioned to do even more than their neighbors are positioned to do for the true good of their society. He wants them to see their unique and strategic position within their communities rather than listen to the party line that seeks to marginalize and minimize their role within their larger culture.

Freedom must come under the control of God's purposes, so Peter adds (καὶ, "and") a prohibition: "do not use your freedom as a covering for evil" (μὴ ὡς ἐπικάλυμμα ἔχοντες τῆς κακίας τὴν ἐλευθερίαν). The prohibition (μὴ, "do not") "denies the thought of the thing, or the thing according to the judgment, opinion, will, purpose, preference, of" God.[152] Peter warns his readers not even to begin considering the possibility of using their freedom for evil purposes.

The noun τὴν ἐλευθερίαν ("freedom") is the cognate of the adjective just used above. The definite article makes specific which freedom is under discussion. Most English translations view it as possessive ("*your* freedom," emphasis added; though cf. NKJV, YLT). The use of the relative adverb ὡς ("as") is the second of its three appearances in this verse. It does not

---

152 Thayer, 408.

introduce a metaphor but continues to express the way Peter's readers are to live (ἔχοντες, "use"). The verb most simply means "to have" or "to hold." The present tense underscores the regular and repeated way believers are to have or to hold their unique freedom as believers in Christ within an earthly political realm. The participle is used to express manner—the way they "hold" their freedom. The way in which they are not to hold out their freedom is as "a covering for evil" (ἐπικάλυμμα...τῆς κακίας). The noun (ἐπικάλυμμα, "a covering") appears only here in the NT. It designates "a stratagem for concealing" something.[153] It essentially describes a pretext or excuse for doing something.[154] Don't justify doing "evil" (τῆς κακίας) by claiming freedom in Christ. The noun means wickedness, depravity, and evil. As such, it stands over against both ἀγαθός ("good," vv.14, 15, 18, 20; 3:6, 10, 11, 13, 16 [2x], 17, 21; 4:19) and καλός ("excellent," "good," 2:12 [2x]; 4:10; cf. 2 Pet. 1:19). It was just used in a compound in verses 12 and 14 (κακοποιῶν, "evildoers").

> **Ministry Maxim**
>
> Freedom from all subjection is the worst kind of bondage.

Paul made a similar argument: "For you were called to freedom, brethren; only do not turn your freedom into an opportunity for the flesh, but through love serve one another" (Gal. 5:13). Indeed, Paul's example may be of help here. He reasons at length in 1 Corinthians 8 and 9 about the role of liberty in Christ, about one's rights and using them to the glory of God. Concerning what rights he might assert as an apostle, Paul said, "we did not use this right, but we endure all things so that we will cause no hindrance to the gospel of Christ" (1 Cor. 9:12), adding, "For though I am free from all men, I have made myself a slave to all, so that I may win more" (v.19). Indeed, "to those who are without law, as without law, though not being without the law of God but under the law of Christ, so that I might win those who are without law" (v.21). Peter similarly exhorts

---

153 BDAG, 2964.

154 Friberg, 164; Thayer, 239.

his readers that rather than using freedom to one's ends, they should make their freedom serve the Master who granted it to them.

In stark contrast (ἀλλ', "but") to the notion of selfish or sinful use of ones freedom, we are to live "as bondslaves of God" (ὡς θεοῦ δοῦλοι). The third use of ὡς ("as") in this verse sets forward the standard by which one's freedom is to be used. The noun δοῦλοι ("bondslaves") is a common one in the NT, being used over 120 times. Some English translations opt for the word "servant" to translate this important word, but this can be misleading (e.g., ESV, NRSV). Greek has other ways to describe a "servant." It is better rendered "bondslave" (ASV; KJV, NKJV, NASU). The word pertains "to being under someone's total control" and thus to one who is "slavish" or "servile."[155] A δοῦλος must yield "unquestioning obedience" to his master and is thus "subservient, enslaved" and "subject" to him in every way.[156] He "serves in obedience to another's will."[157] This enslaved person has come into "a state of being completely controlled by someone" else.[158] A slave has yielded to another. He has lost any personal will as a determining factor of his life and daily choices. These decisions have been surrendered and given over to a master. And in this, they are to "Act as free men." Some live as "slaves of corruption" (2 Peter 2:19), but Peter tells his readers they are to live as "bondslaves of God" (θεοῦ δοῦλοι)—freed by Him to live as they ought and in ways that give life. Paul fundamentally sees himself as a bondslave of Christ (e.g., Rom. 1:1; Gal. 1:10; Phil. 1:1; though cf. δοῦλος θεοῦ, "servant of God" in Titus 1:1) and so identifies other believers (Eph. 6:6; Col. 4:12; 2 Tim. 2:24). James identifies himself as a slave of both God and Jesus Christ (James 1:1). Moses was "the servant of God" (1 Chron. 6:49; 2 Chron. 24:9; Dan. 9:11). Jesus, of course, demonstrated the power of making oneself a servant (Phil. 2:7) for the glory of God (v.11) and the good of others. He was the unique and only "servant of the Lord" (Isa. 52:13–53:12) who subjected Himself to the

---

155 BDAG, 2089.

156 Friberg, 120.

157 Ibid.

158 Louw-Nida, 37.3.

Father in suffering and death (53:10) that He might redeem to Himself a people for His own possession (vv.4–6, 11–12).

P.T. Forsyth put it best, "The first duty of every soul is to find not its freedom but its master."[159] Each soul, having done so, is set free with liberty that can be had in no other way.

> **Digging Deeper:**
> 1. What are the indicators that one can no longer obey earthly political rulers and must "obey God rather than men" (v.13; cf. Acts 5:29)?
> 2. Grade the government under which you currently live regarding its fulfillment of the role of a moral agent of reward and punishment (v.14).
> 3. Discuss this statement with someone: Only a believer in Jesus Christ is free enough to live in submission (vv.15–16).

Verse 17 – "Honor all people, love the brotherhood, fear God, honor the king."

Peter rounds out his instructions concerning relating to the political world in which his readers live. To close his counsel, he issues four commands. The first and fourth deal with those most relationally and spiritually distant to his readers ("all people" and "the king"), and the second and third relate to those closest spiritually and relationally (God and His people). In the chiastic form, the middle two are thus granted prominence. In each case, the object comes first, followed by the imperative verb. The first and fourth demand the same thing from God's people (τιμάω, "honor"), though in the first case, the aorist imperative form is used, and in the fourth, the present imperative.

---

159 Forsyth, 43.

First, Peter commands, "Honor all people" (πάντας τιμήσατε). Peter used the adjective πάντας to open this section (πάσῃ ἀνθρωπίνῃ κτίσει, "every human institution," v.13), and now he uses it as the direct object with which he moves to close the section. He has gone from "every human institution" (Emperor and "governors," vv.13–14) to "all people" (citizens of the Empire). So πάντας ("all people") is sweeping and inclusive, gathering up both genders, people across every social station of life, the entire spectrum of religious belief, and any other categories into which people divide themselves. These we are to "Honor" (τιμήσατε). The verb means first to estimate or fix a value on something (e.g., Matt. 27:9) and then, by extension, to honor or revere someone.[160] It is used repeatedly in the command to honor one's father and mother (Matt. 15:4, 6; 19:19; Mark 7:10; 10:19; Luke 18:20; Eph. 6:2) and then of honor given to God (Matt. 15:8; Mark 7:6; John 5:23; 8:49). It can have the extended sense in which such honor is made manifest through material or financial provision (e.g., Acts 28:10; 1 Tim. 5:3). The financial element is not present here. The valuation of each human being as a bearer of the image of God and giving expression to that value in word and deed is at the heart of Peter's command. The "king" (Emperor) gets no more than "all people," and "all people" are due what is owed to the "king." Social and political stations are not determiners of the "honor" that is due. The determining factor is being a bearer of the image of God.

> **Ministry Maxim**
>
> A Christian looks for how the fear of God defines one's relationships.

The aorist imperative form has generated debate, mainly since the remaining three imperatives are in the present tense. It has been called an ingressive aorist (denoting entry into a state or condition), a gnomic aorist (calling for timeless, general action), a way of indicating "to begin and continue doing" the action prescribed, and an act that picks up its tense from the controlling aorist imperative (Ὑποτάγητε, "Submit") from verse

---

160 BDAG, 7366.

13. But all these face problems.¹⁶¹ Abernathy cites seven different explanations offered by various commentators.¹⁶² Grudem calls it an "unmarked tense," used because Peter wishes "to command the action without specifying anything more about it."¹⁶³ Michaels says it is used to make clear that all four verbs are imperatives. Since the present imperative forms could also be read as indicatives, the first is put in the aorist form to indicate that those that follow should also be read as imperatives.¹⁶⁴ The first is not to be read as a sweeping command fleshed out and made specific by the following three.¹⁶⁵ The chiastic arrangement holds sway. But perhaps, without falling prey to the notion of such a one-and-three arrangement, we could simply say that the opening aorist arrests attention and demands decisive action while the following three imperatives then call to an ongoing state of one's various relationships.

Second, Peter commands, "love the brotherhood" (τὴν ἀδελφότητα ἀγαπᾶτε). The noun (τὴν ἀδελφότητα, "the brotherhood") is used only here and in 5:9 in the NT. As a collective noun, it designates in a concrete sense "a group of people united for a common purpose."¹⁶⁶ A "band of brothers" might capture the sense.¹⁶⁷ The definite article makes specific "the brotherhood" to which Peter refers—believers everywhere, different in location and circumstances, but one through faith in Jesus Christ. Peter never uses the word "church" in his letters, but this term surely points to the same reality. These we are to "love" (ἀγαπᾶτε). The present imperative calls for the ongoing expression of love as a pattern and habit of life. The

---

161 Forbes, 82.

162 Abernathy, 95.

163 Grudem, 130.

164 Michaels, 130.

165 As per the NIV (1984): "Show proper respect to everyone: Love the brotherhood of believers, fear God, honor the king" (cf. also NEB). But how could "God" be subsumed under "everyone"? The NIV has been updated to read: "Show proper respect to everyone, love the family of believers, fear God, honor the emperor."

166 Friberg, 34.

167 Rienecker, 753.

writers of the NT have infused the word group connected with the verb "love" with significant Christian meaning. Their love for Christ, whom they have not seen (1 Peter 1:8), must be extended to one another (1:22).

Third, Peter commands, "fear God" (τὸν θεὸν φοβεῖσθε). Above all others is "God (τὸν θεὸν). Note the definite article, "the [one and only] God." The designation appears thirty-nine times in 1 Peter, with twenty-two of those using the definite article (three of them depending upon textual questions).[168] The noun typically is read as definite even where the definite article is absent, but Peter leaves no doubt. With God, "fear" (φοβεῖσθε) is the only proper posture of the heart. The imperative makes the demand; the present tense underscores the abiding disposition required. Peter has already commanded them to "conduct yourselves in fear" throughout this life (1 Peter 1:17).

The fear of the Lord is the foundation of the OT books of wisdom. It serves as an inclusion wrapping itself around the first nine chapters of Proverbs (1:7; 9:10), as well as the entire collection (Prov. 1:7; 31:30). It is set over against the fear of man (Prov. 29:25). It promises countless benefits for its possessor. It is not only the beginning of knowledge (Prov. 1:7, 29; 2:5) and wisdom (9:10; 15:33), but it instills confidence (14:26) and makes rich (22:4). The fear of the Lord prolongs life (Prov. 10:27), is a fountain of life (14:27), leads to life (19:23), and is rewarded with life (22:4). The fear of the Lord is to join God in His hatred of evil (Prov. 8:13; 16:6, 23:17). One may lose all else, but nothing must stop one from gaining the fear of the Lord (Prov. 15:16).

Isaiah joins the chorus: "He will be the sure foundation for your times, a rich store of salvation and wisdom and knowledge; *The fear of the Lord is the key to this treasure*" (Isa. 33:6, NIV, emphasis added). Oswald Chambers rightly observes: "The remarkable thing about fearing God is that when you fear God, you fear nothing else, whereas if you do not fear God, you fear everything else."[169] Peter would concur: the only other

---

168 θεός with the definite article: 1 Peter 1:3; 2:5 [?], 12, 15, 17; 3:4, 17, 18, 20, 22 [?]; 4:11 [2x], 14, 16, 17 [2x], 19; 5:2, 5 [?], 6, 10, 12.

169 Draper, 216.

usages of the verb in his letters describe the unnecessary and inappropriate fear for the one who fears God (1 Peter 3:6, 14).

After encountering Cornelius the centurion, Peter realized that "in every nation the man who fears Him and does what is right is welcome" to God if they come through faith in Christ (Acts 10:35).

Finally, Peter commands, "honor the king" (τὸν βασιλέα τιμᾶτε). Peter concludes where he began (v.13) with instructions on how to relate to "the king" (τὸν βασιλέα). We saw in verse 13 that while the term could be used of lesser, provincial rulers, in this context, it can only point to the Emperor himself, in the case of the original readers, Nero. The imperative (τιμᾶτε, "honor") is the same as just used with "all people." But here, the present imperative is employed, whereas in the former, the aorist imperative was used. See above for reasons for the aorist imperative there. Here, the present imperative demands ongoing, regular, and abiding action.

So, we see that "the king" (Emperor) is due both subjection (v.13) and "honor" (v.17). Subjection is uniquely due to him because of God's appointment to his role; "honor" is his fundamentally as a bearer of God's image (one among "all people") and then also by virtue of his office. Subjection and honor to governing authorities are due not because of fear of the governing authorities but because of fear of the sovereign God who commands it of His children. Did Peter, in this way, both "honor" Nero and yet also subtly bring him (as one who demanded to be addressed as divine) down to the level of all humans? Whereas "fear" is due to Him who is truly God alone, honor is fitting for "all people," including "the king."

It has been suggested that Peter had Proverbs 24:21 in mind: "My son, fear the LORD and the king; Do not associate with those who are given to change."[170] If so, Peter's change from "fear the LORD and the king" to "fear God, honor the king" is another form of quietly and sagaciously establishing boundaries.[171]

---

170 Bigg, 142; Michaels, 131.
171 Forbes, 83.

> **Digging Deeper:**
> 1. Can you think of one person "beneath" you and one "above" you in terms of power/position to whom you need actively to demonstrate honor? How can you express that to the glory of God?
> 2. In what way are you actively honoring the political leader(s) over you?
> 3 Describe ways that others in your life see the fear of the Lord controlling your relationships.

Verse 18 – "Servants, be submissive to your masters with all respect, not only to those who are good and gentle, but also to those who are unreasonable."

Peter now turns from general instructions for how believers are to live with their governing authorities (vv. 13–17) to how "Servants" (Οἱ οἰκέται) are to relate to their "masters" (τοῖς δεσπόταις).[172] "Servants" (Οἱ οἰκέται) were domestic servants, household slaves. It is used only three other times in the NT (Luke 16:13; Acts 10:7; Rom. 14:4). The plural, as here, can refer to members of the household generally.[173] But here, it clearly refers to those individuals who hold the lowest place in the societal and familial worlds. It is largely equivalent to δοῦλος ("bondslave," cf. 2:16; 2 Peter 1:1, 2:19).[174]

These owe submission "to your masters" (τοῖς δεσπόταις). The word emphasizes the sovereign power and authority of the one designated. The English word *despot* is derived from it, but we tend to use the English word with sinister tones that were not necessarily a part of the Greek root.

---

172 Cf. other NT instruction to slaves in Ephesians 6:5–8; Colossians 3:22–25; 1 Timothy 6:1–2; Titus 2:9–10. A careful study of Philemon will reveal the pastoral wisdom of Paul as he dealt with a master-slave relationship that had been violated but which had potential for reconciliation because of the salvation of both parties (cf. my own *Colossians and Philemon for Pastors*).

173 NIDNTTE, 3:471.

174 TDNT, 2:261; Trench, 34.

It designates "one who has legal control and authority over persons."[175] In their culture, the husband/father of the household held this position over all who dwelt within the home, including especially "Servants." The noun was used of God the Father (Luke 2:29; Acts 4:24; Rev. 6:10) and the Lord Jesus (2 Peter 2:1; Jude 4). But also generally referred to the master of a house (1 Tim. 6:1, 2; 2 Tim. 2:21; Titus 2:9). Peter may have used these rarer terms (Οἱ οἰκέται, "Servants"; τοῖς δεσπόταις, "masters") rather than the more typical (δοῦλος, "servant"; κύριος, "lord")[176] because he reserves δοῦλος for servants of Christ (2:16) and κύριος as a designation of Christ Himself (e.g., 2:13).

The verb (ὑποτασσόμενοι, "be submissive") is the same one used in verse 13 to begin this section outlining the moral, relational duties of believers. See the comments there for more on the word. Here it is in a participial form but probably picks up the force of a command from the imperative form of verse 13.[177] The present tense prescribes this as the abiding and regular posture of "Servants" to their "masters." The passive voice pictures the "masters" as asserting their authority over the "Servants" and the latter complying with the former.

This is to be undertaken "with all respect" (ἐν παντὶ φόβῳ). The phrase "to your masters" (τοῖς δεσπόταις) describes the manner in which submission is to be rendered. We have the noun form (φόβῳ, "fear") of the verb (φοβεῖσθε, "fear") just used in verse 17 where it was used to indicate that "fear" is due to God alone (v.17). But now the obligation is laid upon servants as due to their masters. The word group could be used across a spectrum of meanings, from terror to respect. The present use tends toward the latter. But it is underscored by the use of the adjective παντὶ ("all"). This points not to "all" the fear that might rightly exist along the spectrum but to the entirety of the "fear" that is due by servants to their masters. Ultimately, fear belongs to God alone. Peter has used that as motivation for his readers' obedience ("for the Lord's sake" [διὰ τὸν κύριον] v.13; "fear

---

175 BDAG, 1794.1.

176 As Paul does: Ephesians 6:5–8; Colossians 3:22–25; 1 Timothy 6:1–2; Titus 2:9–10.

177 Wallace, 650–651.

God" [τὸν θεὸν φοβεῖσθε] v.17) and will do so yet again ("for the sake of conscience toward God" [διὰ συνείδησιν θεοῦ] v.19). In reverence of Him we live out our lives under the delegated authorities He places in our lives, rendering to them "all" the respect that the fear of the Lord requires of us. The preposition ἐν ("in") is best understood as indicating attendant circumstances—a servant's submission to his master is to be accompanied with every respect due to a master in their society.[178]

God favors an ordered society. He commands His people first to live within their societal structures in a God-honoring, Christ-exalting way rather than to deconstruct and reconfigure those structures. It is not that He is uninterested in societal and cultural transformation; He is fundamentally interested in the triumph of His Son, which takes place through the gospel's success. Live well within your current societal structures, imperfect and perhaps even evil though they are. This releases the gospel's power in the lives of the individuals within that culture. As the gospel triumphs in life after life its implications and power are

> **Ministry Maxim**
> Submission to God is the foundation of submission in human relationships.

released to have their informative and transformative effect on how those people live together (i.e., their culture and society). The history of God's people proves this reality again and again. Not every culture where Christians have faithfully lived has been transformed, for the gospel is often met with resistance, persecution, and unbelief or hijacked and used for selfish ends. Those cultures continue their downward death spiral until they finally implode. But where the gospel has been largely embraced, the very fabric of society has been remade for the better. The NT repeatedly holds forth the order by which God's transformative power through the gospel is released with life-giving effect—gospel first to individual hearts and as they are reborn, made new, and begin to live in the ongoing transformation of the sanctifying work of the Holy Spirit more and more people come under its transformative powers. Enough people do so, and they

---

178 Harris, 120–121.

begin to live differently. The effect of their salt and light in the larger culture cannot help but bring a response—for ill and death or for good and life.

Peter sets the parameters in which his counsel is to hold sway. He does so through a "not only... but also" formula (οὐ μόνον... ἀλλὰ καὶ). He uses the negation οὐ ("not") and the strong adversative conjunction ἀλλὰ ("but") to set up a dramatic contrast. He uses μόνον ("only") to mark off the circumstances under which such submission would be easier to render and καὶ ("also") to indicate those circumstances under which servants might be prone to excuse themselves from obedience to Peter's directives.

The easier circumstances are when submission and respect are due "to those who are good and gentle" (τοῖς ἀγαθοῖς καὶ ἐπιεικέσιν). Two adjectives are governed by one definite article and are used as substantives ("those who are"). The dative forms signal the object of the submission and respect demanded by Peter. Submission and respect are due first to masters "who are good" (τοῖς ἀγαθοῖς). Peter uses compounded forms of the word group to designate "those who do right" (adjective, v.14) and "doing right" (verb, v.15; cf. also v.20; 3:6, 17), and "doing what is right" (noun, 4:19). He uses the adjective eight times (1 Peter 2:18; 3:10, 11, 13, 16 [2x], 17, 21; cf. also 2 Pet. 2:21). Of the thirteen uses of the word group in 1 Peter every other use (except perhaps 3:10) depicts what is to be true of believers. Peter then may use the adjective to designate believing masters, but we cannot dogmatically so limit the reference.

To this Peter adds (καὶ, "and") a second kind of masters to which submission and respect are due, "those who are... gentle" (τοῖς... ἐπιεικέσιν). This signals not a second kind of master, but a second descriptor of one kind of master. To their goodness is added that they are "gentle." The adjective appears only five times in the NT (Phil. 4:5; 1 Tim. 3:3; Titus 3:2; James 3:17; 1 Peter 2:18). It comes from εἰκός (what is reasonable) and means "equitable, fair, mild, gentle."[179] It denotes one who does not insist "on every right of letter of law or custom" and thus describes that

---

179 Thayer, 238.

which is "yielding, gentle, kind, courteous, tolerant." [180] Spicq says it combines the ideas of "moderation and measure" as well as "goodness, courtesy, generosity" and suggests a translation here of "friendly equilibrium."[181] In Greek literature, generally, it was "an expression for balanced and decent behavior" and "came to be used of a considerate, thoughtful attitude in legal relationships that was prepared to mitigate the rigors of justice, with its laws and claims, in contrast to the attitude that demands that rights, including one's own, should be upheld at all costs."[182]

The more difficult circumstances are when submission and respect must be given "to those who are unreasonable" (τοῖς σκολιοῖς). The word was used literally to describe that which had deviated from what is straight (Luke 3:5). The English word *scoliosis* is derived from this word. As in the only two other occurrences in the NT, it is used here in a figurative sense, describing what is morally bent, twisted, or crooked (Acts 2:40; Phil. 2:15). Some masters are difficult and cruel, not conforming to the straight edge of God's moral standards. Yet even they are due the submission and respect of their believing servants.

> **Digging Deeper:**
> 1. Can you identify a time and a way in which you practiced submission to one with more contextual "clout" even though they were unreasonable"?
> 2. To what modern relationships might the NT instructions to "servants" be rightly applied?

---

180 BDAG, 2950.

181 Spicq, 2:38.

182 NIDNTTE, 2:241.

Verse 19 – "For this *finds* favor, if for the sake of conscience toward God a person bears up under sorrows when suffering unjustly."

Peter now moves to back up what he has instructed "Servants" to do with regard to their "masters" (v.18). The next three sentences (vv.19–21) all begin with γὰρ ("For"), signaling the Apostle's move to explain his demand for submission in their earthly political and domestic relationships (vv.13, 18). The three uses of γὰρ function as an unfolding rationale for such difficult service. Ultimately, Peter turns to Christ's example (v.21), detailing His innocence (v.22), His response to unjust suffering (v.23), and the saving effect which resulted (vv.24–25).

Peter's first line of evidence is "this finds favor" (τοῦτο ... χάρις). The sentence lacks a main verb. Peter no doubt expected his readers to provide the correct verb mentally. English translations generally go with "is" (ESV, KJV, NIV, NRSV, NKJV, YLT), while a couple offer "finds" (NASU, NET). With the possibility of submitting to "unjust" masters (v.18b) established, the demonstrative pronoun (τοῦτο, "this") looks forward, anticipating the expression "bears up under sorrows when suffering unjustly" (v.19b). Such submission "is" or "finds" χάρις. The noun is common in the NT and is generally rendered "grace" (e.g., 1 Peter 1:2, 10, 13; 3:7; 4:10; 5:5, 10, 12). It can be used actively to describe what one freely gives to another, but here it is used passively of what one experiences from another. In this case, it is used in the literary technique of metonymy, substituting an attribute for that which is actually meant—that which brings oneself God's favor, "wins a favorable response,"[183] or becomes a "matter of approval" from God.[184] Peter may be recalling Jesus' similar use of χάρις in Luke 6:32–34, where three times He asks, "what credit is that to you" (ποία ὑμῖν χάρις ἐστίν). Simply stated, Peter is telling us that suffering well under injustice is a means by which God's grace pours into one's life. There is a flavor of grace one tastes in no other way, a depth or dimension

---

183 BDAG, 7895.2.b.

184 Mounce, 1309.

of knowing God that can be had in no other way. This is not to say that suffering earns God's grace, for grace is a free gift (Rom. 5:15–16; 6:23). It is to say that God uses means to give us what He offers without price. In this case the means God uses is suffering well under the heavy hand of an unjust authority. By God's doing, the hand that intends harm unwittingly becomes the arm that extends grace. The servant of God may be assured that in such times "the Spirit of glory and of God rests on" him or her (1 Peter 4:14).

When we keep reading, we discover that verse 20 ends with a similar expression: "this finds favor with God" (τοῦτο χάρις παρὰ θεῷ). Together the two expressions serve as an inclusion, like bookends holding Peter's entire point (vv. 19–20) together as one. Simply stated, the picture is of reward for faithfully bearing up under unjust suffering. Schreiner sees this "grace" or reward as eschatological (1:3–5).[185] This surely is true, but I see here also the rewards of grace in one's present experience even while continuing under the unjust service—founded in a depth of relationship to and with God presently. What one day will be true in all its fullness is already experienced as an earnest through the Spirit (2 Cor. 1:22; 5:5; Eph. 1:13–14).

> **Ministry Maxim**
>
> Under God, the hand that harms opens the way for greater grace.

Peter adds a conditional clause (εἰ ... ὑποφέρει ... τις, "if ... a person bears up under"). The condition is determined as to fulfillment and assumed true; believers in Christ will be required to persevere in the face of threats to their faith. Peter states the matter broadly by using the indefinite pronoun τις ("a person"). This signals that what Peter sets forth now, while applying directly to the matter of slaves (v. 18), is applicable to all God's people when they suffer unjustly. Such "sorrow" befalls all of God's people during their earthly journey, but the singular form signals the individuality of dealing with one's own pain. Indeed, "The heart knows its own bitterness, And a stranger does not share its joy" (Prov. 14:10). The

---

185 Schreiner, 139.

verb is a compound comprised of ὑπό ("under") and φέρω ("to bear," "to carry"). It is used only three times in the NT. Paul used it of the persecutions under which he bore up (2 Tim. 3:11) and the weight of temptation under which every believer must "endure" (1 Cor. 10:13). It depicts one remaining under and carrying a heavy burden. In verse 20, he will call his readers to "endure," twice using a similarly constructed compound verb (ὑπομένω) meaning to remain under. Here the present tense sets forth the ongoing and unremitting nature of the burden being borne. Endurance takes us farther than we desire to go and makes us stay put under more than we ever pictured being able to carry.

To bear *up* implies downward pressure, and that comes from being *under* a weight of "sorrow" (λύπας). It is a word representative of a broad spectrum of experiences that can all be subsumed under pain and sorrow. The plural form here "points to the many and varied difficulties that Christian slaves may experience."[186] Such grief bears down upon one's soul with varying degrees of pressure, but whatever its intensity and precise nature, it is considered the opposite of joy, elation, or happiness.[187] Paul was spared "sorrow upon sorrow" (λύπην ἐπὶ λύπην) when Epaphroditus was brought back to health from the precipice of death (Phil. 2:27). It can come to a believer's life through discipline (Heb. 12:11), broken relationships (2 Cor. 2:1, 3), conviction of sin (2 Cor. 2:7; 7:10), the spiritual lostness of dear ones (Rom. 9:2), and the agony of childbirth (John 16:21).

Here the "sorrow" comes about "when suffering unjustly" (πάσχων ἀδίκως). This is Peter's first use of the verb (πάσχων, "suffering"), but he will now begin to employ it frequently, for a total of twelve times in this letter (1 Peter 2:19, 20, 21, 23; 3:14, 17, 18; 4:1 [2x], 15, 19; 5:10), nearly a third of its total NT usages. Primarily it is used of the sufferings of Christ or His people.[188] This signals the nature of Peter's letter and the direction it will take from this point forward. The participial form is used temporally ("*when* suffering," emphasis added). The present tense

---

186 Forbes, 88.

187 Spicq, 2:418.

188 TDNT, 5:913.

pictures the "suffering" in its present reality, it is happening, and it gives no signal of ending. In this case, it is suffering "unjustly" (ἀδίκως) which is in view. This is the only occurrence of the adverb in the NT. It is placed at the end of the sentence for added emphasis.[189] It pictures the suffering as not conforming to justice and might be rendered "undeservedly"[190] or "wrongfully" (KJV).

A person is pictured suffering in this way "for the sake of conscience before God" (διὰ συνείδησιν θεοῦ). Because the expression συνείδησιν θεοῦ (lit., "conscience of God") is unprecedented elsewhere in the NT, it has given rise to some debate about the Greek text. The NT (and Peter himself) uses the adjective ἀγαθός ("good") with συνείδησις ("conscience," cf. 1 Tim. 1:5, 19; 1 Peter 3:16, 21). This probably motivated an early addition of the word to the text to relieve the tension.[191] The text, as we have it, is surely original. The noun συνείδησις ("conscience") has a breadth of meaning, from an awareness of something to the inward faculty that makes us aware of right and wrong, and on to an "attentiveness to obligation" (what we might call "conscientiousness").[192] Here Peter seems to have in mind the first. He is thinking of the one suffering because[193] he is aware of God's presence and call to faithfulness. The genitive (θεοῦ, lit., "of God") is best understood as objective—it is God of which one is conscious ("mindful of God," ESV; "conscious of God," NIV; "aware of God," NRSV). But it must be said that elements of the verb's other two shades of meaning are not entirely lost here. It is not simply that one is aware of God but that one's conscience speaks to the moral obligation to endure suffering for the Lord's sake.

---

189 Hiebert, 179.

190 BDAG, 129.

191 Cf. Michael's overview of the issues, 133.

192 BDAG, 7053.

193 The preposition διὰ ("for the sake of") is used causally, i.e., "because of," "on account of."

Conscious of God, the faithful sufferer sings with Watts, "Drops of grief can ne'er repay, The debt of love I owe."[194] But in view of Jesus' sufferings for and call upon us, we remain under them for His sake.

Verse 20 – "For what credit is there if, when you sin and are harshly treated, you endure it with patience? But if when you do what is right and suffer *for it* you patiently endure it, this *finds* favor with God."

As in verse 19, Peter again begins with γὰρ ("For") as he continues to build his case for servants being submissive even to masters who are "unreasonable" (v.18). The conjunction calls for thought; it is designed to stimulate reflection and to engage one's powers of reasoning. Peter is inviting his readers to think the thoughts of God with him.

As in verse 19, Peter builds his case by means of a conditional clause, though here he uses two clauses set over against one another in a strong contrast (ἀλλ', "But"). The matter at play is "credit" (κλέος) and "favor" (χάρις) before God as it relates to one's suffering. The first noun (κλέος, "credit") is used only here in the NT. But it arose from the verb κλέω ("to celebrate"); and ultimately is related to the far more common verb καλέω ("to call," "to name"). The noun then fundamentally describes what is spoken about a person. It could be used in the wider Greek literature of a rumor, a report, or news related to someone.[195] And thus, when that report was positive, it could mean glory or fame and served as a "credit" to one's reputation. The interrogative pronoun ποῖον ("what") forms the opening conditional clause into a question. It invites the reader to explore all possibilities for any kind of "credit" that might come to the one about to be described.

Both conditional statements (εἰ … εἰ, "if … if") are considered determined as to fulfillment and assumed true for the sake of the points Peter seeks to make. The crux of both is that those under consideration in each case "endure it with patience" or "patiently endure it"

---

194 Watts, Isaac, "Alas! and Did My Savior Bleed," public domain.

195 Liddell-Scott, 24447.

(ὑπομενεῖτε ... ὑπομενεῖτε). Our present verb ὑπομένω ("endure") follows the similarly constructed ὑποφέρω ("bears up") just used in verse 19. While the compounds are similarly constructed, Michaels says ὑποφέρω (v.19) "refers to a passive kind of endurance (i.e., undergoing or submitting to affliction)," while ὑπμένω (v.20) "means to 'stand one's ground, hold out, endure'" in a more active and positive sense.[196] In verse 19, the verb was in the present tense, underscoring the continual nature of the endurance. Here, however, the future tense is used in both occurrences of the verb, setting this in the hypothetical and inviting the reader to consider what might be the outcome of such endurance.

Peter then puts before us two different ways of enduring hardship. He does so via four participles, used in pairs. All four are used temporally ("when you sin" and "when you do what is right."). The second and fourth, though different verbs, similarly speak of some form of pain (κολαφιζόμενοι, "are harshly treated"; πάσχοντες, "suffer"). The contrast is in the first participle of each pair. Peter thus sets out two different situations calling for enduring pain.

The first picture of endurance is "when you sin and are harshly treated" (ἁμαρτάνοντες καὶ κολαφιζόμενοι). The hypothetical case pictures a time "when you sin" (ἁμαρτάνοντες). The essence of the word is to miss the mark. The present tense may either picture the action as simply taking place or may emphasize that there is a pattern of misbehavior forming. He further (καί, "and") pictures this resulting in being "harshly treated" (κολαφιζόμενοι). The verb means to strike with the fist. It is thus used of the ill-treatment of Jesus, "Then they spat in His face and beat Him with their fists [ἐκολάφισαν]; and others slapped

> **Ministry Maxim**
>
> If suffering must come and endurance be required, let it be for the right reasons.

Him" (Matt. 26:67; cf. Mark 14:65). Paul had been "beaten" (κολαφιζόμεθα, 1 Cor. 4:11, NRSV) because of his faithfulness to Christ. In the Roman world of the time, masters often resorted to beating their servants. The

---

196 Michaels, 140.

verb could also be used of a different kind of suffering that originated from the evil one (2 Cor. 12:7). Peter already has widened the application to not only servants but any who might face some sort of painful consequences of committing sin. There is no great wonder in one being "harshly treated" when they have committed "sin." And there is no great merit in enduring such treatment.

The contrasting (ἀλλ᾽, "But") picture of endurance is "when you do what is right and suffer" (ἀγαθοποιοῦντες καὶ πάσχοντες). As in the first clause, the participle is used temporally ("*when* you do what is right," emphasis added). The verb is repeated here from verse 15; see our discussion there. There, "doing what is right" was to "silence the ignorance of foolish men." Here that hopeful effect has not been realized, and instead of leading to their "silence," it has led to a violent reaction against the well-doing. And thus, the doers of good "suffer" (πάσχοντες). Peter repeats the verb just introduced in verse 19; his theme begins to take form (1 Peter 2:19, 20, 21, 23; 3:14, 17, 18; 4:1 [2x], 15, 19; 5:10). The outcome is lamentable. Peter pictured something more strategic than simply doing what was right. But, as he will later argue, "it is better, if God should will it so, that you suffer for doing what is right rather than for doing what is wrong" (1 Peter 3:17).

The first conditional statement asks a question and invites reflection leading to an answer (ποῖον ... κλέος, "what credit is there?"). The second conditional statement makes a statement and informs the mind (τοῦτο χάρις παρὰ θεῷ, "this finds favor with God"). This phrase is pushed to the end both for emphasis and to form an inclusion with τοῦτο ... χάρις ("this finds favor") in verse 19. Both the demonstrative pronoun (τοῦτο, "this") and the noun (χάρις, "favor") are used as in verse 19; see our comments there. What is added here is what was assumed in verse 19, that the "favor" is found παρὰ θεῷ ("with God"). Peter uses the preposition (παρὰ, "with") five times in his two letters, three with ("God," 1 Peter 2:4, 20; 2 Peter 1:17) and two with κύριος ("Lord," 2 Peter 2:11; 3:8). He uses it both positively (1 Peter 2:4; 2 Peter 1:17) and negatively (2 Peter 2:11). Here it carries the sense of "in the sight of" or "before/in the presence of."[197]

---

197 Harris, 172; cf. TDNT, 5:733.

> **Digging Deeper:**
> 1. Describe the last time you acted specifically because you were aware of God's presence and rule over your life. (v.19)
> 2. How does suffering rightly under unjust treatment grow your soul?
> 3. Can you describe a time you sensed God's pleasure over a step of difficult obedience you took? (v.20)

Verse 21 – "For you have been called for this purpose, since Christ also suffered for you, leaving you an example for you to follow in His steps,"

For a third consecutive sentence (vv.19, 20, 21), Peter begins with γὰρ ("For"). In verse 19, he used it to introduce an explanation of why Christian servants should submit to their masters, regardless of their disposition (v.18). He used it in verse 20 to further elaborate upon the explanation in verse 19, enlarging upon why one ought to submit to contrary masters. Now he uses it again to explain yet further why bearing up under unjust treatment is a part of the believer's call (vv.21–24).

The sentence Peter begins here continues through verse 24. Peter's initial explanation centers on "Christ" (Χριστὸς; cf. αὐτοῦ, "His" to end verse 21). The following three verses all open with the relative pronoun ὅς ("who," v.22; "He," vv.23, 24), continuing the focus upon Jesus. Peter provides a Christocentric answer to the question of unjust suffering.

Peter is blunt, "you have been called for this purpose" (εἰς τοῦτο ... ἐκλήθητε). The demonstrative pronoun τοῦτο ("this") points backward to the theme of patient endurance of unjust suffering, which Peter has been developing (vv.19–20). Such is the very purpose of God for His people (εἰς τοῦτο, "for this purpose"). The preposition (εἰς) with the accusative points to a goal or purpose. The verb (ἐκλήθητε, "you have been called") indicates that this purpose is divinely established. The aorist points to the moment when God extended His gospel call into their lives through the preaching of the gospel. The passive voice indicates that they did not take up the call on their own but that God acted to place this call upon their lives. Peter has already established that God had called them to Himself through the gospel (1:15), and this call included the call to live in holiness of life. God called them out of their spiritual darkness and into His "marvelous light" (2:9). But the darkness hates the light (John 3:19–20) and wars against it, so they should not be surprised that the call out of darkness and into light will involve suffering and require patience. We are called to "inherit a blessing" (1 Peter 3:9), but that will involve non-retaliation ("not returning evil for evil or insult for insult, but giving a blessing instead") and patient endurance under painful trials that may be unjustly heaped upon us. We are called "to His eternal glory in Christ," but this will only come "After you have suffered for a little while" (5:10).

This call comes "since Christ also suffered for you" (ὅτι καὶ Χριστὸς ἔπαθεν ὑπὲρ ὑμῶν). The conjunction ὅτι ("since") is used to designate causality—it is because Christ suffered for you that you are to bear up patiently under unjust suffering. The conjunction καὶ is used adverbially ("also") to indicate that Peter's readers (and any other such Christian sufferers) are not alone in their suffering; Christ suffered as well. "For we do not have a high priest who cannot sympathize with our weaknesses, but One who has been tempted in all things as we are, yet without sin" (Heb. 4:15). Perhaps Peter uses Χριστὸς ("Christ") rather than Ἰησοῦς (Jesus) to set His suffering in the context of His role as Messiah. Peter will, in the next verse, apply one of the Suffering Servant passages to Jesus (Isa. 53:9). The verb (ἔπαθεν, "suffered") is the one just introduced in verse 19 and which will become the thematic thread of the remainder of the letter. There it was Peter's readers who "suffer unjustly," but here it is Christ who suffered. Why did Peter here speak of Jesus' suffering but not His death?[198] The aorist tense views

> **Ministry Maxim**
>
> When life is unfair Jesus has left us an example to copy and footprints to follow.

---

198 Apparently, this so bothered some scribes that it some sought to "correct" the text and so we find a smattering of manuscripts and a few versions that use ἀπέθανεν ("died") instead of ἔπαθεν ("suffered") (cf. Forbes, 90; Jobes, 201; Michaels, 134).

the whole of Jesus' passion as a singular event. Thus, Peter surely was not intending to exclude Jesus' death, but the point at present is about Jesus knowing and sharing the reality of suffering that his readers were currently facing. How are we to understand Peter's intent in using ὑπὲρ ("for")? Harris says, "The preposition ἀντὶ regularly expresses a substitutionary exchange" and "ὑπὲρ usually indicates representation ('on behalf of') or advantage ('for the benefit of')." Yet he identifies several NT passages, this one included, where ὑπὲρ "may bear the dual sense of representation/advantage and substitution" (Rom. 5:6, 8; 14:15; 2 Cor. 5:14–15a; Gal. 3:13; 1 Thess. 5:10; 1 Peter 2:21; 3:18; 1 John 3:16).[199] And all of this Peter makes deeply personal to those reading his letter (ὑμῶν, "you").[200]

In suffering, Jesus was "leaving you an example" (ὑμῖν ὑπολιμπάνων ὑπογραμμὸν).[201] Jesus' death was atoning in nature, as Peter has already made clear (1:18–19) and will again (2:24; 3:18). But here Peter views Christ's sufferings as paradigmatic and precedent-setting for His followers. The noun (ὑπογραμμὸν, "example") is found only here in the NT. It is a compound from ὑπό ("under") and γράφω ("to write"). It was used of "the model of handwriting to be copied by the school boy."[202] One can easily picture the student tracing out each letter below the example provided. The word then came to be used more generally of any "model of behavior as an example to be imitated."[203] Christ laid down the paradigm for patient endurance in unjust suffering. The verb (ὑπολιμπάνων, "leaving") also is found only here in the NT. It is a compound beginning with ὑπό ("under"), but this time added to the root λιμπάνω, a less common form of the verb λείπω ("to leave behind").[204] The resulting compound means

---

199 Harris, 215–216.

200 Some manuscripts have ἡμῶν ("us," cf. KJV, NKJV) instead of ὑμῶν ("you"), but the latter clearly seems to be the superior reading (cf. Forbes, 90; Michaels, 134).

201 Again, some manuscripts have ἡμῖν ("us," cf. KJV, NKJV) rather than ὑμῖν ("you"), but the latter clearly seems to be the superior reading (cf. Forbes, 90; Michaels, 134).

202 Rienecker, 755; cf. TDNT, 1:773.

203 Louw-Nida, 58.59.

204 Thayer, 644.

"to cause to remain subsequent to some temporal reference point."[205] After Jesus suffered, died, rose again, and ascended to the Father's right hand, He left behind not only a people redeemed from their sin and restored to relationship with the Father but a people held under the pattern of His patient endurance. The participle functions to set forth the purpose or result of the main verb ἔπαθεν ("suffered"). The present tense stresses the unending nature of Jesus' example and the moral imperative it lays upon His people. Once again, Peter uses alliteration to add punch to his teaching; note his use of five consecutive words beginning with ὑ- (ὑπὲρ ὑμῶν ὑμῖν ὑπολιμπάνων ὑπογραμμὸν; cf. also 1:4, 19; 2:15; 3:17, 20).

This example was "for you to follow in His steps" (ἵνα ἐπακολουθήσητε τοῖς ἴχνεσιν αὐτοῦ). The verb (ἐπακολουθήσητε, "to follow") is used elsewhere in the NT only in the disputed passage of Mark 16:20 along with 1 Timothy 5:10 and 24. It is a compound, comprised of ἐπί ("upon") and ἀκολουθέω ("to follow"). The resultant meaning is to follow along behind another. Idiomatically, we might picture it as "to walk in the tracks" of or "to follow in the tracks" of another and thus "to behave in the same manner as someone else."[206] The conjunction ἵνα and the use of the subjunctive mood of the verb designate this as a purpose clause. Jesus set out, through the way He suffered, to raise up a people who would behave similarly when suffering unjustly. The aorist tense of the verb pictures specific acts taken to conform to Jesus' pattern of patient endurance under suffering.

The form τοῖς ἴχνεσιν ("His steps") is labeled a dative of rule by Wallace, specifying "the rule or code a person follows or the standard of conduct to which he or she conforms."[207] The genitive (αὐτοῦ, "His"; lit., "the steps of him") is objective, the steps or the manner of life in which Jesus lived. The plural "steps" (τοῖς ἴχνεσιν) sets forth a mental picture of a "line of footprints."[208] The definite article sets them out as those utterly unique footprints left upon the record of human history by none other than the

---

205 BDAG, 7622.
206 Louw-Nida, 41.47.
207 Wallace, 157–158.
208 Rienecker, 755.

Son of God incarnate. We find the record of these "steps" recorded for us in the four Gospels of the NT, explained in the epistles of the NT, taken up in the Book of Acts, and vindicated in Revelation.

Verse 22 – "WHO COMMITTED NO SIN, NOR WAS ANY DECEIT FOUND IN HIS MOUTH;"

Now to Peter's profound introductory statement about the sufferings of Christ (v.21), he adds Scriptural backing—a direct quote from the LXX of Isaiah 53:9.[209] 1 Peter 2:22–25 serves as the ultimate NT identification of Jesus Christ as the fulfillment of Isaiah's Suffering Servant. In verses 22–25, Jobes identifies no fewer than seven possible quotations or allusions to the Suffering Servant of Isaiah 52:13–53:12[210] and Grudem at least five.[211] Jobes may overstate the case but makes the point, saying, "it is only here in the NT that Christ's passion is discussed in terms of Isaiah's prophecy of the Suffering Servant."[212] Peter makes the identification definitive.

Presently Peter quotes from Isaiah 53:9, opening with a relative pronoun (ὅς, "WHO"). As Peter uses it here, it is the first of four parallel relative clauses stretching through verse 22 to the end of verse 24; the antecedent of each relative pronoun is Χριστὸς ("Christ") in verse 21.[213] "The first two clauses focus on Christ's blameless character, the latter two on his saving work."[214] Jesus "COMMITTED NO SIN" (ἁμαρτίαν οὐκ ἐποίησεν). The noun ἁμαρτία ("SIN") is the most frequently used noun

---

209 Peter varies from the LXX only in the addition of the relative pronoun ὅς ("WHO") and substituting ἁμαρτίαν ("SIN") for ἀνομίαν ("lawlessness") (Dubis, 77).

210 Jobes, 194.

211 Grudem, 137.

212 Jobes, 192.

213 We should not suppose, as some have (e.g., Goppelt, 207–210; Davids, 110), that this signals Peter has taken over an early hymn or creedal statement. Who decided Peter was incapable of literary style?

214 Forbes, 90.

in the NT to describe sin. At the root, it describes missing the mark. The verb (ἐποίησεν, "COMMITTED") is the simple and common one meaning "to do." The negation (οὐκ, "NO") is absolute and categorical[215] and forms a "NO ... NOR" (οὐκ ... οὐδὲ) strategy for emphasizing by way of negation that Jesus was utterly undeserving of the suffering He endured. The aorist tense coupled with the negation, indicates Jesus never once acted in sin. When Jesus died on the cross, it was for no "SIN" (ἁμαρτίαν) of His own; He bore "our sins" (τὰς ἁμαρτίας ἡμῶν, v.24).[216]

The sinlessness of Christ is everywhere taught and upheld in the NT. The witnesses all agree. Judas, seeing Jesus' being condemned, admitted to the chief priests and elders of the Jews that he had sinned against "innocent blood" (Matt. 27: 4). Pilate's wife warned him not to act against Jesus, saying, He is a "righteous Man" (Matt. 27:19). The crowds that demanded Jesus' death had no answer when Pilate asked, "what evil has He done?" (Matt. 27:23). They could only cry the louder for His death. One of the criminals crucified next to Jesus came to His defense against the railings of the other criminal, saying, "this man has done nothing wrong" (Luke 23:41). The centurion watching over Jesus' crucifixion exclaimed at His death, "Certainly this man was innocent" (Luke 23:47). The crowds had no answer when Jesus asked, "Which one of you convicts Me of sin?" (John 8:46). Paul testified, "He made Him who knew no sin to be sin on our behalf, so that we might become the righteousness of God in Him" (2 Cor. 5:21). The author of Hebrews declared Jesus was "without sin" (Heb. 4:15) and "holy, innocent, undefiled, separated from sinners" (7:26). John, who knew Jesus as well as Peter did, testified, "in Him there is no sin" (1 John 3:5).

> **Ministry Maxim**
>
> A person's best witness is the record of their deeds and words.

---

215 Thayer, 408.

216 Perhaps Peter substituted ἁμαρτίαν ("SIN") here for the LXX's ἀνομίαν ("lawlessness") in preparation for his statement in verse 24 and to make this very point.

Jesus, as the Suffering Servant, did indeed suffer and die; He did so innocently. He thus stands as the quintessential example of unjust suffering.

"NOR WAS ANY DECEIT FOUND IN HIS MOUTH" (οὐδὲ εὑρέθη δόλος ἐν τῷ στόματι αὐτοῦ). Strictly speaking, δόλος ("DECEIT") was the bait used in catching fish.[217] It came then to be used metaphorically of "taking advantage through craft and underhanded methods."[218] The noun is used eleven times in the NT, designating craft, guile, and fraud. Its ploys play out through false words (1 Peter 3:10). The religious authorities used it in an attempt to gain control over Jesus (Matt. 26:4; Mark 14:1). The unredeemed heart is its source (Mark 7:22). The devil is a liar (John 8:44), the ultimate source of all "deceit" (Acts 13:10). For all these reasons Jesus forsook it and so must all who pledge allegiance to Him (1 Peter 2:1). The verb (εὑρέθη, "WAS...FOUND") is common but stronger than Peter might have used. Vincent says it is "Stronger than the simple *was*, and indicating a guilelessness which had stood the test of *scrutiny*.[219] The aorist tense indicates Jesus was never guilty of even one instance of "DECEIT." The passive voice pictures the deception being discovered by someone listening in on Jesus' words. The expression "IN HIS MOUTH" (ἐν τῷ στόματι αὐτοῦ) means simply "in His speech" or "in His words."

No listener throughout Jesus' life could testify to ever hearing one deceptive word come from His mouth. Jesus declared Himself to be "the truth" (John 14:6). He promised that the one who abides in His word would know the truth and that truth would set him free (John 8:31–32). His testimony was simply, "I tell you the truth" (John 16:7).

When John the Baptist was in prison near the end of his life, he sent his disciples to ask Jesus if he was indeed the one they were expecting. Jesus' response was telling: "Go and report to John what you hear and see" (Matt. 11:4). Jesus' self-certification was to be found in His actions

---

217 Friberg, 119.

218 BDAG, 2074.

219 Vincent, 1:648; cf. Hiebert, 184.

and His words. Peter here underscores that comprehensively Jesus' actions were free of sin and His words were free of deceit. Jesus never sinned and thus never suffered for any sin of His own, and He never sinned in His suffering for our sins. He was for this reason able to serve as "a lamb unblemished and spotless" (1 Peter 1:19) on our behalf and in our stead.

Peter's point in now stressing Jesus' sinlessness is to underscore the injustice of His suffering. We also suffer, and perhaps unjustly, but not because we are without sin. Though we cannot be counted without sin, we must make sure any suffering we do face is not because of our sin.

Verse 23 – "and while being reviled, He did not revile in return; while suffering, He uttered no threats, but kept entrusting *Himself* to Him who judges righteously;"

The second of four relative clauses in verses 22 through 24 is set now before us (ὅς, lit., "*who* while being reviled"). The antecedent remains "Christ" (Χριστὸς, v.21). Peter designates two responses Jesus did not make under the duress of His sufferings and one thing He did make in the face of His persecutions. Each of the negative statements sets forth the conditions of His suffering by way of a temporal participle and then presents what Jesus did not do in the face of this suffering by way of an imperfect tense verb.

Peter looks at what Jesus did "while being reviled" (λοιδορούμενος) and "while suffering" (πάσχων). Both participles are temporal in nature ("while"; many English translations render it with "When"). Both are present tense, underscoring the ongoing, unrelenting nature of the reviling and suffering.

The first verb is used just four times in the NT. It is used of the Jewish leaders' treatment of the blind man whom Jesus healed (John 9:28). It is used of Paul's response to Ananias, the high priest (Acts 23:4). Paul himself testified, "when we are reviled, we bless" (1 Cor. 4:12). In the NT the cognate noun is found three times (1 Tim. 5:14; 1 Peter 3:9 [2x]) and the adjective is used twice as a substantive (1 Cor. 5:11; 6:10). The word-group described a rich part of life within the Greek culture. "In public life in Greece insult and calumny played a considerable part, whether among the heroes in Hom., in political life in the democracies, in comedy, or in the great orators. Not to be susceptible was part of the art of living."²²⁰ "If for Greek writers it was one of the arts of life to know how to insult others or bear insults against oneself, for the believer the suffering of slander and insults is evidence of the cross the Christian disciple is called to bear."²²¹ As Spicq says, "Words lead to blows; insults provoke fights, and blood flows. Christ was subjected to insults and blows, and Christian slaves are urged to imitate his determined silence: 'Abused, he did not abuse in return.'"²²² Peter later uses the noun to instruct his readers in "not returning evil for evil or insult for insult [λοιδορίαν ἀντὶ λοιδορίας], but giving a blessing instead" (1 Peter 3:9). Jesus was reviled while before the Sanhedrin (Matt. 26:67–68; Mark 14:65), by the Roman soldiers (Matt. 27:28–30; Mark 15:17–20) and while on the cross (Matt. 27:39–44; Mark 15:29–32; Luke 23:35–39).

Looking at how Jesus faced such treatment, Peter says, "He did not revile in return" (οὐκ ἀντελοιδόρει). The verb is found only here in the NT. It is a compound, taking as its root the previous verb (λοιδορέω, "to revile") and adding the prefix ἀντί. The preposition ἀντί has a root meaning of being set "over against" something, "opposite" or "facing" that thing. It could then have the sense of "*exchange*, where one object, opposing or distinct from another, is given or taken in return for the other" or "*substitution*, where one object, that is distinguishable from another, is given or taken instead of the other."²²³ Either sense might be in view in the present compound where non-reviling is given in exchange or substituted for the reviling that one has received. The imperfect tense pictures the enduring non-response of Christ under the relentless reviling He faced. As in verse 22, the negation here (οὐκ, "NO") is

> **Ministry Maxim**
>
> Only surrender to our Father enables silence toward our persecutors.

---

220 TDNT, 4:294.

221 NIDNTTE, 3:171.

222 Spicq, 2:408–409.

223 Harris, 49.

absolute and categorical.²²⁴ Jesus' silence is confirmed by the Gospel accounts: before the high priest (Matt. 26:62–63; Mark 14:61), Pilate (Matt. 27:14; Mark 15:5; John 19:9–10), and Herod (Luke 23:9).

The second participle brings us to Jesus "while suffering" (πάσχων). This is the fourth occurrence of the verb Peter introduced in verse 19 and which becomes thematic for the remainder of the letter (1 Peter 2:19, 20, 21, 23; 3:14, 17, 18; 4:1 [2x], 15, 19; 5:10). Again, the present tense pictures the ongoing "suffering" that Jesus underwent. But as Jesus suffered, "He uttered no threats" (οὐκ ἠπείλει). The verb is a compound made up of ἀπό ("from," "away from") and εἰλέω ("to roll up," "to close," "to cover").²²⁵ The verb is used only one other time in the NT, when the Sanhedrin deliberated on how to deal with the preaching of Peter and John. They determined, "let us severely threaten [ἀπειλησώμεθα] them, that from now on they speak to no man in this name" (Acts 4:17, NKJV). Again, the negation is total and without exception (οὐκ, "no") and the imperfect tense underscores the repeated and enduring non-response of Jesus. In contrast to Jesus' non-retaliatory posture, consider Paul's response to the high priest in Acts 23:2–3.

Peter's words here appear to be another allusion to the Suffering Servant of Isaiah 53: "He was oppressed and He was afflicted, Yet He did not open His mouth; Like a lamb that is led to slaughter, And like a sheep that is silent before its shearers, So He did not open His mouth" (Isa. 53:7). The witness of the NT Gospels verifies Peter's words. At Jesus' arrest, when Peter drew his sword to protect Him, Jesus ordered him to put his sword away and offer no resistance (Matt. 26:52). Again and again, we find Jesus refusing to retaliate and holding His tongue (Matt. 26:67–68; 27:11–14, 27–31).

Rather than (δὲ, "but") responding in kind to His persecutors, Jesus "kept entrusting Himself to Him who judges righteously" (παρεδίδου ... τῷ κρίνοντι δικαίως). The verb is a compound made up of παρά ("from") and δίδωμι ("to give"). It appears in the LXX of Isaiah 53:6 and 12, which

---

224 Thayer, 408.

225 Liddell and Scott, 4985, 12724.

may have suggested it to Peter's mind here. The root verb is used by Peter to describe God the Father "who raised Him from the dead and gave [δόντα] Him glory" (1 Peter 1:21; cf. also 5:5). Peter uses the compound in the sense of an official or judicial turning over of sinful angels to judgment (2 Peter 2:4) and of apostates who had "the holy commandment handed [παραδοθείσης] on to them" (v.21). Tellingly, this is the verb used to describe Judas turning Jesus over to the Jews (Matt. 26:15; Mark 14:10; Luke 22:4; cf. Matt. 27:3), the Jews turning Him over to Pilate (Matt. 27:2, 18; Mark 15:1, 10), and Pilate turning Him over to the soldiers (Matt. 27:26; Mark 15:15; Luke 23:25; John 19:16).[226] At each delivery of Jesus down the pipeline of suffering and death He "kept entrusting" to the Father Himself, all that swirled about Him, and all that hung upon His obedience. The imperfect tense is reflected in the translation "*kept entrusting*" (emphasis added), for it depicts the repeated action of Jesus in the face of His tormentors.[227]

There is no object of the action expressed in the Greek text. Just what was Jesus "entrusting" to the Father? The NASU has "Himself" (so also ESV, KJV, NET, NIV, NRSV, NKJV, YLT).[228] Various commentators suggest Jesus' cause,[229] Jesus' case and destiny[230] (cf. NLT, "his case"), the judgment,[231] and his enemies either for judgment[232] or forgiveness.[233] But perhaps it is best to view the matter comprehensively, understanding

---

226 Stibbs, 118–119.

227 Lenski sums up the artful use of verbal tenses in verse 23 by saying, "Here we have three descriptive imperfects which stand out amid the simple aorists of fact. They, too, state facts but present them as on a moving film, the present participles letting us picture the scenes of reviling and suffering, the imperfect verbs letting us dwell on the silent victim as no reviling, no threatening reply issues from his lips" (Lenski, 121).

228 Bigg, 146; Clowney, 119, Davids, 112, Forbes, 91; Lenski, 121, Stibbs, 119.

229 Kelly, 121.

230 Marshall, 94.

231 Goppelt, 212.

232 Michaels, 131, 147.

233 Alford, 4:354.

Jesus to have entrusted Himself and all that concerned Him to the Father, including His cause, destiny, and enemies.[234]

Here was a profoundly personal, deeply spiritual turning over of Jesus' life and very self, along with all that He cared for and faced, to the Father under whose hand He suffered these blows from His enemies. It "was the will of the LORD to crush him; he has put him to grief" (Isa. 53:10, ESV). The present tense here depicts Jesus' ongoing, continuous entrusting of Himself to the Father. Under suffering, a once-and-done consecration does not hold up; it demands a continuous, moment-by-moment, ever-fresh surrender.

Again and again, with each insult and with each blow, Jesus yielded His all to His Father and placed Himself willingly within His plan. With His final breath, "Jesus, crying out with a loud voice, said, 'Father, INTO YOUR HANDS I COMMIT MY SPIRIT.' Having said this, He breathed His last" (Luke 23:46).

In the garden, when the authorities came to arrest Him, Jesus rebuked Peter's attempt at physical violence, "do you think that I cannot appeal to My Father, and He will at once put at My disposal more than twelve legions of angels?" (Matt. 26:53). But he added, "How then will the Scriptures be fulfilled, which say that it must happen this way?" (v.54). Jesus stands as the ultimate example of trusting obedience. He knew the Father's plan of redemption; He understood the demands of the prophetic Scriptures. Jesus entrusted Himself to the Father (cf. Heb. 5:7) and stepped forward to fulfill those Scriptures. In this, He shed light on the path we must walk: "those also who suffer according to the will of God shall entrust their souls to a faithful Creator in doing what is right" (1 Peter 4:19).

The Father is depicted here as "Him who judges righteously" (τῷ κρίνοντι δικαίως). The articular participle is used substantively ("*Him who judges*," emphasis added). The present tense underscores the ongoing discernment of the Father regarding every sentient being in His universe. It is the Father's right, indeed His duty, to judge sin and those who commit

---

234 Grudem, 138; Schreiner, 144.

it. His holiness requires no less. Yet He unfailingly does so "righteously" (δικαίως).

When Abraham interceded over Sodom and asked the Lord's justice in sweeping away the righteous with the unrighteous, he inquired, "Shall not the Judge of all the earth deal justly?" (Gen. 18:25). The question was not concerning the justice of judging sinners, but in sweeping away the righteous with the unrighteous in that judgment. The Lord's answer, again and again, was that if He found the righteous among the wicked, he would "spare the whole place on their account" (18:26, cf. 28, 29, 30, 31, 32). Yet when it came to the judgment of our sins, the Father laid them all upon the supremely innocent one and judged our sins in Him in our place and on our behalf. And this was done as "the demonstration ... of His righteousness ... so that He would be just and the justifier of the one who has faith in Jesus" (Rom. 3:26).

Verse 24 – "and He Himself bore our sins in His body on the cross, so that we might die to sin and live to righteousness; for by His wounds you were healed."

This verse provides the third and fourth occurrences of the relative pronoun (ὅς and οὗ; cf. verses 22 and 23) in the sentence that began in verse 21. The pronouns again find their antecedent in Χριστὸς ("Christ," v.21).

In ordering his words, Peter puts first "our sins" (τὰς ἁμαρτίας ἡμῶν) to emphasize that the sufferings of Christ were not only exemplary (v.21) but atoning; His sufferings and death were for no wrongdoing in Himself, but as an act of substitutionary sacrifice on our behalf. The noun was just used in verse 22, which see. The definite article makes even more specific what "sins" Jesus took upon Himself on the cross. It was for no "SIN" of His own (ἁμαρτίαν, v.22) that Jesus suffered and died; it was for "our sins" (τὰς ἁμαρτίας ἡμῶν). Note the contrast between the singular of verse 22 (He committed not even one sin) and the plural here (the multitude of "our sins"). By here using the first-person plural pronoun (ἡμῶν, "our") Peter counts himself among those so loved and redeemed, standing side-by-side with his readers.²³⁵ These sins "He Himself bore" (αὐτὸς ἀνήνεγκεν). The pronoun αὐτὸς is intensive²³⁶, leading to the translation "He Himself." It was Jesus, the Christ, the second person of the Trinity, the eternal Son, who took our sins upon Himself. Peter thus doubly emphasizes both our culpability for the sins (the definite article and personal pronoun) and the identity of Jesus as the one who bore them (the verbal form and personal pronoun) for us.

Jesus and no other "bore" (ἀνήνεγκεν) the sins we committed. It is a compound made up of ἀνά ("up") and φέρω ("to bear/carry"). It describes the ascent of a mountain (Matt. 17:1; Mark 9:2) and Jesus' ascent into heaven after His resurrection (Luke 24:51). But it was used extensively in the LXX of a priest offering *up* a sacrifice to God on the altar (e.g., Lev. 3:11, 14, 16; 4:10, 19, 26, 31.; cf. Heb. 7:27a; James 2:21). Fittingly, it is used here and elsewhere in the NT to describe Christ's sacrifice of Himself for us on the cross (Heb. 7:27b; 9:28). Jesus made Himself the definitive, "once for all" sacrifice for "our sins" (Heb. 7:27; cf. 9:12; 10:10; 1 Peter 3:18) by offering Himself up to God in death.

Here again, Peter takes us to the Suffering Servant. He combines thoughts from Isaiah 53:4 and 12. "Surely our griefs [τὰς ἁμαρτίας ἡμῶν, "our sins," LXX] He Himself bore [φέρω without the prefix ἀνά]" (v.4a). "Yet He Himself bore [ἀνήνεγκεν] the sin of many, And interceded for the transgressors" (v.12b). The LXX of verses 4 and 12 use both the compounded (ἀναφέρω, v.12) and uncompounded (φέρω, v.4) forms of the Greek verb to render the Hebrew verb נָשָׂא. The Hebrew verb was used "of bearing or carrying" and was "used especially of bearing the guilt or punishment of sin."²³⁷ This led to the matter of "bearing

---

235 Two important manuscripts and minuscules have ὑμῶν ("your") instead of ἡμῶν ("our"), but the overall weight of evidence rests with the first person plural, a form not seen since 1:3 and which may reflect the influence of Isaiah 53:4 (cf. Dubis, 79; Forbes, 92; Michaels, 134; Schreiner, 145).

236 Robertson, *Grammar*, 723.

237 TWOT, 2:601.

the guilt of another by representation or substitution (Lev 10:17) or of the scapegoat (Lev 16:22)."[238]

It is sometimes objected that Peter cannot be speaking of Jesus' making atonement for our sins because the object of the verb is "our sins," and sins are never offered in sacrifice to God.[239] True, sins cannot be offered to God. But Jesus, bearing those sins up to the cross, did offer Himself as the bearer of our sins, our substitute. Jesus took our sins in His body and thus bore them up when He went to the cross. He was the sacrifice; our sins were the cause. He so thoroughly took our sins to Himself ("in His body") that it could be said, "He made Him who knew no sin to be sin on our behalf" (2 Cor. 5:21a). Indeed, "the LORD has caused the iniquity of us all To fall on Him" (Isa. 53:6).

Jesus accomplished this "in His body on the cross" (ἐν τῷ σώματι αὐτοῦ ἐπὶ τὸ ξύλον). God the Son became incarnate, taking a physical body to Himself. This was done so that He might redeem us. He had to be one of us to stand in our place (Heb. 2:17). Our sins were committed bodily, and it had to be "in" (ἐν) a human body that they met God's justice. Jesus' body was prepared for Him by the Father (Heb. 10:5; quoting the LXX of Psa. 40:6 [LXX 39:7]). And "we have been sanctified through the offering of the body [τοῦ σώματος] of Jesus Christ once for all" (Heb. 10:10). Our "sins" are not the offering made to God; Jesus offered Himself to God while bearing "our sins" in His own body.[240]

> **Ministry Maxim**
>
> The Great Physician healed us by taking our wounds upon Himself.

> "Therefore, since the children share in flesh and blood, He Himself likewise also partook of the same, that through death He might render powerless him who had the power of death, that is, the devil, and might free those who through fear of death were

---

238 Ibid.

239 E.g., Michaels, 148; Schreiner, 145.

240 Cf. the argument made by Harris, 144–145.

subject to slavery all their lives. For assuredly He does not give help to angels, but He gives help to the descendant of Abraham. Therefore, He had to be made like His brethren in all things, so that He might become a merciful and faithful high priest in things pertaining to God, to make propitiation for the sins of the people." (Heb. 2:14–17)

Significantly, this happened "on the cross" (ἐπὶ τὸ ξύλον). The noun (ξύλον) literally meant "wood" or the tree from which the wood was taken. It could also signify things made of wood.[241] It is used thus of "clubs" wielded by the party that came to arrest Jesus in the Garden (Matt. 26:47, 55; Mark 14:43, 48; Luke 22:52). But in the mouths of the Apostles, it became the word used for designating the "cross" upon which He died (Acts 5:30; 10:39; 13:29). This was the place that the curse of our sins was laid upon Jesus our substitute. Paul cited Deuteronomy 21:23, which includes the noun, in reference to Christ's saving work on the cross: "Christ redeemed us from the curse of the Law, having become a curse for us-- for it is written, 'CURSED IS EVERYONE WHO HANGS ON A TREE [ἐπὶ ξύλου]'" (Gal. 3:13). It may be that Peter similarly alludes to this verse, which in the LXX reads: κεκατηραμένος ὑπὸ θεοῦ πᾶς κρεμάμενος ἐπὶ ξύλου ("cursed by God is everyone who hangs on a tree"). Tellingly, this is the noun John takes up in the last book of the Bible to describe "the tree of life" (Rev. 2:7; 22:2, 14, 19). The first couple plunged us into sin by defying God and eating of the fruit of the "tree [ξύλον] of knowledge of good and evil" (Gen. 3:3, 6, LXX). We were only delivered from sin by Christ's death upon "the tree" (Acts 5:30; 10:39; 13:29, ESV, KJV, NET, NKJV, NRSV). This opened the way for us to eat forever of "the tree of life" (τοῦ ξύλου τῆς ζωῆς) in fellowship with God.

The interchange of prepositions here is profound. The substitution took place as Jesus offered *up* (ἀνά in compound; ἀνήνεγκεν, "He... bore") Himself as our sin-bearer in our place. This took place "*in* [ἐν] His body" and "*on* [ἐπί] the cross" (emphases added). Our sins were taken by Jesus *in*

---

241 BDAG, 5175.

His own body (human sins committed in our bodies needed to be borne in a human body) and carried *up* to the cross (the place He gave Himself up in sacrifice for us), and there *on* the cross (the place of atonement) His sacrificial death propitiated God, expiated our sins, and set us free from the penalty due to us for them.

The purpose (ἵνα, "so that") of Jesus' substitutionary sacrifice is stated both negatively and positively. First, the negative: Jesus died for us that "we might die to sin" (ταῖς ἁμαρτίαις ἀπογενόμενοι). The verb (ἀπογενόμενοι, "we might die") appears only here in the NT. A compound, it is constructed of the prefix ἀπό ("from," "away from," "out from") and the root verb γίνομαι ("to be born"). It means "to be away from" or "unconnected with."[242] It pictures absolute and complete separation. Here "contrasted with ζήσωμεν, it means 'dead.'"[243] It means "to cease, with a complete and abrupt change."[244] It is thus to "become utterly alienated from our sins."[245] The aorist tense pictures this actually becoming reality. The verb is deponent, so the middle voice should be read as active. The participle may be understood as expressing the means by which one comes to "live" unto righteousness,[246] or it could be temporal, expressing action that precedes its main verb ("we, having died to sins, might live for righteousness," NKJV).[247]

The noun (ταῖς ἁμαρτίαις, "to sin") is repeated from the first clause in this verse, except that instead of being in the accusative form, we now find it in the dative form. Both appear with the definite article, making specific the sins in mind. Both are in the plural, stressing their multiplicity and their humanly inescapable burden. Jesus bore "our sins" (τὰς ἁμαρτίας ἡμῶν) in His body on the cross when He died in order that through Him

---

242 Mounce, 1091.

243 TDNT, 1:687.

244 Louw-Nida, 68.40.

245 Thayer, 60.

246 Dubis, 80.

247 Forbes, 92.

we might die "to sin" (ταῖς ἁμαρτίαις; lit. "to the sins," cf. NIV, KJV, NKJV, NRSV, YLT). The form may be considered a dative of reference; Jesus died for our sins so that we might die with reference to our sins.[248] Jesus' death and resurrection rendered both the guilt (Rom. 3:9–26) and the power of sin (6:6–14) broken. We no longer bear the guilt associated with them (8:1) and are no longer under any necessity to obey them (v.2). When sin's guilt endeavors to blacken the atmosphere of your heart, look to the cross. When sin's power seeks to take power over your thoughts, words, or actions, look to the cross. The work is complete and finished; the freedom is real and present.

The purpose of Jesus' suffering and dying in our place on the cross was that we might "live to righteousness" (τῇ δικαιοσύνῃ ζήσωμεν). In context, the opposite of "to die" (ἀπογενόμενοι) is to "live" (ζήσωμεν). The aorist may be ingressive, "begin to live." As noted above, the verb is qualified by the participle (ἀπογενόμενοι, "to die"), which may designate how one comes to "live" in righteousness or it may express a temporal relationship, one must first die to sin before one can live to righteousness. We have a dative of reference again, to live "with reference to righteousness" (τῇ δικαιοσύνῃ). The definite article signals that "righteousness" which conforms to the character of God, who alone is righteous. Peter uses the noun elsewhere in an ethical sense of conduct that conforms to God's righteousness (1 Peter 3:14; 2 Peter 1:1; 2:5, 21; 3:13). It seems that it is here used in that same sense of moral and ethical conduct, of living "to righteousness." Peter has been telling his readers just what he intends by living in "righteousness" (2:12–20).[249] As with the parallel verb (ἀπογενόμενοι, "we might die"), the aorist depicts the action as actual reality.[250] "The singular 'righteousness,' in contrast to the plural 'the sins,' implies the unitary nature of the new life, marked by daily submissive obedience to God and

---

248 Rienecker, 755; Robertson, *Word Pictures*, 6:106; Dubis (80–81) and Forbes (92) designate it a dative of respect.

249 Michaels, 149.

250 Lenski, 123.

1 Peter 2

His will."[251] As Paul says, "having been freed from sin, you became slaves of righteousness" (Rom. 6:18).

The fourth and final relative clause (οὗ) declares that it is "by His wounds you are healed" (τῷ μώλωπι ἰάθητε). The noun (τῷ μώλωπι, "wounds") "strictly means a cut which bleeds," and thus "the lashing which draws blood." It came then to denote "the weal or discolored swelling left by blow from a fist or whip."[252] The noun is singular but may be considered a collective, and thus English versions translate it with a plural ("wounds").[253] In view of the singular form, Forbes suggests the translation "wounding."[254] The expression serves as a metonymy for the entirety of Jesus' suffering and death, not any one particular part of His Passion, such as His scourging.[255] While Peter has widened the circle of application, he still has servants in view (1 Peter 2:18), and many of them would have such marks upon their bodies after a beating from their masters. But the definite article serves to make specific those "wounds" inflicted upon Jesus during His Passion and which ultimately resulted in His physical death.

The dative (τῷ μώλωπι, "by His wounds") is to be understood as designating means; by means of Jesus' death, which the "His wounds" exemplify, "you are healed" (ἰάθητε). The verb means to restore to a previous condition. It occurs twenty-six times in the NT, only three of which lie outside the record of the Gospels and Acts (Heb. 12:13; James 5:16; 1 Peter 2:24). It was used literally of physical restoration from disease and physical infirmity (Matt. 8:8; Mark 5:29; Luke 9:11; John 4:47; Acts 9:34; James 5:16, etc.) and metaphorically of the spiritual redemption and restoration Christ effects (Acts 28:27; Heb. 12:13). With no mention of physical sickness, our present context clearly identifies Peter's usage as the latter, without denying Jesus' ability to perform

---

251 Hiebert, 188.

252 Rienecker, 755.

253 Hiebert, 189; Lenski, 124.

254 Forbes, 93.

255 Dubis, 81; Forbes, 93; Schreiner, 146.

the former. The aorist tense of the verb is to be understood as ingressive, descriptive of entering a state of healing.[256] The passive voice indicates that it is God, through what Jesus' did on the cross, that effects the healing. The verb rests in the final spot in this extended sentence to place emphasis upon it.[257]

Peter is clearly calling again upon Isaiah 53, this time verse 5: "by His scourging we are healed" (τῷ μώλωπι αὐτοῦ ἡμεῖς ἰάθημεν, LXX). Christ died to atone for our sins. He dealt not partially with only some of the effects of sin but in total. The effects of sin include sickness and ultimately death, in accordance with God's own warning (Gen. 2:17; 3:3). But not all the benefits of Jesus' atoning death are guaranteed to us fully in this life; we will come into some of these entirely only at His Return. The present passage cannot settle the question of healing in the atonement; that must be settled by other passages (e.g., Isa. 53:5; Matt. 8:17).

Digging Deeper:

1. How is our suffering for Christ both like and unlike His suffering for us (v.21)?
2. How does establishing Jesus' innocence in His suffering help Peter make His point (v.22)? How does this help us in rightly applying this in our own suffering?
3. When have you reviled or retaliated when wronged by another (v.23)? What did it achieve?
4. Ask someone close to you to describe how they have witnessed you dying to sin and living to righteousness (v.24).

---

256 Forbes, 93; Wallace, 558–559.

257 Dubis, 81.

Verse 25 – "For you were continually straying like sheep, but now you have returned to the Shepherd and Guardian of your souls."

Peter moves to close the present section (vv.18ff) by way of an explanatory and applicatory comment (γὰρ, "For"). Peter broke off from speaking exclusively to "Servants" (v.18) and, while keeping them in view, began to speak more inclusively about the example and effects of Jesus' sufferings (vv.21–24). Peter now applies his most recent comments (dying to sin and living to righteousness; healing through Christ) to all his readers. He does so by again returning us to the Suffering Servant of Isaiah 53. This time he draws upon Isaiah 53:6a: "All of us like sheep have gone astray, Each of us has turned to his own way." The LXX renders the first clause: πάντες ὡς πρόβατα ἐπλανήθημεν. Peter changes from the LXX's ἐπλανήθημεν ("have gone astray," aorist passive indicative first person plural) to a periphrastic combination of ἦτε ("you were," imperfect active indicative second person plural) and πλανώμενοι ("straying," present passive participle nominative masculine plural).

The first verb (ἦτε, "you were") is in the imperfect tense, describing the abiding pattern of his readers' lives before they met Christ. The second verb (πλανώμενοι,

> **Ministry Maxim**
> The Shepherd became the Lamb to make us His sheep.

"straying") means to be misled or to mislead.[258] It is used by Peter to describe apostates (2 Peter 2:15). The cognate noun πλάνη ("wandering") is used in 2 Peter 2:18; 3:17 and Jude 11; the related noun πλανήτης ("wandering stars") is used in Jude 13. Here the present tense presents this as the regular course of their pre-Christian lives ("*continually* straying,"

---

258 An impressive array of manuscripts substitutes the neuter πλανώμενα for the masculine πλανώμενοι, to conform it to the preceding neuter noun πρόβατα ("sheep"). The result is to make the participle adjectival, modifying πρόβατα ("sheep"). This would yield a rendering of "you were like wandering sheep." The weight of the external evidence rests with the masculine form and the transition to the neuter form is best explained by a scribe's attempt to conform it to the previous noun (Bigg, 149; Dubis, 82; Forbes, 93; Michaels, 134).

emphasis added). The passive voice pictures them at the mercy of every passing whim, passion, or influence. They were, as James said, "like the surf of the sea, driven and tossed by the wind" (James 1:6). Or, to use Paul's language, "children, tossed here and there by waves and carried about by every wind of doctrine, by the trickery of men, by craftiness in deceitful scheming" (Eph. 4:14). The participial form is probably used to designate the manner or habit of their existence (ἦτε, "you were").

Peter, however, does not use the imagery of a storm-tossed sea. Rather he takes up the words of Isaiah 53:6, saying their wandering existence was "like sheep" (ὡς πρόβατα). Sheep are throughout the Bible a stock image of the recalcitrant, willful, insensible, self-absorbed, and vulnerable. Sheep unthinkingly wander from the safety of the flock (Matt. 18:12), blindly fall "into a pit" (Matt. 12:11), and are routinely oblivious to the dangers around them (Matt. 10:16). Sheep are aimless and helpless without leadership and care (Numb. 27:17; 1 Kings 22:17; 2 Chron. 18:16; Ezek. 34:5). Thus Jesus, "Seeing the people ... felt compassion for them, because they were distressed and dispirited like sheep without a shepherd" (Matt. 9:36). Left to themselves "the sheep of the flock will be scattered" (Matt. 26:31, ESV).

In an utter break (ἀλλὰ, "but") with a life of wandering, Peter's readers at the present time (νῦν, "now") "have returned" (ἐπεστράφητε). The verb is a compound made up of ἐπί ("upon") and στρέφω ("to turn"). To turn upon a point in your path and to go the opposite direction is the essence of repentance/conversion ("have turned back," NET; "have turned," NLT). The rendering "returned" need not imply a previous standing with God (which the Gentile readers of Peter's letter did not have), but simply that they were converted, (re)turned to the only One who could save them.[259] Peter recognizes that his readers, though once wandering sheep, heard the voice of their true Shepherd (John 10:16) and turned from their aimless, self-absorbed existence and came to Him for life. The passive voice may reflect the divine initiative in salvation ("are now returned," KJV),[260] or it

---

259 Cf. Forbes, 94; Grudem, 140; Hiebert, 190.

260 Forbes, 94.

may have the force of the middle ("you have turned").²⁶¹ Ironically, however, this same verb that here and elsewhere pictures repentance unto salvation (e.g., Acts 3:19; 2 Cor. 3:16; 1 Thess. 1:9; James 5:19–20) is used later by Peter of apostasy: "It has happened to them according to the true proverb, 'A DOG RETURNS [ἐπιστρέψας] TO ITS OWN VOMIT'" (2 Peter 2:22a; cf. Prov. 26:11; Gal. 4:9).

Him "to" (ἐπὶ) whom they have returned is set forth under two designations.²⁶² Both are governed by one definite article (τὸν, "the"), both pointing to Jesus Christ.²⁶³ First, "the Shepherd" (τὸν ποιμένα). The word is used literally, of course, for those who tend a flock of sheep or goats. But it is also widely used in a metaphorical sense. It is used of national leaders (e.g., Jer. 23:1–4; Ezek. 34:1–10; Zech. 11:16). But ultimately in the OT Yahweh is the true "Shepherd" (e.g., Psalm 23:1; 28:9; 80:1; Isa. 40:11; Jer. 31:10). In the NT Jesus takes this role and is designated "the good shepherd" (John 10:11, 14), "the great Shepherd of the sheep" (Heb. 13:20), and "the Chief Shepherd" (1 Peter 5:4). "Like a shepherd He will tend His flock, In His arm He will gather the lambs And carry them in His bosom; He will gently lead the nursing ewes" (Isa. 40:11). We like sheep have wandered away from God (Isa. 53:6). For this reason, the Suffering Servant became as a lamb (v.7) to redeem us. But now "the Lamb of God" (John 1:29, 36) has triumphed and is depicted as "the Shepherd." The "Shepherd" became a lamb so that He could truly "Shepherd" His sheep. He laid down His life for the sheep (John 10:11, 15) so that He might become the "door of the sheep" (v.7) and they might join the flock of God and come under His care.

---

261 Abernathy, 108; Alford, 4:355.

262 Notice the repetition of the preposition, first in compound (ἐπιστρέφω) and then standing alone (ἐπὶ). Peter depicts his readers stopping *on* (or at) a particular point in their journey, turning around and taking their stand *on* Christ. At root the preposition denotes "position *on* something that forms a support or foundation … implying actual rest on some object" (Harris, 137).

263 This is an example of the Granville Sharp Rule. Two nouns joined by καὶ and with only one definite article that precedes the first noun are to be understood as referring to the same person (Wallace, 270–274).

Jesus said He had come for "the lost sheep of the house of Israel" (Matt. 10:6; 15:24). But he could also say, "I have other sheep, which are not of this fold; I must bring them also, and they will hear My voice; and they will become one flock with one shepherd" (John 10:16). He is unwilling to lose even one of His sheep (Matt. 18:12).

The imagery of shepherding was no doubt powerfully redemptive for Peter. For after his denials of the Lord, Jesus met him on the shore of the Sea of Galilee and gave him a three-fold opportunity to confess his love for Him. It was then that Jesus personally called and restored Peter, commanding him, "Shepherd My sheep" (John 21:16) and "Tend My sheep" (v.17). Peter then called the "elders" of the churches, under "the Chief Shepherd," to function as under-shepherds within their circles of fellowship (1 Peter 5:2–4).

Added (καὶ, "and") to this is the designation "the Guardian" (ἐπίσκοπον). The noun is used four other times in the NT, all of them referring to an office of leadership in the local church (Acts 20:28; Phil. 1:1; 1 Tim. 3:2; Titus 1:7), synonymous with the office of elder. It is a compound comprised of ἐπί ("above," "over") and σκοπός ("one who watches").[264] For this reason, it is often translated as "overseer" (i.e., one who "sees over" God's people). In this case the translation "Guardian" catches the intent for "the focus ... is not upon leadership but upon the role of caring for the believers."[265] And "the oversight of the 'Chief Shepherd' (5:4) has majestic breadth and depth ... The Lord who knows the secrets of our hearts watches over our souls."[266]

The two word groups are joined elsewhere (cf. Acts 20:28; 1 Peter 5:2), suggesting a rich interplay between the terms. "Christ is He who has the fullest knowledge of souls. He knows every inner secret ... He is also the One who gives Himself most self-sacrificingly to care for the souls of the faithful (cf. ἐπισκοπέω in Hb. 12:15). It is for this reason that ποιμήν

---

264 Liddell-Scott, 16156.III.1, 16961, 39191.

265 Louw-Nida, 35.43.

266 Clowney, 126.

and ἐπίσκοπος are so closely related."²⁶⁷ The "Shepherd" stands among His sheep; His presence is their peace. The "Guardian" stands over the flock; His comprehensive vision and intimate insight are their peace. We could not be under better care.

Both as "Shepherd" and "Guardian," Jesus takes responsibility for the care "of your souls" (τῶν ψυχῶν ὑμῶν).²⁶⁸ Here ψυχή designates not simply the immaterial part of a human being but the whole of the life (1 Peter 1:9, 22; 2:11; 3:20; 4:19). The definite article and the personal pronoun work together to make powerfully personal the attention and care of Christ for each one of His people.

> **Digging Deeper:**
> 1. Where and how has your wandering taken you from God?
> 2. Specifically, how are you personally allowing Jesus to shepherd your soul?

---

267 TDNT, 2:616.

268 Some (e.g., Goppelt, 215; Kelly, 125; Marshall, 96; Michaels, 152; Stibbs, 122; cf. "your Shepherd, the Guardian of your souls" NLT) view the second noun (ἐπίσκοπον, "Guardian") as explaining and enlarging upon the first term (ποιμένα, "Shepherd"). In that case they generally see τῶν ψυχῶν ὑμῶν ("of your souls") as connected only to the second term (ἐπίσκοπον, "Guardian"). But because the two word-families are found together elsewhere (cf. Acts 20:28; 1 Peter 5:2; Ezek. 34:11 LXX) it seems best to read them as simply two designations in roughly parallel form and connect "of our souls" to both (cf. Bigg, 149; Davids, 114; Grudem, 140).

1 PETER 3

Verse 1 – "In the same way, you wives, be submissive to your own husbands so that even if any *of them* are disobedient to the word, they may be won without a word by the behavior of their wives,

Peter opens a new section (vv.1–6), this time addressed to "wives" ([αἱ] γυναῖκες).[1] The word can refer to women generally, but since Peter refers to their "own husbands" (τοῖς ἰδίοις ἀνδράσιν), it is clearly a reference to "wives" specifically. Peter's instruction here may be compared to extended instruction by the Apostle Paul in Ephesians 5:22–33, Colossians 3:18–19, and Titus 2:4–5.

The call is for wives to "be submissive" (ὑποτασσόμεναι). The verb is a compound arising from "under" (ὑπό) and "appoint" or "order" (τάσσω). It speaks of authority and submission. It was a military word that described the ranks of soldiers arranging themselves under the leadership of their commander. The participle functions as an imperative (the imperative form in 2:13 extends its influence on the participial forms in 2:18 and here in 3:1). Here, the decision as to whether it is middle or passive voice is difficult. If passive, it may still have a reflexive sense to it.

---

[1] There is some dispute as to whether the definite article is to be considered original or a scribal addition. The meaning is not changed by one's decision.

Thus, in either case, it shows that submission is the wife's voluntary and personal choice. The present tense reveals that the wife is to choose this as an abiding attitude, not simply when it is agreeable to her. Such submission is to be the ongoing pattern of a wife's relationship with her husband.

Peter has already laid this obligation upon all Christian citizens (2:13) and servants (2:18). A broader look at the NT reveals that such submission to authority is required of all. All people are subject to the governing authorities (Rom. 13:1–5; Titus 3:1). Believers are subject to one another (Eph. 5:21). Children are subject to their parents (Luke 2:51). Slaves are subject to masters (Titus 2:9). The church is subject to Christ (Eph. 5:24), as is all else (1 Cor. 15:27–28; Eph. 1:22; Phil. 3:21). No one is exempt from submission to authority.

Peter is not demanding submission of women to men generally, but "to your own husbands" (τοῖς ἰδίοις ἀνδράσιν). As with the previous noun, ἀνήρ can be used generally, in this case, to describe men. Here, however, clearly it is "husbands" who are in view. The definite article (τοῖς) is interpreted as possessive ("your"). Together with the adjective (ἰδίοις, "own") in the attributive position, it underscores the boundaries of the submission in view.

Matters of submission and authority do not imply the superiority of one over the other but reflect a divinely established order which allows all to thrive and flourish. Peter tells a husband to recognize that his wife is "a fellow heir of the grace of life" (v.7), demonstrating spiritual equality. The whole of Scripture testifies that the two are equal in essence, dignity, intellect, and giftedness. Submission, then, is not a statement of worth but of divine assignment and role within God's larger purposes.

A wife's submission to her husband is imperative throughout the NT (Eph. 5:22–24; Col. 3:18; Titus 2:4–5). This is troublesome to many in our contemporary culture with its egalitarian impulses. Some have sought to alleviate their concerns by looking to Ephesians 5 and citing verse 21: "be subject to one another in the fear of Christ." Some argue that this verse, coming immediately before the instructions for a wife to submit to her husband (v.22), reveals the true intent. Paul does not, it is said, envision a male-led relationship but a mutually submissive one. And this is correct if we allow the rest of Ephesians five to inform what Paul meant by his words in verse 21. In what sense is submission a responsibility of both husband and wife? The text makes the answer clear. The husband submits himself to his wife by lovingly, selflessly, and sacrificially taking the initiative to put her needs before his own (Eph. 5:25–33a). This is Christ-like leadership. Robertson quips that while the NT pictures the husband as the head of the home, it does so assuming "the husband has a head and a wise one."[2] The wife subjects herself to her husband through submissive respect (Eph. 5:33b). This affirms that both husband and wife submit to one another. Still, it rightly distinguishes the *way* in which each does so according to the wise and redemptive order established by God.

Peter qualifies the command by way of an adverb (Ὁμοίως). It means something like "likewise," "so," "similarly" or, as here, "In the same way."[3] Peter will use it again in verse 7 with reference to the responsibilities of husbands and in 5:5 of younger men to elders. Thus, the matter of authority and submission is a responsibility laid upon each of God's people, not simply wives. Authority and submission are part of the warp and woof of human relationships as designed by God.[4] The adverb tells us there is a comparison to be drawn. In the present case, it is between the way the wives are to respond to their husbands and something Peter has already stated. The question is, submit "In the same way" as

> **Ministry Maxim**
>
> Submission to legitimate authority is a missional act.

what precisely? How far back does the adverb look for its point of comparison? "In the same way" as all Christian citizens submit to their governing authorities (2:13–17)? "In the same way" as servants submit to their masters, even when they are unjust (2:18–20)? "In the same way" as Christ submitted Himself to the Father in undergoing unjust suffering and ultimately death itself (2:21–25)? It seems best to view the frame of reference

---

2   Robertson, *Word Pictures*, 4:506.

3   BDAG, 5296.

4   For more on authority and submission see the author's *Embracing Authority* (Fearn, Tain: Christian Focus Publications, 2002).

as most immediately referring to Christ (2:21–25). Then secondarily, it may reflect the counsel given to "servants" (2:18–20) and even citizens (2:13–17) as those who also follow Christ's example and submit to those who may or may not be just in their dealings with them. Peter is not in this way saying the relationship of a wife to her husband is the same as that of citizens to their governing leaders or slaves to their masters. They are fundamentally different, but in all three matters, we find the divine imperative for submission and the divine pattern in Christ, though each of the relationships is fundamentally different.

Peter calls for submission to attain a specific purpose (ἵνα + future indicative).[5] The purpose is that their husbands "may be won" (κερδηθήσονται). The verb means "to acquire by effort or investment."[6] The verb is used five times in 1 Corinthians 9:19–22 of Paul's wish to "win" others to faith in Christ. Peter thus encourages a wife's submission to her husband not because it may pay immediate dividends in making her life easier but because it may yet yield something precious—her husband's submission to Christ (cf. the verb in Matt. 18:15). The future tense invites her to make her present submission a faith-investment in hopes of a future return. The passive voice pictures the husband as under the influence of his wife's example, being used by the Holy Spirit to convict his heart.

Peter pictures the husband's surrender to Christ coming about "without a word" (ἄνευ λόγου). The preposition (ἄνευ, "without") is found only three times in the NT (Matt. 10:29; 1 Peter 3:1; 4:9). It indicates separation, but not in a spatial sense.[7] In both of Peter's usages, it is the absence of verbal communication that is in view, "a word" (λόγου, 3:1) and "complaint" (γογγυσμοῦ, 4:9). The expression here means, "without their saying a word"[8] or "without a word being spoken."[9]

---

5   One would expect a subjunctive with ἵνα here with rather than the future indicative, but the later "functions as an equivalent in such purpose clauses" (Dubis, 85).

6   BDAG, 4209; cf. Louw-Nida, 57.189.

7   Harris, 242.

8   Louw-Nida, 89.120.

9   Harris, 243.

A condition qualifies the goal of the husband's salvation: "even if any of them are disobedient to the word" (καὶ εἴ τινες ἀπειθοῦσιν τῷ λόγῳ). The condition (εἴ + future indicative) assumes, for the sake of the argument, the reality of the believing wives being married to unbelieving, "disobedient" husbands. This was not the usual case[10] but was not uncommon (cf. Paul's instruction in 1 Cor. 7:12–16). The καὶ is used emphatically in the condition to stress what would be a worst-case scenario ("even"). Wives should be "submissive" as a standard course of relating to their husbands, but they should do so "even" in the sad scenario that Peter suggests. By "the word" (τῷ λόγῳ), Peter means the gospel (cf. 1 Peter 1:23; 2:8). The verb was already used in 2:8 to describe "those who disbelieve" (2:7). The gospel calls for belief, so to "disbelieve" is to "disobey" the gospel (cf. its use also in 1 Peter 3:20; 4:17). The present tense pictures the abiding nature of the husbands under consideration. The verb is strong, indicating perhaps not simple unbelief but active rejection of and opposition to the gospel.

Peter's point is made more powerfully by his play on words. The wife's refusal to speak "a word" (λόγου) in the face of an unbelieving husband's unjust treatment may be the very thing that opens him to hear again "the word" (τῷ λόγῳ) of the gospel.

Rather than well-worded apologies for the faith, it is "by the behavior of their wives" (διὰ τῆς τῶν γυναικῶν ἀναστροφῆς) that unbelieving husbands are brought to consider seriously the gospel. The preposition διὰ is used to designate the means, instrument, or agency "by" which the unbelieving husbands may be "won." That is, literally translated, "the of the wives' behavior." Peter puts "their wives" (τῶν γυναικῶν; the article understood as possessive, i.e., "their") in the attributive position between the noun and its definite article (τῆς ... ἀναστροφῆς) to stress the new way of life that characterizes such wives. The noun ἀναστροφή ("conduct") is a significant word in Peter's letters, where eight of its thirteen appearances in the NT are found (1 Peter 1:15, 18; 2:12; 3:1, 2, 16; 2 Peter 2:7;

---

10 In Roman-Greco society the wife normally embraced the husband's religion (Clowney, 129; Davids, 115; Forbes, 98; Hiebert, 197; Jobes, 203; Marshall, 98; Michaels, 157; Schreiner, 150).

3:11; cf. the verbal cognate ἀναστρέφω in 1:17). Literally it means "a turning about in place." It then came to designate one's daily behavior.[11] That moment-by-moment conduct is pictured as driven by certain principles[12], for good (1 Tim. 4:12; Heb. 13:7; James 3:13; 1 Peter 1:15; 2:12; 3:1, 2, 16; 2 Peter 3:11) or ill (Gal. 1:13; Eph. 4:22; 1 Peter 1:18). The wickedness of the people of Sodom and Gomorrah drove their behavior (2 Peter 2:7), so the holiness of the One who called them drives believers. Peter has no time for a faith that is mere talk and finds no expression in the way one lives. What fills the heart and possesses the mind is worked out in words and actions (Matt. 12:34; Luke 6:45). This is what makes the apologetic for the gospel so powerful in the lives of recalcitrant husbands. Their wives are not the women they married; they have been fundamentally changed on the inside in such a way that it causes them to behave differently. The wives' responsibility under God is to see that this change casts the gospel in a positive light in their husbands' lives.

Verse 2 – as they observe your chaste and respectful behavior.

Peter says that unbelieving husbands will be "won" for Christ "as they observe" (ἐποπτεύσαντες) their wives' lives. The verb is used elsewhere in the NT only in 2:12 when Peter laid on all believers the obligation to so live, that "because of your good deeds, as they observe [ἐποπτεύοντες] them, [they may] glorify God in the day of visitation." Peter's instruction here to wives is not unusual or confined to only them but is an application of what is required of all followers of Christ. Peter uses the cognate noun to identify himself and James and John as "eyewitness" (ἐπόπται) of Jesus' glory on the Mount of Transfiguration (2 Peter 1:16). The verb itself implies both continuity and intent.[13] It thus suggests that they have regularly observed their wives' behavior and found time and again that "the Spirit of glory and of God rests on" them (1 Peter 4:14). Here, the aorist

---

11   Friberg, 52.
12   BDAG, 566.
13   Louw-Nida, 24.45.

tense depicts the husband's observation of the individual acts of the wife.[14] The participle is usually understood as indicating a temporal relationship to the main verb ("*as* they observe," emphasis added; "when," ESV, NET, NIV; NKJV; NRSV), but some translate it as instrumental ("by," NLT) or causal ("because," CEV).

> **Ministry Maxim**
>
> One's fear of the Lord is both an exhortation and invitation to others.

What they observe is their wife's "behavior" (τὴν ... ἀναστροφὴν). The noun was used in verse 1, which see for more on its meaning. The singular form is probably intended to picture individual acts and the decisions that lead to them. Again and again, in each moment, difficult or not, the wives choose a new path of life. The husbands cannot help but notice.

The behavior the husbands behold is described in two ways, one by a prepositional phrase and the other by an adjective, both of which are in the attributive position between the main noun (ἀναστροφὴν, "behavior") and its definite article (τὴν). In this way, Peter stresses the qualitative nature of the "behavior" of the wives (ὑμῶν, "their"). Their behavior is "chaste" (ἁγνὴν) and also "respectful" (ἐν φόβῳ), which is a reversal of the word order in the Greek text. We will consider them in the order given to us in the original.

The preposition (ἐν, "in") is used to indicate the manner in which one is to conduct one's life.[15] The wife's fear (φόβῳ, "respect") is not set upon her husband and any repercussions he may bring upon her. Instead, it is the fear of the Lord in which she conducts herself. This is clear by the way the phrase is used elsewhere in Scripture. The same phrase (ἐν φόβῳ, "in fear") is used five other times in the NT. Paul uses it of "the fear of God" (2 Cor. 7:1) or Christ (Eph. 5:21). Jude uses it regarding our ministry of mercy to those in sin (Jude 23). Peter has already used it: "If you address as Father the One who impartially judges according to each one's work,

---

14 Some manuscripts have a present participial form of the verb rather than the aorist participle. But the wider support lies with the aorist (Dubis, 85–86; Forbes, 99; Michaels, 154–155).

15 Louw-Nida, 89.84; cf. Abernathy, 43–44.

conduct yourselves in fear [ἐν φόβῳ] during the time of your stay on earth" (1 Peter 1:17, see our comments there). The husband recognizes a beautiful change in his wife's behavior that is not born out of fear of his ill-treatment of her but from a higher, holy fear that longs to please the Lord and, therefore, him as well. This is a powerful ministry and a winsome apologetic for the gospel.

The verbal adjective (ἁγνὴν, "chaste") originally signified "that which awakens religious awe."[16] It describes that which is "awe-inspiring."[17] It is the characteristic quality of Jesus' life (1 John 3:3). It is what Christ finds His Bride to be upon His return (2 Cor. 11:2). It is what older women are to teach younger women (Titus 2:5). It is among the virtues upon which all believers are to let their minds dwell (Phil. 4:8). It is the first mark of divine wisdom (James 3:17). It certainly refers to sexual propriety, but its circle extends to include all the affairs of life. The wife is to so live that her holy fear of God is reflected in her conduct within her home, marriage, and the wider world. This "serves as another reminder that the submission Peter commands must never go so far as to include obedience to demands to do something that is morally wrong."[18]

> **Digging Deeper:**
> 1. Is Peter demanding more of wives than he does of husbands (cf. v.7)?
> 2. In what ways is Peter's instruction to wives like and unlike his instruction to all believers? (vv.1–2)
> 3. How have you seen the witness of deeds win where verbal witness was unwelcome?

---

16 TDNT, 1:123.

17 NIDNTTE, 1:138.

18 Grudem, 147.

Verse 3 – Your adornment must not be *merely* external—braiding the hair, and wearing gold jewelry, or putting on dresses;

Peter continues speaking to "wives," developing what "behavior" will be most likely to win their husbands for Christ (vv.1–2). Just what makes for "chaste and respectful" behavior (v.2)? Peter answers by describing the external (v.3) and internal (v.4) beauty for which wives should strive. He does so by way of a "not...but" (οὐχ...ἀλλ') contrast, verse 3 occupied with the "not" and verse 4 occupied with the contrasting positive.

A relative pronoun (ὧν, "Your") looks back to "your" (ὑμῶν) of verse 2, which ultimately looks back to "wives" ([αἱ] γυναῖκες, v.1) for its antecedent. It is safe to say that Peter would not have applied what he says here only to married women but to females considered more broadly. Yet we must remember the missional purpose of his present counsel to women married to unbelieving, recalcitrant husbands (v.1).

Peter issues a second command to wives (ἔστω, "must...be"). The present imperative with negation (οὐχ) may signal that action already underway be discontinued. The negation (οὐκ, "not") is absolute and categorical.[19] The prohibition relates to a wife's "adornment" (ὁ...κόσμος). The noun κόσμος fundamentally describes that which is well-ordered or arranged.[20] It describes the physical creation (Acts 17:24), humankind which dwells within it (Mark 16:15), as well as that organized system over which the devil presides and which actively opposes God (1 John 5:19). Here, the emphasis is upon the woman as lord over her outward appearance.

> **Ministry Maxim**
> Nothing attracts like that which cannot be put on.

She sets out to establish "order" over her physical features. Our English word *cosmetics* is derived from the original κόσμος. The woman has the power to do with her hair, clothing, face, etc., as she sees fit. But the

---

19 Thayer, 408.
20 BDAG, 4371; Friberg, 235; NIDNTTE, 2:731; TDNT, 3:868; Thayer, 356–357.

women Peter has in mind have come under the reign of a new Master; Jesus is now Lord of every part of their lives, including their bodies (Rom. 6:19; 12:1). The Apostle Paul would ask, "do you not know that your body is a temple of the Holy Spirit who is in you, whom you have from God, and that you are not your own?" (1 Cor. 6:19). He reminds them that they have been "bought with a price" and are responsible now to "glorify God in your body" (v.20). It is theirs to so order their lives and bodies after the wishes and mission of their Master, Jesus.

The noun and its definite article (ὁ ... κόσμος) are separated by a lengthy clause comprised of nine words, all set in the attributive position describing the nature of the "adornment" under question. They define what is "not" (οὐχ) to constitute the wives' ordering of the "beauty" of the physical attributes God has given them.

Such "adorning" is not to be "external" (ἔξωθεν). The adverb of place is used as an adjective.[21] It describes that which is "outside," in this case, descriptive of what can be seen by those around the woman. Does Peter speak absolutely (the woman must never do anything to her "external" members to beautify herself) or inclusively (she must not be concerned only or primarily with making herself beautiful on the outside)? The NASU and NKJV have sided with the latter by adding in italics the word "*merely*." Most English versions allow the unadorned original to stand (e.g., "external," ESV; "outward," NIV) and allow the reader to determine Peter's intent. The last of the three attributive phrases may help us understand the point.[22] The first two ("braiding the hair, and wearing gold jewelry") might be read as absolute prohibitions, but the third ("putting on dresses") cannot, for clearly, women walking around without clothing would violate the Lord's intent. It is likely that Peter is saying the external (whether hairstyles, jewelry, clothing, or the like) is to take second place to the internal and is be made subservient to the King and His Kingdom.

---

21 BDAG, 2825.3.

22 Forbes, 100.

Peter then uses three phrases to address a woman's hair, jewelry, and clothing. All three could be used as tools to make a social (hair, jewelry, and dresses could all be used as signs of status) or sexual (cf. the contrasting "chaste," v.2) statement.

First is "braiding the hair" (ἐμπλοκῆς τριχῶν). The care and styling of "hair" (τριχῶν) is a major part of one's presentation to the world. Here "braiding" (ἐμπλοκῆς) is the concern. The word is used only here in the NT. Peter's concern was probably not the simple three-strand weave of a woman's longer hair, sometimes undertaken for ease of movement and protection of the hair. Rather, he likely has in mind more elaborate plaiting, which often included weaving beads and other ornaments into one's hair and was undertaken to draw attention to oneself.[23]

Second (καὶ, "and") is "wearing gold jewelry" (περιθέσεως χρυσίων). Literally, it is "putting on gold." The first noun is found only here in the NT. It is a compound made up of περί ("around") and θέσις ("setting, placing, arranging").[24] It is used then of putting something around oneself and thus wearing it. Here it is applied to "gold" (χρυσίων). Designating it "jewelry" is an interpretive move by the translators, but probably an accurate one, for to wrap oneself in "gold" is probably to be pictured as putting on rings, bracelets, necklaces, and the like. Certainly, not all such jewelry is wrong, for we read at times of such things in an acceptable light (Gen. 24:22, 30, 47; Job 42:11; Ezek. 16:10–13; Luke 15:22). But ultimately, gold is "perishable" (1 Peter 1:7, 18) while the inheritance the Lord has prepared for all His people is "imperishable" (1:4). In the next verse He will, through Peter, counsel redeemed women to busy themselves with seeking "the imperishable quality of a gentle and quiet spirit, which is precious in the sight of God" (3:4).

Third (ἤ, "or") is "putting on dresses" (ἐνδύσεως ἱματίων). Peter again uses a noun found only here in the NT. It also is a compound, being built of the prefix ἐν ("in") added to the root verb δύω (used with clothes, "get

---

23 Friberg, 147.

24 Liddell-Scott, 20508, 33901.

into," "put on").[25] The noun "dresses" (ἱματίων) is a general one referring to clothing or garments generally, for either gender and of whatever age. In our world of disposable fashions, we fail to comprehend the role clothing played in the ancient near east. Clothing could be a means of investment for the future. It might denote honor, rank, favor, and dignity (e.g., Mark 12:38; James 2:2; Rev. 1:13; 6:11; 7:9; 19:16). The Lord Himself detailed the elaborate and ornate nature of the High Priest's clothing (Exod. 28). Indeed, they were to be made "for glory and for beauty" (28:2, 40). When the father received his prodigal son, he "said to his slaves, 'Quickly bring out the best robe and put it on him, and put a ring on his hand and sandals on his feet'" (Luke 15:22).

The problem was not with dignity and with one's outer presentation confirming that dignity. The problem was the quest for honor by means of one's outward attire. This is a backward orientation and the reverse of Kingdom values. A person is to pursue dignity of character. That dignity cannot help but show up in one's countenance, bearing, carriage, and deportment. But to seek to gain by external adornment what the inner person does not already possess is the sign of a heart not yet fulfilled in its King and caught up with His Kingdom. By contrast, consider how the two women of Proverbs are set before us—madame folly (Prov. 9:13–18) and woman wisdom (Prov. 1:20–33; 8:1–36; 9:1–6; 31:10–31).

In a world bent on demanding the individual's rights, the follower of Jesus Christ, male or female, stands out as one bent first on their responsibility under Christ, bound by His glory and mission. They seek that "which is precious in the sight of God" (1 Peter 3:4). This posture and position affect every area of life. Under the Old Covenant, there were constraints upon the outward appearance of men, including hair (Lev. 19:27; 21:5) and clothing (Deut. 22:5). The Bible clearly continues to lay upon both genders the demand to bring their physical bodies and all that pertains to them under the lordship of Jesus Christ (Rom. 12:1–2; 1 Cor. 6:19–20). Whenever God speaks to one entity (specifically in this case, married women), we must receive God's Word without demanding,

---

25 Liddell-Scott, 14572, 12050.

"What about the others?" As if any of us are positioned to judge God's Word and determine if it is reasonable or acceptable to us.

Paul shared Peter's concern: "Likewise, I want women to adorn themselves with proper clothing, modestly and discreetly, not with braided hair and gold or pearls or costly garments, but rather by means of good works, as is proper for women making a claim to godliness" (1 Tim. 2:9–10). Isaiah sounded a similar alarm (Isa. 3:18–24).

Concerning dress, hairstyling, jewelry, makeup, and other adornments, a godly woman avoids both the extravagant and the erotic. She avoids advertising either the lavish or the sensual. She knows she is a woman and dresses the part (Deut. 22:5), but she increasingly lets her heart and the conduct and words that flow from it make her statement to the world. Her King and His Kingdom have rearranged her understanding of beauty, propriety, and dignity. Godly women aim for beauty but for the right kind of beauty. Simplicity and modesty are cardinal virtues of a Christian woman's values. We miss the Lord's intent if we find here counsel for women to "let themselves go" and become dowdy, drab, and sloven.

Verse 4 – but *let it be* the hidden person of the heart, with the imperishable quality of a gentle and quiet spirit, which is precious in the sight of God.

As the extended relative clause continues (vv.3–4), we now encounter the contrasting (οὐχ … ἀλλ', "not … but") picture of true beauty. It is not outward "adornment" (v.3) that makes for genuine beauty but "the hidden person of the heart" (ὁ κρυπτὸς τῆς καρδίας ἄνθρωπος). When Peter speaks to "wives" (v.1) concerning "the … person" (ὁ … ἄνθρωπος) of their inner being, he uses a masculine noun. This establishes that ἄνθρωπος is not always a gender-specific noun but can refer, as here, more broadly to humans. We are more than bodies; we are persons. While our bodies are the medium through which we encounter and live in the world, they do not represent the totality or even the most fundamental part of who we are. After our bodies die, we live on—somewhere. We are souls in mortal bodies. And it is that inward, incorporeal "person" that is most essential. The physical body is a lamp for "the … person" we are within.

Two qualifiers rest in the attributive position between the noun and its definite article, telling us more about the essence of "the … person" that is most fundamental. That "person" is "hidden" (κρυπτὸς). The adjective denotes that which is concealed or secret.[26] As such, it is the opposite of "external" (ἔξωθεν, v.3). A person's inner being is "hidden" in the sense that it is not subject to the senses—it is not physical, so it cannot be seen; it is not tangible, so it cannot be touched; it is not odorous, so it cannot be smelled; it is not audible, so it cannot be heard. And yet it makes itself known by one's acts and attitude, one's words and ways. That "person" is fundamentally "of the heart" (τῆς καρδίας). The genitive should be understood as appositional or epexegetical; the "person of the heart" is the person we are in our hearts.[27] We cannot be otherwise. Who we are in our hearts is who we truly are, all our "external" efforts notwithstanding. The "of the heart" person is who we are when we are stripped of all else, including our bodies. The "heart" is the seat of one's intellect and rational process, affections and choices, and emotions and feelings. It is where we are either pure (Matt. 5:8) or sinful (v.28). Its reality erupts to the observable world through our words (12:34). Yet it is possible to honor God with our lips even while our hearts are far from Him (15:8). It is the seat of all depravity (v.19). It is the locus of our response to God (22:37); that place where our relationship to Christ is determined (1 Peter 3:15). Paul calls it "our inner man" (Rom. 7:22; 2 Cor. 4:16). In Christ "the old self" is dead and gone, and we have been raised "a new self," which is "being renewed to a true knowledge according to the image of the One who created him" (Col. 3:9–10).

True beauty is to be found "with the imperishable quality" (ἐν τῷ ἀφθάρτῳ) that stands the test of time. Beauty is found not "in" the realm of the physical and external, no matter how spectacular and/or sensual (1 Peter 3:3). It is found "in" (ἐν, "with") the sphere of "the imperishable" (τῷ ἀφθάρτῳ). Peter uses the adjective as a substantive and adds to it the definite article. Peter has already used it to speak of the "imperishable"

---

26 Thayer, 362.
27 Dubis, 88; Forbes, 100.

nature of the gospel-seed by which we have been brought to new life (1:23) and of the nature of our resulting inheritance in Christ (1:4). With the Spirit that gave us new birth continuing to conform us to the image of Christ and with our eternal inheritance set before us as our hope, our hearts are transformed into that which will not perish with the passing of time or the corroding effects of sin. Time and gravity will affect upon the physical body (2 Cor. 4:16) and the things that might adorn it (Matt. 6:19–20). But the person of the heart can abound and grow and thrive, being continually renewed (Rom. 12:2; Eph. 4:23; Col. 3:10) and becoming more beautiful over time. "Therefore we do not lose heart, but though our outer man is decaying, yet our inner man is being renewed day by day" (2 Cor. 4:16).

The effect of this renewing process (sanctification) is that our inner person, our "heart" begins to take on a particular kind of "spirit" (τοῦ ... πνεύματος). This "spirit" is not to be identified as the Holy Spirit.[28] The noun is used to describe the general tenor, disposition, or nature of "the hidden person" we truly are. This, of course, is only possible by the working of the Holy Spirit. The definite article signals that a specific kind of "spirit" is in view. This is set forth in two adjectives joined (καὶ, "and") in the attributive position between the noun and its definite article.

> **Ministry Maxim**
>
> A woman of inward strength possesses a beautiful power with which good looks cannot compete.

This "spirit" is first to be characterized as "gentle" (πραέως). The adjective is found only four times in the NT. It characterizes the heart (Matt. 11:29) and manner of Jesus (21:5) as well as those blessed to live under his reign (Matt. 5:5). Peter, having personally observed Jesus' nature and ways, commends it to women as the adornment of true beauty. It is the fruit of the Holy Spirit's ministry in a person (Gal. 5:23) and is enjoined

---

28 Kelly points out, "since this gentle spirit is commended as pleasing to God, it can hardly be the divine Spirit" (130).

upon all God's people, men and women, married and single (Eph. 4:2; Col. 3:12; James 1:21; 1 Peter 3:15). It is not weakness, but power under control. It depicts a "fine blend of spiritual poise and strength."[29] It "does not show itself when we are wrong, but when we are right... It reveals itself when I am right and when I have the power to hurt someone who is wrong."[30] Gentleness is the ability to accept God's dealings with me without complaint, receive what God allows in my life without wrangling, see the others in my life as tools in God's hand, and to embrace them rather than destroy them. Gentleness means not that I am too weak to do anything about the offenses of others, but that I am strong enough not to do what I want naturally to do about them. It is leaving myself, my rights, my future, and my all in God's hands and trusting Him with them, rather than feeling the need to manipulate things to turn out as I think they should. Gentleness rests upon the triangulation of three great realities: God's sovereignty, love, and wisdom. My life and all its details are surrounded by, under the control of, and being arranged amid these three realities. Gentleness reins in my power because I realize my life is under a greater power, one directed by a ruling, wise, and loving hand. Peter uses the noun form to describe a believer's response to those who ask about their hope (1 Peter 3:15).

In addition (καὶ, "and"), the spirit of beauty is "quiet" (ἡσυχίου). The adjective is found in the NT only here and in 1 Timothy 2:2 where Paul calls for prayer "for kings and all who are in authority, so that we may lead a tranquil and quiet [ἡσύχιον] life in all godliness and dignity." The cognate noun demonstrates that this, too, is a quality required of all God's people (2 Thess. 3:12; cf. its use in Acts 22:2 and 1 Tim. 2:11–12). By "quiet," Peter does not here mean so much audible silence (though cf. "without a word," v.1), but centers on a "mildness of character: a spirit that calmly bears the disturbances created by others and that does not

---

29 Robertson, *Word Pictures*, 1:41.

30 Wiersbe, *Live Like a King*, 71.

itself create disturbances."³¹ It is "the opposite of agitation, impatience, annoyance, notably of compulsive discussion."³²

In short, this woman proves that she is now operating out of a foundation and center that is not of this world or her earthly circumstances. The locus of her life has changed. The circumstances of her home, marriage, and life are now dealt with from an unseen power source which renders her able to engage with her husband (and others) out of a position of strength, not fear or weakness. This newfound power might terrify an unbelieving husband were it not obvious to him, however unimaginable it may seem, that she employs it for his good and not to manipulate or control him. She possesses a beautiful power with which mere good looks cannot compete.

This constitutes beauty "which is precious in the sight of God" (ὅ ἐστιν ἐνώπιον τοῦ θεοῦ πολυτελές). The relative pronoun (ὅ, "which") looks back to "the spirit" (τοῦ ... πνεύματος) or possibly the entirety of verse 4. The verb (ἐστιν, "is") is in the present tense, depicting its abiding, continuous evaluation in the eyes of God. The translation "in the sight of" represents a simpler and more literal "before God" (ἐνώπιον τοῦ θεοῦ). The preposition (ἐνώπιον) can mean both "in the presence of" and "in the opinion of."³³ It is combined with θεός ("God") in the NT to depict His immediate insight and knowledge and our constant examination under His gaze (e.g., Gal. 1:20; 1 Tim. 2:3; 5:4, 21; 6:13; 2 Tim. 2:14; 4:1). Before God's throne and in His estimation such a "spirit" is "precious" (πολυτελές). Spicq says that in "its various usages, this adjective means 'oppressively expensive' or 'rare and luxurious,' even 'sumptuous' ... in any event requiring a major outlay."³⁴ It is used only two other times in the NT, both of which express that which is of high monetary value, whether perfume (Mark 14:3) or clothing (1 Tim. 2:9). Both are telling cross references to Peter's statement here. Given Peter's counsel above in verse 3 the

---

31   NIDNTTE, 2:400.

32   Spicq, 2:183.

33   Harris, 245.

34   Spicq, 3:135.

1 Timothy passage presents an insightful contrast to Peter's evaluation of what is truly valuable. Peter had been sitting in Jesus' presence as that costly vile of perfume was broken and poured upon Him as an anointing. He may have been among those protesting its "waste" (Matt. 26:8; Mark 14:4). It is fitting, then, that Peter uses the same adjective here to describe God's evaluation of what makes a woman truly beautiful, for Jesus' proclaimed, "She has done a beautiful thing to me" (Mark 14:6, ESV, NIV, RSV). Though it was a "beautiful" act, note the fleeting nature of the perfume's fragrance compared to the enduring nature of the blessing pronounced by Jesus upon her (v.9). "Charm is deceitful and beauty is vain, But a woman who fears the LORD, she shall be praised" (Prov. 31:30). Indeed, "man looks at the outward appearance, but the LORD looks at the heart" (1 Sam. 16:7).

> **Digging Deeper:**
> 1. How can the counsel of verses 3–4 be set before the women in your church so as to be understood clearly and received positively?
> 2. Detail ways youth leaders might help girls and young women shape their lives around Peter's counsel.
> 3. Can a Christian woman fulfill these demands while working in the fashion industry? Explain your answer.

Verse 5 – For in this way in former times the holy women also, who hoped in God, used to adorn themselves, being submissive to their own husbands;"

Peter now moves to close his words to "wives" (v.1ff) with an explanatory (γάρ, "For") sentence that looks back to how "the holy women" of the past (v.5) and "Sarah" in particular (v.6) conducted themselves. The γάρ ("For") introduces the two illustrations as evidence that this strategy for "wives" with unbelieving husbands has historical precedent. The καὶ ("also") is adverbial and serves to lay the pattern of these women alongside the counsel Peter has set forth to the believing wives addressed in his letter.

Peter begins with the generalized illustration of "the holy women" (αἱ ἅγιαι γυναῖκες) and how they lived "in former times" (ποτε). They are counted "holy" (ἅγιαι) because they had met Him who alone is holy and had been drawn into the gravitational pull of His grace (1 Peter 1:15–16). As such, they are worthy examples for those who through Christ have become a "holy priesthood" (2:5) and a "HOLY NATION" (2:9). Peter makes them a specific (note the definite article) but indefinite group. Michaels would limit them to the four wives of Abraham, Isaac, and Jacob.[35] He may be correct, but Peter does not confirm his guess.

The adverb οὕτως ("in this way") looks back to what has already been said (vv.1–4) and signifies "in this manner."[36] So "the holy women" of old adorned their lives as Peter called wives reading/hearing his letter to adorn their lives (vv.1–4). He cites how they "used to adorn themselves" (ἐκόσμουν ἑαυτάς). The verb (ἐκόσμουν, "used to adorn") is cognate to the noun just used in verse 3 (κόσμος, "adornment"). See our comments there for more on the word family. The imperfect tense of the verb is used to designate "customary action."[37] The reflexive pronoun (ἑαυτάς, "themselves") indicates the action is taken upon themselves—the subject is also the object of the action.[38]

> **Ministry Maxim**
>
> Submission in marriage says more about one's relationship to God than to one's husband.

These women of the past trusted not in external adornment in dealing with their husbands but focused instead on "the hidden person of the heart" adorned with "a gentle and quiet spirit" (v.4). This constituted them women "who hoped in God" (αἱ ἐλπίζουσαι εἰς θεόν). The articular participle is substantive ("*who*

---

35   Michaels, 164; cf. Forbes, 101.
36   Friberg, 289.
37   Rienecker, 756.
38   Wallace, 350–351; 413–414.

hoped," emphasis added). It designates attendant circumstances. Peter has reminded them that they have been born again into a living hope that is so precisely because it rests upon a Savior who forever lives at the Father's right hand (1:3). Thus, he has told them, "your faith and hope are in God" (1:21). Such hope cannot stay hidden and thus provides all believers an opportunity "to give an account for the hope that is in" them (3:15). Therefore, Peter has already commanded all believers, male and female, married and single, to "fix your hope" (1:13). For wives of unbelieving husbands, that includes taking the prescribed steps Peter has outlined (vv. 1–4). The preposition εἰς ("in") is directional and signifies movement "into" something. Thus their "hope" had moved "into" and was resting exclusively upon God.

This is notable, for Peter does not say their hope was in a superior evangelistic strategy. They did not say, "Words aren't working, so let's switch it up and just act nicer. It will blow our husbands' minds!" (v.2). Rather, they aligned themselves with God through obedience and conformity to His will and trusted to Him their husbands and their opposition to their new faith. It is not that these women chose not "to adorn themselves." It became a matter of that with which they would adorn themselves. They discovered that as it regards the gospel, internal adornment of the heart is more powerful than external adornment of the body.

The corollary to being women "who hoped in God" was "being submissive to their own husbands" (ὑποτασσόμεναι τοῖς ἰδίοις ἀνδράσιν). Their internal rest in God permitted the external submission to their husbands. Their inward "quiet and gentle spirit" (v.4) expressed itself toward God as they set their hope on him (1:13) and toward their husbands as they were "submissive" to them. They could only act relationally toward their husbands because they had acted relationally toward their God. The participle (ὑποτασσόμεναι, "being submissive") describes the way these women "adorned themselves" ("by submitting," ESV, NET, NRSV). The verb was used in verse 1 (cf. 1 Peter 2:13, 18) and creates an inclusion as Peter's counsel to women married to unbelieving husbands is wrapped by this practice. The present tense marks this as their standard mode of operation. The passive voice probably should be read as having the force of the middle—the wives acted upon themselves to live in submission to their husbands. This was a voluntary, personal act of trust in God, not one coerced by the husband. Peter again underscores that this is a choice made by each of the wives regarding how they will relate "to their own husbands" (τοῖς ἰδίοις ἀνδράσιν). It does not speak generally of male/female relationships.

Verse 6 – "just as Sarah obeyed Abraham, calling him lord, and you have become her children if you do what is right without being frightened by any fear."

Peter moves from the general example of "holy women of old" (v.5) to the specific example of Sarah. What "the holy women" of old did (v.5) was "just as" (ὡς) Sarah had done toward Abraham. The conjunction (ὡς) is not intended to signal an exact comparison but introduces an additional example.[39] They "hoped in God," adorning themselves by "being submissive to their husbands." But we are told "Sarah obeyed Abraham" (Σάρρα ὑπήκουσεν τῷ Ἀβραάμ). The verb (ὑπήκουσεν, "obeyed") meant "to answer the door" and thus "to obey as a result of listening."[40] The prepositional prefix (ὑπό, "under") underscores the notion of submission that is present in the word.[41] The aorist tense may be constative, looking at the whole of Sarah's life with Abraham. Or it may look to an event rather than a pattern of ongoing behavior.

When did Sarah thus obey Abraham? Perhaps Peter is looking to her compliance when twice Abraham lied about her being his wife (Gen. 12:11–12; 20:2). But this raises questions. When it comes to submission, whether as citizens to governing authorities (1 Peter 2:13–17), slaves to masters (2:18–20), wives to husbands (3:1–6), or any other legitimate realm of delegated authority, we rightly reserve use of the exception clause that Peter himself employed before the Jewish Sanhedrin (Acts 4:19–20; 5:29). Submission is the right response to legitimate, God-delegated

---

39 BDAG, 8075.2.d.α.

40 Rienecker, 552.

41 Ibid.

authority up until either they require something clearly forbidden by God or they forbid something clearly required by God. Lying is clearly against God's will (e.g., Lev.19:11; Eph. 4:25; Col. 3:9; 1 Tim. 1:10). Peter says Sarah "obeyed" Abraham. Our question, then, is not merely how Sarah might provide cover for Abraham in his lies but how then Peter could cite her as a worthy example of proper submission within marriage. Grudem cites Peter's call for wives to "do what is right" (1 Peter 3:6) as 'a reminder that no acts of disobedience in Sarah's life are to be imitated by Christian wives."[42]

Are submission (vv.1, 5) and obedience (v.6) one and the same? In most circumstances, we can answer in the affirmative, but not in all. Peter calls for submission as the consistently correct response (vv.1, 5). He cites Sarah's obedience as one example of what submission usually looks like. But Peter once found himself in an extreme position where submission and obedience were no longer able to be considered a single entity (Acts 4:19–20; 5:29). An attitude of submission is always possible (by the enabling of the Holy Spirit), but at times strict obedience may not be possible.

Some object that Sarah is not the correct illustration at this point, for her husband was not an unbeliever and did not object to her faith. But Peter probably cites her because of her relationship with her husband even when he was not acting like a believer, which was the case when he deceived regarding his wife. The parallel to Peter's present readers may not be exact, but it was sufficient to make the point.

Sarah obeyed Abraham, "calling him lord" (κύριον αὐτὸν καλοῦσα). The title (κύριον, "lord") was an indicator of deference and respect, not fawning servility. The text is not encouraging the use of the term within marriage today in cultures where the word may carry other connotations. Peter cites it as Sarah's sign of respect and submission to her husband within their culture. The only recorded instance of Sarah referring to Abraham as "lord" is when the Lord appeared to Abraham, promising that He would give him and his wife a child. But Sarah laughed in disbelief at

---

42 Grudem, 150.

the news, saying, "After I have become old, shall I have pleasure, my lord being old also?" (Gen. 18:12). At first blush, Sarah's use of "my lord" (κύριός μου, LXX) on this occasion does not seem to make the point Peter sets forth here. It could be suggested that we must take Peter's reference as a general one, describing not so much her words in any one instance, but the general tenor of her relationship with her husband. But another explanation is possible. It might be that Peter cites Sarah because, even in a low moment of doubt and even when she thought she was talking to no one but herself, she still called her husband "lord." She respected him and acknowledged his position within their relationship. If she then, in one of her lowest moments, did so, then the wives of unbelieving husbands in Peter's day could do the same. This seems more likely to be Peter's intent. The participle (καλοῦσα, "calling") has been variously understood as expressing attendant circumstances to the main verb[43] (ὑπήκουσεν, "obeyed"), the manner in which her obedience was displayed[44], and a temporal connection ("when she called him 'Lord.'").[45] The present tense describes Sarah's consistent and enduring way of relating to her husband.

Peter tells his readers that "you have become her children" (ἧς ἐγενήθητε τέκνα). The relative pronoun (ἧς, "her") reaches back to "Sarah" for its antecedent. The verb (ἐγενήθητε, "you have become") is aorist, looking back to the event of conversion. The verb is deponent, so the passive voice should be read as active.[46] This is probably a signal that Peter's readers were largely Gentile and would have had no claim to Abraham and Sarah apart from the grace of God extended in the gospel of Jesus Christ.[47] Here, the apostle to the circumcised (Gal. 2:8) further reiterates what he learned at

> **Ministry Maxim**
>
> Only fear can displace fear.

---

43 Dubis, 91.
44 Forbes, 102.
45 Michaels, 154, 164.
46 Abernathy, 117.
47 Davids, 121; Hiebert, 203; Kelly, 131.

the home of Cornelius (Acts 10:34–35) and shared with the leadership in Jerusalem, causing them to conclude: "Well then, God has granted to the Gentiles also the repentance that leads to life" (Acts 11:18). Covenant blessings come, not by physical lineage, but by grace, through spiritual rebirth: "it is those who are of faith who are sons of Abraham" (Gal 3:7; cf. 26; 4:21–31; Rom. 4:11; 9:7). Peter has already designated his readers as "children" (τέκνα, 1 Peter 1:14) of God by virtue of the new birth (1:3, 23). Now the wives of unbelieving husbands are designated "children" (τέκνα) of Sarah. Is Peter using the noun in the same sense in both cases? He uses it of what the new birth renders us by nature. He uses it of those who bear a family likeness to Sarah in terms of her relationship with her husband.[48] Covenant grace and standing produce covenant likeness and behavior. Peter may not be choosing between the two but allowing his general reference to include both.

Their affinity, however, to Sarah is contingent, "if you do what is right without being frightened by any fear" (ἀγαθοποιοῦσαι καὶ μὴ φοβούμεναι μηδεμίαν πτόησιν). There is much debate about how to read these two participles. The NASU translates them as conditional statements, as do many English translations (ESV, NIV, NKJV, RSV).[49] Still others have read the participles as instrumental,[50] temporal,[51] imperatival,[52] as indicating the means by which they demonstrate they are Sarah's children,[53] or as signaling result.[54]

The two participles are held parallel by the coordinating conjunction καὶ ("and," ESV, NET, NIV, NRSV). The NASU, however, does not translate καὶ and reads the second participle as qualifying or enlarging upon

---

48 BDAG, 7294.1.a; Friberg, 376; Louw-Nida, 10:36.
49 Wallace, 632–633; Schreiner, 158.
50 Bigg, 153–154.
51 Achtmeier, 216; cf. NET; NLT.
52 Michaels, 166–167.
53 Goppelt, 224.
54 Forbes, 103.

the first participle. It seems best to read them as parallel and complementary statements—the first stating the matter positively ("if you do what is right") and the second stating it negatively ("if you ... do not fear," ESV).

The first participle is "you do what is right" (ἀγαθοποιοῦσαι). Peter has already used the verb to call all God's people to this kind of living (2:15, 20) and will do so again (3:17). What is required of all Christ's people is held again before wives living with unbelieving husbands. The present tense depicts this as the pattern of one's life. Four of the verb's nine appearances in the NT are by Peter (cf. also the cognate adjective in 2:14). It is a compound built of ἀγαθός ("good") and ποιέω ("to do"). "The one who does good [ὁ ἀγαθοποιῶν] is of God; the one who does evil has not seen God" (3 John 11).

The second participle is "do not fear" (μὴ φοβούμεναι, ESV). Peter used the verb to command his readers to "Fear God" (τὸν θεὸν φοβεῖσθε, 2:17). More to his present point, he will use it again to call his readers to fearlessness before their persecutors (3:14). The prohibition (μὴ, "do not") "denies the thought of the thing, or the thing according to the judgment, opinion, will, purpose, preference, of someone."[55] They are not to fear "anything that is frightening" (μηδεμίαν πτόησιν, ESV). The noun (πτόησιν, "that is frightening") is used only here in the NT. In an active sense, it means the act of causing fear, "terrifying," or "intimidation," while in a passive sense, it means "something fearful" or "what is alarming."[56] Either is possible, but given the context, perhaps the passive notion with a meaning of "not fearing human intimidation" best captures the idea.[57] The adjective (μηδεμίαν, "anything"), when used with a noun, as it is here, eliminates all possibilities[58] and marks the negation as emphatic. Peter puts an absolute, total prohibition on wives living in terror of their husband's intimidations. How is this possible? We must connect the command of 2:17 ("Fear God") with Peter's counsel to wives

---

55 Thayer, 408.

56 Friberg, 338.

57 Ibid.

58 BDAG, 4889.

here. When the Lord is seen as bigger than and sovereign over any earthly fear (in this case, an unbelieving husband), then there is a new liberty of life. Proper, healthy fear displaces improper, unhealthy fear. Fear the Lord, and you need fear nothing else; do not fear the Lord, and you may come to fear almost anything.

In this last phrase, Peter may be reflecting the LXX rendering of Proverbs 3:25a (οὐ φοβηθήσῃ πτόησιν, "Do not be afraid of sudden fear").[59] He will quote Proverbs 3:34 later (1 Peter 5:5). Soon Peter, quoting Isaiah 8:12, will similarly exhort his readers, "DO NOT FEAR THEIR INTIMIDATION, AND DO NOT BE TROUBLED."

> **Digging Deeper:**
> 1. Would the appeal to believing women of the past be as powerful an apologetic for Christian women of the twenty-first century as it was for Peter's first century readers (vv.5–6)? Why or why not?
> 2. True or False: Submission in marriage is more a matter of a woman's relationship to God than her relationship to her husband (v.5). Why?
> 3. Are submission (v.5) and obedience (v.6) the same thing? What is the difference, if any?

Verse 7 – "You husbands in the same way, live with *your wives* in an understanding way, as with someone weaker, since she is a woman; and show her honor as a fellow heir of the grace of life, so that your prayers will not be hindered."

As Peter has addressed citizens (2:13–17), servants (2:18–25), and wives (3:1–6), so now he addresses "You husbands" (Οἱ ἄνδρες). The definite

---

[59] Forbes, 103; Michaels, 167; Robertson, *Word Pictures*, 6:110; Schreiner, 158; and compare Peter's "do good" (ESV) to Proverbs 3:27.

article marks this as a vocative. The grace of God in Christ holds a moral imperative over a husband's life with his wife.

The husband "in the same way" (ὁμοίως) as all other groupings within the church must live in a way that keeps the surrounding culture from speaking of them as evildoers because they see their good deeds and are ready to glorify God at Christ's return (2:12). The adverb ὁμοίως was used of wives (3:1), and there we saw that it looked back to Christ for comparison (2:21–25). Here Peter might then secondarily be linking to the instructions to "servants" (2:18–20), citizens (2:13–17), and "wives" (3:1–5). All of them must follow Jesus' example and submit to those who may or may not be just in their dealings with them. Once again, Peter is not insisting that all parallels of citizens, servants, wives, and husbands are exact. His point is that submission is required in every relationship in some fashion and is mandatory wherever and in whatever form it is required. Peter has transitioned from considering believing wives living with unbelieving husbands (3:1) to speaking directly to believing husbands living with their believing wives.

In what way, then, is a husband to practice these things within marriage? First, he is to "live with" (συνοικοῦντες) his wife in a particular way. The verb is found only here in the NT. It is a compound of σύν ("with") and οἰκέω ("to live," "to dwell"). The participle should be understood as having imperatival in force. The present tense sets forth what should be the regular and abiding pattern of the husband's relationship with his wife. The grace (2:4–10) and example of Christ (2:21–25) are to influence and transform every moment of every day and each interaction with his wife as they make a life together.

He is to live with her "in an understanding way" (κατὰ γνῶσιν). The translation represents an effort at rendering the more literal "according to knowledge" (ASV, KJV, YLT). Peter uses the noun (γνῶσιν, "knowledge") only here in the present letter, but he employs it in his second letter to speak of the knowledge of Christ in which the believer is to be constantly growing (2 Peter 1:5, 6; 3:18). What knowledge does Peter have in mind here? And what does it mean for a husband to thus "live with" his wife "according to" (κατὰ; KJV) that knowledge? Harris suggests three possibilities: the knowledge of a Christian "husband-wife relationship in general and sexual relationship in particular," his "knowledge of God's character and will," or "a considerate and tactful manner."⁶⁰ Perhaps Peter is thinking of the husband's knowledge of Christ, meaning his growing relationship with Christ must inform and control how he dwells with his wife. Surely that is true, but is it Peter's specific intent here? Peter's brevity and conciseness of expression leave us with a decision to make. Most English translations opt for some form of relational knowledge between the husband and his wife: "in an understanding way" (CSB, ESV, NASU), "with consideration" (NET), "be considerate" (NIV), "show consideration" (NRSV), "with understanding" (NKJV, NLT). If this is correct, how are we to understand what this knowledge involves and includes?

Peter identifies two markers that tell us if a husband is thinking rightly about his wife and shaping his daily life with her around that knowledge. He twice uses the comparative conjunction ὡς ("as") to set them before us.

The husband is to dwell with his wife "as with someone weaker" (ὡς ἀσθενεστέρῳ σκεύει). The ὡς ("as") sets forward a measure of the husband's knowledge and controls the way in which he is then to live with his wife.⁶¹ The noun (σκεύει, "someone") is more literally "vessel" (note the change of NASB to NASU). It designates "a container of any material used for a specific purpose, with the meaning varying according to the context."⁶² In this context, it depicts a person viewed from the angle of a particular function.⁶³ The function under consideration is her role and relationship as wife and, thus, all that goes into living life with her husband. In this, Peter says, she is comparatively "weaker" (ἀσθενεστέρῳ) than her husband. The comparative signals that both husband and wife are "vessels" crafted by God for His purposes. Of the two, she is the

> **Ministry Maxim**
> How you live with your wife impacts how God will listen to you.

---

60   Harris, 153.
61   Cf. BDAG, 8075.3.a.α.
62   Friberg, 350.
63   BDAG, 6697.3.

"weaker." In what sense can this be accurately stated? Certainly, the typical male is physically stronger than the typical female. Exceptions can be found, but Peter is thinking of the general state of things. Is this all Peter had in mind? The context would suggest that he had in mind also the marriage partner's comparative social strength. As citizens had less social clout and power than their political leaders (2:13–17) and as servants had less social standing and recourse than their masters (2:18–20), so in the first-century Roman world wives had less at their disposal socially and legally in dealing with their husbands. Peter is telling husbands to bear in mind that in terms of raw physical power and social recourse, husbands are in a position to sinfully exercise their will over their wives. This a believing husband must never do. He must transform his every moment with her in light of the knowledge that he possesses inherent advantages over her in terms of physical strength and social power. Mere power plays must not be the means of his living with her.

This is to be his stance toward his wife "since she is a woman" (τῷ γυναικείῳ). The adjective appears only here in the NT. It designates someone or something as feminine.[64] The presence of the definite article signals it is being used as a substantive. She makes up the feminine part of the equation of marriage. He, the male, should rightly calculate what that means. In Peter's words, marriage is an entity comprised of one male and one female in covenant before God for a lifetime (Gen. 2:24; Matt. 19:5–6; Mark 10:7–8).

If this is correct, then to say that the husband must live with his wife "with an understanding of their weaker nature" (HCSB) misses the point. She is not weaker by nature but by circumstances. She is not fundamentally weaker than him, other than typically in physical strength. She is not his inferior by "nature," but he is able, physically and socially, to deal with her by way of power rather than by love. And as one who owes his very existence, presently and eternally, to the love of God through Christ, he must not resort to such tactics. To redeem him, Jesus chose the path of submission to His Father's will and endurance under those who physically,

---

64 BDAG, 1700; Friberg, 102; Thayer, 123.

socially, and religiously claimed power over Him (1 Peter 2:21–25). The husband must be mindful of the position he holds and use it for the purposes of love, service, and his wife's upbuilding.

Secondly, the husband must treat his wife "as a fellow heir of the grace of life" (ὡς καὶ συγκληρονόμοις χάριτος ζωῆς). Again ὡς ("as") sets out the standard of that knowledge which must control a husband's relationship with his wife. He knows her as "a fellow heir" (καὶ συγκληρονόμοις) in Christ.[65] The noun (συγκληρονόμοις, "heir") is a compound made up of σύν ("with") and κληρονόμος ("heir"). It designated "one who receives a possession together with someone else."[66] It is found only three other times in the NT. Abraham, Isaac, and Jacob were all fellow heirs of the same divine promise (Heb. 11:9). Astoundingly, the Gentiles have become fellow heirs with believing Jews (Eph. 3:6). Most stunning of all, believers are designated "heirs of God and fellow heirs with Christ" Himself (Rom. 8:17). The καὶ is used adverbially to indicate that the wife joins her husband as an "heir" of God through Christ. It strengthens the preposition in compound (σύν), further stressing the mutuality of their standing as heirs. More literally it might be rendered, "also a fellow heir." This distinguishes both partners as believers in Jesus. This may indicate that it was less likely that a husband would be married to an unbelieving wife (since wives typically joined their husbands in their religious devotion; though cf. 1 Cor. 7:12) than it was for a believing wife to find herself unequally yoked to an unbelieving husband (3:1–7).

Both husband and wife are heirs "of the grace of life" (χάριτος ζωῆς). Throughout this letter "life" (ζωῆς) is always a result of the new birth (1:3, 23) and the resulting union with the living Christ (2:4–5). A person comes into this "life" only by divine "grace" (χάριτος, 1:2, 10, 13; 2:19, 20; 4:10; 5:5, 10). Peter will close the letter by saying, "I have written to you briefly, exhorting and testifying that" what is written herein "is the true grace of God" and calling his readers to "Stand firm in it!" (5:12).

---

65 Most manuscripts have the nominative plural (συγκληρονόμοι), but the oldest have the dative plural (συγκληρονόμοις). The evidence weighs in favor of the dative (Dubis, 95–96; Forbes, 105; Michaels, 155).

66 Louw-Nida, 57.134.

One of the husband's most basic responsibilities within marriage is to draw upon his inheritance in Christ to enable his wife to live more fully in her inheritance in Christ.

Paul can say, having been "justified by His grace we would be made heirs [κληρονόμοι] according to the hope of eternal life" (Titus 3:7). He declared, "There is neither Jew nor Greek, there is neither slave nor free man, there is neither male nor female; for you are all one in Christ Jesus. And if you belong to Christ, then you are Abraham's descendants, heirs [κληρονόμοι] according to promise" (Gal. 3:28–29). God has blessed all His children "with every spiritual blessing in the heavenly places in Christ" (Eph. 1:3).

Their common standing in Christ requires that the husband "show her honor" (ἀπονέμοντες τιμὴν). The verb is found only here in the NT. It is a compound made up of ἀπό ("away from") and νέμω ("to deal out," "to distribute," to dispense").[67] It thus means to assign or portion out.[68] It marks "a causative relation, with the implication of something deserved"[69] and thus means "to grant that which is appropriate in a relationship."[70] The participle is best understood as indicating the manner in which the husband fulfills the command to "live" with his wife. The present tense marks this as the abiding and regular pattern of the husband's relationship with his wife.

That which the grace of God has made appropriate in the relationship of a believing husband to a believing wife is "honor" (τιμὴν). The noun originally designated "the amount of money or property regarded as representing the value or price of something."[71] It thus signified something's worth or assigned value. Honor is what God the Father spoke over His Son on the mount of transfiguration (2 Peter 1:17). That same "honor" was granted us by His making us the place of His dwelling (1 Peter 2:7), and it is what the grace of God has promised each of His people in fullness at Jesus'

---

67 Liddell and Scott, 5638, 29341.

68 Thayer, 66.

69 Louw-Nida, 90.54.

70 BDAG, 973.

71 Louw-Nida, 57.161.

return (1:7). As those thus honored, we are to "Honor all people," including "the king" (2:17). Though the "honor" given a believing wife is uniquely different from that given to "all people" or to "the king," it too is demanded of the husband. What God has given to us, we should bestow on others.

In a world filled with shame, Christian husbands must not allow anything but "honor" to come to their wives. The husband's job is to make certain that his bride and the watching world understand her value. That value is set in the eyes of Her Master and therefore his valuation of his wife must match Jesus' estimation of her. This valuation and "honor" must be both demonstrated and spoken, lest she or the watching world underestimate her value.

What rides on the husband's faithfulness in this? The couple's earthly happiness? To some extent, yes. But more importantly, Peter says to husbands, live in this way with your wife "so that your prayers will not be hindered" (εἰς τὸ μὴ ἐγκόπτεσθαι τὰς προσευχὰς ὑμῶν). The formula of εἰς τὸ and the infinitive may signal a purpose statement, though perhaps this is better read as indicating a "contemplated result."[72] The negation (μὴ, "not") makes it a negative purpose statement. Something must not happen. The negation is emphatic.

The noun (τὰς προσευχὰς, "prayers") is the common Greek term used to designate one's communication with deity. The plural form makes room for the various forms and functions of prayer, including praise, confession, thanksgiving, petition, and intercession. The definite article underscores prayer's singular significance in the believer's life. It also may signal that Peter is thinking of regular times and practices of prayers established as a discipline of their spiritual lives (lit., "the prayers"). It has been suggested that the plural pronoun (ὑμῶν, "your") makes these the prayers of both husband and wife, probably those lifted to God together. Of course, if there is marital discord, their shared prayer life would be affected. But because the husband is the one being addressed throughout the sentence, it seems more likely that the husbands as a collective group are in view.

The verb (ἐγκόπτεσθαι, "be hindered") is a compound made up of ἐν ("in") and κόπτω ("to cut [off]"). The sense of the word, then, is to

---

72 Hiebert, 207–208.

cut in on or cut off someone or something to become an obstacle that makes further progress difficult and slow. It is used only four other times in the NT, being used of needless rhetoric (Acts 24:4), circumstances that have prevented Paul's travel to Rome (Rom. 15:22), Judaizers' insistence upon circumcision (Gal. 5:7), and the opposition of the evil one (1 Thess. 2:18). So verbal, circumstantial, religious, and spiritual matters may produce a hindrance. But Peter is concerned that marital dysfunction might be added to the list of potential obstacles to one's relationship with God. The husband must see that this does "not" (μὴ) happen. As Peter will soon say using the same noun, "The end of all things is near; therefore, be of sound judgment and sober spirit for the purpose of prayer" (1 Peter 4:7).

In some way, which Peter does not entirely unpack, there is a dynamic connection between a man's relationship with his wife and his relationship with God. A married man can't get far spiritually without God and his wife. How you live with your wife impacts how God will listen to you. No one should risk his prayers being hindered before God. For husbands, this requires living rightly with the wife God has given him. Living wrongly with his wife could produce a breakdown in his relationship with God at its most fundamental and intimate level. Nothing is more precious than our connection to God via prayer. No earthly power-play, in marriage or out of it, is worth threatening that lifeline to God.

Paul also spoke of the relationship between marriage and prayer, though arising from different concerns: "Stop depriving one another, except by agreement for a time, so that you may devote yourselves to prayer, and come together again so that Satan will not tempt you because of your lack of self-control" (1 Cor. 7:5).

> **Digging Deeper:**
> 1. How may it legitimately be said within our culture that a wife is weaker than her husband? How does culture forbid such talk?
> 2. Is Peter being sexist in his words? Why? Why not?
> 3. How would you explain to your children the connection between your prayer life and your relationship to their mother?

Verse 8 – "To sum up, all of you be harmonious, sympathetic, brotherly, kindhearted, and humble in spirit;"

Having instructed specific entities among God's people (2:13–3:7), Peter now issues a new series of exhortations (vv. 8–12) that apply broadly to "all" (πάντες) God's people. He introduces these exhortations with the expression Τὸ δὲ τέλος ("To sum up"). It might literally be rendered, "Now the end." It is most frequently translated as "Finally" (ESV, KJV, NET, NIV, NKJV, NLT, NRSV). It is used elsewhere in the NT in Romans 6:22 and 1 Timothy 1:5. Peter comes to "the end" of the matter of authority, submission, and unjust suffering. He has been majoring in how various groups within the church ought to behave themselves toward the unbelieving who unjustly make life painful for them. But now he turns his attention to how all God's people ought to conduct themselves.

The sentence (running through verse 9) has no main verb, but the translators are right to add the assumed "be" as an imperative. Peter uses five adjectives to set before all God's people that which should characterize them. All are used only here in the NT, except for the fourth, which is only one other time in the NT. All are compound words.

First, God's people should aim to be "harmonious" (ὁμόφρονες). It is a compound made up of ὁμός ("common," "same") and φρήν ("heart," "mind").[73] It depicts like-mindedness, being of one heart and mind, unified, and thus "harmonious." While the word is found only here in the NT, its pages are filled with the concept (e.g., Acts 1:14; 2:46; Rom. 12:16; 15:5–6; 1 Cor. 1:10; Phil. 2:2). Peter, much like Paul (Phil. 2:1–5), is not calling for all God's people to think precisely the same thoughts or hold the same opinions on all things, but to adopt a way of thinking, a certain mindset in which they reason and from which their opinions are formed.

God's people should be "sympathetic" (συμπαθεῖς). This compound is constructed of σύν ("with") and πάσχω ("to experience something").[74] It

---

73   BDAG, 5308; Liddell and Scott, 30812, 45941.
74   Thayer, 596. The root verb is a key one in this letter about suffering (cf. 1 Peter 2:19, 20, 21, 23; 3:14, 17, 18; 4:1 [2x], 15, 19; 5:10).

means "to share the same suffering or emotion" as another and thus to "be compassionate."[75] It marks one "who is affected by the same suffering, the same impressions, the same emotions as another, or who undergoes identical trials, and finally 'sympathizes' with this other person who is in some sort of trouble."[76] While the adjective is found only here in the NT, the cognate verb is used to describe Jesus, who, as our High Priest, is able to "sympathize with our weaknesses" (Heb. 4:15; cf. 10:34). We are to "Rejoice with those who rejoice, and weep with those who weep" (Rom. 12:15).

> **Ministry Maxim**
>
> Begin with others and go from there.

God's people should be "brotherly" (φιλάδελφοι). This may be the NT's only use of the adjective, but the cognate noun (φιλαδελφία, "brotherly love") is frequent, used both for the reality of "brotherly love" (Rom. 12:10; 1 Thess. 4:9; Heb. 13:1) and as the placename of a first-century Mediterranean city hosting a community of believers (Rev. 1:11; 3:7). The compound combines φίλος ("love") and ἀδελφός ("brother"). Peter told his readers, "Since you have in obedience to the truth purified your souls for a sincere love of the brethren [φιλαδελφίαν], fervently love one another from the heart" (1 Peter 1:22). He also enumerated such love as one of the indispensable areas of growth in the Christian life (2 Peter 1:7).

God's people should be "kindhearted" (εὔσπλαγχνοι). The compound is built of the prefix εὖ ("good"), and σπλάγχνον ("bowels"), the latter of which was regarded by the Hebrews as "the seat of the tenderer affections, especially kindness, benevolence, compassion."[77] It depicts sympathetic feelings toward another, which arise from the deepest part of our being. The adjective is found elsewhere in the NT only in Ephesians 4:32, where Paul commands: "Be kind to one another, tender-hearted [εὔσπλαγχνοι], forgiving each other, just as God in Christ also has forgiven you."

---

75 Spicq, 3:320.

76 Ibid.

77 Thayer, 262, 584.

God's people should be "humble in spirit" (ταπεινόφρονες).⁷⁸ The compound is comprised of ταπεινός ("lowly," "humble") and φρήν ("thinking," "understanding").⁷⁹ It means "having a modest opinion of oneself."⁸⁰ Again, while the adjective may be found only here in the NT, the concept is not uncommon. In view of our Savior's pattern of living, we are called "with humility of mind [to] regard one another as more important than ourselves" (Phil. 2:3). No one is "to think more highly of himself than he ought to think; but to think so as to have sound judgment, as God has allotted to each a measure of faith" (Rom. 12:3). We must "give preference to one another in honor" (v.10).

Perhaps there is legitimacy in seeing a chiastic arrangement in these five adjectives.⁸¹ Peter begins and ends (#1 and #5) with one's thinking.⁸² He then moves (#2 and #4) to one's feeling.⁸³ At the center of it all, controlling and radiating outward, regulating one's emotions and thoughts, is love's crowning and binding element.⁸⁴ This might be set out as follows:

"harmonious" (ὁμόφρονες)
   "sympathetic" (συμπαθεῖς)
      "brotherly" (φιλάδελφοι)
   "kindhearted" (εὔσπλαγχνοι)
"humble in spirit" (ταπεινόφρονες)

---

78 A few manuscripts have (φιλόφρονες, "courteous," KJV) instead of (ταπεινόφρονες, "humble in spirit"). But the manuscript evidence supports the present reading.

79 BDAG, 7257.

80 Friberg, 375.

81 Davids, 124; Forbes (108, following Elliot, 603), Goppelt, 232, Schreiner, 164.

82 First, "of one mind" (KJV) and fifth, "a humble mind" (NRSV); Clowney aptly comments, "...if there is to be 'like-mindedness' there must also be 'lowly-mindedness'" (140).

83 Second, "fellow-feeling" (YLT) and fourth, "a tender heart" (ESV, NRSV).

84 At the center: "brotherly love" (ESV), "love of the brethren" (RSV), "love for one another" (NRSV).

Christians are fundamentally an inside-out people. We have been born again (1 Peter 1:3, 23), given a new heart and spirit (Ezek. 18:31; 36:26), and through the new covenant, we have been made new creatures (2 Cor. 5:17). This changes everything. The uniqueness of Christians living together in unity is centered in a fundamental transformation of heart that changes how one thinks, what one values, how one feels, and thus how one acts in relationship. Love planted in the heart is rooted God's loving initiative and sends its shoots into all our relationships to bear fruit.

Each of these qualities was modeled by Jesus: "harmonious" (Phil. 2:1–5), "sympathetic" (Heb. 4:15), "brotherly" (Matt. 11:19; John 15:14–15; Heb. 2:11–14), "kindhearted" (Matt. 15:32; 20:34; Luke 15:20), and "humble in spirit" (Phil. 2:3–5). Each of them is enjoined upon His followers: "harmonious" (Phil. 2:1–5), "sympathetic" (Luke 10:33; Heb. 10:34), "brotherly" (Rom. 12:10; Heb. 13:1; 2 Peter 1:7), "kindhearted" (Eph. 4:32), and "humble in spirit" (Phil. 2:3; Rom. 12:3, 10). Each becomes possible only by the working of God's Spirit (Gal. 5:22–23; Eph. 5:18).

Verse 9 – "not returning evil for evil or insult for insult, but giving a blessing instead; for you were called for the very purpose that you might inherit a blessing."

Peter continues the sentence begun in verse 8, where he sets out the standard for relationships among fellow believers. Here in verse 9, he sets out the basics for relationships with the resolutely unbelieving. He does so by way of a contrast (μὴ ... δὲ, "not ... but"). The contrasting actions are set before us by way of two present-tense participles. There is debate about whether to read these participles as imperatival (ESV, NET, NIV, NLT, NRSV, RSV) or as qualifying the understood command of verse 8, thus designating the manner in which a believer's relationship to the unbelieving is to be demonstrated (KJV, NASU, NKJV, YLT). Even if read as qualifying the mentally-supplied imperative of verse 8, still these participles should be read as having some force of command.

Believers should not be "returning" (ἀποδιδόντες) to the unbelieving in kind for their opposition. The compound verb is made from ἀπό ("from") and δίδωμι ("to give"). Here it has the sense of "give back" or "recompense." It indicates a response in kind, arising from and measured by that which the other party gave. The Lord is the only one in a position to do so, and He will (Rom. 2:6; 2 Tim. 4:14; Rev. 22:12). Believers are forbidden the practice (Rom. 12:17; 1 Thess. 5:15).

Such payback might come in "evil for evil" (κακὸν ἀντὶ κακοῦ). The adjective, used here as a noun, carries the dual sense of moral evil and active harm.[85] Such repayment could also (ἤ, "or") come in the form of "insult for insult" (λοιδορίαν ἀντὶ λοιδορίας). The noun depicts speech that is meant to slander, defame, and injure. The cognate verb was used to describe Jesus' own response, "while being reviled [λοιδορούμενος], did not revile [ἀντελοιδόρει] in return" (1 Peter 2:23). In both cases the preposition (ἀντὶ, "for") means "in return for"[86] and signals reciprocal action, "exact equivalence like 'tit for tat.'"[87]

Rather, believers should be "giving a blessing instead" (τοὐναντίον ... εὐλογοῦντες). The verb is a compound made up of the prefix εὖ ("good") and λογέω ("to speak"). The prefix (εὖ, "good") stands in direct contrast to the κακὸν ("evil") they have received and are tempted to return. Instead of sending back upon the evildoer their own devices, the believer is to draw upon the reservoir of grace and blessing they have received from God and give that back to the one who sought to harm them. "With [the tongue] we bless our Lord and Father, and with it we curse men, who have been made in the likeness of God; from the same mouth come both blessing

Ministry Maxim

Everywhere, to everyone, and in everything, leave grace.

and cursing. My brethren, these things ought not to be this way" (James 3:9–10). The articular adverb (τοὐναντίον, "instead") means "on the other hand."[88] Paul's practice was: "when we are reviled [λοιδορούμενοι], we

---

85 BDAG, 3878.
86 Harris, 50.
87 Robertson, *Grammar*, 573.
88 BDAG, 2588.2; Harris, 244.

bless [εὐλογοῦμεν]" (1 Cor. 4:12). Jesus taught His disciples, "bless those who curse you, pray for those who mistreat you" (Luke 6:28; cf. Matt. 5:44). The wisdom of such a response has long been pressed upon God's people: "Do not say, 'I will repay evil'; Wait for the LORD, and He will save you" (Prov. 20:22).

But what exactly is meant by "blessing"? Note that Peter does not use a noun but a verb. The "blessing" he has in mind is not a *thing* to be given but an action to be undertaken. What does "blessing" look like when enacted? What does it entail? In secular Greek writings of the day, the verb simply meant "to speak well" of someone. But its use in the NT relies not upon secular Greek usage but upon its use in the LXX.[89] The Hebrew concept of blessing was dynamic and powerful. When someone blessed another, they did far more than speak nicely to or about them; they conferred upon them something positive they did not previously possess. "The performance of a blessing involves a word" and symbolic actions (e.g., laying on of the hands) which "confer beneficial power" and "The imparted blessing works unconditionally and irrevocably. It is permanent and can neither be revoked nor rendered ineffective."[90] "Men and things which are blessed are as it were endowed with this power and can transmit it, affecting everything with which they come in contact."[91] Old Testament fathers, patriarchs, kings, prophets, and priests so bless others.[92] In the NT, it is supremely Jesus who blesses (e.g., Matt. 16:17; Mark 10:16; Luke 2:28; 24:50–51).

We were "blessed" by God by being put in union with Christ. This came about as we heard the word of the gospel and believed. God, through the gospel, removed us from under the curse of the broken Law of God. He has made us to reside under His blessing. God has conferred upon us Jesus' own eternal, resurrection life—this is to be blessed indeed. We were so blessed that we might go forth as conduits of the blessing that

---

89 TDNT, 2:755.
90 NIDNTTE, 2:320.
91 TDNT, 2:756.
92 NIDNTTE, 2:320.

comes through the gospel when it is believed. We bless most pointedly as we speak the gospel, in this specific case, to those who persecute us for believing that gospel. We must wed to our proclamation of the gospel those acts which bring into the visible, physical relationship the reality of the gospel's power. The spoken blessing of God's love and grace through Christ thus must be joined to acts of forbearance, service, forgiveness, kindness, grace, and love. This, then, is how to take the blessing of God's grace extended to us through Jesus via the gospel and fulfill our calling to pass that blessing on to others, most especially those who persecute us.

Peter's instruction here signals that what he just said to wives about their witness to their unbelieving husbands "without a word" (1 Peter 3:1) applies situationally. It is not the universal response of Christians to opposition and suffering. Christ's example of silence in the face of His accusers (2:22–23) is a pattern we are to follow (2:21), but so is His explicit instruction to meet defamation with grace-filled verbal responses (Luke 6:28).[93] The child of God will need divinely given wisdom to know which response is most strategically helpful in which situation. The Spirit of God supplies wisdom to know whether to hold the tongue or to speak (Matt. 10:19–20; Mark 13:11; Luke 12:11–12).

For the believer, the reason for this (ὅτι, "for") is "you were called for the very purpose" (εἰς τοῦτο ἐκλήθητε). Does the phrase εἰς τοῦτο ("for the very purpose") refer back to the believer's blessing of their persecutors (ESV, KJV, NIV, NLT, NRSV) or forward to the inheriting of the blessing of God (NASU, NET)? Peter uses the phrase two other times. In 1 Peter 2:21, it looks backward to what was already said; in 4:6, it looks forward to what is about to be said. Some insist that the phrase cannot look backward to the believer's work of blessing persecutors but must look forward to the blessing of God.[94] The rationale is that if it looks backward, it makes a believer's inherited blessing a matter of human works: our inherited blessing from God is the outcome of our blessing those who persecute us. But this misses the Bible's consistent teaching (e.g., 1

---

93 Michaels, 178.

94 E.g., Davids, 126–127; Goppelt, 234–235; Kelly, 136–137; Lenski, 143–144.

Cor. 3:11–15; 2 Cor. 5:10; Eph. 6:8) and of Jesus specifically (e.g., Matt. 16:27; Luke 6:38; Rev. 22:12) with regard to rewards for faithful service. It also misses the larger context of Peter's present letter. He has taken pains to ground all moral instruction in the grace given by God through Christ. He exhausted himself to first delineate the individual believer's identity in Christ (1 Peter 1:1–12) and only then to issue moral imperatives (1:13–2:3). He has done the same regarding believers' corporate identity in Christ (2:4–10), and we now find ourselves amid moral imperatives that rest upon that grace already received (2:11–5:12).

While fine exegetes come out on both sides of the question, it seems most in accord with the present context to read the demonstrative pronoun τοῦτο ("this") as pointing back to the giving of blessing.[95] Spreading grace or "blessing" is "the very purpose" (εἰς τοῦτο) of God for His people. The preposition (εἰς) points to the divinely established goal or purpose behind God's having "called" (ἐκλήθητε) the believer. Peter makes much of the divine call in this letter (1 Peter 1:15; 2:9, 21; 5:10). The aorist tense looks back to that moment when God's call came to them through the gospel. The passive voice indicates God issued the call and set it upon the believer. God has willed that His people suffer for Christ, following His example (1 Peter 2:21) and that amid their suffering, they, as Christ, extend grace and blessing. From the cross Jesus prayed, "Father, forgive them; for they do not know what they are doing" (Luke 23:34). So, too, the believer must give grace in the face of grief and blessing in response to bruising. Believers are to deal in grace, not reprisal. We can do so because we have received and continue to receive from the Lord blessing in the face of our sin. We can do so because our Father can be trusted to work out justice regarding those who harm or defame us (Deut. 32:35; Rom. 12:19).

This is a hard road to walk, but this calling is extended by God "that you might inherit a blessing" (ἵνα εὐλογίαν κληρονομήσητε). The ἵνα with the aorist subjunctive verb signals the purpose of our obedience in

---

[95] For a detailed and technical exegesis see John Piper, "Hope as the Motivation of Love: 1 Peter 3:9–12," NTS 26 (1979–80), 212–231. The entire article can be accessed online at www.desiringgod.org.

blessing when we are mistreated. The noun (εὐλογίαν, "a blessing") is cognate to the verb just used to set forth our duty (εὐλογοῦντες, "giving a blessing"). What we give we will get, just not from the ones to whom we have given it. God is the great rewarder of His people's obedience. The verb (κληρονομήσητε, "you might inherit") is cognate to the noun used to open the letter saying we have been born again to "an inheritance [κληρονομίαν] which is imperishable and undefiled and will not fade away, reserved in heaven for you" (1:4). See the commentary there for more on the concept. And compare what Peter has just said to the husband about his wife being "a fellow heir [συγκληρονόμοις] of the grace of life" (3:7). As indicated in 1 Peter 1:4, this inherited blessing primarily looks to what will be ours in fullness at Jesus' Return. But what will be ours in fullness at His Coming we taste already, as a deposit guaranteed by the present ministry of the indwelling Holy Spirit (2 Cor. 1:22; 5:5; Eph. 1:13–14).

Note the math of God's kingdom. When you receive "evil," subtract "evil" and "insult" and add "blessing." When you give a blessing, God's blessing will multiply. Give a blessing, get a blessing, just not from the one you blessed. Give a blessing, get a blessing, all out of proportion to what you've given.

> **Digging Deeper:**
> 1. Describe how love might control your thinking and feelings to create God-honoring relationships (v.8).
> 2. Who in your life right now needs a blessing they don't deserve? (v.9)

Verse 10 – "For, 'THE ONE WHO DESIRES LIFE, TO LOVE AND SEE GOOD DAYS, MUST KEEP HIS TONGUE FROM EVIL AND HIS LIPS FROM SPEAKING DECEIT.'"

A new sentence begins, but Peter stays on the same theme. His γὰρ ("For") signals that he is offering illustrative material for the point he has been making in verses 9 and 10. It comes in the form of an extended quotation from Psalm 34:12–16 (33:13–117, LXX).[96] The psalm suggests that we have rightly understood Peter's intent in saying that his readers were called to extend a blessing to their persecutors for the purpose of receiving their own blessing from God (v.9). It further suggests that the hoped-for "blessing" from the Lord (v.9b) is not wholly eschatological, but also to be found in this world as a foretaste of that which is to come in fulness at Christ's Return.[97]

Peter quotes the text of the LXX with only slight variations, adaptations that allow him to weave the Psalm into his present context and communication. The quote inverts the order of Peter's logic in verse 9. There he began with the duty of blessing persecutors, reminded them that this was their calling, and ended with the purpose of this being their hope of receiving God's blessing. Here he begins with the anticipated blessing from God in this life (v.10a) and proceeds to the duty of blessing one's persecutors (vv.10b-11) and closes with the Lord as the great judge and rewarder of one's actions (v.12).

The desired blessing is set forward in two phrases. The first looks to "THE ONE WHO DESIRES LIFE" (ὁ γὰρ θέλων ζωὴν ἀγαπᾶν). Peter uses an articular participle as a substantive to set forth "THE ONE WHO DESIRES" (ὁ ... θέλων). The present tense depicts the abiding wish of this one's heart. The verb's meaning can be found along a continuum from wishing to willing. The present usage tends toward the former. It is the desire, longing, and intent of the one under consideration to embrace "life" (ζωὴν). The word describes more than biological existence, heartbeats and brainwaves. It is used for the higher, spiritual life, the life that ultimately can only come from God.

There is a question about how to understand what it is this one desires. The word order might be read, as the NASU has it, "LIFE, TO LOVE AND SEE GOOD DAYS," or it might be read as "to love life and see

---

96   In 1 Peter 2:3 he has already quoted Psalm 34:8.

97   So Clowney,142; Davids, 128; Forbes, 110; Goppelt, 236–237; Hiebert, 216; Jobes, 223–224; contra only eschatological: Alford, 4:360; Dubis, 100; Kelly, 138; Michaels, 180; Schreiner, 166–167 or only in earthly life: Bigg, 157; Grudem, 156–158; Robertson, *Word Pictures*, 6:112.

good days" (ESV; cf. KJV, NASB, NET, NKJV, NLT, NRSV, YLT). We can see that the rendering of the NASU stands apart from most English translations and has even departed from that of the NASB, which had "Let him who means to love life and see good days..." The word order of the Greek text is set out in an A – B – B – A pattern, the elements being noun-infinitive [καὶ, not translated by NASU] infinitive-noun. The question becomes then whether to accept the first noun as standing apart in relation to the participle and the second noun being joined to two infinitives that precede it (NASU) or to read this as a stylistic variation in which there are two pairs of infinitives and their nouns with the order in which they are presented being inverted (most other English translations). It is simplest to read the participle as being qualified by two consecutive infinitive-noun combinations.

The first infinitive (ἀγαπᾶν, "TO LOVE") is present tense and joined to the noun ζωὴν ("LIFE"). It looks at the abiding, broadly defined wish of the heart. The second infinitive (ἰδεῖν, "SEE") is aorist in tense and joined to the noun ἡμέρας ("DAYS"). It expresses the individual, daily, repeated, punctiliar nature of the "GOOD" (ἀγαθὰς) being sought each day as it comes.

The entire clause functions as the subject of the imperative "KEEP" (παυσάτω). The aorist imperative demands action be taken immediately and with urgency ("MUST"). The verb is used fifteen times in the NT. Every other use is in the middle voice, while here we have the active. Therefore, the emphasis is not so much on stopping oneself but on acting to stop or restrain one thing from another.[98]

That which this one must do to enjoy such "blessing" is two-fold, both having to do with speech. This is where Psalm 34 fits with Peter's present concern of believers not responding with a verbal tit-for-tat with persecutors (v.9). First, "KEEP HIS TONGUE FROM EVIL" (τὴν γλῶσσαν ἀπὸ κακοῦ). Added (καὶ, "AND") to this he must keep "HIS LIPS FROM SPEAKING DECEIT" (χείλη τοῦ μὴ λαλῆσαι δόλον). Clearly, "HIS TONGUE" (τὴν γλῶσσαν) and "HIS LIPS" (χείλη)

---

98 Friberg, 304.

represent one's speech. Parallel and complementary are "FROM EVIL" (ἀπο κακοῦ) and "SPEAKING DECEIT" (μὴ λαλῆσαι). The noun κακός ("EVIL") can describe active, moral malevolence as well as disastrous calamity. Peter just used the term to demand there be no "returning evil for evil" (v.9) among Christ's followers. It is used four times across verses 9, 10, 11, and 12. Here being paired with δόλος ("DECEIT"), it marks the words as sinful and their goal as destructive. Originally δόλος designated bait used to catch fish. By extension and used metaphorically, it then described any stratagem, plot or trick used to take in the unsuspecting. It is craft, guile, and fraud. Its ploys are often worked out through false words. It is what the religious authorities used to gain control over Jesus (Matt. 26:4; Mark 14:1). It operates in and arises out of the unredeemed heart (Mark 7:22). The devil is a liar (John 8:44), and he is the ultimate source of all "deceit" (Acts 13:10). Peter has already commanded that all "DECEIT" be put away from their mouths (2:1) and demonstrated that such was never found on the lips of Jesus (2:22). Thus we see what Peter meant by demanding there be no "insult for insult" (v.9) among God's people.

> **Ministry Maxim**
>
> When you speak grace, good goes forth in every direction.

So far, Peter has cited Psalm 34:12 and 13 to help make his point that the hoped-for blessing (v.9) of "LIFE" and "GOOD DAYS" (v.10a) are to be sought along the path of controlled speech (v.10b). In verse 11 he will add four more imperatives the follower of Christ undertakes to obey out of the reservoir of the grace he has received.

Verse 11 – "'HE MUST TURN AWAY FROM EVIL AND DO GOOD; HE MUST SEEK PEACE AND PURSUE IT.'"

Peter continues to cite Psalm 34, this time verse 14 (33:15 LXX). He continues to reproduce the text of the LXX with only slight variations as he adapts it to his present letter. To the command to "KEEP" (παυσάτω) the tongue (v.10), Peter adds four more imperatives. As with the first, these too are all in the aorist tense, demanding urgent action be taken.

First, to enjoy the "blessing" of God (v.9b), "HE MUST TURN AWAY FROM EVIL" (ἐκκλινάτω δὲ ἀπὸ κακοῦ). The δὲ is not translated by the NASU, though notice "And" in the NASB (cf. NET). Again "evil" (κακοῦ) is cited (vv.9, 10, 12) and links the citation of the psalm as an echo of Peter's prohibition against "returning evil for evil or insult for insult" (v.9a). This he must "TURN AWAY FROM" (ἐκκλινάτω ... ἀπὸ). The verb is found only two other times in the NT (Rom. 3:12; 16:17). It is a compound, made up of ἐκ ("from") and λίνω ("to turn aside"). Note the double emphasis resulting from the prefix of the verb (ἐκ, "from") and the preposition (ἀπὸ, "from").[99] Here it means "to cease doing something, with the implication of engaging in some alternative."[100]

> **Ministry Maxim**
>
> Turning *from* must be matched with turning *to* if it is to prove effective.

But the one who seeks God's "blessing" must do more than avoid evil. The psalmist adds (καὶ, "AND") that he must "DO GOOD" (ποιησάτω ἀγαθόν). "GOOD" (ἀγαθόν) stands in direct contrast with "EVIL" (κακοῦ, vv.9, 10, 11, 12). In this context, it reinforces Peter's instruction in "giving a blessing instead" (v.9b) of vengeance for the persecution his readers suffered from their opponents. The verb denotes here the active expression of "GOOD" toward "THOSE WHO DO EVIL" (ποιοῦντας κακά, v.12).

The third and fourth imperatives of this verse are found when the psalmist says: "HE MUST SEEK PEACE AND PURSUE IT" (ζητησάτω εἰρήνην καὶ διωξάτω αὐτήν). The first verb calls upon us to "SEEK" (ζητησάτω). The devil goes about "seeking [ζητῶν] someone to devour" (1 Peter 5:8). In contrast, the search here is for "peace" (εἰρήνην). The verb "SEEK" (ζητησάτω) is reflected in and strengthened by the parallel (καὶ,

---

99 "ἀπὸ merely notes the point of departure, while ἐκ distinctly asserts that one had been within the place or circle before departing" (Robertson, *Grammar*, 561).

100 Louw-Nida, 68.41.

"AND") verb "PURSUE" (διωξάτω). Such seeking and pursuit take the form of extending grace and blessing in the face of harsh treatment.

Verse 12 – "'FOR THE EYES OF THE LORD ARE TOWARD THE RIGHTEOUS, AND HIS EARS ATTEND TO THEIR PRAYER, BUT THE FACE OF THE LORD IS AGAINST THOSE WHO DO EVIL.'"

Peter's citation from Psalm 34 is completed here with his quotation of verses 15 and 16a. He precisely quotes the text of the LXX (33:16–17a, LXX) except for adding ὅτι ("FOR") to adapt it to this letter. It signals that there are reasons behind the five imperatives of verses 10 and 11. Those reasons are three in number, the first two are stated positively, and the third is stated negatively. The three reasons use the metaphor of "THE EYES," "HIS EARS," and "THE FACE."[101] Together they depict the omniscience, favor, and judgment of God. God sees every wrong. God hears every cry. God sends His judgment on all evil.

First, "THE EYES OF THE LORD ARE TOWARD THE RIGHTEOUS" (ὀφθαλμοὶ κυρίου ἐπὶ δικαίους). The precise expression ὀφθαλμοὶ κυρίου ("THE EYS OF THE LORD") is found thirteen times in the LXX, including these great comforts and warnings: "For the eyes of the LORD move to and fro throughout the earth that He may strongly support those whose heart is completely His." (2 Chron. 16:9a). "Behold, the eye of the LORD is on those who fear Him, On those who hope for His lovingkindness" (Psa. 33:18 [32:18, LXX]). "The eyes of the LORD are in every place, Watching the evil and the good" (Prov. 15:3). "The eyes of the LORD preserve knowledge, But He overthrows the words of the treacherous man" (Prov. 22:12). The "LORD" in Psalm 34 is יהוה, but Peter is likely again

> **Ministry Maxim**
>
> Nothing is more determinative in life than the countenance of the Lord.

---

101 Contrast the "TONGUE" and "LIPS" of verse 10.

identifying Jesus (cf. 1 Peter 2:3 citing Psa. 34:8 [33:9, LXX]; 1 Peter 3:15 citing Isa. 8:13).[102]

Here His eyes are "TOWARD THE RIGHTEOUS" (ἐπὶ δικαίους). The preposition (ἐπὶ, "TOWARD") pictures the eyes of God resting "upon" His people. The context identifies "THE RIGHTEOUS" (δικαίους) as those who bear up under persecution without efforts at revenge or payback.

The psalmist adds (καὶ, "AND") a second positive reason for taking up the imperatives of verses 10–11: "HIS EARS ATTEND TO THEIR PRAYER" (ὦτα αὐτοῦ εἰς δέησιν αὐτῶν). While the eyes of the Lord speak of His immediate knowledge, "HIS EARS" (ὦτα αὐτοῦ) remind us of His attentiveness to our cries, whether the silent cries of the heart or the vocalized prayers of the lips. Frequently, especially in the Psalms, the "ears" of the Lord are cited with reference to His listening with favor to the prayers of His people (e.g., Psa. 10:17 [9:38, LXX]; 17:6 [16:6, LXX]). The present expression carries the same comforting notion since the ears of the Lord are said to "ATTEND TO THEIR PRAYER" (εἰς δέησιν αὐτῶν). The preposition (εἰς, "TO") usually carries the idea of "into" but can also be used much as the dative ("to"), as seems to be the case here.[103] Rienecker reports, "The verb from which the noun is derived had the meaning 'to chance upon,' then 'to have an audience w[ith] a king,' to have the good fortune to be admitted to an audience, so to present a petition. The word was a regular term for a petition to a superior, and in the papyri, it was constantly used of any writing addressed to the king."[104] Though it is not the stated reference here, the disciple also should be aware that the Lord knows whether he does "KEEP HIS TONGUE FROM EVIL AND HIS LIPS FROM SPEAKING DECEIT" (v.10) and whether he returns "insult for insult" (v.9) or instead speaks "a blessing" (v.9) over those who oppose him.

---

102 Michaels, 181.

103 Harris, 83.

104 Rienecker, 618–619.

In contrast (δὲ, "BUT") is the final, negatively stated reason for obedience to the commands of verses 10 and 11: "THE FACE OF THE LORD IS AGAINST THOSE WHO DO EVIL" (πρόσωπον ... κυρίου ἐπὶ ποιοῦντας κακά). In the OT, the face of the Lord may shine with favor upon the blessed (Psa. 4:6 [4:7, LXX]). This is reflected in the great blessing of Aaron, "The LORD bless you, and keep you; The LORD make His face [τὸ πρόσωπον αὐτοῦ] shine on you, And be gracious to you; The LORD lift up His countenance [τὸ πρόσωπον αὐτοῦ] on you, And give you peace" (Num 6:24–26). But the face of the Lord also may fall in judgment (Jer. 3:12), or He may hide His face as a sign of disfavor (Psa. 13:1 [12:1, LXX]), which is closer to the idea here. As in the first of the reasons stated in this verse, Peter again uses the preposition ἐπὶ, but here it comes near to the meaning of ἀντὶ and is rightly rendered "AGAINST."

Interestingly, in verse 9, the issue being warned against was "returning evil for [ἀντὶ] evil or insult for [ἀντὶ] insult." Here "THOSE WHO DO EVIL" (ποιοῦντας κακά) would include the persecutors, but also the persecuted who insist on "returning evil for evil or insult for insult" (v.9).

> **Digging Deeper:**
> 1. How can one account for the promised "LIFE" and "GOOD DAYS" (v.10) in the case of martyrdom, which Peter himself would one day face?
> 2. Why is turning from evil never enough, but must be joined with a new pursuit of good (v.11)?
> 3. Explain how the knowledge, favor, and judgment of God (v.12) motivate the persecuted.

Verse 13 – "Who is there to harm you if you prove zealous for what is good?"

At this point, Peter transitions the letter, but just how are we to understand its relationship to what has gone before? He initiates the transition by using the conjunction καί. It is left untranslated by the NASU (also

NIV), but this is a change from the NASB, which translated it "And" (also KJV, NKJV, YLT). Others translate it as "Now" (ESV, NLT, NRSV, RSV) or "For" (NET). Though καί is seldom used as a logical connector, some suggest "Therefore"[105] or "then"[106] as the intent here. Peter wishes to show that what he now says flows naturally out of what he has already said. Up to this point, Peter has only addressed the matter of persecution tangentially (1:6; 2:12, 15, 19; 3:1, 9), but now he will address the matter straight on. Peter has faithfully laid a theological foundation of grace received (1:1–12; 2:4–10) and a moral foundation of obedience expected (1:13–2:3; 2:11–3:12). On this foundation, he moves to address the matter of their suffering for Christ's sake (3:13–5:12).

The transition is made by means of a question: "Who is there to harm you" (τίς ὁ κακώσων ὑμᾶς). Peter states the matter broadly by using the indefinite pronoun τις ("Who"). He poses a rhetorical question to make his point. It could be anyone from any sector of your life with any one of an infinite number of agendas, reasons, purposes, etc. It could be anyone in the crowd of humanity, but what singles them out is their desire "to harm you" (ὁ κακώσων ὑμᾶς). The verb (κακόω) means "to do evil to someone."[107] It is found only six times in the NT, the other five in the book of Acts, where it describes the mistreatment of God's people in Egypt (Acts 7:6) by Pharaoh (v.19), persecution by Herod (12:1), unbelieving Jews in Iconium (14:2), and the citizens of Corinth (18:10). We can thus see that the word identifies suffering experienced in this earthly life, not eschatological suffering at the final judgment. It is related to the adjective κακός ("evil") so prevalent in Peter's thoughts here (1 Peter 3:8, 9 [2x], 10, 11, 12) and the noun κακία ("evil," 2:1, 16), confirming that while Peter is transitioning his line of thought, he will be developing more fully matters already introduced. It thematically

> **Ministry Maxim**
>
> Doing good puts the odds in your favor.

---

105 Schreiner, 169.

106 Clowney, 143; Kelly, 139–140; Michaels, 185.

107 Rienecker, 758.

continues and develops the thought of "THOSE WHO DO EVIL" (ποιοῦντας κακά, v.12b). A future subjunctive participle form is exceedingly rare in the NT, accounting for only thirteen out of the 1,623 future forms found in the NT.[108] The participle is substantival ("*THOSE WHO DO EVIL*," emphasis added).

The question of "harm" revolves around a condition: "if you prove zealous for what is good?" (ἐὰν τοῦ ἀγαθοῦ ζηλωταὶ γένησθε).[109] The condition is formed of the conditional particle ἐάν ("if") and an aorist subjunctive verb (γένησθε, "you prove"). The prospect of the condition's fulfillment is uncertain,[110] not because it is unlikely that his readers will prove to be "zealous for what is good," but because Peter is setting up a hypothetical case. The verb means "to become" and thus pictures his readers at some time and circumstance, proving they have become "zealous" (ζηλωταὶ). The noun is used to designate the other "Simon" among the Disciples as a "zealot" (Luke 6:15; Acts 1:13; cf. 21:20).[111] The root idea of the word is to glow or to burn. Then it describes one who thus boils over in enthusiasm for a particular issue or cause. Some were zealots after the Law (Acts 21:20) as the young Paul proved to be (Acts 22:3; Gal. 1:14). The Corinthians were zealots after certain spiritual gifts (1 Cor. 14:12). All God's people are to be "zealous [ζηλωτὴν] for good deeds" (Titus 2:14). That is Peter's point here (τοῦ ἀγαθοῦ, "what is good"), continuing his call for meeting ill-will and poor treatment with responses that are both good (ἀγαθός, 2:14, 15, 18, 20; 3:6, 10, 11, 16 [2x], 17, 21)

---

108 Dubis, 106; Forbes, 113; Wallace puts the number at twelve (567), but Dubis notes: "Wallace... missed the one in Rom. 8:34."

109 Some find here an intentional reflection of Isaiah 50:9 LXX: ἰδοὺ κύριος βοηθεῖ μοι τίς κακώσει με ("Behold, the Lord will help me: who will harm me?"; e.g., Bigg, 157; Davids, 129; Goppelt, 241; Jobes, 226; Kelly, 140).

110 Most identify this as a third-class condition ("future probable"; Robertson, *Grammar*, 1020). Lenski says the condition "introduces an expectancy" (146–147).

111 Rather than ζηλωταὶ ("zealous") some manuscripts have μιμηταὶ ("imitators," YLT; "followers," KJV), but ζηλωταὶ is represented in "the best and most ancient MSS" and "is clearly to be preferred" (Michaels, 183). Forbes describes it as some scribe's "deliberate attempt to soften a term that came to have quite neg. connotations after the Jewish War of AD 66–70" (Forbes, 113; cf. Michaels, 183).

and beautiful (καλός, 2:12 [2x]; 4:10). The articular adjective is fronted to highlight the contrast between the "good" of the believers and the evil of their persecutors.[112] Peter has already defined what "good" looks like in the context of Christian suffering (2:11–3:9).[113]

Peter's rhetorical question expects the answer "no one." Ordinarily, doing good will be rewarded, not punished. Indeed, this is the very purpose of human government, sent by God "for the punishment of evildoers and the praise of those who do right" (2:14). It is the general point behind the slave's responses to his master (2:18ff) and the wife's behavior toward her unbelieving husband (3:1–6). Now Peter will address the exceptions when Christ's people suffer precisely because they do good. (vv.14ff).

> **Digging Deeper:**
> 1. In your experience does it hold true that those who do good generally aren't treated poorly?
> 2. Judged strictly by your actions, what evidence have you given your neighbors recently that you are "zealous for what is good"?

Verse 14 – "But even if you should suffer for the sake of righteousness, you are blessed. AND DO NOT FEAR THEIR INTIMIDATION, AND DO NOT BE TROUBLED,"

The basic principle stands: people who do good do not normally meet with ill-treatment (v.13). "But" (ἀλλ') what of exceptions to the principle? The ring of this strong adversative introduces a state of affairs ("even if," εἰ καί) that reminds us that things do not always go as they should. The καί is used adverbially ("even"). The NASU translates with "even if," but this actually inverts the order of the Greek text. Robertson holds that the original order is significant. The order of the original is εἰ καί ("if also,"

---

112 Alford, 4:361.
113 Davids, 129.

Darby), not καὶ εἰ ("even if," most English translations). Robertson says, "With καὶ εἰ the supposition is considered improbable," but εἰ καὶ "means 'if also.' Here the protasis is treated as a matter of indifference. If there is a conflict, it makes no real difficulty. There is sometimes a tone of contempt in εἰ καὶ. The matter is belittled."[114]

The condition is formed by εἰ ("if") and an optative verb (πάσχοιτε, "you should suffer"), creating a rare fourth-class condition that renders the condition as a remote possibility, though not at all certain.[115] Comparing the third class condition of verse 13 (ἐὰν ... γένησθε, "if you prove") with this fourth-class condition, Robertson says, "This fourth class condition is undetermined with less likelihood of determination than is true of the third class with the subj[unctive]."[116] Peter will use the same kind of condition in verse 17.[117] The verb occurs twelve times in 1 Peter, more than any other NT book and with almost one-third of its total occurrences (1 Peter 2:19, 20, 21, 23; 3:14, 17, 18; 4:1 [2x], 15, 19). It is used primarily of the sufferings of Christ or of His people.[118] The word becomes the great theme of the letter.

The contemplated suffering is "for the sake of righteousness" (διὰ δικαιοσύνην). The preposition (διὰ) signals the cause of the suffering under consideration ("for the sake of"). Peter postulates a suffering that comes not despite their "righteousness" but precisely because of it. By "righteousness" (δικαιοσύνην), Peter has in mind those things he has been

---

114 Robertson, *Grammar*, 1026; cf. Lenski, 147.

115 Rienecker, 758; Robertson, *Grammar*, 1020–1021; Wallace, 484, 699.

116 Robertson, *Grammar*, 1020.

117 Wallace says, "This text comes as close as any to a complete fourth class condition in the NT. *Prima facie*, the readership of this letter has not yet suffered for righteousness, and the possibility of such happening soon seems remote. The author reinforces this point in v 17, again with the protasis of a fourth class condition: "It is better to suffer for doing good than for doing evil, **if** the will of God *should* so *will* it (εἰ θέλοι τὸ θέλημα τοῦ θεοῦ). Although the occasion of 1 Peter is frequently assumed to involve suffering on the part of the readership, this text seems to argue against that. It is probably better to see the author in the midst of suffering, out of which experience he offers his counsel to believers who may have been insulated from it thus far" (484, emphases original).

118 TDNT, 5:913.

exhorting his readers to do (1:13–2:3; 2:11–3:12). Ultimately, only Jesus is "righteous" (3:18). Yet He went to the cross "so that we might die to sin and live to righteousness [τῇ δικαιοσύνῃ]" (2:24). Peter has just asserted, quoting Psalm 34, that "THE EYES OF THE LORD ARE TOWARD THE RIGHTEOUS [δικαίους]" (3:12).

The protasis (εἰ … πάσχοιτε, "if you should suffer") meets a verbless apodosis (μακάριοι, "you are blessed"). Peter recalls Jesus' teachings from the Sermon on the Mount about what constitutes blessedness (Matt. 5:3–12), particularly with regards to persecution: "Blessed are [μακάριοι] those who have been persecuted for the sake of righteousness, for theirs is the kingdom of heaven. Blessed are [μακάριοι] you when people insult you and persecute you, and falsely say all kinds of evil against you because of Me. Rejoice and be glad, for your reward in heaven is great; for in the same way they persecuted the prophets who were before you" (Matt. 5:10–12; cf. Luke 6:22–23). He will say much the same later in the letter, "If you are reviled for the name of Christ, you are blessed [μακάριοι], because the Spirit of glory and of God rests on you" (1 Peter 4:14). He has already prepared them to seek God's blessing (cf. 1:7; 3:9). The adjective describes being under divine approval and favor. God turns His face toward you and gives you His full attention, favor, affirmation, and grace. When you are "blessed," God smiles upon you.

> **Ministry Maxim**
>
> God's blessing is stronger than the world's hatred.

Peter follows up his conjectural concession and its sure outcome with a quotation from Isaiah 8:12b. Remember, he quoted Isaiah 8:14 in 1 Peter 2:8. This indicates the fundamental nature of Isaiah 8 in Peter's thinking. Peter reproduces the LXX with only minor changes.

Peter substitutes the plural αὐτῶν for Isaiah's singular αὐτοῦ. Isaiah's form is probably to be considered a collective singular, presumably referring to the populace of Judah and Jerusalem who were under threat from a coalition of the Northern Kingdom of Israel and Syria (cf. Isa. 8:4–10). Isaiah 8:12–15 is a personal word from God to Isaiah in the midst of this fearful conflict (cf. v.11). In the context of Isaiah, the point of verse 12 is that the prophet himself should not fear what "these people" fear, meaning the populace of Israel and Judah (the LXX's αὐτοῦ being understood as a subjective genitive, "what they fear"). But Peter's slight change to the plural form αὐτῶν ("THEIR") contextually should be read as an objective genitive (i.e., "do not fear the fear they seek to project upon you").

The only other changes from the LXX are in the way Peter negates the two lines. In the first line, where Isaiah has οὐ μὴ Peter has only μὴ. In the second line, where Isaiah has οὐδὲ μὴ Peter has only μηδὲ. In the first line, Isaiah's double negation (οὐ μὴ) is emphatic, absolute, and complete. The combination of οὐ μὴ and the aorist subjunctive verb "denies a potentiality" and "rules out even the idea as being a possibility."[119] Never, under any condition, should one facing the "INTIMIDATION" of persecutors be subject to "FEAR." Peter's simple μὴ ("NOT") still "denies the thought of the thing."[120] Similarly, in the second line, Isaiah's οὐδὲ μὴ is found sixty-nine times in the LXX, but only once in the NT (Rev. 7:16). Again, Peter simplifies the LXX's combination of οὐδὲ μὴ to a simple μηδὲ.

Two parallel lines set forth the same reality. They are coordinated under a μὴ ... μηδὲ (i.e., "not ... nor") arrangement. First, "AND DO NOT FEAR THEIR INTIMIDATION" (τὸν δὲ φόβον αὐτῶν μὴ φοβηθῆτε). Peter uses a cognate noun and verb that might be set out literally as "And do not fear the fear of them." As we have seen above, the genitive (τὸν ... φόβον αὐτῶν, lit., "the fear of them") surely is an objective genitive, "the fear they inspire" or "the fear they intend."[121] The μὴ with the subjunctive sets the matter out as a prohibition. It carries imperatival force and is used to forbid the occurrence of the contemplated fear.[122] The aorist tense pictures each individual moment and event of fear's encroachment. The verb is deponent, so the passive voice should be read as an

---

119 Wallace, 468–469.

120 Thayer, 408.

121 It could be either the persecutors themselves ("Have no fear of them," RSV) or the fear they seek to instill in the believers ("DO NOT FEAR THEIR INTIMIDATION," NASU). Some see it here as subjective genitive ("do not fear what they fear," NRSV).

122 Wallace, 469.

active.¹²³ This they must counter and refuse. Peter has already counseled his readers to live their lives on this earth in fear of the Lord (1 Peter 1:17; 2:17), knowing that only this proper fear displaces and overcomes inappropriate fear (1 Peter 3:6) and positions us to live in proper respect of others (1 Peter 2:18; 3:2, 16). As Isaiah went on to say in the verse after the one cited here (and to be picked up in Peter's next words, v.15), "It is the LORD of hosts whom you should regard as holy. And He shall be your fear, And He shall be your dread" (Isa. 8:13).

Second, Peter adds, "AND DO NOT BE TROUBLED" (μηδὲ ταραχθῆτε). Like the verb in the first line, this forbids the occurrence ("DO NOT BE TROUBLED"). The verb depicts water that is disturbed or agitated (John 5:4, 7; Ezek. 32:2, 13; 34:18–19), one's stomach similarly upset (Gen. 43:30; 1 Kgs. 3:26; Hab. 3:16), and the cognate noun "mental uncertainty and confusion" (Acts 12:18) and the panic (1 Sam. 5:9) that arises because of "disorders, social disturbances, political agitation, and riots."¹²⁴ Here it likely means something like "uneasiness mixed with fear."¹²⁵ As in the first line, so here, the aorist tense looks at each opportunity to "BE TROUBLED" and forbids the response. The passive voice calls upon the persecuted to refuse the influence of their troublers.

Verse 15 – "but sanctify Christ as Lord in your hearts, always *being* ready to make a defense to everyone who asks you to give an account for the hope that is in you, yet with gentleness and reverence;"

Instead (δὲ, "but") of giving way to "FEAR" or being "TROUBLED" at the painful opposition faced for one's faith in Christ (v.14b), Peter commands his readers to "sanctify" Christ as Lord (κύριον … τὸν Χριστὸν

---

123 Abernathy, 130.

124 Spicq, 3:374.

125 Ibid., 3:375.

ἁγιάσατε).[126] In this Peter continues reflecting the words of Isaiah (Isa. 8:13), though now more loosely than in the previous verse. Peter says, "but sanctify Christ as Lord" (κύριον δὲ τὸν Χριστὸν ἁγιάσατε) while the LXX has, "the Lord Himself fear/sanctify" (κύριον αὐτὸν ἁγιάσατε). Where the LXX has αὐτὸν ("Himself"), Peter has τὸν Χριστὸν ("Christ"). The Greek κύριον ("Lord") is the LXX's rendering of the Hebrew יהוה (Yahweh). With Peter's insertion of "Christ" (τὸν Χριστὸν), he again makes clear his high Christology.

The call is to "sanctify" (ἁγιάσατε) Christ as "Lord" (κύριον). The latter is being placed forward for emphasis. The verb appears only here in Peter's writings, but the cognate noun and adjective also establish sanctification at the heart of Peter's understanding of the Spirit's ministry, the nature of salvation (1 Peter 1:2), the call of the gospel (2 Peter 2:21), the pattern of relationships (1 Peter 3:5), and transformation of life (2 Peter 3:11). The word-group describes the setting apart of something in an exclusive and special relationship. In the context of the things of God, it means to dedicate something to Him and His service. Here then, the notion is of determining in one's heart that Jesus is indeed the "Lord," Yahweh become flesh, who, having suffered and died and risen again, has been set at the Father's right hand as supreme ruler over all things. We cannot make God holy, but we can be certain that He is treated as holy from the core of our being ("Hallowed be Your name," Matt. 6:9). The aorist imperative demands the action be taken immediately, urgently.

The call is thus to afford Jesus that exclusive place "in your hearts" (ἐν ταῖς καρδίαις ὑμῶν). The "heart" is considered the seat of one's being—the locus of all thought, volition, and feeling. Life arises from the "heart," and thus, one is to guard it above all else (Prov. 4:23). One guards the heart best by setting Christ apart there to the exclusive, exalted place of "Lord." We must not read "in your hearts" as meaning merely personally, privately, or inwardly in some secret way. Rather, the idea is that Jesus is proclaimed "Lord" over the whole of one's life, body and existence and is

---

126 The majority text has τὸν θεόν ("God") instead of τὸν Χριστὸν ("Christ," cf. KJV, NKJV, YLT), but the manuscript witness clearly favors τὸν Χριστὸν.

established as such by His rule being extended over that from which one's entire life flows.

The opening words have engendered debate about how to render them. How do the two accusative nouns (κύριον and τὸν Χριστὸν) relate to one another? They are separated only by the postpositive δὲ ("but"). Are they to be read with κύριον ("Lord") as the direct object of the verb (ἁγιάσατε, "sanctify") and τὸν Χριστὸν in apposition to it ("the Lord Christ"; cf. "Christ the Lord," ESV)?[127] Or are we to understand it as an object (τὸν Χριστὸν, "Christ") and its complement (κύριον, "Lord"), yielding a translation of "Christ as Lord" (most English translations)?[128] The wording is ambiguous and either rendering is possible. The forward position of κύριον ("Lord") places special emphasis upon it, seeming to hold it forth as that which is sought in the setting apart of Christ in one's heart. But on the other hand, the Hebrew of Isaiah 8:13 is clearly appositional, supporting a reading here of "the Lord Christ." In the end, the meaning is not significantly altered by either reading.

> **Ministry Maxim**
>
> Christian hope is always illogical to the unhopeful.

Setting Christ as Lord at the command center of one's being will affect life in every direction. With those in opposition, it will position us as "always being ready to make a defense" (ἕτοιμοι ἀεὶ πρὸς ἀπολογίαν). The πρὸς may convey purpose.[129] This "defense" (ἀπολογίαν) is the word from which we get our English word *apologetics*. The word was a technical term from the legal world, describing a verbal defense of oneself or one's position. Paul would use it of his witness for the gospel in his first imprisonment (Phil. 1:7, 16) and the legal process in his final Roman imprisonment (2 Tim. 4:16). But here Peter has in mind not the courtroom (Acts 25:16; 2 Tim. 4:16), but the daily interchanges of life in which people

---

127 Bigg, 158; Dubis, 110; Goppelt, 242; Jobes, 229; Kelly, 142; Lenski, 149; Michaels, 183, 187.

128 Alford, 4:362; Forbes, 115; Schreiner, 173; Vincent, 1:653; Robertson, *Word Pictures*, 6:114; Stibbs, 135.

129 Forbes, 116.

who oppose our faith in Christ demand an accounting for that faith. As Michaels says, "Peter sees his readers as being 'on trial' every day as they live for Christ in a pagan society."[130] One's "defense" of Christian hope does not require scholastic competence but personal witness. It spurs each believer to become "a workman who does not need to be ashamed, accurately handling the word of truth" (2 Tim. 2:15). For "All Scripture is breathed out by God and profitable for teaching, for reproof, for correction, and for training in righteousness, that the man of God may be competent, equipped for every good work" (2 Tim. 3:16, ESV). According to Jesus' own promise, "when they hand you over, do not worry about how or what you are to say; for it will be given you in that hour what you are to say. For it is not you who speak, but it is the Spirit of your Father who speaks in you" (Matt. 10:19–20). Jesus' promise "is meant to rule out worry, not preparation!"[131]

The Spirit-enabled student of the Scriptures may be "always ... ready" (ἕτοιμοι ἀεὶ) for such duty. The adverb ἀεὶ ("always") literally means "through all" and is an idiom that has to do with duration of time that knows no limits.[132] The adjective ἕτοιμοι ("ready") depicts a state of readiness. The NT presses upon believers three things for which they are always to be ready: good works (Titus 3:1; 2 Tim. 2:21), gospel witness (Eph. 6:15; 1 Peter 3:15), Christ's return (Matt. 24:44; Luke 12:40; 1 Peter 1:5).[133] We must thus be perpetually (ἀεὶ, "always") poised (ἕτοιμοι, "ready") to give a Spirit-enabled, Scripture-shaped answer to "to everyone who asks you" (παντὶ τῷ αἰτοῦντι ὑμᾶς). The participle is used substantively (τῷ αἰτοῦντι, "*who* asks," emphasis added). The adjective παντὶ ("everyone") projects the possibilities as wide as possible. At every moment ("always") and with every person ("to everyone"), the believer is to be ready "in season and out of season" (2 Tim. 4:2) to give a reason for their hope.

---

130 Michaels, 188.

131 Marshall, 116.

132 Louw-Nida, 67.86.

133 TDNT, 2:707.

That which they ask of you is "an account for the hope that is in you" (λόγον περὶ τῆς ἐν ὑμῖν ἐλπίδος). Here λόγον ("an account") is used in the sense of making a reckoning, computation, or formal accounting for one's actions ("reason," ESV; "an answer," NET, NIV; "an accounting," NRSV).[134] The preposition περὶ ("for") originally meant "around in a circle" or "on all sides" and came then to mean "about" or "concerning."[135] The accounting sought is for the "hope" (τῆς ... ἐλπίδος) that orbits around and within the believer. Hope (ἐλπίς) is something one is born again into, its living nature derived from the resurrected Christ (1 Peter 1:3, 21). For Peter, the verb (ἐλπίζω, "to hope") is nearly synonymous with exercising faith (1:13; 3:5). Here, the noun has the definite article (τῆς ... ἐλπίδος) specifying and making particular that unique hope that is the birthright of the children of God. In the attributive position, between the noun and its definite article, is the prepositional phrase ἐν ὑμῖν ("in you"). This stresses the qualitative nature of the hope. But just what does it signal? Since the pronoun is in the plural (ὑμῖν, "you"), it might mean "among you." But given Peter's emphasis upon the personal nature of the new birth (1:3, 21), the hope that it confers should probably be seen as equally personal. Thus most English translations render it "in you." If this hope dwells in each heart, it will also be held among God's people.

One's "defense" should be unequivocal, "yet" (ἀλλὰ) take place "with gentleness and reverence" (μετὰ πραΰτητος καὶ φόβου). In the Greek text, this clause is included in verse 16. The adversative ἀλλὰ ("yet") establishes clearly how one's "account" must be rendered to the curious and perturbed unbelievers around them. How one responds to opposition and questioning is as important as with what one responds. This must be accompanied by (μετὰ, "with") two qualities. The first is "gentleness" (πραΰτητος). The word pictures not weakness but meekness. It is power brought under the control of a purpose higher than self-service. It characterized Jesus (Matt. 11:29; 21:5; 2 Cor. 10:1) and becomes real in us only by the working of the Holy Spirit (Gal. 5:23). It is how we receive the word of the gospel

---

134 BDAG, 4605.2.a.

135 Harris, 179–180.

(James 1:21), a sign of heavenly wisdom (James 3:13), to be our constant pursuit (1 Tim. 6:11), that with which we are to clothe ourselves (Col. 3:12), how we are to conduct ourselves in every relationship (Gal. 6:1; Eph 4:2), especially with those who oppose us (2 Tim. 2:25). Paul commanded Titus to teach the believers on Crete, particularly when it came to dealing with unbelieving political authorities, "to malign no one, to be peaceable, gentle [πραΰτητα], showing every consideration for all men" (Titus 3:2). Thus here the "gentleness" for which Peter calls is pictured as directed toward those who oppose and question them. What believers want to do in response is brought under the missional purpose of Jesus (1 Peter 2:9, 12; 3:1), resulting in a restrained, loving, patient response. This "gentleness" rests their fears and concerns in the hands of the sovereign Lord, who rules over and overrules all that takes place in the lives of His children. They have no need to control the situation, only to rest under their Savior's care and take up His purpose.

Added (καὶ, "and") to this is "reverence" (φόβου). Throughout this epistle, Peter consistently designates God as the one to fear rather than man (1 Peter 1:17; 2:18; 3:2, 14). It seems here he has in mind, then, that righteous fear of God which delivers one from the fear of man. This is all the more clear in view of what he has just said in verse 14b. Contextually, it points to that fear of God inherent in reverencing and treating Him as holy ("sanctify Christ as Lord") and which thus takes the power from their intimidators' threats and questions. The fear of the Lord explains the gentleness of a believer's response. Under God's care, His people can leave their persecutors in His hands and need not grasp for control or lash out. With their hope determined and guaranteed by God, they may live at peace in the present, even under the greatest of difficulties.

The same combination was previously demanded of the wife with her unbelieving husband (3:2, 4). This establishes that what was demanded of the wife is not exceptional or additional but simply the general expectation of believers living among unbelievers, now applied within the context of her marriage.

What Peter here calls for from believers can be clearly seen by his own actions when facing opposition. With the words of verse 15 as your guide, read again the account of Peter's answer to the questioners in Acts

2:14–41. Also, compare Paul's response to the charges pressed against him in Acts 25 and 26.[136]

Verse 16 – "and keep a good conscience so that in the thing in which you are slandered, those who revile your good behavior in Christ will be put to shame."

One's "defense" (v.15a) of hope in Christ is to be made not only "with gentleness and reverence" (v.15b) but also in such a way that one is able to "keep a good conscience" (συνείδησιν ἔχοντες ἀγαθήν). The participle (ἔχοντες, "keep," lit., "having") has been described as designating attendant circumstance,[137] being instrumental,[138] or signaling result,[139] but all generally conclude that however it is construed, it carries the force of an imperative. The present tense depicts the ongoing and unending nature of one's hold on "a good conscience" (συνείδησιν … ἀγαθήν). The word "conscience" is a compound, made up of σύν ("with") and εἶδον ("to see," "to perceive"). It is thus a co-knowledge shared with oneself. It points to self-awareness. Paul speaks of "the testimony of our conscience" (2 Cor. 1:12). It is a testimony given to oneself and then passed on to others. The conscience is "the interior faculty for the personal discernment of good and evil, the practical rule of conduct and motive for action."[140] Paul speaks again of a "good conscience" in verse 19. He can speak of "a perfectly good conscience" (Acts 23:1), "a clear conscience" (1 Tim. 3:9; 2 Tim. 1:3), and "a blameless conscience" (Acts 24:16). The conscience is a gift from God but has been distorted through sin. It can be "weak" through immaturity (1 Cor. 8:7), wounded through wrong (v.12), "defiled" by sin (Titus 1:15), and "seared" to the point of insensitivity by repeated rebellion (1 Tim. 4:2). Only God is "good" (Mark 10:18). The conscience

---

136 Cf. Clowney, 149–151.

137 Dubis, 113.

138 Schreiner, 176.

139 Forbes, 117; Storms, 337.

140 Spicq, 3:336.

is, therefore, "good" (ἀγαθήν) only when it accords with the thoughts of God. In this way, it is in tune with reality; it sees as God sees. Paul confessed, "I do not even examine myself. For I am conscious of nothing against myself, yet I am not by this acquitted; but the one who examines me is the Lord" (1 Cor. 4:3b-4). Conscience is a helpful guide only as it is conformed to the written revelation of God (2 Tim. 3:16–17).

Peter already spoke of bearing up under unjust suffering "for the sake of conscience toward God" (1 Peter 2:19; cf. 3:21). He desires no cloud between God and his readers that might obscure His presence, blocking the blessedness of His countenance turned in favor toward them. As they face suffering for Christ's sake, they must have a clear and unobscured fellowship with God, who alone will sustain them.

Peter makes clear the purpose (ἵνα with the subjunctive verb, "so that") of carefully making "gentleness" and "fear" and a "good conscience" a part of their hope-defense. It is not only that his readers might be faithful, but that in the end, their detractors "will be put to shame" (καταισχυνθῶσιν). The verb is a compound derived from κατά ("down") and αἰσχύνη ("shame," "humiliation"). The preposition in compound emphasizes the humbled state of the shamed; their humiliation descends upon them from above. It designates "the shame and disappointment that come to one whose faith or hope is shown to be vain."[141] Peter has used the word before to say that no one who hopes in Christ will "be put to shame" (1 Peter 2:6, ESV). The aorist tense looks to a specific moment in time. The passive voice pictures the unbelieving one being acted upon by another.

> **Ministry Maxim**
>
> A good conscience and good behavior provide a good witness.

What point in time does Peter have in mind for their "shame"? Earlier, he counseled his readers to so suffer that their persecutors might praise God in the end (1 Peter 2:12; cf. 3:1). He has also spoken of so living that his readers might "silence the ignorance of foolish men" (1 Peter 2:15). "God has chosen the foolish things of the

---

141 BDAG, 3972.3.

world to shame [καταισχύνῃ] the wise, and God has chosen the weak things of the world to shame [καταισχύνῃ] the things which are strong" (1 Cor. 1:27). It seems Peter looks for a "shame" that will come in this life, working repentance and faith in Christ. But if that is not to be, Christ will return in glory, being vindicated before all the universe, and those who have not believed will be put to everlasting shame. When Jesus spoke, "all His opponents were being humiliated [κατῃσχύνοντο]" (Luke 13:17). When He returns, all will see that "His name is called The Word of God" (Rev. 19:13). He is the final word from God—the word that fulfills every promise of hope for the believer and the word that silences the folly of all who do not believe.

Peter has in view "those who revile your good behavior in Christ" (οἱ ἐπηρεάζοντες ὑμῶν τὴν ἀγαθὴν ἐν Χριστῷ ἀναστροφήν). The articular participle is used substantively (οἱ ἐπηρεάζοντες, "*those who* revile," emphasis added). The verb means to spitefully abuse, threaten, revile, and "to treat someone in a despicable manner."[142] The present tense pictures the ongoing, steady nature of their actions. The verb appears elsewhere in the NT only in Luke 6:28 when Jesus told His disciples, "bless those who curse you, pray for those who mistreat [ἐπηρεαζόντων] you." This evil, spiteful hatred arises against "your good behavior in Christ" (ὑμῶν τὴν ἀγαθὴν ἐν Χριστῷ ἀναστροφήν). The noun (ἀναστροφήν, "behavior") appears thirteen times in the NT, eight of which are from Peter's pen (1 Peter 1:15, 18; 2:12; 3:1, 2, 16; 2 Peter 2:7; 3:11). It literally means "a turning about in place" and then came to designate one's daily behavior[143], though that moment-by-moment conduct is pictured as driven by certain principles[144], for good (1 Tim. 4:12; Heb. 13:7; James 3:13; 1 Peter 1:15; 2:12; 3:1, 2, 16; 2 Peter 3:11) or ill (Gal. 1:13; Eph. 4:22; 1 Peter 1:18).

For their "conscience" to be "good" (ἀγαθήν; i.e., before God), their "behavior" must be "good" (ἀγαθήν) before the unbelieving world. But it can only be so when it is "in Christ" (ἐν Χριστῷ). Both the adjective

---

142 Ibid., 2919.

143 Friberg, 52.

144 BDAG, 566.

(ἀγαθὴν, "good") and the prepositional phrase (ἐν Χριστῷ, "in Christ") are in the attributive position, between the noun and its definite article (τὴν ... ἀναστροφήν), stressing the qualitative nature of the "behavior." It is "good," but only because it is "in Christ." It can be "good" only as it is "in Christ." The precise phrase ἐν Χριστῷ ("in Christ") occurs seventy-six times in the NT, and all are by Paul except Peter's three usages (1 Peter 3:16; 5:10, 14).[145]

And this should take place "in the thing in which you are slandered" (ἐν ᾧ καταλαλεῖσθε). Peter used the precise expression before (ἵνα ἐν ᾧ καταλαλοῦσιν; 2:12) except that there the verb was active and third person plural, whereas here it is passive and second person plural. The preposition (ἐν, "in") and relative pronoun (ᾧ, "which") assume the presence of a demonstrative pronoun ("the thing"). When joined, they mean "in that which."[146] It all points to something in which, at present, "you are slandered" (καταλαλεῖσθε). The verb is found only five times in the NT (James 4:11 [3x]; 1 Peter 2:12; 3:16). It is a compound made up of κατά ("against") and λαλέω ("to speak"). It means to speak evil of, to slander, to rail against,[147] "to criminate,"[148] to speak ill of, degrade, or defame.[149] The present tense pictures this as a pattern of speech. The passive voice views Peter's readers as being acted upon by their detractors. The Christians are acting (τὴν ... ἀναστροφήν, "behavior") in support of their verbal witness; their detractors merely are talking (καταλαλεῖσθε, "you are slandered"). It appears, therefore, that it is the ethical conduct of the believers that their opponents find so offensive (and which moves them to ask the reason behind their hope), and the form of the opposition at this point is primarily verbal, not physical.

---

145 The general expression occurs 164 times in Paul's letters (Davids, 133; Goppelt, 245; Kelly, 145). John expresses the same concept, but without the precise phrase.

146 BDAG, 5396.1.b.α.

147 NIDNTTE, 3:78.

148 Thayer, 332.

149 BDAG, 3997.

As noted above, the goal in 2:12 is the salvation of their detractors, and we best understand Peter's intent here similarly. So live that those who call you evildoers will be put to shame by your good behavior and may rethink the message of the gospel, believe, and be saved.

> **Digging Deeper:**
> 1. Describe how God has "blessed" you when you have wrongly suffered on His account (v.14).
> 2. How is your hope manifest and evident to the unbelieving around you (v.15)?
> 3. Explain why the state of one's conscience determines the effectiveness of one's witness (v.16).

Verse 17 – "For it is better, if God should will it so, that you suffer for doing what is right rather than for doing what is wrong."

Peter grounds (γὰρ, "For") his counsel in verses 15 and 16 with a summarizing explanation. He presents his line of thought through the formula "it is better ... than" (κρεῖττον ... ἤ). The first component of the formula (κρεῖττον, "better") is the comparative form of ἀγαθός ("good"), found so often in the present context (1 Peter 2:18; 3:10, 11, 13, 16 [2x], 21). He uses the same formula in 2 Peter 2:21. The "better ... than" line of reasoning is familiar from the wisdom literature of the OT (Prov. 12:9; 15:16, 17; 16:8, 19, 32; 17:1; 19:1, 22; 21:9, 19; 22:1; 25:7, 24; 27:5, 10; 28:6), the Gospels (Matt. 5:29–30; 18:8–9; Mark 9:43, 45, 47), the epistles (1 Cor. 7:9; 2 Peter 2:21), and outside the Bible (e.g., Plato).

What is assumed in Peter's line of reasoning is "that you suffer" (πάσχειν). By God's grace, there are seasons when His people do not suffer for their faith, but for Peter's original readers, and far too often in history, that was not the case. The present tense pictures the present nature of their suffering. As they suffer there can be something "better ... than" other possibilities. As Jesus taught, suffering will be a part of His followers' lives (John 15:19; 16:33). There can be something worse than suffering for Jesus. The infinitive functions as the subject of an assumed verb (ἐστιν, "is"). The verb (πάσχω, "to suffer") has become Peter's thematic verb for this letter (1 Peter 2:19, 20, 21, 23; 3:14, 17, 18; 4:1 [2x], 15, 19; 5:10).

If suffering must come, it is "better" that it comes "for doing what is right" (ἀγαθοποιοῦντας). This participle is thrust forward, even before the condition or the main verb, for emphasis. Four of the nine NT usages of the verb are found here in 1 Peter, this being his last (2:15, 20; 3:6, 17). It is a compound built of ἀγαθός ("good") and ποιέω ("to do"). In the first element of the

> **Ministry Maxim**
>
> The value of pain is exposed by what provokes it.

compound, we have expressed again that thematic adjective (ἀγαθός) of which the comparative form was just used to introduce the sentence. The present tense pictures the ongoing nature of the actions of the follower of Christ. Like the one to follow, the participle is used to express cause. Peter pictures suffering that takes place for a certain reason.

Before we come to the contrasting form of suffering, Peter qualifies the first with a condition: "if God should will it so" (εἰ θέλοι τὸ θέλημα τοῦ θεοῦ). Peter loves to alliterate (cf. 1 Peter 1:4, 19; 2:15, 21; 3:20) and does so here once again with the three-fold repetition of words beginning in θ: θέλοι τὸ θέλημα τοῦ θεοῦ.[150] The condition is a rare use of an optative verb in a conditional statement. See our comments on the similar condition above in verse 14. The condition is unfulfilled, and its fulfillment is considered more remote than when other conditional forms are used. This is not because there is little chance of God's people suffering for doing good, for as we have seen, Jesus promised this would be so, and Peter and the rest of the NT authors have confirmed this. It does not call into question the fact of suffering, but just how and when such suffering will occur in their lives.

The expression itself is unusual, being literally rendered "if wills the will of God" (cf. John 7:17). The "will of God" is set out as a substantive that

---

150 Forbes, 119.

acts ("wills") that Christ's people suffer for doing good. We are reminded of and comforted that no suffering ever comes to our lives apart from God's active involvement in it. For some, this raises questions about the goodness of God, provoking questions such as, How can a good God will the suffering of His own people? But such questions assume the highest good to be our own comfort. God wills above all that we are conformed to the image of His Son (Rom. 8:29). It is for this very reason, then, that we are assured "that God causes all things to work together for good [ἀγαθόν] to those who love God, to those who are called according to His purpose" (Rom. 8:28). Where some find reason to disbelieve, others find the greatest comfort in their painful belief.

Peter's wording raises questions about whether God wills the sufferings of His own people. How can He remain a God of love and do so? Elliot seeks a way around this, arguing that it is not God's will that His people suffer, but that they do what is right even if it means suffering.[151] This is an artful dodge, but in the end does not seem to solve the problem. For if they do good and then suffer, God has willed it. Whether it is the cause or the effect, God still sovereignly rules over the entire matter. The statement here seems to say the same thing as in 1:6: "In this you greatly rejoice, even though now for a little while, if necessary [εἰ δέον], you have been distressed by various trials."[152] Peter has already said with regard to patiently enduring suffering, "you have been called for this purpose, since Christ also suffered for you, leaving you an example for you to follow in His steps" (2:21). Furthermore, the Scriptures elsewhere seem to indicate that God does indeed will that suffering be the means to His divine ends—such as effectively proclaiming the suffering Savior through suffering people (cf. Col. 1:24ff). This is the same point Peter has been making that suffering for doing good when patiently endured may win the persecutors to Christ (1 Peter 2:12; 3:1–2). Jesus suffered to bring us to God (3:18) and we are called to suffer patiently in His name so that the gospel of the suffering, dying Savior can come savingly to unbelieving people

---

151 Elliot, 635; cf. Jobes, 232–233.
152 Goppelt, 246.

(2:12, 21; 3:1–2).[153] His suffering and dying were uniquely atoning in nature; ours is proclamatory but essential in disseminating the gospel. We do not solve the problem of theodicy by changing Peter's meaning here. It is not a problem to be solved, but a point of mystery that brings us to our knees in worship before a God so gloriously wise and gracious that He can even subsume evil and suffering to make it serve His purposes of glory and grace.

That which is not "better" is suffering "for doing what is wrong" (κακοποιοῦντας). Again we have a compound: κακός ("evil") and ποιέω ("to do"). The first element (κακός, "evil") stands in direct contrast to the first element (ἀγαθός, "good") in the contrasting participle. Both are built off the verb ποιέω ("to do"). This second participle is held to the end to create a visual, grammatical distance from ἀγαθοποιοῦντας ("doing what is right") and stresses their polarized nature. It, too, is used to express cause, this time of an assumed repetition of the previous infinitive (πάσχειν, "you suffer"). As with the previous participle, the present tense pictures the ongoing nature of their actions.

Jesus used the two compound verbs alongside one another: "I ask you, is it lawful to do good [ἀγαθοποιῆσαι] or to do harm [κακοποιῆσαι] on the Sabbath, to save a life or to destroy it?" (Luke 6:9; cf. Mark 3:4). John too laid the compound verbs alongside one another, declaring, "The one who does good [ὁ ἀγαθοποιῶν] is of God; the one who does evil [ὁ κακοποιῶν] has not seen God" (3 John 11). Peter used the same combination in an adjectival form earlier, saying God appointed governing officials "for the punishment of evildoers [κακοποιῶν] and the praise of those who do right [ἀγαθοποιῶν]" (1 Peter 2:14).

Michaels argues that suffering "for doing what is wrong" is a reference to future, eschatological suffering rather than suffering experienced in this life.[154] After arguing against finding 3:17 "a generalized repetition of 2:20," he cites three reasons for his conclusions. First, he argues that if 3:17 is considered a generalized repetition of 2:20, then it reduces verse 17

---

153 Grudem, 162.

154 Michaels, 191–192; cf. also Forbes, 119.

to a "truism." A truism states something already considered demonstrably true and does not add anything further to the discussion. But this fails on multiple fronts. It fails to recognize that it is the nature of proverbial statements to simplify. It does not add to the argument set forth precisely because it is not trying to do so; it is the nature of the genre employed. It further ignores the value and multiplied examples of the nature of repetition in the Scriptures as a pedological technique. Does the fact that Peter basically repeats what he has already said somehow immediately make it untrue? Does not repetition often do precisely the opposite, marking a statement as worthy of extra note? And if verse 17 basically repeats a point already made, isn't that note precisely what we would expect here after a sustained line of reasoning before verse 18 moves us in a different, complementary direction? He is repeating what he earlier said specifically to slaves (2:18ff) and applying it now more broadly to all God's people. As in 2:20, it opened the door to a theological exploration of Jesus' sufferings and death (2:21–25), so it serves similarly here in 3:17 (cf. 3:18–22).[155] Second, Michaels notes that the "better...than" proverbial form appears in the NT and says its form is consistent: a word for "good" or "better," two infinitives expressing the actions or experiences being weighed against each other, and a word of comparison. What he does not note, however, is that this is not the form we find in 3:17 (we have two participles instead of two infinitives). He states that the NT "better...than" proverbial statements are consistently eschatological, which may be true enough, but he fails to recognize that the OT examples (which he admits do exist) do not always speak of eschatological realities (e.g., Prov. 3:14; 12:9; 15:16, 17; 16:8, 19; 17:1). What is to say Peter followed the NT examples rather than the OT examples? Has he not frequently cited and alluded to OT Scriptures throughout this letter? Finally, Michaels says the context supports the eschatological interpretation of verse 17. In support, he cites particularly 3:10–12 (a quotation from Psalm 34). But in his haste to argue that 3:17 does not reflect 2:20, he admits the context supports the opposite of his eschatological interpretation.

---

155 Clowney, 153–154.

The worst thing Peter can think of is not suffering but suffering for the wrong reason. He has touched already on this theme (2:20; 3:1–2) and will continue to do so, later commanding: "Make sure that none of you suffers as a murderer, or thief, or evildoer, or a troublesome meddler; but if anyone suffers as a Christian, he is not to be ashamed, but is to glorify God in this name" (1 Peter 4:15–16).

> **Digging Deeper:**
> 1 Are you more comforted or confused by the fact that God may will the suffering of His own people? Why?
> 2 Can you identify a time you brought pain upon yourself because of your own behavior rather than your faith in Christ?

Verse 18 – "For Christ also died for sins once for all, *the* just for *the* unjust, so that He might bring us to God, having been put to death in the flesh, but made alive in the spirit;"

Having begun to directly address the matter of persecution (3:14–17), Peter now cites Jesus' unjust suffering (3:18–22). This reflects the pattern Peter used when he spoke to servants about submission to unbelieving masters (2:18–20) and then cited Jesus' suffering (2:21–24). This serves not only to hold up Christ as our example in suffering but also to ground our responses to such suffering in the grace of God extended to us in Christ. Whether in obeying commands or enduring suffering, Peter founds his exhortations on Christological, theological, and redemptive bedrock. The course Peter runs through verses 18–22 will be grammatically complex, and several parenthetical thoughts will take the reader aside momentarily, but the overall thrust is that though Christ suffered and died (v.18a), He was raised to life (v.18b), and ascended to the Father's right hand (vv.19a, 22a) where He sits utterly triumphant over all His foes (v.22b). In the difficult and complex statements of verses 19–21, we must not lose sight of the primary point of Jesus' overcoming, universal victory.

Because of Jesus' victory over all opposing forces, believers can meet suffering knowing that ultimately in Christ they too will triumph.

The opening ὅτι ("For") connects what he says here to what he has just been saying. In verse 17, Peter reiterated the basic premise that suffering for doing good is better than suffering for doing bad (cf. 2:20). Now, as an explanatory, supporting illustration, he returns to speak of the sufferings, death, resurrection, and ascension of Jesus (3:18–22). The sentence Peter begins here runs through verse 20.

Peter sets the matter out plainly: "Christ...died for sins" (Χριστὸς...περὶ ἁμαρτιῶν ἔπαθεν). There is a question related to the text here. Is the verb ἀπέθανεν ("died," NASU, RSV) or ἔπαθεν ("suffered," ESV, KJV, NET, NIV, NRSV, NLT, NKJV, YLT)?[156] Peter uses the latter twelve times in this letter, more than any other NT book. He never elsewhere uses ἀποθνήσκω ("to die"). The manuscript evidence favors ἀπέθανεν ("died"), but the context of the letter lends support to ἔπαθεν ("suffered"). It might be argued that scribes would be more likely to change ἀπέθανεν ("died") to ἔπαθεν ("suffered") because of Peter's propensity toward the latter verb. But it might also be argued that the latter verb's multiplied use argues for its likelihood here. It might also be maintained that later scribes changed "suffered" to "died" to conform it to standard NT phraseology for what was done "for sins." In the end, a definitive answer eludes us, but we do well to remember that when Peter speaks of Jesus' sufferings, he does not imagine only those things that lead up to the moment of death but includes all that Jesus underwent leading up to and including His death. The meaning is not greatly altered, whichever verb we view as the original. As presented in our Greek text, the verb is in the aorist tense, picturing the whole of Jesus' sufferings and death as a singular whole and pointing to them as the sole ground of hope for sinners. Notably, Peter speaks as he does of Jesus' sufferings and death, for he was the one who opposed Jesus when He began to disclose His coming passion to the Disciples (Matt. 16:22; Mark 8:32). What he once opposed he now champions as the sole ground of hope.

---

156 Cf. the similar issues at 2:21 and our discussion there.

When the preposition (περὶ, "for") is used with either ἁμαρτίας or ἁμαρτιῶν in conjunction with a word denoting sacrifice or sacrificial offering, the sense of the prepositional phrase is 'to atone for sin(s)" or simply "for sins(s)."[157] In light of the appearance of ὑπὲρ in the next clause Harris notes that "ὑπὲρ is more common with persons and περὶ with things," as seems to be the case here in verse 18.[158]

Peter used καὶ ("also") adverbially to note that Jesus' sufferings and death were like what he had just told his readers they must face for His sake. There was likeness of His sufferings and theirs, but there were also infinite differences. Peter now speaks of the uniqueness of Jesus' sufferings and death.

Jesus' death was "once for all" (ἅπαξ). While the adverb could point simply to that which occurred one time, it was used in the NT to designate "the uniqueness of Christ's work as something which cannot be repeated."[159] It was used this way in Hebrews 9:26–28. In contrast to the High Priest, who had to appear repeatedly in God's presence in the Holy of Holies (v.25), "now once [ἅπαξ] at the consummation of the ages" Jesus "has been manifested to put away sin by the sacrifice of Himself" (v.26).

> **Ministry Maxim**
>
> Jesus' triumph after suffering injects hope into our suffering.

In our present passage, the adverb combined with the aorist tense of the verb emphasizes the singularity Jesus' sufferings and death as contrasted not only with the repeated offerings of the High Priest throughout time but also with the ongoing nature of the suffering of Peter's readers. Theirs are present and ongoing. Jesus' was past and is complete. Theirs may go on throughout life; Jesus' was accomplished, finished, complete, and perfect. The adverb designates "the historical and unrepeatable nature of God's redemption in Christ."[160] Spicq says, "Christ offered

---

157 Harris, 183; cf. BDAG, 5803.1.g.

158 Harris, 211.

159 TDNT, 1:382.

160 NIDNTTE, 1:343.

himself and died one single time for sins, and it is indeed true that this oblation was perfect and unique, so that there is no need for it to be renewed. But if this translation suggests the definitive quality of Christ's sacrifice, it does not sufficiently emphasize that it is absolute, complete; it takes *hapax* too exclusively as an adverb of quantity and inadequately reflects the word's etymology. *Hapax* may be an old nominative whose root is found in *peg-ny-mi,* 'to fasten by driving well in, to drive into the ground, fasten by assembling, fix by compacting, solidifying, crystallizing, jelling, being congealed.'"[161] He then summarizes and applies, saying, "On the theological plane, to say that the sacrifice of Christ is 'compact' would mean that it includes all of its effects (and its commemorations?), like the spring which contains potentially the whole river."[162]

When Jesus died for us, it was "*the* just for *the* unjust" (δίκαιος ὑπὲρ ἀδίκων). Neither noun has the definite article, so it more literally reads "just for unjust." Peter thus emphasizes the qualitative nature of each. But both may still be considered definite.[163] Jesus is "just" (δίκαιος); we are "unjust" (ἀδίκων). He is rightly related to the Father; we are at enmity with Him. He is without sin (1 Peter 2:22); we have sinned. He stands under the Father's favor; we stand under His judgment. He fulfilled the Law and all the righteous demands of God; we have been lawless, independent, and reckless. God, in forbearance and patience, "sends rain on the righteous and the unrighteous [δικαίους καὶ ἀδίκους]" (Matt. 5:45). In the end, He will raise "both the just and the unjust [δικαίων τε καὶ ἀδίκων]" (Acts 24:15, ESV) and all will stand before Him. Peter uses a singular form to speak of Jesus (δίκαιος, "just") but a plural one to speak of us (ἀδίκων, "unjust"). "Christ is in the 'righteous' category all by himself. 'Unrighteous' refers to everyone else."[164] The Suffering Servant of Isaiah 53 is called "the Righteous One" (δίκαιον; 53:11; cf. the title used of Christ in Acts 3:14; 7:52; 22:14; cf. 1 John

---

161 Spicq, 1:142.

162 Ibid., 1:143.

163 Robertson, *Grammar*, 757.

164 Forbes, 122.

2:1) and is said to "justify many" (δικαιῶσαι). Through His sufferings and death, the Suffering Servant would make others what He Himself already was. He did this by offering Himself "for" (ὑπὲρ) us. As in 2:21 (see our comments there), we recognize that "ὑπὲρ usually indicates representation ('on behalf of') or advantage ('for the benefit of')." Yet here ὑπὲρ "may bear the dual sense of representation/advantage and substitution" (Rom. 5:6, 8; 14:15; 2 Cor. 5:14–15a; Gal. 3:13; 1 Thess. 5:10; 1 Peter 2:21; 3:18; 1 John 3:16).[165]

Jesus died for a purpose (ἵνα and the subjunctive verb; "so that'), that He might bring us to God" (ὑμᾶς προσαγάγῃ τῷ θεῷ). The verb is a compound made up of πρός ("to") and ἄγω ("to bring"). It is used only three other times in the NT (Luke 9:41; Acts 16:20; 27:27). It could be used across a spectrum of meaning, variously denoting "the bringing of a person before a tribunal or presenting him at a royal court or the ritual act of bringing sacrifice to God or the consecration of persons to God's service."[166] The aorist tense looks to the definitive, decisive deliverance into relationship with God. That Jesus had to "bring us to God" means of course that we were estranged from Him. Jesus made the sacrifice which enabled reconciliation between God and "us" (ὑμᾶς).[167] Peter underscored how profoundly personal this work of Jesus must be for each one.

Jesus reconciled us to His Father by a two-fold action, set out by a μὲν... δὲ formula (i.e., "on the one hand... but on the other hand"). The two actions are set before us in two aorist passive participles. Both qualify προσαγάγῃ τῷ θεῷ ("He might bring us to God") and are probably to be considered instrumental/means (Jesus brought us to God by means of His death and resurrection).[168] Both emphasize accomplished action. Both picture Jesus being acted upon from outside—in the first,

---

165 Harris, 215–216.

166 Rienecker, 759.

167 One manuscript has no pronoun at all; others have ἡμᾶς ("us") and others ὑμᾶς ("you"). The second plural form (ὑμᾶς, "you") is more in keeping with the surrounding context (vv.13–17; Dubis, 117; Forbes, 122; Michaels, 195; cf. NET, NIV, NLT, NRSV).

168 Dubis, 117; Forbes, 122.

by His enemies; in the second, by His Father. Both are followed by dative singular nouns. In addition to the intended contrast, the "pairing of the two participial expressions by the use of μὲν ... δὲ has the effect of subordinating the first to the second: 'though put to death in the flesh, he was made alive in the Spirit.'"[169]

A great deal of debate has circled around these two statements, and interpretations run across a broad spectrum. Let's establish what seems to be clear before diving into the questions that remain. Clearly, Peter provides us with two parallel statements that are in some way contrasted with one another. The parallel forms indicate that we should interpret them in parallel ways. Though there is debate as to the particulars, it seems clear that Peter is speaking in the first statement of Jesus' death and in the second of His resurrection. Beyond these more obvious points, let us consider the specific words and statements.

First, Jesus is set before us as "having been put to death in the flesh" (θανατωθεὶς ... σαρκὶ). The verb is used eleven times in the NT. In eight of the other ten occurrences, it refers to physical death (Matt. 10:21; 26:59; 27:1; Mark 13:12; 14:55; Luke 21:16; Rom. 8:36; 2 Cor. 6:9). In the other two occurrences, it used metaphorically of having died to the Law (Rom. 7:4) and putting to death "the deeds of the body" (Rom. 8:13). We may safely conclude that here Peter intends the physical death of Jesus.

This took place "in the flesh" (σαρκὶ), that is to say, bodily, as it pertains to physical, earthly life. Jesus physically died. As to this world and what fills it, Jesus was separated and removed from it through death. His burial bore witness to this fact. The chief priests and Council sought false testimony against Jesus "that they might put Him to death [θανατώσωσιν]" (Matt. 26:59; cf. Mark 14:55). They "conferred together against Jesus to put Him to death [θανατῶσαι]" (27:1). This they accomplished by turning Jesus over to the Roman authorities who crucified Him.

Second, Jesus was "made alive in the spirit" (ζωοποιηθεὶς ... πνεύματι). This verb also appears eleven times in the NT. It is a compound comprised

---

169 Michaels, 205; cf. Jobes, 240.

of ζωός ("alive," "living") and ποιέω ("to do," "to make").[170] It referred to the giving of life where once death reigned (John 5:21 [2x]; 6:63; Rom. 4:17; 8:11; 1 Cor. 15:22, 36, 45; 2 Cor. 3:6; Gal. 3:21). In Romans 8:11 the verb appears in parallel with and as synonymous with the verb more regularly used of Jesus' resurrection (ἐγείρω). This eliminates the possibility that Peter refers here to what remained true of Jesus after He died and before He was raised from the dead. The Bible credits all three members of the Trinity with giving life (John 5:21; 6:63; 10:18). Jesus spoke of being able to raise Himself to life again after death (John 2:19), but consistently the Scriptures attribute Jesus' resurrection to the working of the Father (e.g., Acts 2:24; 3:15; 5:30; Rom. 6:4; Gal. 1:1; Eph. 1:20; Col. 2:12; Heb. 13:20). This leads us to conclude the passive here functions as a divine passive, God the Father being the one bringing to pass Jesus' resurrection.

But just what does Peter intend by "in the spirit" (πνεύματι)? Some translations find here a reference to God the Spirit, the third member of the Trinity (KJV, NIV, NKJV, NLT). This would require, however, that the two datives be understood as functioning in different senses—the former as depicting the sphere of reference and the second as designating instrumentality or means ("by," KJV, NKJV). While not impossible, it is less likely that two datives set forth in such proximity and as clearly parallel would be expected to be understood in different ways. It is both simpler and truer to the actual text to see the two datives as functioning in the same way with their respective participles. If the first ("in the flesh") pointed to the sphere wherein Jesus' death was realized (bodily, with regard to the physical world), then it stands to reason that "in the spirit" here means spiritually, as regards the immaterial world.

---

170 BDAG, 3398.

In this way, both nouns would be considered datives of reference or respect.[171] With respect or in reference to the concrete world, as to things physical, Jesus died; as to the immaterial world, as to things spiritual, Jesus was made alive. This latter need not exclude Jesus' body, for He received a glorified, resurrection body (1 Cor. 15). Jesus "was declared the Son of God with power by the resurrection from the dead, according to the Spirit of holiness, Jesus Christ our Lord" (Rom 1:4). Since the Holy Spirit is the effective power in the realm of all things spiritual, there might be room for a tentative acknowledgment of those who translate "Spirit" rather than "spirit" (KJV, NIV, NKJV, NLT).

Verse 19 – "in which also He went and made proclamation to the spirits *now* in prison,"

Peter continues the sentence he began in verse 18. But now he takes a couple of steps away from the trajectory of thought he began there and will ultimately pick up and complete in verse 22 with the note of Christ's complete triumph over all opposing forces. While arriving at a unified understanding of verses 19 through 21 has eluded interpreters throughout Church history, we need not be in doubt about Peter's primary point. Through His death, resurrection, and ascension, Jesus has triumphed over all evil, particularly those malevolent spiritual forces at the root of mankind's rebellion (v.22). Verses 19 through 21 need thorough and careful exploration. The waters often have been clouded rather than cleared by long and hotly debated exegesis and interpretation. We do well to keep

---

171 So Clowney (157–158), Davids (138), Forbes (123), Goppelt (253), Hiebert (239), Jobes (242), Kelly (151), Marshall (121–123), Michaels (204). Some who argue for both datives as signifying the realm or sphere of the activity come close to the same idea (e.g., Grudem, 163–164; Robertson, *Grammar*, 523; Storms, 12:338–339). Others argue for both to be datives of agency (i.e., put to death by human beings; raised by the Holy Spirit, but this strains the wording of the first) or both as datives of means (Lenski, 158). Still others argue that nothing requires the two datives be interpreted alike (e.g., Wallace claims "poetic license" to interpret them differently, 343). Some among them say the first is a dative of respect/reference and the second a dative of agency (Dubis, 117–118; Schreiner, 184); others that the first is a dative of sphere and the second a dative of means (Wallace, 155, 166). Other options abound.

ever before us Peter's primary point. The comments that follow with relationship to verses 19 through 21 are designed to help us explore Peter's challenging words, but the expositor's path should not be lost—the message is Jesus' complete triumph (vv.19–22).

Peter uses a relative clause (ἐν ᾧ, "in which") to set out something of the breadth of Jesus' triumph. Establishing the antecedent of the relative pronoun (ᾧ, "which") is a key to understanding Peter's point. It is simplest to find it in "spirit" (πνεύματι) in verse 18. Others believe the phrase here is to be understood as pointing to cause ("for which reason," "because of this") and thus looks back upon the entire previous clause (v.13). Still others read the phrase as temporal ("on which occasion," "meanwhile") and may or may not find necessity in identifying a specific antecedent.[172] All are possible syntactically. The addition of the accompanying preposition ἐν ("in") creates a combination (ἐν ᾧ) used by Peter five times in this letter (1:6; 2:12; 3:16, 19; 4:4). The combination of the two "connects w[ith] the situation described in what precedes" and means "*under which circumstances = under these circumstance*"[173] or "*as far as this is concerned*" (i.e., the "spirit" of v.18).[174] It points to the circumstance or condition under which something took place (i.e., Jesus' transition from death to life, v.18).[175] Despite arguments to the contrary, the simplest and most straight forward option seems best—the relative pronoun finds its antecedent in πνεύματι ("spirit") in verse 18 and the combination ἐν ᾧ ("in which") indicates under what conditions or in what sphere (i.e., in reference to the spiritual world; having been raised out of death to resurrection life) Jesus took the action outlined here in verse 19.

The καὶ is used adverbially ("also") as it was in verse 18 and will be again in verse 21. Here it indicates what Jesus did in addition to ("also") being raised victoriously over all in the spiritual realm. That is, "He...made

---

172 NET Bible; Wallace, 343.
173 BDAG, 5391.1.k.γ.
174 Ibid. 2581.7.
175 Ibid.

proclamation" (ἐκήρυξεν). The verb (κηρύσσω, "to preach") is used over sixty times in the NT and is one of its standard words for proclamation of the gospel. The word describes the activity of one sent as an authorized and commissioned representative of a higher authority. Such a one delivers an authoritative message and does so as if the ruling power were present personally to speak the word. The aorist tense sets Jesus' proclamation forth as a singular, decisive event. The verb is pushed to the end of the clause for emphasis.

"He ... made proclamation" (ἐκήρυξεν) is qualified by the participle πορευθεὶς ("went"). The word simply stresses movement from one area to another. Peter uses it again in verse 22 of Jesus' ascension, saying Jesus "is at the right hand of God, having gone [πορευθεὶς] into heaven." The context thus moves us to understand it the same way here. Peter is thus not describing something that happened between Jesus' death and resurrection, but a proclamation that Jesus made after He was raised from the dead (cf. our comments on v.18 above). Here the participle may be understood as temporal ("when ... going," Dubis, 105, 121). It simply designates that Jesus completed the journey that made possible His proclamation. The aorist tense views the action as punctiliar. The verb is deponent, so the passive voice should be understood as active.

This proclamation was "to the spirits now in prison" (τοῖς ἐν φυλακῇ πνεύμασιν). The "spirits" in view are specified by the presence of the definite article (τοῖς ... πνεύμασιν). The noun is the same one just used in verse 18 to designate that in which Jesus was raised to life. So now alive triumphantly in reference to and in the realm of all that is "spirit," Jesus naturally made a proclamation of victory there. But here, Peter has a specific subset of "spirits" in view, those "now in prison" (ἐν φυλακῇ). The prepositional phrase is in the attributive position between the noun and its definite article, further indicating the nature of the "spirits" in view.

Questions abound! What is the precise identity of these "spirits"? What did they do to warrant being put "in prison"? Where is this "prison"? Who put them there? And when? It is right to seek answers to these questions.

No answer will silence all debate.[176] In a passage as debated as this one, we must, as Marshall says, seek the answer that "is the least difficult."[177]

As to the identity of these "spirits," there are generally three views. Some identify the "spirits" simply as those who had died by that time. But there is little evidence that the noun πνεῦμα ("spirit") in the plural is used to refer to human beings without some qualification (e.g., Heb. 12:23). In the NT, it typically refers to spiritual beings, frequently wicked ones. Peter more typically uses ψυχή ("soul") to reference the immaterial in humans.[178]

Others take a similar tack but limit the human "spirits" in view to those who resisted and remained in unbelief during Noah's day (cf. 20). This suffers from the same weaknesses as the previous view. In this camp are those who believe the pre-incarnate Son of God made His proclamation by the Holy Spirit operating in Noah as he preached to his contemporaries and prepared the ark. This might receive some support from 1 Peter 1:11, which speaks of "the Spirit of Christ within" the OT prophets. Others of this mind believe that between Jesus' death and resurrection, He descended into hell to preach to the "spirits" of these folks. Some believe this was an announcement of victory, others an offer of salvation. In the latter case, the Scripture is clear, "it is appointed for men to die once and after this comes judgment" (Heb. 9:27). There are no second chances at salvation after physical death. In either case, we might ask, why would Jesus make such a proclamation only to a limited group?

Others believe these refer to those "spirits" described in Genesis 6:1–5, reflecting a widespread contemporary Jewish interpretation of those

---

176 Many rightly cite Luther on this passage: "A wonderful text is this, and a more obscure passage perhaps than any other in the New Testament, so that I do not know for a certainty just what Peter means" (168).

177 Marshall, 127.

178 Davids, 139; Dubis, 120; Forbes, 124; Jobes, 250; Michaels, 206–207; contra Grudem, 215–219; Clowney, 157–164.

events, particularly in the book of 1 Enoch. This appears to be Peter's understanding of the events in 2 Peter 2:4 as well as that of Jude (Jude 6). Peter there linked those events (2 Peter 2:4) with the events of the Flood (2:5), a connection he appears to make here as well (1 Peter 3:19–20). Given Peter's proclivity to so understand the events of Genesis 6 and to combine with them the events of the Flood (Gen. 7–8), it seems most likely that he is also doing so in the present context.

We return then to answer the questions raised above. What is the precise identity of these "spirits"? Though debate will continue, it seems both simplest and clearest to understand them as those wicked spirits operative in the era of world history that found its climax in the Flood of Noah's day. What did they do to warrant being put "in prison"? They engaged in unprecedented evil with human beings (Gen. 6:1–2) and were likely the driving forces behind the violence that precipitated the divine judgment of the flood (6:5–7, 11–12). Where is this "prison"? This is not addressed by Peter here, but elsewhere Peter tells us God "cast them into hell and committed them to pits of darkness, reserved for judgment" (2 Peter 2:4), and Jude adds that He "has kept [them] in eternal bonds under darkness for the judgment of the great day" (Jude 6). As "spirits," their location is not a matter to be understood spatially but relationally and spiritually in terms of relationship to and distance from God. Who put them there? God did, to vindicate His justice and to preserve a line of grace that might eventuate in an offer of salvation to Adam's fallen race. And when? It is sufficient to say generally, around the time of the Flood (v.20).

> **Ministry Maxim**
>
> There is no realm or place in which Christ's triumph is not complete.

Questions remain. Debate will continue. Faithful expositors aim for what they believe most likely to be the understanding of Peter's original readers and proclaim that in a way that supports the Apostle's overall point: Jesus' complete triumph through death, resurrection, and ascension to the right hand of the Father (vv.18–22) and this to encourage his readers that they may be faithful in their suffering, for Christ's triumph is also theirs.

Verse 20 – "who once were disobedient, when the patience of God kept waiting in the days of Noah, during the construction of the ark, in which a few, that is, eight persons, were brought safely through *the* water."

Peter's challenging sentence begun in verse 18 continues to unfold. Using a participle, Peter designates those "who were once disobedient" (ἀπειθήσασίν ποτε). The dative form points toward those to whom Christ "preached" (v.19), and its antecedent is found in the "spirits" of verse 19. But what particularly is he saying about them, and what role does the participle play in this? Does he use the participle attributively ("who once were disobedient"; cf. NIV, NKJV, NLT, NRSV, YLT), adverbially to express temporal action ("after they were disobedient," NET), or causally ("because they formerly did not obey," ESV)? If used attributively it would normally be accompanied by the definite article, but its absence, in this case, may be explained by the ellipsis created by Peter's grammar.[179] The aorist tense looks back to that era surrounding the Flood and views the actions as representative of that point in time. It is made up of the verb πείθω ("to convince") with the alpha-privative for negation. It designates the one who refuses to be convinced, to believe, to obey. Four of the verb's fourteen NT uses are by Peter. It can describe those who "are disobedient to the word" of the gospel (τῷ λόγῳ ἀπειθοῦντες, 2:8) and husbands who do not believe (ἀπειθοῦσιν τῷ λόγῳ, "are disobedient to the word," 3:1). Ultimately Peter uses it to speak of coming judgment and asks "what will be the outcome for those who do not obey the gospel of God? [ἀπειθούντων τῷ τοῦ θεοῦ εὐαγγελίῳ]" (4:17). The adverb ποτε ("once"; "formerly," ESV, NKJV, RSV; "long ago," NET, NIV, NLT; "in former times," NRSV; "sometime," KJV, YLT) serves to underscore that a particular era and its actions are under consideration. Its specifics are identified by the ὅτε ("when") clause that follows.

The disobedience of these wicked "spirits" went on "when the patience of God kept waiting" (ὅτε ἀπεξεδέχετο ἡ τοῦ θεοῦ μακροθυμία) for

---

179 Dubis, 32, 122; Forbes, 126.

repentance by those influenced by them. The verb (ἀπεξεδέχετο, "kept waiting") is in the imperfect tense, signaling the ongoing extension of God's patience over time. The verb is deponent, so the middle voice should be read as having an active voice.[180] The verb's first appearance in extant Greek literature is in the NT, and it may have been coined by one of the first-century believers.[181] It is found eight times in the NT, six of which are from the pen of Paul. In all six, the Apostle uses it with regard to the return of Jesus Christ and the fullness of salvation into which He will bring His people at that time (Rom. 8:19, 23, 25; 1 Cor. 1:7; Gal. 5:5; Phil. 3:20). It is a double compound: ἀπό ("from"), ἐκ ("out of"), and δέχομαι ("to receive"). The prepositions in compound "indicate the eager but patient waiting."[182] Burton explains that the first preposition (ἀπό, "from") "intensifies the verb," while the second (ἐκ, "out of") "indicates 'to be receiving from a distance,' i.e., 'to be intently awaiting.'"[183]

Here again, Peter is alliterating for rhetorical effect (cf. 1 Peter 1:4, 19; 2:15, 21; 3:17). By using a verb with an alpha-privative prefix and a compound verb beginning with the prefix ἀπό ("from") he creates a dramatic assonance and contrast between the disobedience (ἀπειθέω) and the waiting (ἀπεκδέχομαι).

Here "the patience of God" (ἡ τοῦ θεοῦ μακροθυμία), by way of a metonymy, is personalized and made to stand for God Himself. The personal designation (τοῦ θεοῦ, "of God") is placed in the attributive position between the noun (μακροθυμία, "patience") and its definite article (ἡ, "the") to stress the particular quality being demonstrated in His "waiting." The emphasis on *divine* "patience" here underscores and strengthens the already intensive nature of the previous verb (ἀπεξεδέχετο, "kept waiting").

This disobedience in the face of divine longsuffering unfolded "in the days of Noah" (ἐν ἡμέραις Νῶε). Noah lived for 950 years (Gen. 9:29); the Flood did not come until he was 600 years of age (7:6; 9:28). Genesis

---

180 Abernathy, 138.

181 Hellerman, 223.

182 Rienecker, 559.

183 Cited by Rienecker, 515.

6:3 may be read as indicating the building of the ark took 120 years, during which time apparently Noah also preached to the wicked populace that surrounded him (2 Peter 2:5). We are specifically told it was "during the construction of the ark" (κατασκευαζομένης κιβωτοῦ) that "the patience of God kept waiting." The genitive absolute "focuses the patience of God on the time taken to construct the ark."[184] The present tense of the verb (κατασκευαζομένης, "during the construction") stresses the ongoing nature of God's forbearance. The passive voice pictures the ark itself being brought to reality under God's command by Noah's hands. The participle is probably to be understood as temporal (i.e., "*during* the construction," emphasis added).[185] The verb is a compound made up of κατά ("down") and σκευάζω ("to make ready"). The prepositional prefix may add a sense of the thoroughness of the preparation. For those 120 years, God refused to judge the overt, swelling wickedness of Noah's generation (Acts 14:16; 17:30; Rom. 2:4; 3:25). God did not immediately act against either the angelic rebels or the human sinners they influenced, but "waited patiently" before unleashing His judgment. Some argue that the cryptic description of "the sons of God" cohabitating with "the daughters of man" (Gen. 6:1–7) cannot be located with confidence within the days of Noah. But the Biblical text presents it in precisely this way, for the genealogy of Genesis 5 is constructed to lead us to the introduction of Noah (5:28–32). Then we have the account of the wicked antediluvian world (Gen. 6:1–7), which is immediately followed by the unfolding of Noah's life (6:8–10:32).

It was the ark "in which a few" (εἰς ἣν ὀλίγοι) found refuge. The preposition εἰς ("in") designates their entry into and location within the ark.[186] The pronoun ἣν ("which") designates the ark itself as the place in which they found safety from God's judgment in the Flood. Compared to the larger population of humanity at the time, Noah and his family were only

---

184 Forbes, 126.

185 Wallace states that ninety percent of the time the participle in a genitive absolute construction is temporal (655; cf. Dubis, 122).

186 Harris suggests the εἰς here encroaches upon the meaning of ἐν, being thus used to designate the location of Noah and his family within the ark (84–85).

"a few" (ὀλίγοι). The saved were "few" compared to those who faced judgment. But they were, individually speaking, significant, for Peter moves to specify, "that is, eight persons" (τοῦτ' ἔστιν ὀκτὼ ψυχαί) who were saved. The "eight" (ὀκτὼ) were Noah, his wife, their three sons and their wives (Gen. 7:7).[187] They are designated as ψυχαί ("persons"). Here, as throughout 1 Peter, ψυχή is used to speak of individuals as whole persons, not merely their immaterial component. In light of the debate in verse 19 (see above), this is significant as it reminds us that Peter's (and the NT's) preferred way of referring to a person is as a "soul" (ψυχή), not a "spirit" (πνεῦμα).

> **Ministry Maxim**
>
> There is a wideness in God's mercy where only the repentant few dwell.

The readers of Peter's letter were "aliens" (1 Peter 1:1) and "strangers" (2:11) on this earth, no doubt few in number compared to the unbelieving that surrounded them. Peter's emphasis on the minority saved in Noah's day would encourage them on their own.

Nestled in the ark Noah and his family "were brought safely through the water" (διεσώθησαν δι' ὕδατος). The verb is a compound made up of διά ("through") and σῴζω ("to save"). The preposition that is found here as a prefix stands alone as the next word in the sentence—adding emphasis to the idea of being utterly delivered "through" and ultimately out of the waters of the Flood. The root verb appears in the next verse (σῴζει, "saves") in application to Peter's readers. The compound is used eight times in the NT, especially of Paul being delivered through many dangers (Acts 23:24), particularly his shipwreck (27:43, 44; 28:1, 4). It is also used of the healing only Jesus can effect (Matt. 14:36; Luke 7:3). The preposition strengthens the sense of the root verb, and the compound has a sense of "to rescue completely from danger."[188] The aorist tense pictures the dramatic point at which Noah and his family were rescued from the

---

187 "The mention of 'eight persons' is one of many New Testament examples where seemingly minor details in the Old Testament are quoted as historically reliable" (Grudem, 170).

188 Louw-Nida, 21.29; cf. Robertson, *Grammar*, 560.

waters of the Flood. The passive voice pictures God, by means of the ark, acting on their behalf.

The preposition (δι', "through") may convey a double entendre, being used both in a local sense ("through water") and an instrumental sense ("by means of water").[189] In such a case, Peter would be saying both that Noah and his family were rescued *from* ("through") the waters that drowned all other life forms and that they were saved *by means* of those waters from the evil that the waters were used to judge. In his second letter, Peter reminds his readers that ". . . the earth was formed out of water and by water" and that it was then later "through [these same waters that] the world at that time was destroyed, being flooded with water" (2 Peter 3:5–6). In verse 21, Peter will apply these things to the waters of baptism. The waters of baptism are used both to symbolize union with Christ in His death (Rom. 6:3) and, emerging up out of them, union with Him in His resurrection life (v.4). The same waters that picture the death of the old man/life (vv.6–7), picture our being brought through to resurrection life (vv.8–11; cf. the use of διά in a similar context in 1 Cor. 10:1–2).

Peter was in good company in using Noah as an encouragement to his believing contemporaries. Other NT authors did much the same. "By faith Noah, being warned by God about things not yet seen, in reverence prepared [κατεσκεύασεν] an ark for the salvation of his household, by which he condemned the world, and became an heir of the righteousness which is according to faith" (Heb. 11:7). Noah's obedience in building the ark and gathering his household into it was an act of faith ("By faith"), obedience ("being warned"), and worship ("reverence"). Jesus warned that "the coming of the Son of Man will be just like the days of Noah. For as in those days before the flood they were eating and drinking, marrying and giving in marriage, until the day that Noah entered the ark, and they did not understand until the flood came and took them all away; so will the coming of the Son of Man be." (Matt. 24:37–39; cf. Luke 17:26–27, 30)

The complex lines of verses 18–20 can become confusing as we try to keep straight the many explanations that have been floated over the years

---

189 Davids, 142–143; Harris, 42; Hart, 60; Kelly, 159; cf. Michaels, 213.

concerning their meaning. We do well to keep Peter's overall point plainly in view—Jesus has triumphed over all wicked forces (v.22) by way of His death, resurrection, and ascension (vv.18–19a, 22). This is intended as an encouragement to believers who themselves suffer unjustly and must find the strength to remain faithful to Christ. Knowing that He, too, suffered and even died, but ultimately triumphed and promised to bring His own people into His triumph sustains suffering believers in their trial of faith. The point of verses 19b and 20 is that Jesus triumphed over even the worst of all wicked spirits and in the darkest of times. In union with Him, we too may triumph in all the wickedness that confronts us.

> **Digging Deeper:**
> 1. How is Jesus' suffering more than an example for us in our suffering (v.18)?
> 2. What principles should guide faithful expositors of God's Word in handling difficult texts such as this one (vv.19–20)?

Verse 21 – "Corresponding to that, baptism now saves you—not the removal of dirt from the flesh, but an appeal to God for a good conscience— through the resurrection of Jesus Christ,"

Peter begins a new sentence but continues the complex line of thought he began in verse 18. Having just spoken of the "water" (ὕδατος) of the flood (v.20b), Peter continues by saying, "Corresponding to that" (ὃ καὶ ... ἀντίτυπον). The neuter singular relative pronoun (ὃ, "that") and the previous noun (ὕδατος, "water") agree in gender and number.[190] Baptism under the new covenant is designated by Peter as "Corresponding to" (ἀντίτυπον) the waters of the Flood. The type-antitype relationship

---

190 The nominative form of the relative pronoun (ὃ, "which") is better attested than the dative (ᾧ) which appears to be a scribe's effort to simplify the difficult syntax.

was one of correspondence. The type left its imprint (the antitype) when struck.[191] The type, or original in this case, was the "water" of the Flood. That was, by God's design, to find its "Corresponding" antitype in Christian baptism. The word is used elsewhere in the NT only in Hebrews 9:24, where the Tabernacle/Temple was the antitype of the original type in God's presence. Here the καὶ is left untranslated (but cf. "And," NASB; cf. NIV, NET, NLT, NRSV).

Peter flatly declares, "baptism now saves you" (ὑμᾶς ... νῦν σῴζει βάπτισμα). The adverb νῦν ("now") contrasts the present realities under the new covenant with the ancient world of the Flood. Though the ages are different and the worlds distant from one another, there remains an imprint of that Flood upon the new covenant people. The plural personal pronoun (ὑμᾶς, "you") establishes Peter's readers—and all other new covenant people—in relationship to the "few" (ὀλίγοι) of Noah's family (v.20).[192] They were only "eight persons" (ὀκτὼ ψυχαί) compared to the entire human race of their day. So, Peter's readers are outnumbered and overwhelmed among the unbelieving populace of the world in their day.

Despite the differences, there is a similarity, for "baptism ... saves" (σῴζει βάπτισμα) as the waters of the Flood saved Noah and his family. This simple statement is, for some, a paradigmatic guide to Christian life and ministry; for others, it is treated as a near-misstatement that must be explained away. A key to understanding Peter's intent is the meaning of the verb "saves" (σῴζει). A quick check of any Greek lexicon will reveal that the verb has a remarkable breadth of meaning. It was the verb of choice to describe Peter's cry to Jesus after he had stepped out of the boat onto the water and began to sink: "Lord, save [σῶσόν] me!" (Matt. 14:30). It was used to describe God bringing the people of Israel out of Egypt under Moses' leadership (Jude 5). It was used to describe physical healing from bodily disease (Mark 5:34). And, of course, it was widely

---

191 TDNT, 8:246.

192 Some manuscripts have ἡμᾶς ("us") instead of ὑμᾶς ("you"). The evidence is fairly evenly distributed between the two options but seems to tip in favor of the latter as is evident in most English translations (though cf. "us" in KJV, NKJV, YLT). In either case the meaning is not greatly affected.

used of salvation from sin, God's judgment, and into eternal life. Our quest is to discover in what sense Peter used the verb here. He employed the verb only one other time in this letter, and there it describes salvation from God's judgment through the gospel (1 Peter 4:18). But such a small sample size makes it tenuous to insist upon a similar meaning here. The immediate context must inform us.

But before we look back to the surrounding context, we should let Peter finish his statement. By way of an emphatic "not ... but" (οὐ ... ἀλλὰ) construction Peter explains what he does not mean and what he does mean by "baptism now saves you." He begins by explaining what baptism is not. It is "not the removal of dirt from the flesh" (οὐ σαρκὸς ἀπόθεσις ῥύπου). The negation (οὐκ, "not") is absolute and categorical.[193] The noun (ῥύπου, "dirt") is used only here in the NT. It refers to "dirt as refuse" as opposed to soil.[194] It can describe something "that is sticky and greasy,"[195] or "a dark viscous juice," such as ear wax.[196] In the LXX, it is used both of physical filth and debased moral character.[197] The genitive (ῥύπου, "dirt") is to be regarded as objective, signifying that which is to be removed. Here his thoughts are upon how it might appear on "the flesh" (σαρκὸς). It may be tempting to read σάρξ in the Pauline sense of that immaterial something in fallen humanity that tends away from God and His Law. But Peter consistently uses it of physical flesh (1 Peter 1:24; 3:18; 4:1, 2, 6), and that appears to be the best understanding of the term here. The noun ἀπόθεσις ("the removal of") is used only here and in 2 Peter 1:14. There it is used metaphorically of death under the imagery of taking down and putting away a

> **Ministry Maxim**
>
> Baptism is a Christ-exalting, Spirit-dependent response of faith to God's grace in Jesus.

---

193 Thayer, 408.

194 BDAG, 6532.1.

195 Spicq, 3:227.

196 BDAG, 6532.3.

197 NIDNTTE, 4:220.

tent. Here it simply describes the removal of something. The preposition in compound (ἀπό, "from") emphasizes the getting rid of or removal of something away "from" the person. The essence of baptism is not the rote application of external rites. It is not the application of water to the body that saves. Salvation is not a matter of ritual or outward act.

Peter now explains what baptism is; this is in strong contrast (ἀλλὰ, "but") to what it is not. Let there be no mistake. Baptism is "an appeal to God" (ἐπερώτημα εἰς θεόν). The noun (ἐπερώτημα, "an appeal") is used only here in the NT. In literary Greek, it meant to ask a question, and in the LXX, to make a request of God.[198] It also was used in the sense of making a pledge or promise and thus designated "the content of what is promised."[199] Thus "pledge" (CSB, HCSB, NET, NIV; "promise," NCV) rather than "appeal" may be a better rendering. Such could take the form of a "response" (NLT; cf. "answer," KJV, NKJV) to a question or inquiry, thus a pledge made in response to questions. In the latter sense, the noun became a technical term for the establishment of a contract and indicated the "'pledge' or 'undertaking' given by one of the parties in answer to formal questions addressed to him."[200] It came then to indicate one's "agreement to conditions or demands."[201] Historical evidence reveals that in the early church, candidates for baptism were asked a series of questions about their relationship with Christ. They would respond accordingly, pledging their allegiance to Christ in dependence upon the enabling Holy Spirit. The present context of unjust suffering and anticipating the exhortations of 4:1–3 all support this understanding of the word here. In baptism, the candidate, in view of God's saving grace, is pledging a life of discipleship and obedience to Christ in reliance upon His Spirit. It becomes then "an expression of the repentance that baptism itself represents."[202]

---

198 Spicq, 2:34.

199 Louw-Nida, 33.162; 33.288.

200 Rienecker, 760.

201 Ibid.

202 Dubis, 127.

Thus, whatever else Peter may mean, this points to baptismal candidates of an age to understand questions about their faith and to respond personally to confess that faith. The words indicate that individuals capable of reasoned faith and confession of that faith are in view.

The "pledge" ("appeal") offered in baptism is made to God "for a good conscience" (συνειδήσεως ἀγαθῆς). The word "conscience" is a compound, made up of σύν ("with") and εἶδον ("to see," "to perceive"). This is the third time Peter has used the word in this letter (cf. 1 Peter 2:19; 3:16; see our comments there). The Bible describes several conditions in which one's conscience may be found. Negatively, one may have a weak conscience because of immaturity (1 Cor. 8:7, 10), a wounded conscience through being wronged (1 Cor. 8:12), a defiled conscience because of unconfessed sin (Titus 1:15), or a seared conscience through repeated rebellion against God (1 Tim. 4:2). Positively, one's conscience may be clear (1 Tim. 3:9; 2 Tim. 1:3), blameless (Acts 24:16), perfect (Heb. 9:9), or, as here, "good" (1 Tim. 1:5, 19; 1 Peter 3:16). The word is frequent in Hebrews where it is made clear that rituals are powerless to cleanse the conscience (Heb. 9:9; cf. 10:1–2). Such cleansing comes only through the death and resurrection of Jesus Christ (9:14; 10:22).

We must decide just how the genitive form (συνειδήσεως ἀγαθῆς, "good conscience") is to be understood in relationship to ἐπερώτημα ("appeal"). Since we have seen the likely intent of ἐπερώτημα is "pledge," reading the present genitive as objective ("*of* a good conscience," KJV, NET, NIV, NKJV, YLT, emphasis added) is required (instead of subjective, "*for* a good conscience," emphasis added). As ῥύπου ("dirt") in the previous, parallel expression is read as objective (ῥύπου, "dirt"), so here συνειδήσεως ("conscience") is as well.[203] The expression thus "makes explicit the content of the pledge or appeal."[204] The "pledge" of baptism is made by the candidate from a conscience already cleansed by Christ and His saving work and in promise of a life of discipleship, living with a "good conscience" by God's grace and the enabling of His Spirit. The "pledge"

---

203 Forbes, 130.

204 Dubis, 126.

made in baptism is thus a Christ-exalting, Spirit-dependent response of faith to God's grace made real in the death, resurrection, and ascension of Jesus Christ (vv.18, 19, 22).

Accordingly, salvation is "through the resurrection of Jesus Christ" (δι' ἀναστάσεως Ἰησοῦ Χριστοῦ). We must connect the use of the preposition διά ("through") here to its use both independently and in compound in verse 20. While there it may have carried a bit of double entendre, here clearly is used instrumentally to designate the means by which one is "saved." Ultimately it is not the physical act of baptism (the mere application of water to the body) that "saves," but the triumph of Jesus Christ through His death and resurrection. That resurrection is the basis of new life for the believer (1 Peter 1:3). As Noah and his family were saved through and by the flood waters that brought judgment against that generation of sinners and their sin (v.20, see comments above), so we are saved by the crucified, risen Lord Jesus Christ. In union with Christ, we are brought through the judgment of our sins that fell upon Him as our substitute (1 Peter 2:24; 3:18) and then brought into new, eternal, resurrection life with Him who is now lives forever more (1:3; 3:18) at the Father's right hand (3:18, 22). Rituals cannot cleanse the conscience (Heb. 9:9). Only the death and resurrection of Jesus can do that (9:14; 10:22). While Peter does say, "Baptism now saves you," he immediately qualifies what he means. Ultimately, eternal salvation from sin is not found in the act of baptism but in one's union with Christ in His death and resurrection, a union that is to be depicted in baptism. To the degree that one's baptism rightly depicts one's entire dependence upon Him who died and rose again, it reflects and bears witness to the salvation of God. In baptism, we bear witness to our union with Christ in His death and resurrection (Rom. 6:4).

So, just what does Peter mean by "baptism now saves you"? The context insists that we find the answer in the salvation of Noah and his family from the Flood. So we ask, from what precisely were Noah and his family saved? From God's wrath expressed in the Flood, yes. But why was His wrath poured out? To judge sin, yes. But more precisely, God's wrath was sent to wipe clean all remnants of a generation so wicked that He had to remove them and begin again with humanity. It was not judgment merely against individual sins and the sinners who committed them, but against an entire system of evil that was at work, a system driven and advanced by wicked "spirits" (vv.19) over which Jesus is now utterly victorious (v.22). Noah and his family alone, out of all the peoples of the earth, rejected that system and the "spirits" that drove it. He was saved from that system and the judgment God brought upon it by passing through the waters of the Flood.

Is there a "corresponding" parallel in the believer's life today wherein we can link baptism and the flood? There is, and Ephesians 2:1–7 helps us understand it. We are each born into this world dead toward God (v.1), under the influence of Satan (v.2), and captive to an organized system he oversees in opposition to God (vv.2–3). How might one escape that system and its controlling power? Through the grace of God in which He places one in union with Jesus Christ in His death, resurrection, and ascension (vv.4–6). Through repentant faith in Jesus Christ as our substitute on the cross and as our resurrected Lord, we are saved from our sins, the devil and his kingdom, and from the wrath of God that must come upon them (vv.8–9). When that happens, we are counted in God's eyes as having already died, risen, and ascended to His right hand. We are already considered to be in Christ, even as he reigns presently over all demonic powers (1:19–23). This is precisely where Peter will take us in the next verse (1 Peter 3:22). One's baptism formally bears witness to that great salvation, personally received.

It is not that baptism saves one eternally. But in our baptism, we formally and officially declare to all that we belong to Jesus Christ by God's grace and live now in the victory Christ has won. Baptism is the confession and testimony that, by God's grace, we have been removed out of the sinful Satan-controlled world system and been brought into Christ's Kingdom (Col. 1:13–14). Peter's reference to "baptism" may be counted as an example of the literary device metonymy, in which a thing is referred to by means of something with which it is closely associated in some way.[205] In this case, physical baptism is used when the actual saving reality

---

205 Dubis, 125.

is the death, resurrection, and ascension of Jesus, the benefits of which one enters by divine grace in repentance and faith.

Looking back to verse 18 we realize that Peter is already circling back to his main point—that through His death, resurrection, and ascension Jesus has triumphed over all opposing forces and, in union with Christ, Peter's readers may be certain they will share in His triumph. In verse 22 Peter completes the circle and places an exclamation point behind Christ's victory.

Verse 22 – "who is at the right hand of God, having gone into heaven, after angels and authorities and powers had been subjected to Him."

Peter now concludes the extended, complex, and challenging line of thought he began in verse 18. He does so by returning to the main theme of Jesus' triumph over all challengers.

The relative pronoun (ὅς, "who") finds its antecedent in "Jesus Christ" (Ἰησοῦ Χριστοῦ) at the end of verse 21. The present tense verb (ἐστιν, "is") holds forth what is abidingly, enduringly, presently true. Jesus "is at the right hand of God" (ἐστιν ἐν δεξιᾷ [τοῦ] θεοῦ). The preposition ἐν is used in the locative sense ("at"). To be "at the right hand" (ἐν δεξιᾷ) is to be in a position of incomparable privilege, honor, authority, and power. To be thus at the right hand "of God" ([τοῦ] θεοῦ)[206] is to be at the highest point of all reality, exalted over all things.[207] As Jesus prepared to ascend to that place, He told His disciples, "All authority has been given to Me in heaven and on earth" (Matt. 28:18; cf. Luke 10:22; John 3:35; 13:3; 17:2). This was prophesied (Psa. 110:1; 109:1 LXX; cf. Psa. 8:6) and has been fulfilled following Jesus' death, resurrection, and ascension. Jesus applied the prophecy to Himself (Matt. 22:44; Mark 12:36; Luke 20:42).

---

206 There is question as to the genuineness of the definite article (τοῦ) but θεός is often considered definite even without the article, so the meaning is unchanged either way.

207 "Instead of the qualifier τοῦ θεοῦ ... sometimes we find 'of the Mighty One' (Mt 26:64; Mk 14:62), 'of God Almighty' (Lk 22:69), 'of the Majesty in heaven' (Heb 1:3), 'of the throne of God' (Heb 12:2), or 'of the throne of the Majesty in heaven' (Heb 8:1)" (Harris, 107).

In Peter's first sermon on the day of Pentecost, he declared that not only was Jesus alive from the dead (Acts 2:31–32) but that He had ascended and was seated at the Father's right hand (vv.33–35), in fulfillment of the prophecy of Psalm 110:1. And thus the session of Jesus at the Father's right hand became a ubiquitous theme in the teaching of the early church (Mark 16:19; Rom. 8:34; Eph. 1:20; Col. 3:1; Heb. 1:3, 13; 8:1; 9:24; 10:12; 12:2).

Jesus now sits at the Father's right hand, exercising His authority and deploying His power to guide all things to the end appointed by the Father. "But now we do not yet see all things subjected to him" (Heb. 2:8). But when Jesus has accomplished this, "then comes the end, when He hands over the kingdom to the God and Father, when He has abolished all rule and all authority and power. For He must reign until He has put all His enemies under His feet. The last enemy that will be abolished is death. For HE HAS PUT ALL THINGS IN SUBJECTION UNDER HIS FEET. But when He says, 'All things are put in subjection,' it is evident that He is excepted who put all things in subjection to Him. When all things are subjected to Him, then the Son Himself also will be subjected to the One who subjected all things to Him, so that God may be all in all" (1 Cor. 15:24–28).

Davids explains, "Peter is well aware... that while Jesus may now sit and potentially control the powers, he has yet to bring them all decisively into subjection... what was potentially won at the cross began to be exercised in the resurrection and will be consummated in the return of Christ."[208]

Jesus' presence and activity "at the right hand of God" is a reality because of his "having gone into heaven" (πορευθεὶς εἰς οὐρανόν). Jesus died (1 Peter 3:18a) and rose (v.18b) and ascended to heaven (v.19a). The verb used here (πορευθείς, "having gone") is the same one used in verse 19a (πορευθεὶς, "He went"). Clearly, here Jesus' ascension is in view and, as argued above, this likely means that Jesus' ascension is also intended in verse 19. The repetition of the verb here also signals that Peter is returning

---

208 Davids, 147.

to the theme he began to set forth in verses 18 and 19a and that verses 19b-21 must be read in light of the overall theme of the utter and complete triumph of Christ. The aorist tense sets this forth as a historical, objective reality. The verb is deponent, so the passive voice should be read as active.[209] The participle is temporal and depicts action that clearly preceded Jesus' being seated at the right hand of God. Luke says Jesus was "carried up" (ἀνεφέρετο) into heaven (Luke 24:51). His compound verb is made up of ἀνά ("up") and φέρω ("to bear/carry") and is likewise in the passive voice. He says further than Jesus was "lifted up" (ἐπήρθη) from among the disciples (Acts 1:9). Here too, he uses a compound verb, this time made up of ἐπί ("on," "upon") and αἴρω ("to lift up") and again in the passive voice.

Jesus went "into heaven" (εἰς οὐρανόν). The preposition depicts Jesus' movement "into" (εἰς) that realm. From the vantage point of the disciples, "a cloud received Him out of their sight" (Acts 1:9). From heaven's perspective, Jesus came to the realm of the Father's dwelling, to His immediate presence, to His throne. One need not press for further precision as to the spatial location of "heaven." Our current categories of thinking and understanding of the dimensions of reality prohibit us from having a more exact understanding.

In this exaltation and session, Jesus sits at the pinnacle of all things. "For in subjecting all things to him, He left nothing that is not subject to him" (Heb. 2:8). But "it is evident that He is excepted who put all things in subjection to Him" (1 Cor. 15:27). The NT regularly specifies that Jesus' sovereign rule includes triumphing over all spiritual beings (e.g., Eph. 1:21; Col. 2:10).

Peter thus designates specifically that Jesus sat down "after angels and authorities and powers had been subjected to Him" (ὑποταγέντων αὐτῷ ἀγγέλων καὶ ἐξουσιῶν καὶ δυνάμεων). All three terms apparently represent various classifications and ranks of angelic, spirit beings. The three are found in various combinations in different places throughout the NT. We may deduce that there is organization and design among the angelic ranks,

---

209 Abernathy, 142.

both holy[210] and wicked. But to draw fine distinctions or to create a detailed hierarchy of an angelic organization is to infer more than the terms allow us. We can be sure there are differentiations among them, but just how they relate to and are distinguished one from the other is a matter of speculation. What is clear is that the subjugation is total. The Bible speaks of their subjugation to Christ both as a present reality, as here (cf. Eph. 1:20–22; Col. 2:10, 15), and also as one that is being presently accomplished in the world (Heb. 2:7–8) and to be completed at His Coming (1 Cor. 15:24; Phil. 2:10). It is not always clear when they refer to what we would deem good angels or to wicked fallen angels/spirits. Here, given the reference to "the spirits now in prison" (v.19), Peter surely has in mind at least the wicked variety. All those under consideration would have been at least originally classified as "angels" (ἀγγέλων), probably the broadest term of the three. They are then also described as "authorities" (ἐξουσιῶν) who, by the right of the devil as "the god of this world" (2 Cor. 4:4; cf. John 12:31; 14:30; 1 John 5:19), exercise their impressive "powers" (δυνάμεων) in service of his wicked kingdom.

> **Ministry Maxim**
>
> Christ is triumphant over all things, even the evilest, so my trust in Him will be vindicated.

All "angels" (ἀγγέλων) are created beings who were originally brought into being to serve God and those who inherit His salvation (Heb. 1:14). If Revelation 12:4 is understood as descriptive of Satan's original rebellion, as many as one-third of the angels sided with him and became wicked. These beings are often described in the NT as both "authorities" (ἐξουσιῶν; 1 Cor. 15:24; Eph. 1:21; 2:2; 3:10; 6:12; Col. 1:16; 2:10, 15) and "powers" (δυνάμεων; Rom. 8:38; 1 Cor. 15:24; Eph. 1:21).

The aorist tense verb (ὑποταγέντων, "had been subjected") views the subjection as immediate and complete. The majority of English translations read it as a passive voice (ASV, ESV, KJV, NASB, NKJV, NRSV,

---

210 Compare Revelation 4–5 for the layers of angelic beings around the throne of God and Jesus as the only one able to approach Him who sits on the throne.

YLT), though some translate it as a middle voice (CSB, HCSB, NET, NIV, RSV).²¹¹ The participle expresses the result of Christ's ascension to the Father's right hand in glorious triumph. Peter has already used the verb in 2:13, 18; 3:1, 5 (also in 5:5), and we must read it here in light of the theme he has established. What the wicked "spirits" (v.19) by force have been made to do toward Christ, God's people are to practice toward one another, not by force but by the compelling beauty of grace (2:4–10). These spirits' subjugation is not merely an administrative matter but personal, for it is "to Him" (αὐτῷ; i.e., Christ) that they have been subjected. "Their subjection to Christ is undoubtedly the content of his proclamation (1 Peter 3:19)."²¹²

Why does Peter state these things? His original readers faced painful persecution, whether as a present reality or a future probability. He wrote to strengthen the resolve of their faith for the trials they faced. The Christ for whom they maintain their testimony of faith in painful suffering (1 Peter 3:13–17) has already suffered unto death for them (v.18a), risen victoriously from death and every foe (v.18b), and has gone back to heaven (vv.19a, 22a), proclaiming over all the dark forces His utter triumph (v.19b), and in heaven has taken His seat at the right hand of God as the sovereign authority over all things (v.22b). He reassures them that "even the evil powers behind the rulers who persecuted Christians had been subdued, and the final outcome was not in question."²¹³ They can say with Paul, "I am convinced that neither death, nor life, nor angels, nor principalities, nor things present, nor things to come, nor powers, nor height, nor depth, nor any other created thing, will be able to separate us from the love of God, which is in Christ Jesus our Lord" (Rom. 8:38–39).

Though Peter does not develop the idea here, Paul could say that God has made what is true of Jesus to be true of His people as placed in union with Him. He "raised us up with Him, and seated us with Him in the heavenly places in Christ Jesus" (Eph. 2:6). But as Harris notes, when

---

211 Dubis, 128.

212 Storms, 343.

213 Keener, Be Prepared to Suffer for Doing Good section, last para., 1 Peter 3:22.

applied to believers, "he does not add 'at his right hand [ἐν δεξιᾷ αὐτοῦ],' a phrase that is applied to Christ in a comparable statement in Eph 1:20. Christ's exalted status cannot be shared. Angels stand or fall down in worship in God's presence; the enthroned Son sits."[214]

Let us pause now to make certain that amid the complex and difficult lines of verses 19–22 we do not lose Peter's point. In the face of unjust suffering (3:13–17) the believer finds solace and strength in the fact that Jesus also suffered and died unjustly (v.18a), but He was raised from the dead by His Father (v.18b) and has ascended back to His right hand in glory, triumphant over all wicked forces that bring suffering and pain upon His people (vv.19a, 22). Even the worst of the wicked spirits have been overcome in His triumph (vv.19b-20a), and He is able to rescue His own from the judgment of sin (vv.20b-21).

Digging Deeper:
1. Using the text of verse 21 how could you answer one who says "'baptism now saves you' proves the doctrine of baptismal regeneration"?
2. How does the knowledge of a triumphant, living Savior in the presence of God on our behalf help us in times of unjust suffering (v.22)?

---

[214] Harris, 107.

1 PETER 4

Verse 1 – "Therefore, since Christ has suffered in the flesh, arm yourselves also with the same purpose, because he who has suffered in the flesh has ceased from sin,"

The logical connector οὖν ("Therefore") continues the line of thought Peter has been developing and draws logical implications from it. To what precisely is Peter referring? Given that Peter cites the suffering of Christ as the basis for what he is about to command ("since Christ has suffered in the flesh"), it seems that he looks back over the whole of 3:18–22, in which he outlined Jesus' suffering unto death (v.18a), His resurrection (vv.18b, 21b), and His ascension (vv.19a, 22a) as the basis for His complete triumph over all foes (v.22b).

The command is to "arm yourselves" (ὑμεῖς ... ὁπλίσασθε). The verb is found only here in the NT, though the general concept is prevalent (e.g., Rom. 13:12; 2 Cor. 6:7; 10:4; Eph. 6:11–17; 1 Thess. 5:8). In wider Greek literature, it could be used variously of food preparation, putting a horse in harness, and of arming soldiers.[1] Here the military side of the metaphor is primary. The aorist imperative underscores the urgency of the need for action. The middle voice calls for action to be taken upon

---

1 Liddell and Scott, 31032.

oneself, so here it means to "prepare oneself."[2] The personal pronoun (ὑμεῖς) is emphatic both by its mere presence and its forward position.

That with which we are to arm ourselves is "with the same purpose" (τὴν αὐτὴν ἔννοιαν). The noun ἔννοια ("purpose") appears in the NT only here and in Hebrews 4:12, where it points to the "the thoughts and intentions [ἐννοιῶν] of the heart." It is rendered variously as "way of thinking" (ESV, NCV), "attitude" (NET, NIV, NLT), "intention" (NRSV), "thought" (RSV), "mind" (ASV, KJV, NKJV, YLT), "understanding" (CSB), and "resolve" (HCSB). It designates "the content of mental processing" and thus an individual thought, bit of knowledge, or insight.[3] It is "the mental conception that follows consideration or deliberation."[4] It thus designates "a particular manner or way of thinking."[5] Peter looks for the "same" (αὐτὴν) way of thinking to be ours "also" (καὶ). It is not far from Paul's "Have this attitude in yourselves which was also in Christ Jesus" (Phil. 2:5).

> **Ministry Maxim**
>
> Christ is the pattern for our thinking in both suffering and sanctification.

The ground of this is that "Christ has suffered in the flesh" (Χριστοῦ ... παθόντος σαρκὶ).[6] The clause is thrust forward for emphasis, picking up on the theme of His unjust suffering (2:21–25; 3:18–22). The participle (παθόντος, "has suffered") continues holding forth one of Peter's keywords in this letter (2:19, 20, 21, 23; 3:14, 17, 18; 4:1 [2x], 15, 19; 5:10). The aorist tense sets out Jesus' passion as whole, accomplished, and complete. The participle is causal ("*Since* Christ has suffered," emphasis added). Because Jesus suffered in the flesh unjustly, we who also suffer in

---

2   NIDNTTE, 3:535.

3   BDAG, 2665.

4   Friberg, 151.

5   Louw-Nida, 30.5.

6   Some manuscripts add ὑπὲρ ἡμῶν ("for us"). Still others add ὑπὲρ ὑμῶν ("for you"). But early manuscripts with the absence of both clauses lend support to the shorter reading and make the clauses appear as efforts at clarification by later scribes. We adopt the shorter reading as original.

the flesh unjustly ought to adopt His same way of thinking, for He has triumphed over all foes precisely by suffering, dying, rising, ascending, and reigning. We, by His grace, share in His triumph. He will cause all our sufferings to end in triumph and vindication through the resurrection of the dead at His Coming.

Jesus' suffering was accomplished "in the flesh" (σαρκὶ), an echo of the earlier "having been put to death in the flesh" (θανατωθεὶς … σαρκι; 3:18). It reminds us that when Peter mentions Jesus' suffering, he means it to include His death. And it stands over against (note the μὲν … δὲ formula in 3:18) His being "made alive in the spirit" (ζωοποιηθεὶς … πνεύματι; 3:18; cf. v.21), having ascended (vv.19, 22), and being seated at the Father's right hand (v.22).

The reason we ought to adopt Jesus' way of thinking in our suffering is "because he who has suffered in the flesh has ceased from sin" (ὅτι ὁ παθὼν σαρκὶ πέπαυται ἁμαρτίας). The conjunction ὅτι marks this as a clause expressing a causal relationship ("because"). But just who does Peter have in mind? A variety of views have been espoused. Some apply it to Christ, citing the parallel between Χριστοῦ … παθόντος σαρκὶ ("Christ has suffered in the flesh") and ὁ παθὼν σαρκὶ ("he who has suffered in the flesh") and viewing ὅτι as expressing the content of the "the same purpose" (τὴν αὐτὴν ἔννοιαν), instead of introducing a causal relationship.[7] Other interpretations are found among those who understand the ὅτι as causal. Some find in the statement a hint that there is purifying value in suffering itself. Others say that suffering helps bring sinful impulses under control. Others say the statement points to death (and some, to martyrdom) as the only thing that ultimately enables one to have "ceased from sin."[8] And still others view the sufferings as indicating the believer's union with Christ in His death and resurrection and find a parallel in Romans 6:6–7.[9]

---

7   Clowney, 169–170; Davids, 149; Michaels, 226–229.

8   Lenski, 179–180.

9   Clowney, 170–171; Rienecker, 761; Stibbs, 148–149.

It seems unlikely that it refers to Jesus, despite vigorous protestations to the contrary.[10] In what reasonable sense could Jesus be said to have "ceased from sin"? Jesus is without sin, as Peter has made a point of emphasis (1 Peter 1:19; 2:22; 3:18).

The context (especially vv.2ff) makes it more likely that Peter is expressing a true principle of the one who believes in Jesus. This then holds in parallel the statement of Christ's suffering (Χριστοῦ ... παθόντος σαρκὶ, "Christ has suffered in the flesh") and this description of His followers' suffering (ὁ παθὼν σαρκὶ, "he who has suffered in the flesh"). This latter line holds forth "the same way of thinking" (τὴν αὐτὴν ἔννοιαν; ESV) as Christ's. By "he who has suffered in the flesh" (ὁ παθὼν σαρκὶ), Peter has in mind Christ-followers who, like Christ, suffer unjustly in an evil world. The singular form does not require identifying this with Christ but is a generalized way of picturing the one who adopts this way of thinking and acting. The participle is used substantively ("*he who* has suffered," emphasis added). The aorist tense has in view the event of painful suffering, whatever it may involve. Like Christ's suffering, this one's is also "in the flesh" (σαρκὶ).

The very fact that such a one suffers for righteousness' sake is an indication that he "has ceased from sin" (πέπαυται ἁμαρτίας). The verb is used fifteen times in the NT. Every occurrence of the verb is, as here, in the middle voice (except for 1 Peter 3:10, where it is in the active voice). The middle voice lends the sense of stopping oneself from something. The perfect tense emphasizes the state or condition of having settled one's disposition toward "sin." The singular form ἁμαρτίας ("sin") pictures sin as an act, as an individual transgression of God's law and will. For Peter, the noun depicts the act of sin, not a sin principle, as so often with Paul.[11] The genitive form here may emphasize separation "from" sin.[12] The point is not that believers may attain sinless perfection but that their willingness to suffer for Christ demonstrates that they have chosen a path of

---

10   E.g., Clowney, 169–170; Davids, 149; Michaels, 226–229.

11   Bigg, 167.

12   Wallace, 107–109.

righteousness rather than sin. They have decided and adopted a way of thinking that values obedience more than self-expression and sin.

It has been suggested that Peter has in mind something analogous to Paul's statement in Romans 6: "… knowing this, that our old self was crucified with Him, in order that our body of sin might be done away with, so that we would no longer be slaves to sin; for he who has died is freed from sin" (vv.6–7).[13] If so, this would understand Peter's "has suffered" as including one's death toward sin. This would require a meaning for one's death to sin that, of necessity, would be different than Christ's death with regard to sin, for, tempted in every way just as we are (Heb. 4:15), He never sinned (1 Peter 1:19; 2:22; 3:18).

In any case, Peter's point is not that the pain of suffering overrides the allurements of lust and sin (thus giving rise later to extreme expressions of self-mutilation and harm) or that there is redemptive value in one's sufferings (only Christ's provided that, 1 Peter 1:18–19; 2:24; 3:18). It reads too much of Paul into Peter's words to find the latter echoing the former's view of union with Christ in death to sin as in Romans 6:6–7. Peter's point is simply that one's willingness to suffer unjustly proves that one has genuinely turned from sin and is following Christ.

Verse 2 – "so as to live the rest of the time in the flesh no longer for the lusts of men, but for the will of God."

Peter's sentence continues with an extended purpose clause expressed by εἰς τὸ and the infinitive βιῶσαι ("to live").[14] The introductory formula (εἰς τὸ) opens the clause, and the infinitive is held to the end of the sentence for emphasis. The aorist tense depicts how the one under consideration intends to live in the moment, with each challenge, temptation, opportunity, and demand. The qualitative nature of each decision is set

---

13   Rienecker, 671.
14   Alford, 4:371; Davids, 150; Dubis, 132; Forbes, 137; Grudem, 175; Kelly, 169; Michaels, 223, 229; Rienecker, 761; Schreiner, 201; Stibbs, 149; cf. ASV, CSB, ESV, HCSB, KJV, NKJV, NRSV; contra those who read the infinitive clause as expressing result: Bigg, 167; Hiebert, 258–259; Lenski, 180; cf. NIV.

forth by a stark μηκέτι...ἀλλὰ ("no longer...but") contrast. The negation (μηκέτι, "no longer") marks the option as unthinkable; the contrast is blunt and bold (ἀλλὰ, "but").

That which is in play is how one will live "the rest of the time in the flesh" (τὸν ἐπίλοιπον ἐν σαρκὶ...χρόνον). The distance between the definite article (τὸν, "the") and its noun (χρόνον, "time") is great, and it has led to speculation as to whether it belongs to the adjective ἐπίλοιπον ("remaining") or to the noun χρόνον ("time"). Though the distance between the noun and definite article is significant, it is unlikely that Peter used the definite article to substantivize the adjective. Rather, we should read the adjective in the attributive position, emphasizing the qualitative nature of the "time" under consideration. The noun (χρόνον, "time"; cf. 1:17, 20; 4:3) designates a finite space or span of time, whether that be specific or indefinite.[15] The definite article marks out a definite period. Furthermore, the verb Peter uses (βιῶσαι, "to live") is used only here in the NT and designates life as lived on the earth.[16] Peter is clearly thinking of a portion of his readers' personal, earthly lifespans.

In the attributive position also is the prepositional phrase ἐν σαρκὶ ("in the flesh"). Peter uses the noun σάρξ ("flesh") six times in this immediate context (3:18, 21; 4:1 [2x], 2, 6). In 3:18, Peter says that Jesus died a bodily, physical death. Baptism is not the application of water to the human body to remove dirt (3:21). Jesus suffered in a very real, human, physical body (4:1a). His followers often must also suffer in their physical, earthly bodies (4:1b). Here, that which the noun clearly designates is the bodily, earthly life of the individual. The adjective (ἐπίλοιπον, "remaining") designates "a part that remains from a whole" and thus what is "left" or "remaining."[17] Peter thus has in view that portion of one's

> **Ministry Maxim**
>
> As a believer the rest of your life is already under contract.

---

15   Mounce, 732.

16   Friberg, 91.

17   BDAG, 2984.

earthly life left after conversion. He pictures the time between one's conversion and one's entrance fully into God's presence, either through death or at Christ's Return.

Throughout this time, that which such a one refuses is "the lusts of men" (ἀνθρώπων ἐπιθυμίαις). The noun ἐπιθυμία is a morally neutral term, designating any strong and overwhelming desire. Among Paul's nineteen uses of the noun, it is used in a negative sense in every case except Philippians 1:23 and 1 Thessalonians 2:17. Peter's eight uses of the noun are always in a negative sense, describing passions that characterized them prior to conversion. They were undertaken in ignorance (1 Peter 1:14) and were fleshly (2:11), human (4:2), unredeemed (4:3), worldly (2 Peter 1:4), corrupt (2:10), fleshly (2:18), and personal (3:3). The plural form sets forth these "lusts" in their diversity and combined power; some of them are enumerated in verse 3. The plural noun ἀνθρώπων designates any such "lusts" in the human race without being gender specific. The genitive form (ἀνθρώπων, "of men") is subjective, designating the lusts that characterize fallen humanity of either sex.

By way of contrast, that which such a one embraces is "the will of God" (θελήματι θεοῦ).[18] Peter speaks both of God's will (1 Peter 2:15; 3:17; 4:19) and "the will of man" (θελήματι ἀνθρώπου, 2 Peter 1:21). God's will is to suffer for doing good (1 Peter 3:17; 4:19) and, by continuing to do good even while suffering, to silence the unbelieving (2:15). All this is in view in the present sentence where Christ's suffering unjustly is in view (3:18) and made programmatic for His followers (4:1) who are called to break with human sinfulness (vv.2–3). Both dative nouns, ἐπιθυμίαις ("lusts") and θελήματι ("will"), "express the rule by which the man shapes his life."[19] There may be an intended contrast between the plural ἀνθρώπων ἐπιθυμίαις ("the lusts of men"), the latter of which Peter will further develop with a series of plural nouns in verse 3, and the

---

18 By placing ἀνθρώπων ("of men") before ἐπιθυμίαις ("lusts") and θεοῦ ("of God") after θελήματι ("will") Peter uses the distance via word order to emphasize the divide between "men" and "God" (cf. Alford, 4:371; Dubis, 131).

19 Bigg, 167; cf. Dubis, 131; Forbes, 137; Hiebert, 259.

singular θελήματι θεοῦ ("will of God").[20] Stibbs comments, "The Christian life, if rightly ordered, can enjoy a unity and an integration impossible to sinners. For there is only one true God; and for His people He has at any one time only one will. By contrast sinners are distracted and pulled first this way and then that by desire to satisfy the varied appetites which dominate those in whose company they find themselves."[21]

> **Digging Deeper:**
> 1. What does it mean for you to "arm" yourself "with the same purpose" as Christ right now in your workplace? Neighborhood? Family (v.1)?
> 2. How can verse 2 help you make the point that the greater issue is not how long one's life is, but with what shall it be consumed?

Verse 3 – "For the time already past is sufficient *for you* to have carried out the desire of the Gentiles, having pursued a course of sensuality, lusts, drunkenness, carousing, drinking parties and abominable idolatries."

Peter moves to elaborate upon (γὰρ, "For") his point that his readers should live out their remaining time in this life for "the will of God" rather than "the lusts of men" (v.2).

With the noun ὁ ... χρόνος ("the time"), Peter picks up its use in verse 2, where it is used to designate the remaining portion of one's mortal life. Peter now uses the word to depict the other side of one's life, that portion up until this moment. The definite article marks it out as specific, designating that portion of one's life that was lived before conversion to Christ.

For Peter's readers, that time was "already past" (παρεληλυθὼς). The perfect tense pictures it as having come to an end and is gone forever.

---

20 Hiebert, 259; Stibbs, 149; contra, Michaels, 229.
21 Stibbs, 149.

Time cannot be retrieved. The verb is a compound comprised of παρά ("beside") and ἔρχομαι ("to come, "to go"). Used literally, it can simply describe movement ("pass by") in reference to a fixed vantage point (cf. Matt. 8:28; Mark 6:48). But it is often used metaphorically, as it is here. Presently it means "to no longer be available" for something.[22] Peter uses the verb to remind us that one day "the heavens will pass away" (2 Peter 3:10). So too the days of our lives up to this moment have passed by us, never to be retrieved and now unavailable to us. It is the first of three perfect tense verbs in this verse, all of which "emphasize the thought that this past of theirs is a closed chapter; that part of the story is over and done."[23]

That portion of life was more than "sufficient" (ἀρκετός) for the purposes of rebellious, independent sinfulness. The adjective designates that which "is sufficient for some purpose" and satisfies that purpose.[24] Peter understates the matter but, by doing so, communicates strongly that it was not only "sufficient" but "far more than sufficient."[25]

That of which our past is already full and for which it is no longer available is "to have carried out the desire of the Gentiles" (τὸ βούλημα τῶν ἐθνῶν κατειργάσθαι).

Having just spoken of the "will [θέλημα] of God" (v.2; cf. 2:15; 3:17), Peter uses a near synonym to describe "the desire [βούλημα] of the Gentiles." The word groups were used almost evenly in the LXX, but by the time of the NT, the former far outpaced the latter. The verbal form is found about five times as often as its counterpart. Our present noun is found only three times in the NT (Acts 27:43; Rom. 9:19; 1 Peter 4:3). Great debate swirls around the distinction, if any, in the meaning of the two words. Thayer, while noting the varying opinions, says βούλομαι "seems to designate the will which follows deliberation" and θέλω "the will which proceeds from inclination."[26] Given the infrequency of the

---

22 BDAG, 5688.2.
23 Rienecker, 761.
24 Louw-Nida, 59.45.
25 Dubis, 133; Forbes, 138.
26 Thayer, 286.

use of the present noun and Peter's exclusive use of θέλημα when speaking of the will of God, he surely intends a contrast and distinction between the two.²⁷

The "desire of the Gentiles" is a rough equivalent of "the lusts of men" (ἀνθρώπων ἐπιθυμίαις, v.2).²⁸ It is, as the end of this verse shows, a life independent of God and His Law, defining their deities and pursuing their own ends (cf. "lawless idolatry," ESV). It found expression in their "former lusts," carried out in their "ignorance" (1 Peter 1:14), the "futile way of life inherited from" their "forefathers" (v.18). Most Peter's readers would have been Gentiles (τῶν ἐθνῶν, "the Gentiles"). Now, however, through Christ, they are "a chosen race, a royal priesthood, a holy nation, a people for God's own possession" (1 Peter 2:9, NASB). Peter thus used the term "the Gentiles" now to designate not ethnicity but unbelief.

This they once "carried out" (κατειργάσθαι). The verb is a compound comprised of κατά ("down") and ἐργάζομαι ("to work"). The preposition in compound either intensifies the root verb or emphasizes the downward motion of the effort²⁹, perhaps then being "perfective" in that it "views the linear progress down to the goal" and thus means "work on to the finish."³⁰ It means, then, "to do something with success and/or thoroughness."³¹ The perfect tense underscores that sense and pictures their efforts as a completed state of affairs. The verb is deponent, so the middle voice should be read as an active. The infinitive is epexegetical to ἀρκετός, clarifying just what is meant by "sufficient."³²

Peter thus depicts his readers' past as "having pursued a course of" (πεπορευμένους ἐν) sin. This is the verb just used to describe Jesus' ascension back to heaven after His resurrection (3:19, 22). Now it depicts

---

27 Forbes, 138.
28 Michaels, 230.
29 Thayer, 339.
30 Rienecker, 552.
31 Louw-Nida, 42.17.
32 Dubis, 133; Forbes, 138; Robertson (*Grammar*, 1076) calls the infinitive "complementary" to the adjective.

these sinners' descent into sin. The perfect tense depicts their former state within the grip of the sins about to be enumerated. The verb is deponent, and thus the middle voice should be read as active. The preposition (ἐν) denotes the sphere of debauchery in which they walked before conversion to Christ.

He uses six plural nouns (the last of which has an adjectival qualifier) to designate the pattern of behavior characteristic of unredeemed Gentiles (cf. Rom. 13:13; Gal. 5:19–21). The plural forms underscore the multiplicity of expressions each may find. The first five involve the unfettered indulgence of the appetites. The first two have to do with sexual abandon, and the next three involve excessive indulgence in alcohol. The final item deals with idolatry, "the taproot of the evils portrayed" in the other five terms.[33]

The first is "sensuality" (ἀσελγείαις). Four of its ten NT appearances are in Peter's letters (cf. 2 Peter 2:2, 7, 18; cf. Jude 4). "In the NT only the older and sensual sense of 'voluptuousness' or 'debauchery' is relevant," and here it has the nuance of "sexual excess."[34] It arises, said Jesus, from the corruption of the sinful human heart (Mark 7:22). Paul identifies it as one of "the works of the flesh" (Gal. 5:19) that characterizes the unregenerate (Eph. 4:19). Paul sees it, as does Peter, as the opposite of living in light of Christ's return and our standing before Him (Rom. 13:12–13). It is "unbridled lust, excess, licentiousness, lasciviousness, wantonness, outrageousness, shamelessness, insolence."[35] It stands as the opposite is ἐγκράτεια ("self-control," 2 Peter 1:6).[36] The plural form points to the varied and multiple expressions of sensuality that occur when accountability is abandoned. Fritzsche views the plural as indicating "wanton (acts or) manners, as filthy words, indecent bodily movements, unchaste handling of males and females, etc."[37]

---

33 Hiebert, 261.
34 TDNT, 1:490.
35 Thayer, 79.
36 Davids, *Handbook*, 67.
37 As quoted by Thayer, 79–80.

Next in Peter's list of infamous things is "lusts" (ἐπιθυμίαις). The noun is a morally neutral term, designating any strong and overwhelming desire, but here it has negative, sinful connotations. Peter used it in verse 2 to describe those degrading impulses common to the fallen human condition. Here, coupled with ἀσελγείαις ("sensuality"), the meaning is more narrowly focused on the indulgence of sexual urges.

Third Peter lists "drunkenness" (οἰνοφλυγίαις). The word occurs only here in the NT. It is a compound made up from οἶνος ("wine") and φλύω ("to bubble up"), the latter signaling overflow or excess. It may be used "of the individual occurrences of drunkenness."[38] The noun was "used for a debauch; no single word rendering it better than this; being as it is an extravagant indulgence in potations long drawn out."[39]

To this, Peter added "carousing" (κώμοις). The noun appears elsewhere in the NT only in two of Paul's lists of vices where it is designated one of "the works of the flesh" (Rom. 13:13; Gal. 5:21), the opposite of allowing the Spirit to bear His fruit in one's life (Gal. 5:22–23). It originally denoted dinner parties, but because of excessive drinking, these often turned immoral. They were "drinking parties involving unrestrained indulgence in alcoholic beverages and accompanying immoral behavior."[40] As "a drunken dinner party,"[41] it often "ended in the party parading the streets crowned, bearing torches, singing, dancing, and playing frolics."[42] Trench observes that the term combines the notions "of riot and of revelry."[43]

> **Ministry Maxim**
> Jesus ascended to heaven to rescue those who descended into sin.

---

38 BDAG, 5241.

39 Trench, 227.

40 Louw-Nida, 88.287.

41 Spicq, 2:355.

42 Liddell and Scott, 25728.

43 Trench, 227.

To this, Peter adds "drinking parties" (πότοις). The noun appears only here in the NT. In Greco-Roman culture, it "was customary for literati to hold banquets at which topical discussions were featured, with participants well lubricated with wine." But in the present case, it is likely that Peter "has less sophisticated participants in mind."[44] In combination with the other terms, the word here "suggests something less sophisticated and more along the lines of wild and frenzied drinking bouts."[45]

Added (καὶ, "and") to these are "abominable idolatries" (ἀθεμίτοις εἰδωλολατρίαις). The noun (εἰδωλολατρίαις, "idolatries") is a derogatory term found four times in the NT. It is counted among the works of the flesh (Gal. 5:20). Believers are called upon to flee from it (1 Cor. 10:14) and to put it to death (Col. 3:5). Idolatry is distinctively "the desire of the Gentiles" and representative of all those who do not worship the Lord is truth. The adjective (ἀθεμίτοις, "abominable") is used only here and in Acts 10:28 in the NT. It is constructed of the alpha-privative for negation and the noun θέμις, that which is laid down by custom, law, or divine decree.[46] It thus can designate that which is unlawful. Such is the case in Acts 10:28 where Peter explained to Cornelius and his guests "how unlawful [ἀθέμιτόν] it is for a man who is a Jew to associate with a foreigner or to visit him." The word could also bridge from a matter's legality to its moral repugnance and thus mean "disgusting" and "unseemly" because it breaks the bonds of decency.[47] English translations vary between the legal ("lawless," CSB, ESV, HCSB, NRSV, RSV; "unlawful," YLT; "wanton," NET) and the morally disgusting ("abominable," ASV, KJV, NASU, NKJV; "detestable," NIV; "terrible," NLT). To the Righteous One and those who are shaped after His heart, idolatry is "abominable" precisely because it is unlawful and contrary to His nature.

---

44 BDAG, 6114.
45 NET Bible.
46 Liddell and Scott, 20346.
47 BDAG, 158.2.

Verse 4 – "In *all* this, they are surprised that you do not run with *them* into the same excesses of dissipation, and they malign *you*;"

Peter's concern with the believer's break with a life of pagan debauchery continues and is wrapped up in the phrase ἐν ᾧ ("In all this"; cf. 1 Peter 1:6; 2:12; 3:16, 19). The relative pronoun (ᾧ, "this") references the break believers have made with their pagan past and its indulgent practices (v.3). The preposition (ἐν) can be either understood as describing the sphere of the unbelievers' surprise ("in"; cf. KJV, NKJV, YLT) or the cause of it ("So," NET).

The outcome of believers' break with a life of sin is that "they are surprised" (ξενίζονται). The "they" is "the Gentiles" (v.3), the unbelieving people who surround Peter's readers. When used transitively, the verb depicts hospitality, what one extends when visitors arrive unannounced (Acts 10:6, 18, 23, 32; 21:16; 28:7; Heb. 13:2). Used intransitively, as here, it means something new and strange (Acts 17:20) or that which surprises, its meaning here and in verse 12 where it appears again.[48] A believer's new patterns of living in holiness come to the unbelieving as a stranger, taking them by surprise and leaving them uncertain of how to engage them. The present tense pictures the ongoing dismay they feel. The passive voice pictures them being affected by the new lives of holiness that the believers display.

> **Ministry Maxim**
>
> Our mere non-participation is enough to cause offense to sinners.

In the first-century world of Peter's readers, the basic fabric of civic and social life was intertwined with pagan religious observances that often involved idolatrous elements and sinful excesses. Anyone who ceased to participate was perceived as anti-social and a threat to the health of society. In such a world, morality quickly became inverted, holiness being denounced as evil, evil being touted as for the public good. Jews generally refused such

---

48   Friberg, 432.

involvements and were, from the beginning, regarded as anti-social. But for Gentiles who embraced faith in Jesus, their new allegiance tore them from the fabric of life into which they had been woven from their earliest days. Old acquaintances were forsaken as sinful indulgences were now rejected. Once a friend of the community, they were now seen as its enemy.

That which astonishes them is "that you do not run with them" (μὴ συντρεχόντων ὑμῶν) any longer. The negation (μὴ, "not") echoes the previous "no longer [μηκέτι] for the lusts of men" (v.2) and finds that commitment now lived out in the daily lives of Peter's readers. Again, it is an unequivocal negation. The verb is a compound made up of σὺν ("with") and τρέχω ("to run"). It is found elsewhere in the NT only in Mark 6:33 and Acts 3:11, where it is used literally of people running together toward some place or toward someone. Here it is used metaphorically of the mad rush of pursuing sin together with others of like heart. The participle may be understood as temporal ("when you do not join them," ESV; cf. NET, NLT) or explanatory ("that you do not run with them"; cf. KJV, NIV, NKJV, NRSV). Once Peter's readers ran headlong with their compatriots after the lifestyle described in verse 3. Now they no longer do so. They have a new heart with a new passion after holiness. The change has been difficult for their former partners in sin to understand and adjust to.

That pursuit was "into the same excess of dissipation" (εἰς τὴν αὐτὴν τῆς ἀσωτίας ἀνάχυσιν). The preposition εἰς depicts the unbelievers' rush not just *to* but "into" a life of sin. They dive in and go deep, all restraints removed. They abandon themselves to indulgence (cf. "plunge into," NLT). That "into" which they dive is "the...excess" (τὴν...ἀνάχυσιν). The noun is found only here in the NT and never appears in the LXX. It comes ultimately from the prefix ἀνά ("up") and the verb χέω ("to pour out")[49], with the prefix perhaps having the sense of "pouring out until it rises up and runs over." Indeed, the word is well translated as "the flood" (ESV, NET, NKJV, NLT). The term was used in classical Greek of the incoming tide filling the tidepools and low spots along the shore.[50] The

---

49 Liddell and Scott, 46565.

50 Alford, 4:372; Vincent, 1:661.

definite article marks it as a particular lifestyle and pursuit. Their course of life is "an impetuous plunge into an open sewer."[51] Two qualifiers sit in the attributive position between the noun and its definite article, each more fully describing the quality of "the flood" into which the unbelieving abandon themselves.

The first qualifier is the noun "dissipation" (ἀσωτίας). It arises ultimately from σῴζω ("to save") with the alpha-privative added for negation. It thus depicts one who is considered unsavable.[52] It is used elsewhere in the NT only in Ephesians 5:18 and Titus 1:6. It concerns "behavior which shows lack of concern or thought for the consequences of an action."[53] The adverbial counterpart to our noun is used in the NT only to describe the lifestyle of the prodigal son (ἀσώτως, "loose living"; Luke 15:13). And "the word *prodigal* refers to the one who has only the sole vicious tendency to destroy his means of subsistence."[54] Trench notes that "The waster of his goods will be very often a waster of everything besides, will lay waste himself—his time, his faculties, his powers; and, we may add, uniting the active and passive meanings of the word, will be himself laid waste; he at once loses himself, and is lost."[55] Such dissipation "is very often associated with drinking binges during festivals"[56] (cf. Eph. 5:18) and thus is appropriate for the life described by the six nouns in verse 3. The definite article (τῆς) here also makes that connection specific.

The pronoun αὐτὴν, used as an adjective ("same"), is also in the attributive position, emphasizing the qualitative nature of the excesses the believers not only indulge but in which they expect to be joined. It underscores the sense of mutuality inherent in the prefix (σὺν, "with") of the verb.

---

51 Michaels, 233.
52 NIDNTTE, 1:437.
53 Louw-Nida, 88.96.
54 Spicq, 1:121, emphasis original.
55 Trench, 56–57.
56 Spicq, 1:121.

Their surprise is not simply passive dismay, It becomes active assault: "they malign you" (βλασφημοῦντες). Non-participation may be read as judgment; judgment may look like opposition. Opposition to the community's accepted lifestyle is an attack on life as the community knows and values it. This must be dealt with. They often do so through verbal attacks (1 Peter 2:12, 15; 3:9, 16; 4:14). We derive our English word "blaspheme" from this root. It means to "slander, *revile, defame, speak* irreverently/impiously/disrespectfully *of or about.*"[57] The participle here designates this as the result of the believers' lifestyle change. Most English versions view this as an action taken against believers, thus providing "you." But reviling those who follow Christ is tantamount to blaspheming Him whom they love, and blaspheming Christ is also a denunciation of those who love Him. So ultimately, both the Lord and His people are subsumed in the hatred of the world (John 15:20). The present tense pictures this as a reality that is not likely to change. Peter will use the verb to speak of those who blaspheme "the way of the truth" (2 Peter 2:2), "angelic majesties" (2:10), and "where they have no knowledge" (2:12). Those who believe a maligned gospel will themselves also be maligned.

Verse 5 – "but they will give account to Him who is ready to judge the living and the dead."

Peter's plural relative pronoun (οἵ, "they") looks back to "they" who "are surprised" at the believers' new lifestyle (v.4). These opponents of the gospel and its people "will give account" (ἀποδώσουσιν λόγον). The compound verb is made up of ἀπό ("from") and δίδωμι ("to give"). Peter used it in 3:9 of the kind of recompense one desires to make to one who has harmed them. But here, it has a legal sense of "to meet a contractual or other obligation" and thus to "pay out" what is due.[58] Each human, created by God and living in His world, owes Him an "account" (λόγον) and will be required to provide it. Most simply λόγος means "a word." Here

---

57 BDAG, 1500.b.
58 Ibid., 910.2.

the singular form points to a particular appointment and a particular report. All of one's life must be gathered up in that moment, and a single report given that covers it all. No one will escape the necessity of standing before God and making "a formal accounting"[59] of one's life. The books will be closed on each one's life. Before they can be closed, God requires a closing statement by each one. Then He renders His verdict on what will come of this one based upon how one has lived and therefore accounted for their response to the grace God has extended to him.

> **Ministry Maxim**
>
> Only one word can sufficiently account for anyone's life.

"So then each one of us will give an account of himself to God" (Rom. 14:12). In that day, "each one will bear his own load" (Gal. 6:5). The future tense of Peter's verb looks to a time yet to come, and God has already appointed that day (Acts 17:31), a day when He "will judge the secrets of men" (Rom. 2:16). None will escape that accounting for "there is no creature hidden from His sight, but all things are open and laid bare to the eyes of Him with whom we have to do" (Heb. 4:13). "Then I saw a great white throne and Him who sat upon it, from whose presence earth and heaven fled away, and no place was found for them. And I saw the dead, the great and the small, standing before the throne, and books were opened; and another book was opened, which is the book of life; and the dead were judged from the things which were written in the books, according to their deeds" (Rev. 20:11–12).

Each one's accounting will be made "to Him who is ready to judge" (τῷ ἑτοίμως ἔχοντι κρῖναι). The participle with the definite article is used substantively (τῷ ... ἔχοντι, "to *Him who* is," emphasis added). It may more literally be rendered "to the one having." It references as Judge either God the Father (Rom. 14:10; 1 Peter 1:17; Rev. 20:11–12) or God the Son (Matt. 16:27; 25:31–46; John 5:22, 27; Acts 10:42; 17:31; Rom. 2:16; 2 Cor. 5:10; 2 Tim. 4:1; Jude 14–15). Earlier, Peter designated the Father as Judge (1 Peter 1:7; 2:23), but he also links the judgment with Jesus'

---

59 Ibid., 4605.2.a.

Return (1:13; 5:4). Jesus said, "not even the Father judges anyone, but He has given all judgment to the Son" (John 5:22). If applied to Christ, "Judge adds the crowning feature to the glories of the exalted Savior set forth in 3:22."[60] The present tense of the participle underscores His present and continual readiness to undertake this at any moment.

That which He has or "is" is denoted by the adverb ἑτοίμως in the attributive position ("ready"). It is used only two other times in the NT and, in both cases, appears in combination with the same verb (Acts 21:13; 2 Cor. 12:14). In all three, an infinitive (here κρῖναι, "to judge") indicates that which one stands "ready" to do.[61] The cognate adjective was used in 3:15: "always being ready [ἕτοιμοι] to make a defense to everyone" who asks about their hope. Of particular note is that the cognate adjective (Matt. 24:44; Luke 12:40; cf. 1 Peter 1:5) and verb (Luke 12:47; Rev. 19:7; 21:2) are used of readiness for Jesus' Return, a similar note being sounded by Peter here. That for which He is prepared is "to judge" (κρῖναι). The aorist tense denotes the definite, decisive, eternally defining nature of the moment.[62] The readiness is held continuously; the judgment will take place in a moment. Peter has already denoted God as "him who judges righteously" (1 Peter 2:23) and that He does so "impartially… according to each one's work" (1:17).

What is paid out (ἀποδώσουσιν, "will give") is a response in kind. It arises from and is measured by what the other party has done. It is just, commensurate, and appropriate. Believers are never to undertake such work (Rom. 12:17; 1 Thess. 5:15; 1 Peter 3:9), only the Lord can do so, and He will (Rom. 2:6; 2 Tim. 4:14; Rev. 22:12).

He will judge both "the living and the dead" (ζῶντας καὶ νεκρούς). This is a standard NT expression for the universality of accountability to God (Acts 10:42; 2 Tim. 4:1; cf. Rom. 14:9). The two terms are held in coordinate relationship by the conjunction καὶ ("and"). Yet the two are expressed in different ways. The latter is an adjective, here used as a

---

60 Hiebert, 264.
61 Forbes, 141.
62 Alford, 4:373.

substantive (νεκρούς, "the dead"). The former is a participle used substantively (ζῶντας, "the living"). The present tense denotes the nature of their existence at the time of Christ's Return. In the Greek text, neither carries the definite article, though it may still be considered definite ("*the* living and *the* dead," emphasis added).[63] The point of the expression is that no one escapes their appointment at the throne. There will be no hiding in the shadows of death to avoid standing before God. All will have to "account" for the life they lived in this world and will receive judgment as to their existence in the next. Similarly, those living at Jesus' Return will face judgment just as surely as will those who previously died and will, at His Coming, appear before the throne of God to bring an "account" for their lives.

Truth exists, and it is not the product of a social construct. The squishy ideology of our pluralistic, relativistic age will face the blunt force of objective, undeniable truth at the throne of God. Jesus warned, "an hour is coming, in which all who are in the tombs will hear His voice, and will come forth; those who did the good deeds to a resurrection of life, those who committed the evil deeds to a resurrection of judgment" (John 5:28–29). Paul declared before the Roman governor Felix, "there shall certainly be a resurrection of both the righteous and the wicked" (Acts 24:15; cf. Luke 14:14). Long before Jesus and the Apostles, Daniel prophesied, "Many of those who sleep in the dust of the ground will awake, these to everlasting life, but the others to disgrace and everlasting contempt" (Dan. 12:2). Peter will soon remind his readers, "The end of all things is near" (1 Peter 4:7a). The Lord stands "ready to judge" all who have ever lived.

Peter sets before us an end-time reversal of what has transpired within time.[64] Earlier it was unbelievers who demanded an accounting from believers for clinging to what appears to be an irrational hope (1 Peter 3:15). At the end of time, however, it is unbelievers who are called before

---

63 Robertson, *Grammar*, 793.

64 Beare, 181; Clowney, 174; Elliot, 729; Forbes, 140–141; Hiebert, 264; Michaels, 234; Schreiner, 204.

God's throne where they must "give account" for their lives on this earth and their response to Christ—either as the cornerstone of God's people or as the "stone of stumbling" and "rock of offense" (1 Peter 2:7–8, NASB). "Therefore those who do not receive Him as their Saviour, must face Him as their Judge."[65]

> **Digging Deeper:**
> 1. How can you best help someone realize that "the time already past is sufficient" for their pursuit of sin (v.3)?
> 2. Why does your non-participation so enrage sinners (v.4)? Why are they not content in their own indulgence?
> 3. What "word" will you speak before the Lord when He asks for an account of your life (v.5)?

Verse 6 – "For the gospel has for this purpose been preached even to those who are dead, that though they are judged in the flesh as men, they may live in the spirit according to *the will of* God."

Peter presents evidence (γὰρ, "For") to back up his insistence that all people will stand before God to "give account" for their lives (v.5). As exhibit A, he sets out something God did with a specific "purpose" in mind. He will set "this purpose" (εἰς τοῦτο) out in the remainder of the sentence. The clause is placed at the front of the sentence for emphasis and to pique the readers' interest and urge them to watch for what is said next. The purpose will be fully expressed in the second half of the sentence and is signaled by "that" (ἵνα). But first, Peter must set up that statement, and to do so, he reminds his readers that "the gospel has been preached even to those who are dead" (καὶ νεκροῖς εὐηγγελίσθη). It comes as no surprise to Peter's readers that "the gospel has been preached" (εὐηγγελίσθη). The

---

65 Stibbs, 150–151.

verb is a compound made up of εὖ ("good") and ἀγγέλλω ("to announce"). The root verb is used in the NT only when Mary Magdalene came to Jesus' Disciples "announcing [ἀγγέλλουσα] to the disciples, 'I have seen the Lord'" (John 20:18). But the compound for is used over fifty times and is the standard NT way of expressing the proclamation of the good news of the gospel. Peter has already used it to remind his readers of "those who preached the gospel [εὐαγγελισαμένων] to you" (1 Peter 1:12). And to remind them that the everlasting "word" of which Isaiah prophesied (Isa. 40:6–8) "is the word which was preached [εὐαγγελισθὲν] to you" (1 Peter 1:25).

There is nothing surprising to Peter's readers about the gospel being preached. But he sets before the verb in an emphatic position the fact that this took place "even to those who are dead" (καὶ νεκροῖς). Peter's simple statement has engendered endless debate and called forth a great deal of commentary. But, as so often is the case, the simplest understanding is the best. The gospel was preached not only to Peter's readers (1 Peter 1:12, 25), but "even" (καὶ) to those among them who died after they heard the gospel. The conjunction is used adverbially and emphatically ("even") to indicate a unique subset of those to whom the gospel was preached. By "those who are dead" (νεκροῖς), Peter does not mean that the gospel was preached somehow to people after they died. Peter just used the noun (v.5) to divide humanity into two groups—those who, from the perspective of the time of Jesus' Return, were either alive or had already died by that time. It makes sense then that he used it again here to speak of those who, from the time perspective of this letter, had already died. To read Peter as referring to gospel preaching to people after death would be a violation of the present context. Furthermore, we wonder how this would encourage believers to remain faithful and live holy lives in the face of unjust suffering. Why not, then, just give way to sin and the pressures of society and count on a second opportunity at the gospel after death? Furthermore, it is out of step with this letter's understanding of salvation as well as that of the whole of Scripture. Similarly, it does not refer to those who are "dead" spiritually, for this would require two different understandings of the same noun within the same sentence. Also, this would require the present tense of the verb because, certainly, the gospel was continuing to be preached to the spiritually dead, but what we have is an aorist tense, indicating a specific and complete proclamation of the gospel. The meaning, rather, is that those who had heard the gospel believed it and then subsequently died before the time of Peter's writing. This understanding best coordinates the two uses of νεκρός ("dead") in such close proximity.

Peter now moves to fully explain the "purpose" of which he has already spoken (ἵνα, "that"; "so that," NET, NIV, NRSV). That purpose is set before us by way of contrast using a μὲν ... δὲ (typically, "on the one hand ... on the other hand") formula.

The first element (μὲν) is translated by most English translations as a concession: "though they are judged in the flesh as men" (κριθῶσι ... κατὰ ἀνθρώπους σαρκὶ; but cf. KJV, NIV, NKJV). The aorist tense of the verb (κριθῶσι, "they are judged") pictures the event. The passive voice depicts them as being acted upon by another who passes the judgment and brings it to pass. The subjunctive mood pairs with ἵνα to indicate a purpose clause. Despite (δὲ) this act of judgment, "they may live" (ζῶσι). The judgment was a judgment of physical death. But this death was not able to keep them from life. The present tense contrasts the point action of the previous aorist verb. They "live" presently, continuously, and without end. Later, Peter will picture judgment beginning with the house of God (4:17a) as a purifying process before that judgment falls in destruction upon the enemies of the gospel and God's people (vv.17b-18).

> **Ministry Maxim**
>
> Every time the gospel is spoken life and death hang in the balance.

The two clauses contain a pair of contrasting elements. The judgment took place "in the flesh" (σαρκὶ). They live "in the spirit" (πνεύματι). The two dative singular nouns are positioned at the end of their respective clauses and indicate the realm in which the action took place.[66] The judgment took place "in the flesh," in the physical body, and related to the life of that body. The judgment

---

66 Forbes, 142; cf. Wallace who identifies them as datives of respect, identifying "the frame of reference" within which the respective actions took place (144–146).

against sin is death. In warning Adam and Eve away from sinful independence, God said, "in the day that you eat from it you will surely die" (Gen. 2:17). Death came immediately to their relationship to God and began to work its processes in their bodies as well so that it can be rightly said, "the wages of sin is death" (Rom. 6:23). These who had heard the gospel of Jesus Christ and found eternal life in Him had since that time physically died. Given God's verdict against sin, it appeared to the world they had been judged. What had faith in Christ gained them? They died as all men do. Yet, Peter tells us, they live on "in the spirit," in the realm of spiritual, eternal, divine life.

That this is the correct understanding of Peter's words here is confirmed by the fact that both nouns in precisely the same forms were already used in 3:18, where they were applied to Jesus.[67] He, "having been put to death in the flesh" (σαρκὶ) was "made alive in the spirit" (πνεύματι). There they referred to Jesus' physical death upon the cross and His subsequent resurrection from the dead. Here, we rightly understand Peter as referring to people who physically died after hearing and believing the gospel but who continued unendingly in the resurrection life provided them in Christ.

The second contrast is seen in that these people faced judgment "as men" (κατὰ ἀνθρώπους), and yet they live "according to the will of God" (κατὰ θεόν). The English text obscures what is set out clearly in the Greek original. Peter uses κατὰ twice in parallel, contrasting clauses. A more literal rendering makes it clear: "according to [κατὰ] men" and "according to [κατὰ] God" (YLT; cf. NIV). While this clearly sets out the parallelism, it leaves one wondering just what these two clauses mean. The NASU understands the two occurrences of κατὰ to be used differently ("as" and "according to"). Some translations try to render them with identical expressions in both cases: "the way" (ESV), "by...standards" (NET), "according to" (KJV, NIV, NKJV, YLT), "as" (NRSV), "like" (RSV). Clearly, there is little consensus regarding just how they should be understood or translated. Generally, the preposition is used to indicate

---

67 Cf. also the use of σαρκὶ in 4:1 [2x] and 2.

correspondence or conformity.[68] But that to which correspondence or conformity is found is different in each case, so it is difficult to preserve the parallelism in English. On the one hand, the judgment of death came according to "men" (ἀνθρώπους). Those who believed the gospel have, like all other humans, succumbed to physical death. Yet they presently and continuously live according to "God" (θεὸν). Corresponding to and in conformity with the sentence passed upon all "men" (i.e., human beings), these that Peter and his readers have in mind are "dead" physically. Their experience is in conformity to that which all humans face. Yet, corresponding to and in conformity with the promise of "God" in the gospel of Jesus Christ, they now continuously "live" in His presence. Their present spiritual reality is in conformity to that of God, who lives eternally. And this is because of Jesus' resurrection from the dead and their union with Him. Jesus' words have become true, "because I live, you will live also" (John 14:19).

Digging Deeper:
1. How does Peter's reasoning in verse 6 feed our urgency in sharing the gospel?
2. What response would you give to someone who says the universal fact of physical death disproves the power of the gospel (v.6)?

Verse 7 – "The end of all things is near; therefore, be of sound judgment and sober *spirit* for the purpose of prayer."

Peter has been making a point about the importance of time in his readers' lives. He reminded them that "the time already past" (v.3) has been spent in independence from God and has been filled up with enough sin. Now

---

68   Harris, 152.

"the rest of the time in the flesh" should be devoted to God and His will (v.2). They have chosen in the present to honor God with their obedience even if it proves painful (v.4) because the time will come when all will stand before God to give an account (v.5).

Picking up on these time sequences, Peter declares, "The end of all things is near" (Πάντων δὲ τὸ τέλος ἤγγικεν). Many English translations do not render the conjunction δὲ (but cf. "But," KJV, NKJV; "For," NET; "Now," HCSB). Just how to render the conjunction is a challenge. But Peter clearly transitions at this point, though he does so by building upon the urgency established by his reflections upon our sinful past, our meaningful present, and our future accountability before God's throne.

Peter speaks expansively, calling before our minds "all things" (Πάντων) and wants us to consider "the end of" (τὸ τέλος) them. Our understanding of "all things" (Πάντων) should be all-encompassing. Peter thrust it to the beginning of the sentence for added emphasis. He has a vision "in which the heavens will pass away with a roar and the elements will be destroyed with intense heat, and the earth and its works will be burned up" (2 Peter 3:10). This encompasses everything above us ("the heavens"), all that is beneath and around us ("the earth"), and all that mankind has done, accomplished, produced, and brought forth throughout history ("and its works").

Peter wants us to contemplate "the end of" (τὸ τέλος) all these things. The noun marks the last point in the duration of something and, thus, "the end of" that period. It points to conclusion, fulfillment of purpose, consummation, and completion, not simply cessation.[69] The presence of the definite article is telling and signals that Peter has in view that "end" in which "all things" will have found their appropriate place, whether in judgment or in salvation. Indeed, Peter has in mind "the end of" this created order. As it signals judgment, Peter speaks later of how "all these things are thus to be dissolved" (2 Peter 3:11, ESV). He says, "the heavens will be destroyed by burning, and the elements will melt with intense heat" (v.12). The end will involve "the removing of those things which can be shaken, as of created things, so that those things which cannot

---

69 NIDNTTE, 4:479.

be shaken may remain" (Heb. 12:27). As it signals salvation, Peter has worked to set his readers' eyes upon the longed-for fulfillment of Christ's work on their behalf (1 Peter 1:3–9, 13; 2:12). Peter has already alerted his readers to the fact that they live in the "last times" (1:20), the period that began when Jesus was raised from the dead (1:3; 3:21–22).

This "end" is "near." But what precisely does Peter mean by "is near" (ἤγγικεν)? Nearness is a relative matter. One thing can be nearer than something else, yet still further from it when compared to another thing. Earth is nearer to the sun than Jupiter, but it is farther from the sun than Mercury. The verb can refer to one coming near to death (Phil. 2:30), of physical proximity to something (Acts 9:3; 10:9; 21:33; 22:6; 23:15), of time in relation to the sovereign plan of God in fulfilling a promise (Acts 7:17), and relationally and experientially in drawing near to God (Heb. 7:19; James 4:8). It is used elsewhere, as it is here, in an eschatological sense: "you see the day drawing near" (Heb. 10:25) and "the coming of the Lord is near" (James 5:8). Paul uses the cognate preposition to remind that "now salvation is nearer [ἐγγύτερον] to us than when we believed" (Rom. 13:11). The Father "has fixed a day in which He will judge the world" (Acts 17:31). If indeed the coming of Christ, and thus "the end of all things," is a fixed point established by God's sovereign will, then it is "nearer" to us now (and with each passing day) than it was yesterday. But that still says nothing definite about just now "near" it is in terms of time as we understand it. But the certainty of its approach and the uncertainty of the time of its arrival both call for prudent living in the present. In his second letter, Peter reminds his readers that "with the Lord one day is like a thousand years, and a thousand years like one day" (2 Peter 3:8) and that "The Lord is not slow about His promise, as some count slowness" (v.9). In the end "the day of the Lord will [have] come like a thief" (v.10).

> **Ministry Maxim**
>
> Pray always in the shadow of the clock.

Peter here uses the verb in the perfect tense, indicating that "the end" of all things as we know them has come near to us, and we continue abidingly in that state of nearness; "the end" is waiting, impending, looming. With Jesus' coming, death, resurrection, and ascension, "the last days" have come upon the earth (Acts 2:17; Heb. 1:2; James 5:3). All that remains is the proclamation of the gospel to all the peoples of the earth and "then the end will come" (Matt. 24:14).

From these sobering contemplations, Peter draws a logical deduction (οὖν, "therefore"). He will outline a series of behaviors that reflect an awareness of one's life lived under the looming "end of all things" (vv.7b-11). Thus "Not drunken debauchery and license, but sober clear-headedness, marks the Christian (4:7). Love, not lust, fills his heart (4:8); the Christian home is open for hospitality, not orgies (4:9). Ministry replaces exploitation (4:9–11)."[70]

These considerations of time and accountability call us to "be of sound judgment and sober spirit" (σωφρονήσατε ... καὶ νήψατε). First, we should "be of sound judgment" (σωφρονήσατε). The verb is used six times in the NT (Mark 5:15; Luke 8:35; Rom. 12:3; 2 Cor. 5:13; Titus 2:6; 1 Peter 4:7). It could be used to describe one who is "in his right mind" (Mark 5:15; Luke 8:35) as opposed to the insanity of demon-possession. But in the bulk of its uses, the verb has the sense of having a self-controlled mind which enables a person to live a self-controlled life. The aorist imperative presses urgently for our obedience.

In addition (καὶ, "and"), we should "be of ... sober spirit" (νήψατε). This verb also appears six times in the NT, half of which are by Peter (1 Thess. 5:6, 8; 2 Tim. 4:5; 1 Peter 1:13; 4:7; 5:8). Used literally, the word could describe being free from intoxicants and, given the sins of indulgence and drunkenness Peter called out in verse 3, it might be tempting to read it that way here.[71] But in all its NT usages, it is used figuratively (and so also here, be of "sober *spirit*," emphasis added). It means then to "be free fr[om] every form of mental and spiritual 'drunkenness', fr[om] excess, passion, rashness, confusion, etc." and thus to be "be well-balanced" and "self-controlled."[72] Again the aorist imperative demands action be undertaken immediately and urgently. Do we have here a reflection of Jesus' words to Peter in the Garden: "Keep watching and praying

---

70 Clowney, 177.

71 Dubis, 140; Forbes, 146.

72 BDAG, 5098.

that you may not come into temptation; the spirit is willing, but the flesh is weak" (Mark 14:38; cf. Luke 21:36)?

The verbs, so closely related to one another in their meaning, may form a hendiadys, making a singular point through two commands. With both verbs, Peter is echoing a theme he began earlier in the letter: "Therefore, prepare your minds for action, keep sober in spirit, fix your hope completely on the grace to be brought to you at the revelation of Jesus Christ" (1 Peter 1:13).

The next phrase (εἰς προσευχάς, "for the purpose of prayer") is to be read with both preceding verbs, not simply the latter (e.g., "be soberminded, then, and watch unto the prayers," YLT; cf. KJV). Peter states the reason for taking these steps. The preposition (εἰς) generally denotes the entry into something and here sets forth the purpose or goal toward which the actions are taken ("for the purpose of").[73] That objective is "prayer" (προσευχάς). In Peter's only other use of the noun, he is also concerned for that which might hinder the prayers of Christian married men (1 Peter 3:7, see the comments there for more on the noun). The plural form indicates both the diversity of forms in which prayer is expressed (including praise, confession, thanksgiving, petition, and intercession) and the repeated nature of its practice. Prayer is both a weapon to be wielded (Eph. 6:17–18) and that which we fight to protect. Davids well says, "proper prayer is not an 'opiate' or escape, but rather a function of a clear vision and a seeking of even clearer vision from God."[74] Prayer is both why we stay sober-minded and how we stay sober-minded.

Verse 8 – "Above all, keep fervent in your love for one another, because love covers a multitude of sins."

"Above all" (πρὸ πάντων). The preposition πρὸ means "before" and here emphasizes priority, not in time, but importance (cf. James 5:12).[75] The

---

73 Harris, 83, 88.

74 Davids, 157.

75 Harris, 185; Robertson, *Grammar*, 623.

adjective (πάντων, "all") is repeated from verse 7. As there, we should read it here as inclusive of "all" that makes up the present reality. "All" will find its appointed "end" at the return of Christ and the throne of God. In this light, there is nothing in all creation that is more important than what Peter now sets before his readers.

Top priority is given to what happens "in your love for one another" (τὴν εἰς ἑαυτοὺς ἀγάπην). Peter is describing life rightly lived in light of the impending "end" of all things found in either judgment or salvation. In verse 7, he dealt with matters as they relate to oneself ("be of sound judgment and sober spirit") and God ("for the purpose of prayer"). Now in verses 8 through 11, he focuses on Christian relationships[76] as signaled by his use of the reflexive pronoun ἑαυτοὺς (vv.8, 10) and the reciprocating pronoun ἀλλήλους (v.9). Both forms emphasize the mutuality of the action—the former in which the subject of the action participates in the action itself (lit., "the into yourselves love"[77]) and the latter emphasizes the back-and-forth nature of the interchange ("one another").[78] The preposition εἰς ("for") signals the extension of love into the arena of mutual relationships among Christian believers. The entire phrase ("for one another") is in the attributive position between the noun and its definite article (τὴν ... ἀγάπην), thus denoting the nature of the "love" that is under consideration. This is Peter's first use of this significant NT noun (cf. 1 Peter 5:14; 2 Peter 1:7), but he has used the verb extensively throughout this letter (1:8, 22; 2:17; 3:10; cf. 2 Peter 2:15). In 2 Peter 1:7 he makes ἀγάπη the crowning virtue of eight that must be added continually in ever-greater measures to one's Christian life. There he makes ἀγάπη one extension beyond φιλαδελφία ("brotherly kindness"). Perhaps it can best be said that ἀγάπη is at the very heart of God's love toward us and is thus the highest level of love we can have for one another.

---

76 "... the fact that verses 8–11 (consisting of a series of participles) are grammatically dependent on the imperatives of verse 7 ... implies that the duties now enumerated naturally flow out of the believer's personal relationship to God" (Hiebert, 271).

77 Hiebert, 271.

78 Wallace, 350–351.

Peter desires his reader to "keep fervent" (ἐκτενῆ ἔχοντες) in their love for one another. The verb is a participle in form (ἔχοντες); the NASU does not translate it (cf. "maintain," NRSV; "hold," RSV; "have," KJV, NKJV; "having," YLT). It means simply "having" or "holding." But it can carry the sense of "having" or "holding" to protect. The participial form may describe attendant circumstances (that which is to be going on at the same time as their clear-headed praying, v.7b), but it probably also borrows the power of command from the two imperatives in verse 7. The present tense makes this the enduring and continual responsibility of believers living rightly in the light of "the end of all things."

> **Ministry Maxim**
>
> Concentrate on love or you'll be consumed by bitterness.

The love that we are to continually live in with one another is characterized by the adjective ἐκτενῆ ("fervent"). It is used in the NT only of Jesus in Gethsemane praying "very fervently" (Luke 22:44). The cognate adverb is used in 1 Peter 1:22 also of love ("fervently love one another from the heart") and elsewhere in the NT only of the "fervent" prayer being made by the church for Peter while he was in prison (Acts 12:5). It is "used of tension of the will and means 'tense,' 'resolute,' 'eager'"[79] and thus signals "intensity without negligence or failing."[80]

The reason (ὅτι, "because") to apply such effort and endurance is because of what "love" (ἀγάπη) accomplishes. Its faithful and full exercise "covers a multitude of sins" (καλύπτει πλῆθος ἁμαρτιῶν). The verb (καλύπτει, "covers") is in the present tense, depicting the ongoing nature of the covering of "love." Originally the word carried the notion of hiding or burying something in the earth.[81] It was used literally of the storm-tossed waves covering the boat in which were Jesus and the Disciples (Matt. 8:24; cf. Luke 8:16; 23:30). But it was also used metaphorically (Matt. 10:26; 2 Cor. 4:3 [2x]). James uses it in similar terms to Peter: "he

---

79 TDNT, 2:465.

80 Spicq, 1:461.

81 TDNT, 3:558.

who turns a sinner from the error of his way will save his soul from death and will cover [καλύψει] a multitude of sins" (James 5:20).

Indeed, Peter demands that such love conceals "a multitude of sins" (πλῆθος ἁμαρτιῶν). The noun ("multitude") designates an indefinitely large number. It is used of the host of angels that appeared to the shepherds announcing Jesus' birth (Luke 2:13), of the swelling throngs that flocked to Jesus in His season of popularity (e.g., Mark 3:7–8; Luke 6:17; 19:37), of the miraculously large catch of fish (Luke 5:6), and of the stars in heaven (Heb. 11:12). Here the genitive noun ἁμαρτιῶν ("sins") marks that which is so innumerable. Peter has used the noun already to indicate that Jesus had no sins of His own (1 Peter 2:22) but that our sins were laid upon Him at the cross (2:24) so that He might remove them from us and reconcile us to God (3:18). Considering this great grace, the believer has determined to be done with sin (4:1). And now in the face of the "sins" of others, has decided to swallow them up in "love."

But just whose sins are covered? Some early church fathers[82] believed it was the sins of the one extending the love, and down through the ages, there have been those who followed them.[83] They have looked for support from Luke 7:47. Though some try to avoid the implication, this smacks of merited forgiveness rather than the gospel of free grace. This defies Peter's emphasis on salvation coming only because of Christ's redemptive, substitutionary atoning death (1 Peter 2:22–24; 3:18) in harmony with the entire NT. Upon closer examination, in fact, we discover that the word appears in the LXX with the sense of covering as forgiveness of sin. It is so used in Psalm 84:3 (85:3 MT; 85:2 English) in parallel with the forgiving of iniquity. It also appears in the LXX of Nehemiah 3:37 (3:37 MT; 4:5 English) in a similar sense.[84] In both cases, the Greek renders a Hebrew verb that is also used elsewhere for the forgiveness of sins (e.g., Psa. 32:1). It appears rather that the sins covered are committed by those

---

82 Goppelt cites Tertullian, Clement of Alexandria, and Origen (298).

83 E.g., Kelly, 178; TDNT, 3:559; Spicq, 2:247–248. Spicq goes so far as to say, "in the NT, *agape* has the value of an expiatory sacrifice" (2:248).

84 Dubis, 141; NIDNTTE, 2:613.

who are being loved, though they sinfully wronged the lover.[85] Certainly, our love for another who has wronged us does not "cover" their sin in the sense of atoning for it but in the sense of burying it and removing it from consideration in our relationship. And in such cases, our "love" by means of forgiveness testifies to the one source of true forgiveness, Jesus Christ.

Peter appears to be recalling Proverbs 10:12: "Hatred stirs up strife, But love covers all transgressions" (as also does James 5:20). Here we see that "The righteous man covers over and hides from view the personal offenses committed against him. Rather than pulling these wrongs out to public view and responding in kind, the righteous throws a wet blanket over the flame of another's sin against him. Rather than calling down judgment on the one who wrongs us, we are to personally absorb the wrong in the cushion of our love."[86] This is a theme that runs throughout the Bible. "He who covers a transgression seeks love, But he who repeats a matter separates intimate friends" (Prov. 17:9). "A man's discretion makes him slow to anger, And it is his glory to overlook a transgression" (Prov. 19:11). Love "is not provoked, does not take into account a wrong suffered" and it "bears all things, believes all things, hopes all things, endures all things" (1 Cor. 13:5, 7).

Perhaps Peter's counsel here is not far from what Paul called for from the Colossian believers when he told them to put on Christian virtues, "bearing with one another, and forgiving each other, whoever has a complaint against anyone; just as the Lord forgave you, so also should you" (Col. 3:13). In small, fledgling congregations any rift in a relationship could threaten the entire Christian presence in a city. The first line of defense was "bearing with one another," simply absorbing one another's irritations in grace and refusing to let them become an issue. Where such irritations rose to the level of sin which could not be ignored, there were to be efforts at reconciliation which resulted in "forgiving each other" just as "the Lord forgave you." Jesus taught the path to be taken in such instances (Matt. 18:15–22; cf. Gal. 6:1–5). The basic irritants we all bring

---

85   NIDNTTE, 2:616.

86   Kitchen, *Proverbs: A Mentor Commentary*, 223.

to relationships should be smothered in grace. The sins that we commit should be dealt with and forgiven.

Some fires are only extinguished by suppression—denying the flames access to the oxygen that would feed it into an inferno. So also grace suffocates from the beginning those sparks which might ignite a destructive fire in our relationships.

After Jesus instructed His disciples in the matter of forgiving one another, Peter asked, "Lord, how often shall my brother sin against me and I forgive him? Up to seven times?" Jesus answered him, "I do not say to you, up to seven times, but up to seventy times seven" (Matt. 18:21, 22). Many may be the "sins" (ἁμαρτιῶν), but greater yet shall be the "love" shown in forbearing and forgiving each one.

Verse 9 – "Be hospitable to one another without complaint."

The clause contains no verb, so the translators have rightly understood an imperative ("Be"). That which is required is "hospitable" (φιλόξενοι) service to others. The adjective is used only three times in the NT. The other two usages are in lists of qualifications for church leaders (1 Tim. 3:2; Titus 1:8; cf. the cognate noun in Rom. 12:13; Heb. 13:2). It is a compound word made up of φίλος ("love") and ξένος ("strange," "foreign"), meaning "stranger-loving." This is compared to the more common brotherly love (φιλαδελφία), which Peter himself has emphasized (1 Peter 1:22; 2 Peter 1:7 [2x]; cf. 1 Peter 3:8). With "hospitable" service there is no payback, no family duty, no bloodlines to obligate. There is no earthly human reason to love the stranger, only a heavenly one. Peter shows us that being "hospitable" is not to be left to the leaders of the church but practiced by all its members.

> **Ministry Maxim**
>
> Grudging hospitality is an oxymoron.

Hospitality was a vivid and regular part of Hebrew society. Community residents were almost under obligation to take in the traveling stranger who stopped in the city for a night of rest. Hospitality was a profound part of the expansion of the gospel as believers spread out across the Mediterranean world (3 John 5–8; cf. 2 John 10). Churches met in homes as well. They relied on the generous hospitality of the homeowners (Rom. 16:3–5, 23; 1 Cor. 16:19; Col. 4:15; Philem. 2). Jesus placed hospitality not only on the horizontal plane of human relationships but revealed a vertical and spiritual dimension to this ministry as well (Matt. 25:31–46). Peter uses the plural form of the word here to emphasize the multiplicity of expressions or the repeated practice of hospitality.[87] Sadly, hospitality has fallen on hard times in a day when privacy and individuality are valued above community.

As in verses 8 and 10, he uses here the preposition εἰς ("to"), but here he combines it with the reciprocal pronoun ἀλλήλους ("one another") instead of the reflexive pronoun (ἑαυτοὺς, "one another") found in both those verses. The resulting meaning is largely the same.

We are to display a "hospitable" spirit "without complaint" (ἄνευ γογγυσμοῦ). The preposition (ἄνευ, "without") is found only three times in the NT (Matt. 10:29; 1 Peter 3:1; 4:9). It indicates separation, but not in a spatial sense.[88] In both of Peter's usages, it is the absence of verbal communication that is in view—a "word" (λόγου) in 3:1 and here vocalized "complaint" (γογγυσμοῦ). The noun is used only four times in the NT. The people of Israel grumbled about Jesus (John 7:12). The Hellenistic Jews of Jerusalem grumbled when there were inequities in the distribution of food among the believers (Acts 6:1). Paul told believers in Philippi to "Do all things without grumbling [γογγυσμῶν] or disputing" (Phil. 2:14). In the LXX the word is used to describe the murmurings of Israel (e.g., Exod. 16:7, 8 [2x], 9, 12; Numb. 17:20, 25). It may thus describe "whispering"[89] and a half-voiced, under-the-breath kind of muttering that sows seeds of disgruntlement in the soil of other hearts.

Peter clearly recognized the practice of hospitality as going to the core of one's view of personal space, possessions, time, and energies. Implicit in his words is also the recognition that hospitality was particularly a point of vulnerability to those who wished to take advantage of the goodwill

---

87 Hiebert, 273.

88 Harris, 242.

89 BDAG, 1667.

and generosity of believers. Thus, in one of the churches' earliest extant, extra-biblical documents, leaders provided the larger Christian community with guidelines in the practice of hospitality, particularly as it related to traveling gospel workers. The Didache may date to as early as A.D. 100 and regulated expectations regarding hospitality, including a maximum stay of two days, or perhaps at most three. Beyond this, Christian visitors were to find work and support themselves. It was a maxim that a failure to do so was evidence of ulterior, non-gospel motives.[90] Thus both grace and discernment are necessary for the practice of hospitality, but if an error is made, let it be on the side of joyful, willing grace.

Verse 10 – "As each one has received a *special* gift, employ it in serving one another as good stewards of the manifold grace of God."

Peter reminds his readers that "each one has received a special gift" (ἕκαστος ... ἔλαβεν χάρισμα). The noun χάρισμα ("a special gift") is used seventeen times in the NT; this is the only use outside of Paul's letters. It can refer to the free gift of salvation in Christ (Rom. 5:15, 16; 6:23), to divine enablement worked out in the believer by the Holy Spirit (Rom. 12:6; 1 Cor. 1:7; 12:4, 9, 28, 30, 31), and more generally of favor extended (2 Cor. 1:11). Jesus, just before He ascended, spoke of "the promise of My Father" (Luke 24:49). Shortly afterward that promise was referred to more specifically as "the gift of the Holy Spirit" (Acts 2:38). Fundamentally, the gift is the Holy Spirit Himself. The contextual connection of "gift" and the Spirit in 2 Timothy 1:6 and 7 (cf. v.14) and elsewhere (Rom. 1:11; 1 Cor. 1:7; 12:4, 31) seems to confirm this. The Spirit is the gift. We often speak of a spiritual gift as the ability to "do" something, treating it almost as an objective thing we possess. It seems more in accord with the teaching of Scripture to see the Spirit as the gift and the newly imparted ability as simply the way the Holy Spirit sovereignly chooses to express Himself through the individual. A

---

90 www.thedidache.com (XII.2–5).

spiritual gift is simply the Holy Spirit being Himself uniquely through an individual believer, as He wills (1 Cor. 12:11). All believers receive the Holy Spirit (Rom. 8:9; Titus 3:5–6). The Holy Spirit chooses how He expresses Himself in and through the individual.

This divine giftedness is true of "each one" (ἕκαστος) in the body of Christ, none being excepted. Everyone within the body of Christ "has received" (ἔλαβεν) some such gift from the Lord. The aorist tense makes definite the giving; it refers not to a process or development but to a point at which the gift was bestowed. All are given the same Spirit upon conversion; not all receive the same expression or gifting of the Spirit. None, however, are without some gifted expression of the Spirit through them.

Every such gift is given that we might "employ it in serving one another" (εἰς ἑαυτοὺς αὐτὸ διακονοῦντες). The giftings of the Holy Spirit are not given for self-indulgence or self-gratification but for "serving" (διακονοῦντες). Peter used the verb of the service performed by the prophets of old for those of us on this side of the cross and resurrection: "they were not serving themselves, but you" (1 Peter 1:12). He will use the verb again in verse 11. Here the present tense sets forth the abiding nature of spiritual gifts. They continually focus on others within the body of Christ. The participial form parallels the participle in verse 8 and similarly carries the force of a command picked up from the imperatives in verse 7.

Each one's gift is to be used "in" (εἰς) serving the larger body of Christ and its individual members. As he did in verses 8 and 9, Peter combines εἰς with either a reflexive (vv.8, 10) or a reciprocal pronoun (v.9). Here again, the preposition εἰς ("for") signals the extension of service into the arena of mutual relationships among Christian believers. See our comments above on verse 8 for Peter's use of the reflexive pronoun (ἑαυτοὺς, "one another"). Hiebert observes that the pronoun "stresses the mutual benefit of the gifts...God has made the members interdependent; that which benefits others has a reflexive benefit for us."[91] Here the combination εἰς ἑαυτοὺς αὐτὸ διακονοῦντες means literally, "serve it to one another"[92] or

---

91 Hiebert, 275.

92 Dubis, 143.

"serve one another with it."[93] The neuter singular pronoun αὐτὸ ("it") designates the individual gift a believer may have "received" from God.

This we seek to do "as good stewards of the manifold grace of God" (ὡς καλοὶ οἰκονόμοι ποικίλης χάριτος θεοῦ). The word "stewards" (οἰκονόμοι) originally referred to the manager of a household or estate. His responsibility was placed upon him by the owner of the house, and the steward was held responsible for the welfare of that household and its goods (Luke 12:42; 16:1–8). Peter reminds us that the grace God pours into our lives is not ultimately for our own indulgence or merely for our own benefit but was given that it might be stewarded in relationship to others for God's glory. The steward lives under the awareness that one day he will give an accounting for his care of this good deposit from the Lord. The term is used of apostles and other church leaders (1 Cor. 4:1), including local church elders/overseers (Titus 1:7). But here, the plural form makes clear that all God's people serve in such a role. Peter views the church as "the household of God" (1 Peter 4:17), and thus the image is apt. Faithfulness is the one indispensable quality of a "good" (καλοὶ) steward (Matt. 24:45; Luke 12:41–42; 1 Cor. 4:2).

> **Ministry Maxim**
> Grace received is a gift to pass on.

Peter uses two comparatives, καθὼς ("as") and ὡς ("as"). The former is a comparative that means "to the extent or degree to which"[94] or "in proportion as."[95] In the manner and measure with which we have received God's grace in our individual lives, so we are to distribute this grace to others for His glory.[96] "Freely you received, freely give" (Matt. 10:8). The latter (ὡς) marks the manner in which something is to be

---

93 BDAG, 229.2.a.

94 Ibid., 3843.2.

95 Thayer, 315; contra Dubis who calls it a marker of cause (143).

96 Kenyon observes that there is "a balance between engiftment and responsibility" (quoted by Hiebert, 274).

done.[97] The common picture of the household manager ("stewards") sets the standard.

Peter uses two cognate words, χάρισμα ("a special gift") and χάριτος ("grace"). For Peter χάρις ("grace") is largely synonymous with salvation (1 Peter 1:2, 10, 13; 3:7). Such grace is already ours (1:10), continues to become ours more and more in this life (1:2), and yet will be only fully experienced at Jesus' Return (1:13). God's grace is "manifold" (ποικίλης). The adjective originally described that which is many-colored. It points to the variety and diversity of ways "grace" finds expression in the lives of His people. The inflow of God's "grace" comes to us all in "manifold" circumstances and ways, but in God's plan, it always brings with it "a ... gift" that is designed not for our benefit alone, but to be passed on to others for their good and to God's glory. The way God works His grace *in* us is linked to how He wishes to bring His grace *through* us to others. In fact, Peter used the adjective earlier to describe the vast variety of ways that trouble comes to a believer's life (1:6), but now he reminds us that the grace of God can be just as varied. No trial comes, but there is a perfect grace to match it; no grace comes to us without a corresponding outlet for the strengthening of others.

In writing to the Corinthian believers of the χάρισμα ("gift") of God, Paul provided a listing of potential expressions (1 Cor. 12:7–10). He wrote similarly, but more briefly, to the Romans (Rom. 12:6–8). Peter does not enumerate the specific "manifold" ways God's grace is to be a "gift" to one another beyond the categories of serving and speaking (1 Peter 4:11). Given the use of the adjective ποικίλος ("manifold") for both trials (1:6) and grace (4:10) perhaps Peter views a connection between the two. Does he approach Paul's sentiment regarding the connection between the grace we receive from God in our trials and the comfort God continues to pass along to others through us?

"Blessed be the God and Father of our Lord Jesus Christ, the Father of mercies and God of all comfort, who comforts us in all our affliction so that we will be able to comfort those who are in any affliction with the

---

97 BDAG, 8075.1.

comfort with which we ourselves are comforted by God. For just as the sufferings of Christ are ours in abundance, so also our comfort is abundant through Christ. But if we are afflicted, it is for your comfort and salvation; or if we are comforted, it is for your comfort, which is effective in the patient enduring of the same sufferings which we also suffer; and our hope for you is firmly grounded, knowing that as you are sharers of our sufferings, so also you are sharers of our comfort" (2 Cor. 1:3–7).

Digging Deeper:
1. Nearly 2,000 years ago Peter announced, "the end is near." How can you answer the one who says God's Word cannot be taken seriously because of the time that has passed between then and now (v.7)?
2. Describe a way in which you've covered another's sin against you (v.8).
3. Why do you think hospitality has suffered in our culture (v.9)?
4. List some of the varied ways God's grace has come to your life. Can you list some of the varied ways He pours His grace through you to others (v.10)?

Verse 11 – "Whoever speaks, *is to do so* as one who is speaking the utterances of God; whoever serves *is to do so* as one who is serving by the strength which God supplies; so that in all things God may be glorified through Jesus Christ, to whom belongs the glory and dominion forever and ever. Amen."

Peter elaborates upon what he meant in verse 10 by each one receiving a special gift to be stewarded in service to other believers. Whereas Paul at times enumerated many individual gifts (Rom. 12:6–8; 1 Cor. 12:8–10), here Peter focuses only on two broad functional categories of gifting. Both categories are set before us by the repeated conditional clause εἴ τις

("Whoever"). In both cases, it literally means "if anyone." In each case, the condition (εἴ, "if") is assumed true—the churches to which Peter writes are made up of those who speak or serve.[98] The indefinite pronoun (τις, "whoever") broadens the consideration to the entire breadth of the members of Christ's church in any given locale. The entire church is under consideration, and everyone who makes it up. All believers should both speak (1 Peter 3:15–16) and serve (2:15; 3:13, 17; 4:10) in the name of the Lord. Yet by God's sovereign will (1 Cor. 12:11), He may gift them for effectiveness in one more than the other.

The first category includes anyone who "speaks" (λαλεῖ). The verb is the common NT way of referencing human vocalization. The present indicative pictures the action as ongoing and actual. But Peter has more in mind than simple human speech or conversation. He is thinking of those who, as a ministry to the body, make use of their words. Paul may have included in this category ministries such as a "word of wisdom," a "word of knowledge" (1 Cor. 12:8), prophecy, tongues, interpretation of tongues (v.10), teaching (Rom. 12:7), and exhortation (v.8). But we should not imagine that these exhaust the ways God uses the words of His people in edification.

Every word that comes from every believer's mouth is to be "only such a word as is good for edification according to the need of the moment, so that it will give grace to those who hear" (Eph. 4:29). But God has particularly endowed some within the body of Christ to make their words especially effective in strengthening His people. When this is the case, such a one is to speak "as one who is speaking the utterances of God" (ὡς λόγια θεοῦ). The expression lacks a verb, and most commentators agree an imperative is called for ("is to do so"; cf., "let him speak," NASB; "let it be with," NET; "they should do so," NIV;

> **Ministry Maxim**
>
> Failure to glorify God is as much a sin of commission as of omission.

---

98   Cf. Acts 6:1–4 for the early church's application of these two categories in the context of an early conflict. Cf. Romans 12:7.

"must do so," NRSV). The noun (λόγια, "the utterances") in the singular means simply "a saying" or "an utterance," especially from God. It is found only four times in the NT, all in the plural form. In the OT, it is used to denote the word of God.[99] It is similarly used in the NT, where it refers to the Law of God given through Moses (Acts 7:38), the promises of God in Scripture (Rom. 3:2), and the Scriptures in their totality (Heb. 5:12). We should understand the genitive (θεοῦ, "of God") as subjective, the word that comes from God. The ὡς ("as") identifies the manner in which the speaking is to be set forth. Peter means not "'as Scripture speaks,' with sincerity and gravity"[100] but "speak as if delivering the very oracles of God."[101]

The Second Helvetic Confession declares: "We believe and confess the canonical Scriptures of the holy prophets and apostles of both Testaments to be the true Word of God, and to have sufficient authority of themselves, not of men. For God himself spoke to the fathers, prophets, apostles, and still speaks to us through the Holy Scriptures." But then it goes on to make the remarkable statement:

> "THE PREACHING OF THE WORD OF GOD IS THE WORD OF GOD. Wherefore when this Word of God is now preached in the church by preachers lawfully called, we believe that the very Word of God is proclaimed, and received by the faithful; and that neither any other Word of God is to be invented nor is to be expected from heaven: and that now the Word itself which is preached is to be regarded, not the minister that preaches; for even if he be evil and a sinner, nevertheless the Word of God remains still true and good."[102]

---

99 TDNT, 4:138.

100 Bigg, 174; cf. Grudem, 183.

101 Michaels, 250.

102 www.ccel.org/creeds/helvetic.htm

One must note it is not simply preaching (standing up and talking about religious matters) which is accounted as the Word of God, but the preaching *of the Word of God* that then comes to the hearer as the Word of God. It is only as preaching is in conformity to the written Word of God that it is constituted the Word of God to the hearers. That proclamation which takes as its substance the very words of the holy Scriptures and in submission to them and shaped by them and set forth under their authority, in faithfulness reproducing them to their hearers by the enabling of the Holy Spirit is to those hearers the very Word of God. Then, and only then, may you "speak as though God himself were speaking through you" (NLT) because, by His Spirit through His written Word, He is "speaking through you." "This admonition is ... at the same time a promise: Human speech can and will become ... speech that comes from God."[103] Indeed, "what the Christian spokesman enunciates, if he is faithful, is God's word; he does not simply repeat the divine message, but God speaks through him."[104] Paul said, "as from God, we speak" (2 Cor. 2:17). He preached "as though God were making an appeal through" him (2 Cor. 5:20). We take up "the word of God" as that which "is living and active and sharper than any two-edged sword, and piercing as far as the division of soul and spirit, of both joints and marrow, and able to judge the thoughts and intentions of the heart" (Heb. 4:12). We speak the gospel with an expectation of God the Spirit producing through it the regeneration of those who hear (1 Peter 1:23–25).

This is not to say that God imparts new revelation through the faithful, Spirit-anointed preacher. He makes the canonical, already-given revelation of the written Word of God contemporary, alive, present, powerful, and personal to those who hear it. God has spoken with finality through His Son. He has closed the canon of Scripture. But, thankfully, He has not ceased to speak.

What a humbling thing it is to speak the Word of God! What a solemn responsibility, what a fearful undertaking, what a high calling, what

---

103 Goppelt, 304.

104 Kelly, 180.

a tremulous boldness to hold forth the written Word of God! "Whoever speaks, is to do so as one who is speaking the utterances of God."

We should not limit this to words spoken from behind a pulpit. Wherever God's Word is spoken faithfully to others—in evangelism, counseling, Bible studies, testimonies, etc.—God Himself speaks to people. We should not limit this to recognized clergymen. But neither should we discount the God-ordained place and importance of gathering as God's people regularly to sit under the exposition of God's written Word (Acts 2:42a; 1 Cor. 14:26; 1 Tim. 4:6, 11–16; 2 Tim. 4:1–2). God's people should gather in expectation of hearing God speak to them through the reading and exposition of the Scriptures.

The second functional category of giftedness he suggests includes anyone who "serves" (διακονεῖ). The condition again is assumed as true—those to whom Peter writes were serving others. The verb is the same one just used in verse 10 (see our comments there). We thus note that all God's gifts, whatever their exact nature or the form they take, are for serving others (1 Cor. 12:7). But among the panoply of gifts God gives His people, there are some that especially focus upon serving. Perhaps among those gifts enumerated by Paul, this would include at least service, leadership, mercy, helping, and administration. The present tense pictures the unfolding and ongoing nature of the service.

Such a one is to serve thus "as one who is serving by the strength which God supplies" (ὡς ἐξ ἰσχύος ἧς χορηγεῖ ὁ θεός). Again the clause lacks a verb, and an imperative should be supplied (e.g., "one who is serving"; "let him do so," NASB; "do so," NET; "should do so," NIV; "must do so," NRSV). The preposition ἐξ ("by") serves as "a marker of the source from which ... something is physically or psychologically derived."[105] It is, more literally, "out of" the supplied strength of God that one ministers. In this case, that which is derived is "strength" (ἰσχύος). The noun is used of something inherent to the human condition, which is to be brought to bear in fulfilling the first and greatest commandment of loving God (Mark 12:30, 33; Luke 10:27). But it is also used to designate something that

---

105 Louw-Nida, 89.3.

is God's alone (2 Thess. 1:9; Rev. 5:12; 7:12) and yet which He expresses toward and shares with His people (Eph. 1:19; 6:10). It is in these latter senses that Peter uses it, for when serving others becomes difficult, human "strength" will wane. Only then can the divinely given "strength" enable us to continue in deference to the needs of others.

This strength is specified as that "which God supplies" (ἧς χορηγεῖ ὁ θεός). The relative pronoun ἧς ("which") finds its antecedent in ἰσχύος ("strength"). The verbal noun "supplies" (χορηγεῖ) ("supplies") is used only one other time in the NT, in 2 Cor. 9:10, where it denotes the open-handed supply of God to His servants. Originally the word denoted one who outfitted a chorus with all they needed to perform, but later it came to be used more generally of defraying the costs of something and to supply all that is needed. Peter used the compounded verbal form in 2 Peter 1:5. The generous supplier is "God" (ὁ θεός) Himself.

Perhaps we may conclude that just as the words spoken are God's very words to those who listen, so the service which takes place "by the strength which God supplies" involves God's very presence and grace touching those who receive the service. God is present extending life through the speaking that takes place by His Spirit; God is present extending life-giving grace through acts of service that take place by His power. God's people become the conduits of God's words and grace through words spoken and actions taken.

The speaking takes place by the word God has given in the Bible ("of God"); the serving takes place "by the strength which God supplies" through His Spirit. Both categories of gifts mentioned by Peter—speaking and serving—find their origin in Jesus. On the same evening when He spoke the Upper Room Discourse (John 13–17), He took the towel and washed His disciples' feet (John 13:1–20).

In both cases, Peter assigns a purpose for the action (ἵνα plus subjunctive, "so that"). It is that "God may be glorified" (δοξάζηται ὁ θεός). The present tense reminds us that glory is unceasingly God's. The passive voice pictures God being thus "glorified" as His people speak His Word and serve one another out of His supplied strength. The God (θεοῦ) who gives His Word, the God (ὁ θεός) who strengthens, is the God (ὁ θεός) who receives glory through the speaking and service which He empowers His people to perform.

This is to be so "in all things" (ἐν πᾶσιν). The prepositional phrase is thrust forward for emphasis. The form of the adjective πᾶσιν could be read as either masculine ("in everyone"[106]) or neuter ("all *things*," emphasis added). Virtually all English translations opt for the neuter, and it is most appropriate in this context. The statement, of course, includes "all things" without limit (Eph. 4:6; Col. 1:18; 3:11), but here it most immediately includes all that His people do for His sake through their speaking and serving. There is not one thing, however minute and seemingly trivial, in which God is not to be glorified "through Jesus Christ" (διὰ Ἰησοῦ Χριστοῦ). The διὰ ("through") signals intermediate agency.[107] The Father gave all authority over to the Son (Matt. 28:18; Luke 10:22; John 3:35; 13:3; 17:2) to bring all things in submission to Himself (Rev. 5). When that happens, "then comes the end, when He hands over the kingdom to the God and Father, when He has abolished all rule and all authority and power" (1 Cor. 15:24). Jesus "must reign until He has put all His enemies under His feet" and "When all things are subjected to Him, then the Son Himself also will be subjected to the One who subjected all things to Him, so that God may be all in all" (vv.25, 28).

God is the one "to whom belong the glory and dominion forever and ever" (ᾧ ἐστιν ἡ δόξα καὶ τὸ κράτος εἰς τοὺς αἰῶνας τῶν αἰώνων). The precise referent of the relative pronoun (ᾧ, "to whom") is not entirely clear. It could be either "Jesus Christ,"[108] who is the closest possible referent, or it could be "God" (ὁ θεός),[109] who has already had glory ascribed to Him in the sentence. Scripture rightly ascribes glory to both, and ultimately as members of the one Godhead, there is no need to differentiate

---

106 Clowney, 187.

107 Wallace, 433–434.

108 E.g., Bigg (176), Grudem (183), Hart (73), Jobes (283), Marshall (144–145), Michaels (253), Stibbs (157), Robertson, *Word Pictures* (6:126), Schreiner (216).

109 E.g., Alford (4:377), Davids (162), Dubis (145), Forbes (150), Goppelt (306), Hiebert (277–278), Kelly (181), Storms (349).

the glory of one over against the other. The present tense verb (ἐστιν, "belong") sets out the eternal, abiding, unchanging reality of "the glory and dominion" (ἡ δόξα καὶ τὸ κράτος) that is due. The indicative mood sets this out as reality (cf. "belongs," NASU, "belong," ESV, NET, NRSV, NKJV), as opposed to an optative which would mark it as a prayer-wish ("be," NIV).[110]

The peculiar "glory" (note the definite article) is His, presently, eternally, abidingly. To fail to glorify God is not simply to fail to give Him something He deserves but to try to steal what He already rightly possesses.

Peter is also concerned with the "dominion" (τὸ κράτος) of God. The noun designates "the possession of force or strength that affords supremacy or control."[111] It "refers to strength regarded as abundantly effective in relation to an end to be gained or dominion to be exercised."[112] God possesses this uniquely (again, note the definite article) and eternally (1 Tim. 6:16; 1 Peter 5:11; Jude 25; Rev. 1:6; 5:13).

The formula εἰς τοὺς αἰῶνας τῶν αἰώνων ("forever and ever") designates the duration of eternity. "The added genitive τῶν αἰώνων simply emphasizes the unendingness or eternality already expressed by εἰς τοὺς αἰῶνας (or εἰς τὸν αἰῶνα). But the two juxtaposed plurals suggest that from one perspective, eternity may be considered an interminable accumulation of endless 'ages.'"[113] The phrase is found often in the NT, especially in doxological statements as we have here (Gal. 1:5; Phil. 4:20; 1 Tim. 1:17; 2 Tim. 4:18; Heb. 13:21; Rev. 1:6, 18; 4:9, 10; 5:13; 7:12; 10:6; 11:15; 15:7; 19:3; 20:10; 22:5).

Peter marks this doxological outburst with a solemn and sealing "Amen" (ἀμήν). The expression was carried over directly from Hebrew, which was long used to acknowledge "a word which is valid, and the validity of which is binding for me."[114] Peter concludes both of his letters this

---

110 Dubis, 145; Forbes, 150; Hart, 73; Michaels, 253; Storms, 349.

111 Friberg, 236.

112 Rienecker, 523–524.

113 Harris, 95; cf. TDNT, 1:199.

114 TDNT, 1:335–337.

way (1 Peter 5:11; 2 Peter 3:18), and Paul often ended his expressions of praise similarly (Rom. 1:25; 9:5; 11:36; 16:27; Gal. 1:5; Eph. 3:21; Phil. 4:20; 1 Tim. 1:17; 6:16). Used in this way it means something like "so it is," "so be it" or "may it be fulfilled."[115] All who read (or heard) these words would be moved to reciprocate with their own affirming "Amen."

Some have speculated that Peter's doxology at this point signals the original ending of the letter, with the remainder of the book as we know it added later. But doxologies often appear within the body of NT letters rather than at the end (Rom. 11:36; Gal. 1:5; Eph. 3:21; Rev. 1:6; 5:14; 7:12).

> **Digging Deeper:**
> 1. Has God given you an inclination more toward speaking or serving? How have others confirmed this?
> 2. Identify a time you sensed God speaking or actively working through you. What made the difference on that occasion?

Verse 12 – "Beloved, do not be surprised at the fiery ordeal among you, which comes upon you for your testing, as though some strange thing were happening to you;"

The doxology of verse 11 signaled not the end of the letter but the closing of a line of thought Peter had been developing. He now once again addresses his readers as "Beloved" (Ἀγαπητοί), signaling that he is launching a new line of thought. He previously used the term in 2:11, where he was transitioning from the expression of his readers' corporate identity in Christ (2:4–10) to imperatives for godly living based on that grace (2:11–5:12). Now, within that overall section, he transitions from his general exhortations about living in God's grace in the last days (4:1–11) to a

---

115 Thayer, 32.

return to the matter of unjust suffering as followers of Christ (4:12–5:12; cf. 3:9–22).

Peter immediately issues a prohibition; "do not be surprised" (μὴ ξενίζεσθε). The present imperative with the negation (μὴ, "do not") can be read as demanding action that is underway be discontinued, but this need not necessarily be the case. The passive voice depicts the surprise overtaking them as their present trial befalls them. The verb was used in verse 4 to describe unbelievers' surprise that believers no longer run with them in sin. Here it is used of the surprise of believers that their unbelieving neighbors inflict pain upon them for their new pattern of choices. Mutual surprise has overtaken their network of relationships, offense being taken, and painful reaction being the result. The verb meant literally "to show hospitality," to entertain someone as a guest.[116] So Peter is making a play on his call for the practice of hospitality in verse 9. There the word was a compound of φίλος ("love") and ξένος ("strange," "foreign"), the latter of which is the cognate adjective (which Peter will use at the end of this present verse) to our present verb. They are to welcome one another as believers into their homes and share their lives and goods. Likewise, when "the fiery ordeal" of suffering for their faith walks through the door of their lives and makes itself at home, they are not to be thrown off. Metaphorically, the verb meant "to surprise or astonish by the strangeness and novelty of a thing."[117] Peter calls upon his readers to not be taken aback by the new and unwanted guest of suffering that has invited itself into their lives.

> **Ministry Maxim**
>
> The only surprise in Christian suffering is when there is none.

Peter refers to their suffering as "the fiery ordeal among you" (τῇ ἐν ὑμῖν πυρώσει). The noun (τῇ ... πυρώσει, "the fiery ordeal") depicts the process of burning, and it is used elsewhere in the NT only of the burning in judgment of the city of Babylon (Rev. 18:9, 18; cf. 1 Peter 5:13).

---

116 BDAG, 5163.1.

117 Thayer, 432.

It is used in the LXX of Proverbs 27:21 to describe the use of fire to try and test the purity of precious metals.[118] Such imagery is common in the OT (e.g., Psa. 66:10; Zech. 13:9; Mal. 3:1–4). In this way, Peter sets forth their painful suffering as something controlled by and used by God for the testing, purifying, and certifying of their faith. The definite article indicates the specifics of their present trial—unknown to us but well-known to them and the Lord. The prepositional phrase (ἐν ὑμῖν, "among you") in the attributive position further magnifies the forcible entrance of this unwelcome guest into their midst.

Their "fiery ordeal" could be explained in earthly, circumstantial, relational terms. All of which were painful. But spiritually, it had a purpose. Peter describes it as that "which comes upon you for your testing" (πρὸς πειρασμὸν ὑμῖν γινομένη). The preposition πρὸς ("for") here carries the ideal of a goal (aiming at or striving toward something) and, thus, ultimately of "design" or "destiny" behind the thing with which it is connected.[119] That which thus carries a sense of "design" and "destiny" in their lives is the "testing" (πειρασμὸν) with which they are presently being faced. The noun can depict either a temptation to fall into sin or a trial by which the true character and nature of something are revealed. Peter always uses it in this latter sense (1 Peter 1:6; 2 Peter 2:9). Interestingly, in 1:6, the trials are described as "various," using the same adjective (ποικίλος) he just used to describe the "manifold" grace of God (v.10). Peter is returning to the themes that have dominated the letter. Yes, they are facing a painful, "fiery ordeal." But it is not a rude stranger that has forced its way into their lives and thus ought to shock them. It is a tool in the hand of their sovereign Lord, and they should face it with the confidence that He is only allowing it in His love and using it for their good. It brings out "the proof of your faith" (1:7).

This trial, says Peter, "comes upon you" (ὑμῖν γινομένη). The verb means "to be" or "to become." The present tense pictures the real-time

---

118 Elsewhere in Biblical literature it is used only in Amos 4:9 of God's discipline of His wayward people.

119 BDAG, 6247.3.c.β.

reality of their pain. The verb is deponent, so the middle voice should be read as active. The participle may be attributive and connected to τῇ ἐν ὑμῖν πυρώσει ("the fiery trial among you")[120] or causal and connected with μὴ ξενίζεσθε ("do not be surprised").[121]

Armed with this insight, suffering believers are not to be shocked "as though some strange thing were happening to you" (ὡς ξένου ὑμῖν συμβαίνοντος). Now we meet the adjective (ξένου, "some strange thing"), used here as a substantive and the subject of the participle, which forms part of the compound verbs found early in this verse (and in v.4) and in verse 9. It denotes something foreign, odd, and out of place because unknown, unfamiliar, or unnatural. It serves prominently in Jesus' description of the final judgment and is used to describe Himself (Matt. 25:35, 38, 43, 44). The comparative (ὡς, "as though") sets up the comparison that is to be avoided. The "fiery ordeal" is no stranger, not because it is a welcome and familiar friend, but because of who allowed it, sent it, rules it, and uses it to His own ends. The verb is a compound made up of σύν ("with") and βαίνω ("to stand"). It is used "of circumstances coming together to form an event."[122] It occurs eight times in the NT, often in dramatic circumstances (Mark 10:32; Luke 24:14; Acts 3:10; 20:19; 21:35; 1 Cor. 10:11; 2 Peter 2:22). Jesus used it to set before His disciples the coming events of His approaching arrest, trial, death and resurrection (Mark 10:32). It is used to describe the two disciples on the road to Emmaus reflecting on the events of Jesus' life and death (Luke 24:14). Paul used it to reflect upon the trials he had faced (Acts 20:19). Here Peter is inviting his readers to see the painful events that have come to them (ὑμῖν, "to you") as directed and controlled by the sovereign hand of the Lord who loves them. The present tense invites them to see God's hand active in the events that may have been transpiring even at that moment.

---

120 Dubis, 147.

121 Bigg, 176; Forbes, 154.

122 Friberg, 361.

Verse 13 – "but to the degree that you share the sufferings of Christ, keep on rejoicing, so that also at the revelation of His glory you may rejoice with exultation."

The sentence continues from verse 12. There Peter's readers were commanded, "do not be surprised" (μὴ ξενίζεσθε) now in strong contrast (ἀλλὰ, "but") he sets before them the positive action they are to undertake instead: "keep on rejoicing" (χαίρετε). The present imperative demands action be taken continually, repeatedly, as a pattern of life. The two occurrences of the verb in this verse constitute Peter's only use. However, notice how Peter and the other Apostles, after being arrested and released, "went on their way from the presence of the Council, rejoicing [χαίροντες] that they had been considered worthy to suffer shame for His name (Acts 5:41).

The rejoicing is to take place "to the degree that you share the sufferings of Christ" (καθὸ κοινωνεῖτε τοῖς τοῦ Χριστοῦ παθήμασιν). The conjunction functions adverbially (καθὸ, "to the degree that"). It is a compound made up of κατά ("according to") and the relative pronoun ὅς ("who," "which," "what").[123] It is only found three other times in the NT (Rom. 8:26; 2 Cor. 8:12 [2x]). It points to proportionality. It signals that "how much you share Christ's sufferings is how much you can rejoice."[124]

We have seen that Peter views "the sufferings of Christ" (τοῖς τοῦ Χριστοῦ παθήμασιν) as including His death. He was himself a "witness of the sufferings of Christ" (1 Peter 5:1). He saw Jesus suffer and die. Yet somehow, he can say to his readers, now decades after the fact, that they "share" (κοινωνεῖτε) in them in some way.

Nothing was insufficient or incomplete regarding Christ's atoning work on the cross. There is no redemptive merit in the things which Peter's readers suffered. Nor is there any such merit in anything endured or suffered by any other. Once for all, Christ alone bore the penalty of our sins, making perfect atonement that can never be supplemented, augmented, or improved upon.

---

123 Robertson, *Grammar*, 967.

124 Louw-Nida, 78.53.

The verb (κοινωνεῖτε, "you share") means to "share" something or "have a share" in something. The cognate noun was used in three ways in the NT: *participation* (association by shared experience; 1 Cor. 10:16; Phil. 1:5; 2:1; 3:10), *fellowship* (association by shared life; 1 Cor. 1:9; 2 Cor. 6:14; 13:14 [13]; Gal. 2:9), and *giving* (association by shared goods, i.e., a gift/contribution; Rom. 15:26; 2 Cor. 8:14; 9:13), though the line of demarcation between the first two is not always easily drawn.[125] Peter's use of the verb here tends toward the first two shades of meaning. But in what way do we have a share in Jesus' sufferings?

Jesus' sufferings are complete redemptively (no further atonement is possible or necessary). But they are not complete missionally—for He continues to use the sufferings of His Body to advance the gospel He established through His sufferings, death, resurrection, ascension, session, and glorification. Paul thus can say, "Now I rejoice in my sufferings for your sake, and in my flesh I do my share on behalf of His body, which is the church, in filling up what is lacking in Christ's afflictions" (Col. 1:24).[126]

Jesus was right to say, just before He died, "It is finished!" (John 19:30). The sole hope of any soul before God is the substitutionary death and resurrection of Jesus Christ on their behalf. What, then, does Peter mean by telling his readers they may "share the sufferings of Christ"? Jesus left nothing incomplete regarding the atonement for our sins, but in His earthly life and ministry, He did not complete everything regarding the advancement of that message. He commissioned His disciples to complete the great commission (Matt. 28:19–20). This, He was clear to say, would involve suffering (Acts 9:16; 14:22; Rom. 8:17; 1 Thess. 3:3; 2 Tim. 3:12; 1 Peter 5:10). There is no merit in such hardship, but it is nevertheless a part of the suffering necessary for the gospel to advance, the Kingdom to spread, and the church to grow (2 Cor. 1:5–8; 2 Tim. 2:9–10). In this, Paul was glad to "do [his] share" (Col. 1:24). We must each be ready to carry our load in this regard. So too, Peter here can

---

125 TDNT, 3:798–809.

126 Cf. the author's *Colossians and Philemon for Pastors*, 132–137.

speak of how "you share the sufferings of Christ." Indeed, Paul told others, "the sufferings of Christ are ours in abundance" (2 Cor. 1:5). Such "fellowship" is real, for, as Paul discovered even at his conversion, when His Body suffered, Christ suffered (Acts 9:4). And Paul longed to know Christ, including "the fellowship of His sufferings" (Phil 3:10). Indeed, Peter's choice of the present tense (κοινωνεῖτε, "share") underscores the immediacy and constancy of the shared experience and shared life between the Lord and His servant.

How shall we understand the genitive τοῦ Χριστοῦ ("of Christ")? It is often understood as subjective, the sufferings which Christ experienced. Perhaps Peter intends nothing more by his expression than he meant by calling his readers to follow Christ's example in suffering (1 Peter 2:12–24).[127] But we must consider Peter's entire statement. If the suffering is merely by example (v.13a), then is the promised rejoicing at His return also detached and exemplary? Don't the Scriptures offer us more when they say Christ "will transform the body of our humble state into conformity with the body of His glory" (Phil. 3:21)? Is there not more than a detached, observed, and reflective joy and glory involved?

Dubis argues that the genitive may be understood attributively and thus reflect the concept of the "messianic woes"[128] developed in the intertestamental period and by Rabbis from seed-thoughts scattered throughout the OT. The notion understood all time to be divided into two great eras—the present evil age and the age to come. The transition from one age to the next was understood to include great suffering by the people of God (Rom. 8:18–25). These sufferings were necessary if the age to come was to ever dawn in the fullness of its promise. Some conceived of a pre-determined amount of necessary suffering, though not all embraced this view.

> **Ministry Maxim**
>
> In divine hands there is an eventual proportionality to suffering and joy.

---

127 Forbes, 155; Michaels, 262.

128 Dubis, 148.

Paul may have had these "messianic woes" in mind when he penned Colossians 1:24, and Peter may here as well. This was the milieu into which both men were born and in which they were raised. Surely their newfound faith in Christ brought a maturing and refining in their understanding of these "woes," but it seems unlikely that this understanding was abandoned entirely. It was thus in this sense that Paul (cf. Rom. 5:3) and we, as commanded here, might rejoice in our sufferings, for suffering means progress toward the return of Christ and the dawn of the new age. Neither Paul's nor Peter's nor our sufferings are atoning, for that work had been finished entirely by Christ. Nevertheless, the sufferings of Christ's obedient people perform a definite service, to borrow Paul's words, "on behalf of [Christ's] body." They play a vital part in moving events along to the fulfillment of the Messiah's sufferings and the dawning of the age to come. All believers are encouraged to think in these terms (Rom. 8:18–25).

Peter sets forth the reason (ἵνα, "so that") for their obedient rejoicing even in painful trials: "at the revelation of His glory you may rejoice with exultation" (ἐν τῇ ἀποκαλύψει τῆς δόξης αὐτοῦ χαρῆτε ἀγαλλιώμενοι). The conjunction καί is used adverbially ("also"), indicating that our share in Jesus' sufferings does not stand alone as the sole or final word on our lives but that we anticipate "also" great joy. The verb (χαρῆτε, "you may rejoice") is in the subjunctive mood and joined to ἵνα in marking a purpose clause. The verb is deponent, so the passive voice should be read as an active voice. The aorist tense sets forth the rejoicing as an actual event occurring at a point in time, "with finality, with utter completeness" at Christ's return.[129]

The participle ἀγαλλιώμενοι ("with exultation") modifies χαρῆτε ("you may rejoice"). The two verbs are largely synonymous, but ἀγαλλιάω may add "the idea of exulting, jubilating, skipping and bubbling over with shouts of delight."[130] It was used as Peter began his letter with a call to rejoicing (cf. 1:6, 8). The participle may signal the manner of the

---

129 Lenski, 204.

130 Ibid.

rejoicing and intensifies the main verb ("overjoyed," NIV; "the wonderful joy," NLT).[131] In using both verbs here, Peter may be recalling Jesus' instruction to "Rejoice [χαίρετε] and be glad [ἀγαλλιᾶσθε]" (Matt. 5:12) in the face of persecution. But there we learn that "persecution places us in the company of the persecuted prophets... here it places us in the company of Christ himself."[132] Significantly, both verbs appear together again in Revelation 19:7: "Let us rejoice [χαίρωμεν] and be glad [ἀγαλλιῶμεν] and give the glory to Him, for the marriage of the Lamb has come and His bride has made herself ready."

This rejoicing will take place "at the revelation of His glory" (ἐν τῇ ἀποκαλύψει τῆς δόξης αὐτοῦ). The preposition ἐν ("at") is used temporally to signal the time of "the revelation" (τῇ ἀποκαλύψει), which earlier he referred to as "the revelation of Jesus Christ" (ἀποκαλύψει Ἰησοῦ Χριστοῦ, 1:7, 13). The revelation will consist "of His glory" (τῆς δόξης αὐτοῦ). Peter has consistently held "glory" before his readers as both belonging to God/Christ alone (1:11, 21; 4:11) and as their ultimate hope in Christ (1:7). And he will continue to do so (4:14; 5:1, 4, 10). Here it is Christ's own glory, now fully unveiled, that is in view. But in 1:7, the revelation of Jesus will result in His people receiving, among other things, "glory." When Jesus comes in His glory, He will make His children share that "glory" with Him (Phil. 3:21; Col. 3:4). At that time, those who have died with their faith in Jesus will find that what has been "sown in dishonor" will be "raised in glory" (1 Cor. 15:43). Even now, our present suffering "is producing for us an eternal weight of glory far beyond all comparison" (2 Cor. 4:17).

Peter, then, warns his readers away from surprise over unjust suffering for their faith (v.12) and calls upon them to rejoice now in such suffering so that they might rejoice even more rapturously with and in Christ at His unveiling (v.13). Rejoice now in pain with anticipation of rejoicing then in bliss.

---

131 Forbes, 155; Dubis, 148–149.

132 Lenski, 203.

> **Digging Deeper:**
> 1. Does understanding God's purpose in permitting suffering in His peoples' lives take any of the sting out of it (v.12)? Why or why not?
> 2. How does present joy in pain prepare us for greater joy in bliss (v.13)?

Verse 14 – "If you are reviled for the name of Christ, you are blessed, because the Spirit of glory and of God rests on you."

In addition to calling for "rejoicing" and "exultation" (v.13), Peter declares to his readers: "you are blessed" (μακάριοι). There is no verb, "you are" being added by the translators. The adjective (μακάριοι) stands bare and alone and is more powerful for its starkness. Peter used the same solitary form to say: "But even if you should suffer for the sake of righteousness, you are blessed" (1 Peter 3:14). Here again, Peter reflects Jesus' teachings about what makes for blessedness (Matt. 5:3–12), particularly with regards to persecution: "Blessed are [μακάριοι] those who have been persecuted for the sake of righteousness, for theirs is the kingdom of heaven. Blessed are [μακάριοι] you when people insult you and persecute you, and falsely say all kinds of evil against you because of Me. Rejoice and be glad, for your reward in heaven is great; for in the same way they persecuted the prophets who were before you" (Matt. 5:10–12; cf. Luke 6:22–23). The adjective describes being under divine approval and favor. Blessedness is found when God turns His countenance toward you and gives you His full attention, His favor, His affirmation, and His grace. You are "blessed" when God smiles upon you.

> **Ministry Maxim**
> God never allows a grief that is not accompanied by a greater glory.

Yet, as in 3:14, their state of blessedness is conditional. It is true only "If you are reviled for the name of Christ" (εἰ ὀνειδίζεσθε ἐν ὀνόματι Χριστοῦ). The condition in 3:14 was cast in a rare form indicating only the possibility of the need to "suffer for the sake of righteousness." Here, however, the reality is assumed to be true. The present tense of the verb pictures the current reality for his readers. Peter believes his readers are currently being "reviled for the name of Christ." The verb has a range of meanings from "simple reproach to cursing and blasphemy, with invective, mockery, affront, insult, and abuse included in between."[133] On the cross, Jesus was the object of the reviling of the Jews and even the criminals who hung next to Him (Matt. 27:44; Mark 15:32; Rom. 15:3). Jesus promised this would be the lot of His followers but assured them that this would not interrupt their blessedness, but rather magnify it (Matt. 5:11; Luke 6:22). It is helpful to place Peter's present word alongside the other vocabulary he uses throughout the letter to describe the opposition his readers faced: λοιδορέω ("to revile"; 2:23) and λοιδορία ("reviling," 3:9 [2x]), ἐπηρεάζω ("to mistreat," 3:16), καταλαλέω ("to speak against," 2:12; 3:16) and καταλαλιά ("slander," 2:1).[134] In this we can see that the nature of the opposition they were presently facing was primarily verbal, along with the social ostracizing that comes with such treatment. There is little to prove that his readers were facing the active threat of martyrdom, though those days may have been yet before them. It was now, rather, that the present verbal assault came precisely "for the name of Christ" (ἐν ὀνόματι Χριστοῦ). To come or to act in the name of another is to stand in their place, bear their authority, and enact their will (e.g., Acts 16:18; 2 Thess. 3:6). Jesus is He who comes in the name of the Lord (Matt. 21:9, 39; Mark 11:9; Luke 13:35; 19:38; John 12:13) and was, for this reason, pronounced "blessed" by the crowds at His Triumphal Entry (Matt. 21:9, 39). But soon, the cheers turned to jeers as Jesus was condemned and crucified. Those who believe in Him petition the Father in Jesus' Name (e.g., John 14:13–14; 15:16), have been sent out in His Name (John 20:21), have authority to speak and act in His Name so as to fulfill His Commission (e.g., Acts 3:6; 16:18), but also must suffer reproaches from those who despise His Name. Here

---

133 Spicq, 2:586.

134 Forbes, 156.

ἐν ὀνόματι Χριστοῦ ("for the name of Christ") is equivalent to Jesus' "because of Me" (ἕνεκεν ἐμοῦ, Matt. 5:11).

Peter provides the reason there should be no fretting in such circumstances. It is "because" (ὅτι) at such times another reality of greater force also comes upon them: "the Spirit of glory and of God rests on you' (τὸ τῆς δόξης καὶ τὸ τοῦ θεοῦ πνεῦμα ἐφ' ὑμᾶς ἀναπαύεται). Peter's repetition of the definite article τὸ has occasioned much discussion. Also debated is whether the first occasion of τὸ serves as the definite article for πνεῦμα ("Spirit") or as a shorthand link back to τῆς δόξης ("glory") in verse 13.[135] But it is unnecessary to read the definite article that way, for the connection is made sufficiently by the repetition of the noun τῆς δόξης here in verse 14. We read both occasions of τὸ as connected to the final noun of the clause πνεῦμα, the article being "repeated in order to make each of the genitives stand out separately."[136] This moves us then to read the two definite genitive nouns (held in parallel relationship by καί, "and") as attributive, showing us just what Peter means by "the Spirit."

First, the Spirit under consideration is "of glory" (τῆς δόξης).[137] Second, it is the Spirit "of God" (τοῦ θεοῦ).[138] The entire clause may read literally as "the of the glory and of the God Spirit." The first does indeed continue the idea of God's glory from verse 13, now telling us "the glory" that Christ will make us to share with Him at His Return (v.13) is already upon us through the present ministry of the Holy Spirit. The joy that will be universal at the full revelation of Jesus' glory (v.13) is a present and personal reality by the Spirit's ministry to each believer (v.14), especially so in the midst of suffering for the sake of Jesus' Name. Paul tells us that the Holy Spirit "is the down payment of our inheritance, until the redemption of

---

[135] Schreiner argues for the latter (221), following Achtemeier (309).

[136] Lenski, 206.

[137] Some manuscripts add "of power" (καὶ δυνάμεως or καὶ τῆς δυνάμεως) after "of glory" and before "of God." But the addition appears to be an effort to ease what some scribes may have felt is an abrupt and awkward combination (cf. Michaels, 256; NET Bible; Schreiner, 221).

[138] Robertson says the second τὸ serves to make both definite articles emphasize their respective noun and that πνεῦμα ("Spirit") is to be understood with τῆς δόξης ("of glory") (*Grammar*, 767, 785).

God's own possession, to the praise of his glory" (Eph. 1:14, NET; cf. 2 Cor. 1:22; 5:5).

The Spirit is then also denoted as none other than the "of God" (τοῦ θεοῦ) Spirit. That is to say, the third Person of the Trinity, God the Spirit (1 Peter 1:2, 11–12). The third Person of the Trinity is generally understood as the active agent of the Godhead, the one moving, working, activating, and making actual the will of God the Father through God the Son. The glory of God is made known wherever the Spirit of God is present and active. Peter points, then, to one Spirit, that fully divine third member of the Godhead, the revealer of God in His glory. Note the Trinitarian emphasis in this verse as Peter specifies all three members of the Godhead (as he did also in 1:2).

Peter's great point is that this very Spirit, the Spirit of God that will radiate the unveiled glory of God to all of creation at the Return of God the Son (v.13), already now "rests on you" (ἐφ᾽ ὑμᾶς ἀναπαύεται). The verb is a compound made up of ἄνα ("on") and παύω ("to make to rest"). The verb used transitively means simply "to cause to cease" and thus to rest from activity (e.g., Matt. 26:45; Mark 6:31).[139] It can also mean "to refresh" (e.g., 1 Cor. 16:18; 2 Cor. 7:13; Philem. 7, 20). In the middle voice, as we have it here, it can mean "to remain at rest" or "rest upon."[140] And thus, here with the preposition (ἐφ᾽, "on") means to settle or rest upon something.

The preposition ἐπί ("upon") with the accusative (as it is here) is used throughout the NT to designate some blessing that comes or rests upon God's people: the word of God (Luke 3:2), the kingdom of God (Matt. 12:28; Luke 10:9), the grace of God (Luke 2:40), the Holy Spirit (Luke 2:25; Acts 1:8; 2:17–18; 10:45; Titus 3:6), and the power of Christ (2 Cor. 12:9).[141] This, Peter says, has become the reality of "you" (ὑμᾶς). The plural encompasses all Peter's believing readers, then and now.

---

139 TDNT, 1:351.

140 Ibid.

141 Harris, 138.

The verb was, at times, further compounded by adding the additional prefix ἐπί ("upon").[142] It was used in the LXX when the Shekinah descended upon the Tabernacle to meet with Moses and to cause the Spirit to rest upon seventy of the elders (Numb. 11:25–26). The sons of the prophets who had previously been disciples of Elijah saw Elisha take up their master's mantel, strike the waters of the Jordan and cross over on dry land. They exclaimed, "The spirit of Elijah rests on Elisha" (2 Kings 2:15). In the NT, it is used of the disciples' blessing resting upon a home and its inhabitants when they are received well (Luke 10:6).

Stephen serves as an apt illustration of what Peter sets forth here. He was a man known to be full of the Holy Spirit (Acts 6:5, 10), who faced intense persecution (6:9–15; 7:57–56), even unto death (vv.59–60). It is said of him in the extremity of his persecution, "being full of the Holy Spirit, he gazed intently into heaven and saw the glory of God, and Jesus standing at the right hand of God" (v.55).

But here Peter appears to reflect Isaiah 11:2, where the simple compound is found: "The Spirit of the LORD will rest [ἀναπαύσεται] on Him, The spirit of wisdom and understanding, The spirit of counsel and strength, The spirit of knowledge and the fear of the LORD." This, Isaiah says, would prove true of "the stump of Jesse," the "branch from his roots" (11:1, 10). From the perspective of the Apostles, this was fulfilled in Jesus (Matt. 1:1; Acts 13:23; Rom. 15:12). Peter believed it was the Spirit of Christ who spoke to and through the prophets (1 Peter 1:10–12). Peter transitions from the future tense of the LXX (ἀναπαύσεται, "will rest") to the present tense (ἀναπαύεται, "rests") to indicate that the passage has been fulfilled in Jesus and that now what is true of Him is true also for all who are in Him through faith. The same Spirit that rested upon Jesus now rests upon His people, even and especially in their suffering.

Some early manuscripts add κατὰ μὲν αὐτοὺς βλασφημεῖται, κατὰ δὲ ὑμᾶς δοξάζεται ("on their part the is evil spoken of, but on your part he is glorified") to end the sentence. Among major English translations, the

---

142 Some manuscripts use the double compound form here in 1 Peter 4:14, though the simple compound appears to be the original text.

KJV, NKJV, and YLT include the extra lines. Among modern commentators, Michaels stands nearly alone in defending the longer addition.[143]

In all the debate about textual issues and how grammar is to be understood, let us not miss this remarkable fact—in this life, at one and the same moment, both glory and suffering may abide upon the believer. It is in this present tension that we are called upon to hold our faith in Jesus and to hold out faith in Jesus to the watching world. Suffering and pain will fall away at Christ's Return. The present foretaste of glory will only grow larger, infinite in fact. Let us rejoice in the glory, for it shall triumph in the end.

> **Digging Deeper:**
> 1. How have you experienced both the presence of pain and intimacy with Christ at one and the same time?
> 2. How would you counsel a hurting believer, so they find deeper intimacy with God amid their pain?

Verse 15 – "Make sure that none of you suffers as a murderer, or thief, or evildoer, or a troublesome meddler;"

With all his talk about the blessedness of suffering for Christ (vv.12–14), Peter now pauses to clarify that particular kind of suffering that he has in mind. He distinguishes suffering that is not joined by God's blessing (v.15) and that suffering which is (v.16). In this, he is largely restating his instruction from 2:19–20 and 3:13–17.

The NASU does not translate γάρ (but cf., "for," YLT; "But," ESV, KJV, NET, NKJV, NRSV, RSV). The NIV and NLT take what follows as a conditional clause ("If... should not," NIV; "if... however... must not"). The γάρ most likely introduces verses 15 and 16 as an expansion upon and explanation of Peter's insistence in verse 14 that their suffering must be "for the name of Christ."

---

143 Abernathy, 160; Michaels, 265–266; contra. Schreiner, 222.

Peter commands, "Make sure that none of you suffers" (μὴ ... τις ὑμῶν πασχέτω). This is the first element of a μὴ ... δὲ contrast the spans verses 15 and 16. The negation (μὴ) with the combination of the singular indefinite pronoun (τις) and plural personal pronoun (ὑμῶν) serves to cast the command as wide as possible and yet to demand that not even one single individual from that total number be found in the condition outlined. It is a total prohibition. There is to be none among the followers of Christ who "suffers" (πασχέτω) for the wrong reasons. The verb is found twelves time in 1 Peter and forms one of the main themes of the letter (see our comments on 2:19). The present imperative with the negation (μὴ) forms an absolute prohibition, forbidding even a single exception.

> **Ministry Maxim**
>
> Nosiness may nix God's blessing.

Peter provides four possibilities of that which is to be shunned. They are divided into two groups by the repeated use of ὡς ("as"). All four lack the definite article, emphasizing the qualitative nature of each.

The first grouping includes three items, coordinated by the repeated use of ἢ ("or") between the listed items. First is "a murderer" (φονεὺς). The word describes exactly what we would expect, one who commits homicide, who takes the life of another. Such a one is a violator of the sixth commandment. At an earlier time, Peter used the word to describe Barabbas, whom the Jews asked Pilate to release instead of Jesus (Acts 3:14). Stephen used the word to describe what the Jews had done to Jesus (7:52).

The second is "thief" (κλέπτης). It describes precisely what the English word suggests. Our English word *kleptomaniac* (i.e., one who does not restrain himself from repeated theft) is a derivative. Peter used the noun again in 2 Peter 3:10, but only by analogy for the Lord's coming ("the day of the Lord will come like a thief"). This person is a violator of the eighth commandment.

Third is "evildoer" (κακοποιός). The adjective is used as a substantive. It is a compound made up of κακός ("evil") and ποιέω ("to make"). Peter used the word in 1 Peter 2:12 and 14 for the only other two occurrences of the word in the NT (see our comments on 2:12). The cognate verb is found in 1 Peter 3:17. It is the opposite of Peter's repeated emphasis on believers going about doing good (1 Peter 2:15, 20; 3:6, 11, 17; 4:19).

A second occurrence of ὡς ("as") before the fourth item seems to indicate that Peter will now advance his case on a slightly different basis. The first two items in the list are violations not only of God's moral law but of the laws of the land. The third serves as a catchall to gather up all other such violations.

The fourth item is "a troublesome meddler" (ἀλλοτριεπίσκοπος). The word is a compound constructed of ἀλλότριος ("another's") and ἐπίσκοπος ("overseer").[144] The word is found only here in the NT and LXX and nowhere else in Greek literature prior to this letter. However, ἀλλότριος is used in other compound words and always "denotes an activity which is foreign to the doer, or which is not his concern."[145] Thayer thinks this compound refers "to those who, with holy but intemperate zeal, meddle with the affairs of the Gentiles — whether public or private, civil or sacred — in order to make them conform to the Christian standard)."[146] But most understand it to refer to someone who makes other people's business their own. It designates a "busybody," someone who annoyingly and without invitation sticks his/her nose into other people's affairs. If this indeed is the case, "Peter must have had in mind a pernicious kind of meddling, for the person in view is classed with murderers and thieves."[147] Paul warned of younger widows who "learn to be idle, as they go around from house to house; and not merely idle, but also gossips and busybodies, talking about things not proper to mention" (1 Tim. 5:13). He similarly warned the entire church in Thessalonica, telling them to "attend to your own business" (1 Thess. 4:11) and warns "that some among you are leading an undisciplined life, doing no work at all, but acting like busybodies" (2 Thess. 3:11). Consider Jesus' example when "Someone in the crowd said to Him, 'Teacher, tell my brother to divide the family inheritance

---

144 Cf. the use of the uncompounded noun applied to Christ in 1 Peter 2:25 and the kindred verb ἐπισκοπέω ("to give attention to") in 5:2.

145 TDNT, 2:622.

146 Thayer, 29; cf. Vincent, 1:664.

147 NIDNTTE, 1:256.

with me,'" He responded, "Man, who appointed Me a judge or arbitrator over you?" (Luke 12:13–14).

Did Peter really think that some among the believers in Asia Minor were tempted to murder or theft? Perhaps, but it seems more likely that, while he was serious about those sins, he was setting up a progression that moved from those things which are most clearly sinful to that which may be, in many eyes, less clearly sinful.[148] How then are we to understand the specific intent of these four as robbers of a sufferer's blessing? Perhaps Peter is doing nothing more than sweeping the gamut of all possible sins, from the most obviously egregious to those more easily excused. Bigg suggests regarding the final item, "Peter is not adding another offence, but summing up all possible offences in a comprehensive et cetera. 'Neither as a murderer, nor thief, nor evildoer, nor, in a word, as a bad Christian.'"[149] Forbes suggests, "The use of ὡς highlights this final term, not so much as something less criminal (as Michaels 268), but as an activity more subtle and probable."[150]

Verse 16 – "but if *anyone suffers* as a Christian, he is not to be ashamed, but is to glorify God in this name."

Now Peter sets out the second half of the μὴ ... δὲ contrast he began in verse 15. He has warned his readers away from suffering for any kind of wrongdoing (v.15) and now sets forth that suffering which brings with it God's blessing (cf., v.14).

The contrast to suffering for any of the sins suggested in verse 15 is "if *anyone suffers* as a Christian" (εἰ ... ὡς Χριστιανός). The verb is missing but is to be supplied by the reader in coordination with verse 15. Because there

> **Ministry Maxim**
>
> It is impossible to glorify Christ apart from bearing His Name.

---

148 Hiebert, 289; Jobes, 288.

149 Bigg. 179.

150 Forbes, 159.

is no verb, one has to take an educated guess at the nature of the condition (εἰ, "if"), though it seems plain that, like the conditional statement in verse 14, it is a first-class condition which is assumed for the sake of the argument to be true. Just what Peter means by "as a Christian" (ὡς Χριστιανός) is settled by the expression "for the name of Christ" (ἐν ὀνόματι Χριστου) in verse 14. It also anticipates "in this name" (ἐν τῷ ὀνόματι τούτῳ) at the end of this verse. The name or title "Christian" (Χριστιανός) is used only three times in the NT. It was first applied to the followers of Jesus in Antioch (Acts 11:26) and later was upon the lips of the pagan ruler Agrippa (26:28). It was not a self-chosen designation, but one applied derisively to believers by the unbelieving around them. The actual word is a Latinized form that tags someone as a partisan or follower of the one designated by the name. In this fashion, we have "Herodians" (Ἡρῳδιανῶν; Matt. 22:16; Mark 3:6; 12:13), followers or partisans of Herod. The word "Christian," thus, originally meant "follower of Christ" or "partisan of Christ." Originally, it was not a complimentary term, but Christ's followers embraced it from the second century.[151]

If the designation "Christian" fits, he who suffers "is not to be ashamed" (μὴ αἰσχυνέσθω). Peter now initiates another μὴ ... δὲ contrast ("not ... but"). The verb is used five times in the NT (Luke 16:3; 2 Cor. 10:8; Phil. 1:20; 1 Peter 4:16; 1 John 2:28), where it appears only in only the middle/passive voice. Here the middle voice seems to point to an inward sense of embarrassment or shame. The present imperative with negation amounts to an absolute prohibition against at any time being "ashamed" of bearing the name "Christian." Jesus said, "For whoever is ashamed of Me and My words in this adulterous and sinful generation, the Son of Man will also be ashamed of him when He comes in the glory of His Father with the holy angels" (Mark 8:38). Paul's testimony was, "I am not ashamed; for I know whom I have believed and I am convinced that He is able to guard what I have entrusted to Him until that day." (2 Tim. 1:12).

---

151 Thayer, 672.

In contrast (δὲ, "but"), he "is to glorify God" (δοξαζέτω ... τὸν θεόν). This has been one of Peter's clarion calls throughout 1 Peter (1:8; 2:12; 4:11). The present imperative demands the action be undertaken regularly, consistently, habitually, and as a pattern of life. The two imperatives are juxtaposed one over against the other in the order of the Greek sentence so that the contrast between being ashamed and glorifying God is heightened even further.

We are to bring glory to God "in this name" (ἐν τῷ ὀνόματι τούτῳ), which means not "Christ" (v.14) per se, but more specifically "Christian" (Χριστιανός) as at the beginning of the present verse.[152] But, given the meaning of the latter, it amounts to the same thing. The preposition (ἐν, "in") indicates the sphere within which one brings glory to God. Enveloped in all it means to belong to and follow Christ and to be known as such, bringing glory to Him.

> **Digging Deeper:**
> 1. What does Peter's grouping of sins in verse 15 tell us about the seriousness of nosiness?
> 2. Do you believe the term "Christian" continues to serve as a good identifier of Christ's people (v.16)? Why or why not?
> 3. Do you prefer another designation as a follower of Christ? Why?

---

152 Some later manuscripts have μέρει ("matter") instead of ὀνόματι ("name"), but the latter is found in the earliest manuscripts we possess. It is argued that it would be highly unlikely for a scribe to change from ὀνόματι to μέρει, but the other way around is sustainable given the use of ὀνόματι in verse 14. Yet the manuscript evidence weighs in favor of retaining ὀνόματι ("name"). (Dubis, 153; Forbes, 159; contra. Michaels, 256–257, 269–270).

Verse 17 – "For *it is* time for judgment to begin with the household of God; and if *it begins* with us first, what *will be* the outcome for those who do not obey the gospel of God?"

Peter begins a sentence that will run through verse 19. Verse 17 faces the challenge of an ellipsis, wherein a couple of verbs are expected to be supplied by the reader. Yet the basic sense is clear. What Peter sets out here serves as the reason (ὅτι, "For") specifically for his call to glorify God as those who bear the name "Christian" (v. 16) and perhaps more broadly for all he has said about suffering for Christ in verses 12–16.

That reason has to do with the pivotal time in which they live: "it is time for judgment to begin" ([ὁ] καιρὸς τοῦ ἄρξασθαι τὸ κρίμα). The genitive neuter definite article (τοῦ) stands alone and is attracted to the infinitive.[153] The infinitive (ἄρξασθαι, "to begin") can mean "to rule" or "to govern," but here has the sense of initiating something. The aorist tense points to a definite starting point. The middle voice pictures the initiative coming about by the unfolding events of God's redemptive plan. Thus, the reader will assume rightly that it is God, by nature of His sovereign rule and providential work in salvation history, that has launched the initiative. That which God has initiated is "time" ([ὁ] καιρὸς).[154] The word for "time" (καιρός) designates an opportune or seasonal time, a "time" that is advantageous for the fulfillment of some purpose.[155] Peter used the noun four times, always in the singular (1 Peter 1:5, 11; 4:17; 5:6). Peter sees his present day as one highly significant "time" in the unfolding of God's final program for the ages (τοὺς αἰῶνας τῶν αἰώνων, 1 Peter 4:11; cf. 1:25; 5:11). It is the "time" in God's unfolding plan for "judgment" (τὸ

> **Ministry Maxim**
>
> Judgment has already been put in motion—how will you survive?

---

153 Cf. Robertson, *Grammar*, 512, 1061, 1076.

154 There is debate as to whether the definite article (ὁ) is original or not. The evidence is evenly divided. The meaning is not greatly affected either way (Dubis, 154; Michaels, 257).

155 Thayer, 318.

κρίμα, lit., "the judgment") to take place. The word did not necessarily indicate a penal verdict or punishment but could simply depict the action of a judge.[156] That seems to be the case here. In fact, he will speak of such judgment in two senses, here as painful but purifying discipline for the believing (v.17a) and as retribution for the unbelieving (vv.17b-18).

That it here points to the former is made clear in that the inauguration, launching, or starting point for God's judgment is "with the household of God" (ἀπὸ τοῦ οἴκου τοῦ θεοῦ). The preposition (ἀπὸ, "with") might have been better rendered "from" (YLT; "at," ESV, KJV, NKJV), signaling the starting point "at" or "from" which God's judgment will move out in wider and wider circles until it takes in all people.[157]

What does Peter mean by "the household of God"? Does he speak relationally (i.e., the family of God) or conceptually (i.e., the temple of God)? Given the context of Peter and the theme of verses 12–16, it seems more likely to be the latter. In 1 Peter 2:4–5, we were introduced to the radical notion that we, the people of God, through the New Covenant in Jesus, are now the temple of God's dwelling. This is an image held forth throughout the NT (1 Cor. 3:16; 2 Cor. 6:16; Eph. 2:21–22; Heb. 3:6; 10:21–22). So, yes, Peter includes the relational element (for he does address redeemed people) but also is thinking primarily conceptually (a dwelling place of God). So, instead of "the household of God," a translation of "the house of God" (KJV, NET, NKJV, YLT) is more appropriate. And to this end, Peter has indicated that the time of purification through suffering has come upon God's people (1 Peter 1:6–7) in order that they might become a vessel fit for His dwelling. Under other imagery, the Apostle Paul speaks of God at work now to purify the Bride of Christ for His Son so that at His Return, "He might present to Himself the church in all her glory, having no spot or wrinkle or any such thing; but that she would be holy and blameless" (Eph. 5:27).

---

156 BDAG, 4406.3.

157 "In general, when expressing spatial relations, ἀπὸ denotes motion from the edge or surface of an object" (Harris, 57).

In Peter's reasoning from narrower to wider, from God's people to those who refuse to be God's people, there is, perhaps, an allusion to the prophecy of Ezekiel 9:6: "'Utterly slay old men, young men, maidens, little children, and women, but do not touch any man on whom is the mark; and you shall start from My sanctuary.' So they started with the elders who were before the temple." General judgment is coming, so let it "start from My sanctuary" and with "the elders."[158]

Jeremiah was called to announce God's wrath upon "all the nations" (Jer. 25:15, 17), even naming them one by one, starting with Jerusalem (vv.18–26). And when the nations refused to drink the cup of God's wrath (vv.27–28a), he is to tell them, "You must drink!" (v.28b, ESV). The reason being: "For behold, I am beginning to work calamity in this city which is called by My name [i.e., Jerusalem], and shall you be completely free from punishment?" (v.29a; 32:29 LXX).

In Malachi's day, the people demanded God bring about justice by judging their oppressors (Mal. 2:17). God said that, as promised, He would send "the messenger of the covenant" to deal out justice. "But," asks the prophet, "who can endure the day of His coming? And who can stand when He appears? For He is like a refiner's fire and like fullers' soap" (3:2). Indeed, says Malachi, "He will sit as a smelter and purifier of silver, and He will purify the sons of Levi and refine them like gold and silver, so that they may present to the LORD offerings in righteousness" (v.3). God will begin with His own people, purifying and refining them in holiness. "Then I will draw near to you for judgment," and sentence will be passed upon all who are not truly His people (v.5).

In Amos's day, the Israelites complained that the day of the Lord had not come (Amos 5:18), but the prophet warned them that day would mean not mere retribution for their enemies but painful purifying for them (vv.18–24).

In the NT, the Apostle Paul told the Roman believers, "The wrath of God *is being revealed* from heaven against all the godlessness and

---

158 Note that Peter will immediately "exhort the elders among you" in 1 Peter 5:1–4 (cf. Grudem, 189–190).

wickedness of people, who suppress the truth by their wickedness" (Rom. 1:18, NIV, emphasis added). The time for judgment has come. But he argues for two and a half chapters that this serves not only to pronounce condemnation for the ungodly sinner but draws a circle around all the people of the earth "so that every mouth may be closed and all the world may become accountable to God" (Rom. 3:19). He told the Corinthian believers that "when we are judged, we are disciplined by the Lord so that we will not be condemned along with the world" (1 Cor. 11:32).

Peter now extends his rationale (δὲ, "and") through a conditional statement. The conditional particle (εἰ, "if") is joined to an assumed present indicative verb ("begins," ESV, NASU, NIV, NKJV, NLT, NRSV; "starts," NET; "first," YLT) and thus yields a first-class condition which is assumed to be true for the sake of the point Peter is making. The protasis assumes God's judgment is in motion and "begins with us first" (πρῶτον ἀφ' ἡμῶν). The adverb πρῶτον ("first") designates that which is "first in a series involving time, space, or set."[159] In this case, it is "first" in the order of two kinds of judgment—one inaugural move to purify God's people (v.17a) and a second which envelops the entire unbelieving world in judgment (v.17b-18). The preposition (ἀφ', "with") is used as it was just above, in the sense of outward movement "from" (YLT), the starting point of God's people. It is telling that Peter switches from his use of the second person plural ("you"), now using "us" (ἡμῶν) rather than "you" (ὑμῶν).[160] Peter has not used a first-person plural pronoun since 2:24. But here he steps into the circle of judgment with his readers and all who name the name of Christ. No one—not even an apostle—is free from the purifying work of God among His people.

Peter expects no debate about the arrival and inauguration of God's judgment with the people of God in a process of purification and sanctification. It is an accepted fact. On the established ground that God has

---

159 Louw-Nida, 60.46.

160 Some manuscripts do have ὑμῶν ("you") rather than ἡμῶν ("us"), but the weight of evidence rests clearly with ἡμῶν and the alternate appears to be an effort to conform the text to the use of the second person plural throughout the preceding context. (Michaels, 256–257).

already inaugurated a movement of judgment that has begun with His people in discipline and refinement, then, he wonders aloud, "what will be the outcome for those who do not obey the gospel of God?" (τί τὸ τέλος τῶν ἀπειθούντων τῷ τοῦ θεοῦ εὐαγγελίῳ). The apodosis is stated as a rhetorical question (τί, "what") to emphasize the horror of the possibility set forth. There is again an ellipsis, and a verb must be mentally supplied ("will be"). Peter queries about "the outcome" (τὸ τέλος) of these events for the unbelieving. Whereas καιρός (see above) pointed to an eschatologically ripe "time," τὸ τέλος points to the goal toward which an act has moved from the beginning. It thus designates the appointed end, "the outcome" of the καιρός moment. The καιρός inaugurates a new movement of action, τέλος is the designed end toward which it has traveled from the beginning. We have, then, the critical, eschatologically ripe moment ([ὁ] καιρὸς, "time"), the initiation of its work (ἄρξασθαι, "to begin"), and the appointed finale of its destination and arrival (τὸ τέλος, "the outcome"). Jesus' death and resurrection brought forth the first, the sending of the Spirit and formation of the body of Christ brought about the second, and the third will be realized upon Jesus' Return.

And what, Peter wonders, will this mean "for those who do not obey" (τῶν ἀπειθούντων)? The participle is used as a substantive ("*those who* do not obey," emphasis added). This is now the fourth time Peter has used this verb (1 Peter 2:8; 3:1, 20; 4:17). The verb is a strong one, indicating perhaps not simple unbelief but active rejection of and opposition to the gospel. The present tense depicts a sustained pattern of disobedience to the gospel's call. The genitive form means "*of* those who disobey" (cf. KJV, NET, NKJV, RSV) and is here set forth by "for."

Ultimately, that which is disobeyed is "the word" (τῷ λόγῳ, 1 Peter 2:8; 3:1) which is shorthand for the fuller designation Peter uses here: "the gospel of God" (τῷ τοῦ θεοῦ εὐαγγελίῳ), as extended and expounded in the written "word" of God. The word order could more literally be rendered as "the of the God gospel." The genitive τοῦ θεοῦ ("of God") could be understood either objectively (the gospel God has sent) or subjectively (the gospel that is about God). Sitting in the attributive position, between the noun and definite article (τῷ ... εὐαγγελίῳ), it signals the message of good news that comes from and centers in God's great, gracious work of salvation through Jesus Christ. This divine "gospel" has built into it a call of command to come to God in humility, confession, repentance, and faith to receive the good that is held forth by the announcement of the gospel. Peter characterized his readers' response to the gospel's call as "obedience to the truth" (1 Peter 1:22; cf. 1:2, 14). To fail to obey this call must bring to pass the horror of judgment from which God, through His Son, offers to free us. Having rejected the call of the gospel, all that remains is "a terrifying expectation of judgment" (Heb. 10:27).

Peter does not draw the line at those who do not believe the gospel but at those "who do not obey the gospel" (v.17). Do you *believe* the gospel? It is an important question, surely. But do you *obey* the gospel? Peter asks because if you don't obey the gospel, it is likely you have not truly believed the gospel.

Peter reasons if purifying, refining, sanctifying judgment (v.17a) is how God deals with those who stand under the blood of Christ, if this is how God deals with those who have run to Christ for refuge from God's wrath (and have found it) if this is how God deals with those who have been washed of their sins and have been declared righteous in His sight, what of those who have not (v.17b)?

In the words of Julia Ward Howe's hymn, we find the response befitting believers in the face of such news:

> He has sounded forth the trumpet
> That shall never call retreat;
> He is sifting out the hearts of men
> Before His judgment seat;
> Oh, be swift, my soul, to answer Him;
> Be jubilant, my feet;
> Our God is marching on.[161]

---

161 *The Battle Hymn of the Republic*, Julia Ward Howe, 1862.

Verse 18 – "AND IF IT IS WITH DIFFICULTY THAT THE RIGHTEOUS IS SAVED, WHAT WILL BECOME OF THE GODLESS MAN AND THE SINNER?"

Having looked to the prophets for the basic categories of his thinking (see above in verse 17), Peter now further (καὶ, "AND") grounds his line of thought in the OT by citing Proverbs 11:31 from the LXX. The LXX varies a bit from the Hebrew text, which reads, "If the righteous will be rewarded in the earth, How much more the wicked and the sinner!" The LXX has changed the sense of the verse to read "If the righteous be scarcely saved." The Hebrew emphasizes reward in this life, and the LXX emphasizes the outcome of the last judgment.[162]

The protasis sets out the condition: "IF IT IS WITH DIFFICULTY THAT THE RIGHTEOUS IS SAVED" (εἰ ὁ δίκαιος μόλις σῴζεται). The condition (εἰ, "IF") is, as in verses 14, 16, and 17, of the first class and assumed true for the establishing of Peter's line of thinking. We have met "THE RIGHTEOUS" (ὁ δίκαιος) before in 1 Peter 3:12 (in a quote from Psalm 34:15) and 3:18, where it designates Christ Himself. The verb σῴζω ("SAVED") was already met in 1 Peter 3:21. Here, the present passive form looks at the abiding safety of being thus rescued by God through Christ.

The heart of the LXX's change from the Hebrew text of Proverbs 11:31 is the adverb μόλις ("with difficulty"). It is translated variously: "scarcely" (ASV, ESV, KJV, NKJV, RSV, YLT), "barely" (NET, NLT), "hard" (NIV, NRSV), "with difficulty" (CSB, HCSB). In the LXX, it has the sense of "with difficulty" or "hardly."[163] It is used six times in the NT. Four appear in Acts, describing the difficulty of personal circumstances (Acts 14:18; 27:7, 8, 16). It also appears in Romans 5:7: "For one will hardly [μόλις] die for a righteous man; though perhaps for the good man someone would dare even to die." There the sense seems to be that of rarity rather than difficulty. Here the sense of difficulty seems to remain.

---

162 TDNT, 4:736.

163 Ibid.; Thayer, 417.

But in just what sense are we to understand this difficulty as it relates to the salvation of the righteous? Is Peter stressing the difficulty of the purifying trials that those redeemed by God must pass through to enter the next life with God?[164] Or is he emphasizing that it is only at the highest of prices that the righteous have been redeemed to God?[165] In support of the first, Peter has stressed again and again the necessity of believers enduring unjust suffering for Christ's sake (1 Peter 1:6–7; 2:19–20; 3:1, 9, 13–14; 4:1, 12–19). Paul says, "Through many tribulations we must enter the kingdom of God" (Acts 14:22) and "All who desire to live godly in Christ Jesus will be persecuted" (2 Tim. 3:12). But in support of the second line of thought we have Peter's insistence of the high and singular price of the blood of God's own Son (1 Peter 1:18–19; 2:24).

> **Ministry Maxim**
>
> The price of redemption and discipleship signal the price of unbelief.

But, one wonders, must we choose between these two options? Could something of both be in Peter's words?[166] Given that Peter has already emphasized both points, it seems wise to hear echoes of both in his current expression.

It was "WITH DIFFICULTY" that we were redeemed. Look at the humility it took from God the Son to become man, and that, in the lowliest of fashions. Look at what obedience cost Him in the course of His earthly life. Look at the agony of His prayer in the Garden. Look at the scorn, derision, and shame heaped upon Him as He stood before His accusers. Look at the sufferings of His scourging, abuse, and crucifixion. Behold the agony of His cry, "MY GOD, MY GOD, WHY HAVE YOU FORSAKEN ME?" (Matt. 27:46). Look at the "precious blood, as of a lamb unblemished and spotless" being poured out to death (1 Peter 1:19) to redeem us.

---

164 Bigg, 181; Clowney, 195; Davids, 172; Goppelt, 333–334; Hiebert, 293; Jobes, 294; Kelly, 194; Lenski, 212–213; Michaels, 272; Schreiner, 228; Stibbs, 163; Storms, 352.

165 Barnes, 199.

166 Forbes, 162; MacArthur, 258.

Being purchased at such an infinite price, still only "WITH DIFFICULTY" will anyone finally arrive home to God, safe in His eternal Kingdom. Look at the "DIFFICULTY" of choosing the narrow gate over the broad and easy way (Matt. 7:13–14; Luke 13:23–24). Look at the "DIFFICULTY" of the "many tribulations" through which "we must enter the kingdom of God" (Acts 14:22). Look at the "DIFFICULTY" of daily taking up your cross and following Jesus. Look at the "DIFFICULTY" of hearing our Master say, "In the world you will have tribulation" (John 16:33). Look at the "DIFFICULTY" of being told "in advance that we were going to suffer affliction" for Christ's sake (1 Thess. 3:4). Hear the "DIFFICULTY" in the call to "join … in suffering for the gospel" (2 Tim. 1:8). Indeed, Jesus Himself said, entry into the Kingdom of God is not a just a "DIFFICULTY," but a human impossibility! Yet Jesus also promised that "What is impossible with men is possible with God" (Luke 18:27, ESV).

The protasis, thus, sets before us both the high price of our redemption and the difficult course of our discipleship. The apodosis answers with another rhetorical question (cf. v.17): "WHAT WILL BECOME OF THE GODLESS MAN AND THE SINNER?" (ὁ ἀσεβὴς καὶ ἁμαρτωλὸς ποῦ φανεῖται). The two adjectives are used as substantives. Both are governed by one definite article (ὁ, "THE … THE") and coordinated by καὶ ("AND"), making this an example of the Granville Sharp Rule—the two substantives basically synonymous and describe not two different kinds of individuals, but one and the same person identified by two words.[167] The singular forms are generic, designating a particular class of individuals. The verbal query (ποῦ φανεῖται, "WHAT WILL BECOME OF") is more literally, "where will appear?" The future tense looks to that time of the end after Jesus has come and His judgment is complete. It echoes, "what will be the outcome for those who do not obey the gospel of God?" (v.17b). It is a question about destiny. The question is rhetorical, but the answer that hangs obvious in the air, upspoken, and for that reason, even more ominous, is that they will find no place in the Kingdom of God.

---

167 Alford, 4:380; Dubis, 156; Forbes, 162; Wallace, 270–290.

They must dwell eternally "away from the presence of the Lord and from the glory of his might" (2 Thess. 1:9).

Peter makes his point through a pair of contrasts. "THE RIGHTEOUS" (ὁ δίκαιος) is set over against "THE GODLESS MAN AND THE SINNER" (ὁ ἀσεβὴς καὶ ἁμαρτωλὸς). In the present context, "THE RIGHTEOUS" would be anyone who "suffers as a Christian" (v.16) and is a part of "the household of God" (v.17a). "THE GODLESS MAN AND SINNER" would be identified as "those who do not obey the gospel of God" (v.17). They may be "a murderer, or thief, or evildoer, or a troublesome meddler" (v.15). So too the certainty of "IS SAVED" (σῴζεται) stands opposite of the uncertainty of "WHAT WILL BECOME OF" (ποῦ φανεῖται).

The answer that is expected in response to Peter's rhetorical question's uncertainty is that such people will also face God's judgment. Theirs will not be the first, measured, refining installment of divine judgment. It will be the final, unrestrained outpouring of His wrath. Their judgment will not be for purification that they might be presented to Christ as His prepared Bride (Eph. 5:25–32). They will face the judgment of God apart from the saving merits of Jesus.

Here the Apostle Paul would add his amen, for he has gone on record with another suffering body of believers regarding their suffering at the hands of unbelievers.

> For after all it is only just for God to repay with affliction those who afflict you, and to give relief to you who are afflicted and to us as well when the Lord Jesus will be revealed from heaven with His mighty angels in flaming fire, dealing out retribution to those who do not know God and to those who do not obey the gospel of our Lord Jesus. These will pay the penalty of eternal destruction, away from the presence of the Lord and from the glory of His power, when He comes to be glorified in His saints on that day, and to be marveled at among all who have believed-- for our testimony to you was believed. (2 Thess. 1:6–10)

Consider, if it took Christ to free us, what of those who refuse God's one sacrifice for sin? What will become of those who dare to stand before this infinitely holy God in their unrighteousness? If God so deals with us who stand before Him in the merits of His Son's perfect life, what will become of those who stand before Him in the demerits of their own sinfulness? If God so deals with us who stand before Him with our confidence in the sacrificial death of Christ on our behalf, what will become of those who stand before Him in the confidence of their own actions? If God so deals with us who stand before Him with our hope set upon a risen Savior, what will become of those who must face death on their own? If God so deals with us who stand before Him, hearing our ascended, glorified Savior pleading the sufficiency of His life, death, and resurrection on our behalf, what will become of the one who goes there without an Advocate?

Verse 19 – "Therefore, those also who suffer according to the will of God shall entrust their souls to a faithful Creator in doing what is right."

Peter now gathers up the thoughts of verses 12–18 and draws a logical conclusion (ὥστε καὶ, "Therefore"). In fact, verse 19 might be read as a summation of the entire letter to this point.[168] The combination ὥστε καὶ is found four other times in the NT (Acts 5:15; 19:12; 1 Cor. 7:38; Gal. 2:13). The καὶ ("also") may be understood as qualifying either ὥστε ("Therefore")[169] or οἱ πάσχοντες ("those...who suffer")[170]

---

168 Forbes says it "virtually encapsulates everything that the author has said so far concerning suffering" (163); Grudem says, "In this one verse is summarized the teaching of the entire letter" (191).
169 Michaels, 272–273; Schreiner, 229; YLT.
170 Alford, 4:380; Goppelt, 334; Hart, 75; Hiebert, 294; Jobes, 295; Kelly, 194; Lenski, 213; ASV, NASU.

or παρατιθέσθωσαν ("shall entrust").[171] Most English versions leave it untranslated.

Peter is concerned for "those who suffer according to the will of God" (οἱ πάσχοντες κατὰ τὸ θέλημα τοῦ θεοῦ). Peter continues the now-familiar theme of suffering. The verb is the familiar and thematic πάσχω. This is now the eleventh of its twelve uses in the letter (see our comments on 2:19). The participle is used substantively ("*those who* are suffering," emphasis added). The present tense pictures the immediate and ongoing reality of the suffering.

Peter is specifically concerned with those who embrace their suffering "according to God's will" (κατὰ τὸ θέλημα τοῦ θεοῦ). On His part, God has willed it; He has "for a little while" found their suffering "necessary" for His sovereign purposes (1 Peter 1:6).[172] Now on their part they must be certain it befalls them "unjustly" (2:19) and they face it with endurance (2:20), after the pattern of Jesus' suffering (2:21; 3:18; 4:1), without retaliation (2:23), "for the sake of righteousness" (3:14), and for doing good (3:17). He is not thinking of that suffering which might come for sin (2:20), doing wrong (3:17), or as "as a murderer, or thief, or evildoer, or a troublesome meddler"

> **Ministry Maxim**
>
> He who willed you into existence can be trusted in how He deals with you now.

(4:15). Peter has already told his readers it "is the will of God that by doing right you may silence the ignorance of foolish men" (2:15), that "it is better, if God should will it so, that you suffer for doing what is right rather than for doing what is wrong" (3:17), and he has called them "to live the rest of the time in the flesh no longer for the lusts of men, but for the will of God" (4:2).

The path forward in unjust suffering is that those who suffer "shall entrust their soul" (παρατιθέσθωσαν τὰς ψυχὰς αὐτῶν) to God Himself. The verb (παρατιθέσθωσαν, "shall entrust") means simply "place beside"

---

171 Bigg, 181.

172 Cf. "if wills the will of God" (lit. rendering of εἰ θέλοι τὸ θέλημα τοῦ θεοῦ, 3:17).

or "place before," but in the middle voice, as here, it carries the sense of entrusting or committing something to someone for safekeeping.[173] The term came out of commerce, where a person placed their wealth on deposit with another and into their care.[174] Paul used the cognate noun of that which God entrusts to us as His servants (1 Tim. 6:20; 2 Tim. 1:12, 14). The present imperative calls for continually, throughout the suffering, putting one's soul on deposit with God. In this, we have Jesus' own example, for He used the verb with His last breath to entrust Himself to God, praying, "Father, INTO YOUR HANDS I COMMIT [παρατίθεμαι] MY SPIRIT" (Luke 23:46; cf. Psa. 31:5; 30:6, LXX). Indeed, Peter tells us, using a different but kindred verb, Jesus "uttered no threats, but kept entrusting [παρεδίδου] Himself to Him who judges righteously" (1 Peter 2:23). Here, as throughout 1 Peter, the term "souls" (τὰς ψυχὰς) designates not some immaterial subset of the person, but represents the whole of their being. That this must be a deeply personal and individual act is highlighted by the use of the personal pronoun (αὐτῶν, "their").

We are to put ourselves on deposit "to a faithful Creator" (πιστῷ κτίστῃ). The expression is pushed forward for emphasis. The noun (κτίστῃ, "Creator") is found only here in the NT. However, the kindred verb κτίζω ("to create") is used fifteen times. In the NT, the verb is used either of God's original creation (Matt. 19:4; Mark 13:19; Rom. 1:25; 1 Cor. 11:9; Eph. 3:9; Col. 1:16 [2x], 1 Tim. 4:3; Rev. 4:11 [2x], 10:6) or of the new creation He brings about through Jesus Christ (Eph. 2:10, 15; 4:24; Col. 3:10). The emphasis here may be upon the former, but Peter speaks to people who have undergone the latter. As new creatures in Christ, they can trust their Creator to deal with them wisely according to His will. As "Creator," He is sovereign over all that He has brought into being. He not only brought into being all things but preserves and keeps by His providence all He has created. As "faithful," He has graciously revealed Himself and His purposes to His creatures. He keeps His word. He fulfills His promises. He does what He says. He does not deviate from

---

173 Friberg, 298; cf. TDNT, 8:162–164.

174 Robertson, 4:565.

His purposes. He was under no obligation to reveal His purposes and promises to us but having done so, He bound Himself to fulfill them. Thus, when we share by His grace in those purposes and promises, we can cast ourselves upon Him, knowing that we are safe with Him. You may be confident in "casting all your anxiety on Him, because He cares for you" (1 Peter 5:7).

How exactly is this transaction to take place? In prayer? Surely that is involved (cf. Psa. 31:5; Luke 23:46). But Peter says specifically it takes place "in doing what is right" (ἐν ἀγαθοποιΐᾳ). The noun (ἀγαθοποιΐα, "doing what is right") is used only here in the NT, but it joins a number of other ἀγαθ- words used a total of thirteen times throughout the letter (ἀγαθοποιός, "doing good," 2:14; ἀγαθοποιέω, "to do good," 2:15, 20; 3:6, 17; ἀγαθός, "good," 2:18; 3:10, 11, 13, 16 [2x], 17, 21). It is as we live "in" (ἐν) the realm or sphere of active obedience to the will of God ("doing what is right"), despite what it may cost us, that we are "entrusting ourselves" to our faithful Creator. Continual obedience is the path of continual trust.

> **Digging Deeper:**
> 1. What is your current "fiery ordeal" (v.12) and how is it serving to purify your faith (v.17a)?
> 2. How have you experienced the "DIFFICULTY" of discipleship to Jesus (v.18)?
> 3. Stop right now for a few minutes and item by item "entrust" yourself and your life again to your "faithful Creator" (v.19).

1 PETER 5

Verse 1 – "Therefore, I exhort the elders among you, as *your* fellow elder and witness of the sufferings of Christ, and a partaker also of the glory that is to be revealed,"

Peter transitions at this point in the letter, yet he draws logical conclusions from what has gone before (οὖν, "Therefore").[1] As we noted in 4:17 when Peter told his readers, "it is time for judgment to begin with the household of God," it is likely he was drawing upon Ezekiel 9:6.[2] It issues a call for all-inclusive judgment upon the unbelieving, the believing separated by a special mark (v.6a). Yet the judgment is to "start from My sanctuary" (v.6b), the Temple of God in Jerusalem. God narrowed the field from the eventual judgment of the unbelieving to the preliminary judgment that would begin at the Temple. He narrowed it then once more by saying, "they started with the elders who were before the temple" (v.6c). This signals that Peter is not simply now throwing in some thoughts on a new topic but is continuing the theme upon which he has been dwelling. Judgment will come to the unbelieving (1 Peter

---

1   There is some debate about the text here. Some manuscripts have the definite article (τοὺς), including NA[28] and UBS[5], while still others have the conjunction (οὖν, "Therefore") followed by the definite article. The conjunction standing alone, however, is probably the more difficult reading and for that reason should be retained (Forbes, 165; cf. Dubis, 159).

2   Cf. Dubis, 159; Forbes, 166; Grudem, 192–193; Jobes, 300; Michaels, 279; Schreiner, 230.

4:17b), it will begin with the new temple of God, His people (v.17a), and thus they should not be surprised by the suffering they face, for it is part of God's refining process in their lives (vv.12–19). Furthermore, the elders must prepare to lead through the "fiery ordeal" (4:12) that they and their fellow believers face. Universal judgment is coming. But it will come first to the believing as a refining and purifying work of God. And it will come first to those who stand at the head of the believing, "the elders" (Πρεσβυτέρους). "Therefore" (οὖν), by way of one extended sentence that runs through verse 4, Peter turns his attention to preparing these men to lead God's people through the "fiery ordeal" that lies ahead.

Peter thus addresses the "elders among you" (Πρεσβυτέρους... ἐν ὑμῖν). The adjective is used as a substantive (Πρεσβυτέρους, "elders") and stands first for emphasis. The word originally spoke of men of advanced age, but regarding leadership, it is a carryover from the Jewish roots of the church. In the synagogue, elders were the leaders. The word then came to refer to the church's leaders rather than simply the chronological age of an individual. Paul appointed elders for every church established during his first missionary journey (Acts 14:23). Paul left Titus on Crete that he might "appoint elders in every city" (Titus 1:5). See 1 Timothy 3 and Titus 1 for the qualifications of those able to so serve the local church.

In verse 2, Peter will use a verb (ἐπισκοπέω) cognate to the noun ἐπίσκοποι ("overseers"), which is used elsewhere as interchangeable with πρεσβύτεροι ("elders," cf. Acts 20:17, 28; Titus 1:5, 7). Both terms describe one office in the NT church. The title "overseers" (ἐπίσκοποι) may describe the duty of the office, while "elders" (πρεσβύτεροι) depicts the honor and dignity of the office. The command to "shepherd" (ποιμάνατε, v.2) the flock of God may describe the work of those who hold the office. In the NT, elders are regularly spoken of in a plurality (cf. Acts 11:30; 14:23; 20:17; 1 Tim. 4:14; 5:17; Titus 1:5; James 5:14).

Peter dubs them the elders who are "among you" (ἐν ὑμῖν). The elders are individuals that exist as a part of the local body. They stand among the people who make up that body. They live out their lives amid the people of God. Notably, Peter says to the larger body of believers that these men are "among you" (ἐν ὑμῖν), and as he turns to address the elders themselves, he says they are to shepherd the flock of God that is "among you" (ἐν ὑμῖν, v.2). There is a mutuality and shared life between elders and the people of the flock. The elders live and minister among the people, and the people live surrounded by the body of the elders.

To these elders, Peter says, "I exhort" (παρακαλῶ). There is an interesting dynamic being played out here. Peter speaks to the entirety of the people who make up the churches to which he writes and tells them that he is now speaking to the elders among them. Peter does not merely exhort the elders. He does so in the presence of all the people among whom they live and minister and whom they are called to lead. In effect then, in the presence of God (for whom Peter speaks) and before the people of the churches, Peter addresses the elders and issues an exhortation concerning the fulfillment of their calling. Note the multiple layers of accountability—God, His apostle, His people.

The verb is a regular feature in the NT. It is a compound constructed from καλέω ("to call") and παρά ("beside"). Most literally, it might mean "to call alongside," but its emphasis can vary from encourage and comfort on one end of the spectrum to exhort and implore on the other end. The context of each use must determine where on this continuum of meaning the author intends to anchor that particular use of the verb.

> **Ministry Maxim**
>
> The honors, responsibilities, and demands of leadership are best when shared.

As we survey all Peter says to these elders, we find both encouragement (v.4) and exhortation (vv.2–3). The specific exhortation will be found in the imperative "shepherd" (ποιμάνατε, v.2a), and the specific encouragement will come in the promise "you will receive" (κομιεῖσθε, v.4). While Peter here singles out the elders for exhortation, he has already so exhorted all his readers: "Beloved, I urge [παρακαλῶ] you as aliens and strangers to abstain from fleshly lusts which wage war against the soul" (1 Peter 2:11). And Peter characterizes the entirety of 1 Peter as an exhortation: "…I have written to you briefly, exhorting [παρακαλῶν] and testifying that this is the true grace of God. Stand firm in it!" (5:12b). Peter speaks in the first person for one of the few times in this letter (cf. 2:12; 5:12).³

Peter makes his exhortation to the elders from three bases. First, he addressed them "as your fellow elder" (ὁ συμπρεσβύτερος). The noun is found only here in the NT and is the earliest known usage of the term in Greek literature. It is a compound comprised of σύν ("with") and πρεσβύτερος ("elder"). Typically, elders were designated as existing in a plurality and were designated to operate as pastoral leaders over a specific congregation (Acts 14:23; 20:17). Peter and John (2 John 1; 3 John 1) both, however, used the term of themselves and it appears to have in these instances a wider application. Michaels observes, "an 'apostle' is in some sense an 'elder' to the entire Christian community in the world, not to one church in particular."⁴ Peter, then, addresses these "elders" as something of a peer. He has already denoted his apostleship (1 Peter 1:1), but here he stands on level ground with these pastoral leaders and speaks to them of their common calling, appointment, accountability, and responsibility. Peter understands the demands that rest upon them as those charged with the leadership and care of Christ's people.

Second (καί, "and"), Peter speaks to them as a "witness of the sufferings of Christ" (μάρτυς τῶν τοῦ Χριστοῦ παθημάτων). This is now the sixth time in this letter Peter has mentioned the sufferings of Christ (1:11; 2:21, 23; 4:1, 13; 5:1). He identifies himself here as a "witness" (μάρτυς) of those sufferings. The construction (one definite article assigned to two nouns that are connected by καί) indicates that only one person is in view here. Peter was at one and the same time "a fellow elder" and a "witness." The noun μάρτυς ("witness") is a telling self-designation for Peter. It identifies one who faithfully and truthfully testifies as to their experience. And this Peter had done (Acts 2:32; 3:15) and now was doing so again in this letter. But the word also came to identify one who does so even unto death, and thus μάρτυς became our English word *martyr*.

---

3   Forbes, 166.
4   Michaels, 280.

Jesus had named Peter the rock (John 1:42) and identified his confession as the rock upon which the church would be built (Matt. 16:16–18). Peter had been the clear and obvious leader of the disciples from the beginning being named first in every list of the disciples. Yet, here he did not say, ' I exhort you as one of the few who were present when Jesus unveiled His glory and Moses and Elijah appeared to Him" (Matt. 17:1–8) or "I exhort you as the only one Jesus invited to walk on the water with Him" (Matt. 14:22–29) or "I exhort you as one of the few asked by Jesus to go with Him into the home where He raised the little girl from the dead" (Mark 5:35–43). Peter did not call upon any one of the numerous other privileges he had experienced in relationship to Jesus. Rather, he spoke as one who had seen the sufferings of Christ with his own eyes. He had observed the way the Jewish leadership dealt with Jesus. He knew of their plots against Him. He had been there as, time and again, Jesus warned the disciples of His impending sufferings and death. He was in the garden as Jesus agonized in prayer. He was there when the arresting party came. He saw his Master manhandled by the soldiers. He "followed … at a distance" as they dragged Him through the darkened streets of Jerusalem (Matt. 26:58; Mark 14:54; Luke 22:54). He followed right into the courtyard of the High Priest and observed the injustice of His trials. There Jesus' words to him came true as Peter three times denied he knew Him. Across the courtyard, piercing through the mayhem unfolding around Him, Jesus, from the depths of His suffering, met the eyes of Peter (Luke 22:61). We are told that Peter then "went out and wept bitterly" (Matt. 26:75). Whether Peter found his way back and observed anything more of Jesus' trials, the brutality against Him, His crucifixion or death is a matter of debate among scholars. But for Peter's purposes here, it does not matter. For μάρτυς ("witness") need not necessarily imply eyewitness, but faithful reporter of the truth. Peter was witness to at least a majority of Jesus' sufferings. He has proven to be a faithful "witness" of His Master's sufferings.

Peter saw Jesus' suffer. He knew that Jesus had died. He was able to find his way to Jesus' tomb. And Peter proved not only a faithful "witness" to Jesus' suffering unto death but beheld Him alive from the dead on more than one occasion. In one of those encounters, Jesus had restored Peter to ministry after his painful betrayal, calling him to shepherd His sheep (John 21:15–17). There Jesus had also told Peter this would one day cost him his life (vv.18–19). Since that day, Peter, who once vehemently opposed Jesus' talk of suffering (Matt. 16:22), had used every opportunity to cast others' eyes upon Jesus, knowing that his service as "witness" (μάρτυς) to Christ's sufferings would one day become his service as *martyr* for Christ's glory. In this, too, Peter was identifying with his fellow elders, for they also had to prove faithful witnesses to Christ's sufferings—by their proclamation and by their living.

Third, Peter calls out to them as "a partaker also of the glory that is to be revealed" (ὁ καὶ τῆς μελλούσης ἀποκαλύπτεσθαι δόξης κοινωνός). The noun (ὁ … κοινωνός, "a partaker") designates "one who fellowships and shares something in common with another."[5] It means "fellow" or "participant" and is especially "adapted to express inner relationship."[6] It can describe business (Luke 5:10) or ministry (2 Cor. 8:23; Philem. 17) partners, a kind of union experienced in worship (1 Cor. 10:18, 20), or the bond between believers who share together in persecution (2 Cor. 1:7; Heb. 10:33). Significantly, in his only other use of the noun Peter told the readers of his second letter than through God's promises "you may become partakers [κοινωνοὶ] of the divine nature" (2 Peter 1:4). This will factor in significantly as we seek to determine just what Peter means here by "the glory" (τῆς … δόξης). Peter here chose the masculine noun (κοινωνός) over the feminine form of the noun (κοινωνία) and the verbal form (κοινωνέω).[7] The feminine noun is abstract, while the masculine form is used concretely and refers to participants or partners.[8]

A long intervening phrase in the attributive position separates the noun and its definite article. The phrase amounts to an adverbial use of the conjunction καὶ ("also"), a participle (μελλούσης, "is about"), an

---

5 Friberg, 233; cf. TDNT, 3:804.

6 NIDNTTE, 3:798.

7 The feminine noun and the verbal form are found nineteen times each; in contrast the masculine noun is found ten times.

8 Hafemann, Scott, "'Divine Nature' in 2 Pet 1,4 Within its Eschatological Context", Biblica, vol.94 (2013), 94–95.

infinitive (ἀποκαλύπτεσθαι, "to be revealed"), and a noun (τῆς ... δόξης, "the glory").

That of which Peter is a "partaker" is "the glory" (τῆς ... δόξης). Peter not only observed and now bears witness to the sufferings and death of Christ, but he has already become a "partaker" of Christ's glory, as had his readers (1 Peter 1:8; 4:14). The definite article designates this as a particular "glory." He, along with James and John, beheld Jesus' glory on the Mount of Transfiguration (Matt. 17:1–8; Mark 9:2–8; Luke 9:28–36), and it continued to have a powerful effect upon Peter (2 Peter 1:16–18). That may be present here, but only as a fire already lit and lighting the way forward to an even greater experience. Peter uses the noun ten times in this letter. The "glory" of mortal flesh is fleeting (1:24). God's gospel call from the beginning has been "to His eternal glory in Christ' (5:10). Jesus suffered and died but, beginning with His resurrection, He dwells presently in glory (1:11, 21). He sent His Holy Spirit so His people can already share in a foretaste of that glory (4:14; cf. 2 Cor. 1:22; 5:5; Eph. 1:14). As His people serve one another by the gifts of the Spirit operative in them, He is glorified (4:11). At Jesus' Return His glory will be fully unveiled, and His people will share fully in its radiance with Him (1:7; 4:13; 5:4).

This "glory" is, then, both present experience and future hope, now only a foretaste, then in fullness. The term "partaker" points to the former, while the phrase "that is to be revealed" points toward the latter. The articular participle (μελλούσης, "is about") is used attributively, the glory of which Peter already tastes "is about" to reach a new, fuller dimension. The present tense underscores the continuous readiness of this "glory" to be unveiled. Peter has already warned, "The end of all things is near" (1 Peter 4:7).

The infinitive (ἀποκαλύπτεσθαι, "to be revealed") is in the present tense and again underscores the present readiness of that "glory" for its full revelation. The passive voice indicates that its revelation depends upon another, in this case, the Father's timing in sending His Son the second time.

Peter is not only a "witness" to Christ's "sufferings" but "also" (καὶ) a "partaker" of His subsequent and soon-to-be fully revealed "glory." It would appear, then, that by designating himself as a "partaker" of God's glory Peter is speaking both of a present reality in his life by the Spirit ("partaker") as well as a future hope to be entered into at Jesus' Return ("that is to be revealed"). As a "fellow-elder," a "witness" of Jesus' sufferings, and as a "partaker" of His glories, Peter directly addresses the elders of the churches to which he now writes. In all three terms, Peter establishes common ground with the "elders" among those to whom he writes. He understands the unique demands of leading and serving God's people in times of distress and suffering. While the elders were not privileged as eyewitnesses of Jesus' sufferings (1 Peter 1:8), they too must prove faithful as witnesses to Jesus' sufferings and triumph. Peter and the elders together live presently in the down payment of Christ's glory by the Holy Spirit and hold steadfastly to the hope of sharing fully in His glory at Him coming.

Verse 2 – "shepherd the flock of God among you, exercising oversight not under compulsion, but voluntarily, according to *the will of* God; and not for sordid gain, but with eagerness;"

Peter's specific exhortation now comes to the fore: "shepherd the flock of God" (ποιμάνατε τὸ ἐν ὑμῖν ποίμνιον τοῦ θεοῦ). The verb has in mind "the whole office of the shepherd, the guiding, guarding, folding of the flock, as well as the finding of nourishment for it."[9] It was used prophetically of the Messiah (Matt. 2:6; cf. Micah 5:2) and also of the risen, glorified Jesus' ministry to martyrs (Rev. 7:17) and the nations (19:15; cf. 12:5). Jesus forgave a repentant Peter his denials and commanded him, "'Shepherd [ποίμαινε] My sheep'" (John 21:16). This encounter surely was in Peter's mind as he penned these words. Paul used the verb to indicate that shepherding is at the heart of the call of local church elders/overseers: "Be on guard for yourselves and for all the flock, among which

> **Ministry Maxim**
>
> Elders must be close enough to the flock to shepherd them and distant enough to oversee them.

---

9 Trench, 86.

the Holy Spirit has made you overseers, to shepherd [ποιμαίνειν] the church of God which He purchased with His own blood'" (Acts 20:28). Peter makes this an imperative. He leaves this not as an option for local church elders (1 Peter 5:1) but as part and parcel of their ministry. The aorist tense may be ingressive, "take up the task of shepherding."[10]

The object of the elders' shepherding ministry is "the flock" (τὸ ... ποίμνιον). The noun is kindred to the verb just used (ποιμάνατε, "shepherd").[11] The noun was used in the OT of God's people Israel (e.g., Jer. 13:17; Zech. 10:3). Jesus endearingly addressed His disciples as "little flock" (Luke 12:32). Paul spoke to the elders of Ephesus about those under their charge (Acts 20:28–29). They must be guarded (v.28) from "savage wolves" who would devour them (v.29). The "flock" is "the church of God," those "He purchased with His own blood" (v.28). In the NT the noun always appears in the singular form, a collective singular referring to the body of those who are God's through Jesus Christ. Peter is presently dealing with pluralities—multiple elders caring for a collective "flock." He is not disinterested in individual shepherds or the sheep placed under their charge but sees each one undertaking their duties shoulder to shoulder with others similarly called, all caring for sheep in the context of their relationship to all God's other sheep. The elder/overseer/shepherd must somehow find the balance between concern for individual "sheep" and the care for and welfare of the entire "flock." As a "flock," God's people need tender care (Luke 12:32), oversight, shepherding, protection (Acts 20:28–29), and examples (1 Peter 5:3).

This "flock" is qualified in two ways. It is identified as "of God" (τοῦ θεοῦ). The genitive is subjective—the flock which belongs to or originates with God. In the case of the cognate accusative, "If the accusative has a modifier (either adjective or genitive), the overall construction is more

---

10 Rienecker, 765.

11 It is designated a "cognate accusative," "a direct object which has the same root or at least contains the same idea as the verb of which it is the direct object. The cognate accusative functions as an internal object of a verb, whereas what is usually called a direct object is an external object. This category employs the substantive without a preposition" (Brooks and Winbery, 50; cf. Dana and Manty, 94; Wallace, 189–190).

emphatic."[12] The flock is also "among you" (ἐν ὑμῖν). As the elders are "among you" (i.e., the "flock," v.1) so he can say to the elders, "the flock of God" is "among you" (i.e., surrounded by divinely called spiritual leaders). By divine design, there is among His people a mutuality of dwelling among (ἐν ὑμῖν) one another. The "flock" is the charge of the elders/overseers/shepherds, not the possession. God owns "the flock" and calls and appoints the leaders. They are accountable to God as stewards both of His people and His appointment. The prepositional phrase (ἐν ὑμῖν, "among you") is placed attributively between the article and noun, pointing "to a close characteristic relation between the shepherds and the sheep."[13]

This shepherding involves "exercising oversight" (ἐπισκοποῦντες).[14] We have here the verbal form of ἐπίσκοπος ("overseer," Acts 20:28; Phil. 1:1; 1 Tim. 3:2; Titus 1:7), which Peter uses of Jesus in 2:25 where it is translated "Guardian" and combined with ποιμένα ("Shepherd"). The verb is a compound made up of "over" (ἐπί) and "to look at or after" (σκοπέω).[15] As overseers, the elders are charged with providing "oversight" of "the flock of God." The participle qualifies the imperative "shepherd," indicating the way they will fulfill the command. The present tense underscores the continual nature of the work of shepherding God's people.

As to dignity and character, these men are "elders" (v.1). As to function and role, they shepherd God's people by overseeing them (v.2).

Through three emphatic positive-negative contrasts, Peter sets forward the proper manner of this shepherding ministry of oversight (μὴ ... ἀλλὰ, μηδὲ ... ἀλλὰ, μηδ' ... ἀλλὰ; vv.2b-3). The negation (μὴ, μηδὲ) forbids any thought or consideration of the matters introduced.[16] The strong

---

12 Wallace, 189.

13 Hiebert, 303.

14 A few manuscripts do not include this verb, though it has generally wide and significant inclusion among important manuscripts. Its inclusion is supported by the fact that it is found in early manuscripts and has a broad representation among the manuscripts.

15 Liddell and Scott, 16958 and 39184; The root verb appears in the NT in Luke 11:35, Romans 16:17, 2 Corinthians 4:18, Galatians 6:1, Philippians 2:4, and 3:17.

16 Thayer, 408.

adversative ἀλλά ("but") in each case introduces the emphatically positive contrasting virtue to be embraced.

The first contrasting pair begins with "not under compulsion" (μὴ ἀναγκαστῶς). The adverb is found only here in the Bible, but the cognate verb (ἀναγκάζω, "to force," "to compel") is found nine times (e.g., Matt. 14:22; Luke 14:23; 2 Cor. 12:11; Gal. 2:3, 14). Our verb indicates doing something out of obligation, unwillingly, under constraint, or by force. While the work of an elder is worthy of one's desire (1 Tim. 3:1), one enters the office only by appointment by God and His people (e.g., Acts 14:23; Titus 1:5). The added busyness to one's schedule, the dangers of leading the church when facing persecution, the emotional strain of caring for souls, the relational pressure of unreasonable expectations, and a host of other factors might make an elder act "under compulsion" rather than glad willingness. The pressures to "perform" in ministry can come from many directions—personal ego, past wounds, cultural expectations, board pressures, ecclesiastical authorities, peer pressure, competitive spirit, financial need, career advancement, shame, pride, the congregation, etc. Each may exert its unique pressure, and any can descend to arm-twisting.

In emphatic contrast (ἀλλά, "but") is shepherding the flock "voluntarily" (ἑκουσίως) and "according to the will of God" (κατὰ θεόν). The adverb (ἑκουσίως, "voluntarily") is found in the NT only here and in Hebrews 10:26, where it refers to willfully chosen sin. It denotes that which is voluntary, willing, and of one's own accord.[17] In such a case the impetus to action arises from internal considerations ("voluntarily"), not external pressures or goading ("under compulsion"). One so motivated continues in his service regardless of response, recompense, reward, or remuneration. Such can say with his Master, "My food is to do the will of Him who sent Me" (John 4:34). To serve out of such motives is to act "according to the will of God" (κατὰ θεόν), or more literally, "according to God."[18] The preposition κατά ("according to") signals simple correspondence between two things. We are

---

17 Ibid., 198.

18 Some later manuscripts do not include κατὰ θεόν, but the strongest and earliest manuscripts do include it and we should consider it original (cf. Davids, 178; Michaels, 276–277).

to act toward others as God has acted toward us (Eph. 4:32). God acted out of the love that is His by nature, not because of the loveliness of the object. God operated out of His own internal nature, not the external attractiveness of the object of His love. "Freely you received, freely give" (Matt. 10:8).

The second and third contrasts switch from the simple negation (μὴ, "not") to the compounded form μηδὲ ("not"). It is comprised of μὴ ("not") with δὲ ("and"). Elders are to serve "not for sordid gain" (μηδὲ αἰσχροκερδῶς). The adverb appears only here in the Bible. It is a compound made up of αἰσχρός ("shameful") and κέρδος ("a gain"). Paul used both roots when he instructed Titus about those "teaching things they should not teach for the sake of sordid [αἰσχροῦ] gain [κέρδους]" (Titus 1:11). Paul held overseers (Titus 1:7) and deacons (1 Tim. 3:8) to the same standard, using the cognate adjective (αἰσχροκερδής, "fond of dishonest gain"). Peter's present exhortation concerning an elder's motives regarding financial gain is balanced by other NT exhortations to the congregation regarding an elder's right to reasonable remuneration (1 Cor. 9:3–14; 1 Tim. 5:17–18). Faithfulness and generosity on the part of the congregation and contentment and purity on the part of the elder are the paths of godliness. One serving as an elder might seek remuneration in many forms, from financial to social, psychological, emotional, and mental. But to serve simply for payday (whatever the currency) is shameful. Paul set the example when he said, "But whatever things were gain [κέρδη] to me, those things I have counted as loss for the sake of Christ" (Phil. 3:7).

Rather, in stark contrast (ἀλλὰ, "but"), elders should serve "with eagerness" (προθύμως). Again, this adverb appears only here in the NT, but the cognate adjective appears in Romans 1:15: "So, for my part, I am eager [πρόθυμον] to preach the gospel to you also who are in Rome" (elsewhere in the NT only Matt. 26:41; Mark 14:38). The cognate noun is used five times in the NT (Acts 17:11; 2 Cor. 8:11, 12, 19; 9:2). It is a compound comprised of the prefix πρό ("before") and θυμός ("the soul," "the mind," "*a strong passion or emotion of the mind*"[19]). "The word

---

19 Mounce, 1171.

is extremely strong and expresses enthusiasm and devoted zeal."[20] Elders must be passionate, motivated people—not after selfish reward, but in service of God and others.

Verse 3 – "nor yet as lording it over those allotted to your charge, but proving to be examples to the flock."

Peter continues to expound upon the way the shepherding oversight of the elders is to be carried out (vv.1–2). He now adds a third contrasting, explanatory pair to the two pairs in verse 2. The elders are to exercise their oversight "nor yet as lording it over those allotted to your charge" (μηδ' ὡς κατακυριεύοντες τῶν κλήρων). The comparative ὡς ("as")[21] with the negation (μηδ', "nor") designates the manner in which the oversight of the elders is not to take place.[22]

The elders are forbidden from "lording it over" (κατακυριεύοντες) those under their care. The verb is a compound made up of κατά ("down") and κυριεύω ("to be lord or master of people or of a country").[23] It thus has the sense of ruling with a heavy, authoritarian hand. It is "to lord it over someone, to domineer, to exercise complete control."[24] The participle expresses the manner in which elders are not to practice oversight of the people. The prohibition against "lording it over" those under the elders' care implies that there was a legitimate authority which they did carry and must not harm (1 Thess. 5:12; 1 Tim. 5:17; Heb. 13:17). Jesus, however, made clear that the pattern for His servants was that of humble

---

20 Rienecker, 765.

21 To Peter's delight in alliteration (cf. 1 Peter 1:4, 19; 2:15, 21; 3:17, 20) we might add assonance. He may have used ὡς partly for the literary effect of its echo of four adverbs in verse 2, all of which end in -ως (ἀναγκαστῶς, "under compulsion"; ἑκουσίως, "voluntarily"; αἰσχροκερδῶς, "for sordid gain"; προθύμως, "with eagerness"). (cf. Michaels, 285).

22 BDAG, 8075.1.b.α.

23 Liddell and Scott, 22914, 25640.

24 Rienecker, 765.

service, not executive power (Matt. 20:25–28; Mark 10:42–45; Luke 22:24–27).²⁵

Elders are forbidden to do so with "those allotted to your charge" (τῶν κλήρων). The expression is more literally "of the lots." The singular designated "a small object (pebble, twig, potsherd, etc.) thrown to determine a choice or assign a portion."²⁶ But here, in the plural, it identifies those to whom the lot fell, the people who make up "the flock of God" in each location and under the care of specific elders.²⁷ This came about not by some blind toss of the dice but according to God's sovereign will. "The lot is cast into the lap, But its every decision is from the LORD" (Prov. 16:33).

> **Ministry Maxim**
> Elders lead best by demonstrating what a disciple looks like.

With this knowledge the elders undertake their service with a profound sense of accountability to the one who called them to their task, who modeled how to fulfill it, who assigned them their portion of "the flock of God," and who is "the Chief Shepherd" (v.4) of these people.

Instead (ἀλλά, "but") of "lording it over" the flock, the elders should be "proving to be examples to the flock" (τύποι γινόμενοι τοῦ ποιμνίου). The verb (γινόμενοι, "proving to be") means simply "to become." The present tense sets it forth as the constant object of the elders' pursuit. One-and-done will not suffice; examples must perpetually prove themselves to be worthy of that status. Like its parallel participle, the participle designates how the elders' shepherding oversight is to take place. That which they are thus to be is "examples" (τύποι). The noun could be used technically to describe a "type" (Rom. 5:14; 1 Cor. 10:6 [cf. v.11]), an official "standard" against which something is measured (Rom. 6:17), and, as here, an

---

25 Cf. "The Authority of God and the Church" in *Embracing Authority*, John A. Kitchen (Inverness: Christian Focus Publications, 2002), 77–96.

26 Friberg, 232.

27 Note the parallelism of "the lots" (τῶν κλήρων) and "the flock" (τὸ ... ποίμνιον, v.2; τοῦ ποιμνίου, v.3). The churches/flock made up of the people of God are the "lots" assigned to the elders. The word choice suggests "the idea of divine appointment of these particular people to these particular elders" (Jobes, 306; cf. Goppelt, 347; Michaels, 286).

"example" (Phil. 3:17; 1 Thess. 1:7; 2 Thess. 3:9; 1 Tim. 4:12) or "model" (Titus 2:7) in matters ethical and moral.[28] And this "to the flock" (τοῦ ποιμνίου). The genitive is objective; the elders are to be examples to the flock under their charge.[29] They are "the flock of God" (v.2), ultimately under the care of "the Chief Shepherd" (v.4), but immediately overseen by the elders as under-shepherds. The elders thus live to model what discipleship to Jesus, godly manhood, and Christ-honoring leadership looks like.

Elders rightly shepherd the flock of believers placed under their charge by God through exercising oversight with the right *mindset* ("not under compulsion, but voluntarily, according to the will of God," v.2a), *motive* ("and not for sordid gain, but with eagerness," v.2b), and *manner* ("nor yet as lording it over those allotted to your charge, but proving to be examples to the flock," v.3). "The three negative attitudes might be summarized as love of praise, love of profit, and love of power."[30]

Verse 4 – "And when the Chief Shepherd appears, you will receive the unfading crown of glory."

Peter adds (καὶ, "And") a final promise to round out his address to the leaders of the congregations. The promise will be fulfilled only "When the Chief Shepherd appears" (φανερωθέντος τοῦ ἀρχιποίμενος). The participle (φανερωθέντος) is understood rightly as temporal ("*When*...appears," emphasis added). The verb is used frequently throughout the NT and depicts the act of making visible that which has heretofore been unseen.[31] Peter uses it to speak both of Christ's first advent (1 Peter 1:20) and, as here, of His Second Advent. The aorist tense depicts

> **Ministry Maxim**
>
> To shepherd under the Chief Shepherd is the greatest of all callings.

---

28 Spicq, 3:387.
29 Forbes, 169; Robertson, *Word Pictures*, 6:131.
30 Storms, 354.
31 Mounce, 439.

the decisive moment in which Christ will appear, bringing an end to the present age and ushering in the Kingdom of God in its fullness. The passive voice pictures the Christ as being acted upon, His Father, who alone knows the day and hour of Jesus' Return (Matt. 24:36; Mark 13:32), unveiling His Son to the world in all His glory.

Jesus is now "the Chief Shepherd" (τοῦ ἀρχιποίμενος) and will appear as such at that time. The imagery of a shepherd (ποιμήν) is found frequently throughout the Bible. The word is used literally for those who tend the flock, but it is also widely used in a metaphorical sense. National leaders were viewed as shepherds of the people (e.g., Jer. 23:1–4; Ezek. 34:1–10; Zech. 11:17), even when their faith was not genuine (Isa. 44:28). Moses and David were both shepherds in the literal (Moses: Exod. 3:1; David: 2 Sam. 7:8) and metaphorical senses of the word (Moses: Psa. 77:20; Isa. 63:11; David: 2 Sam. 5:2; Psa. 78:70–72). But ultimately Yahweh is the true "Shepherd" (e.g., Psalm 23:1; 28:9; 80:1; Isa. 40:11; Jer. 31:10). Through the prophets, God promised a new Shepherd who would care for His people with truth and justice (Ezek. 34:23; 37:24). Jesus fulfills these promises and is designated "the good shepherd" (John 10:11, 14), "the great Shepherd of the sheep" (Heb. 13:20), and, here, "the Chief Shepherd" (1 Peter 5:4). Peter has already reminded us that "you were continually straying like sheep, but now you have returned to the Shepherd and Guardian of your souls" (1 Peter 2:25). Jesus will ever serve as our Shepherd: "the Lamb in the center of the throne will be their shepherd, and will guide them to springs of the water of life; and God will wipe every tear from their eyes" (Rev. 7:17).

Here the title is unique (τοῦ ἀρχιποίμενος, "the Chief Shepherd"). The noun (ἀρχιποίμην) is a compound made up of ἀρχι (that which is first or highest in order, rank, or prominence) and ποιμήν ("shepherd"), the prefix implying superiority.[32] The definite article further marks Jesus as unique and in a class of His own. Jesus is "Chief" of all shepherds who came before Him or surrounded Him during His earthly life. He is "Chief Shepherd" as the fulfillment of the divine prophecies of a

---

32 Liddell and Scott, 6612, 6634.

coming, ultimate Shepherd. But Jesus is also "Chief Shepherd" over all the elders who "shepherd the flock of God" to which Peter now writes (1 Peter 5:1–3). Peter emphasizes that the elders (v.1), in their duty of shepherding the people of God (vv.2–3), are truly under-shepherds. They "must carry out their duty in union with Christ, the 'chief of pastors,' in conformity with his instructions and his example."[33]

The promise to faithful elders is that at the return of Christ, "you will receive the unfading crown of glory" (κομιεῖσθε τὸν ἀμαράντινον τῆς δόξης στέφανον). The verb (κομιεῖσθε), "you will receive") was already used by Peter when he spoke of "obtaining [κομιζόμενοι] as the outcome of your faith the salvation of your souls" (1 Peter 1:9). The verb is used ten times in the NT, most of the time in an eschatological context related to receiving or obtaining (Matt. 25:27; 2 Cor. 5:10; Eph. 6:8; Col. 3:25; Heb. 10:36; 1 Peter 5:4) as it does here. In the active voice, it simply means "to bring" (Luke 7:37), but in the middle voice, as we have it here, it means to "carry off," "get (for oneself)," or "receive."[34] Thus the idea of "personal appropriation and enjoyment" is involved.[35] It is used of receiving wages, a return on an investment (Matt. 25:27), and the fulfillment of a promise (Heb. 10:36; 11:39). It is also used of recompense or reward—either positively (Eph. 6:8; 1 Peter 5:4), negatively (Col. 3:25), or either (2 Cor. 5:10). Here, the future tense looks forward to that time "when the Chief Shepherd appears." The middle voice "indicates special interest or involvement of" the elders "in the activity or outcome."[36]

That received will be "the unfading crown of glory" (τὸν ἀμαράντινον τῆς δόξης στέφανον). The noun designated the laurel wreath placed upon the head of the victor in the athletic games of Greece. Athletes complete "to receive a perishable wreath," but believers serve to gain "an imperishable" one (1 Cor. 9:25). Thus, throughout the NT, the noun

---

33 Spicq, 1:209.
34 BDAG, 4337.3.
35 Stibbs, 80.
36 Forbes, 169.

is coupled with genitive nouns to describe the reward anticipated by faithful believers. We read of the "crown of exultation" (1 Thess. 2:19), the "crown of life" (James 1:12; Rev. 2:10), a "crown of righteousness" (2 Tim. 4:8), and a "crown of twelve stars" (Rev. 12:1). Jesus wore the crown of thorns (Matt. 27:29; Mark 15:17; John 19:2, 5), but is now "crowned with glory and honor" (Heb. 2:9) and is thus able to make His own wear the crown of victorious salvation.

In the attributive position, between the noun and its definite article (τὸν … στέφανον, "the … crown"), are two qualifiers. The genitive (τῆς δόξης, "of glory") is appositional or epexegetical—the crown consists of the glory which Jesus will bestow upon faithful elders (cf. "the glory that is to be revealed, v.1).[37] The definite article makes explicit that this is not some secondary, reflective "glory." It is God's own glory, now somehow by the miracle of His grace made to reside in and through our fully redeemed bodies (Phil. 3:21).

This "glory" is "unfading" (ἀμαράντινον). The adjective is found only here in the NT. The adjective means *"composed of amaranth,"* which is a flower that "never withers or fades, and when plucked off revives if moistened with water."[38] It thus serves as "a symbol of perpetuity and immortality."[39] It is derived from the kindred adjective found in 1:4: "to obtain an inheritance which is imperishable and undefiled and will not fade away [ἀμάραντον], reserved in heaven for you." All that is human and of human origin will fade and fail (1:24), but that which is of divine origin "will not fade away" (1:4).

---

37 Robertson, *Grammar*, 498.
38 Thayer, 30; cf. BDAG, 372.
39 Thayer, 30.

> **Digging Deeper:**
> 1. How does Peter's example in referring to himself (v.1) demonstrate how we as leaders in Christ's church should think about and present ourselves?
> 2. How is your struggle for the right mindset, motive, and manner of leadership different now than earlier in your service as an elder (vv.2b-3)? Which are you struggling with most at the present time?
> 3. How do you balance shepherding God's people (v.2) but also living actively as a sheep under the care of "the Chief Shepherd" (v.4)?

Verse 5 – "You younger men, likewise, be subject to *your* elders; and all of you, clothe yourselves with humility toward one another, for GOD IS OPPOSED TO THE PROUD, BUT GIVES GRACE TO THE HUMBLE."

Having addressed the elders (5:1–4), Peter turns first to address "young men" (v.5a) and then "all of you" (v.5bff). Having previously singled out citizens (2:13–17), servants (2:18–25), wives (3:1–6), and husbands (3:7) for instruction and exhortation appropriate to their station in life, Peter now addresses "You younger men" (νεώτεροι). The adjective is used here as a substantive and is comparative.[40] The adjective is masculine in form but most English translations do not limit the call to males ("men," though cf. NLT) but render it with something gender-neutral like "you who are younger" (ESV, NET, NIV, NRSV; cf. KJV, NKJV, YLT). But within the culture it would be more likely to be the young males that might chafe openly under the leadership of their "elders." Compared to "the elders" (v.1), these are "younger." The designation may have to do with a chronology of years but also their spiritual development, maturity, and character. The former is more likely to be the emphasis here because "all of you"

---

40 BDAG, 5065.3.b.β.

(πάντες) will soon broaden Peter's reference to taking in the whole of the congregation. Peter may again be following the lead of Ezekiel 9:6 (see comments above on 4:17 and 5:1), where both "elders" (πρεσβυτέροις) and the "younger" (νεώτεροι) are mentioned.[41]

The adverb "likewise" (Ὁμοίως) means something like "so," "similarly," "in the same way," or as here, "likewise."[42] Peter used it in 3:1 with reference to a wife's submission to her husband and in 3:7 with reference to the responsibilities of husbands. Thus, in each case, the matter of authority and submission is central to its use. The responsibility of submission to authority is laid upon each of God's people. Authority and submission are part of the warp and woof of human relationships as designed by God. The adverb tells us there is a comparison to be drawn. In 3:1, the comparison looked back to Christ's submission (2:21–25) but was probably secondarily linked to the instructions to "servants" (2:18–20), citizens (2:13–17), and "wives" (3:1–6). But to what does it look back here? The emphasis on submission in 2:13–3:5 forms a general backdrop for Peter's exhortation here, but specifically, it seems to look back to the accountability of elder-shepherds (5:1–3) to Christ, "the Chief Shepherd" (v.4). Just as the elders live submissively to "the Chief Shepherd," so the younger members of the flock are to live submissive to His under-shepherds, the elders.

The command "be subject to your elders" (ὑποτάγητε πρεσβυτέροις) represents the sixth and final time that Peter uses the verb in this letter, having called for submission by citizens (2:13), servants (2:18), wives (3:1, 5), as well as noting the submission of demonic spirits to the triumphant Christ (3:22). The verb is a compound built from ὑπό ("under") and τάσσω ("to order," "to appoint," "to arrange"). It carries the connotation of authority and the order that results from

> **Ministry Maxim**
>
> God's hand is opened to you to the degree you bow beneath it.

---

41 Dubis, 164; Schreiner, 236.

42 BDAG., 5296.

arranging life under it. The aorist imperative demands action be taken at once. The passive voice may point to their yielding to the authority of the elders, giving the sense of "be subjected to your elders." But there is nothing here to indicate a heavy-handed demand for submission "to your elders" (πρεσβυτέροις). The expression is more generic than that, simply "to elders" (YLT). There is nothing in the Greek text corresponding to "your." Some understand this as a general reference to the older members of each church fellowship rather than to the "elders" as office-bearers. Some cite 1 Timothy 5:1, where both key nouns are found together, as supporting evidence. It must be said, however, that the context there controls the idea of general age groups within the church (cf. v.2). Here Peter has clearly been using πρεσβύτερος in the technical sense of elders within the church (1 Peter 5:1–4). Paul does get around to using it in that sense in 1 Timothy 5, but not until verse 17. Here the context must control how we read the term and that points toward understanding it as a reference to the body of believing men who form the "elders" of the churches to whom Peter writes. Peter's words in verses 1–4 inform what he intends here.

We should stop to question why Peter feels the need to issue this brief but pointed demand for the "younger" to be submissive to the "elders." Given the overall message of the letter, one wonders if, under the pressures of suffering for the sake of Christ, the "younger" were at odds over how to respond to those who opposed them and made life difficult. Did they feel a more proactive, aggressive response was called for? Were there potential fracture lines within the congregations along the line of age demarcation? Peter did not fill out for us the background of this command. But church history and experience may tell us that stressors (of whatever kind) within the church often expose potential lines of fracture between age groups. It behooves the elders to lead well in a Christ-like way; it falls to the "younger" to submit to the shepherding oversight and leadership of their elders.

After his brief exhortation to the "younger," Peter turns to add (δὲ, "and") a fuller exhortation to "all of you" (πάντες). The exhortation continues through verse 12, effectively closing the letter, save for the final greetings (vv.13–14). By "all of you" (πάντες), Peter means the entire congregation: men, women, citizens (2:13–17), servants (2:18–20), wives (3:1–6), husbands (3:7), elders (5:1–4), and the "younger" (5:5). Peter used the adjective similarly in 3:8 where he turned the letter from addressing individual groups within the churches (2:13–3:7) to open a section where he addressed "all of you" (πάντες, v.8). Similarly, here, as he turns to close the letter, Peter addresses everyone who makes up the congregations to whom he writes. He thrusts the adjective forward to the head of the sentence to make it emphatic.

The universal exhortation is to "clothe yourselves" (ἐγκομβώσασθε). The verb is found only here in Biblical literature, though the concept is found elsewhere (cf. Gal. 3:27; Eph. 4:24; 6:11–17; Col. 3:10, 12; 1 Thess. 5:8). The verb is a compound ultimately derived from ἐν ("in") and κόμβος ("band," "knot").[43] It means to bind something to oneself.[44] The aorist imperative form demands action be taken at once and with urgency. The verb is a deponent, and thus the middle voice should be read as an active voice.[45] The word is akin to the word for "the large apron that workers or slaves fitted or fastened to their tunics to protect them."[46] Perhaps in Peter's mind, there is a remembrance from the Upper Room of Jesus' humility when He took a towel and "girded himself" and washed the Disciples' feet (John 13:4ff). Peter was singled out for the lesson of the towel and basin (vv.8–10), but all were called to follow Jesus' example of humble service (vv.14–15).

That with which one is to so "clothe" oneself is "humility toward one another" (ἀλλήλοις τὴν ταπεινοφροσύνην). Peter previously used the reciprocal pronoun (ἀλλήλοις, "toward one another") to call upon them to love "one another" (1:22), to practice hospitality to "one another" (4:9), and will use it again to call them to greet "one another" with a holy kiss (5:14). Presently, however, his concern is "humility" (τὴν ταπεινοφροσύνην). The noun is found seven times in the NT, the other six used by Paul (Acts

---

43   BDAG, 2194; Thayer, 166.

44   Liddell and Scott, 12353.

45   Abernathy, 173.

46   Spicq, 1:405.

20:19; Eph. 4:2; Phil. 2:3; Col. 2:18, 23; 3:12). It is a compound made up of ταπεινός ("humble") and φρήν ("heart," "mind"). The first root appears in the OT quotation Peter will introduce at the end of this verse. The compound does not occur in the LXX, but ταπεινός does, and frequently. The non-Christian world used ταπεινός negatively, but with the coming of Christ, the word was transformed. Jesus called out, "Take My yoke upon you and learn from Me, for I am gentle and humble [ταπεινός] in heart" (Matt. 11:29a). Robertson can thus say, "It is the crowning social grace and is Christian in origin and spirit."[47] The compound form is generally used in a positive sense, as it is here, to describe "a quality of voluntary submission and unselfishness *humility, self-effacement*."[48] But it can also be used in a pejorative sense, meaning "a misdirected submission in cultic behavior *self-abasement, (false) humility, self-mortification*" (cf. Col. 2:18, 23).[49] But clearly, Peter has the positive sense in mind. The presence of the definite article marks this as literally "*the* humility," perhaps underscoring that this is the preeminent characteristic of Christ in His first coming (cf. Phil. 2:5–8) and thus should be found in all His people.

Peter now provides the ground (ὅτι, "for") upon which he can issue this demand. In doing so, he cites Proverbs 3:34: "GOD IS OPPOSED TO THE PROUD, BUT GIVES GRACE TO THE HUMBLE" ([ὁ] θεὸς ὑπερηφάνοις ἀντιτάσσεται, ταπεινοῖς δὲ δίδωσιν χάριν). He quotes the LXX precisely, except that he replaces the LXX's κύριος with [ὁ] θεὸς ("GOD")[50], a change James also makes when he quotes the proverb (James 4:6).

In its original context, the proverb is the third of four reasons not to imitate or envy the violent (Prov. 3:31–35). The LXX has significantly nuanced the first line of the proverb from "Do not envy a man of violence" to "GOD IS OPPOSED TO THE PROUD." God responds to us based

---

47 Robertson, *Paul's Joy in Christ*, 120.
48 Friberg, 375.
49 Ibid.
50 There is a question about the definite article here. But James 4:6 includes it and it seems best to understand it as original here as well.

on our response to Him and others. Scoffing will draw not His indifference, but His scoffing at us (Prov. 1:22, 26). Even the strongest man who shakes his fist at heaven draws heaven's laughter and derision (Ps. 2:1–5). The Lord responds to us in kind (Psa. 18:25–26). So, whether in pride or in violence, God sets Himself up in opposition to the one who resists Him. The call here is to humility by all God's people before God and one another. God will array Himself in all His omnipotence against the one who willfully rises to assert his will over God's. Could there be greater folly?

Here "THE PROUD" (ὑπερηφάνοις) is a compound often said to be constructed from ὑπέρ ("over," "above") and φαίνω ("to bring to light") and to designate "one who shows himself above his fellows."[51] But others see the etymology of the word as obscure.[52] What is clear is that it designates the haughty, proud, and arrogant. It is found five times in the NT. Beyond its use in James 4:6, it appears in two of Paul's vice lists (Rom. 1:30; 2 Tim. 3:2) and, significantly, in Mary's Magnificat: "He has scattered those who were proud [ὑπερηφάνους] in the thoughts of their heart" (Luke 1:51). The cognate noun is found but once in the NT (Mark 7:22).

God "IS OPPOSED TO" (ἀντιτάσσεται) all such. The compound, comprised of ἀντί ("against") and τάσσω ("to arrange," "to put in order"), means "to set in array against."[53] The contrast between "be subject" (ὑποτάγητε) and "IS OPPOSED TO" (ἀντιτάσσεται) is stark. Both are built off the root τάσσω ("to arrange," "to put in order"), but the prefixes move in opposite directions: ὑπό ("under") and ἀντί ("against"). The former pictures one willingly submitting to God's authority, while the latter pictures God rising "against" the one who refuses to bow "under" His authority. The image of the latter comes into focus when we imagine a nation turning out its entire military against an enemy. God does so actively, presently, and continuously, as the present tense indicates. The middle voice depicts God as taking counsel with Himself in deciding to array all His omnipotent powers and all the resources at His disposal in a

---

51 Trench, 102; cf. Thayer, 641.
52 TDNT, 8:526; cf. Spicq, 3:391.
53 Friberg, 59.

pitched battle against the arrogant. Again, we must ask, could there be any greater folly than to resist the Lord?

The proverb makes its point by way of a contrasting (δὲ, "BUT") second line in which God "GIVES GRACE TO THE HUMBLE" (ταπεινοῖς... δίδωσιν χάριν). Both the object (ταπεινοῖς, "THE HUMBLE") and the divine response (δίδωσιν χάριν, "GIVES GRACE") stand emphatically over against those of the first line. The noun (ταπεινοῖς, "THE HUMBLE") is one of the roots of ταπεινοφροσύνην ("humility") used just above in this verse. There it stressed the inward thoughts or disposition that make for such "humility," while here, it designates the one who has embraced such a heart. For more on the word, see above our comments on the compound word. "THE PROUD" (ὑπερηφάνοις) shine the light upon themselves in order to exalt themselves over others; "THE HUMBLE" (ταπεινοῖς) does his work in the interior of his heart and mind to decide who and what he is and then relates to others appropriately out of that self-understanding.

To such God "GIVES GRACE" (δίδωσιν χάριν). This is God's continuous, ongoing, abiding posture toward the humble, as the present tense underscores. Peter's intention in this letter has been to set out "the true grace of God" (5:12). Here, he tells us that the "God of all grace" (5:10) causes His grace to overflow (1:2) to His people, amid and even through suffering (2:19–20), as we await the final delivery of the fullness of grace at Jesus' return (1:13). We position ourselves to receive this ministry of grace through the practice of active humility.

The difference is incalculable between "IS OPPOSED" (ἀντιτάσσεται) and "GIVES" (δίδωσιν), between "THE PROUD" (ὑπερηφάνοις) and "THE HUMBLE" (ταπεινοῖς), and between "GRACE" (χάριν) and facing the omnipotence of God arrayed in infinite might against you. When one arranges one's life in submission to God, the floodgates of grace are opened from the throne, and all we require in our time of need is supplied (Heb. 4:16). When one refuses to do so, God Himself arrays Himself in active opposition against everything the rebellious one attempts. The "mighty hand of God" (v.6) will be arranged in opposition to you or opened to supply you. It just depends on how you choose to posture yourself in relation to it.

> **Digging Deeper:**
> 1. How have you chafed under the leadership of those older than you? What was your complaint? How did you practice (or fail to practice) submission in those situations?
> 2. Describe how in the past week you have demonstrated active humility toward another.

Verse 6 – "Therefore humble yourselves under the mighty hand of God, that He may exalt you at the proper time,"

Peter draws a logical deduction (οὖν, "Therefore") from his citation of Proverbs 3:34 (in v.5). Given the options of living under God's open, giving hand or facing the opposing force of His omnipotence (v.5), the only reasonable choice is to "humble yourselves" (Ταπεινώθητε). The verb is cognate to the noun just used in verse 5 (ταπεινοῖς, "the humble"). Here the aorist imperative demands action be taken at once. Given the options, do whatever is necessary to become one of "the humble." When James quoted Psalm 3:34 (James 4:6), he immediately followed it with the command "Submit therefore to God" (ὑποτάγητε οὖν τῷ θεῷ, v.7), but followed it up with precisely the same command we have here (ταπεινώθητε, "humble yourselves"). Jesus humbled Himself on our behalf (Phil. 2:8); in response, we humble ourselves before Him.

> **Ministry Maxim**
>
> The divine hand under which you bow is the delivering hand which will bless you.

The passive voice of the verb depicts the humbling coming at the will of another: "allow yourselves to be humbled."[54] Be humbled before God in His might, glory, and grace. "Peter was not calling for passive resignation or a forced humiliation, but for a voluntary acceptance of the

---

54 Raymer, 2:856; Wallace, 441.

humiliating circumstances that befell the readers under God's permissive will."[55] Thus, Peter demands "not just passive resignation but active co-operation" with God's will.[56] Peter specifies it as humbling ourselves "under the mighty hand of God" (ὑπὸ τὴν κραταιὰν χεῖρα τοῦ θεοῦ). The expression is familiar in the OT, especially in conjunction with God's deliverance of Israel from Egypt (e.g., Exod. 3:19; 32:11; Deut. 3:24; 1 Kings 8:42; Ezek. 20:33, 34; Dan. 9:15).

The demand that the younger "be subject" to the elders (v.5) used a compound verb built from ὑπό ("under") and τάσσω ("to order," "to appoint," "to arrange"). Now the preposition prefixed is used independently (ὑπὸ, "under"). We must subject ourselves "under" God and "under" those authorities He places over us in life, whether in the nation where we reside (1 Peter 2:13–17), the marriage in which we live (3:1–7), or the church in which we serve and worship (5:1–5).

Peter speaks of the will (2:15; 3:17; 4:19), the patience (3:20), the Spirit (4:14), the household (4:17), the gospel (4:17), the flock (5:2), and the grace "of God" (τοῦ θεοῦ; 5:12). Jesus, we are told, "is at the right hand of God" (3:22). Here too it is "the...hand" (τὴν...χεῖρα) of God that is in view. The "hand" is the most active part of the body and the one by which most things are accomplished. It thus figuratively speaks of action and often is associated with power.[57] The "hand of God" designates "the embodiment of divine power."[58] Here it is designated as "mighty" (κραταιὰν). The adjective is used only here in the NT. The cognate noun (κράτος), however, is found twelve times. Peter uses the noun in two doxologies, referring to God's "dominion" (1 Peter 4:11; 5:11). Almost half of its usages are found in combination with δόξα ("glory"; Col. 1:11; 1 Peter 4:11; Jude 25; Rev. 1:6; 5:13). The noun is used in the NT only of God's power (except in Heb. 2:14). It points to "the possession of force

---

55 Hiebert, 311.

56 Stibbs, 170.

57 NIDNTTE, 4:644.

58 Ibid., 4:645.

or strength that affords supremacy or control"[59] or, as Robertson puts it, "perfect strength."[60] It is "the inherent strength which displays itself in the rule over others."[61] Here "the hand of God" is seen operating either against the proud or on behalf of the humble.

There is a purpose (ἵνα and aorist subjunctive, "that") behind the humility which Peter demands. It is that "He may exalt you at the proper time" (ὑμᾶς ὑψώσῃ ἐν καιρῷ). The verb (ὑψώσῃ, "He may exalt") is used of Jesus, both on the cross (John 3:14; 8:28; 12:32, 34) and in His ascension (Acts 2:33; 5:31). It was with an "uplifted [ὕψωσεν] arm" that God brought the people out of Egypt (Acts 13:17).

Peter promises that "at the proper time" (ἐν καιρῷ), lifting will follow humbling. The phrase is literally and simply "in time." The precise expression is also used in the NT to point to the time for eating (Matt. 24:45; Luke 12:42), the time of one's temptation (Luke 8:13), and the final harvest as directed by the Lord (Matt. 13:30). The only other NT occurrence of the phrase is by Peter when he said Christ's people are being preserved "for a salvation ready to be revealed in the last time [ἐν καιρῷ ἐσχάτῳ]" (1 Peter 1:5). But here it has no qualifying adjective. Because of this ambiguity, we should read the aorist tense of the verb as picturing the event of the uplifting without limiting it to the resurrection and glorification that comes at Jesus' Return, although that will be the final, climactic expression of this grace. But also, throughout life, where His people humble themselves under God's hand, He moves to lift them up.

The hope is accentuated by the placement of the plural personal pronoun (ὑμᾶς, "you") before the verb, thus emphasizing it and designating it as true of all God's people and yet deeply personal.

Peter applies to his readers what he had heard from Jesus: "Whoever exalts [ὑψώσει] himself shall be humbled; and whoever humbles himself shall be exalted [ὑψωθήσεται]" (Matt. 23:12; cf. Luke 14:11; 18:14). Time and again God has proven His ability and willingness to enforce

---

59 Friberg, 236.

60 Robertson, 4:476.

61 Rienecker, 566.

this principle: "He has done mighty deeds with His arm; He has scattered those who were proud in the thoughts of their heart. He has brought down rulers from their thrones, And has exalted [ὕψωσεν] those who were humble" (Luke 1:51–52).

When you bow "under" (ὑπὸ) God's hand, He uses it to "exalt" (ὑψώσῃ) you in the grace of His favor and the wisdom of His timing. With God, the way up is always down.

Verse 7 – "casting all your anxiety on Him, because He cares for you."

Many English translations begin a new sentence with verse 7 (e.g., NIV, NLT, NRSV, RSV), but in the Greek text, the sentence continues from verse 6. Those who begin a new sentence with verse 7 generally render the participle as an imperative. But the participial phrase qualifies the command to "humble yourselves" (Ταπεινώθητε) under God's hand (v.6). The verb (ἐπιρίψαντες, "casting") is used elsewhere in the NT only in Luke 19:35, where Jesus' disciples "threw [ἐπιρίψαντες] their coats on the colt and put Jesus on it." It is a compound made up of ἐπί ("upon") and ῥίπτω ("to cast out/off/forth").[62] The participial form expresses the means by which one humbles oneself under God's mighty hand (v.6).[63] "Humbling oneself is not a negative act of self-denial per se, but a positive one of active dependence on God for help."[64]

That which is cast is one's "anxiety" (τὴν μέριμναν). The noun is used only five other times in the NT, three of which appear in the parallel accounts of Jesus' parable of the soils. The seed that falls upon the rocky soil finds that the "worry [μέριμνα] of the world" chokes it out and renders it "unfruitful" (Matt. 13:22; cf. Mark 4:19; Luke 8:14). Jesus used it

---

62 Liddell and Scott, 16898, 38310.

63 Forbes, 175; Grudem, 202; Hiebert, 313; NET Bible; Storms, 356; Wallace, 630. Others read the participle as expressing attendant circumstances (Dubis, 167; Jobes, 313) or result (Forbes, 176).

64 Wallace, 630.

to warn, "Be on guard, so that your hearts will not be weighted down with ... the worries [μερίμναις] of life, and that day will not come on you suddenly like a trap" (Luke 21:34). The "anxiety" here is not simply a generalized concept, but specific, being designated so by the presence of the definite article. Each one bears a unique, personal, singular burden. "The heart knows its own bitterness, And a stranger does not share its joy" (Prov. 14:10). Each one must roll their anxiety upon the Lord. Indeed, the anxiety is deeply personal (ὑμῶν, "your"). For Peter's original readers, this included worries and fears arising from persecution.

> **Ministry Maxim**
>
> God's care invites our casting so He can carry our worries.

We are to be entire in our commitment of these things to the Lord, for it is to be "all" (πᾶσαν) of our anxiety. Only when "all" our anxiety is transferred to Jesus does the care of Jesus begin to become palpable. The entire phrase πᾶσαν τὴν μέριμναν ὑμῶν ("all your anxiety") is made emphatic by being placed forward before the participle.[65]

Peter may well call upon Psalm 55:22 for the thought: "Cast your burden upon the LORD and He will sustain you; He will never allow the righteous to be shaken" (54:23, LXX). There the psalmist is oppressed by a multitude of enemies, facing "the pressure of the wicked" (v.3). But even worse is that his "familiar friend" (v.13) has joined them. The distress is eating him up, even killing him (vv.4–5).

The enemy "has put forth his hands against" the psalmist (v.20), but God's servant resides under "the mighty hand of God" (1 Peter 5:6). His enemies "bring down trouble upon" him (v.3). He wishes for wings that he might "fly away" (v.6). But God's mighty hand will "exalt" (1 Peter 5:6) the one who trusts in Him.

Peter's readers faced growing resistance from the Roman government and culture. They too were distressed and must heed the psalmist's counsel. Like the psalmist, they too must cast their anxiety upon the Lord and

---

65 Forbes, 175; Hiebert, 313.

rest under God's mighty hand, waiting for that moment when He will lift him up.

Peter is probably also reflecting and applying what He heard Jesus teach (Matt. 6:25–34 and Luke 12:24–31).

Peter gives a reason (ὅτι, "because") why we should do so. It is not primarily to avoid being crushed by "the mighty hand of God" but because "he cares for you" (αὐτῷ μέλει περὶ ὑμῶν). The phrase is more literally, "to him a care for you." The verb μέλω ("he cares") means to be the object of someone's care.[66] The present tense stresses God's continual concern for His child. The preposition (περὶ, "for") was just met as the prefix of the compound verb ἐπιρίψαντες ("casting"), doubling the emphasis. You are to cast your care "upon" (περὶ, KJV, NASB, NKJV, YLT) God because His care rests "upon" (is "for") you.

> **Digging Deeper:**
> 1. How have you experienced God's "mighty hand" in your life (v.6a)? How have you humbled yourself beneath it?
> 2. Describe how God has reversed the direction and circumstances of your life as you have humbled yourself before Him (v.6b).
> 3. How does anxiety work directly against one's experience of the love of God? (v.7)

Verse 8 – "Be of sober *spirit*, be on the alert. Your adversary, the devil, prowls around like a roaring lion, seeking someone to devour."

Having addressed his readers' orientation and responsibilities toward God (v.7), Peter now addresses their orientation to the opposing spiritual world (vv.8–9). In verse 8, he issues two imperatives that are followed by an

---

66 Liddell-Scott, 27720.

explanation. In verse 9, he will follow up with another imperative and explanation.

The first imperative is "Be of sober spirit" (Νήψατε). This is now the third time Peter has made this call (1 Peter 1:13; 4:7). Half of all the verb's NT appearances are by Peter's pen (cf. 1 Thess. 5:6, 8; 2 Tim. 4:8). The word, used literally, could describe being free from intoxicants. But all its NT usages are figurative (and so here, of "sober *spirit*"). Metaphorically, it means to "be free fr[om] every form of mental and spiritual 'drunkenness', fr[om] excess, passion, rashness, confusion, etc." and thus to be "be well-balanced" and "self-controlled."[67] The aorist imperative demands immediate and urgent action be undertaken. The aorist may be considered ingressive, calling his readers to begin the action for which he calls. Peter may be recalling Jesus' words to him in the Garden: "Keep watching and praying that you may not come into temptation; the spirit is willing, but the flesh is weak" (Mark 14:38; cf. Luke 21:36).

The second imperative demands Peter's readers "be on the alert" (γρηγορήσατε). A literal use of the verb calls for one to be or stay awake. Figuratively, as here, it means to be on the alert or to be watchful. Along this line, we might say, "Keep your eyes open!"[68] Again, the aorist imperative demands urgent, immediate action and is ingressive in import. They are to waste no time and give all effort in establishing a pattern of sober-mindedness and alertness regarding the opposing spiritual world in which they exist. In the Gospels, it is used either in eschatological warning to "be alert" for the coming of Christ (Matt. 24:42, 43; 25:13; Mark 13:34, 35, 37; Luke 12:37) or, as with the previous verb, in Christ's call to the disciples to pray with Him in the Garden (Matt. 26:38, 40, 41; Mark 14:34, 37, 38). Paul uses it regarding the vigilance of church leadership in watching over the flock under their charge (Acts 20:31), as a call to

> **Ministry Maxim**
>
> Only a fool ignores evil that is personal, active, and destructive.

---

67 BDAG, 5098.

68 Ibid., 1689.2.

alertness in the last days (1 Thess. 5:6, 10), and more generally in a call to all believers (1 Cor. 16:13).

The same two verbs appear together in 1 Thessalonians 5:6: "so then let us not sleep as others do, but let us be alert [γρηγορῶμεν] and sober [νήοωμεν]." Restfulness (v.7b) does not relieve us of the demands of vigilance (v.8a). Nor does vigorous vigilance (v.8a) negate the peaceful rest of the child of God (v.7a).

The reason[69] for Peter insisting on these things is we have an "adversary" (ὁ ἀντίδικος). The word is a compound made up of ἀντί ("against") and δίκη ("right"/"justice"). In its other NT usages, it designates a legal opponent at court (Matt. 5:25 [2x]; Luke 12:58; 18:3). But this technical meaning slowly generalized until it could designate an opponent outside the realm of the legal word, as it does here. The definite article marks this one as the believers' paramount "adversary." His antipathy is deeply personal (ὑμῶν, "Your").

In apposition to "adversary" (ὁ ἀντίδικος) is "the devil" (διάβολος). Technically an adjective, in the NT, the word often functions as a noun. In the NT, it is generally accompanied by the definite article, but here it is anarthrous. But the absence of the article should not dissuade us from reading it as definite, for it is used here as a title for our "adversary."[70] Furthermore, given that it stands in apposition to a noun with the definite article, this too should be read as definite.[71] As an adjective, it means slanderous (e.g., 1 Tim. 3:11; 2 Tim. 3:3; Titus 2:3), but as a substantive, as it is here, it designates a slanderer. In the LXX, it normally translates the Hebrew שָׂטָן ("Satan"), which similarly designates the evil one as the slanderer of God's people.[72] "The work of the adversary always implies an

---

69 Some manuscripts contain ὅτι ("because") at this point of transition between the two imperatives and the explanatory words that follow in the rest of verse 8. It is likely that a scribe felt the need to smooth what seemed an abrupt bit of grammar. The shorter text (without ὅτι) is unadorned and makes the same point more powerfully for its abruptness.

70 Wallace, 249; Robertson, *Grammar*, 794–795.

71 Dubis, 168.

72 BDAG, 1831.2; NIDNTTE, 4:265.

attempt on the part of the διάβολος to separate God and man."[73] The one "who is called the devil and Satan" is also designated "the accuser of our brethren" (Rev. 12:9, 10). The OT account of the High Priest Joshua standing before the Lord with "Satan [ὁ διάβολος] standing at his right hand to accuse him" (Zech. 3:1) illustrates the evil one's role. Similarly, the strategy of the evil one before God regarding Job illustrates his basic mode of operation (Job 1–2).

Thank God "we have an Advocate" at the Father's right hand (1 John 2:1) who lives forever (Heb. 7:25) to counter the evil one's every accusation and to confirm that "there is now no condemnation for those who are in Christ Jesus" (Rom. 8:1)!

Our enemy "prowls around" (περιπατεῖ), says Peter. This is the common verb meaning "to walk." The present tense depicts the evil one's regular, constant, and persistent pursuit of bringing down the children of God. Significantly, the compounded form of the verb, ἐμπεριπατέω ("walk about"), is used of the devil in Job 1:7 and 2:2.[74]

His prowling is "like a roaring lion" (ὡς λέων ὠρυόμενος). The phrase precedes the verb, giving it extra emphasis. The use of ὡς signals a coming descriptor of the verb's action. The noun λέων ("lion") casts him as ferocious, dangerous, and terrifying. No fewer than six different words are used in the OT to describe this beast. It is used frequently in the OT and depicts a fearsome, overwhelming terror. Standing out is the example of Daniel in the lions' den (Dan. 6; Heb. 11:33). Paul's persecutors are pictured as such (2 Tim. 4:17). Here it is his "roaring" (ὠρυόμενος) that stands out. The verb is found only here in the NT, though it is more frequent in the LXX (e.g., Judg. 14:5; Psa. 104:21 [103:21, LXX]; Zeph. 3:3). In fact, Peter's imagery may rest upon that of Psalm 22:13 (21:14, LXX): "They open wide their mouth at me, As a ravening and a roaring lion." The participial form depicts the "roaring" as characteristic of the devil as "a lion." The present tense underscores this as an ongoing, even basic tactic of the evil one.

---

73 TDNT, 2:73.

74 Dubis, 169.

In the natural world, a lion's roar is used to announce his presence and to warn all contenders of his might. Yet it is used not only to intimidate but also to paralyze its prey. So too, the evil one uses intimidation and fear as one weapon in his arsenal of tactics. We might say that his basic strategy is that of lying (John 8:44). He also uses temptation (Matt. 4:3; 1 Thess. 3:5). If these fail, he turns to fear and intimidation.

Within the context of the letter, we should probably understand the roaring of the evil one as represented in the threats of persecution that were currently being unleashed upon the readers of Peter's letter. In this, Peter reminds his readers that while they face terrifying earthly realities, the hand behind them is not of this world and is unspeakably evil. "Put on the full armor of God, so that you will be able to stand firm against the schemes of the devil. For our struggle is not against flesh and blood, but against the rulers, against the powers, against the world forces of this darkness, against the spiritual forces of wickedness in the heavenly places" (Eph. 6:11–12).

We do well to note that elsewhere Jesus is designated "the Lion that is from the tribe of Judah" (Rev. 5:5). His is the right to rule (cf. Gen. 49:9–10), not only the kingdom of Judah, but all things (Matt. 28:18). The devil is a usurper and a want-to-be. His roar is fearsome, but in all things and at all times, he answers to the Lion who rules all things. When even an angel of God "cried out with a loud voice, as when a lion roars" (Rev. 10:3), he trembled.

The evil one goes about "seeking someone to devour" (ζητῶν [τινα] καταπιεῖν). There is a textual question about the presence and form of τινα ("someone"). It is absent in a few manuscripts. Other manuscripts have the interrogative pronoun τίνα ("whom"). Because the earliest manuscripts lack accent points, the issue is complicated further. Given the evidence, it seems likely some form, accented or unaccented, should be considered original. The meaning is changed little if we opt for τινα ("someone") or τίνα ("whom"). There is also variance between subjunctive καταπίῃ and the infinitive καταπιεῖν. In the end, any answer is tentative, but it seems the evidence goes with τινα καταπιεῖν ("someone to devour").[75]

---

75 Forbes, 177; NET Bible.

The participle (ζητῶν, "seeking") describes the manner of the evil one as he goes about his malevolent work.[76] Peter already used the verb of the one who loves life, commanding him to "seek" (ζητησάτω) peace, turning away from evil (1 Peter 3:11). The evil one works for death, and instead of seeking peace, he seeks "to devour" (καταπιεῖν) anyone in his path. The infinitive denotes the purpose of the devil's seeking.[77] The verb is a graphic one. The compound is made up of κατὰ ("down") and πίνω ("to drink"). It is the verb used to describe Jonah being swallowed whole by the great fish (Jonah 2:1; 1:17 English). It is used of the earth swallowing up water (Rev. 12:16), of the waters of the Red Sea overwhelming the Egyptians (Heb. 11:29), and of one swallowing a camel (Matt. 23:24). "It depicts the total destruction of the victim."[78] Spiritually, death is "swallowed up" in the victory of the risen Christ (1 Cor. 15:54), and at His return, our mortal bodies will be "swallowed up" by life (2 Cor. 5:4). The evil one, ever the anti-Christ (1 John 2:18, 22; 2 John 7), in a dark parody of Christ's overwhelming victory, wants to swallow down to death and damnation all whom he is able. The present tense of "seeking" underscores the ceaseless pursuit of the evil one, while the aorist of "devour" pictures the singular event of the destruction he pursues.

Jesus warned Peter, "Satan has demanded permission to sift you like wheat" (Luke 22:31). Peter now warns all within the reach of his pen that the same enemy also desires their destruction. After His warning, Jesus set Peter's heart at rest: "but I have prayed for you" (v.32). Gratefully, "The Lord who prayed for Peter prays for us" (Rom. 8:34; Heb. 7:25; 1 John 2:1–2).[79]

---

76 Dubis, 169.
77 Ibid.
78 Hiebert, 315.
79 Clowney, 215.

Verse 9 – "But resist him, firm in *your* faith, knowing that the same experiences of suffering are being accomplished by your brethren who are in the world."

Peter continues addressing his readers' stance toward the evil one at work (vv.8–9). The use of the relative pronoun (ᾧ, "him") keeps the focus on the "devil," our "adversary" (v.8). To the two aorist imperatives of verse 8, Peter now adds a third: "resist" (ἀντίστητε). As with the previous two imperatives, the aorist calls for urgent action and is ingressive in that it demands they begin what must become the pattern of their lives. The verb is a compound made up of ἀντί ("against") and ἵστημι ("to stand"). James uses the same word in the same sense: "Resist [ἀντίστητε] the devil and he will flee from you" (James 4:7). It could be used both of the resistance of the evil one and his forces against the gospel and its workers as well as the resistance of those workers against his efforts. So Paul uses it of demonically inspired human opposition to his ministry (2 Tim. 3:8 [2x]; cf. "escape from the snare of the devil, having been held captive by him to do his will," 2:26; cf. also 4:15). Where Peter and James command God's people to "resist," Paul commanded them to "stand," each time using the uncompounded form ἵστημι (Eph. 6:11, 13, 14). He commands: "Take up the full armor of God, so that you will be able to resist [ἀντιστῆναι] in the evil day, and having done everything, to stand firm" (Eph. 6:13). If you do not stand *against* (ἀνθίστημι) the evil one you will not stand (ἵστημι) at all.

Let us not lose sight of the point that there is a personal (ᾧ, "him") enemy of God's people. It is no vague, impersonal force that resists God and His people and which they must resist in return. We face a personal being, one evil in the highest degree. His wickedness is beyond human imagination. He is a murderer and a liar (John 8:44). He is a thief and a destroyer (10:10). He deals in death (Heb. 2:14–15). Destruction is all that satisfies him. Hosts of wicked minions serve him and carry out his will (Eph. 1:21; 6:12; Col. 2:15). He rules a dark kingdom that is the opposite of all that is good and righteous and life-giving (Col. 1:13). Evil is never just a matter of detached ethical and moral questions. Evil is rooted in a personal being, and thus the battle against evil will always be deeply personal.

Peter qualifies the command with two clauses. The first is verbless, but we should probably mentally provide a participle like ὄντες ("being"). If this is the correct assumption, the clause would be understood as identifying how we are to "resist" the devil. This happens by being "firm in the faith" (στερεοὶ τῇ πίστει). The adjective (στερεοὶ, "firm") is used only four times in the NT. It is used of the "solid food" (Heb. 5:12, 14) of God's Word that gives life, grows, and sustains God's people. It is used of the mind and knowledge which God possesses regarding His people (2 Tim. 2:19). The word pertains "to being solid or firm in contrast with that which is soft or liquid."[80]

"Forever, O LORD, Your word is settled in heaven" (Psa. 119:89). "THE WORD OF THE LORD ENDURES FOREVER" (1 Peter 1:25). "Heaven and earth will pass away, but My words will not pass away" (Matt. 24:35). "The firm [στερεὸς] foundation of God stands" (2 Tim. 2:19). This is what Peter means by "faith" (τῇ πίστει). The definite article makes specific that it is not faithfulness in general nor a subjective spirit of trust that is needed. It is "the faith which was once for all handed down to the saints" (Jude 3) by Jesus, through the Holy Spirit working in the Apostles and their designates to pen the words of the NT. Our trust is required, but Peter at this moment is calling not so much for the personal, subjective side of trust (which is addressed in the adjective στερεοὶ, "firm") as he is identifying the one solid, enduring foundation upon which we must plant our feet and from which we must never be moved. The dative case designates the locus of our restful trust ("*in* the faith," KJV, NIV, NKJV, YLT, emphasis added).

> **Ministry Maxim**
>
> Victory comes not by running from, but resistance to the devil.

Let our trust in the Word of God match its own enduring, immovable, inviolable nature. Let our faith rest solidly and enduringly upon the foundation of God's knowledge of us and of the demands His holy nature presses upon us. We have as our example Jesus' resistance of the devil in

---

80 Louw-Nida, 79.7.

the wilderness (Matt. 4:1–11; Luke 4:1–13). Thus we "Resist the devil." And the promise is that when we do, "he will flee from you" (James 4:7). Just as "the devil … departed from" Jesus (Luke 4:13, NASB).

The second clause to qualify the command to "resist" does not tell us how to fulfill the command but identifies that which will be necessary in order to do so. It involves "knowing" (εἰδότες) something about the battle we are in. Peter uses οἶδα twice as often (1 Peter 1:18; 5:9; 2 Peter 1:12, 14; 2:9) as γινώσκω (2 Peter 1:20; 3:3). There is debate as to any difference in meaning between οἶδα and γινώσκω. The two can be used interchangeably without significant variance in meaning, but at times οἶδα emphasizes cognitive knowledge which "is present to the mind," while γινώσκω "denotes … a knowledge grounded in personal experience."[81] The participle is best understood as indicating what causes one to be able to successfully "resist" the devil ("because you know," NET, NIV; "for," NRSV).[82]

That knowledge that helps one to find success in the spiritual battle manifested in earthly persecution is "that the same experiences of suffering are being accomplished by your brethren who are in the world" (τὰ αὐτὰ τῶν παθημάτων τῇ ἐν [τῷ] κόσμῳ ὑμῶν ἀδελφότητι ἐπιτελεῖσθαι). By "the same experiences of suffering" (τὰ αὐτὰ τῶν παθημάτων; lit., "the things of the sufferings"), Peter probably does not demand exact correspondence. In one place, persecution takes the form of ridicule and shame. In another, perhaps legal action in the courts, in yet another physical violence, and in yet another location, it may take a different form yet. The precise details may differ, but they alike are "suffering" (τῶν παθημάτων). While the details may differ, the details matter. The panoply of sufferings faced by Jesus' followers is known in their specifics. The use of definite articles with both the pronoun and noun serve to emphasize the particular details that Peter's readers were experiencing. The word group is central to Peter's letter (πάθημα, 1 Peter 1:11; 4:13; 5:1, 9; πάσχω, 2:19, 20, 21, 23; 3:14, 17, 18; 4:1 [2x], 15, 19; 5:10).

---

81 Thayer, 118.
82 Forbes, 178.

Whatever Peter's readers are facing, so are their "brethren" (τῇ ... ἀδελφότητι). The noun is used only here and in 2:17 in the NT. It is a collective noun, and as such designates in a concrete sense "a group of people united for a common purpose."[83] As we saw earlier, the expression "band of brothers" might capture the sense.[84] The term is not gender-specific to males but includes believers of both sexes. The definite article makes specific "the brotherhood" to which Peter refers—believers everywhere, different in location and circumstances, but one through faith in Jesus Christ and the suffering it brings. Though he does not employ the word "church" anywhere in this letter, Peter here points to the same reality under a different name.

Who are these "brethren"? The noun is qualified in two ways, both of which are in the attributive position between the noun and its article. They are "in the world" (ἐν [τῷ] κόσμῳ). Paul and John use the word of the evil system set up against God and His people (e.g., Eph. 2:2; 1 John 2:15–17), but Peter uses it of this created order (1 Peter 1:20; 5:9) and even of a person's adorning of their body (3:3). The acceptance or rejection of the definite article (τῷ) as original does not alter the intent or meaning of Peter's words. God's people are "in" (ἐν) the world. Because the devil is still "the god of this world" (2 Cor. 4:4; cf. John 12:31; 16:11) and "the whole world lies in the power of the evil one" (1 John 5:19) this means God's people are momentarily still within reach of his tether.

They are "your" (ὑμῶν) brothers and sisters. Peter considers his readers within the circle of the "brethren." Through faith in Jesus Christ, they have become a part of "THE PEOPLE OF GOD" (2:10). God's people are their "family." Peter is making the point Paul also made in a larger context: "No temptation has overtaken you but such as is common to man" (1 Cor. 10:13a).

Located both in "the world" and within the circle of the "brethren," Peter's readers have a share in the suffering not only that they face but which their brothers and sisters in Christ endure in every place where they exist.

---

83 Friberg, 34.

84 Rienecker, 753.

These sufferings "are being accomplished" (ἐπιτελεῖσθαι) by these brothers and sisters. It is a compound verb comprised of ἐπί ("on"/"upon") and τελέω ("to bring to an end," "to complete," "to finish"). It means "*to bring to an end, accomplish, perfect, execute, complete.*"[85]

It is used to complete an act of giving (Rom. 15:28; 2 Cor. 8:6, 11 [2x]), sanctification (2 Cor. 7:1; Gal. 3:3), God's work of salvation (Phil. 1:6), the construction of the Tabernacle (Heb. 8:5) and the performance of priestly duties (9:6). God has a specific end in mind when He allows His people to suffer. We do not often understand those purposes or when that end will have been reached, but knowing our God is sovereign, we know such purposes exist, and it is our duty to see them "accomplished."

Paul could tell the Colossians, "Now I rejoice in my sufferings for your sake, and in my flesh I do my share on behalf of His body, which is the church, in filling up what is lacking in Christ's afflictions" (Col. 1:24). No one, not even an apostle, can add anything to the redemptive perfection of Jesus' sacrifice. Jesus' sufferings on our behalf are not "lacking" in anything to secure us to God and to bring us into His grace and glorification in His presence. But Paul could speak missionally and programmatically of something "lacking in Christ's afflictions." Paul knew intimately the connection between Christ, the living Head, and His people, the Church. When, before conversion, he persecuted Christ's followers, Jesus stopped him in his tracks and asked, "why are you persecuting Me?" (Acts 9:4). After conversion, God showed Paul that while the securing of salvation can never be improved, augmented, supplemented, or made more complete, the advance of the gospel not only will involve suffering but only advances through Christ's suffering people. Only willing, joyous, suffering people can tell convincingly of a Savior who suffered unto victory. So, writing to the Colossians from a prison cell, Paul could rejoice in his sufferings, knowing that Christ was using them to advance the very gospel he was called to proclaim.

There are things to be "accomplished" through the suffering you and the people of God with whom you are associated face. The present tense

---

85 Thayer, 244.

of the verb stresses that not a moment of suffering goes by but what it is bringing to pass God's sovereignly appointed work. The form should be read as a passive voice. It depicts God as accomplishing this work in and through His children as they endure suffering for His sake.

In these exhortations and challenges, "Peter is obviously here seeking to do what the Lord told him to do after his own recovery from failure, namely, to strengthen his brethren" (Luke 22:31–32).[86]

> **Digging Deeper:**
> 1. How may we remain "sober" and "alert" to the evil one and his ways without getting out of balance (v.8)?
> 2. In what way have you faced the devil's hatred and destructive wrath (v.8)?
> 3. What can we do to make people alert to the devil and his efforts without either driving them away or overly frightening them (v.8)?
> 4. List practical, Biblical ways that believers can "resist" the devil and his forces (v.9). How might you train others in these things?

Verse 10 – "After you have suffered for a little while, the God of all grace, who called you to His eternal glory in Christ, will Himself perfect, confirm, strengthen *and* establish you."

As Peter begins a new sentence, he uses δὲ to make the transition. The NASU does not translate δὲ (but cf. NASB and most English translations, "And"; "But," CEV, KJV, NKJV). Having underscored the reality of suffering among all God's people (v.9b), Peter now, by way of a promise, assures his readers of God's final victory worked out in their lives (v.10). Whereas the focus of verse 8 and 9 was the devil, in verses 10 and 11 it returns to rest upon "the God" (Ὁ … θεὸς) of all grace. The final victory (vv.10–11) is contrasted with the present spiritual warfare (vv.8–9).

---

86 Stibbs, 172.

God's final grace (vv.10–11) stands over against the devil's present harassment (vv.8–9). And thus, Peter brings the main body of his letter to a close on a high note of promise (v.10) and praise (v.11), gathering up and completing thoughts with which he began the letter and has developed throughout.

The main thrust of this sentence is that "the God of all grace" (Ὁ … θεὸς πάσης χάριτος), despite their suffering, will keep His promise to completely save His people. How are we to understand the genitive χάριτος ("of… grace")? Certainly, grace is of the very nature of God. And all grace derives from and is delivered by God through Jesus Christ. Grace has been a theme of Peter's letter (1 Peter 1:2, 10, 13; 2:19, 20; 3:7; 4:10; 5:5, 10, 12). From the grace Peter wishes for his readers presently (1:2) to the full and final expression of grace at Jesus' return (1:13), all God does He does in grace. He gifts and empowers His people that they all might know "the manifold grace of God" (4:10). Wherever God encounters humility, He pours out grace (5:5). Peter's entire letter is an exposition of "the true grace of God" (5:12).

But God is not simply the "God of… grace," but the God of "all" (πάσης) grace. He "has blessed us with every spiritual blessing in the heavenly places in Christ" (Eph. 1:3). God is the reservoir of all grace. There is no grace outside of Him. All grace resides in and arises from God's own nature. It is His good pleasure to extend this grace to His people. "God is able to make all grace abound to you, so that always having all sufficiency in everything, you may have an abundance for every good deed" (2 Cor. 9:8). And He "gives to all generously and without reproach" (James 1:5). "Thanks be to God for His indescribable gift" of grace to us in His Son (2 Cor. 9:15)! God ever and always deals in "grace that can meet every need and prevail in every situation."[87]

It is the God of all grace "who called you" (ὁ καλέσας ὑμᾶς). We thus enter this grace only at God's initiative. God introduced this grace in our lives by His call (1 Peter 2:9), and He brings it to completion at His Son's return (1:13). Everything is grace, from the divine initiative of calling to

---

87 Clowney, 218.

the divine consummation at Jesus' return. We are assured, then, that this same God who called us through the gospel will uphold us and fulfill His purposes presently in our suffering. The articular participle (ὁ καλέσας, "who called") is used substantively and attributively. The aorist tense views the decisive and effective event of God's call through the gospel.

The completion of God's call and the surety of His keeping are assured because, from the beginning, His call was "to His eternal glory in Christ" (εἰς τὴν αἰώνιον αὐτοῦ δόξαν ἐν Χριστῷ ['Ἰησοῦ]).[88] The phrase "in Christ" (ἐν Χριστῷ) may be understood to qualify either δόξαν ("glory") adjectively or ὁ καλέσας ("who called") adverbially.[89] The proximity of ἐν Χριστῷ makes it an attractive option, but grammatically it is more likely that it is to be connected with ὁ καλέσας ("who called"). The qualifiers of "glory" (τὴν ... δόξαν) are placed in the attributive position between the noun and its definite article: it is the "of Him" (αὐτοῦ) and "eternal" (αἰώνιον) "glory." It is "in Christ" that God calls us to Himself. Through union with His Son in His death and resurrection, we are bought to share in God's own "glory."

Note also the interplay between εἰς ("to") and ἐν ("in"). Generally, εἰς emphasizes movement "into" while ἐν emphasizes presence "in." God calls His people "into" the shared experience of His glory by placing us "in" Christ and, through that union, making us ever share with Him in His glory.

Peter uses four verbs to set out the "grace" which He gifts to the humble (v.5).[90] All are future tense, indicating that while God works presently in and through His people (4:10) to accomplish much of these things in one another's lives, in the end, it is God who will have brought the work of salvation to a complete end. We should, then, read these future

---

88 Many manuscripts add Ἰησοῦ ("Jesus"), but the shorter text is probably the original due to the greater likelihood of a scribe adding to the divine name, rather than subtracting from it (Michaels, 293).

89 Dubis, 171.

90 Some manuscripts have only three verbs, but these are "probably accidental omissions due to the similar verb endings" (Michaels, 293). Some manuscripts change the indicatives to the optative mood. But Michaels calls these "secondary stylistic modifications" (ibid.).

indicative verbs as describing the grace God works out in His people's lives here and now, even (and perhaps *especially*) in times of suffering, but also as that process that will be brought to glorious completion at the revelation of His Son, perfecting these graces in our lives forever.

First, God "will Himself perfect" His people (αὐτὸς καταρτίσει). "Himself" (αὐτὸς) is emphatic and marks God as the active agent in each of these actions. God personally carries out these fulfillments of His gospel promise. Even when He uses secondary means, God's hand does the work. The verb is a compound composed of κατά ("against") and ἄρτιος ("complete," "suitable," "exactly fitted").[91] The preposition in prefix signifies that it is "against" a standard that something is made "perfect" or to which it is "exactly fitted." In secular writings, the word was used in the medical world of setting a broken bone and in the nautical world of "repairing and refitting a damaged vessel."[92] In the NT, it is used of mending fishing nets (Matt. 4:21; Mark 1:19). It is descriptive of the end goal of discipleship; the disciple being fitted in exactness to his master (Luke 6:40). It describes the church's work of restoring a sinning member (Gal. 6:1). Those "whom He foreknew, He also predestined to become conformed to the image of His Son" (Rom. 8:29). And "these whom He predestined, He also called; and these whom He called, He also justified; and these whom He justified, He also glorified" (v.30). "Faithful is He who calls you, and He also will bring it to pass" (1 Thess. 5:24).

> **Ministry Maxim**
>
> Present suffering becomes only "a little while" when held alongside "eternal" grace.

Second, God "will ... confirm" (στηρίξει) His people. The verb derives from the same root as ἵστημι ("to stand"), which Peter has just used in compound in verse 9 (see above). Used literally it depicts "setting up something so that it remains immovable."[93] Luke used it metaphorically

---

91 Liddell and Scott, 6553.
92 Rienecker, 766.
93 Friberg, 356.

of the resolute nature of Jesus' determination to go to Jerusalem (Luke 9:51). It could also be used to describe making something inwardly firm and solid.[94] It is an act of God (1 Thess. 3:13; 2 Thess. 2:17; 3:3). It is the express intent of a spiritual leader as he shepherds the flock under his charge (Rom. 1:11; 1 Thess. 3:2). It was, in fact, the personal charge of Jesus to Peter: "when once you have turned again, strengthen your brothers" (Luke 22:32). But it is also the responsibility of the individual disciple (James 5:8) and of the community of believers (Rev. 3:2). In fact, it includes all of this, God working through a spiritual leader's ministry to his people (Rom. 16:25) and dependent upon their obedient response. Peter can also speak of it as a completed work: "I will always be ready to remind you of these things, even though you already know them, and have been established [ἐστηριγμένους] in the truth which is present with you" (2 Peter 1:12).

Thirdly, God will "strengthen" (σθενώσει) His people. The verb appears only here in the NT and means "to cause to be more able."[95] It is to "cause someone to be or to become more able or capable, with the implication of a contrast with weakness."[96] The faithful of old "from weakness were made strong" (Heb. 11:34). Paul learned that "power is perfected in weakness" (2 Cor. 12:9). Jesus "was crucified because of weakness, yet He lives because of the power of God." And thus "we also are weak in Him, yet we will live with Him because of the power of God" (2 Cor. 13:4). When we die, our bodies are "sown in weakness," but at Christ's coming our bodies are "raised in power" (1 Cor. 15:43).

Finally, God will "establish" (θεμελιώσει) His people. Literally, the verb meant to provide something with a foundation, to lay a foundation or thus to found something (Matt. 7:25). Then figuratively, it describes "providing a firm base for belief or practice" and can be translated with words such as establish, strengthen, settle, cause to be firm or unwavering."[97]

---

94 BDAG, 6826.2.

95 Friberg, 348.

96 Louw-Nida, 74.14.

97 Friberg, 196.

All four verbs point to God's stabilizing work in His people through grace. Each contributes its own nuance of meaning, but they exhibit "significant semantic overlap"; one man suggests the paraphrase: "God will make everything right beyond your wildest dreams."[98]

While God is even now working out these processes in our lives, the fullness of all this awaits the coming of Christ. These things will all happen "After you have suffered for a little while" (ὀλίγον παθόντας). This is Peter's final usage of the verb that has formed the central vein of this letter (1 Peter 2:19, 20, 21, 23; 3:14, 17, 18; 4:1 [2x], 15, 19; 5:10). Here, the aorist tense pictures our suffering not as a process but gathers it up and views it as an event, one that will have an end. The participle is temporal (παθόντας, "*After* you have suffered," emphasis added). There will be an "After" to your suffering! The temporal usage of the participle is confirmed by the adverbial use of the adjective ὀλίγον ("for a little while"), which appears before the participle for emphasis.[99] The "little while" (ὀλίγον) of suffering stands in contrast to the "eternal" (αἰώνιον) glory to be ours at Christ's unveiling.[100] From the vantage point of "After," all the suffering—the seemingly interminable pain and agony—will appear to us as having gone on only "for a little while."

Peter uses the adverb as an inclusion to the letter.[101] He began by telling his readers, "you greatly rejoice, even though now for a little while [ὀλίγον], if necessary, you have been distressed by various trials (1 Peter 1:6). He reminds them now that "After you have suffered for a little while [ὀλίγον]" Christ will bring to pass all the promised salvation of God (5:10). Peter thus signals that hope comes from perspective. Loss of perspective intensifies suffering. When our pain appears big and God's promises appear small, pain only intensifies. When the promises of God are large in our view, pain does not disappear, but it takes its place, finds its measure, and is exposed for what it is—a "momentary, light affliction"

---

98 Dubis, 172.

99 Ibid.

100 Forbes, 179.

101 cf. 1 Peter 3:20 and 5:12 where it is used as an adjective.

that "is producing for us an eternal weight of glory far beyond all comparison" (2 Cor. 4:17). Paul, with perspective in place, could rightly say, "I consider that the sufferings of this present time are not worthy to be compared with the glory that is to be revealed to us" (Rom. 8:18). Such perspective does not minimize present pain but restores the greatness of the salvation that puts pain in its place and will one day eliminate it altogether. The people of God put pain in its proper place by clinging to the promises of God.

From the first initiative of grace through God's calling, throughout this life of being strengthened and upheld by His hand amid suffering, and culminating in our entrance into "eternal glory," we are held securely by "the God of all grace."

Verse 11 – "To Him *be* dominion forever and ever. Amen."

Having completed his letter, save for one final explanation and exhortation (v.12) and the final greetings (vv.13–14), Peter now seals his epistle with a doxology of praise. So "a doxology of adoration responds to the promise" of grace.[102]

Peter's concern is "dominion" (τὸ κράτος).[103] Here the word denotes "the possession of force or strength that affords supremacy or control."[104] "The word refers to strength regarded as abundantly effective in relation to an end to be gained or dominion to be exercised."[105] God possesses this uniquely (note the presence of the definite article) and eternally (1 Tim. 6:16; 1 Peter 4:11; Jude 25; Rev. 1:6; 5:13). It is a fitting expression after the exhortation to humble oneself under "God's mighty [κραταιὰν] hand" in verse 6 and the promise of verse 10 with its four verbs all describing

---

102 Goppelt, 366.

103 Some manuscripts add ἡ δόξα ("the glory"). This, however, appears to be the clear effort of a scribe to conform the present text to that of the previous doxology in 4:11. But here Peter has just mentioned δόξα ("glory") in verse 10.

104 Friberg, 236.

105 Rienecker, 523–524.

in nuanced ways the stabilizing, strengthening, confirming, saving work of God. May this God of glory and grace reign forever and in all things!

"At the time Peter wrote these words, to all human appearances it must have seemed that to Rome instead belonged the dominion forever."[106] Yet by faith, Peter ascribes such "dominion" over all things "To Him" (αὐτῷ). Contextually, this points to "the God of all grace," who through Christ has promised to complete the salvation He has put in motion through Him (v.10). The dative makes this an implicit call for all creation to come under God's rule. The "dominion" is already His, but Peter's expression intends to call everyone who reads or hears his words to gladly attribute to God His rightful due and to express it not only with their lips but by their lives lived in submission "To Him." The verb is absent in the Greek text, but the reader is expected to mentally provide it. Whether it should be an optative ("be," e.g., ESV, NASU, NIV, NRSV) or indicative ("is," NCV, YLT; cf. "belongs," NET) is a matter of debate among translators. The former is a prayer-wish of that for which Peter longs; the latter a statement of present reality. Peter's previous doxology has the indicative ἐστιν ("is," 4:11), and thus it seems best to mentally supply an indicative here as well.

> **Ministry Maxim**
>
> What God's grace promised God's power will perform.

The phrase τὸ κράτος εἰς τοὺς αἰῶνας ("be dominion forever and ever") is repeated verbatim from 1 Peter 4:11. See our comments there. While here, Peter uses the abbreviated εἰς τοὺς αἰῶνας rather than the longer εἰς τοὺς αἰῶνας τῶν αἰώνων of 4:11, there is no appreciable difference in meaning, and thus it is rendered "forever and ever" in both.[107]

Here, as in his previous doxology, Peter marks his praise with "Amen" (ἀμήν). The expression came directly from Hebrew, where it acknowledged "a word which is valid, and the validity of which is binding

---

106 Jobes, 317.

107 Many manuscripts add τῶν αἰώνων, but this also appears to be an attempt to conform the text to that of 4:11.

for me."[108] Both of Peter's letters conclude with an "Amen" (1 Peter 5:11; 2 Peter 3:18; cf. Jude 25). Paul often climaxed his expressions of praise similarly (Rom. 1:25; 9:5; 11:36; 16:27; Gal. 1:5; Eph. 3:21; Phil. 4:20; 1 Tim. 1:17; 6:16). It means something like "so it is," "so be it" or "may it be fulfilled."[109] Those who read (or heard) these words in faith would reciprocate with their own affirming "Amen."

> **Digging Deeper:**
> 1. How can you effectively convince others of the "little while" of their suffering and the "eternal" nature of their salvation in Christ (v.10)?
> 2. How does knowledge of and rest in the sovereign reign of God (v.11) help us in times of temporal suffering?

Verse 12 – "Through Silvanus, our faithful brother (for so I regard *him*), I have written to you briefly, exhorting and testifying that this is the true grace of God. Stand firm in it!"

The name "Silvanus" (Σιλουανοῦ) is mentioned in the NT on three other occasions, all in association with the Apostle Paul (2 Cor. 1:19; 1 Thess. 1:1; 2 Thess. 1:1). We are probably correct in identifying him the "Silas" (Σιλᾶς) of the book of Acts (15:22, 27, 32, 34, 40; 16:19, 25, 29; 17:4, 10, 14, 15; 18:5), the latter being a contracted form of the more formal Silvanus. He appears to have been a Roman citizen (Acts 16:37). He was initially identified with the church in Jerusalem and was their selection, along with Judas Barsabbas, to accompany Paul and Barnabas in bearing the letter from the Jerusalem Council to the churches of Antioch, Syria, and Cilicia (Acts 15:21–35). Having completed this mission, Silas traveled and ministered with Paul during his second

---

108 TDNT, 1:335–337.

109 Thayer, 32.

missionary journey (Acts 15:36–18:23) after Barnabas and Paul sharply disagreed about inviting John Mark along again. Along the way, in Lystra, they took on Timothy as well (Acts 16:1–3). The three of them (joined later by Luke in Troas, cf. Acts 16:10ff) traveled and announced the gospel broadly across Asia Minor, Macedonia, and Achaia. It is in conjunction with Paul and Timothy that he is mentioned at the head of the letters to the Thessalonian believers (1 Thess. 1:1; 2 Thess. 1:1) and as having preached Jesus Christ among the Corinthians (2 Cor. 1:19). In Philippi he, along with Paul, was seized (16:19), attacked, beaten with rods (v.22), imprisoned (v.24), miraculously delivered (v.25). In Thessalonica they were run out of town (17:10). Silvanus thus lived up to the original assessment of those in Jerusalem who identified him as a leading man among the brothers (Acts 15:22) and a prophet who consistently "encouraged and strengthened the brethren" (v.32). He has been thus associated mostly with the ministry of the Apostle Paul, but his relational roots to the Apostle Peter probably went back to his time with the church in Jerusalem. At some unknown point, he reconnected with the Apostle Peter, and thus his name appears here. Having ministered extensively with Paul across a major portion of Asia Minor, he was surely a valuable resource to Peter in penning and disseminating this letter to the believers there.

> **Ministry Maxim**
>
> Wrapped into the grace-gift is the gifted ability to stand firm in it.

The fact that Peter can say it was "through" (Διὰ) Silvanus "I have written to you" (ὑμῖν ... ἔγραψα) could refer to his service to Peter as an amanuensis in taking down the letter, or it could refer to his role as a courier of the letter to its recipients in Asia Minor (1:1). The more traditional understanding has been that Silvanus served as amanuensis for Peter in taking down this letter. The Apostle Paul, at times, employed the services of another in penning down his words (e.g., Rom. 16:22). It is possible that Peter did something similar with this letter. If this is the case, no clear answers are to be found regarding the level of involvement Silvanus may have had in forming and shaping the letter. Whether he served as a secretary taking down the Apostle's words in strict dictation or was given a freer hand in personally framing Peter's thoughts cannot now be known.

More recent scholarship has insisted that it points not to Silvanus's role as an amanuensis but his service as the carrier of the letter to its addressees.[110] Support is found in the actions of the Jerusalem Council. Having reached an agreement about their response to the question of the Law (and circumcision in particular) as it relates to Gentile believers in Jesus, they wrote a letter to express their decision. Then, along with Paul and Barnabas, they selected "Judas called Barsabbas, and Silas, leading men among the brethren" (Acts 15:22) and "They wrote this letter by them" (γράψαντες διὰ χειρὸς αὐτῶν, v.23a, NKJV). Note particularly the use of διὰ ("by"). It is clear from the context that none of the four men named penned the letter but that it was "by their hand" that the letter was delivered to its intended audience. This lends credence to the possibility that the similar language used here of one of those original men is used in much the same way.

Still others suggest that Silvanus may have served both as amanuensis and courier.[111] Wherever one deems the weight of evidence to lie, we can be confident that, whatever the details of Silvanus' role, as with "All Scripture," 1 Peter "is breathed out by God and profitable for teaching, for reproof, for correction, and for training in righteousness" (2 Tim. 3:16, ESV). As with the OT Scriptures, so too with this letter, "men moved by the Holy Spirit spoke from God" (2 Peter 1:21)

The verb (ἔγραψα, "I have written") is an example of the epistolary aorist. From the vantage point of the readers of the letter, it had been written previously, though at the precise moment these lines were being penned, the letter was not yet quite complete.

Most English translations connect ὑμῖν ("to you") with the verb ἔγραψα ("I write"), but there is a great distance between the two in the original word order. While this is not impossible grammatically, it seems

---

110 E.g., Dubis, 173; Forbes, 183; Grudem, 206–207; Hiebert, 326–327; Jobes, 320; Lenski, 229; Michaels, 306; Schreiner, 248–249.

111 E.g., Bigg, 195; MacArthur, 228; Raymer, 2:857; Robertson, *Word Pictures*, 6:134; Stibbs, 175.

far better to connect ὑμῖν ("to you") with τοῦ πιστοῦ ἀδελφοῦ ("the faithful brother"), which immediately follows in the Greek text (cf. "a faithful brother unto you," NKJV; "to you the faithful brother," YLT). The effect is to stress that in his role in the letter's composition and/or delivery (see above), Silvanus has proven "faithful" to the recipients of the letter, proving to be a "brother" to them.[112]

What Peter tells us here confirms the witness of the rest of the NT as to the character of Silvanus. Peter adds his witness here to that earlier witness of the believers in Jerusalem (Acts 16:22, 32), telling his readers that Silvanus "is our faithful brother" (τοῦ πιστοῦ ἀδελφοῦ). Somewhat surprisingly, this is the only use of the noun (τοῦ ... ἀδελφοῦ) in this letter (though cf. the use of the collective noun ἀδελφότης, in 5:9). Peter will use it in addressing the recipients of his second letter (2 Peter 1:10) and as a designation for the Apostle Paul (3:15). In the attributive position emphasizing the quality of Silvanus as a "brother," is the adjective "faithful" (πιστοῦ). Here it means "trustworthy, faithful, dependable, inspiring trust or faith"[113] rather than "believing." That Silvanus is a believer is a given in the minds of both Peter and his readers. But the adjective could be used "of persons who show themselves faithful in the transaction of business, the execution of commands, or the discharge of official duties."[114] In this sense, Peter uses it to designate the character of Silvanus. Note the presence of the definite article (τοῦ ... ἀδελφοῦ). Some read the definite article as a possessive ("our brother"; cf. NASU, NKJV). But perhaps Peter is holding forth Silvanus as, literally, "*the* faithful brother" of whom they had perhaps heard previously. The testimony they have heard about this man's faithfulness is true.

To this assessment, Peter adds his own authoritative, confirming witness: "(for so I regard him)" (ὡς λογίζομαι). The verb comes from the world of mathematics and stresses the logical and ordered nature of the thinking. Here it represents a personal view or opinion of something, or

---

112 Dubis, 173–174.

113 BAGD, 664.

114 Thayer, 514.

in this case, someone, after considered reflection (cf. Rom. 8:18; 1 Cor. 4:1).[115] The present tense sets this out as Peter's abiding view of Silvanus. The verb is deponent, so the middle voice should be read as active.[116] This personal word of testimony would underscore the standing of Silvanus among those to receive the letter. If he was also to carry the letter to its intended audiences, this also might further exhort them to receive him with grace and treat him with honor while among them.

Peter bears witness also to the nature of the letter to which we have given ourselves in study. These five chapters constitute in Peter's mind as having written only "briefly" (δι' ὀλίγων). Peter has used the adjective four times, both adverbially to designate a length of time (1 Peter 1:6; 5:10) and adjectivally to designate relative size in numbers (3:20) or size (5:12). The preposition (δι') is used to express means: "as my vehicle in conveying my meaning."[117] Peter is signaling that he had much more he could have said and perhaps desired to say, but the concise expression he has given us in 1 Peter is a faithful witness of his message. Peter was there when Jesus told the Disciples, "I have many more things to say to you, but you cannot bear them now" (John 16:12), and perhaps he felt something of those constraints in penning this letter. The author of the letter to the Hebrews admitted, "we have much to say" (Heb. 5:11) but felt constraints in what he could communicate in that letter. Indeed, he closed the letter by adding: "I urge you, brethren, bear with this word of exhortation, for I have written to you briefly" (Heb. 13:22).

In these pages, Peter views himself as "exhorting and testifying" (παρακαλῶν καὶ ἐπιμαρτυρῶν). The two present tense participles designate Peter's purpose in the present letter. The first, "exhorting" (παρακαλῶν), is a compound built from the verb καλέω ("to call") and the prepositional prefix παρά ("beside"). At root, it means "to call alongside," but its meaning may vary from encourage and comfort to exhort and implore. The context of any given usage will determine where the author intends the

---

115 BDAG, 4598.3.

116 Abernathy, 181.

117 Alford, 4:387.

meaning to land along this spectrum of meaning. Here Peter seems to use the verb in the stronger sense. Peter feels the weight of the dark hour in which he and his contemporaries live. Urgency surges through his exhortations in this letter. Peter only used the verb twice before, once when he said, "I urge [παρακαλῶ] you as aliens and strangers to abstain from fleshly lusts" (2:11), and again when he said, "I exhort [παρακαλῶ] the elders among you" (5:1). But he views the letter as filled with such urgings as he pressed home the implications of the gospel of the grace of God in Jesus Christ.

To this is added (καὶ, "and") "testifying" (ἐπιμαρτυρῶν). The verb is used only here in the NT.[118] It too is a compound, made up of ἐπί ("upon") and μαρτυρέω ("to bear witness"). The resulting word means to attest something, "to supply evidence that" something is true, and "to confirm that fact by evidence."[119]

To this second participle, then, Peter adds "that this is the true grace of God" (ταύτην εἶναι ἀληθῆ χάριν τοῦ θεοῦ). By "this" (ταύτην), Peter apparently refers in some way to what has gone before in this letter. He is giving apostolic verification (cf. 1 Peter 1:12) that what he has held before God's people is indeed "the true grace of God" (ἀληθῆ χάριν τοῦ θεοῦ). From his opening blessing (1:2) to this final command (5:12), everything about this letter has circled around the "grace" of God in Christ (1:10, 13; 2:19, 20; 3:7; 4:10; 5:5, 10). This divine grace realized in Jesus Christ was long predicted (1:10), secured at the cross and in the resurrection (1:19–21; 2:21–24; 3:18–22) of Jesus, is presently available (3:7; 4:10; 5:5), but will only be fully realized at Jesus' Return (1:13). It is "the grace of life" (3:7), "manifold" in its varied forms and expressions (4:10). It comes only to the humble (5:5) and arises entirely from God's own nature (5:10).

---

118 Though Hebrews 2:4 has the double compound συνεπιμαρτυρέω: σύν ("with") + ἐπί ("upon") + μαρτυρέω ("to bear witness").

119 Rienecker, 767.

As Peter closes his letter, he offers one last command: "Stand firm in it!" (εἰς ἣν στῆτε).[120] The preposition εἰς ("in") can sometimes shade toward the more traditional meaning of ἐν. This appears to be the case here, where we should understand it in a locative sense, describing the sphere "in" which Peter's readers are to take their stand.[121] Perhaps the expression has "the pregnant force of entering *into* and standing fast *in*.[122] The relative pronoun ἣν ("it") finds its reference in "the true grace of God" as expressed in Peter's letter. The verb (στῆτε, "Stand firm") is the root of the compound word in verse 9 and translated "resist": ἀντί ("against") and ἵστημι ("to stand"). Peter commands his readers to stand against the devil (v.9) and to "Stand firm" in the grace of God (v.12). Here, the aorist imperative urgently demands action at once and yet also may be considered ingressive, commanding them to now reestablish their stand in the grace of God as a way of life.

Verse 13 – "She who is in Babylon, chosen together with you, sends you greetings, and *so does* my son, Mark."

Peter now closes the letter by sending and commanding greetings. These greetings serve to bind together a widely dispersed body of believers, many of whom would not have met one another, but the knowledge of whose fellowship strengthens their resolve to stand firm in the common grace they share in Christ (v.12).

The greetings, firstly, come from "She who is in Babylon" (ἡ ἐν Βαβυλῶνι). The reference to "Babylon" (Βαβυλῶνι) has been the cause of much speculation. The NT uses it literally of the earthly kingdom that took Judah into exile (Matt. 1:11, 12, 17 [2x]; Acts 7:43). The only other NT usages are found in Revelation (Rev. 14:8; 16:19; 17:5; 18:2, 10, 21)

---

120 Some manuscripts have the perfect indicative (ἐστήκατε) instead of the aorist imperative (στῆτε). The KJV, NKJV, and YLT follow the former; most English translations follow the latter. The imperative has the better manuscript support (Forbes, 185; Michaels, 305).

121 Harris, 85.

122 Vincent, 1:673.

where it appears to be used figuratively. By the time of the NT era, the ancient kingdom of Babylon had been long since defunct, and the capital city was a non-player on the world stage. A Roman military fortress in Egypt near present-day Cairo also went by the name Babylon. But there is no evidence that Peter was present there or that the recipients of the letter would have recognized Peter's intent in naming it. There is no record of Peter having ever visited either that area or city. There is ample evidence, historical and traditional, that Peter did visit the city of Rome before his death.

For this reason, most modern scholars understand Peter's reference to "Babylon" as a figurative way of referring to Rome. Like Babylon of old, in Peter's day, Rome was the most powerful nation on earth. Like Babylon of old, Rome, both the Empire and the city, were the center of ungodliness. Like Babylon of old, Rome was, for Peter, a place of dislocation and even exile (cf. 1 Peter 1:1; 2:11) from his homeland.[123] Like Babylon of old, Rome too would fold and disappear from the scene. Peter may have been motivated in his cryptic reference by the fact that he wanted to conceal his location from the authorities who would have loved to lay hands on one of Jesus' chief apostles. Yet he knew that those to whom the letter was addressed would recognize both the location from which he wrote and the spiritual implications of his designating it "Babylon." To those being persecuted by the powers of Rome, Peter's designation was a signal that the persecutors would not ultimately win but that God's Kingdom would prevail. To those finding themselves increasingly "aliens and strangers" (1 Peter 2:11) living in exile away from their true homeland in God's presence, Peter's reference signaled that he too understood their heavenly homesickness. Peter's reference would fortify his readers to remain faithful under the painful trials brought upon them by representatives of Rome.

The article ἡ ("She who") is feminine and singular in form. While it is possible it refers to an individual and probably well-known woman

---

123 Forbes, 185; In Βαβυλῶνι ("Babylon") we may have another inclusion, matching διασπορᾶς ("the dispersion," ESV) in 1:1 (Goppelt, 375; Jobes, 323; Michaels, 311).

living in Rome,[124] it is far more likely that Peter intended his readers to understand the singular as a collective, the reference being to the church in Rome (cf. 2 John 1, 13).[125]

The triumph of the Kingdom would ultimately come only at Jesus' Return, but already God has called out a people for His glory from the very heart of the evil Empire. There were there those "chosen together with you" (συνεκλεκτὴ). The adjective is found only here in the NT. It is a compound comprised of σύν ("with") and ἐκλεκτός ("chosen," "select"). The root adjective (ἐκλεκτός) is used frequently throughout the NT to refer to the elect of God (e.g., Matt. 22:14; 24:22; Luke 18:7; Rom. 8:33; 1 Peter 1:1; 2:9). Peter also uses it of Christ Himself (1 Peter 2:4, 6). The use of the adjective in 1:1 and of the compound form here form an inclusion wrapping the entire letter in the electing love of God.[126] All of them, those scattered across Asia Minor and those living in Rome, were together "in Christ" (5:10), the elect of God, and as such, have been made by God "chosen together" by His grace.

These, then, now send "greetings" (Ἀσπάζεται). The verb is found almost sixty times in the NT, forty of which appear in extensive listings in Paul's letters (e.g., twenty-one times in Rom. 16:3–23).[127] The verb means just what we would expect it to, "to greet" or "to welcome" another. The present tense looks not simply to one-and-done compliance to a social requirement upon encountering one another but to an ongoing lifestyle of welcome toward one another. The middle voice has an active meaning. The verb is thrust to the head of the sentence for emphasis. The Apostle Paul frequently used the indicative to convey his

> **Ministry Maxim**
>
> Physical location does not define one's identity, electing grace does.

---

124 Some have suggested Peter's wife as a possibility (E.g., Alford, 4:388; Bigg, 197).
125 Some manuscript read ἐκκλησία ("church") after Βαβυλῶνι ("Babylon"), but the evidence is against its genuineness (cf. KJV, NLT; NRSV; YLT).
126 Dubis, 176; Forbes, 185.
127 NIDNTTE, 1:427.

own personal greetings or those of others who are with him (e.g., Rom. 16:21–23; 1 Cor. 16:19–20; 2 Cor. 13:12; Phil. 4:21–22; Col. 4:10, 12, 14; Titus 3:15). If "Babylon" is a cover for Rome, then we do well to note Paul's twenty-five uses of the verb in Romans 16, bespeaking the breadth and depth of relationships enjoyed there among the believing.

Added (καὶ, "and") to this, these greetings from the wider body of believers in Rome are the individual greetings of "my son, Mark" (Μᾶρκος ὁ υἱός μου). Mark's home in Jerusalem had early been a center of Christian life and ministry, a place Peter frequented, and it would have been well-known (Acts 12:12–17). Mark had been chosen to travel with Paul and Barnabas on their first missionary journey (Acts 13:5). Not long later, however, he left Paul and Barnabas and returned to Jerusalem (13:13). At the beginning of the second missionary journey, Barnabas insisted upon bringing Mark along again. But this led to a division between himself and Paul (15:37–39). Whether this was because of Barnabas's heart as an encourager (4:36) or because Mark was his "cousin" (Col. 4:10), we cannot be certain. Approximately twelve years passed between their separation and Paul's first surviving mention of Mark (Col. 4:10).[128] We can see from that reference that Mark was Paul in his first imprisonment in Rome. Over a decade later, during Paul's second imprisonment, the Apostle longed for the ministry of Mark (2 Tim. 4:11). Clearly, Paul's opinion of Mark changed, and he spoke of him positively (cf. also Philem. 24). We are not certain of the time-relationship between Paul's mentioning Mark in conjunction with his Roman imprisonments and this reference to Mark by Peter, who appears to write from Rome. Perhaps Mark spent any intervening time in ministry in Rome. It is likely that Mark wrote the Gospel bearing his name from the city of Rome.

Peter identifies Mark as "my son" (ὁ υἱός μου). Clearly, Peter did not intend this in a biological sense. Rather, it pointed to a close spiritual and ministerial relationship. Paul spoke similarly of Timothy (1 Tim. 1:18; 2 Tim. 1:2) but used different terminology. Peter's precise Greek expression is found when at Jesus' baptism, a voice from heaven spoke and said:

---

128 Lightfoot, 234.

"This is My beloved Son [ὁ υἱός μου], in whom I am well-pleased" (Matt. 3:17; cf. Mark 1:11; Luke 3:22). Beyond this, it is an expression with which Peter would have had some history. He was there on the mountain when a voice came out of the engulfing cloud and announced, "This is My beloved Son [ὁ υἱός μου], with whom I am well-pleased; listen to Him!" (Matt. 17:5; cf. Mark 9:7; Luke 9:35), an event that was indelibly imprinted upon his heart and mind (2 Peter 1:17). The only other NT usage of this precise wording is in the mouth of the father when his prodigal son returned home: "this son of mine [ὁ υἱός μου] was dead and has come to life again; he was lost and has been found" (Luke 15:24).

Does any of this play into Peter's use of the expression regarding Mark? The inclusion of Mark as the only individual from whom Peter extends greetings may simply reflect who was at hand when he was completing and sending the letter. But it may also be evidence of an interesting bit of pastoral strategy.

It had been precisely as Paul, Barnabas, and Mark stepped onto the soil with the intent of entering Asia Minor that Mark had turned back (Acts 13:13). This had a lasting, though not permanent, effect on Paul's relationship to Mark (Acts 15:37–39). Did this also have an enduring effect upon Mark's relationship to the churches of Asia Minor? We have no record of that fact, but certainly, Paul had to work through the issue, which took him some time (Col. 4:10; Philem. 24; 2 Tim. 4:11).

And what are we to make of the juxtaposition here of Silvanus (v.12) and Mark (v.13)? It was, after all, Silvanus whom Paul selected as his ministry partner (Acts 15:40) after he and Barnabas had fallen out over Mark's participation in Paul's second missionary journey (vv.36–39). After the sad division between Paul and Barnabas, how did Mark feel about Silvanus? How did Silvanus regard Mark? We do not know, but the two were apparently together in the glad and peaceful company of the Apostle Peter as this letter was being written.

These are questions and conjectures, admittedly. But as we read here Peter's greetings from Mark, one wonders if Peter saw in Mark a reflection of himself—one who had once failed (Matt. 26:69–75; Mark 14:66–72; Luke 22:55–65; John 18:25–27) but had later been restored to ministry (John 21:15–19). For whatever reason, Peter conveyed greetings as he did, demonstrating a humble, grace-filled heart that longs to see God's people well-connected in the fellowship of the Spirit in the Name of Christ.

Digging Deeper:
1. How does Peter's purpose of "exhorting and testifying" via this letter inform us about the form and function of our preaching should take (v.12)?
2. How should the fact that one's location ("in Babylon") does not limit one's spiritual fellowship ("chosen together with") shape how you think of other believers (v.13)? In what way does this affect how your church should view other bodies of believers?

Verse 14 – "Greet one another with a kiss of love. Peace be to you all who are in Christ."

Peter, as Paul often does (e.g., Rom. 16:3, 5–16; 1 Cor. 16:20; 2 Cor. 13:12; Phil. 4:21; Col. 4:15; 1 Thess. 5:26; Titus 3:15), now employs the imperative form of the verb just used in verse 13 (ἀσπάσασθε, "Greet"). He uses it to command the recipients of his letters to thus "greet" others in the Body of Christ (cf. Heb. 13:24). See above in verse 13 for more on the verb. Here the aorist imperative demands that action be taken at once, perhaps immediately upon the conclusion of the reading of this letter. The second-person plural form demands that the entire body of the church fulfill the command. The reciprocal pronoun "one another" (ἀλλήλους; cf. Rom. 16:16; 1 Cor. 16:20; 2 Cor. 13:12) calls for the back-and-forth exercise of the greetings among the members of their fellowships.

The greeting is to be carried out "with a kiss of love" (ἐν φιλήματι ἀγάπης). A "kiss" (φίλημα) was a customary and expected greeting within Jewish culture (Luke 7:45). It was a sign of solidarity and fellowship within the early churches. Paul designated it as "holy" (Rom. 16:16; 1 Cor. 16:20; 2 Cor. 13:12; 1 Thess. 5:26), while Peter marks it as "of love" (ἀγάπης). Whereas Paul consistently used the dative form of the adjective (ἁγίῳ, "holy"), Peter uses the genitive noun (ἀγάπης, "of love"). In this way, Peter designated not so much the quality of the kiss ("holy") but that from which it arose ("of love"). The birthplace of this greeting-kiss is the love of God expressed to His people in Jesus Christ (John 3:16) and magnified in and through them by the Holy Spirit (Rom. 5:5) and now expressed as the binding element of their relationships to one another (1 Peter 1:22; 2:17; 4:8).

"Peace be to you all who are in Christ" (Εἰρήνη ὑμῖν πᾶσιν τοῖς ἐν Χριστῷ). The blessing of "Peace" (Εἰρήνη) shows up at the beginning of all Paul's epistles (e.g., Rom. 1:7; 1 Cor. 1:3; 2 Cor. 1:2) and sometimes in their ending (e.g., Gal. 6:16; Eph. 6:23). Peter opens and closes with it here (1 Peter 1:2; 5:14) and in his second letter (2 Peter 1:2; 3:14). Yet the precise expression "Peace be to you" (Εἰρήνη ὑμῖν) is found elsewhere only on the lips of the resurrected Jesus (Luke 24:36; John 20:19, 21, 26).

> **Ministry Maxim**
>
> A spoken blessing is a blessing in itself.

The exact expression τοῖς ἐν Χριστῷ ("who are in Christ") is found elsewhere in the NT only in Romans 8:1: "Therefore there is now no condemnation for those who are in Christ Jesus [τοῖς ἐν Χριστῷ]" (Rom. 8:1). Is there anything that could bring more "Peace... to you" than knowing there is no condemnation for those who are in Christ Jesus? Peter is both liberal and inclusive (ὑμῖν πᾶσιν, "you all") and limited and exclusive in his blessing, for it is only for those "who are in Christ Jesus" (τοῖς ἐν Χριστῷ). Such peace exists only for those who are "in Christ," but for all who are "in Christ."[129]

With his final wish of peace, Peter concludes the letter in which he has counseled his readers about how to meet the hostility of an unbelieving world. It is only those "who are in Christ Jesus" (τοῖς ἐν Χριστῷ) that have

---

[129] Some more recent manuscripts add "Jesus" and "amen" at the end of the sentence. But this is not represented in the earlier and best manuscripts, suggesting it was a later addition by a scribe or an adaptation for liturgical purposes.

the foundation and resources to abide in peace amid tribulation. It is only as we "Stand firm in" (v.12) that grace that we can continue to "glorify God" (4:16).

Digging Deeper:
1. Is verbally speaking "Peace" over another simply a nice relational gesture or does it have some actual effect upon the other (v.14)?
2. How might you begin to utilize such a benediction in relationship to others?

APPENDIX A

PREACHING AND TEACHING 1 PETER

Preaching is one of the great privileges of a pastor. The NT has much to say about faithfully preaching God's Word. It is my conviction that expository preaching should be the regular practice of every local church pastor.[1] Of course, even among those of similar belief, there is not always consensus on just what constitutes expository preaching. Similarly, each pastor is comfortable preaching passages of different lengths and series of varying duration. Local circumstances also permit (or require) sermon series of differing lengths.

What follows are suggestive attempts at projecting both preaching series and their individual sermons. First, I offer an exegetical outline of 1 Peter. Then I offer three possibilities for preaching the letter—a single message covering the entire book, a shorter series of messages, and a more extended series of messages. These may, of course, be expanded even further. You may divide the letter differently than I have suggested here. I hope these suggestions will provide fodder for your preaching these portions of sacred Scripture. It is your duty as a servant of God to wrestle with

---

[1] See the author's *Revival in the Rubble* (chapter 10), *Embracing Authority* (chapter 9), and *He is Able* (chapters 11–15) for more on the primacy and practice of expository preaching.

the text of Scripture until God brings you forth with a message for His people, which arises from His Word.

"I solemnly charge you in the presence of God and of Christ Jesus, who is to judge the living and the dead, and by His appearing and His kingdom: preach the word; be ready in season and out of season; reprove, rebuke, exhort, with great patience and instruction" (2 Tim. 4:1–2).

EXEGETICAL OUTLINE

I. **Grace given personally in Jesus Christ. (1:1–12)**
   A. Identity by grace. (1:1–2)
      1. Who the recipients are. (1:1)
         a. They are chosen.
         b. They are aliens.
         c. They are scattered.
      2. How they know their identity. (1:2)
         a. They were foreknown by God the Father. (1:2a)
         b. They were set apart by God the Spirit. (1:2b)
         c. They were redeemed by God the Son. (1:2c)
   B. Perspective by grace. (1:3–12)
      1. The magnitude of their salvation. (1:3–5)
         a. A living hope. (1:3)
         b. An incorruptible inheritance. (1:4)
         c. A secure people. (1:5)
      2. The significance of their trial. (1:6–9)
         a. Their trial purifies their faith in Christ. (1:6–7)
         b. Their trial personalizes their experience of Christ. (1:8–9)
      3. The privilege of their salvation. (1:10–12)
         a. The prophets envy them. (1:10–12a)
         b. The angels envy them. (1:12b)

II. **Imperatives for godliness. (1:13–2:3)**
   A. Set your hope. (1:13)
      1. With prepared minds. (1:13a)
      2. With sober spirits. (1:13b)

 B. Be holy. (1:14–16)
  1. Rejecting former lusts. (1:14)
  2. Reflecting Him who called. (1:15–16)
 C. Fear God. (1:17–21)
  1. Because God is your judge. (1:17)
  2. Because of the price of your redemption. (1:18–19)
  3. Because of Christ's obedience. (1:20–21)
 D. Love one another. (1:22–25)
  1. Because of your purifying conversion. (1:22)
  2. Because of your transformative regeneration. (1:23–25)
   a. Regeneration by God's imperishable word. (1:22–23a)
   b. Regeneration by God's living word. (1:23b)
   c. Regeneration by God's enduring word. (1:23c-25)
 E. Long for God's word. (2:1–3)
  1. By laying aside all sin. (2:1)
  2. Like newborn babies. (2:2)
  3. Because you have tasted God's goodness. (2:3)

III. Grace given corporately in Jesus Christ. (2:4–10)
 A. Corporate foundation. (2:4–8)
  1. A new temple. (2:4–5a, 6–8)
   a. Christ the living stone. (2:4a)
   b. Christ the cornerstone. (2:4b, 6–7)
   c. Christ the stumbling stone. (2:8)
  2. A new priesthood. (2:5b)
 B. Corporate identity. (2:9–10)
  1. A chosen race. (2:9a)
  2. A royal priesthood. (2:5b, 9b)
  3. A holy nation. (2:9c)
  4. A new people. (2:9d-10)

IV. Imperatives for godliness. (2:11–5:12)
 A. Living among unbelievers. (2:11–4:11)
  1. The sensory world. (2:11–12)
   a. Abstain from fleshly lusts. (2:11)
   b. Keep your behavior excellent. (2:12)
  2. The political world. (2:13–17)

a. Living in subjection to authorities. (2:13–15)
   b. Living in freedom with yourself. (2:16)
   c. Living in responsibility toward others. (2:17)
3. The domestic world. (2:18–25)
   a. Submit respectfully. (2:18–19)
   b. Suffer rightly. (2:20)
   c. Step reverently. (2:21–25)
      i. Jesus spoke no sin. (2:22–23a)
      ii. Jesus submitted to God. (2:23b)
      iii. Jesus substituted on our behalf. (2:24)
      iv. Jesus shepherds our souls. (2:25)
4. The marital world. (3:1–7)
   a. Instructions to wives. (3:1–6)
      i. The wife's submission. (3:1–2)
      ii. The wife's adornment. (3:3–4)
      iii. The wife's pattern. (3:5–6)
         aa. The example of women of old. (3:5)
         bb. The example of Sarah. (3:6)
   b. Instructions to husbands. (3:7)
      i. Live with your wife according to knowledge. (3:7a)
      ii. Honor your wife as a fellow heir. (3:7b)
5. The painful world. (3:8–22)
   a. Relationships within the Christian fellowship. (3:8)
   b. Relationships within the opposing world. (3:9–22)
      i. Blessing in the face of cursing. (3:9)
         aa. This is illustrated from Psalm 34:12–16. (3:10–12)
      ii. Suffer for righteousness. (3:13–17)
         aa. Good as a guard against suffering. (3:13)
         bb. Good as a reason for suffering. (3:14, 17)
         cc. Witness in the face of suffering. (3:15–16)
            (i). These qualities illustrated from Christ's life. (3:18–22)
               (aa). Christ's Passion—willing substitution. (3:18a)

                (bb). Christ's Triumph – triumphant resurrection. (3:18b-21)
                (cc). Christ's Reign – victorious session. (3:22)
    6. The dying world. (4:1–11)
        a. Separate from the spiritually dying. (4:1–6)
            i. Separated thinking. (4:1)
            ii. Separating choosing. (4:2–3)
            iii. Separated preparing. (4:4–6)
        b. Serve the spiritually living. (4:7–11)
            i. Though alert prayer. (4:7)
            ii. Through glad hospitality. (4:8–9)
            iii. Through gifted service. (4:10–11)
                aa. The stewarding of God's gifts. (4:10)
                bb. The showing of God's gifts. (4:11a-b)
                    (i). The gift of speaking. (4:11a)
                    (ii). The gift of serving. (4:11b)
                cc. The significance of God's gifts. (4:11c)
B. Suffering at the hand of unbelievers. (4:12–5:12)
    1. Serving in suffering. (4:12–19)
        a. The norm of suffering. (4:12)
        b. The hope in suffering. (4:13)
        c. The enabling in suffering. (4:14)
        d. The purpose in suffering. (4:15–18)
            i. God is purifying His people. (4:17a)
            ii. God will judge the lost. (4:17b-18)
        e. The rest in suffering. (4:19)
    2. Serving in leading. (5:1–11)
        a. Elders who lead. (5:1–4)
            i. The elders' identity. (5:1)
                aa. A shared calling. (5:1a)
                bb. A shared foundation. (5:1b)
                cc. A shared glory. (5:1c)
            ii. The elders' duty. (5:2–3)
                aa. Shepherd God's flock. (5:2a)

                (i). With the right mindset. (5:2b)
                (ii). With the right motive. (5:2c)
                (iii). With the right manner. (5:3)
            iii. The elders' reward. (5:4)
        b. People who follow. (5:5–11)
            i. Younger men: Be subject to the elders. (5:5a)
            ii. All God's people. (5:5b-11)
                aa. Be humble. (5:5b-7)
                bb. Be sober. (5:8)
                cc. Be resolute. (5:9)
                dd. Be hopeful. (5:10)
                ee. Be worshipful. (5:11)
    C. A final imperative: Stand in grace! (5:12)
V. **Conclusion. (5:13–14)**
    A. Final greetings. (5:13–14a)
        1. Greetings extended. (5:13)
            a. Greetings from the church in "Babylon." (5:13a)
            b. Greetings from Mark. (5:13b)
        2. Greetings commanded. (5:14a)
    B. Final benediction. (5:14b)

EXPOSITIONAL OUTLINES

Single message

New Life in Christ
A new identity yields a new life.
I. I am, therefore, I do. (1:1–2:3)
   A. God has given me a new identity in Christ. (1:1–12)
      1. I am chosen. (1:1a)
      2. I am exiled. (1:1a)
      3. I am scattered. (1:1b-2)
      4. I am saved. (1:3–5)
      5. I am suffering. (1:6–9)
      6. I am privileged. (1:10–12)
   B. God has given me a new responsibility in Christ. (1:13–2:3)
      1. I set my hope. (1:13)
      2. I aim to be holy. (1:14–16)
      3. I fear God. (1:17–21)
      4. I love others. (1:22–25)
      5. I desire God's Word. (2:1–3)
II. We are, therefore, we do. (2:4–5:11)
   A. God has given us a new collective identity in Christ. (2:4–10)
      1. We are God's temple. (2:4–5a)
      2. We are God's priests. (2:5b-8)
      3. We are a chosen race. (2:9a)
      4. We are a royal priesthood. (2:9b)
      5. We are a holy nation. (2:9c)
      6. We are a new people. (2:9d-10)
   B. God has given us new collective responsibilities in Christ. (2:11–5:11).
      1. We live among unbelievers. (2:11–4:11)
         a. In our society. (2:11–12)
         b. In our nation. (2:13–17)
         c. In our workplace. (2:18–25)
         d. In our marriages. (3:1–7)

    e. In our world. (3:8–4:11)
2. We serve God and others. (4:12–5:11)
    a. We serve in suffering. (4:12–19)
    b. We serve in leading. (5:1–11)

Shorter Series (6 messages)
Series title: Living a New Life

#1   **1:3–21 Living Hopefully**
Jesus transforms our future.

I. **The greatness of our salvation. (1:3–5)**
    A. Unlimited mercy. (1:3a)
    B. Unending life. (1:3b)
    C. Undying hope. (1:3c)
    D. Undiminishing inheritance. (1:4)
    E. Unfailing security. (1:5)
II. **The significance of our trial. (1:6–9)**
    A. Our trials purify our faith in Christ. (1:6–7)
    B. Our trials personalize our experience of Christ. (1:8–9)
III. **The desirability of our position. (1:10–12)**
    A. The prophets envy us. (1:10–12a)
    B. The angels envy us. (1:12b)
IV. **The excellence of our calling. (1:13–21)**
    A. We are called to hope. (1:13)
    B. We are called to holiness. (1:14–21)

#2   **1:22–2:3 Living Simply**
Jesus simplifies our lives.

I. **Love for the people around us. (1:22–25)**
    A. Love's mutuality. ("love one another," 1:22c)
    B. Love's source. ("a sincere love," "from the heart," 1:22a, b)
    C. Love's intensity. ("fervently," 1:22d)
    D. Love's origin. (1:22–25)

1. From God's vantage point. (1:23–25)
2. From man's vantage point. (1:22)

II. Long for the word given to us. (2:1–3)
 A. The passion. ("long for the pure milk of the word," 2:2b)
 B. The picture. ("like newborn babies," 2:2a)
 C. The pursuit. ("that by it you may grow in respect to salvation," 2:2c)
 D. The pull. ("if you have tasted the kindness of the Lord," 2:3)
 E. The price. ("putting aside all …" 2:1)

#3 **2:4–25 Living Faithfully**

Jesus transforms the roles in which we live.

I. Life in relationship to our Savior. (2:4–10)
 A. Jesus is the source of our identity. (2:4–5)
  1. He is a "living stone." (2:4)
  2. We are "living stones." (2:5)
 B. Jesus is the source of our destiny. (2:6–8)
 C. Jesus is the source of our activity. (2:5b, 9b)
  1. Offer spiritual sacrifices. (2:5b)
  2. Fulfill a special mission. (2:9b)

II. Live in relationship to our country. (2:11–17)
 A. Life in the spiritual war zone. (2:11)
  1. The war raging within me. (2:11)
  2. The war raging around me. (2:12)
 B. Life in the political war zone. (2:13–17)
  1. Motive: "for the Lord's sake." (2:13a)
  2. Master: "to every human institution." (2:13b–14)
  3. Mission: "such is the will of God." (2:15a)
  4. Method: "that by doing right." (2:15b-16)
  5. Maxims. (2:17)

       a. If we treat everyone like an emperor, then the emperor is treated like everyone else. (2:17a, d)
       b. Only God deserves to be feared. (2:17c)
       c. Christian relationships are unique. (2:17b)
III. **Life in relationship to our employers. (2:18–25)**
    A. The Path of Success. (2:18–20)
       1. Successful actions.
          a. Submission. (2:18a)
          b. Endurance. (2:19b-20)
       2. Successful attitudes.
          a. The fear of God. (2:18b-19a)
          b. The calling of God. (2:21a)
       3. Successful outcomes. (2:12, 15, 19)
          a. Your employer's salvation. (2:12)
          b. Your employer's silence. (2:15)
          c. Your employer's salute. (2:19a)
    B. The Path of the Savior. (2:21–25)
       1. Christ's sufferings as example. (2:21–23)
          a. A pattern to be copied. (2:21a)
          b. A path to be followed. (2:21b-23)
       2. Christ's sufferings as salvation. (2:24–25)
          a. Freedom from bondage. (2:24a)
          b. Healing from sickness. (2:24b)
          c. Shepherding from waywardness. (2:25)

#4   **3:1–22 Living Together**
Jesus transforms our relationships.

I. **Relationship within our homes. (3:1–7)**
    A. A wife's gospel strategy. (3:1–6)
       1. Submission vs. control. (3:1a)
       2. Conduct vs. words. (3:1b-2)
       3. Internal vs. external. (3:3a, 4a)
       4. Character vs. cosmetics. (3:3, 5–6)
       5. Rest vs. fear. (3:6b)

  B. A husband's gospel strategy. (3:7)
    1. A shared life: "live with your wives."
    2. A shared mind: "in an understanding way."
    3. A shared calling: "as with someone weaker."
    4. A shared honor: "show her honor."
    5. A shared inheritance: "as a fellow heir of the grace of life."
II. Relationship outside our homes. (3:8–17)
  A. In relationship to fellow believers. (3:8)
    1. Thinking: "harmonious" & a "humble in spirit."
    2. Feeling: "sympathetic" & "kindhearted."
    3. Committing: "brotherly."
  B. In relationship to unbelievers. (3:9–12)
III. Relationship above our homes. (3:13–22)
  A. In relationship to the transforming Jesus. (3:13–17)
    1. A life of submission: "sanctify Christ as Lord" (3:15a)
    2. A life of hope: "an account for the hope that is in you." (3:15c)
    3. A life of readiness: "always being ready to make a defense to everyone who asks you." (3:15b)
    4. A life of gentleness: "gentleness." (3:15d)
    5. A life of respect: "reverence." (3:15e)
  B. In relationship to the triumphant Jesus. (3:18–22)
    1. Jesus' obedience brings us to God. (3:18)
    2. Jesus' obedience broadcast His triumph. (3:19–20)
    3. Jesus' obedience brought Him to the throne. (3:21–22)

#5 **4:1–19 Living Aligned**

Jesus aligns our lives to reality.

I. Jesus gives us a life apart. (4:1–6)
  A. Separate yourself in your thinking. (4:1)
  B. Separate yourself in your choosing. (4:2–3)
  C. Separate yourself in your preparing. (4:4–6)

II. Jesus gives us a life ahead. (4:7–11)
  A. Reclaim your prayer life. (4:7)
    1. Pray with the end in view. (4:7a)
    2. Pray with your mind controlled. (4:7b)
  B. Rekindle your Christian relationships. (4:8–9)
    1. Shared grace. (4:8)
    2. Shared life. (4:9)
  C. Refocus your divine service. (4:10–11)
    1. God has given something to you: "As each has received a special gift." (4:10a)
    2. God gave it to you, but it is for other people: "employ it in serving one another." (4:10b)
    3. God holds you responsible to make sure it helps others: "as good stewards." (4:10c)
    4. God's gifts to you are unique: "of the manifold grace of God." (4:10d-11a)
    5. God's gifts all have one goal: "so that in all things God may be glorified." (4:11b)

III. Jesus gives us a life alert. (4:12–19)
  A. Suffering is a test to pass. (4:12)
  B. Suffering is a fellowship to enter. (4:13–14)
  C. Suffering is a choice to make. (4:15–16)
  D. Suffering is a judgment to face. (4:17–18)
  E. Suffering is an opportunity to seize. (4:19)

#6   5:1–14 Living boldly
Jesus frees us to live boldly.

I. Leading through the fire. (5:1–4)
  A. A leader's experience. (5:1)
    1. I lead best when I stand among you. (5:1a)
    2. I lead best when I focus on Christ. (5:1b)
    3. I lead best when I speak from experience. (5:1c)

 B. A leader's calling. (5:1–2)
  1. I must lead out of maturity: "I exhort the elders among you." (5:1a)
  2. I must lead out of responsibility: "exercising oversight." (5:2b)
  3. I must lead out of familiarity: "the flock of God among you." (5:2a)
 C. A leader's method. (5:2c-3)
  1. I must lead with the right mindset: "not under compulsion." (5:2c)
  2. I must lead with the right motive: "not for sordid gain." (5:2d)
  3. I must lead with the right manner: "nor yet as lording it over those allotted to your charge." (5:3a)
 D. A leader's perspective. (5:4)
  1. I will meet with accountability. (5:4a)
  2. I will meet with reward. (5:4b)

II. Walking through the fire. (5:5–14)
 A. Walk humbly. (5:5–7)
  1. Our humility. (5:5a, 6a)
  2. God's hand. (5:5b-7)
   a. God's opposing hand. (5:5b)
   b. God's giving hand. (5:5c)
   c. God's ruling hand. (5:6a)
   d. God's lifting hand. (5:6b-7)
 B. Walk alertly. (5:8–9)
  1. Be alert in thinking. (5:8)
  2. Be alert in posture. (5:9)
 C. Walk steadfastly. (5:10–12)
  1. Rooted in the past: "the God of all grace, who called you." (5:10b)
  2. Confident about the future: "to His eternal glory in Christ, will Himself, perfect, confirm, strengthen and establish you." (5:10c)

3. Faithful in the present: "After you have suffered for a little while." (5:10a)
4. Resilient in the process: "Stand firm." (5:12b)
D. Walk unitedly. (5:12–14)
1. Walk in the apostolic gospel. (5:12a)
2. Walk in wider fellowship. (5:13)
3. Walk in local fellowship. (5:14)

Longer Series (15 messages)
Series title: Gospel Grace in a Godless World

#1   **1:1–2 Gospel Identity**
God's grace changes everything about us.

I. **Who am I? (1:1)**
   A. I am chosen. (1:1c)
   B. I am an exile. (1:1a)
   C. I am scattered. (1:1b)
II. **How did I get here? (1:2)**
   A. I was foreknown by God the Father. (1:2a)
   B. I was set apart by God the Spirit. (1:2b)
   C. I was redeemed by God the Son. (1:2c)

#2   **1:3–12 Gospel Perspective**
The gospel opens our eyes.

I. **We see the magnitude of our salvation. (1:3–5)**
   A. We have been given a living hope. (1:3)
   B. We have been given an incorruptible inheritance. (1:4–5)
II. **We see the significance of our trials. (1:6–9)**
   A. Our trials purify our faith in Christ. (1:7)
   B. Our trials personalize our experience of Christ. (1:8–9)

III. We see the desirability of our position. (1:10–12)
  A. The prophets envy us. (1:10–12a)
  B. The angels envy us. (1:12b)

#3 1:13–21 Gospel Stability
The gospel stabilizes our lives.

I. Looking forward: Set your hope. (1:13)
II. Looking upward: Be holy. (1:14–16)
III. Looking backward: Fear God. (1:17–21)

#4 1:22–2:3 Gospel Simplicity
The gospel simplifies life.

I. A new love for the people around us. (1:22–25)
  A. Love's mutuality: "love one another." (1:22)
  B. Love's source: "from the heart" & "a sincere love of the brethren" (1:22)
  C. Love's intensity: "fervently." (1:22)
  D. Love's origin. (1:22–25)
     1. From God's vantage point (1:23–25)
     2. From man's vantage point. (1:22)

II. A new longing for the word given to us. (2:1–3)
  A. The passion: "long for the pure spiritual milk." (2:2b)
  B. The picture: "Like newborn infants." (2:2a)
  C. The pursuit: "that by it you may grow up into salvation." (2:2c)
  D. The pull: "if indeed you have tasted that the Lord is good." (2:3)
  E. The price: "So put away all." (2:1)

#5 2:4–10 The Gospel-defined Life
The gospel redefines one's life.

I. Jesus is the source of our identity. (2:4–5)
  A. He is a "living stone." (2:4)
  B. We are "living stones." (2:5)

II. **Jesus is the source of our destiny. (2:6–8)**
  III. **Jesus is the source of our activity. (2:5b, 9b)**
  A. We offer spiritual sacrifices. (2:5b)
  B. We fulfill a special mission. (2:9b)

#6 **2:11–17 Gospel Citizenship**
The gospel produces better citizens.

  I. **Life in the spiritual war zone. (2:11)**
  A. The war raging within me. (2:11)
  B. The war raging around me. (2:12)
  II. **Life in the political war zone. (2:13–17)**
  A. Motive: "for the Lord's sake." (2:13a)
  B. Master: "to every human institution." (2:13b-14)
  C. Mission: "such is the will of God." (2:15a)
  D. Method: "that by doing right." (2:15b-16)
  E. Maxims (2:17)
  1. If we treat everyone like an emperor, then the emperor is treated like everyone else. (2:17a, d)
  2. Only God deserves to be feared. (2:17c)
  3. Christian relationships are unique. (2:17b)

#7 **2:18–25 Gospel Employees**
The gospel opens the way to heavenly success at work.

  I. **The path of success. (2:18–20)**
  A. Successful actions.
  1. Submission. (2:18a)
  2. Endurance. (2:19b-20)
  B. Successful attitudes.
  1. The fear of God. (2:18b-19a)
  2. The calling of God. (2:21a)
  C. Successful outcomes. (2:12, 15, 19)
  1. Your employer's salvation. (2:12)
  2. Your employer's silence. (2:15)
  3. Your employer's salute. (2:19a)

II. The path of the Savior. (2:21–25)
  A. Christ's sufferings as example. (2:21–23)
    1. A pattern to be copied. (2:21a)
    2. A path to be followed. (2:21b-23)
  B. Christ's sufferings as salvation. (2:24–25)
    1. Freedom from bondage. (2:24a)
    2. Healing from sickness. (2:24b)
    3. Care in our lostness. (2:25)

#8 **3:1–7 Gospel Marriage**
The gospel transforms marriages.

I. A wife's gospel strategy. (3:1–6)
  A. Submission vs. control. (3:1a)
  B. Conduct vs. words. (3:1b-2)
  C. Internal vs. external. (3:3a, 4a)
  D. Character vs. cosmetics. (3:3, 5–6)
  E. Rest vs. fear. (3:6b)
II. A husband's gospel strategy. (3:7)
  A. A shared life: "live with your wives."
  B. A shared mind: "in an understanding way."
  C. A shared calling: "as with someone weaker."
  D. A shared honor: "show her honor."
  E. A shared inheritance: "as a fellow heir of the grace of life."

#9 **3:8–17 Gospel Blessing**
The gospel aligns us to receive God's blessing.

I. Life in relationship to fellow believers. (3:8)
  A. Thinking: "harmonious" & "a humble spirit."
  B. Feeling: "sympathy" & "kindhearted."
  C. Committing: "brotherly."

II. Life in relationship to unbelievers. (3:9–12)
   A. Do not give in kind. (3:9a)
   B. Do give in grace. (3:9b)
      1. Scripture's promise of blessing. (3:10–12)
III. Life in relationship to the Lord. (3:13–17)
   A. A life of submission: "sanctify Christ as Lord" (3:15a)
   B. A life of hope: "an account for the hope that is in you." (3:15c)
   C. A life of readiness: "always being ready to make a defense to everyone who asks you." (3:15b)
   D. A life of gentleness: "gentleness." (3:15d)
   E. A life of respect: "reverence." (3:15e)

#10   **3:18–22 Gospel Triumph**
Following Jesus leads us to share in His triumph.

I. Jesus' obedience brings us to God. (3:18)
II. Jesus' obedience broadcast His triumph. (3:19–20)
III. Jesus' obedience brought Him to the throne. (3:21–22)

#11   **4:1–6 Gospel Separation**
The gospel imparts a life apart.

I. Separate yourself in your thinking. (4:1)
II. Separate yourself in your choosing. (4:2–3)
III. Separate yourself in your preparing. (4:4–6)

#12   **4:7–11 Gospel Perspective**
The gospel sets our eyes on eternity.

I. Perspective reclaims our prayer life. (4:7)
   A. Pray with the end in view. (4:7a)
   B. Pray with your mind controlled. (4:7b)
II. Perspective rekindles our Christian relationships. (4:8–9)
   A. Shared grace. (4:8)
   B. Shared life. (4:9)

III. Perspective refocuses our divine service. (4:10–11)
  A. God has given something to you: "As each has received a special gift." (4:10a)
  B. God gave it to you, but it is for other people: "employ it in serving one another." (4:10b)
  C. God holds you responsible to make sure it helps others: "as good stewards." (4:10c)
  D. God's gifts to you are unique: "of the manifold grace of God." (4:10d-11a)
  E. God's gifts all have one goal: "so that in all things God may be glorified ..." (4:11b)

#13 **4:12–19 Gospel Suffering**
The good news of the gospel includes news about suffering.

I. Suffering is a test to pass. (4:12)
II. Suffering is a fellowship to enter. (4:13–14)
III. Suffering is a choice to make. (4:15–16)
IV. Suffering is a judgment to face. (4:17–18)
V. Suffering is an opportunity to seize. (4:19)

#14 **5:1–4 Gospel Leadership**
The gospel produces godly leaders.

I. A gospel leader's experience. (5:1)
  A. I lead best when I stand among you. (5:1a)
  B. I lead best when I focus on Christ. (5:1b)
  C. I lead best when I speak from experience. (5:1c)
II. A gospel leader's calling. (5:1–2a)
  A. I must lead out of maturity: "I exhort the elders among you." (5:1a)
  B. I must lead out of responsibility: "exercising oversight." (5:2b)
  C. I must lead out of familiarity: "the flock of God among you." (5:2a)

III. A leader's method. (5:2b-3)
   A. I must lead with the right mindset: "not under compulsion." (5:2c)
   B. I must lead with the right motive: "not for sordid gain." (5:2d)
   C. I must lead with the right manner: "nor yet as lording it over those allotted to your charge." (5:3)
IV. A leader's perspective. (5:4)
   A. I will meet with accountability. (5:4a)
   B. I will meet with reward. (5:4b)

#15 5:5–14 Gospel Journeying
Through the gospel, Jesus will lead us home.

I. The gospel enables us to walk humbly. (5:5–7)
   A. Our humility. (5:5a, 6a)
   B. God's hand. (5:5b-7)
      1. God's opposing hand. (5:5b)
      2. God's giving hand. (5:5c)
      3. God's ruling hand. (5:6a)
      4. God's lifting hand. (5:6b-7)
II. The gospel enables us to walk alertly. (5:8–9)
   A. Be alert in thinking. (5:8)
   B. Be alert in posture. (5:9)
III. The gospel enables us to walk steadfastly. (5:10–12)
   A. Rooted in the past: "the God of all grace, who called you. (5:10b)
   B. Confident about the future: "to His eternal glory in Christ, will Himself, perfect, confirm, strengthen and establish you." (5:10c)
   C. Faithful in the present: "After you have suffered for a little while." (5:10a)
   D. Resilient in the process: "Stand fast." (5:12b)

IV. The gospel enables us to walk unitedly. (5:12–14)
    A. Walk in the apostolic gospel. (5:12)
    B. Walk in wider fellowship. (5:13)
    C. Walk in local fellowship. (5:14)

APPENDIX B

A TOPICAL INDEX TO THE MINISTRY MAXIMS

What follows is a topical index of the Ministry Maxims found in each verse of the commentary. In many cases, each verse could have multiple Ministry Maxims formulated for it, so this does not serve as a comprehensive index of all 1 Peter teaches. Rather this index serves as a quick guide to locating some of its teaching on various subjects, as capsulated in the Ministry Maxims. These topics may provide a starting point in dealing with issues in your personal study or training church leaders.

Accountability – 4:5
Aliens – 1:1
Anxiety – 5:7
Authority – 2:14, 17, 18; 3:1; 5:5, 6, 11
Atonement – 2:24; 4:18
Baptism – 3:21
Beauty – 3:3, 4
Bless/blessing – 3:9, 10, 14; 4:14, 15, 16; 5:6, 14
Christ – 1:19; 2:4
    Ascension of – 3:22
    Death of – 2:24; 3:18; 4:18
    Example of – 2:21

      Glory of, glorification – 1:21; 4:13, 16
      Non-retaliation of – 2:23
      Rejection of – 2:7; 4:18
      Resurrection of – 3:18
      Return of – 4:5, 7
      Shepherd – 2:25; 5:4
      Silence of – 2:23
      Sinlessness of – 2:22
      Suffering of – 2:21, 22, 23, 24; 3:18; 4:1, 13
      Triumph of – 3:19, 22

Christian – 4:16
Church/Body of Christ – 1:23; 2:5, 10; 4:17; 5:2, 3
Citizen(s) – 2:13, 14, 15
Clothing – 3:3, 4
Complain – 4:9
Conscience – 3:16
Cross – 1:11, 18, 19; 2:24, 25; 4:18
Death – 1:24; 4:6
Devil/demons – 3:19, 22; 5:8, 9
Elders – 5:1, 2, 3
Elect/election – 1:1, 20; 2:4, 9; 5:13
Endurance – 2:20, 21
Evil – 2:14; 3:19; 5:8, 9
Faith/trust – 1:9, 21, 22; 2:4, 6, 8, 23; 3:5, 21, 22; 4:19; 5:7, 12
Faithfulness – 1:13; 4:16; 5:12
Fear – 3:6, 14; 5:7
Feelings – 1:1, 10, 17; 5:7
Flesh – 2:11
Forgiveness – 4:8
Freedom – 2:16; 4:2
Gentleness – 3:4
Glory/glorification – 1:7, 8, 11; 2:9, 12; 4:11, 14
God –
      Attention of – 3:12
      Creator – 4:19

　　　　Faithfulness – 1:21; 5:11
　　　　Face of – 3:12
　　　　Fear of – 1:17; 2:17; 3:2, 6
　　　　Glory of – 4:11, 14, 16
　　　　Grace of – 5:10, 12, 13
　　　　Hand of – 5:6
　　　　Holiness – 1:15, 16
　　　　Judge/judgment – 1:17; 3:12, 20; 4:5, 17; 4:18
　　　　Knowledge of – 3:12
　　　　Love of – 2:11; 5:7
　　　　Power of – 5:11
　　　　Sovereignty of – 2:8
　　　　Will of – 2:15; 4:2, 19
Good deeds – 2:15, 20; 3:8
Gospel – 1:22, 25; 2:3, 4
Government – 2:13, 14, 17
Grace – 2:3, 9, 19, 20; 3:12; 4:10; 5:5, 10, 11, 12, 13
Hair – 3:3
Healing – 2:24
Holy Spirit – 1:12; 4:14
　　　　Gifts of – 4:10
Hope – 1:3, 5, 10, 13, 21; 2:6; 3:15, 18; 4:13; 5:11
Honor – 2:17
Hospitality – 4:9
Humility – 5:5, 6
Identity – 1:1; 2:5, 9, 10, 11; 4:16; 5:13
Inheritance – 1:4, 5
Joy/rejoicing – 1:6, 8
Judgment – 2:7, 8; 4:7, 17
Leadership – 5:1, 2, 3
Life –
　　　　Brevity of – 1:24, 25
　　　　Eternal – 4:6
　　　　Purpose of – 2:5; 4:2
Love – 1:22; 2:17; 3:8; 4:8

Lusts – 2:11; 4:3
Marriage –
      Husband – 3:1, 5, 7
      Wife – 3:1, 2, 3, 4, 5, 6
Mercy – 2:10; 3:20
Obedience – 1:14, 22; 2:20; 3:6; 4:2
Opposition – 2:15; 3:15; 5:8, 10
Persecution – 2:15, 20, 23; 3:9, 13, 14, 17; 4:4, 18; 5:10
Perspective – 5:10
Prayer – 3:7; 4:7
Preaching – 1:12; 4:6, 11
Pride – 5:5
Promise(s) – 1:13; 5:11
Providence – 1:20; 2:13, 19; 4:19
Punishment – 2:14
Redeem/redemption – 1:2, 18, 19; 2:9, 24, 25; 3:1; 4:18
Regeneration – 1:3, 4, 20, 23
Relationships – 2:17, 18; 3:3, 8, 9; 4:8, 9, 15; 5:14
Repentance – 3:20; 4:3
Resurrection – 1:3, 21
Revenge – 3:9
Reward – 2:14; 5:4
Salvation – 1:2, 5, 9, 10, 11; 2:2, 8; 4:7
Sanctification/holiness – 1:11, 14, 15, 16, 17, 18, 24; 2:1, 2, 3, 11, 12, 16, 21, 22, 24; 3:2, 4, 8, 11; 4:1, 2, 3, 4, 17
Scripture – 1:10, 12, 23, 24, 25; 2:2, 3, 6
Second Coming – 1:6, 7, 8, 9, 13; 2:12
Security – 1:4; 2:25
Service – 2:5, 15, 16; 3:8; 4:2, 10, 11; 5:2
Shepherd – 5:2, 4
Silence – 2:23
Sin – 2:11; 4:8, 11, 15
Slander – 2:12, 15; 4:4
Sojourners – 1:1
Speech – 3:10

Submission – 1:14; 2:13, 16, 18, 20, 23; 3:1, 5, 6; 4:19; 5:5, 6, 7
Suffering – 1:6, 8, 11; 2:12, 19, 20, 21, 22, 23; 3:9, 13, 14, 15, 17; 4:1, 4, 12, 13, 14, 15, 16, 18, 19; 5:9, 10
Time – 4:7
Trials/testing – 1:6; 2:20; 4:14; 5:7, 8, 12
Trinity – 1:2
Unbelief – 2:7, 8; 2:12; 4:18
Witness – 2:9, 12; 3:1, 2, 4, 9, 13, 15, 16
Words – 3:10, 15
Works – 2:12, 15; 3:16
World – 2:11, 15
Worship – 2:5, 9, 12

APPENDIX C

ANNOTATED BIBLIOGRAPHY

This annotated bibliography is provided to help pastors determine how to invest their money in commentaries before preaching 1 Peter. I believe a pastor should interact with the Greek text at the greatest depth his training and available tools afford him. My comments come from this perspective.

As I prepare to preach a book of the NT I seek several commentaries that work closely and carefully with the Greek text, engage in technical discussions, and provide in-depth insights into the original text. I then look for two or three commentaries that are more exegetical or theological in nature. Finally, I want one or two that are more expositional or homiletical in character. After my own exegetical work, I work through the commentaries in that order. Those in the first category help me with analysis (taking the pieces apart). Those in the second category assist in the transition from analysis to synthesis (putting the pieces back together). Those in the last category help me move from text to message. To that end, then, I would want to have (in addition to this current volume!):

Technical Commentaries: Forbes (though not quite fitting the category),

Michaels.

Theological/exegetical Commentaries: Grudem, Jobes, Schreiner.

Expositional Commentaries: Clowney, Samra.

In the annotations that follow, my observations are personal reflections, and each reader may come to different conclusions about a given commentary.

Abernathy, David. *An Exegetical Summary of 1 Peter.* 2nd ed. Dallas: SIL International, 2008.

> Not a commentary in the usual sense, this volume was prepared with Bible translators in mind. It gathers insights from sixteen commentaries and reference works along with ten different English translations in addition to the Greek text. It presents the findings in a verse-by-verse format under two headings: "Lexicon" and "Question" (in which various answers to key questions related to the text are provided). It "makes more sources of exegetical help available than most translators have access to" (6). It can be helpful in quickly surveying the exegetical options on key questions concerning the text of Scripture. A bit pricy for a volume of only 184 pages, but it may be money well spent for the busy pastor with limited resources and time.

Achtmeier, Paul J. *1 Peter.* Philadelphia: Fortress Press, 1996.

> A highly regarded technical commentary, lauded for its scholarship. At over 400 pages in length, Achtmeier is thorough. He favors pseudonymous authorship and a late date of composition in the 80s or 90s. Those still exercising their Greek muscles will find good gain from this volume. It is not inexpensive, so consider your resources.

Alford, Henry. *Alford's Greek Testament: An Exegetical and Critical Commentary.* 5 vols.

> Grand Rapids, Michigan: Baker Book House, reprint 1980 from the 1871 version. Based on the Greek text. Its age limits its usefulness, but there are occasional gems to be found here.

Barbieri, Louis A. *First and Second Peter*. Everyman's Bible Commentary. Chicago: Moody Publishers, 2003.

> Conservative. Dispensational. Simple. Perhaps helpful for Sunday School teachers and lay Bible study leaders.

Barclay, William. *The Letters of James and Peter*. The Daily Study Bible. Edinburgh: The Saint Andrew Press, 1958, 1960, 1961, 1964.

> Barclay is not always where we would like him to be on some matters, but he occasionally provides helpful background material.

Bartlett, David Lyon. *1 Peter*. New Interpreter's Bible, vol. XII. Abingdon Press, 1998.

> The commentary is part of a single volume covering Hebrews through Revelation. Bartlett was educated and taught at Yale Divinity School and later at Columbia Theological Seminary (Georgia). He was ordained by the American Baptist Churches, USA. Conservative expositors will find elsewhere a better return for their dollars and time.

Beare, F.W. *The First Epistle of Peter*. Oxford: Blackwell, 1947.

> Does not believe Peter to be the author and argues for a late date of composition. He represents the historical-critical school of thought, casting doubt on the text, the author, the date of composition, and the purpose of the letter.

Bentley, Michael. *Living for Christ; First and Second Peter*. Welwyn Commentary Series. Durham, England: Evangelical Press, 1990.

> Affirms Petrine authorship. A basic introduction to the themes of 1 Peter from a Reformed perspective. It appears this volume has been replaced in the series by the volume by William VanDoodewaard (see below).

Best, Ernest. *1 Peter*. New Century Bible Commentary. Grand Rapids: William B. Eerdmans, 1982.

> Adopts a critical approach to Scripture. Denies Petrine authorship, suggesting pseudonymous authorship. He concedes that it may have arisen from the Petrine school of thought and dates it in the 80s or 90s. There might be some help here, but one can find as much elsewhere.

Bigg, Charles. *A Critical and Exegetical Commentary on The Epistles of St. Peter and St. Jude*. The International Critical Commentary. Edinburgh: T.&T. Clark Limited, 1903.

> Bigg believes the present letter was "the work of an 'interpreter,' likely Silvanus (5–6). Considering its age, the volume does still yield help to the careful student of the Greek text of 1 Peter, but with limited resources one should look to a newer volume that will prove more essential.

Blum, Edwin A. *1, 2 Peter and Jude*. The Expositor's Bible Commentary, v.12. Grand Rapids: Zondervan Publishing House, 1981.

> In the 2012 update to this series this volume has been replaced by one by J. Daryl Charles (see below). Blum earned his Th.D. from Dallas Theological Seminary (to go with a D. Theol. from the University of Basel). He went on to a long teaching career at DTS. The series is designed specifically for the preaching pastor and, though often the comments are not as extensive as one might like, it proves helpful at some points.

Boring, M. Eugene. *1 Peter*. Abingdon New Testament Commentaries. Nashville: Abingdon Press, 1999.

> Takes a critical approach to Scripture. Argues for pseudonymous authorship seeing the text as a mashup of Pauline and Petrine traditions.

Brown, John. *The First Epistle of Peter*. New York: Robert Carter & Brothers, 1851.

A nineteenth century classic from a man of remarkable hunger for God's Word. Read his biography first and you will appreciate his commentaries even more. Obviously dated, but Reformed, devout, and warmhearted. Exhaustive (and exhausting) at 800 pages! The entire work is available as a downloadable text: www.monergism.com.

Cedar, Paul A. *James, 1, 2 Peter, Jude*. The Communicator's Commentary. Vol. 11. Lloyd J. Ogilvie, Gen. Ed. Waco: Word Books, 1984.

The series calls on those noted as good communicators of the Bible and offers insights to those who would communicate the Bible to others. This volume strives to combine "exposition, illustration, and application" of these four NT books (9). It probably won't help you much with the text of 1 Peter itself, but you may find help in plotting your preaching through 1 Peter.

Charles, J. Daryl. *1 Peter*. The Revised Expositor's Bible Commentary, vol. 13. Grand Rapids: Zondervan, 2006.

This volume replaced the volume by Edwin A. Blum in the original 1976 edition of this series (see above). Charles also wrote the commentary for 2 Peter and Jude in the Believers Bible Commentary series (see Erland Waltner below). The author writes from a pacifist perspective. This is a marked shift from the author of the original volume who is in the Dallas Theological Seminary tradition. Embraces Petrine authorship. As with the original EBC, because of the nature of the series and being bound together in one volume with the commentary on other NT letters, the comments sometimes leave one wishing for more, but what is provided can be helpful.

Clark, Gordon H. *Peter Speaks Today: A Devotional Commentary on First Peter*. Philadelphia: Presbyterian and Reformed Publishing Company, 1967.

> Simple, non-technical expositions of the letter with a stress on each passage's connection to the larger Biblical witness. Carson says Clark "can be thoughtful, sometimes frustrating, almost never humble, but occasionally a useful supplement to the standard works."[1]

Cleave, Derek. *1 Peter*. Focus on the Bible. Fearn, Tain: Christian Focus Publications, 1999.

> This volume appears to have been replaced the 2013 offering by Paul Gardner in this series (see below). Conservative. Reformed. Affirms Petrine authorship. The series aims to be readable, reliable, and relevant and this contribution achieves that aim. Solid, basic commentary. May help in bridging from the study to the pulpit.

Clowney, Edmund. *The Message of 1 Peter: The Way of the Cross*. The Bible Speaks Today. Downers Grove, Illinois: InterVarsity Press, 1988.

> Clowney deals with the text thematically and theologically, from a Reformed perspective. His strength in Biblical theology shines through here as he helps us read 1 Peter in the flow of the whole of God's revelation and purpose, giving significant insight into its OT connections. He will prove helpful in both your early stages of projecting a series as well as your work in individual passages. Clowney packs a great deal into an economy of words. One of my essential texts on this letter.

Craddock, Fred B. *First and Second Peter and Jude*. Westminster Bible Companion. Louisville: Westminster John Knox Press, 1995.

> The series is "intended to help the laity of the church read the Bible more clearly and intelligently" (ix). Comments are based on the NRSV.

---

[1] D.A. Carson, *New Testament Commentary Survey* (Grand Rapids: Baker Academic, 2007), 139.

Agnostic on the matter of Petrine authorship, considering the matter irrelevant (13). Believes Peter was dead by the time 2 Peter was written (92). Conservative expositors will invest their resources elsewhere.

Cranfield, C.E.B. *The First Epistle of Peter*. London: SCM Press, 1950.

Accepts Petrine authorship. Typical of Cranfield's well-received commentaries. Though the work is somewhat dated, there is good help to be found here.

Cunningham, Robert C. "1 Peter" in *The Complete Biblical Library – Hebrews-Jude*. Thoralf Gilbrant, international ed. Ralph W. Harris, exec. ed. Springfield, IL: World Library Press, Inc., 1989. WORD*search* CROSS e-book.

The series, covering the entire OT and NT and consisting in total of thirty-nine volumes, involved over 500 scholars and took over twenty years to complete. It endeavors to mine the original texts and make their riches available to those with little to no knowledge of the original languages. It provides, "verse-by-verse commentary that is useful for a basic understanding of every Old and New Testament verse." It is strong in comparative translations, with over 100 different translations employed in the NT commentaries. It may prove helpful to those without training in theology or the original languages.

Davids, Peter H. *The First Epistle of Peter*. The New International Commentary on the New Testament. Grand Rapids: William B. Eerdmans Publishing Company, 1990.

Admits it is impossible to "demonstrate that Peter could *not* have written the letter" (7) but constructs a scenario where the composition falls heavily upon Silvanus. Davids is helpful in making OT connections throughout the letter. I often found it helpful but place it in my second tier of essential commentaries on 1 Peter.

Donelson, Lewis R. *I and II Peter and Jude*. New Testament Library. Philadelphia: Westminster John Knox Press, 2010.

> Argues for pseudonymous authorship and a date in the last decade of the first century.

Doriani, Daniel M. *1 Peter*. Reformed Expository Commentary. Phillipsburg: P&R Publishing, 2014.

> Pastoral, Christ-centered expositions of the letter. Doriani is also the editor of the NT volumes in the series. Reformed, conservative, faithful, and doctrinal. Provides a good example of exposition and thus may aid in the step from exegesis to preaching.

Dubis, Mark. *1 Peter: A Handbook on the Greek Text*. Waco: Baylor University Press, 2010.

> Like all volumes in this series, it "is designed to guide" the reader "through the intricacies of the Greek text" (ix). It proceeds verse-by-verse through the text of the letter. It offers virtually no theological reflection. It is a valuable aid to the pastor as he works personally with the text of Scripture and before he turns to other commentaries. I found great help here. One may compare the similarly designed contribution by Greg W. Forbes in the *Exegetical Guide to the Greek New Testament* (see below).

Elliot, John H. *I Peter*. The Anchor Yale Bible Commentaries. New Haven: Yale University Press, 2007.

> The series is broadly ecumenical; Elliot himself was Lutheran. The volume is the result of a lifetime of Petrine studies. He denies Petrine authorship. At almost 1,000 pages the conservative pastor with a full church ministry schedule will likely find it too daunting to work through on any consistent basis.

Feldmeier, Reinhard. *The First Letter of Peter: A Commentary on the Greek Text*. Waco: Baylor University Press, 2008.

> Feldmeier is a German Protestant scholar; this volume of over 330 pages was translated into English by Peter H. Davids (see above). The introduction alone is 115 pages long. Though this is a substantial contribution to the literature on 1 Peter, the preaching pastor will probably want to invest his dollars and time elsewhere.

Fleagle, Arnold R. *First Peter: Strategic Imperatives for Suffering Saints*. The Deeper Life Pulpit Commentary. Camp Hill, Pennsylvania: Christian Publications, 1997.

> A brief devotional commentary from one with a holiness background.

Forbes, Greg W. *1 Peter*. Exegetical Guide to the Greek New Testament. Nashville: B&H Publishing Group, 2014.

> Not a commentary in the usual sense, yet, as with each volume in the series, it "aims to close the gap between the Greek text and the available tools" and "aims to provide all the necessary information for understanding the Greek text" (xvi). The book proceeds on a paragraph-by-paragraph basis offering at each stop the Greek text, structural analysis, discussion of each phrase, various translations of key words, suggested topics for further study with a bibliography, and homiletical suggestions. Compare this volume with that of Mark Dubis (see above). I was helped greatly by both volumes, but if I had to choose one, I would select Forbes since it includes insight into sentence structure, specific bibliographical suggestions on each section, and brief homiletical suggestions.

Gardner, Paul. *1 & 2 Peter and Jude: Christians Living in an Age of Suffering*. Focus on the Bible. Fearn, Tain: Christian Focus Publications, 2013.

> This volume appears to have replaced the 1970 offering by Cleave in this series (see above). Conservative. Reformed. Faithful. Affirms Petrine authorship of both letters.

Goppelt, Leonhard. *A Commentary on 1 Peter*. Grand Rapids: William B. Eerdmans Publishing Company, 1993.

> Goppelt was a well-respected German Lutheran scholar. He did not believe Peter to be the author of the letter. He evidences a lifetime of research behind the commentary, but the comments are mired in the historical-critical school of thought and his assumptions as a devotee of Gerhard von Rad. I had high expectations for the volume but found myself consistently disappointed.

Green, Joel B. *1 Peter*. Two Horizons Bible Commentary. Grand Rapids: William B. Eerdmans, 2007.

> Affirms Petrine authorship. Arminian in perspective. Provides paragraph-by-paragraph commentary and theological exploration and integration. Green serves as the NT editor for the series and his work reflects well the aims of the series. The volume's strength may be found in its stimulus to explore the letter theologically.

Grudem, Wayne A. *1 Peter: An Introduction and Commentary*. Tyndale New Testament Commentaries, vol. 17. Downers Grove, Illinois: InterVarsity Press, 1988, 2009.

> The relative brevity of this volume is disproportionate to its helpfulness. Grudem is a conservative scholar and careful exegete. He is reformed in perspective. He accepts Petrine authorship. In difficult texts, where opinions may vary, he weighs the options and argues the case for his view clearly and thoroughly. You will want this volume at hand as you preach through 1 Peter.

Harink, Douglas. *1 and 2 Peter*. Brazos Theological Commentary. Ada, Michigan: Brazos Press, 2009.

> The series includes authors from Protestant, Catholic, and Orthodox traditions. The authors must affirm the Nicene Creed. Harink teaches at The King's University in Edmonton, Alberta.

Hartin, Patrick J. *James, First Peter, Jude, Second Peter*. New Collegeville Bible Commentary. Collegeville, Minnesota: Liturgical Press, 2006.

A contemporary Catholic treatment of these letters of Paul. It is no surprise then that the comments are based upon the New American Bible.

Helm, David R. *1 & 2 Peter and Jude: Sharing Christ's Suffering*. Preaching the Word. Wheaton: Crossway, 2008.

The author is the Executive Director of the Charles Simeon Trust, and it comes, therefore, as no surprise that he offers excellent examples of contemporary exposition through 1 Peter. Can be helpful when it comes time for homiletical work. Reformed.

Hiebert, D. Edmond. *First Peter*. Chicago: Moody Press, 1984, 1992.

Hiebert at his best—solid exegetical outline, depth without crushing detail, theologically conservative, exegetical skill, pastoral wisdom. I own and use with benefit every commentary Hiebert wrote.

Hillyer, Norman. *1 and 2 Peter, Jude*. New International Biblical Commentary. Peabody, Massachusetts: Hendrickson Publishers, 1992.

After pastoring several churches in England, Hillyer served as librarian at Tyndale House in Cambridge. He affirms Petrine authorship. He covers all three letters in around 250 pages of commentary. A concise, conservative commentary that touches insightfully on the key issues without becoming mired in technical matters. Carson calls it "sane and sensible."[2] See the next entry.

Hillyer, Norman. 1 & 2 Peter, Jude. Understanding the Bible Commentary. Grand Rapids: Baker Books, 1981.

See Hillyer's listing just above. The Understanding the Bible Commentary series is a rebranding of the New International Biblical

---

2   Carson, 138.

Commentary (by Hendrickson Publishers), so, this is basically the same text as that in the previous entry.

Henry, Matthew. *Matthew Henry's Commentary on the Whole Bible: Complete and Unabridged in One Volume.* Peabody, Massachusetts: Hendrickson Publishers, Inc., 1991.

Dated, but devotionally warm and thus sometimes helpful in homiletical development.

Horrell, David G. *1 Peter.* New Testament Guides. Sheffield: Sheffield Academic Press, 2008.

Horrell teaches NT at Exeter University in England. He has contributed a brief volume (114 pages) that is not so much a commentary on the text as an introduction designed to help undergraduate students learn how to approach the letter.

Hort, F.J.A. *The First Epistle of St Peter: I.1-II.17.* New York: Macmillan, 1898.

Hort was born in Ireland but was educated and taught in England. He was raised in a conservative Christian environment but during his education drifted toward more liberal views of the Bible. He joined B.F. Westcott in publishing a critical edition of the Greek NT. The present work covers only the first portion of the letter, being published posthumously. Affirms Petrine authorship.

Hunter, A.M. – "1 Peter" in The Interpreter's Bible, vol. 12. George Arthur Buttrick, ed. Nashville: Abingdon-Cokesbury Press, 1957.

This was replaced in The New Interpreter's Bible by the work of David Lyon Bartlett (see above). Carson calls Hunter's contribution "useful."[3]

---

3 Ibid.

Ironside, Henry A. *James and 1 and 2 Peter*. Ironside Expository Commentaries. Grand Rapids: Kregel, 2008.

> Classic devotional expositions from a much-loved Bible teacher from a previous generation. Warm, but dated. Expend your resources elsewhere.

Jobes, Karen H. *1 Peter*. Baker Exegetical Commentary on the New Testament. Grand Rapids: Baker Academic, 2005.

> A well-received work of more recent scholarship. Jobes accepts Petrine authorship. She offers an extensive introduction (57 pages) that thoroughly interacts with the relevant questions. It thus serves as a good source for the busy pastor to identify and digest the larger discussion on introductory matters. The comments themselves demonstrate depth of thought, thorough research, and a sensitive heart. I was frustrated at times trying to locate comments on specifics parts of the original text (and sometimes found there were none as the discussion had been caught up in larger questions suggested by the text). Yet there is great help here for the exegetical preacher. I recommend making this an essential commentary for your work in the text.

Kelly, J.N.D. *The Epistles of Peter and Jude*. Black's New Testament Commentaries. London: Adam & Charles Black, 1969, 1976.

> A renowned British scholar. He is undecided as to Petrine authorship. Some use of the Greek and where it is found it is transliterated for those without proficiency in the original language. The commentary on 1 Peter covers approximately 180 pages. One will find some help here but can find more elsewhere.

Keener, Craig S. *1 Peter: A Commentary*. Grand Rapids: Baker Academic, 2021.

> This is a substantial work reflective of great care and meticulous study. Keener offers his own translation of 1 Peter. In a forty-page introduction, Keener takes seventeen of those pages to thoroughly discuss the matter of authorship. He concludes that "it seems significantly likelier

than not that this letter was authored by Peter." He provides over 400 pages of commentary on the text of the letter. He extensively compares Peter's letter to ancient Jewish and Greco-Roman texts, perhaps more often that the local church pastor will find helpful. The bibliography is vast, covering almost 100 pages. This is a careful, thoughtful commentary that will prove helpful to the pastor-expositor who is willing to wade through some extensive background information that will not directly apply to his preaching.

Kistemaker, Simon J. *Epistles of Peter and the Epistle of Jude*. New Testament Commentary. Grand Rapids, MI: Baker Book House, 1987.

Kistemaker provided six volumes to the New Testament Commentary series begun by William Hendriksen. This is a conservative, solid commentary of the letters from a Reformed perspective. Valuable and helpful.

Leaney, A.R.C. *The Letters of Peter and Jude*. Cambridge Bible Commentaries on the New Testament. Cambridge: Cambridge University Press, 1966.

Based on the New English Bible. Suggests that 1 Peter may be pseudonymous. Connects rebirth with baptism and suggests that it is not the historical factualness of Jesus' resurrection that is in view in 1:3, but "the conquest of death and evil which Christ communicates to his followers" (18). The pastoral expositor can look elsewhere.

Leighton, Robert. *An Obedient and Patient Faith: An Exposition of 1 Peter*. Greenville: Calvary Press, 1999.

A Puritan devotional commentary by a highly-regarded Scottish bishop and scholar. The commentary was published posthumously in two volumes, appearing in 1693 and 1694. You can access the entire work online: https://archive.org/details/practicalcomment01leig.

Leighton, Robert and Griffith Thomas. *1 and 2 Peter*. Crossway Classic Commentaries. Wheaton: Crossway, 1999.

Leighton's portion on 1 Peter is condensed version with updated language of his longer, two volume commentary (See just above).

Lenski, R.C.H. *The Interpretation of the I and II Epistles of Peter, the three Epistles of John, and the Epistle of Jude*. Minneapolis: Augsburg Publishing House, 1966.

A classic Lutheran commentator. Because of its age some newer developments are not touched upon, yet often helpful and intriguing on the Greek text. Helpful in giving a Lutheran perspective on difficult passages (e.g., 1 Peter 3:18–22). Occasionally the source of a valuable nugget of insight.

Lumby, J. Rawson. *The Epistles of St. Peter*. The Expositor's Bible. Hodder and Stoughton, 1893.

Expositions by an English cleric and scholar of a bygone era. He affirms Petrine authorship of both letters. The expositions are dated and have been surpassed by other more recent works.

Luther, Martin, *Commentary on the Epistles of Peter and Jude* (Grand Rapids: Kregel Publications, 1982).

Classic. Luther being Luther.

MacArthur, John. *MacArthur New Testament Commentary – 1 Peter*. Chicago: Moody Press, 2004. WORDsearch CROSS e-book.

As is typical for MacArthur's commentaries the introduction is brief. As always, he provides strong work in the text, is conservative and consistent. One will want to have a good technical commentary on hand, but this is a valuable resource for the preaching pastor.

MacLeay, Angus. *Teaching 1 Peter: Unlocking 1 Peter for the Bible Teacher*. Fearn, Tain, Ross-shire, Scotland: Christian Focus Publications, 2008.

> The series aims to combine into one volume Biblical commentary and homiletical assistance. Deals faithfully and conservatively with the letter. The depth of the commentary is limited, but the volume's usefulness comes in helping the expositor faithfully bridge from exegesis to pulpit.

Marshall, I. Howard. *1 Peter*. The IVP New Testament Commentary Series. Downers Grove, Illinois: InterVarsity Press, 1991.

> A brief offering from a well-respected British scholar with a voluminous output of written works. He is Arminian in persuasion. The size limits dictated by the series have left us with a shorter volume and less detail than one might have wished for. The goal of the series is to present "the heart of each New Testament author's message" along with addressing the most difficult exegetical issues in each Biblical book. Marshall accepts the letter's witness to Petrine authorship. The volume is not on my essential list for the pastoral exegete but may prove helpful.

McKnight, Scot. *1 Peter*. NIV Application Commentary. Grand Rapids: Zondervan, 1996.

> The series aims to help the reader bridge the gap between the present century and the first century. I have found some individual volumes to be more helpful in that regard that others. In 2014 McKnight converted to Anglicanism. Early on he embraced and wrote prolifically on the emerging church, though later he broke ways with the movement. Affirms Peter as the author, perhaps with some "polishing" from Silvanus (28).

Meyer, F. B. *Tried by Fire: Expositions of the First Epistle of Peter*. London: Marshall, Morgan and Scott, 1950 reprint.

> Thirty-one pastoral expositions by a warm-hearted, and much-loved preacher from the past. May be helpful in seeing how Meyer outlines each message and makes pastoral applications.

Michaels, J. Ramsey. *1 Peter*. Word Biblical Commentary, vol. 49. Waco: Word Books, 1988.

I find the format of the series frustrating at times, but Michaels provides one of the better technical commentaries on the letter. He is agnostic about Petrine authorship. While you may not always agree with his conclusions, Michaels consistently provides helpful analysis and insight into the text exegetically. You will want to have this volume at hand as you study and preach through 1 Peter.

Michaels, J. Ramsey. *Word Biblical Themes: 1 Peter*. Dallas: Word Publishing, 1989.

Michaels (see just above) offers here a briefer (106 pages) series of theological reflections on various themes throughout 1 Peter. The pastoral expositor can bypass this volume in favor of his commentary.

Miller, Donald G. *On This Rock: A Commentary on First Peter*. Princeton Theological Monograph Series. Allison Park, Pennsylvania: Pickwick Publications,1993.

Aimed at the pastor but gives evidence of being familiar with the academic issues. Ninety-six of its 373 pages are given to introductory matters. Finds no compelling arguments against Petrine authorship. Thorough, thoughtful expositions. Good on application. This volume may be helpful as one moves toward application and homiletical matters.

Moffat, James. *James, Peter, and Jude*. The Moffat New Testament Commentary. London: Hodder and Stoughton, 1928.

A Scottish theologian of a previous generation. His commentary is based on his own translation of the Greek text. Affirms Petrine authorship, as dictated to Silvanus. Helpful in its day, but now dated. The entire volume is available for free download: https://www.bestbiblecommentaries.com/free-pdf-james-commentary/.

Mounce, Robert H. *A Living Hope: A Commentary on 1 and 2 Peter*. Eugene: Wipf and Stock, 2005.

> An esteemed conservative scholar who has left us highly respected commentaries on Romans (New American Commentary) and Revelation (New International Commentary on the New Testament). He served on the translation teams for the NIV, NLT, and ESV. Affirms Petrine authorship. The commentary is brief (approx. 150 pages) and largely expositional. It provides a quality outline of the letter and verse by verse commentary. It will prove helpful to the preaching pastor.

Nisbet, Alexander. *1 and 2 Peter*. Geneva Series of Commentaries. Edinburgh: The Banner of Truth Trust, 1982.

> The author was a Covenanting minister from the 1600's. Reformed in theology.

Osborne, Grant R. *1 Peter*. Cornerstone Bible Commentary. Carol Stream: Tyndale House Publishers, 2011.

> Written from an Arminian perspective. Based on the NLT. The goal of the series is exegetical and theological reflection on the text that is made accessible. I have at times found the series helpful at times, but often find it wanting on many details of the text.

Philips, John. *Exploring the Epistles of Peter: An Expository Commentary*. John Phillips Commentary Series. Grand Rapids: Kregel, 2005.

> Philips' forte lies in the strong outlines he provides, and the present volume is no exception. His alliterative approach may or may not appeal to you, but in either case you may find helpful insights into how to expound the letter in classical fashion.

Powers, Daniel G. – *1 & 2 Peter, Jude: A Commentary in the Wesleyan Tradition*. New Beacon Bible Commentary. Kansas City: Beacon Hill Press of Kansas City, 2010.

A strong, up-to-date commentary from a Wesleyan-holiness perspective. Affirms Petrine authorship. Each section considers the relevant text under three headings: "Behind the Text" (historical and literary context, sociological and cultural issues, literary features), "In the Text" (verse-by-verse exposition), and "From the Text" (theological significance, history of interpretation, use of the OT in the NT, interpretation of the later church, application). Any Greek is transliterated. The pastoral expositor will find good help here. Carson calls it "impressive."[4]

Raymer, Roger M. "1 Peter." *The Bible Knowledge Commentary: New Testament*, John F. Walvrood and Roy B. Zuck, Editors. Colorado Springs: Victor Books, 1983.

Solid, conservative, evangelical. Good as far as it goes, but too brief to be of substantive help to the serious expositor.

Rees, Paul S. *Triumphant in Trouble: Studies in I Peter*. Westwood, New Jersey: Fleming H. Revell Company, 1962.

Expositions of Peter's first letter given during a conference. Rees was for twenty years the pastor of First Covenant Church of Minneapolis and a past president of the National Association of Evangelicals. Simple, practical, passionate expositions from a previous era.

Ross, J.M.E. *The First Epistle of Peter: A Devotional Commentary*. London: The Religious Tract Society, 1918.

Twenty-five simple, devotional expositions through the letter. The author gives no effort to dealing with critical matters. Dated and now surpassed by more recent works.

Samra, James G. *James, 1 and 2 Peter, and Jude*. Teach the Text Commentary Series. Grand Rapids: Baker Academic, 2016.

Written by a pastor who holds an M.Th. from Dallas Theological

---

[4] Carson, 147.

Seminary and a Ph.D. from Oxford University. Designed specifically to help the pastor preach and teach the text of Scripture. Following your personal study of the text, you will want to use more thorough-going technical and exegetical commentaries first, but you may find this volume helps you bridge from the study to the pulpit. Each NT letter is broken into suggested preaching pericopes, the "big idea" of each pericope is stated, and key themes are set out. Then the context and structure of the passage are discussed, followed by verse-by-verse commentary. Finally, the theology of the text is explored before suggestions for preaching, illustrating, and applying the passage are set out. There is good help here.

Sanchez, Juan. *1 Peter for You*. Epsom, U.K.: The Good Book Company, 2016.

Solid, faithful, Reformed expositions of the letter. Practical and helpful as examples of how to handle the text.

Schreiner, Thomas R. *1, 2 Peter, Jude*. The New American Commentary, v.37. Nashville: B&H Publishing Group, 2003.

Reformed. Affirms Peter as the author of the letter. Strong both exegetically and in theological reflection on the text. Make this one of your on-hand and often-consulted exegetical/theological commentaries as you work your way through the letter.

Selwyn, Edward Gordon. The *First Epistle of Peter: The Greek Text with Introduction, Notes, and Essays*. London: MacMillan, 1946.

Believes Peter to be the author. Interacts extensively with the Greek text. You frequently will find Selwyn in the footnotes of other commentaries. This was the standard among scholarly commentaries based on the Greek text until Achtmeier's volume. You may find a copy helpful if it can be obtained without great expense.

Senior, Donald. *1 Peter*. Sacra Pagina. Collegeville, Minnesota: Liturgical Press, 2003.

> Senior is the president and professor of NT at Catholic Theological Union, Chicago. Believes in pseudonymous authorship.

Skaggs, Rebecca. *1, 2 Peter and Jude Through the Centuries*. Blackwell Bible Commentaries. Hoboken: Wiley-Blackwell, 2020.

> A sizeable contribution at 326 pages. Expensive. From the publisher: "Each chapter includes an overview of central issues and topics, a selection of ancient readings with interpretations, and a brief survey of modern scholarship on the subject. Illuminating how readings vary across historical periods and interpretive communities." The expositor will invest his limited resources elsewhere.

Skaggs, Rebecca. *The Pentecostal Commentary on 1 Peter, 2 Peter, Jude*. The Pentecostal Commentaries. Cleveland: Pilgrim Press, 2004.

> As the title states this commentary seeks to interpret the letter from a Pentecostal perspective. It is a slight volume, coming in at only 176 pages.

Sproul, R.C. *1–2 Peter*. St. Andrews's Expository Commentary. Wheaton: Crossway, 2011.

> Faithful expositions from a Reformed perspective by a beloved defender of the faith. Helpful in thinking through the text theologically and in making the transition from exegesis to sermon crafting.

Stibbs, Alan M. and Andrew F. Walls. *The First Epistle General of Peter*. Tyndale New Testament Commentaries. Grand Rapids: William B. Eerdmans Publishing Company, 1959, 1981.

> This volume was replaced and surpassed by Grudem's newer contribution to the series (see above). Stibbs provided the commentary and Andrew F. Walls contributed the introduction. It represents fine

British evangelical scholarship from its era. The authors affirm Peter's authorship of the letter. The volume's brevity means one should look elsewhere for detail on individual verses, but it does a fine job of developing the letter as a whole and how each section contributes to that whole. Valuable, though surpassed by Grudem.

Storms, Sam. "1 Peter" in *Hebrews-Revelation*. ESV Expository Commentary, vol. 12. Wheaton: Crossway, 2018.

The series emphasizes passage-by-passage exposition of each book. Reformed. Affirms Petrine authorship. For the relative brevity of the commentary, one is surprised by the value packed in the economy of words. A good outline of each section of the letter is provided and insightful comments are provided on each verse. There is good help here for the pastor who practices expository preaching.

William VanDoodewaard. *1 & 2 Peter: Feed My Sheep*. Welwyn Commentary Series. Durham, England: Evangelical Press, 2017.

This has replaced the original 1990 volume by Michael Bentley in this series (see above). A warmly Christ-centered exposition from a Reformed perspective. Affirms Petrine authorship of both epistles. The strength of the volume is its care in dealing with the text of Scripture and its pastoral application for readers today.

Walls, David. *I & II Peter, I, II & III John, Jude*. Holman New Testament Commentary. Nashville: Broadman & Holman, 1999.

Simple, straight-forward help to teach or preach the text of 1 Peter. Comments are based on the NIV. The design of the series keeps the comments from being extensive or detailed, but comment on each verse is provided. Each section has its main point stated and closes by setting out the principles held forth in that section as well as suggestions for application to life. Suggested teaching outlines are provided. The value of the volume will be found as one makes the turn from exegesis to sermon-crafting.

Waltner, Erland and J. Daryl Charles. *1 and 2 Peter, Jude*. Believers Church Bible Commentary. Harrisonburg, Virginia: Herald Press, 1996.

> Waltner provides the commentary on 1 and 2 Peter from a conservative Mennonite perspective. Sizeable at 336 pages. Affirms Petrine authorship. His pacifist stance provides an interesting background to a letter that addresses the suffering of God's people.

Watson, Duane F. and Terrance Callan *First and Second Peter*. Paideia Commentaries on the New Testament. Grand Rapids: Baker Academic, 2012.

> The series was prepared for theological students and aims to help them ground any contemporary understanding of NT texts to their original settings. Not a verse-by-verse commentary but takes the text in larger rhetorical units. Authors in this series variously represent Protestant, Catholic, and Orthodox perspectives. The preaching pastor can find better resources for his investments.

Vinson, Richard B. *1 and 2 Peter, Jude*. Smyth & Helwyns Bible Commentary. Macon: Smyth & Helwyns, 2010.

> Believes in pseudonymous authorship. Vinson contributed the volume on Luke in the same series. Each volume in the series takes a "multimedia" approach and includes maps, art, and drawings to illustrate the truths of the text. Additionally, each volume comes with a CD-ROM which allows the reader to access digital resources.

Wiersbe, Warren W. *The Bible Exposition Commentary: New Testament*, vol. 2. Colorado Springs: Victor Books, 2001.

> Wiersbe's reputation as an outstanding Bible teacher who faithfully opens the Scriptures for hungry hearts is well deserved. Technical information is not Wiersbe's focus, the size and nature of the volume necessitates other emphases. He regularly provides some insightful and helpful homiletical tidbit.

Witherington III, Ben. *Letters and Homilies for Hellenized Christians: A Socio-Rhetorical Commentary on 1–2 Peter*. Downers Grove: IVP Academic, 2016.

Witherington, a prolific scholar, examines the letters from an Arminian perspective. It is a massive contribution, coming in at 432 pages. As the subtitle indicates, the letters are examined using socio-rhetorical methodologies. The author teaches at Asbury Seminary and is ordained by the United Methodist Church.

www.ingramcontent.com/pod-product-compliance
Lightning Source LLC
Chambersburg PA
CBHW060748230426
43667CB00010B/1480